S0-DOQ-440

The Charlie Chan Film Encyclopedia

The Charlie Chan Film Encyclopedia

by Howard M. Berlin

McFarland & Company, Inc., Publishers
Jefferson, North Carolina, and London

Frontispiece: Chang Apana, the real Charlie Chan (courtesy Honolulu Police Department)

Library of Congress Cataloguing-in-Publication Data

Berlin, Howard M., 1946–
The Charlie Chan film encyclopedia / by Howard M. Berlin.
p. cm.
Includes bibliographical references and index.
ISBN 0-7864-0709-3 (library binding : 50# alkaline paper) ∞
1. Charlie Chan films—Encyclopedias. I. Title.

PN1995.9.C37 B47 2000
791.43'651—dc21 99-56163
CIP

British Library Cataloguing-in-Publication data are available

Manufactured in the United States of America

McFarland & Company, Inc., Publishers
Box 611, Jefferson, North Carolina 28640
www.mcfarlandpub.com

This encyclopedia is dedicated to
the many fans who, fifty years later,
still keep the interest in Charlie Chan alive
and have made this work a worthwhile endeavor.

壽福

(Long life and happiness)

Contents

Introduction

Who or what is a Charlie Chan fan? Is it someone who carefully programs the VCR for the late night (or early morning) reruns on television? Is it someone who struggles to possess the complete collection of *Charlie Chan* films on videotape, even though it is currently impossible? Is it someone who trades Chan trivia and aphorisms with friends and others on the Internet? Is it someone who shows 16mm *Charlie Chan* films at a local library and, just before Charlie Chan is to reveal the killer, stops the film and has the audience try to guess the identity of the murderer? If this were a multiple choice test, the best answer would be "all of the above." As Charlie Chan would say, "Humbly admit to same," and I personally have 41 of the 47 films (six films are considered to be "lost"). My wife and children think I'm nuts.

Earl Derr Biggers penned his first novel, *House Without a Key*, in 1925. Forty-seven movies and six Charlie Chans later, fans of the best-known Oriental detective have been around for quite a long time. My first recollection of *Charlie Chan* movies is from television in the late 1950s, even before I was a teenager. Since then there have been periods of strong interest and decline. However, the VCR changed all of that for me. I could record my own copies and enjoy them whenever I liked. I was in seventh heaven.

The Charlie Chan Film Encyclopedia contains virtually everything you wanted to know about Charlie Chan films in an A to Z accumulation of over 1,900 entries of facts, characters, actor and crew biographies, filmographies, and plot summaries, plus over 270 of Charlie's famous aphorisms and 88 movie stills, photographs of actors and actresses, and illustrations. All told, you will find very few facts missing. If they have stuck in your memory, they're probably here.

The arrangement is completely alphabetical. With some exceptions, alphabetical order is followed along normal dictionary and encyclopedic lines. "Mc" is alphabetized as though spelled "Mac." Entries that begin with numbers in numerical form are placed in numerical order at the beginning of the particular letter. Entries beginning with an abbreviation are alphabetized as if they were spelled out (e.g., "Mr." is alphabetized as "mister"). For some proper names (both English and foreign) I have tried to use a "best guess" spelling, particularly when the word is fictitious or is not definitively documented elsewhere.

In writing this book, the intent was to make *The Charlie Chan Film Encyclopedia* the reference bible for *Charlie Chan* lovers everywhere, with something inside for everyone. Some fans just enjoy Charlie's pearls of wisdom; others like to identify famous actors and actresses who may have been relative unknowns when they appeared in a Chan film, such as Rita Cansino (later Rita Hayworth). Some know their favorite scenes and dialogue by heart. Other fans simply enjoy seeing the films over and over again, and thanks to unedited commercial videotapes, cable television movie channels, and 16mm films, they now have that opportunity. Since the series has lasted so many years (despite its obvious character and racial stereotypes), Charlie Chan still appeals to a wide audience, both here and abroad.

A number of concerns arose when I first thought of writing *The Charlie Chan Film Encyclopedia.* First, I wondered if *Charlie Chan* fans would appreciate such a detailed breakdown of the series, but I felt that nearly everyone who watches the *Charlie Chan* films frequently thinks of something he or she would like to check. For many of the entries it was necessary to check a number of reference books, a task that was sometimes easier said than done. Many of these books are very popular (some even considered "classics") and were often the ones that had been stolen from public libraries or had pictures and pages neatly (and not-so-neatly) removed by individuals who could be characterized as no better than selfish and irresponsible thieves.

The aim of this encyclopedia is to bring together information from many sources, both published and Internet, into a single volume. I knew that I could assemble a great deal of the detailed data from my own copies of the movies, literary sources, and modern technology (the Internet, with its movie databases, *Charlie Chan* web sites, and message boards, makes vast amounts of information readily available with the click of a mouse button). Despite the information highway and all the other resources available, some sources nevertheless contain factual and spelling errors, and there was no well-organized *Charlie Chan* reference in a single place. After all, inquiring minds want to know.

A second concern was how to handle what little information and details exist on the first two pre–Oland silent films—*The House Without a Key* (1925) and *The Chinese Parrot* (1927)—as well as the four early Fox films considered to be "lost"—*Charlie Chan Carries On* (1931), *Charlie Chan's Chance* (1932), *Charlie Chan's Greatest Case* (1933), and *Charlie Chan's Courage* (1934). The answer was, "The best I can."

A third concern was whether to include the later Chan movies and TV series such as the movie *The Return of Charlie Chan* (1971) with Ross Martin; the 1957 television series *The New Adventures of Charlie Chan* starring J. Carrol Naish; and the Peter Ustinov spoof, *Charlie Chan and the Curse of the Dragon Queen* (1981). As the sole honorable judge and jury, I decided against it. In many ways I am a traditionalist. The original *Charlie Chan* movies, if nothing else, were black and white films made for the big screen. They were not comedies or satires, although they did have their moments of comic relief. With very few exceptions, the original screen series was a virtual continuum of movies released over an 18-year period. Like it or not, the later candidates failed to measure up to my standards.

When researching biographic information about actors and actresses, sources very often were at odds with each other regarding dates of birth. When such discrepancies occurred, I usually cited the earlier date, taking the position that film stars will try to make themselves seem younger rather than older. In some cases, doubtful dates are prefaced by "c." (circa), and unknown dates of birth or death are marked by an asterisk (*).

For each *Charlie Chan* film, cast and crew lists, running times, release dates, etc., were primarily obtained from the *American Film Institute Catalog of Motion Pictures Produced in the United States*, on-screen credits, sources contemporaneous to the film's production, and later dated sources. In cases where a film is known by more than one title, the title used in this book is the one that the film is cataloged under in the *American Film Institute Catalog of Motion Pictures Produced in the United States.* Release dates are assumed to be national release dates as determined from studio records or release charts of *The Motion Picture Herald.* In the cast lists, brackets are sometimes placed around portions of certain on-screen credits. If, for example, a character's name in the on-screen credits was simply "Fletcher" but the film states a full name or professional title, i.e., Arthur Fletcher, the credit will appear as "[Arthur] Fletcher."

Most of the films produced after 1934 have a Production Code Administration (PCA, a.k.a. the "Hays Office") certification number listed. These numbers were issued to films that adhered to standards of the Motion Picture Production Code.

This book could not have been written without the assistance of those who provided needed stills and photos, advice, and factual information. "Raspberries" and "Bronx cheers" go to those few individuals and institutions who never bothered to respond to my requests and inquiries. For those who were considerate in sharing their time and resources, I would like to acknowledge the assistance of the following:

• *Organizations and Companies*
American Film Institute, Lawrence Berkeley Laboratories, Honolulu Police Department, Eddie Brandt's Saturday Matinee, Boeing Company, Jesse Owens Foundation, and Everett Collection.

• *Individuals*
Jessica Berlin (my daughter), John Betancourt, Bob Boatman, Steven Brown, Ed Carr, Gary Crawford, Joseph S. Devaney, Paul Dial, Christopher Ellis, Robert J. Hiza, John Hunt, Ed Kasprowicz, Virginia Kay, Jim Knoppow, Claude Litton, Glenn Malme, Paula McHale, Steve Owens, James Robert Parish, Don Rogers, Sheila Sacks, Bruce Salem, Richard Salomon, Kurt Schmidt, Stephen Wong, and the many individuals on the Charlie Chan Message Board on the Internet.

Unlike several of the review articles and movie guides which have assigned some sort of numerical rating to each film, I have chosen not to follow this practice, for such a system is far too subjective in my opinion to be useful here. For the record, my favorite actor playing Charlie Chan is Warner Oland. My favorite Chan film is *Charlie Chan at Treasure Island*, with *Charlie Chan in Egypt* (and its opening title music from *Swan Lake*) a close second. I think the worst *Charlie Chan* movie is *The Trap*, although probably several others are close behind in this category. My favorite aphorism is, "Mind like parachute—only function when open!" (from *Charlie Chan at the Circus*), which I often place at the beginning of exams in many of the college courses I teach.

Hopefully, I have done my homework better than the villains did theirs in the films, for they are always caught and are sometimes greeted with Charlie Chan's damning accusation, "You are murderer!" As for this book, both my Jewish grandmothers would often say when giving a present or gift, "Enjoy. Use it well!" I hope you enjoy this book as much as I did writing it, and will use it well. As Charlie Chan often says, 多謝, translating to, "Thank you, so much."

HOWARD M. BERLIN
Wilmington, Delaware
Fall 1999

The Encyclopedia

A

A-469W Case number for Gravelle's escape from the Rockland State Sanitarium (whose case is assigned to Sgt. Kelly) in *Charlie Chan at the Opera* (1936).

AAA Funeral Parlor Funeral parlor owned by shady undertaker Mr. Grail in *The Shanghai Chest* (1948).

A.C. Initials on a briefcase recovered from the sunken ship S.S. *Nestor*, in *Charlie Chan's Secret* (1936). From the briefcase's contents, Charlie Chan concludes that these initials must be that of the missing Allen Colby.

Abdul Dr. Zodiac's assistant (portrayed by Trevor Bardette in his first of two *Charlie Chan* roles) in *Charlie Chan at Treasure Island* (1939). Rhadini has Abdul pose as Dr. Zodiac when he appears at the Temple of Magic to accept a public challenge. While Rhadini is levitating Eve Cairo during one of his illusions, Rhadini murders Abdul to lead the police into believing that Dr. Zodiac is now dead. Charlie Chan demonstrates how Rhadini used his magic wand as a blowgun to kill Abdul and then wounded himself to deflect suspicion.

abracadabra Magical incantation intended to ward off evil spirits and thought to possess magical powers when spoken. It was first employed in the Middle East in the occult ceremonies of the second-century Gnostics. Now, "abracadabra" is merely gibberish frequently used in popular magic and conjuring.

In *Black Magic* (1944), Birmingham Brown is given a magic book, *How to Disappear: Vanishment Made Easy*, by Mr. Johnson who is very eager to turn his job as the Bonners' butler over to Birmingham. Johnson tells Birmingham that the book is "guaranteed to make you go from where you is to ain't where you was, in a flash," when you snap your fingers and say the magic word, abracadabra. When Birmingham asks if it works, Johnson, who can't wait to leave, snaps his fingers and says, "abracadabra," and exits.

Academy Awards None of the 47 *Charlie Chan* films ever received an Academy Award nomination by The Academy of Motion Picture Arts and Sciences. However, five actors and 35 crew members who had worked on the Chan series were honored with at least one Oscar nomination for other films, in addition to two Technical Achievement Awards and two Medal of Commendation/ Honorary Awards. Of those Oscar nominees, Thomas K. Little received the most nominations (21) for his art direction and production designs, six of which resulted in Oscars. Richard Day received 20 nominations, seven of which were awarded Oscars. *See* table, page 6.

Ace Casino El Paso, Texas, casino as mentioned in *Charlie Chan at the Circus* (1936). On May 30, 1935 (Declaration Day, now Memorial Day), Joe Kinney and Tom Holt are caught cheating at cards at the casino and Holt kills the sheriff. *See also* **May 30, 1935**.

Academy Awards

Actors	Nominations
Warner Baxter	1 (1 Oscar)
William Demarest	1
Ray Milland	1 (1 Oscar)
J. Carroll Naish	2
H.B. Warner	1

Crew Members	Nominations
Joseph H. August	2
William Austin	1
Jerome Cady	1
Charles G. Clarke	4
Irving Cummings	1
William S. Darling	7 (3 Oscars)
Richard Day	20 (7 Oscars)
Haldane Douglas	1
William Fox	1
Karl Hajos	2
Bernard Herzbrun	1
Percy Ikerd	1
Harry Jackson	1
Clint Johnston	1
Edward J. Kay	5
Harry M. Leonard	1
George Leverett	1
Sonya Levien	2 (1 Oscar)

Crew Members	Nominations
John F. Link, Sr.	1
Thomas K. Little	21 (6 Oscars)
Louis Loeffler	2
Otho Lovering	1
Rudolph Maté	5
Herschel McCoy	2
Joseph MacDonald	3
Barney McGill	1
Bess Meredyth	2
Virgil Miller	1
Emil Newman	1
Ernest G. Palmer	4 (1 Oscar)
David Raksin	2
Aaron Rosenberg	1
Harry Warren	11 (3 Oscars)
Gordon Wiles	1 (1 Oscar)
Joseph C. Wright	12 (2 Oscars)

Technical Achievement Award

Daniel B. Clark	1
Charles G. Clarke	1

Medal of Commendation/Honorary Award

Charles G. Clarke	1
Ralph Morgan	1

Acuff, Eddie (June 3, 1908, Caruthersville, Arkansas–December 17, 1956, Hollywood, California) American stage and screen character actor who appeared in over 170 films. Acuff portrays the suspicious sailor in Manolo's Cabaret in *Charlie Chan in Panama* (1940).

The brother of country and western singer Roy Acuff, Eddie Acuff drifted to Hollywood in the early 1930s, where he almost immediately secured day-player work at Warner Bros. studios. From his debut as a marine orderly in *Here Comes the Navy* (1934), Acuff showed up in film after film as reporters, photographers, deliverymen, sailors, shop clerks, and the occasional Western comical sidekick. Acuff's most memorable acting stint occurred after Irving Bacon left Columbia's *Blondie* series. From 1946 through 1949, Acuff made nine *Blondie* appearances as the hapless mailman who was forever being knocked down by the eternally late-for-work Dagwood Bumstead.

Adams, Betty U.S. Olympic Team member (portrayed by Pauline Moore in her first of three *Charlie Chan* roles) and girlfriend of Olympic pole vaulter Richard Masters in *Charlie Chan at the Olympics* (1937). During the Olympic Games' opening ceremonies, Adams sees that Lee Chan has been kidnapped and rushes back into the Olympic Stadium to tell Charlie Chan what has happened.

Adams, John Alias for Jan Van Horn, who has been a guard at the Sixth National Bank for eight years, in *The Shanghai Cobra* (1945). Adams uses the fictitious name of R. Rogers to hire Ned Stewart, a private detective, to follow his daughter Paula Webb, who he feels may be in danger.

Adelaide Member of Cole King's variety troupe (portrayed by Tanis Chandler in her second of two *Charlie Chan* roles) in *The Trap* (1947). Marcia threatens to reveal that Adelaide is secretly married to the troupe's physiotherapist, George "Doc" Brandt.

adrenaline Also called epinephrine, the hormone drug Dr. Ainsley tells Charlie Chan he is going to give Mrs. Russell as a heart stimulant after she is found strangled in *Charlie Chan in Reno* (1939). When Charlie Chan uncovers that Ainsley falsified the death certificate of Mrs. Russell's husband, Wayne Russell, three years ago, Chan rushes to stop Ainsley and, after Jimmy grabs the syringe, requests that its contents be analyzed. The police laboratory later reports that the syringe contained a deadly poison instead of adrenaline.

Adrian, Iris (May 29, 1913, Los Angeles, California–September 17, 1994) American character actress (real name: Iris Adrian Hostetter) and former Ziegfeld Follies dancer who appeared in over 120 films, often cast as a gum-chewing, wisecracking or tawdry blonde. Adrian portrays follies dancer Wanda LaFern in *The Sky Dragon* (1949).

Iris Adrian started her career in a Broadway chorus, but her big break was the Ziegfeld Follies of 1931 which brought her success in comedy revues and nightclubs. Actor George Raft brought her to Hollywood in 1934 where she made her movie debut as Goldie in his movie, *Rhumba* (1935). This led to dozens of other supporting roles and a few big ones. She remained active in the movies during the 1960s and '70s, mostly in comedies. One of her last roles was that of the receptionist Dottie in the short-lived television series *The Ted Knight Show* (1978).

Aerodrome du Bourget Paris airport where Charlie Chan arrives in *Charlie Chan in Paris* (1935). Bourget is a Paris suburb, and the airport is the same one at which Charles Lindbergh landed his plane, *Spirit of St. Louis*, after the first transatlantic flight in 1927.

Agnew, Tom Radio announcer (portrayed by Ted Osborn) for *The Crime League* broadcasts in *Charlie Chan at the Wax Museum* (1940). Agnew is really "Butcher" Degan, having changed his appearance through facial surgery performed by Dr. Cream. *See also* **Degan, "Butcher."**

Aguirre, Nita Female spy (portrayed by Carol Forman in her first of two *Charlie Chan* roles) in *Docks of New Orleans* (1948). Aguirre teams together with Grock and André Pereaux to prevent Simon Lafontaine and his syndicate partners from shipping poisonous gas to South America.

Lafontaine is suspicious of Aguirre from the start when she gives him a phony letter of introduction from a man named Brennan, an acquaintance of Lafontaine. When they meet the following day, Brennan tells Lafontaine that he had never met Miss Aguirre. She is later introduced to Charlie Chan as a Countess and cousin of Pereaux, himself posing as Mr. Fernand. However, Chan knows all about her true identity from police files.

Ahmad, Edfu Arnold household servant (portrayed by Nigel De Brulier) in *Charlie Chan in Egypt* (1935). Tom Evans tells Charlie Chan that Ahmad claims that he is a direct descendant of the High Priest Ahmeti.

Because he is the one who buys the cigarettes for Carol Arnold that are found to contain the drug mapuchari, and when both Professor Arnold and his nephew Barry Arnold are murdered, Ahmad is thought by Fuad Soueida and Professor Thurston to be the one behind all of these events and flees when accused. Chan, however, correctly reasons that Edfu Ahmad's fanatical devotion to his ancestors was mistaken as a motive for murder.

Ahmeti One of the most powerful High Priests of the 21st Dynasty whose tomb and mummy are discovered by Professor Arnold in *Charlie Chan in Egypt* (1935). When using an x-ray machine to examine the Ahmeti mummy inside its sealed mummy case, Charlie Chan inquires of Tom Evans whether or not Ahmeti died a violent death. Evans says that Egyptian records tell that Ahmeti died a natural death at 78 years old.

On the x-ray screen, Evans shows Chan the necklace around Ahmeti's neck with the identifying cartouche. However, Charlie keenly observes that the mummy inside also has what appears to be a bullet near its heart.

Philip Ahn

Concluding that the mummy could not be that of Ahmeti, they open the mummy case and remove the wrappings from the mummy's head only to discover that it is the body of Professor Arnold, who Professor Thurston claimed was at Napata.

Ahn, Philip (March 29, 1911, Los Angeles, California–February 28, 1978, Los Angeles, California) Korean-American actor, sometimes also credited as Philson Ahn. In two *Charlie Chan* roles, Ahn portrays Wing Foo, Charlie Chan's son-in-law, in *Charlie Chan in Honolulu* (1938) and Capt. Kong, the skipper of the *Shanghai Maid*, in *The Chinese Ring* (1947).

Philip Ahn had roles in over 100 films and, although he was of Korean descent, he usually played Chinese or Japanese-named characters. He was perhaps best known as Master Kahn in the *Kung Fu* television series from 1972 to 1975.

Aiken, Joseph E. Sound engineer for five *Charlie Chan* films at Twentieth Century–Fox: *Charlie Chan in Honolulu* (1938), *City in Darkness* (1939), *Charlie Chan in Panama* (1940), *Charlie Chan's Murder Cruise* (1940), and *Murder Over New York* (1940).

Ainsley, Dr. Bachelor physician of the Hotel Sierra (portrayed by Ricardo Cortez in his first of two *Charlie Chan* roles) in *Charlie Chan in Reno* (1939). In 1936, Jeanne Bently murdered her husband, Wayne Russell, and Dr. Ainsley was the attending physician who falsified the death certificate to indicate that Russell died from a heart attack. Since that time Ainsley has been blackmailing Jeanne Bently.

Near the movie's conclusion, Ainsley tells Charlie Chan he is going to give Mrs. Russell an injection of adrenaline as a heart stimulant after she is found strangled, but son Jimmy grabs the syringe and Charlie requests that the contents of the syringe be analyzed. The police laboratory later reports that the syringe contained a deadly poison instead of adrenaline, and Ainsley is arrested for attempted murder and blackmail.

Albright, Hardie (December 16, 1903, Charleroi, Pennsylvania–December 7, 1975, Mission Viejo, California) American stage and screen character actor (real name: Hardy Albrecht) who appeared in over 50 films. Albright portrays Walter Meeker in *The Jade Mask* (1945).

Born to a family of vaudevillians, Hardie Albright studied drama at Carnegie Tech and took classes at The Art Institute of Chicago before embarking upon a theatrical career. He made his New York debut with Eva Le Gallienne's company in 1926, and his motion picture bow in 1931. Though typed as a virile, athletic leading man, there was always an air of dishonesty surrounding Albright's performances which better suited his playing unsympathetic roles.

Since one of his trademarks was a fixed, insincere grin, it is altogether appropriate that one of his last roles was as the double-crossing Smiley Williams in *Angel on My Shoulder* (1946). His final film appearance was as Carl Blackburn in exploitation producer Kroger Babb's notorious *Mom and Dad* (1948), a quickie "sex education" movie. After his film career, Albright made several appearances on television shows such as *Gunsmoke*, *Rawhide*, and *Perry Mason*. In his last years, Hardie Albright wrote several informative textbooks on the art of acting, and also taught drama classes at UCLA.

Alderson, Erville (September 1, 1882, Kansas City, Missouri–August 4, 1957, Glendale, California) American character actor who appeared in over 100 films and had roles in two *Charlie Chan* movies. Alderson portrays court clerk Walter Somerville in *The Shanghai Chest* (1948) and Professor Scott in *The Feathered Serpent* (1948).

Aldridge, Katharine (July 9, 1917, Tallahassee, Florida–January 12, 1995, Rockport, Maine) Model and magazine cover girl who appeared in over 20 films, sometimes credited as Kay Aldridge or Katherine Aldridge. She portrays Laura Thursday in *Dead Men Tell* (1941).

Alex "The sloppy fellow" burglar (portrayed by George Davis in his last of three *Charlie Chan* roles) in *City in Darkness* (1939). Alex and "Gentleman" Max break into Petroff's house and wait in the cellar for Petroff to go to bed before attempting to rob the house. While waiting, they find a bottle of cognac (Napoleon brandy) and drink it. Unlike his fastidious partner Max, who drinks from a glass, the uncouth Alex drinks directly from the bottle and spills brandy on himself.

Alexander, J. Grubb American screenwriter, sometimes credited as J.G. Alexander, who has written over 40 silent and early sound films, including *The Chinese Parrot* (1927).

J. Grubb Alexander began his film career in 1914, and his best-known silent screen credits include two of director Paul Leni's finest efforts—*The Man Who Laughs* (1927) and *The Chinese Parrot* (1927). After the arrival of talkies, Alexander signed on at Warner Bros. where he remained until he closed out his career in 1932.

Algard Building Location (in Room 211) where Ralph Brett makes phone calls to talk to his unknown espionage ring superior in *The Scarlet Clue* (1945).

Ali The head digger (portrayed by John George in his first of two *Charlie Chan* roles) in *Charlie Chan in Egypt* (1935). In the movie's prologue, Ali mysteriously collapses and dies when Ahmeti's tomb is opened by Professor Arnold and Ali looks inside through a small opening.

aliases Throughout the series, many characters used aliases. On three occasions Charlie Chan himself was incognito—posing as the house boy Ah Kim in both *The Chinese Parrot* (1927) and *Charlie Chan's Courage* (1934), and as Fu Yuen in *Charlie Chan in Panama* (1940). In *Castle in the Desert* (1942), even a U.S. Army carrier pigeon (number 13576) was given the alias Ming Toy by Charlie. *See* table, below.

Allen, Capt. San Francisco policeman (portrayed by Al Bridge in his second of two

Aliases

Movie	Real Name	Alias(es)
The Chinese Parrot	Charlie Chan	Ah Kim
	Jerry Delaney	P.J. Madden (in disguise)
Charlie Chan Carries On	Jim Everhard	John Ross
The Black Camel	Arthur Mayo	Tarneverro
	Mrs. Denny Mayo	Anna

[table continued]

Movie	Real Name	Alias(es)
Charlie Chan's Courage	Charlie Chan	Ah Kim
	Henry Maydorf	Thaddeus Gamble
	Jerry Delaney	P.J. Madden (in disguise)
Charlie Chan in London	Paul Frank	Geoffrey Richmond
	Capt. Seeton	Philips
Charlie Chan in Paris	Henri Latouche	Marcel Xavier (in disguise)
	Max Corday	Marcel Xavier (in disguise)
Charlie Chan in Shanghai	unknown	James Andrews
Charlie Chan in Honolulu	Elsie Hillman	Carol Wayne
	Mike Hannigan	Detective Arnold
Charlie Chan at Treasure Island	Paul Ellson	Paul Essex
	Stuart Salisbury	Thomas Gregory
	Fred Rhadini	Dr. Zodiac (in disguise)
City in Darkness	Tony Madero	Antonio Castille
Charlie Chan in Panama	Reiner	Jennie Finch
	Charlie Chan	Fu Yuen
	Emil Manolo	Ramon Gonzales
	Kathi von Czardas	Kathi Lenesh
Charlie Chan's Murder Cruise	Jim Eberhardt	Professor Gordon
Charlie Chan at the Wax Museum	"Butcher" Degan	Tom Agnew (after surgery)
Murder Over New York	Paul Narvo	Keith Jeffrey (after surgery)
	Mrs. Paul Narvo	Patricia West, Miriam Shaw, Lucy Millard, Dorothy Cochran
	Ramullah	Aga Singh, Rewa Singh, Rayadrolu Khan, Gunga Subba
Dead Men Tell	Charles Parks	Charles Thursday
	unknown	Bill Lydig
Charlie Chan in Rio	Lola Wagner	Lola Dean
	Alfredo Cardoza	Alfredo Marana
	Barbara Cardoso	Helen Ashby
Castle in the Desert	Cesare Borgia	Watson King
	Lucrezia della Borgia	Lucy Manderley
Charlie Chan in the Secret Service	Fraulein Manleck	Mrs. Winters
	Philipe von Vegon	Luiz Philipe Vega
Black Magic	Norma Duncan	Nancy Woods
	Chardo the Great	Paul Hamlin
The Jade Mask	Lloyd Archer	Walter Meeker (in disguise)
The Scarlet Clue	Ralph Brett	Rolf Brot
	Cooper	Carper, Cauper
	Janet Carter	Hulda Swenson
The Shanghai Cobra	Special Agent Hume	Bradford Harris
	Jan Van Horn	John Adams (after surgery), R. Rogers
	Paula Webb	Pauline Webster
Shadows Over Chinatown	Craig Winfield	Jeff Hay
	Mary Conover	Mary McCoy
	Joe Thomas	Jack Tilford
	Mike Rogan	Mike Roberts, Mickey Roberts, Marty Roman
Dangerous Money	Theodore M. Layne	Mr. Whipple
	Joseph Murdock	Mrs. Whipple (in disguise)
Docks of New Orleans	André Pereaux	Fernand, Citron, Boronoff, Grumbauer
The Golden Eye	Lt. Mike Ruark	Vince O'Brien
The Sky Dragon	Marie Burke	Connie Jackson
	Andrew J. Smith	Andy Barrett

Charlie Chan roles) in *Shadows Over Chinatown* (1946). Allen's commanding officer is Chief Brannigan.

Allen, Fred Film director and editor of almost 60 films, including four *Charlie Chan* films: *Charlie Chan at the Olympics* (1937), *Charlie Chan in Reno* (1939), *Charlie Chan in Panama* (1940), and *The Chinese Cat* (1944).

Allen, Joe, Jr. Actor who portrays ship purser George Brace in *Dangerous Money* (1946).

Allen, John Henry Black actor who portrays Warren Fenton's stable boy "Streamline" Jones in *Charlie Chan at the Race Track* (1936).

Allwyn, Astrid (November 27, 1909, South Manchester, Connecticut–March 31, 1978, Los Angeles, California) Swedish-American leading lady in over 40 films, often typecast as dark-purposed femme fatales, black widows, and "other women." Allwyn portrays Janice Gage in *Charlie Chan's Secret* (1936).

Before retiring from films in 1943, one of her largest roles was as the calculating daughter of Claude Rains in Frank Capra's *Mr. Smith Goes to Washington* (1939). Allywn was married to actor Robert Kent, who portrays Victor Karnoff's secretary and brother-in-law, Gordon Chase, in *Charlie Chan at Monte Carlo* (1937).

"Aloha Oe" Well-known Hawaiian love song, meaning "Farewell to You," whose words and music were written by Queen Lili'uokalani in 1878. It is the closing song in *The Black Camel* (1931).

alternative titles During production, *Charlie Chan* films often had one or more working titles. When released, many films also had different on-screen titles or were advertised with secondary titles. *See* table, below.

Alvin, John (1917–) Actor who portrays Vic Armstrong, the nephew of Judge Wesley Armstrong, in *The Shanghai Chest* (1948).

Alyn, Kirk (October 8, 1910, Oxford, New Jersey–March 14, 1999, The Woodlands, Texas) Character actor (real name: John Feggo, Jr.) who appeared in 20 films, sometimes also

Alternative Titles

Original Title	Alternative Title(s)
Charlie Chan's Secret (1936)	*Charlie Chan in San Francisco*
Charlie Chan in Reno (1939)	*Death Makes a Decree*
Charlie Chan at Treasure Island (1939)	*Charlie Chan at the World's Fair*
City in Darkness (1939)	*Charlie Chan in City in Darkness*
Charlie Chan's Murder Cruise (1940)	*Charlie Chan's Cruise, Chan's Murder Cruise, Chan's Cruise, Charlie Chan's Oriental Cruise*
Murder Over New York (1940)	*Charlie Chan in City in New York*
The Chinese Cat (1944)	*Murder in the Fun House*
Black Magic (1944)	*Murder Chamber, Charlie Chan in the Murder Chamber, Meeting at Midnight* (reissue title)
The Jade Mask (1945)	*Mystery Mansion*
The Scarlet Clue (1945)	*Robot Murder*
The Red Dragon (1945)	*Charlie Chan in Mexico*
Dark Alibi (1946)	*Fatal Fingerprints, Fatal Fingertips, Charlie Chan in Alcatraz*
Shadows Over Chinatown (1946)	*Corpus Delicti, The Mandarin's Secret*
Dangerous Money (1946)	*Hot Money*
The Trap (1947)	*Murder in Malibu Beach*
The Chinese Ring (1947)	*The Red Hornet*
Docks of New Orleans (1948)	*Charlie Chan in New Orleans*
The Shanghai Chest (1948)	*Murder by Alphabet*
The Golden Eye (1948)	*The Mystery of the Golden Eye*
The Sky Dragon (1949)	*Murder in the Air*

credited as Jack Fago and Kirk Allyn. He portrays Sgt. Reynolds in *The Trap* (1947) and also played the dual role of Clark Kent and Superman in *Superman* (1948) and *Atom Man vs. Superman* (1950).

americium Americium is a radioactive metal whose symbol is Am, and is the 95th element in the series of the periodic table. In *The Red Dragon* (1945), Charlie Chan reveals that it was Marguerite Fontan's uncle in Czechoslovakia who discovered the 95th element and formula for the atomic bomb and died preventing the Nazis from using his discovery.

Americium does not occur naturally and was synthesized for the first time in 1944 when scientists bombarded plutonium-239 with helium ions and obtained the isotope americium-241. The known isotopes of americium are radioactive. Usable amounts of Am-241 are obtained by bombardment of plutonium-241 in nuclear reactors. Because it emits strong gamma radiation, Am-241 is used in various types of measuring devices and in radiography. *See also* **95th element**; **Seaborg, Glenn T**.

Ames, Leon (January 20, 1902, Portland, Indiana–October 12, 1993, Laguna Beach, California) American character actor (real name: Leon Waycoff) who appeared in over 120 films, often as harassed or kindly fathers and suave professional men. Ames portrays gangster Buzz Moran in *Charlie Chan on Broadway* (1937).

Leon Ames began his stage career as a sleek, dreamy-eyed matinee idol in 1925 and was still billing himself under his real name, Leon Waycoff, up until 1935. His best early leading role was as the poet-hero Pierre Dupin in *Murders in the Rue Morgue* (1932). He played many a murderer and caddish "other man" before he was cast as the kindly, slightly befuddled patriarch Mr. Alonzo Smith in *Meet Me in St. Louis* (1944). He would play essentially this same character throughout the rest of his career, starring on television as Clarence Day, Sr., in *Life with Father* (1953–55) and as Stanley Banks in *Father of the Bride* (1961–62). In 1963 he replaced the late Larry Keating in the role of Alan Young's neighbor, Gordon Kirkwood, on *Mr. Ed*.

In 1933 Ames was one of the founding members of the Screen Actors Guild and gained a reputation amongst producers as a political firebrand, which may have been why his roles diminished in size during the next few years. Ironically, when Ames was president of SAG, his conservatism and willingness to meet management halfway incurred the wrath of the union's more liberal wing. In spite of all this, he received the Life Achievement Award in 1981 from the Screen Actors Guild. Offscreen, Ames was the owner of a successful, high profile Los Angeles automobile dealership.

Anderson, John Shady insurance investigator (portrayed by Paul Maxey) in *The Sky Dragon* (1949). Anderson, working with airline stewardess Marie Burke and William French, who is the president of the Apex Insurance and Bonding Company, schemes to rob an airplane shipment of $250,000.

When the plane lands at the airport and the police are there to check everyone, Anderson, known to Lt. Ruark, departs the plane with the money hidden in the shoulders and lining of his overcoat which he carries folded over his arm. He then exchanges coats with French before they both come inside the plane to get the details of the missing money shipment French's company insured. French is now carrying the stolen money and is not searched because he wasn't on the plane when the money was stolen.

Years ago, Anderson and his assistant Ed Davidson investigated a confidence scheme at a crooked airline operation that involved Wanda LaFern, Andrew Barrett, and his wife Connie Jackson, alias Marie Burke. However, Connie disappeared with $60,000 which was never recovered. Barrett was eventually tracked down and arrested by Davidson and sent away to prison for three years on evidence gathered by Anderson. Once her husband was in prison, Anderson took Connie Jackson on as a partner in his criminal activities.

Having killed five people, Anderson is

perhaps the most prolific multiple murderer of all the *Charlie Chan* villains. During Flight 17, when the money shipment is stolen, Anderson murders both Ben Edwards (the shipment's courier) and Ed Davidson (Anderson's associate). He shoots and kills ex-con Andrew Barrett in Charlie Chan's house, claiming self-defense when Barrett threatens Chan with a gun. He also murders pilot Don Blake in Wanda LaFern's dressing room in the Gayety Theatre by fracturing his skull. Finally, during Chan's reconstruction of the money shipment heist onboard the plane, Anderson shoots and kills his other partner in the scheme, Connie Jackson (alias Marie Burke), again claiming self-defense when she panics and draws a gun from her handbag.

Anderson, William H. Sound recordist for six *Charlie Chan* films at Twentieth Century–Fox, and *Mr. Moto's Gamble* (1938), a reworked version of the never-completed *Charlie Chan at the Ringside.*

Charlie Chan filmography: *Charlie Chan in Honolulu* (1938), *Charlie Chan in Reno* (1939), *Charlie Chan at Treasure Island* (1939), *City in Darkness* (1939), *Charlie Chan in Panama* (1940), *Charlie Chan's Murder Cruise* (1940).

Andrews, James U.S. government agent (code number 53) who is working with British secret agent Sir Stanley Woodland to investigate opium smuggling in *Charlie Chan in Shanghai* (1935). After Woodward is murdered because he probably knew too much, an impostor, portrayed by Russell Hicks in his first of three *Charlie Chan* roles, represents himself as Andrews and arrives in Shanghai to continue the investigation of Secret Assignment File 457N. The impostor also wants to learn what information Chan really has.

Charlie later finds out that this James Andrews is an impostor and is the real leader of the opium smuggling ring. From information he requested from the U.S. government, Chan learns that the real James Andrews was murdered several weeks earlier in San Francisco and neither smoked nor drank liquor. In his room, the hospitable Chan asks the impostor if he would like a cigarette and some Scotch, both of which he eagerly accepts.

Andrews, Stanley (August 28, 1891, Chicago, Illinois–June 23, 1969, Los Angeles, California) American stage and screen character actor who appeared in over 230 films. Appearing in two *Charlie Chan* movies, Andrews portrays Inspector Vessey (unbilled) in *Dead Men Tell* (1941) and Theodore Von Scherbe in *Docks of New Orleans* (1948).

Stanley Andrews moved from the stage to the movies in the mid–1930s, where at first he was cast in steadfast, authoritative roles. He became familiar to regular moviegoers in a string of performances as ship captains, doctors, executives, military officials and construction supervisors. By the early 1950s Andrews had broadened his range to include grizzled, old, western prospectors and aging sheriffs. This led to his most lasting contribution to the entertainment world—the role of the Old Ranger on the long-running syndicated television series *Death Valley Days*. Beginning in 1952, Andrews introduced each episode, doing double duty as commercial pitchman for 20 Mule Team Borax until 1963 when the U.S. Borax company decided to alter its corporate image with a younger spokesperson—a 51-year-old actor named Ronald Reagan.

Andriot, Lucien N. (November 19, 1892, Paris, France–March, 1979) Cinematographer of over 120 silent and sound films. He was also the cinematographer for *Charlie Chan at the Opera* (1936) and *Mr. Moto's Gamble* (1938), a reworked version of *Charlie Chan at the Ringside* that was never completed.

Angel, Heather (February 9, 1909, Oxford, England–December 13, 1986, Santa Barbara, California) Leading lady (real name: Heather Grace Angel) who appeared in over 50 films and portrays Carlotta Eagan in *Charlie Chan's Greatest Case* (1933). Angel also appeared in six *Bulldog Drummond* films from

1929 to 1939, five of which featured her in the role of Phyllis Clavering.

Anna Shelah Fane's maid (portrayed by Violet Dunn) in *The Black Camel* (1931). Anna is the widow of Denny Mayo, the actor her mistress Shelah murdered three years earlier during a mad love affair.

Note: The character Anna loosely parallels that of Helen Ashby in *Charlie Chan in Rio* (1941).

Anthony, Walter (February 13, 1872, Stockton, California–May 1, 1945, Hollywood, California) Writer of titles, subtitles, and scripts for nearly 60 silent and sound films. He designed the titles for *The Chinese Parrot* (1927).

Subtitles were a necessity in silent films, and they went down easier with audiences if they were attractively designed. This job fell to such experts in the field as American-born Walter Anthony, who began designing titles in 1922. Moving up the professional ladder in the mid–1920s, Anthony started writing the titles as well as the scripts for movies such as *The Sea Hawk* (1924), *The Cat and the Canary* (1927), and the silent version of *All Quiet on the Western Front* (1930).

He then went to work for Warner Bros., remaining there until 1935. After a long period of inactivity, Walter Anthony popped up at the Paramount short subjects unit, writing scripts for such series as *Popular Science* and *Unusual Occupations* from 1940 to 1945.

Antoine Petroff's butler (portrayed by Pedro de Córdoba) in *City in Darkness* (1939). Antoine was wounded when fighting in World War I at Verdun and walks with a limp. He returns to Petroff's house after seeing his son Henri off to the army and overhears Petroff making plans to sell ammunition to France's enemies with forged clearance papers. He takes the papers from Petroff's desk and then struggles with Petroff, killing him with a gunshot. Although he will have to stand trial for the murder, he is told by Romaine that he is to receive the Croix de Guerre for his bravery. *See also* **Croix de Guerre**.

anxiety neurosis In psychoanalytic theory, the occurrence of episodes or attacks of one or more bodily sensations (heart palpitations, rapid shallow breathing, a feeling of tightness in the throat and chest, a queasy feeling in the stomach, a flushed face, coldness in the hands and feet), followed by longer periods of listlessness and fatigue.

The topic of anxiety neurosis occurs twice in *Charlie Chan* films. In *Dead Men Tell* (1941), Gene LaFarge (a patient of Dr. Bonney) has a fear of facing unpleasant situations, and his impulse is to run away from problems. In *Castle in the Desert* (1942), Dr. Retling, a physician who prefers not to qualify himself as a psychiatrist, tells Charlie Chan that Paul Manderley suffers from anxiety neurosis and dreads scandal.

Apana, Chang (1871–1933) The real-life Chinese police detective who lived on Punchbowl Hill in Honolulu and on whom Earl Derr Biggers patterned his *Charlie Chan* novels. Biggers created his famous fictional detective character based on Apana's remarkable achievements as a detective. He incorporated some of these in his immensely popular novels about the islands, starting with *The House Without a Key* in 1925.

Chang Apana was born in 1871, and his education was scant, having never attended school. He neither read nor wrote English or his native Chinese language. The only language he read was Hawaiian, which he spoke fluently. Prior to joining the police department in 1898, Apana was a cowboy.

As a police officer, Detective Apana was fearless and energetic and was one of the most colorful characters to emerge from the rolls of the Honolulu Police Department. He carried scars on his face and body as a result of encounters while performing his duty. Veteran officers often told stories of his daring feats, especially relating to the early days of Chinese immigration to the islands when there was much opium smuggling. The hoodlums all feared Apana, for he was the only man on the force allowed to carry a whip. Apana retired in 1932 after serving 34 years and died a year later in 1933. He is buried at

Warner Oland (right) and Chang Apana when they met in Honolulu during the filming of *The Black Camel* (Everett Collection).

the Manoa Chinese Cemetery in Honolulu. *See also* **Biggers, Earl Derr; Chan, Charlie**.

Apartment 26 Apartment number of Princess Mei Ling in *The Chinese Ring* (1937). The apartment is located at Grant Avenue and Bennett Place in San Francisco's Chinatown.

Apartment 36 Apartment number of Mary McCoy, alias Mary Conover, who lives in the Randolph Apartments in *Shadows Over Chinatown* (1946).

Apartment 44 Apartment number of June Preston at the Roxbury House in *Murder Over New York* (1940).

Apex Detective Agency One-man detective agency operated by Ned Stewart in *The Shanghai Cobra* (1945).

Apex Insurance and Bonding Company Insurance company, whose president is William E. French, in *The Sky Dragon* (1949). French's company insured the shipment of the $250,000 that is stolen on Flight 17 to San Francisco, and over which two persons are killed.

aphorisms Short, pointed sentences expressing a truth or precept. In the movies, Charlie Chan (especially Warner Oland's Chan) was famous for his many pithy proverbs and pearls of wisdom. Some authors have referred to these also as Chanograms, Chanisms, and Biggersisms.

Charlie Chan Carries On (1931)
[As obtained from published reviews]

"Advice after mistake is like medicine after

dead man's funeral."—to Inspector Duff and Pamela Potter

"Each man think own cuckoos better than next man's nightingales."—to Inspector Duff

"Good wife best household furniture."—to Mark Kennaway

"Man seldom scratches where does not itch." —to Patrick Tait

"Only very brave mouse make nest in cat's ear."—to Inspector Duff and Pamela Potter

"Time will not press, and talk will not cook rice."—to Captain Keane

"Too late to dig well after honorable house is on fire."—to Mrs. Chan

The Black Camel (1931)

"Alibi have habit of disappearing like hole in water."—to Alan Jaynes

"Always harder to keep murder secret than for egg to bounce on sidewalk."—to Tarneverro

"Can cut off monkey's tail, but is still monkey."—to Kashimo

"Death is a black camel who kneels unbidden at every gate. Tonight, black camel has knelt here."—to Wilkie Ballou

"Even bagpipe will not speak when stomach is empty."—to the Chief of Police

"Learn from hen. Never boast about egg until after egg's birthday."—to Jimmy Bradshaw

"Only very clever man can bite pie without breaking crust."—to Julie O'Neil and Jimmy Bradshaw

"Secret of this case harder to determine than alley cat's grandfather."—to Kashimo

"Soap and water never can change perfume of Billy goat."—to Kashimo

"Sometimes difficult to pick up pumpkin with one finger."—to Tarneverro

"Way to find rabbit's residence is to turn rabbit loose and watch."—to Tarneverro

Charlie Chan's Chance (1932)

[As obtained from published reviews]

"My day's work has been useless as life preserver for fish."

"This is unexpected as squirt from aggressive grapefruit."

Charlie Chan in London (1934)

"Case like inside of radio—many connections, not all related."—to Geoffrey Richmond

"If you want wild bird to sing—do not put him in cage."—to Sgt. Thacker

"No time to expose lies—must expose truth." —to Geoffrey Richmond

"To know occupants of house—must look in backyard."—to Sir Lionel Bashford

Charlie Chan in Paris (1935)

"Canary bird out of cage may fly far."—to Henri Latouche

"Cannot see contents of nut until shell is cracked."—to Victor Descartes

"Eyes of kitten open only after nine days." —to Lee Chan

"Faith is best foundation for happy future." —to Victor Descartes

"Good detective never ask what and why until after he see."—to Lee Chan

"Hasty conclusion like gunpowder—easy to explode."—to Inspector Renard

"Joy in heart more enjoyable than bullet." —to Lee Chan

"Kindness in heart better than gold in bank." —to Henri Latouche

"Mud turtle in pond more safe than man on horseback."—to Yvette Lamartine

"Must turn up many stones to find hiding place of snake."—to Paul Lamartine

"Only foolish man waste words when argument is lost."—to Inspector Renard

"Perfect case like perfect doughnut—has hole. Optimist only sees doughnut—pessimist sees hole."—to Inspector Renard

"Silence big sister to wisdom."—to Yvette Lamartine

"Youth tonic for old blood."—to Yvette Lamartine

Charlie Chan in Egypt (1935)

"Cannot read printing in new book until pages cut."—to police chief Soueida

"Courage greatest devotion to ones we love." —to Carol Arnold

"Drop of water on thirsty tongue more precious than gold."—to Snowshoes

"From life to death is reach of man."—to Tom Evans

"Hasty conclusion easy to make—like hole in water."—to Tom Evans

"Impossible to prepare defense until direction of attack is known."—to John Thurston

"Insignificant molehill sometimes more important than conspicuous mountain."—to Tom Evans and Carol Arnold

"Journey of life like feather on stream—must continue with current."—to Snowshoes

"Kind thoughts add favorable weight in balance of life and death."—to Nayda

"Theory like mist on eyeglasses—obscures facts."—to Dr. Racine

"Waiting for tomorrow waste of today."—to Tom Evans

Charlie Chan in Shanghai (1936)

"Beauty of poppy conceal sting of death." —to James Andrews

"Cold omelet like fish out of sea—does not improve with age."—to Lee Chan

"Dreams like liars—distort facts."—to Lee Chan

"Hasty conclusion like hind leg of mule—kick backward."—to Ivan Marloff

"Holiday mood like fickle girl—privileged to change mind."—to reporters

"Long journey always start with one short step."—to James Andrews

"Motive like end of string, tied in many knots. End may be in sight but hard to unravel."—to Col. Watkins

"Old excuse like ancient billy goat—has whiskers."—to Lee Chan

"Only foolish dog pursue flying bird."—to James Andrews

"Shot in dark sometimes find eye of bull." —to Lee Chan

"Silence best answer when uncertain."—to Lee Chan

"Spider does not spin web for single fly." —to James Andrews

Charlie Chan's Secret (1936)

"Best place for skeleton is in family closet." —to Dick Williams and Fred Gage

"Finding web of spider does not prove which spider spin web."—to Henrietta Lowell

"Greeting at end of journey like refreshing rain after long drought."—to Henrietta Lowell

"Hasty deduction like ancient egg—look good from outside."—to Baxter

"If strength were all, tiger would not fear scorpion."—to Dick Williams and Inspector Morton

"If tongue in tower bell could speak—will have solution."—to Inspector Morton

"Like child who play with matches—get burned."—to Inspector Morton

"Necessity is mother of invention but sometimes stepmother of deception."—to Henrietta Lowell

"Perhaps woman's intuition, like feather on arrow—may help flight to truth."—to Henrietta Lowell

"Wheel of fate has many spokes."—to Dick Williams

"Unknown danger like summer lightning—strike where least expected."—to Dick Williams

"When pilot unreliable—ship cannot keep true course."—to Henrietta Lowell

"When weaving net—all threads counted." —to Janice Gage

"With proper lever baby's fingers can move mountain."—to Inspector Morton

Charlie Chan at the Circus (1936)

"Cannot tell where path lead until reach end of road."—to Lt. Macy

"Curiosity responsible for cat needing nine lives."—to Lee Chan

"Enemy who misses mark like serpent—must coil to strike again."—to Lt. Macy

"Evidence like nose on anteater."—to Lee Chan

"Facts like photographic film—must be exposed before developing."—to Tiny and Tim

"Free tickets to circus like gold ring on merry-go-round—make enjoyment double."—to Joe Kinney

"Frightened bird very difficult to catch."—to Lt. Macy

"Give man plenty of rope—will hang self." —to Lt. Macy

"Guilty conscience only enemy to peace and rest."—to Mr. Gaines

"Inquisitive person like bear after honey—sometime find hornet's nest."—to Lt. Macy

"Man who seek trouble never will find it far off."—to Lady Tiny

"Mind like parachute—only function when open."—to Lt. Macy

"One grain of luck sometimes worth more than whole rice field of wisdom."—to Lt. Macy

"One ounce of experience worth ton of detective books."—to Lee Chan

"Question without answer like far away water—no good for nearby fire."—to Holt

"Silent witness sometimes speak loudest." —to Lt. Macy

"Size of package does not indicate quality within."—to Lady Tiny and Colonel Tim

Charlie Chan at the Race Track (1936)

"Confucius say no man is poor who have worthy son."—to Lee Chan

"Easy to criticize—most difficult to correct."—to Warren Fenton

"Foolish rooster who stick head in lawn mower end in stew."—to Lee Chan

"Good wife best household furniture."—to Bruce Rogers and Alice Fenton

"Hasty conclusion like toy balloon—easy blow up, easy pop."—to Lee Chan

"Long road sometimes shortest way to end of journey."—to Warren and Alice Fenton

"Man who flirt with dynamite sometimes fly with angels."—to Lee Chan

"Man with gun like lightning—never strike twice in same place."—to Lee Chan

"Rabbit run very fast but sometimes turtle win race."—to George Chester

"Roots of tree laid in many directions."—to Lee Chan

"Surprise attack often find enemy unprepared."—to Lee Chan

"Suspicion often father of truth."—to Charlie Chan's Chief of Police

"Truth sometimes like stab of cruel knife." —to Catherine Chester

"Useless talk like boat without oar—get no place."—to Lee Chan

"When play cannot see man who deal cards—much wiser to stay out of game."—to Lee Chan

Charlie Chan at the Opera (1936)

"Humility only defense against rightful blame." —to Inspector Regan

"Luck happy combination of foolish accidents."—to Sgt. Kelly and Inspector Regan

"Madness twin brother of genius because each live in world created by own ego—one sometimes taken for other."—to Gravelle

"Man who ride on merry-go-round often enough finally catch brass ring."—to Lee Chan

"Politeness golden key that open many doors." —to Sgt. Kelly and Inspector Regan

Charlie Chan at the Olympics (1936)

"A good fisherman, like clever merchant, knows lure of bright colors."—to Charlie Jr.

"All play and no work make Charlie Chan very dull policeman."—to Arthur Hughes

"Danger like light on end of moving train—now safely past."—to Lee Chan

"Envelope like skin of banana—must be removed to digest contents."—to Lee Chan

"Fish in sea like tick on dog—always present but difficult to catch."—to Charlie Jr.

"Good hunter never warn tiger of trap."—to Mr. Hopkins and Cartwright

"Hasty accusation like long shot on horse race—odds good but chances doubtful."—to Mr. Hopkins and Cartwright

"Have never met Santa Claus either but accept gifts from same."—to Lee Chan

"Hope is sunshine which illuminate darkest paths."—to Inspector Strasser

"Last step ease toil of most difficult journey."—to Mr. Hopkins and Cartwright

"Like toupee on bald head—used for cover-up."—to Lee Chan

"Only foolish man will not acknowledge defeat."—to Charles Zaraka and Yvonne Roland

"Piece of string with hook on one end—optimist on other"—to Dr. Burton and Chief Scott

"Race not always won by man who start first."—to Chief Scott

"Truth like football—receive many kicks before reaching goal."—to Mr. Hopkins

"When all players hold suspicious cards, good idea to have joker up sleeve."—to Lee Chan

Charlie Chan on Broadway (1937)

"Camera remember many things human eye forget."—to Inspector Nelson

"Murder case like revolving door—when one side closed, other side open."—to Inspector Nelson and Murdock

"New York like mouth of great river—many reefs in channel to break small sightseeing boat from Honolulu."—to Lee Chan

"One cabin too small for two detectives." —to Lee Chan

Charlie Chan at Monte Carlo (1937)

"Car with new spark like flea on puppy dog—make both most active."—to Inspector Jules Joubert

"Destination is never reached by turning back on same."—to Lee Chan

"Present case like too many cocktails—make very bad headache."—to Inspector Jules Joubert

"Remember in future that tongue often hang man quicker than rope."—to Lee Chan

Charlie Chan in Honolulu (1938)

"As mind is fed with silent thought, so should body absorb its food."—to Chan family

"Bait only good if fish bite on same."—to Jimmy Chan

"Caution very good life insurance."—to Jimmy Chan

"Making bedfellow of serpent no guarantee against snakebite."—to Detective Arnold

"Opinion like leaf in hot water—both need time for brewing."—to Detective Arnold

"When money talks, few are deaf."—to Capt. Johnson and Jimmy Chan

Charlie Chan in Reno (1939)

"Charming company turn lowly sandwich into rich banquet."—to Vivian Wells

"If want wild bird to sing—do not put him in cage."—to Sheriff Fletcher

"Man yet to be born who can tell what woman will or will not do."—to Curtis Whitman

"Tombstone often engraved with words of wisdom."—to Sheriff Fletcher

"When searching for needle in haystack, haystack only sensible location."—to Mrs. Russell

"Words cannot cook rice."—to Curtis Whitman

Charlie Chan at Treasure Island (1939)

"If befriend donkey, expect to be kicked." —to Jimmy Chan

"If request music, must be willing to pay fiddler."—to Pete Lewis and Fred Rhadini

"Obvious clues, like tricks in magic, usually prove deceptive."—to Jimmy Chan

"One scholar in family better than two detectives."—to Jimmy Chan

"Swelled head sometimes give police more cooperation than criminal mistake."—to Jimmy Chan and Pete Lewis

City in Darkness (1939)

"A wise man questions himself—a fool, others."—to Santelle and Pierre

"Already hands of watch reach out to grasp new day."—to Marcel

"Beware of spider who invite spider into parlor."—to Romaine and Antoine

"Bird never divide worm until safe in nest." —to Marcel

"First war profiteer like early bird—look for big fat worm."—to Santelle and Romaine

"Patience big sister to wisdom."—to Marcel

"Quite evident that sugar daddy attract many butterflies."—to Marcel

"Truth only path out of tangled web."—to Marie Dubon

Charlie Chan in Panama (1940)

"Bad alibi like dead fish—cannot stand test of time."—to Jimmy Chan

"Man without relatives is man without trouble."—to Jimmy Chan

Charlie Chan's Murder Cruise (1940)

"Better a father lose his son than a detective his memory."—to Jimmy Chan

"Better ten times a victim than let one man go hungry."—to Professor Gordon and beggar

"Life has been risked for jewels far less valuable than friendship."—to Dr. Suderman and Professor Gordon

"Man can more safely search for gold if world thinks he dig ditch."—to Jimmy Chan
"Memory of Number Two son still elusive—like soap in bathtub."—to Jimmy Chan
"To speak without thinking is to shoot without aiming."—to Jimmy Chan
"Truth like oil—will in time rise to surface." —to Dr. Suderman
"When Chinese emperor have eight suspects of murder, he solve problem very quickly—chop off eight heads—always sure of getting one criminal."—to Professor Gordon and Dick Kenyon
"Young man's explanation like skin of sensitive woman—very thin."—to Paula Drake

Charlie Chan at the Wax Museum (1940)

"Any powder that kills flea is good powder." —to Jimmy Chan
"Every bird seek its own tree—never tree the bird."—to Dr. Otto Von Brom
"Justice like virtue—bring its own reward." —to Mrs. Joe Rocke
"Knowledge only gained through curiosity."—to Inspector O'Matthews
"Mice only play when cat supposed to be in bed."—to Inspector O'Matthews
"Suspicion is only toy of fools."—to Jimmy Chan
"Truth speak from any chair."—to Lily Latimer
"Will imitate woman and change mind." —to Dr. Cream

Murder Over New York (1940)

"British tenacity with Chinese patience like royal flush in poker game—unbeatable." —to Inspector Hugh Drake
"Coincidence like ancient egg—leave unpleasant odor."—to Jimmy Chan
"Confidence of favorite son like courage of small boy at dentist—most evident after tooth extracted."—to Inspector Vance
"Desire to live still strongest instinct in man." —to David Elliot
"Door of opportunity swing both ways."—to Jimmy Chan
"Fresh weed better than wilted rose."—to Jimmy Chan
"Happy solution never see light of truth kept in dark."—to Patricia West
"Needle can be found when correct thread located."—to Inspector Hugh Drake
"Nut easy to crack often empty."—to Jimmy Chan
"One man with gun have more authority than whole army with no ammunition." —to Jimmy Chan
"Same leopard can hide under different spots."—to Patricia West
"Thought at present like dog chasing own tail—getting no place."—to Jimmy Chan
"Wishful thinking sometimes lead to blind alley."—to Inspector Vance

Dead Men Tell (1941)

"Bullet from killer easier to take than bullet from Number Two son."—to Jimmy Chan
"Man has learned much who has learned how to die."—to Patience Nodbury
"Message sometimes hide in magic of practical joke."—to Steve Daniels and Jed Thomasson
"Swallow much but digest little."—to Jimmy Chan
"Trouble is like first love—teach many lessons."—to Jimmy Chan and Dr. Bonney

Charlie Chan in Rio (1941)

"Biggest mistakes in history made by people who didn't think."—to Chief Souto and Jimmy Chan
"Prefer not to walk across before coming to bridge."—to Bill Kellogg
"Slippery man sometimes slip in own oil." —to Jimmy Chan
"Sweet wine often turn nice woman sour." —to Chief Souto
"To one who kill, life can suddenly become most precious."—to Helen Ashby

Castle in the Desert (1942)

"Caution sometimes mother of suspicion." —to Dr. Retling
"Desert without Indians very safe."—to Madam Lily Saturnia
"Guardhouse excellent guarantee for offspring."—to Jimmy Chan
"Guilty conscience like dog in circus—many tricks."—to Paul Manderley

"Man who fears death die a thousand times." —to Madam Lily Saturnia

"Man without enemies like dog without fleas." —to Madam Lily Saturnia

"Sharp wit sometimes better than deadly weapon."—to Watson King

"Theory like thunderstorm—very wet."—to Jimmy Chan

Charlie Chan in the Secret Service (1944)

"If man place himself in way of finger of suspicion, must not be surprised if he receive poke in eye."—to Paul Arranto

"Detective without curiosity is like glass eye at keyhole—no good."—to Luiz Vega

"Suspicion like rain—fall on just and unjust."—to Paul Arranto

"When alibi pushed at me—always suspect motive in woodpile."—to Luiz Vega

The Chinese Cat (1944)

"Expert is merely man who make quick decisions—and is sometimes right."—to Dr. Paul Rednick

"Fear you are weak limb to which no family tree may point with pride."—to Tommy Chan

"Once you have large family, all other troubles mean nothing."—to Sgt. Harvey Dennis and Leah Manning

"Manning case like modern highway—sooner or later come to detour."—to Tommy Chan and Birmingham Brown

"Manning case like puzzle—wrong pieces appear."—to Tommy Chan

"Never start anything until I see end of road." —to Dr. Paul Rebnik

"You talk like rooster who think sun come up just to hear him crow."—to Tommy Chan

"Your assistance about as welcomed as water in a leaking ship."—to Tommy Chan

Black Magic (1944)

"Shady business do not make for sunny life."—to Justine Bonner

The Jade Mask (1945)

"Murder know no law of relativity."—to Sheriff Mack

"No barber shave so close but another barber find some work to do."—to Sheriff and Officer Godfrey

The Scarlet Clue (1945)

"So many fish in fish market—even flower smell same."—to Capt. Flynn

The Shanghai Cobra (1945)

"Cannot sell bear skin before shooting bear." —to Tommy Chan

"Even wise man cannot fathom depths of woman's smile."—to Ned Stewart

"Mice will never play so long as cat is in house."—to Inspector Harry Davis

"Too many hands sometimes destroy pudding."—to Ned Stewart

The Red Dragon (1945)

"Like Chinese army, Chinese ink cannot be wiped out."—to Luis Carvero

Dark Alibi (1946)

"Do not think of future—it come too soon." —to June Hartley and Hugh Kenzie

"Earthquake may shatter the rock but sand upon which rock stood still right there in same old place."—to June Hartley and Hugh Kenzie

"No experiment failure until last experiment success."—to Anthony Morgan and Mr. Thompson

"One small wind can raise much dust."—to Anthony Morgan and June Hartley

Shadows Over Chinatown (1946)

"Never bait trap with wolf to catch wolf." —to Mary Conover and Joseph Thompson

"Number Two son like flea on dog—must have fine-toothed comb to find same." —to Birmingham Brown

"Sleep only escape from yesterday."—to Mrs. Conover

"Sometime surgeon's scar speak louder than fingerprints."—to Capt. Allen

Dangerous Money (1946)

"Good hunter never break twig under foot." —to Capt. Black

"Good wife's place should be at mate's elbow in time of trouble."—to Tao and Laura Erickson

"Guilty mind sometimes pinch worse than ancient boot of torture."—to George Brace and Rona Simmonds

"Kangaroo reach destination by leaps and bounds."—to Capt. Black

"Tiger going away from village is never feared." —to Capt. Black

The Trap (1947)

"Leisurely hunter have time to stalk prey, but hunter in haste must set trap."—to Jimmy Chan and San Toy

The Chinese Ring (1947)

"Death, my son, is the reckoning of heaven. In this case, most complicated reckoning."—to Tommy Chan

"Luck happy chain of foolish accident."—to Sgt. Davidson

"Man who ride on merry-go-round all the time sooner or later must catch brass ring."—at movie's end

"Man who ride on tiger cannot dismount." —to Birmingham Brown

"Politeness golden key to many doors."—to Sgt. Davidson

"Strange events permit themselves the luxury of occurring in strange places."—to Sgt. Davidson

"Successful detective one upon whom luck shows smiling countenance."—to Sgt. Davidson

"Woman not made for heavy thinking, but should always decorate same like blossom of plum."—to Sgt. Davidson and Peggy Cartwright

Docks of New Orleans (1948)

"Death one appointment we must all keep and for which no time set."—to Capt. McNalley

"Even lemon grown in shade will ripen in the end."—to Tommy Chan and Capt. McNalley

"He who goes in after tiger must pay price." —to Pereaux, Nita Aguirre, and Grock

"He who squanders today talking about yesterday's triumph have nothing to boast of tomorrow."—to Pereaux and Nita Aguirre

"He who takes whatever gods send with smile has learned life's hardest lesson. I personally find it difficult to achieve that smile." —to Tommy Chan and Simon Lafontane

"Ships with too many pilots have difficulty reaching port."—to Capt. McNalley

The Shanghai Chest (1948)

"Certain facts seem to gleam clear like snow on distant mountain top."—to Phyllis Powers

"Happiest walk in life of mailman are on holiday."—to Lt. Ruark

"Hardly worth exhibiting puzzle until more pieces fit together. Much must still be checked, but patience are virtue one must hug to bosom."—to Lt. Ruark

"Sometimes muddy waters when stirred sufficiently bring strange things to surface."—to Lt. Ruark

"Surprised detective might as well clutch iron ball and dive in lake."—to Lt. Ruark

The Golden Eye (1948)

"People who listen at keyhole rarely hear good of themselves."—to Tommy Chan

"Small investigation sometimes bring large amount of knowledge."—to Pete

The Feathered Serpent (1948)

"Confucius say that only children and fools open their mouths when they have nothing to say."—Lee Chan to Tommy Chan

"Man who improve house before building solid foundation apt to run in very much trouble."—to Tommy Chan

"Sometimes human tissue tell more than human lips."—to Professor John Stanley

"Very difficult to estimate depth of well by size of bucket."—to Professor Paul Evans

The Sky Dragon (1949)

"Case very much like photographic negative—proper development sometimes bring interesting things to light."—to Wanda LaFern

"Ideas planted too soon often like seeds on winter ground—quickly die."—to Lt. Ruark

"Innocent act without thinking—guilty always make plans."—to Lt. Ruark and Tim Norton

"Tired man's idea sometimes very much like child's nightmare—easily dispelled by bright light of day."—to Lt. Ruark

"Wise playwright plan ahead so that movement of actors does not disturb play." —to John Anderson

Apia Capital and only city of Western Samoa, an independent state in the South Pacific and the location of the gravesite of writer Robert Louis Stevenson. In *Dangerous Money* (1946), Rona Simmonds tells Charlie Chan that she is traveling to Apia to visit the Robert Louis Stevenson shrine.

Appleby, Dorothy (January 6, 1906, Portland, Maine–August 9, 1990, Long Island, New York) Character actress who appeared in over 30 films and portrays the dancer Nardi in *Charlie Chan in Paris* (1935).

APV1 Identification number of the airplane in which Charlie Chan lands at Paris' *Aerodrome du Bourget* in *Charlie Chan in Paris* (1935).

Archer, Lloyd The stepson of Mr. Harper and husband of Stella Graham (portrayed by Jack Ingram) in *The Jade Mask* (1945). When first introduced to Charlie Chan, Archer claims he wanted to get back both the house and the gas formula that Mr. Harper, his stepfather, stole from his real father.

When in vaudeville with his wife, Lloyd Archer was a quick change artist and ventriloquist who could impersonate anyone. Archer cunningly kills police officer Jim Kimball, Mr. Harper, Walter Meeker, Roth, and Michael Strong (the last two while disguised as Meeker). Archer also tries to kill his wife by telling her how to gain entrance to Harper's secret room but not telling her that the desk is a death trap when opened.

Area D, Block 21 Map location of the Berlin residence of Charles Zaraka, where Lee Chan is being held hostage in *Charlie Chan at the Olympics* (1937). *See also* **BP-41**.

Armstrong, Judge Wesley Uncle of Vic Armstrong in *The Shanghai Chest* (1948). The judge (portrayed by Pierre Watkin) was in charge of the trial of Tony Pindello, who was framed for murder and sentenced to be executed in the gas chamber at San Quentin. However, the Judge now has evidence that Pindello was probably innocent and wrongly executed.

To make it appear as part of an alphabet-type serial revenge killing by the already dead Tony Pindello (whose fingerprints were found at the murder scene), Judge Armstrong was the first person murdered by Ed Seward.

Armstrong, Mr. Bank president of the San Francisco branch of the Exchange Specie Bank of Peiping in *The Chinese Ring* (1947). In his attempt to embezzle some of the $1 million Princess Mei Ling has on deposit at his bank (by forging her Chinese signature on checks), Armstrong (portrayed by Byron Foulger) murders the Princess, her maid Lilly Mae Wong, and a little Chinese boy.

Armstrong, Vic Nephew of Judge Wesley Armstrong in *The Shanghai Chest* (1948). When his uncle is murdered, Vic is arrested because of a disagreement about money he and his uncle had had earlier that day. After the argument, Judge Armstrong called his lawyer, Ed Seward, and arranged to meet him the next morning to have Vic written out of his will.

The police find the younger Armstrong standing over his uncle's body holding the murder weapon, a knife. Armstrong is later released when it is found that the fingerprints of Tony Pindello, who was recently executed for murder, are also found at the scene.

Arnold, Barry Paranoid, high-strung brother of Carol Arnold in *Charlie Chan in Egypt* (1935). Arnold (portrayed by James Eagles in his first of two *Charlie Chan* roles) is crippled from an accident ten years ago when a large stone toppled onto his foot. He blames his father, Professor Arnold, for bringing him and his sister to Egypt.

Fearing that Barry has information that could expose him after learning of the death of his father, Professor Thurston (Barry's uncle) ingeniously murders Barry by placing a thin-walled glass tube of poison gas inside Barry's violin. When Barry plays a certain note on the instrument later that evening, the vibration from the violin's sound breaks the glass and the poison gas escapes through the sound vents and is inhaled by Barry, killing him instantly.

Arnold, Carol The daughter of Professor Arnold and the fiancée of Tom Evans in *Charlie Chan in Egypt* (1935). Her uncle, Professor Thurston, tells Carol (portrayed by Pat Paterson) that her father had supposedly found evidence of a royal burial ground at Napata in the Upper Nile and went there to investigate, but has not been heard from for some time. Carol becomes despondent and now takes medication prescribed by Dr. Racine for her anxiety.

Arnold, Detective Joe Alias of wanted murderer Mike Hannigan (portrayed by Richard Lane) in *Charlie Chan in Honolulu* (1938). Hannigan murdered the real Detective Arnold in Shanghai, and his body was pulled from the Yangtze River. Now posing as Detective Arnold, Hannigan is on the *Susan B. Jennings* with fellow murderer Johnnie McCoy under the guise of extraditing McCoy to the United States. However, Charlie Chan has already recognized Hannigan from a police wanted-poster received earlier from San Francisco and knows he is an impostor.

Arnold, Mr. The high-strung stage manager portrayed by Maurice Cass in *Charlie Chan at the Opera* (1936).

Arnold, Professor Archeologist (portrayed by George Irving in his first of two *Charlie Chan* roles) who leads an expedition near Luxor and discovers the tomb of Ahmeti in *Charlie Chan in Egypt* (1935). At the request of the French Archeological Society, which financed Arnold's expedition, Charlie Chan comes to Egypt to see Professor Arnold and find out why some treasures of the Ahmeti tomb have recently found their way to several private European collections and the Berlin Museum in violation of the agreement between Arnold and the Society.

When Arnold's brother-in-law, Professor Thurston, shows Charlie some of the tomb's treasures in the laboratory, Charlie becomes interested in Ahmeti's mummy case, noticing that the varnish around the seal is not quite dry. Rather than open the case at first, Thurston, Chan, and Tom Evans use the laboratory's x-ray machine to view the mummy's remains. On the x-ray screen, Evans shows Chan the necklace around Ahmeti's neck with the identifying cartouche. However, Charlie keenly observes that the mummy has what appears to be a bullet near its heart. Concluding that the mummy could not be that of Ahmeti, they open the mummy case and remove the wrappings from the mummy's head only to discover that it is the body of Professor Arnold who Thurston claimed was at Napata. Arnold was murdered by Professor Thurston after Thurston finally discovered the secret entrance of the tomb's treasure room and wanted to keep the secret to himself.

Arranto, Inez The sister (portrayed by Gwen Kenyon) of Paul Arranto in *Charlie Chan in the Secret Service* (1944).

Arranto, Paul The brother (portrayed by George J. Lewis in his first of three *Charlie Chan* roles) of Inez Arranto in *Charlie Chan in the Secret Service* (1944). Arranto was injured in an accident some months ago and remains in a wheelchair to find out what certain political enemies would do if they believed that he would not enter politics again.

arsenic Deadly poison used in making herbicides and pesticides. In both *The Chinese Parrot* (1927) and its remake, *Charlie Chan's Courage* (1934), arsenic is put in the bird feed used to kill Tony, the talking parrot.

Arthur, Art (1912–April 23, 1985, Riverside, California) American screenwriter and television writer who began his career as a theater columnist for a Brooklyn newspaper and wrote the story which served as the basis for *Charlie Chan on Broadway* (1937). While in the service during World Ward II, Arthur penned the script for the Oscar-winning short subjects documentary, *Seeds of Destiny.* The Oscar was awarded to the U.S. War Department in 1946.

Ashby, Helen Lola Dean's secretary (portrayed by Kay Linaker in her last of four

Charlie Chan roles) in *Charlie Chan in Rio* (1941). Ashby is really Barbara Cardosa, the widow of Manuel Cardozo who was murdered in Honolulu by Lola Dean. Ashby plans with her brother-in-law Alfredo Cardoza, posing as the psychic Alfredo Marana, to extract a confession from Dean about the murder.

Note: The character Helen Ashby loosely parallels that of Anna (Mrs. Denny Mayo) in *The Black Camel* (1931).

assistants In almost every film, Charlie Chan has one or more assistants, which are not always by his choice. They often serve as comedic foils and, when not getting in Charlie's way, do on occasion provide needed assistance in gathering clues and helping to get Charlie out of tight spots. Most of the assistants are his children (Lee, Jimmy, Tommy, Eddie, Willie, Charlie Jr., Frances, and Iris). They are always self-appointed and think they are capable detectives like their honorable father.

In the Monogram films when Charlie Chan is a private detective with no official ties to the Honolulu police, he also has a chauffeur along (Birmingham Brown or Chattanooga Brown). Only once is a policeman, named Kashimo, specifically assigned as his (inept) assistant. Of the 41 films that are not considered lost, there are only four in which Chan has no assistant—*Charlie Chan in London* (1934), *Charlie Chan in Egypt* (1935), *Charlie Chan's Secret* (1936), and *City in Darkness* (1939).

Asther, Nils (January 17, 1897, Malmö, Sweden–October 13, 1981, Stockholm, Sweden) Suave Swedish leading man who appeared in over 50 films and who portrays Professor Paul Evans in *The Feathered Serpent* (1948).

Nils Asther was trained at the Royal Dramatic Theater, and his European film career flourished under the tutelage of Swedish director Mauritz Stiller, who also nurtured the talents of Greta Garbo. Brought to the U.S. in 1926, Asther played all-American leads in such films as *The Cardboard Lover* (1927) and *Our Dancing Daughters* (1928). In the talkies Asther was now everyone's favorite indeterminate foreigner, utilizing his exotic accent and Continental manners in both heroic and villainous roles in American and British films.

Astor Hotel New York hotel where a banquet is held by the New York police in honor of Charlie Chan's arrival in *Charlie Chan on Broadway* (1937).

Ateliers Metallurgiques The name of the bonds, each 250,000 francs, which are owned by Victor Karnoff in *Charlie Chan at Monte Carlo* (1937). Karnoff ships $1 million of these bonds to Paris to be sold, but Renault, the bank messenger, is killed (along with Karnoff's chauffeur Ludwig) by Karnoff's brother-in-law and secretary Gordon Chase, who steals the bonds. Although stolen, the bonds nevertheless are insured against theft.

Atrash, Dauod (David) Luxor pharmacist (portrayed by John Davidson in his first of two *Charlie Chan* roles) in *Charlie Chan in Egypt* (1935). Charlie Chan observes that the medicine prescribed by Dr. Racine for Carol Arnold's anxiety over her father's absence comes from Atrash's pharmacy.

Chan visits Atrash at his pharmacy and inquires about the medicine that Dr. Racine prescribes for Carol Arnold, and is told that it is a mild sedative. Also, Charlie asks if Atrash dispenses mapuchari, which Chan notices was in the cigarettes smoked by Miss Arnold. Atrash then replies that he does not dispense the drug.

Atwill, Lionel (March 1, 1885, Kent, Croyden, England–April 22, 1946, Pacific Palisades, California) British-born stage and screen actor (real name: Lionel Alfred William Atwill) who appeared in nearly 75 films. In two *Charlie Chan* roles, he portrays Cliveden Compton in *Charlie Chan in Panama* (1940) and Dr. Suderman in *Charlie Chan's Murder Cruise* (1940).

Lionel Atwill, whose nickname was "Pinky," was born into wealth and educated at London's prestigious Mercer School where he originally planned to pursue a career as an architect. Instead, he became a stage actor,

Lionel Atwill

working steadily from his debut at age 20, most often in the plays of Ibsen and Shaw. Establishing himself in America, Atwill continued his stage work, supplementing his income with silent film appearances, the first being as Courtenay Urquhart in *Eve's Daughter* (1918). Atwill's rich rolling voice made him a natural for talking pictures. Following a pair of Vitaphone short subjects in 1928, he made his debut bow in *The Verdict* (1932).

Most effective in roles as an aristocratic villain, Atwill found himself appearing in numerous melodramas and horror films, including the classic *Mystery of the Wax Museum* (1933). Atwill's career was threatened in 1940 when it was revealed that he'd hosted an orgy at his home, complete with naked guests and pornographic films. Atwill lied to protect his party guests at his trial and was convicted of perjury. The resulting scandal made Atwill virtually unemployable at most studios, but he found a semipermanent home at Universal Pictures, which at the time was grinding out low budget horror films.

Lionel Atwill died in the middle of the production of the 1946 Universal film *Lost City of the Jungle*. Viewers watching the movie today will no doubt notice how Atwill's character of Sir Eric Hazariasturns often turns his back to the camera, allowing the producers to cover his absence with a stand-in.

August, Joseph H. (April 26, 1890, Idaho Springs, Colorado–September 25, 1947, Culver City, California) Cinematographer for nearly 130 silent and sound films, including *The Black Camel* (1931) and *Charlie Chan's Chance* (1932).

After graduating from the Colorado School of Mining, Joseph August became an assistant cameraman in 1911 for Thomas Ince and was soon promoted to first cameraman. He then worked as the regular cinematographer of Reginald Barker, William S. Hart, and other directors throughout the silent era. In 1918 he was a co-founder of the elite American Society of Cinematographers (A.S.C.), an association for the promotion of excellence in motion picture photography. He later went on to work on some of John Ford's most famous films. He served as a Navy commander in Iceland and the Pacific during World War II. In 1947, while filming *Portrait of Jennie*, he collapsed and died on the set.

August was nominated for two Academy Awards in the Best Cinematography, Black-and-White category for *Gunga Din* (1939) and *Portrait of Jennie* (1948).

Austin, Lois (1908–1957) Character actress who appeared in over 25 films, including three *Charlie Chan* movies. Austin portrays wardrobe mistress Mrs. Thorn in *The Trap* (1947), Cartwright's landlady (unbilled) in *The Shanghai Chest* (1948), and Mrs. Margaret Driscoll in *The Golden Eye* (1948).

Austin, William (June 12, 1884, Georgetown, British Guyana–June 15, 1975, Orange County, California) Actor (real name: William Crosby Piercy Austin) in over 60 silent and sound films, and film editor of over 80 films, including *Dangerous Money* (1946). In 1953 Austin was nominated for an Academy

Award in the Best Film Editing category for *Flat Top* (1952).

Avalanche Racehorse owned for four years by Major Gordon Kent and then given to his son-in-law George Chester in *Charlie Chan at the Race Track* (1936). Trained by Bagley, Avalanche is the number four horse ridden by jockey "Tip" Collins in the Melbourne Cup in Australia and crosses the finish line first. However, Collins intentionally fouls Stardust during the race on orders of Bagley, who is part of a racetrack gambling ring headed by Chester.

Avalanche is then disqualified from the race and Stardust, as the second-place finisher, is declared the winner. The track stewards feel that Collins should have been able to prevent Avalanche from "pulling wide" and is barred from further racing for two years. However, Kent strongly feels that a racetrack gambling ring had paid his jockey to throw the race and vows to get to the bottom of it by sending his old friend Charlie Chan a telegram.

While on the S.S. *Oceanic* traveling to America, Kent is killed in Avalanche's stall in the ship's forward hold. Kent's death is first classified as an accident when the ship's doctor thinks that Kent was kicked in the head by Avalanche, but Chan's investigation while the ship is docked in Honolulu proves that Kent was murdered instead. Despite the death of his father-in-law, Chester continues with plans of taking Avalanche to California and entering him in the Santa Juanita Handicap.

After leaving Honolulu, one of Chester's henchmen purposely starts a small fire in the ship's stable area to create a distraction whereby the horses Avalanche and Gallant Lad are switched. They somewhat resemble each other after some coloring dye is applied to change their appearances, but Gallant Lad's owner, Warren Fenton, is not fooled. Knowing that the real Avalanche is the better horse of the two and that Gallant Lad is virtually unknown in America, Fenton lets the switch remain. Because Gallant Lad is now a "ringer," Fenton figures he can win a lot of money by betting on an unknown long shot. Just before the race, Charlie Chan realizes that the horses were switched and now reverses the pair so that they will be running under their true names.

Because of the publicized threats against Avalanche, none of the jockeys are willing to ride Avalanche in the Santa Juanita Handicap. However, Eddie Brill steps up to Chester and offers to ride Avalanche. Brill does win the race, but Avalanche stumbles and falls immediately after crossing the finish line from the effects of a tranquilizer dart fired by Al Meers. However, both Brill and Avalanche are later found to be uninjured.

Aztec Temple of the Sun Lost Aztec temple located near the village of San Pablo at the foot of the Diablo Mountains in *The Feathered Serpent* (1948). Professor Henry Farnsworth leads an expedition to search for Aztec ruins which reportedly hold a vast treasure of jade and gold in the tomb of King Kannick.

B

Bagley The trainer of the racehorse Avalanche which is owned by George Chester in *Charlie Chan at the Race Track* (1936). Bagley (portrayed by Gavin Muir) is part of a racetrack gambling ring headed by Chester.

Bailey, William N. (September 26, 1886–November 8, 1962, Hollywood, California) Actor, sometimes also credited as Bill Bailey and William Norton Bailey, who appeared in almost 90 silent and sound films. Bailey portrays the policeman Harris (unbilled) in *Charlie Chan's Secret* (1936) and also appears in the first *Charlie Chan* silent movie, *The House Without a Key* (1925).

baksheesh From the Turkish *bahsis*, a Middle-Eastern term meaning a "tip" or "gratuity," as used by the dragoman in *Charlie Chan in Egypt* (1935).

Ballou, Rita Rita (portrayed by Marjorie White in her second of two *Charlie Chan* roles) is the Hollywood friend of actress

Shelah Fane and wife of Wilkie Ballou in *The Black Camel* (1931).

Ballou, Wilkie Wilkie (portrayed by Richard Tucker) is the Hollywood friend of actress Shelah Fane and husband of Rita Ballou in *The Black Camel* (1931).

banderilla Spanish word for a small dart with a ribbon used for baiting bulls. In *The Red Dragon* (1945), Alfred Wyans buys a bottle of Red Dragon Chinese black indelible ink from artist Iris Ling, telling her that the ink is for his *banderillas*.

When looking for clues in Wyans office, Charlie Chan asks police Inspector Luis Carvero the exact meaning of *banderilla*, and Carvero replies that it can be a small flag or ribbon. Both then deduce that Wyans was referring to his typewriter's ribbon, with which he wrote the secret research papers using the indelible ink so that it was hidden by the typewriter ribbon's normal ink.

Banque Lamartine *see* **Lamartine Bank**

Barclay, Joan Attractive American leading lady who appeared in over 50 films. Barclay portrays Paula Webb, alias Pauline Webster, in *The Shanghai Cobra* (1945).

Joan Barclay was first seen on screen as an unbilled chorus girl in the Warner Bros. movie *Golddiggers of 1933* (1933). After a year's worth of bit roles at Warners, Barclay was signed by quickie producer Sam Katzman. From 1934 to 1942 she played the lead in the two-film serials *Shadows of Chinatown* (1935, as Joan Whiting) and *Blake of Scotland Yard* (1937, as Hope Mason). Barclay also appeared with Bela Lugosi as Alice Saunders in *Black Dragons* (1942) and as Alice Wentworth in *The Corpse Vanishes* (1942).

She was briefly contracted by RKO in the mid–1940s where she landed a sizable role as Joan, a baseball player's wife, in *Ladies Day* (1943), in addition to parts in lesser known films. Barclay returned to Monogram Pictures for her final screen appearance in *The Shanghai Cobra* (1945).

Bardette, Trevor (November 19, 1902, Nashville, Arkansas–November 28, 1977, California) American character actor who appeared in over 100 films, often in villainous roles as gangsters and rustlers. In two *Charlie Chan* roles, Bardette portrays Abdul the Turk in *Charlie Chan at Treasure Island* (1939) and a Hindu businessman (unbilled) in *Murder Over New York* (1940).

Barelli, Enrico Baritone opera star in Mme. Lilli Rochelle's San Marco Opera Company in *Charlie Chan at the Opera* (1936). Barelli, portrayed by George Gaye, sings the role of Mephisto in the opera *Carnival* and, although married to Mme. Anita Barelli, is romantically involved with Mme. Rochelle, whose jealous husband, Mr. Whitely, has both followed by a private detective.

It was years earlier that Barelli and Mme. Rochelle locked Gravelle, her husband and also an opera singer, in his dressing room during a Chicago opera house fire and left him for dead. Years later, Gravelle confronts Barelli, ties him up, and takes his place as Mephisto in the opera, during which Barelli is murdered by his wife.

Barelli, Madame Anita Second soprano in Mme. Lilli Rochelle's San Marco Opera Company in *Charlie Chan at the Opera* (1936). Portrayed by Nedda Harrigan, Mme. Barelli is married to baritone Enrico Barelli. Constantly humiliated in public by both her husband and Mme. Rochelle, Mme. Barelli murders both during the opening night performance of *Carnival*, but Gravelle, an escapee from a sanitarium, is first blamed.

Bari, Lynn (December 18, 1913, Roanoke, Virginia–November 20, 1989, Goleta, California) Attractive actress (real name: Marjorie Schuyler Fisher, a.k.a. Marjorie Bitzer) who appeared in over 100 films. Bari portrays Marie Dubon in *City in Darkness* (1939) and also plays newspaper reporter Penny Kendall in *Mr. Moto's Gamble* (1938), a reworked version of *Charlie Chan at the Ringside* that was never completed.

The stepdaughter of a minister, Lynn Bari entered films as an unbilled chorus girl in *Dancing Lady* (1933), for which she was hired more for her high cheekbones than her dancing ability. Later that same year she signed a contract with Fox studios, inaugurating a decade-long association with that studio. Though she yearned for parts of substance, the brunette actress was generally limited to "B" pictures and pin-up poses. However, one of her rare leading roles in an "A" picture was playing Claire Harris opposite Henry Fonda in *The Magnificent Dope* (1942).

Only a few of her later films made full use of Bari's talents. The best of her screen roles in the 1950s was as Piper Laurie's social-climbing mother, Harriet Blaisdell, in *Has Anybody Seen My Gal?* (1952). On television, Bari portrayed Connie Conway in *The Detective's Wife* (1950) and Gwen Allen in *Boss Lady* (1952).

Barrat, Robert H. (July 10, 1891, New York, New York–January 7, 1970, Hollywood, California) American stage and screen character actor who appeared in over 140 films, often as a villain in westerns. Barrat portrays the double murderer Capt. Johnson of the *Susan B. Jennings* in *Charlie Chan in Honolulu* (1938).

When actor Robert Barrat moved from stage to films in the early 1930s, he found himself twice blessed. He was dignified-looking enough to portray business and society types, but also athletic enough to get down and dirty in barroom-brawl scenes. An ardent physical fitness advocate in real life, Barrat was once described by his friend and frequent co-worker James Cagney as having "a solid forearm the size of the average man's thigh."

The actor's size and menacing demeanor served him well when pitted against such comparatively pint-sized comedians as the Marx Brothers in *Go West* (1940), where he portrayed Red Baxter. When not intimidating with his muscle power, Barrat was fond of playing roles that called for quaint, colorful accents, such as Captain Ferring in *Wonder Bar* (1934).

Barraud, George British-born writer and actor who appeared in almost 15 films. Barraud portrays hunt secretary Air Force Major Jardine in *Charlie Chan in London* (1934).

Barrett, Andy Shady ex-con (portrayed by Lyle Talbot) who uses the alias Andrew J. Smith when traveling with sister-in-law Wanda LaFern on Flight 17 in *The Sky Dragon* (1949).

Charlie Chan finds out from fingerprints that Barrett is a commercial pilot and eight years earlier had married Wanda's younger sister, Connie Jackson. The three were involved in a confidence scheme involving a crooked airline operation, after which Connie made off with $60,000 that was never recovered. Barrett was arrested by Ed Davidson and sent away to prison for three years on evidence gathered by John Anderson. When confronted by Chan about his past, Barrett tries to bargain with him while holding a gun, but is shot and killed by Anderson, who claims self-defense.

Barrie, Mona (December 18, 1909, London, England–1964) Demure, soulful-eyed stage and screen actress (real name: Mona Smith) who appeared in almost 50 films. She portrays Lady Mary Bristol in *Charlie Chan in London* (1934).

Although born in England, Mona Barrie was educated in Australia. She worked steadily on stage in both her native and adopted country before coming to America with a Fox studio contract in 1933. Not quite charismatic enough to become a star, Mona prospered as a second lead, frequently cast as a woman of mystery or a wronged wife. She also displayed an unsuspected flair for deadpan comedy in her virtually wordless portrayal of a haughty movie queen in W.C. Fields' *Never Give a Sucker an Even Break* (1941).

Barry, Wesley (August 10, 1907, Los Angeles, California–April 11, 1994, Fresno, California) Actor, producer, director, and assistant director of over 60 silent and sound films, including four *Charlie Chan* entries: *Dangerous Money* (1946), *The Shanghai Chest* (1948), *The Golden Eye* (1948), and *The Sky Dragon* (1949).

Bartlett, Talbot Local assayer (portrayed by Bruce Kellogg in his second of two *Charlie Chan* roles) in *The Golden Eye* (1948). Although Charlie Chan is introduced to Bartlett as an Oriental curio dealer selling jade to Mr. Manning, Bartlett nevertheless knows Charlie as the famous Chinese detective. He reminds Chan that he played first base on Number One son Lee's high school baseball team and was a former customs inspector in Honolulu.

Now in Arizona as an assayer, Bartlett is the leader of a gold smuggling operation at Manning's Golden Eye Mine. Fearing that his man Driscoll would be captured and reveal all the details about the smuggling, Bartlett shoots and kills Driscoll under the pretext of stopping him from getting away from Chan and Lt. Ruark. With Evelyn Manning's father murdered, Bartlett then plans to marry Evelyn and take over the mine.

Barton, Denny Professional gambler (portrayed by G.P. Huntley) in *Charlie Chan at the Race Track* (1936).

Bashford, Sir Lionel British Home Secretary (portrayed by David Torrence in his first of two *Charlie Chan* roles) in *Charlie Chan in London* (1934). Bashford's name is again mentioned in a later movie, *Charlie Chan in Shanghai* (1935), when a reporter remarks that Chan and Shanghai police commissioner Col. Watkins had previously met each other at Scotland Yard at the time of Sir Lionel Bashford's murder.

Bates Judge Armstrong's butler (portrayed by Olaf Hytten) in *The Shanghai Chest* (1948).

Batwa Tribe Pygmoid people (also referred to as Twa) who are indigenous inhabitants of modern-day Rwanda and Burundi and comprise less than 1 percent of either country's population.

In *Charlie Chan at Treasure Island* (1939), there is a statue of an African pygmy in the lobby of Rhadini's Temple of Magic. With the statue is a sign reading, "Pigmy Hunter (Batwa Tribe)."

Baxter Bumbling Colby family butler (portrayed by Herbert Mundin) who reluctantly assists Charlie Chan in *Charlie Chan's Secret* (1936). Like some of Chan's assistants in the series' later films (Birmingham Brown in particular), Baxter is seen as the ultimate coward, petrified of his own shadow and hesitant to have anything to do with death or situations that are the least bit spooky.

Baxter, Warner (March 29, 1891, Columbus, Ohio–May 7, 1951, Beverly Hills, California) Handsome leading man (real name: Warner Leroy Baxter) of stage and screen who appeared in over 110 silent and sound films. Baxter portrays famed explorer Col. John Beetham in *Behind That Curtain* (1929).

Although born in Ohio, Warner Baxter was raised in San Francisco by his widowed mother where, following the earthquake of 1906, they lived in a tent for two weeks. He worked as a farm implement salesman in his late teens before turning his hobby of amateur theatricals into a lifelong profession. By 1910 he was in vaudeville and from there came Broadway plays and movies. Alternating between stock company assignments and civilian jobs during the World War I years, Baxter reportedly made his first film in 1914, though he'd later list *Her Own Money* (1922) as his official screen debut.

As a matinee idol in the silents, Baxter came to prominence as the Cisco Kid in his first talkie, *In Old Arizona* (1929), for which he won a Best Actor Oscar. He went on to star with Myrna Loy as Jackson Durant in *Penthouse* (1933), as Dan Brooks in *Broadway Bill* (1934), and (in what many consider his best role) as Dr. Samuel Mudd, the doctor who treated Lincoln's assassin, in *The Prisoner of Shark Island* (1936). That year his $284,000 income topped the industry. Sporting a dashing mustache and decked out in evening clothes, Baxter cut quite a figure in such films as *To Mary—With Love* (1936) and *Wife, Doctor and Nurse* (1938).

From 1943 to 1949 he starred as Dr. Ordway in ten movies from the popular *Crime Doctor* "B"-picture series at Columbia. He had suffered a nervous breakdown and the shooting schedules were easy on him. One year after completing his final film, *State Penitentiary* (1950), Warner Baxter died of pneumonia as a result of cranial surgery which was intended to relieve his long struggle with arthritis.

Bay City Escort Bureau San Francisco escort bureau acting as a cover for murder and insurance fraud which is investigated by Charlie Chan in *Shadows Over Chinatown* (1946). Run by Craig Winfield (alias Jeff Hay) and Joan Mercer, the escort bureau convinces some of their escorts to marry wealthy older men who then mysteriously die on their honeymoons. The beneficiaries then disappear after the death benefits are paid. Mary Conover once worked at the escort bureau but was frightened and left after Mike Roberts began suggesting that it was possible for her to become a wealthy widow.

Bayne, Gloria Radio actress (portrayed by Janet Shaw in her first of two *Charlie Chan* roles) and roommate of Diane Hall in *The Scarlet Clue* (1945). Bayne tells her boss, radio station manager Ralph Brett, that she knows he stole Diane's car during the time he murdered an enemy agent named Rausch. She tries to blackmail Brett with this information in return for more money and better acting roles.

Before she can tell Charlie Chan anything about Rausch's murderer, Bayne is murdered by Mrs. Marsh after inhaling a gas from a radio actuated gas pellet inside a radio studio stage microphone and then smoking a cigarette, the combination of which produces a deadly poison.

The Bear Went Over the Mountain Children's song sung by Lee Chan while taking a shower in Charlie Chan's hotel room in *Charlie Chan in Shanghai* (1935).

Beaudine, William, Sr. (January 15, 1892, New York, New York–March 18, 1970, Canoga Park, California) Nicknamed "One-Shot," Beaudine was a writer, actor, and director of over 170 movies. He directed four of the six *Charlie Chan* films at Monogram starring Roland Winters.

William Beaudine broke into films in 1909 as a jack-of-all-trades for director D.W. Griffith, and directed his first film in 1915. His best silent film was also one of his least typical, *The Canadian* (1926). Making a successful transition to sound, Beaudine gained a reputation for swiftness and efficiency, earning him the nickname of "One Shot" Beaudine. He accepted an offer to make films in England in 1934, spending three years there.

Upon returning to Hollywood, Beaudine found that he'd been largely forgotten, and was forced to restart his career at the bottom. Beaudine was also once the head of the Directors Guild of America and directed the following television series: *Lassie* (1954), *Broken Arrow* (1956), *Naked City* (1958), and *The Green Hornet* (1966). At the time of his retirement in 1967, William Beaudine was the oldest active director in Hollywood.

Charlie Chan filmography: *The Chinese Ring* (1947), *The Shanghai Chest* (1948), *The Golden Eye* (1948), *The Feathered Serpent* (1948).

Beck, Thomas (December 29, 1909, New York, New York–September 23, 1995, Miami

Thomas Beck (Everett Collection)

Shores, Florida) American actor who often played the role of a young bachelor in four *Charlie Chan* films. Beck portrays Victor Descartes in *Charlie Chan in Paris* (1935), Tom Evans in *Charlie Chan in Egypt* (1935), Bruce Rogers in *Charlie Chan at the Race Track* (1936), and Phil Childers in *Charlie Chan at the Opera* (1936).

Thomas Beck was but one of a legion of pleasant, unassuming young men who were signed to Twentieth Century–Fox contracts in the mid–1930s. In his short film career, Beck also portrayed the village priest opposite Shirley Temple in *Heidi* (1937). He worked to promote the Screen Actors Guild and improve working conditions for actors, and left movie work in 1939 at age 30 after Fox reduced his salary for his political activities with the Guild. Beck successfully pursued a number of business ventures before retiring to Florida in the early 1970s. In 1995 he died of Alzheimer's disease and heart ailments.

Beddoe, Don (July 1, 1891, Pittsburgh, Pennsylvania–January 19, 1991, Woodland Hills, California) American stage and screen character actor (real name: Donald T. Beddoe) who appeared in over 160 films, and who portrayed Frederick Ross in *Charlie Chan's Murder Cruise* (1940).

Don Beddoe was raised in Cincinnati, Ohio, where his father headed the Conservatory of Music. Although he started out in journalism, he took an interest in theater and became involved first with amateur companies and then with professional theater troupes. He debuted on Broadway in 1929 in *Nigger Rich*, which starred Spencer Tracy, and kept up a decade-long career on the stage.

In films, Beddoe appeared in a wide range of supporting roles in literally scores of movies, often as either a fast-talking reporter or as a mousy sort. He became one of the most familiar faces in Hollywood movies, despite remaining almost unknown by name outside the industry. Following service in the Army Air Corps during the Second World War, he continued to work steadily in small roles and as a comedy foil to such Columbia short subject stars as The Three Stooges, Andy Clyde, and Charley Chase. Beddoe also often appeared on television shows such as *Perry Mason*, *Rawhide*, *Gunsmoke*, *Maverick*, and *Bewitched*.

Note: Some sources give birth years of 1888, 1889, and 1903.

Bedell The secretary (portrayed by Perry Ivins in his second of two *Charlie Chan* roles) to Albert Dufresne at the Lamartine Bank in *Charlie Chan in Paris* (1935).

Beetham, Col. John Famed British explorer (portrayed by Warner Baxter) who is an old flame of Eve Mannering in *Behind That Curtain* (1929). Beetham goes to India to do some research in the desert and embarks on a four-month caravan from India to Teheran, Persia (Iran).

***Behind That Curtain* (novel)** The third *Charlie Chan* novel written by Earl Derr Biggers and published by Bobbs-Merrill in 1928. The novel was serialized in *The Saturday Evening Post* from March 31 to May 5,

The cover of an early edition of *Behind That Curtain*, written by Earl Derr Biggers in 1928 (courtesy Don Rogers).

"The desert gives and the desert takes," says Boris Karloff (in his first talkie role) to Warner Baxter in *Behind That Curtain* (Everett Collection).

1928, and was the basis for the 1929 film of the same name. It was later remade as *Charlie Chan's Chance* (1932).

***Behind That Curtain* (1929)** The first *Charlie Chan* film produced by the Fox Film Corporation.

Source: based on the novel *Behind That Curtain* by Earl Derr Biggers (Bobbs-Merrill, 1928), which was serialized in *The Saturday Evening Post* from March 31 to May 5, 1928. Original Copyright: Fox Film Corporation, June 28, 1929; LP506. Copyright Renewed: August 16, 1956; R176233. Release Date: June 28, 1929. Sound: Movietone. Film: b&w; 35mm; 10 reels; 8,320 feet. Running Time: 91 minutes.

Presenter: William Fox. Producer: Irving Cummings. Scenario: Sonya Levien and Clarke Silvernail. Screen Version: George Middleton. Photography: Conrad Wells, Dave Ragin, and Vincent Farrar. Film Editor: Alfred DeGaetano. Settings: William S. Darling. Sound: G.P. Costello. Costumes: Sophie Wachner. Assistant Director: Charles Woolstenhulme.*

Cast

Warner Baxter	*as*	Col. John Beetham
Lois Moran		Eve Mannering
Gilbert Emery		Sir Frederic Bruce
Claude King		Sir George Mannering
Philip Strange		Eric Durand
Boris Karloff		Sudanese servant
Jamiel Hassen		Habib Hannah
Peter Gawthorne		Scotland Yard inspector
John Rogers		Alf Pornick
C. Montague Shaw		Hilary Galt
Finch Smiles		Galt's clerk
Mercedes De Velasco		Nunah
E.L. Park		Charlie Chan

Plot Summary: Eve Mannering, the niece of the wealthy Sir George Mannering, marries Eric Durand, a fortune hunter,

*Unbilled.

against her uncle's wishes. Durand kills Hilary Galt, a lawyer and investigator hired by her uncle to examine Durand's past. Upon discovering the plot after they are married and movie to India, Eve leaves Durand and joins an old family friend, Col. John Beetham, an explorer who is about to begin a four-month desert expedition from India to Persia.

Fearing Beetham will implicate himself in her affairs after Beetham is questioned about the murder by Sir Frederic Bruce of Scotland Yard, Eve flees Persia and comes to San Francisco. Sir Frederic Bruce is attracted to the case by a mysterious pair of Chinese slippers found on the victim's body, a gift from Beetham. His investigation leads to a lecture hall where Beetham is speaking, and there Durand is revealed to be the murderer and is killed evading the law.

Note: *Behind That Curtain* was also released in a silent film version in 1929 and was later remade as *Charlie Chan's Chance* (1932).

"Behind That Curtain Lies the Mystery of the East" Title of Col. John Beetham's talk about his explorations in the Persian Desert given at San Francisco's Cosmopolitan Club in *Behind That Curtain* (1929).

belaying pin A removable wooden or metal pin in the rail of a ship or boat, around which ropes can be fastened. In *Dead Men Tell* (1941), Bill Lydig is about to strike Jimmy Chan over the head with a belaying pin but stops when he catches sight of Gene LaFarge watching.

Belden, Charles S. (April 21, 1904–November 3, 1954, Woodland Hills, California) Screenplay writer of four *Charlie Chan* films at Twentieth Century–Fox, and *Mr. Moto's Gamble* (1938), a reworked version of *Charlie Chan at the Ringside* that was never completed.

Charles Belden was the man responsible for the three-act play *The Mystery of the Wax Museum*, which, though never produced in New York, was memorably filmed twice by Warner Bros., the second time as the 3-D classic *House of Wax* (1953). Most of Belden's time was spent at Warner Bros., contributing additional dialogue for already-completed screenplays. He was also brought in to punch up the script for Universal's *Dracula's Daughter* (1936), adding some welcome comic relief. Belden's other screenwriting credits include several of producer Harry Sherman's *Hopalong Cassidy* westerns.

Charlie Chan filmography: *Charlie Chan at the Opera* (1936), *Charlie Chan on Broadway* (1937), *Charlie Chan at Monte Carlo* (1937), *Charlie Chan in Honolulu* (1938).

Belescu Shady wartime profiteer (portrayed by Noel Madison) and business associate of Petroff in *City in Darkness* (1939). As the middleman who works for a commission, Belescu is supposed to deliver clearance documents to Charlotte Ronnell so that illegal ammunition can be shipped out of France on the ship *Medusa* before war is declared.

When forced at gunpoint by Ronnell to turn over the papers without receiving his payment, Belescu gives Ronnell an envelope with blank papers instead and leaves before Ronnell discovers the deception. However, Ronnell later shoots and kills Belescu.

Bellamy, Madge (June 30, 1900, Hillsboro, Texas–January 24, 1990, Upland, California) American all-purpose actress (real name: Margaret Derden Philpott) who appeared in almost 60 films. Bellamy portrays Becky Fothergill in *Charlie Chan in London* (1934).

Madge Bellamy got her start in theater working with a stock company in Denver. Put under a personal contract by a Broadway producer, she received her big break when she replaced Helen Hayes in the Broadway play *Dear Brutus*. Her success as a stage actress led to her being signed by Fox Pictures.

After appearing in a number of silent films in the early '20s, she was best remembered for her performances as Lorna Doone in *Lorna Doone* (1922) and as Miriam Marsh in *The Iron Horse* (1924). A strong will contrasted with her screen image of innocence and led to disagreements over roles. She had been cast in a number of films each year and was in Fox's first talkie feature as Sally Quail in *Mother Knows Best* (1928). However, her refusal to work in the film *The Trial of Mary Dugan* (1928), which was bought expressly for her, led to her contract with Fox being terminated.

It would be three years until she returned to the screen as Madeleine Short Parkerin in the cult favorite *White Zombie* (1932) with Bela Lugosi, but her career was not going anywhere. For the next few years she appeared in a small number of low budget films, and by 1936 her film career was over. In 1943 she shot her lover, millionaire A. Stanford Murphy, after he jilted her to marry another woman. (The shooting was not fatal, and Madge received a suspended sentence and was placed on probation.)

Benbow, Elmer Portrayed by John Swor, Elmer is a member of Dr. Lofton's around-the-world tour in *Charlie Chan Carries On* (1931).

Benbow, Mrs. Wife (portrayed by Goodee Montgomery) of Elmer Benbow and member of Dr. Lofton's around-the-world tour in *Charlie Chan Carries On* (1931).

Bently, George Mining engineer (portrayed by Morgan Conway) and estranged husband of Jeanne Bently in *Charlie Chan in Reno* (1939).

Bently, Jeanne Bitchy New York socialite (portrayed by Louise Henry in her second of two *Charlie Chan* roles) in *Charlie Chan in Reno* (1939). Bently is staying at the Hotel Sierra in Reno, Nevada, to obtain a divorce from her current husband. In the hotel, she runs into Mary Whitman, also at the hotel for the same reason, and whose husband Bently plans to marry.

Later that evening, Bently is murdered by the hotel's social director, Vivian Wells, but Mary Whitman is accused of the crime. Charlie Chan finds out that in 1936 Jeanne Bently murdered her then-husband, Wayne Russell, and Dr. Ainsley was the attending physician who falsified the death certificate to indicate that Russell died from a heart attack. Since that time Ainsley had been blackmailing Jeanne Bently.

Berkeley Building Building in which Charles Edwards has his magic supplies office (Room 726) in *Black Magic* (1944). It is located across the street from the Chalmont Building, from which Mrs. Justine Bonner, under a hypnotic trance, walks off the roof and falls to her death.

Berlin German capital city and site of the 1936 Olympic Games. Berlin is the location setting for much of *Charlie Chan at the Olympics* (1937).

Best, Bettie Actress who portrays Cole King's variety troupe member Winifred in *The Trap* (1947).

Best, Deannie Actress who portrays Phyllis Powers, Judge Armstrong's secretary, in *The Shanghai Chest* (1948).

Best, Willie (May 27, 1916, Sunflower, Mississippi–February 27, 1962, Hollywood, California) Goggle-eyed black comic actor who appeared in almost 100 films and unfortunately perpetuated the stereotype of the black man who was frightened by his own shadow. Nicknamed Sleep 'n' Eat, Willie Best was known for his roles as a shuffling, illiterate, superstitious porter, stable boy, or chauffeur.

In the *Charlie Chan* films by Monogram, Best portrays Chattanooga Brown (the cousin of Birmingham Brown), who (like Birmingham) is Charlie's chauffeur in *The Red Dragon* (1945) and *Dangerous Money* (1946). Best also appeared in a brief, unbilled role as himself in *The Shanghai Chest* (1948). Besides movies, he also appeared regularly in several television shows such as Stu Erwin's *The Trouble with Father* (1950), *My Little Margie* (1952), and *Waterfront* (1954). *See* photo, page 36.

Beverley, Helen Actress of English- and Yiddish-language films who portrays Norma Ducan (alias Nancy Woods) in *Black Magic*

Years before his appearance as Chattanooga Brown, Willie Best (right) appeared with Bill "Bojangles" Robinson in the Shirley Temple movie *The Littlest Rebel* (1935).

(1944). Beverley was once married to actor Lee J. Cobb.

Big Ben Porter (portrayed by Dudley Dickerson) on the S.S. *Newcastle* in *Dangerous Money* (1946).

Biggers, Earl Derr (1884, Warren, Ohio–April 5, 1933, Pasadena, California) American crime novelist, playwright, and creator of Charlie Chan. Biggers was born to Robert and Emma (née Derr) Biggers and graduated from Harvard in 1907. According to Jon Tuska's *The Detective in Hollywood*, Biggers apparently preferred storytellers like Rudyard Kipling and Richard Harding Davis to the classics.

Biggers' first job was that of writing a humorous column for the *Boston Traveler*, although he did not much care for it and was soon promoted to drama critic. In 1913 he wrote a mystery novel, *The Seven Keys to Baldpate*, published by Bobbs-Merrill, which was so successful it was adapted into a long-running Broadway play by George M. Cohan and became the basis for four films of the same name (1917, 1925, 1929, and 1945). His wife commented that her husband employed no secretaries, notes, or research files, nor did he ever keep copies of his work.

While vacationing in Honolulu in 1919, and wanting to write a mystery novel set there, Biggers read a newspaper article about a case effectively solved by two Honolulu detectives named Chang Apana and Lee Fook. Biggers had never before heard of an Oriental

Novelist Earl Derr Biggers, the creator of Charlie Chan.

detective and was intrigued by the concept, so much so that a character for a book began to form in his mind.

Beginning with the January 24, 1925, issue of *The Saturday Evening Post*, *The House Without a Key* was serialized before the original hardcover publication about Charlie Chan of the Honolulu Police Department made its first appearance and became an instant success. Biggers received letters from readers all over the country who wanted another Charlie Chan story, although he never intended to write a series.

From that point on, Sergeant Chan of Punchbowl Hill traveled the globe solving crimes and fastly becoming a celebrity. These adventures were chronicled in five more books by Biggers: *The Chinese Parrot* (1926), *Behind That Curtain* (1928), *The Black Camel* (1929), *Charlie Chan Carries On* (1930), and *Keeper of the Keys* (1932), all of which were published by Bobbs-Merrill and serialized in *The Saturday Evening Post*.

By the end of the Chan novels, Biggers had promoted Charlie to Inspector Chan of the Honolulu Police. All of Biggers' novels were transformed into films, with the sole exception of *Keeper of the Keys*, which was made into a three-act Broadway play and opened on October 18, 1933, at the Fulton Theatre. One possible reason for why *Keeper of the Keys* never made it to film was that the play closed after only three weeks—the same year Biggers died from a heart attack.

"Biggest Little City in the World" Official slogan of Reno, Nevada, seen in *Charlie Chan in Reno* (1939).

Billings, Sgt. Local Washington, D.C., policeman in *Charlie Chan in the Secret Service* (1944). Billings is an old friend of Charlie Chan from Hawaii and the U.S. Marines. When George Melton is found dead, Billings is part of the police detail that stands guard outside the house with orders to keep unauthorized persons outside.

Bixby, Professor Alias used by Fred Rhadini disguised as a bearded Berkeley psychology professor to gain entrance to Dr. Zodiac's mansion in *Charlie Chan at Treasure Island* (1939).

Black, Capt. Commander of the S.S. *Newcastle* (portrayed by Joseph Crehan in his second of two *Charlie Chan* roles) in *Dangerous Money* (1946).

Black, Samuel Bank guard at the Sixth National Bank who is the third bank employee to be murdered with cobra venom in *The Shanghai Cobra* (1945). Paula Webb, another bank employee, notices Black talking with H.R. Jarvis and she begins to follow Black to Joe's Coffee Shop. The cobra venom is on a pin that appears when Black pushes the coin return button on the coffee shop jukebox after it fails to play the song he requested ("The Blue Danube").

***The Black Camel* (novel)** The fourth *Charlie Chan* novel written by Earl Derr Biggers and published by Bobbs-Merrill in 1929. The novel was serialized in *The Saturday Evening Post* from May 18 to June 22, 1929, and was the basis for the 1931 film of the same name, which was unofficially remade as *Charlie Chan in Rio* (1940). *See* photo, page 38.

The cover of an early edition of *The Black Camel*, written by Earl Derr Biggers in 1929 (courtesy Don Rogers).

***The Black Camel* (1931)** The third *Charlie Chan* film produced by the Fox Film Corporation.

Source: based on the novel *The Black Camel* by Earl Derr Biggers (Bobbs-Merrill, 1929), which was serialized in *The Saturday Evening Post* from May 18 to June 22, 1929. Original Copyright: Fox Film Corporation, May 7, 1931; LP2301. Copyright Renewed: June 4, 1958; R215878. Passed by the National Board of Review. Production: mid–April to early May, 1931. Release Date: June 7, 1931. Sound: Western Electric System. Film: b&w; 8 reels; 6,560 feet. Running Time: 67 or 71 minutes.

Presenter: William Fox.* Associate Producer: William Sistrom. Director: Hamilton MacFadden. Assistant Director: Sam Wurtzel. Screenplay and Dialogue: Barry Conners, and Philip Klein. Adaptation: Hugh Strange. Contract Writer: Dudley Nichols.* Cameramen: Joe August and Dan Clark. Settings: Ben Carré. Film Editor: Al DeGaetano.* Costumes: Dolly Tree.* Sound Engineer: W.W. Lindsay, Jr. Business Manager: W.F. Fitzgerald.*

Cast

Warner Oland	*as*	Charlie Chan
Sally Eilers		Julie O'Neil
Bela Lugosi		Tarneverro [alias for Arthur Mayo]
Dorothy Revier		Shelah Fane
Victor Varconi		Robert Fyfe
Murray Kinnell		Smith
William Post		Alan Jaynes
Robert Young		Jimmy Bradshaw
Violet Dunn		Anna [alias for Mrs. Denny Mayo]
J. M. Kerrigan		Thomas MacMasters
Mary Gordon		Mrs. MacMasters
Rita Rozelle		Luana
Otto Yamaoka		Kashimo
Dwight Frye		Jessop
Richard Tucker		Wilkie Ballou
Marjorie White		Rita Ballou
C. Henry Gordon		Van Horn
Robert Homans*		Chief of Police
Louise Mackintosh*		Housekeeper
Hamilton MacFadden*		Movie director

Plot Summary: Motion picture star Shelah Fane is filming a movie in Honolulu. She consults the mystic Tarneverro, her spiritual advisor, to decide if she should marry Alan Jaynes, a wealthy globetrotter she met on the boat to Hawaii. During a crystal ball session, Shelah confesses that three years earlier she fell in love with her co-star, Denny Mayo, and that she was in his house the night he was murdered. Agitated after the consultation, Shelah tells Julie O'Neil, her protégé, that she cannot now marry Alan.

Anna, Shelah's maid, brings Shelah some orchids from stage actor Robert Fyfe (who is appearing in town) but is greatly upset when she sees Shelah tearing up a photograph of Denny Mayo. That evening, just before a

**Unbilled.*

dinner party Shelah is giving, Julie and Jimmy Bradshaw (a tourist bureau employee who wants to marry Julie) find Shelah stabbed to death in her pavilion. Julie then has Jimmy Bradshaw remove Shelah's emerald ring from her finger.

During his investigation, Inspector Charlie Chan of the Honolulu police finds the orchids crushed next to Shelah's body, with their pin missing. After Chan's blundering assistant Kashimo finds the ripped photograph of Mayo, both Tarneverro and Julie hide pieces of it. When Kashimo brings in a beach bum who calls himself Smith and whose shoes match the footprints found outside the pavilion, Fyfe, Shelah's ex-husband, then confesses that he killed her. However, Chan deduces that Fyfe could not have been at the pavilion when the murder took place. Needing money, Smith, who is an artist, threatens Fyfe that he will tell what he overheard Shelah say in the pavilion unless Fyfe buys one of his paintings. After Fyfe gives him $100 and promises to pay $200 more, an unseen assailant (Jessop) shoots Smith on the beach.

At Jimmy Bradshaw's urging, Julie confesses to Chan that she took the emerald ring because it contains an inscription from Mayo. She says that Shelah had wanted to keep their relationship a secret. Chan learns from an Australian couple, the MacMasters, that Tarneverro is really Denny Mayo's brother, Arthur.

Before Smith dies from his gunshot wound, he tells Chan that he heard Shelah tell Fyfe that she confessed to Tarnevarro that she killed Denny Mayo. Robert Fyfe confirms this and says that after Shelah had found out that Mayo had a wife in England, she shot him during a quarrel. Fyfe says he confessed to her murder only because he loved her and wanted to protect her memory. Smith also reveals that he took a diamond pin from the pavilion, which Chan notices has a part missing.

Chan later searches Shelah Fane's house and finds a scratch mark on the floor under the dinner table that he believes was made by the shoe in which the missing piece of the pin is probably still lodged, and that Shelah's murderer must have sat in the chair nearest the scratch mark. Chan has the suspects sit where they sat the previous night. Tarneverro sits in the chair next to the scratch, but Chan learns that later the previous night, the maid Anna sat in the same chair.

Chan looks at her shoe and finds the piece of the diamond pin in the shoe's heel. Anna then reveals that she is really Mrs. Denny Mayo and admits to killing Shelah. Tarneverro confesses that he came to Hollywood to find his brother's murderer, and that when Shelah confessed to him, he told Anna. As Chan goes to arrest Anna, Jessop, the butler (who loves Anna) pulls a gun. After a brief struggle, Chan disarms him. Jessop then admits he shot Smith because he knew too much.

Notes: The novel *The Black Camel* was originally published serially in *The Saturday Evening Post* from May 18 to June 22, 1929. Of the entire *Charlie Chan* series, *The Black Camel* was the only film to be shot entirely on location in Honolulu, and was the first of three films directed by Hamilton MacFadden. *The Black Camel* was unofficially remade as *Charlie Chan in Rio* (1940), which coincidentally had MacFadden in a minor acting role.

Black Hook Nickname for Matthew Nodbury (the pirate grandfather of Miss Patience Nodbury), who was hanged for piracy and murder in *Dead Men Tell* (1941). Miss Nodbury claims that Black Hook drew a map to show the location of a $60 million treasure buried on Cocos Island.

Nodbury tells Charlie Chan that Black Hook had a peg leg and a hook, and relates the legend of how the ghost of Black Hook appears to each of the Nodburys as they are about to die. After Miss Nodbury retires to her cabin, Jed Thomasson masquerades as Black Hook. Nodbury then hears the tap of a peg leg and the scratching of a hook on her door. When she opens the door and sees what she believes to be the ghost of Black Hook, Nodbury, having a weak heart, dies of a heart attack and the impostor takes her piece of the map.

***Black Magic* (1944)** The third *Charlie Chan* film produced by Monogram Pictures Corporation.

Alternate Titles: *Charlie Chan in Black Magic*; *Charlie Chan: Meeting at Midnight*; and *Meeting at Midnight* (reissued by Associated Artists, Ltd.). Working Titles: *Murder Chamber* and *Charlie Chan in the Murder Chamber*. Source: based on the character "Charlie Chan" created by Earl Derr Biggers. Original Copyright: Monogram Pictures Corporation, July 15, 1944; LP12737. Copyright Renewed: June 16, 1972; R530967. Production: May 3 to mid–May, 1944. Release Date: September 9, 1944. Sound: Western Electric Mirrophonic Recording. Film: b&w; 5,822 feet. Running Time: 64–65 minutes.

Producers: Philip N. Krasne and James S. Burkett. Director: Phil Rosen. Assistant Director: Bobby Ray. Original Screenplay: George Callahan. Director of Photography: Arthur Martinelli. Art Director: Dave Milton. Film Editor: John Link. Set Decorations: Al Greenwood. Musical Director: David Chudnow. Musical Score: Alexander Laszlo. Sound Recording: Max Hutchinson. Production Manager: Dick L'Estrange. Camera Operator: Dave Smith.* Assistant: Monty Steadman.* Still Photography: Earl Crowley.* Special Effects: M.B. Kinne.* Wardrobe: Harry Bourne.* Script Girl: Marie Messinger.* Props: Sammy Gordon* and Ralph Martin.* Grips: Lew Dow* and George Booker.* Gaffer: Joe Wharton.*

Cast

Sidney Toler	*as*	Charlie Chan
Mantan Moreland		Birmingham Brown
Frances Chan		Frances Chan
Joseph Crehan		Inspector Matthews
Helen Beverley		Norma Duncan [alias Nancy Woods]
Jacqueline deWitt		Justine Bonner
Geraldine Wall		Harriet Green
Ralph Peters		Officer Rafferty
Frank Jaquet		Paul Hamlin [a.k.a. Chardo]
Edward Earle		Dawson
Claudia Dell		Vera Starkey
Harry Depp		Charles Edwards
Charles Jordan		Tom Starkey
Dick Gordon		William Bonner

**Unbilled.*

Plot Summary: While holding a séance at his home, phony psychic William Bonner asks for questions from those present. After an unknown voice asks what happened in London on October fifth, 1935, the lights are extinguished and Bonner is found murdered.

Bonner's wife Justine summons Inspector Matthews of the homicide bureau, and he orders all those present at the Bonner house to headquarters for questioning. The suspects at the séance are Justine Bonner, Harriett Green, Paul Hamlin, Charles Edwards, Nancy Woods, newly hired butler Birmingham Brown, and Charlie Chan's daughter, Frances Chan. When the coroner notifies Inspector Matthews that the bullet has disappeared from Bonner's body, Matthews then forces Charlie Chan into joining the investigation by threatening to hold his daughter in jail as a suspect.

After studying the interviews with the suspects, Chan asks to speak to Nancy Woods and informs Matthews that she is using an alias because the monogram on her purse reads "ND" and her real name is Norma Duncan. Confronted with her lie, Norma claims that she used the alias to infiltrate Bonner's séance and prove that Bonner drove her father to commit suicide.

At the Bonner house, Justine Bonner communicates to séance assistants Tom and Vera Starkey through an intercom linked to their hidden room. When Frances, who has come to visit Birmingham Brown at the Bonner house, overhears the conversation, she alerts her father. Hurrying to the house, Chan discovers the secret room hidden behind a cabinet in the séance parlor. The subjects are reassembled at police headquarters and Chan reveals that Mr. Hamlin and Mrs. Green were both being blackmailed by Bonner, and that Mrs. Bonner had threatened to kill her husband because of his infidelity. Chan then asks if anyone can identify who asked the mysterious question about London, to which no one replies.

Later, Norma Duncan sends Chan a message to come to her hotel, but when Chan enters her room, he finds her in a trance. Just then, the lights go out, a gun is fired, and the assailant runs out the door. Awakened from her trance, Norma is unable to remember what happened to her. Puzzled, Chan sends a cable to Scotland Yard. Later, at the Bonner house, Frances and Birmingham again overhear Mrs. Bonner asking the unseen séance assistants, Tom and Vera, for their help, and Frances decides to follow Mrs. Bonner when she leaves the house.

Following Mrs. Bonner to the Berkeley building, Frances meets her father and Inspector Matthews there and finds Mrs. Bonner's glove outside a closed door. Mrs. Bonner, now in a trance, ascends to the rooftop of a building across the street where a voice coaxes her to jump from the ledge. After she plunges to her death, Chan notices a peculiar stain on her coat and takes it to the police lab for analysis. The coroner identifies the substance as manasterol, a powerful mind-control drug that renders its victims helpless. He then gives Chan several pills that contain the antidote to the drug.

Announcing that Mrs. Bonner committed suicide out of remorse for murdering her husband, Matthews declares the case closed. However, Chan rejects Matthews' conclusion and returns to search the office room in front of which Mrs. Bonner's glove was found. There Chan is slugged from behind, manacled, and hypnotized by an unseen assailant who orders him to climb to the roof and jump. After swallowing one of the antidote pills, Chan proceeds to the same roof as Mrs. Bonner.

Meanwhile Frances is concerned when she is unable to locate her father and notifies Inspector Matthews' assistant, Officer Rafferty. Together they hurry to the Berkeley building and trace Chan to the roof. As Chan totters unsteadily on the ledge, the antidote begins to work and he comes out of his trance just as Frances and Rafferty appear. When Rafferty hands Chan the response from his telegram request to Scotland Yard, Chan reconvenes a séance at the Bonner house.

That night, Chan exposes Tom and Vera Starkey in their secret room and then challenges the séance participants to answer a series of word association questions. Charlie asks the fateful question about October fifth, 1935, the lights go out, and a gunshot is fired. Turning the lights back on, Chan produces a cable from Scotland Yard telling that on October fifth, 1935, Chardo, a famous magician, was gravely injured in a car accident. Chan relates that Chardo's wife, Justine, had just run away with his assistant, William Bonner. After undergoing plastic surgery to alter his appearance, Chardo determined to make Justine and Bonner pay for their betrayal. Chan then extracts from his chair a bullet made from frozen blood, thus explaining the disappearing bullet that killed Bonner. Addressing Paul Hamlin as Chardo, Chan then seizes the cigar case in which is hidden the spring gun used to kill Bonner.

Note: Michael R. Pitts, in *Famous Movie Detectives*, states that *Black Magic* is the only entry of the *Charlie Chan* series that is in the public domain, being sold to collectors under the reissued title *Meeting at Midnight*. The Bonner house used for the séances is the same one previously seen in Monogram's *The Invisible Ghost* (1941), starring Bela Lugosi.

Blackmer, Sidney (July 13, 1896–October 5, 1973, New York, New York) Suave American stage and screen actor who appeared in over 200 silent and sound films, sometimes also credited as Sydney Blackmer. He portrays industrialist Victor Karnoff in *Charlie Chan at Monte Carlo* (1937).

Sidney Blackmer had planned to study law at the University of North Carolina, but football and amateur theatricals held more interest for him. Heading east to make his fortune as an actor, Blackmer accepted day work at various film studios in Fort Lee, New Jersey, reportedly appearing in the pioneering Pearl White serial *The Perils of Pauline* (1914).

After making his Broadway bow in 1917, Blackmer served as a lieutenant in World War I. His star-making stage role was the title character in *The Mountain Man* (1921). Eager to have a go at all branches of entertainment,

Sidney Blackmer (Everett Collection)

Blackmer sang on radio in the 1920s and participated in the first experimental dramatic presentations of the Allen B. DuMont television series.

In films, Blackmer was usually cast as a smooth society villain, such as the "Big Boy" in *Little Caesar* (1931). He also appeared in both sinister and sympathetic roles in a handful of Shirley Temple pictures. Blackmer is perhaps best remembered for his portrayals of President Theodore Roosevelt in over a dozen films, including *This Is My Affair* (1937) and *My Girl Tisa* (1948). In 1950 Blackmer won the Tony Award for his portrayal of the drink-sodden "Doc" in the William Inge play *Come Back, Little Sheba.* For several years, Blackmer served as the national vice president of the Muscular Dystrophy Association.

Blake, David Political economist (portrayed by Barry Bernard) who works for the Department of Political Economy in *Charlie Chan in the Secret Service* (1944). Charlie Chan remarks to Blake that the morning's newspaper wrote that what David Blake doesn't know about economics would fill many books.

Blake, Don Co-pilot of Flight 17 (portrayed by Joel Marston) in *The Sky Dragon* (1949). Listening outside Wanda LaFern's dressing room door in the Gayety Theatre, Blake overhears Wanda LaFern and Marie Burke (a.k.a. Connie Jackson) talking, and discovers the true facts about their past and the theft of $250,000 aboard the plane. When Wanda leaves her dressing room for her number on stage, Blake enters the dressing room and confronts Connie. He is then knocked unconscious by John Anderson and suffers multiple fractures of the skull. He later dies in a hospital without regaining consciousness.

Blake, Hal The head animal trainer for the Kinney & Gaines Combined Circus (portrayed by Tom McGuire) in *Charlie Chan at the Circus* (1936). Blake is romantically involved with trapeze artist Louise Norman and often does not get along with the circus' co-owner, Joe Kinney.

Blake, Larry J. (c. 1914–May 25, 1982, Los Angeles, California) Character actor who appeared in 50 films and portrays press agent Rick Daniels for Cole King's variety troupe in *The Trap* (1947).

Blake, Oliver (April 4, 1905, Centralia, Illinois–February 12, 1992, California) Lanky, long-nosed, stage and screen character actor (real name: Oliver Prickett) who appeared in over 45 films. Blake portrays Hank (Wigley) who owns the Mojave Wells Hotel in *Castle in the Desert* (1942).

Oliver Blake acted on stage under his given name of Oliver Prickett. From the mid-1920s onward, Blake was a fixture at the Pasadena Playhouse, where his brother Charles was managing director and his sister Maudie was a resident character actress. At the Playhouse he starred in such productions as *Charley's Aunt*, and also taught classes for first-year students.

He entered films in 1941 and was confined to bit roles. One of his more visible screen assignments was as dour-faced Indian neighbor Geoduck in Universal's *Ma and Pa Kettle* series. An apparent favorite of comedian

Bob Hope, Blake showed up in a variety of roles in several Hope farces, notably as the world's most emaciated Santa Claus in *The Seven Little Foys* (1955). On television Oliver Blake played the recurring role of Carl Dorf in the 1956 sitcom *The Brothers.*

Blandick, Clara (June 4, 1881, on an American ship, Hong Kong–April 15, 1962, Hollywood, California) Character actress who appeared in almost 120 films and portrays Minerva Winterslip in *Charlie Chan's Greatest Case* (1933). Blandick is best remembered for her portrayal of Dorothy's Aunt Em in *The Wizard of Oz* (1939). Suffering from severe arthritis and impending blindness, she one day fixed her hair, dressed up in her best outfit, placed her favorite photos and memorabilia around her room, and committed suicide by overdosing on sleeping tablets.

Blane, Sally (July 11, 1910, Salida, Colorado–August 27, 1997, Palm Springs, California) American actress (real name: Elizabeth Jane Young) who appeared in nearly 70 silent and sound films and portrays Stella Essex in *Charlie Chan at Treasure Island* (1939).

Throughout her career, Sally Blane would be better remembered as the older sister of film star Loretta Young. She not only looked just like Loretta (with lighter hair) but she also tended to play the same type of roles. Her two other sisters, Polly Ann and Georgiana, were also actresses. When her parents separated, her mother took the children to live with her married sister in Hollywood. The four Young children were quite photogenic and had no trouble securing $3.50 per day in the movies as extras. After convent school, Elizabeth Jane resumed her film work under the studio-imposed name of Sally Blane and appeared as leading lady in *The Collegians*, a series of youth-oriented two-reel comedies.

In 1929 Sally and sister Loretta were among the "WAMPAS Baby Stars," a group of promising young actresses promoted for publicity purposes by the Western Association of Motion Picture Advertisers. Loretta was dedicated to becoming a full-fledged star, but Sally lost interest in pursuing fame early on, settling instead for the life of a freelance working actress. Occasionally she'd obtain the lead in an upper-echelon picture like *Advice for the Lovelorn* (1933) or *The Silver Streak* (1934). For the most part however, Sally Blane was content to appear in less demanding low-budget westerns and crime melodramas.

In 1935 Blane married actor-director Norman Foster, who directed three *Charlie Chan* films, including *Charlie Chan at Treasure Island* (1939) featuring Blane. She then virtually retired to raise a family. In 1939 Loretta Young insisted that all her sisters appear as her fictional sisters in *The Story of Alexander Graham Bell*, which was the only time Sally co-starred with her three sisters.

Bleifer, John (July 26, 1901, Zawiercie, Poland–January 24, 1992) Actor who appeared in over 40 films, often seen as sinister European types in the pre-war films of Twentieth Century–Fox. Bleifer portrays Ludwig, Victor Karnoff's murdered chauffeur, in *Charlie Chan at Monte Carlo* (1937). During the war, Bleifer alternated between playing fascist villains and hapless refugees. Active until the early 1980s, Bleifer portrayed Ben-Dan in *QB VII* (1974) and a rabbi in *The Frisco Kid* (1979).

Bliss, Capt. Eldorado policeman (portrayed by Wade Boteler in his first of two *Charlie Chan* roles) in *Charlie Chan's Courage* (1934). Bliss and Constable Brackett are called in to investigate the murder of Louie Wong.

Note: Capt. Bliss is mentioned in Earl Derr Biggers' novel *The Chinese Parrot*, which served as the basis for *Charlie Chan's Courage* (1934). However, the film credits of *The Chinese Parrot* (1927), as given in the *American Film Institute Catalog of Motion Pictures Produced in the United States*, do not list the character.

bloody heelprint When Brett murders Rausch in *The Scarlet Clue* (1945) he accidentally steps in some blood, leaving a heelprint at the murder site which is noticed by

Charlie Chan. Chan sees another bloody heelprint when at the Cosmo Radio Center and concludes that "Killer is someone who walk here recently. Perhaps someone we all see."

"The Blue Danube" Number 10 song requested by Samuel Black from the jukebox in Joe's Coffee Shop in *The Shanghai Cobra* (1945). When a different song plays instead, Black tells Lorraine, the voice from the jukebox, that the song is not what he requested. Lorraine then tells Black to push the coin return button and his money will be refunded. When he does so, he is stuck by a protruding pin covered with cobra venom, which kills him minutes later on the street.

Blystone, Jasper (1900–September 25, 1965, Hollywood, California) Assistant director of nearly 15 films, including three *Charlie Chan* entries at Twentieth Century–Fox: *Charlie Chan at the Olympics* (1937), *Charlie Chan in Reno* (1939),* and *Charlie Chan at the Wax Museum* (1940).*

Blystone, John G. (December 2, 1892, Rice Lake, Wisconsin–August 6, 1938, Beverly Hills, California) Writer and director of over 50 silent and sound films. Blystone was the director for *Charlie Chan's Chance* (1932).

After graduating from the University of Wisconsin, John Blystone tried his luck as an actor but turned to writing and directing. One of his first films as director was Buster Keaton's *Our Hospitality* (1923), even though Keaton probably did most of the directing himself. Through his working relationship with western star Tom Mix, Blystone earned a lucrative contract at Fox Studios.

Unobtrusive and easygoing, Blystone worked best with actors and screenwriters who tended to dominate their productions. Keaton and comedian Will Rogers both appreciated Blystone's willingness not to get in their way. Even Laurel and Hardy had Blystone direct two of their features, *Swiss Miss* (1938) and *Block-Heads* (1938), with the understanding that Blystone would merely yell "action" and "cut" and then leave the two comedians on their own.

Less than a month after completing *Block-Heads*, the 45-year-old Blystone died of a heart attack. Blystone was the brother of both character actor Stanley Blystone, who appeared in four *Charlie Chan* films, and Jasper Blystone, who was the assistant director for three *Charlie Chan* films.

*Unbilled.

Blystone, Stanley (August 1, 1894, Rice Lake, Wisconsin–July 16, 1956, Hollywood, California) Good-looking character actor (real name: William Stanley Blystone) who appeared in over 170 films, often as a policeman or in villainous roles. In four unbilled *Charlie Chan* roles, Blystone portrays a policeman in both *Charlie Chan at the Olympics* (1937) and *Charlie Chan in Reno* (1939), a court bailiff in *Charlie Chan at the Wax Museum* (1940), and a fingerprint technician in *Murder Over New York* (1940). Blystone was the brother of director John G. Blystone and assistant director Jasper Blystone.

Entering films in 1915, the burly, muscular, mustachioed Blystone excelled in curt, villainous roles, such as the crooked ringmaster in Tom Mix's *The Circus Ace* (1927). In the talkie era, Blystone was busiest doing two-reel comedies at RKO, Columbia, and the Hal Roach studios, often cast as brutish authority figures at odds with the comedy leads. In the Three Stooges' *Half Shot Shooters* (1936), he plays the sadistic Sgt. McGillicuddy. Blystone was en route to Desilu Studios to play a small role on the television series *Wyatt Earp* when he collapsed on the sidewalk and died of heart failure.

Blythe, Betty (September 1, 1893, Los Angeles, California–April 7, 1972, Woodland Hills, California) Supporting actress (real name: Elizabeth Blythe Slaughter) who appeared in nearly 95 silent and sound films and portrays Mrs. Manning in *The Chinese Cat* (1944).

Formerly an art student at USC, Betty

Blythe began as a stage actress. After touring Europe and the States, she entered films in 1917. Blythe was then brought to Hollywood's Fox Studios as a replacement for screen vamp Theda Bara. As famous for her revealing costumes as for her dramatic skills, Blythe became a star in such exotic silent films as *The Queen of Sheba* (1921) and *She* (1925). Although her stage training helped her in the transition to talkies, her facial features had matured rather rapidly, and she was soon given only supporting roles.

Betty Blythe spent most of the 1940s in touring companies of Broadway hits like *The Man Who Came to Dinner* and *Wallflower*, and supplemented her income by giving acting and diction lessons. Blythe's final screen appearance was an unbilled one-line bit in the "Embassy Ball" sequence in *My Fair Lady* (1964), in which she was photographed by her favorite cameraman from the silent days, Harry Stradling.

Boggs, Robert One of George Kirby's two butlers (portrayed by Leyland Hodgson) in *Murder Over New York* (1940). Boggs was once arrested in England some years ago for a crime he did not commit. Hugh Drake thinks he recognizes him and sends a request to Scotland Yard for further information. When a cablegram does arrive after Drake's murder, Jimmy Chan sees Boggs in the kitchen steaming open the envelope, fearing the exposure of his previous arrest would make him the prime suspect for Drake's murder.

Bogotá Capital city of Colombia. In *City in Darkness* (1939), Charlie Chan sees Tony Madero's fake passport identifying him as Antonio Castillo from Bogotá. Sensing that the Castillo identity is a phony, Chan remarks that he had once been in Bogotá and liked the view of the river from the mountain. He then asks the bogus Castillo the name of the river, to which Castillo replies, "The Colombia River." Chan then exposes Castillo as a fraud as Bogotá is an inland city and has no river.

Bolton, Mary Newspaper reporter for *The Daily Record* (portrayed by Marguerite Chapman) who helps persuade Charlie Chan to appear on Dr. Cream's weekly *The Crime League* radio broadcast in *Charlie Chan at the Wax Museum* (1940).

Boltz, Raymond, Jr. Set designer for four *Charlie Chan* films at Monogram: *The Trap* (1947), *The Shanghai Chest* (1948),* *The Golden Eye* (1948),* and *The Sky Dragon* (1949).*

Bon Ton Burlesque Company Burlesque company in which Grace Gortner performed as a chorus girl and was romantically attracted to its manager, Craig Winfield, in *Shadows Over Chinatown* (1946).

Bonanova, Fortunio (January 13, 1893, Palma de Mallorca, Spain–April 2, 1969, Woodland Hills, California) Dashing former opera singer, impresario, and stage and screen actor who appeared in over 70 films. Bonanova portrays Inspector Luis Carvero in *The Red Dragon* (1945).

A law student at the University of Madrid, Bonanova switched his major to music and attended Madrid's Real Conservatory and the Paris Conservatory. He inaugurated his operatic career as a baritone at the age of 17. By age 21 he was in films, producing, directing and starring in a silent production of *Don Juan* (1921). He spent most of the 1920s singing at the Paris opera and writing books, plays, and short stories. He arrived in America in 1930 to co-star with Katherine Cornell on Broadway. At the invitation of his friend Orson Welles, Bonanova portrayed the feverish singing teacher, Signor Matisti, in Welles' *Citizen Kane* (1941).

Bonner, Justine Jealous wife (portrayed by Jacqueline deWitt) of William Bonner and partner in a phony séance and psychic business in *Black Magic* (1944). When in London years ago Justine Bonner was an assistant to the magician Chardo the Great. She ran off

**Unbilled.*

with William Bonner, Chardo's assistant, and married him.

Mrs. Bonner is jealous of Harriet Green, with whom her husband is having an affair. She is murdered by her ex-husband (as Paul Hamlin) when he has her walk off the roof of a building while in a hypnotic trance under his control.

Bonner, William Phony psychic and medium (portrayed by Dick Gordon) who holds séances in *Black Magic* (1944). During one séance, Bonner is startled by an unfamiliar voice who repeatedly asks the question, "What happened in London the night of October fifth, 1935?" When a scream is heard and the lights come on, Bonner is found dead, killed by a bullet that entered his heart but didn't pass through his body and can't be found. Furthermore, the bullet is shot by a gun no one heard and no one has found. Bonner was once an assistant to a magician named Chardo the Great when in London years ago. There he ran off with Chardo's wife Justine, and they were later married.

Bonney, Dr. Anne Psychoanalyst (portrayed by Lenita Lane in her first of two *Charlie Chan* roles) who is treating Gene LaFarge for his anxiety in *Dead Men Tell* (1941).

"Bopsy loves Toots" Inscription on the inside of a gold wedding band belonging to a member of the audience during Fred Rhadini's magic act in *Charlie Chan at Treasure Island* (1939). Rhadini hosts a party in honor of San Francisco's Golden Gate International Exposition, and Eve Cairo, who is Rhadini's mind-reading assistant, is able to read Rhadini's mind as he holds the ring.

Borden, Eugene (March 21, 1897, Paris, France–July 21, 1972, California) Character actor of stage and screen who appeared in almost 70 films, often as unbilled headwaiters, porters, pursers, and coachmen. In four *Charlie Chan* roles at Twentieth Century-Fox: Borden portrays Johnny Burke's henchman, Louis, in *Charlie Chan on Broadway* (1937); a hotel clerk (unbilled) in *Charlie Chan at Monte Carlo* (1937); a French gendarme in *City in Darkness* (1939); and night club host Armando in *Charlie Chan in Rio* (1941).

Borgia, Cesare (September, 1475–March 12, 1507) The illegitimate son of Rodrigo Cardinal Borgia, who later became Pope Alexander VI. Cesare Borgia was perhaps the most ruthless prince of the Italian Renaissance and was the apparent model for Niccolò Machiavelli's *The Prince*.

Created a cardinal by his father in 1493, Cesare had a younger sister, Lucrezia, and he renounced his ecclesiastical career in 1498. With the death of Alexander VI in 1503, Cesare was imprisoned by the new pope, Julius II. He later escaped to Spain where he fought for the royal house of Navarre, into which he had married, until he was killed in a skirmish near Viana, Spain.

In *Castle in the Desert* (1942), the 15th century Cesare Borgia is the subject of Paul Manderley's book. Manderley wants to live and think like him. A modern-day Cesare Borgia arrives (using the alias Watson King) who possesses many similarities to his Renaissance namesake. He is Lucy Manderley's (née Princess Lucrezia della Borgia) long lost younger stepbrother, who was once acquitted on a charge of poisoning someone, was reportedly killed many years ago in the Spanish War, but is still alive.

Lucy shows Charlie Chan an old photograph of her and Cesare, who has a noticeable scar on the left side of his forehead. However, Mme. Saturnia says that he is alive, which is confirmed by Brenda Hartford who says that Cesare wrote to her husband a month ago asking for money. *See also* **King, Watson**.

Borgia, Lucrezia (April 18, 1480–June 24, 1519) The younger sister of Prince Cesare Borgia and illegitimate daughter of Rodrigo Cardinal Borgia, who later became Pope Alexander VI. For political reasons, Lucrezia's father arranged three marriages for her, and she was renowned as a master of political intrigue as well as a patron of the arts. Rumors of her participation in her family's poison plots have never been proved.

In *Castle in the Desert* (1942), Lucy Manderley, who is married to the wealthy and reclusive historian Paul Manderley, is also Princess Lucrezia della Borgia. Having some similarities to the Renaissance namesake, Lucy is the older stepsister of Cesare Borgia, who she was told was killed many years ago in the Spanish War but is still alive. *See also* **Manderley, Lucy**.

Bosworth, Hobart (August 11, 1867, Marietta, Ohio–December 30, 1943, Glendale, California) American character actor, director, screenwriter, and producer (real name: Hobart Van Zandt Bosworth) of nearly 160 silent and sound films, who portrays the dual roles of Philip J. Madden and his impersonator, Jerry Delaney, in *The Chinese Parrot* (1927).

Hobart Bosworth ran away to sea at age 12, taking up acting six years later. He made several starring appearances on Broadway before being forced to quit acting after temporarily losing his voice. His film career began with a starring role in the Selig Company's *The Power of the Sultan* (1907), thought to be the first dramatic film to have been shot on the West Coast. Bosworth went on to act, direct, produce, and/or write many more Selig one-reelers.

He formed his own production company in 1913 when he directed and starred (as Wolf Larsen) in the ambitious seven-reel feature film *The Sea Wolf* (1913). He spent more than a decade as a leading Hollywood star, then began taking supporting roles in the 1920s, often playing heavies. His career continued successfully into the sound era and he remained on-screen up to his death in 1943.

Boteler, Wade (October 3, 1891, Santa Ana, California–May 7, 1943, Hollywood, California) Stocky stage and screen character actor who appeared in over 250 silent and sound films, often as a policeman. In two *Charlie Chan* roles, Boteler portrays Capt. Bliss in *Charlie Chan's Courage* (1934) and Lt. Macy in *Charlie Chan at the Circus* (1936).

Wade Boteler was in practically every "B" western made between 1930 and 1935, often cast as a hard-hearted sheriff or crooked land baron. Affecting an Irish brogue, Boteler was also in demand for policeman roles, notably as Inspector Queen in the *Ellery Queen* film, *The Mandarin Mystery* (1936).

Bourbon Street Garage New Orleans garage near St. Louis Street holding the stolen car of Simon Lafontaine in *Docks of New Orleans* (1948).

On orders of Pereaux, Grock attempts to kidnap Simon Lafontaine in front of Charlie Chan's house after he seeks Chan's help. Grock poses as Lafontaine's driver, but when Tommy and Birmingham find the real driver unconscious, Grock speeds away before he can be stopped and caught. Grock later parks the stolen car in the Bourbon Street Garage, whose attendant, "Mobile" Jones, is a friend of Birmingham's and to whom Birmingham owes money.

Bowan, Professor Spiritualist advisor (portrayed by Arthur Edmund Carewe) to Henrietta Lowell in *Charlie Chan's Secret* (1936). With his assistant Carlotta as a medium, Bowan conducts séances at Colby House to enable Henrietta Lowell, a devout believer in psychic phenomena, to be in contact with her dead brother Bernard Colby, whose spirit acts as a "guide" to the world beyond and delivers information about the missing Allen Colby.

When the face of a very dead Allen Colby appears during the séance, Charlie Chan's investigation reveals that much of what transpires at the séance is a result of trickery. Henrietta Lowell then instructs her lawyer to remove Bowan and Carlotta from her will, denying them a $100,000 endowment they were to receive upon her death to continue their psychic research. Also as a result of the trickery, the police now suspect Bowan and Carlotta of murdering Allen Colby.

bowienite Poison placed by Emil Manolo in R.J. Godley's cigarettes in *Charlie Chan in Panama* (1940).

Boyd, Mildred Black actress who portrays Marguerite Fontan's maid, Josephine, in *The Red Dragon* (1945).

Boyle, Walden Actor who plays the unbilled role of George "Doc" Brandt in *The Trap* (1947).

BP-41 Control identification number used by the Berlin police in *Charlie Chan at the Olympics* (1937). Charlie Chan places a "homing pigeon" transmitter inside a look-alike remote control box for an airplane guidance system to locate where his kidnapped son Lee is being held. The Berlin police use direction-finding equipment to determine the transmitter's precise location. Three cars report their direction finder's readings as:

Car 37—north by northeast, 2 points east
Car 46—west by southwest, 6 points south
Car 49—south by southeast, 1 point south

After drawing the points on a city map, Inspector Strasser orders all police cars to converge on Area D, Block 21.

Brace, George Purser on the S.S. *Newcastle* (portrayed by Joe Allen, Jr.) who is engaged to Rona Simmonds in *Dangerous Money* (1946). Brace has falsified a travel visa for his fiancée, for which Rona is now being blackmailed by P.T. Burke.

Bracey, Sidney (1877, Melbourne, Victoria, Australia–August 5, 1942, Hollywood, California) Character actor of stage and screen who appeared in almost 140 silent and sound films, sometimes also credited as Sidney Bracy. Bracey portrays a ship's steward aboard the S.S. *Oceanic* in *Charlie Chan at the Race Track* (1936).

The son of actress Clara T. Bracey and lyric tenor Henry Bracey, Sidney Bracey began his own stage career at the turn of the century. By 1910 he was starring in American film productions at the old Kalem Studios. Eventually his short, thin stature worked against his credibility as a virile lover, and Bracey became a character player in silent features.

Bracey was a particular favorite of comedian Buster Keaton, who was among the first to recognize Bracy's potential in low-key "gentleman's gentleman" roles. Bracy continued playing butlers, valets, and stewards into the early 1940s, and was also prominently featured in such short subjects as *Our Gang's Second Childhood* (1936) and *Three Smart Boys* (1937).

Brackett, Constable Eldorado policeman (portrayed by DeWitt C. Jennings) who, with Capt. Bliss, is called in to investigate the murder of Louie Wong in *Charlie Chan's Courage* (1934).

Note: Brackett is mentioned in Earl Derr Biggers' novel *The Chinese Parrot*, which serves as the basis for *Charlie Chan's Courage* (1934). However, the film credits of *The Chinese Parrot* (1927) in the *American Film Institute Catalog of Motion Pictures Produced in the United States* do not list the character.

Brade, T.M. Portrayed by Ivan Simpson, the son of the man from whom Dan Winterslip stole jewels and gold 35 years ago while working as a boat mate in *Charlie Chan's Greatest Case* (1933).

Bradley, Truman (February 8, 1905, Missouri–July 28, 1974, Los Angeles, California) Character actor who appeared in nearly 30 films and had roles in two *Charlie Chan* movies. Bradley portrays Captain Kane, skipper of the *Suva Star*, in *Dead Men Tell* (1941) and Paul Wagner in *Charlie Chan in Rio* (1941). After finishing his career in films, Bradley was the host and narrator for the *Science Fiction Theater* (1955) television series and was Burns and Allen's well-known radio announcer.

Bradshaw, Jimmy Fast-talking, quick-witted publicity director for the local tourist bureau (portrayed by Robert Young) in *The Black Camel* (1931). Bradshaw is romantically attracted to Julie O'Neil.

Brady, John Film editor for *Castle in the Desert* (1942).

Brand, Harry (Unbilled) director of publicity for *Dead Men Tell* (1941), *Charlie Chan in Rio* (1941), and *Castle in the Desert* (1942).

Brandish, Joseph International smuggler (portrayed by Barton Yarborough) posing as an oil salesman in *The Red Dragon* (1945). In his attempts to obtain Alfred Wyans' secret research papers that describe a new 95th element, he murders Walter Dorn, Wyans, and the Countess Irena, each time using an ingenious, radio-controlled fired bullet.

Brandt, George "Doc" Physiotherapist (portrayed by Walden Boyle) for Cole King's variety troupe in *The Trap* (1947). Now using a false name, Brandt is a former physician who was accused of his wife's murder six years ago; although the charges were dropped, his career was ruined.

King's girlfriend, Marcia, threatens to reveal that Brandt and Adelaide are secretly married (and also hints that she knows Brandt's real identity). With the case solved, Charlie Chan assures Brandt that the Board of Medical Examiners will reinstate his medical license and he will be free to practice under his real name.

Brasno, George (1911–1982) Midget actor (42 inches tall) who appeared in about seven films with his equally diminutive sister Olive Brasno. With his sister as his dancing partner, George Brasno portrays the circus entertainer Colonel Tim in *Charlie Chan at the Circus* (1936).

Brasno, Olive (1917, Old Bridge, New Jersey–January 25, 1998, Lakeland, Florida) Midget actress (40 inches tall) who appeared in about seven films with her equally diminutive brother George Brasno. With her brother as her dancing partner, Olive Brasno portrays the circus entertainer Lady Tiny in *Charlie Chan at the Circus* (1936).

At the age of 10, Olive Brasno was performing with her brothers and sisters on the back of a family truck when she was spotted by a talent scout. She first performed in local shows and then turned to vaudeville. Brasno reportedly turned down an offer of $75 a week playing a munchkin in *The Wizard of Oz* (1939) because she was making $150 a week in vaudeville. She went on to perform in movies with her brother George, sharing the stage (as herself) with Jimmy Durante in *Carnival* (1935) and Shirley Temple in *Little Miss Broadway* (1938).

Brayton, Margaret Actress who portrays Cole King's variety troupe member Madge Mudge in *The Trap* (1947).

Brecher, Egon (February 16, 1885, Czechoslovakia–August 12, 1946, Hollywood, California) Character actor of stage and screen who appeared in 80 films and portrays Ulrich, the surly caretaker of Colby House, in *Charlie Chan's Secret* (1936).

As a Czech stage actor and director, Egon Brecher came to Hollywood in 1929 and appeared in foreign-language versions of American films. Briefly a fixture of mid–1930s horror films, Brecher could be seen as the majordomo in *The Black Cat* (1934) and as the coroner in *Mark of the Vampire* (1935). In *Werewolf of London* (1935) it was Brecher's duty (in the role of an unbilled Himalayan priest) to intone the venerable "There are some things it is better not to bother with!" He worked steadily in the espionage films of the 1940s, as his Slavic accent was well-suited to both noble and villainous roles.

Brent, Evelyn (October 20, 1899, Tampa, Florida–July 4, 1975, Los Angeles, California) American character actress (real name: Mary Elizabeth Riggs) of stage and screen who appeared in over 100 silent and sound films, sometimes credited as Betty Riggs or Dorothy Riggs. Brent portrayed the impostor nun nurse Sister Teresa in *The Golden Eye* (1948).

Born in Florida, Evelyn Brent was raised in New York by her widowed father. As a teenage model, Brent began appearing in films at the Popular Plays and Players studio in Fort Lee, New Jersey. After World War I she traveled to England where she worked in films and on stage. She returned to the U.S. and established herself in exotic, dangerous roles, notably in the late silent efforts of director Josef von Sternberg. Luckily, Evelyn's voice matched her screen image perfectly and she had no trouble adjusting to talkies.

Unfortunately, her earliest talkie starring efforts were box-office failures, and by the mid–1930s she was consigned to secondary roles. She took occasional sabbaticals from Hollywood to tour in vaudeville, and finished up her acting career in "B" movies at Monogram. She then worked as an actor's agent in the 1950s.

Brent, George (March 15, 1904, Shannonsbridge, Ireland–May 26, 1979, Solana Beach, California) Suave leading man (real name: George Brendan Nolan) of stage and screen who appeared in almost 90 films, typically in gentlemanly, romantic roles. Brent portrays Captain Ronald Kene in *Charlie Chan Carries On* (1931).

George Brent played opposite all of Warners' greatest actresses, including Barbara Stanwyck and Olivia de Havilland. He was best known for his work with Bette Davis, with whom (according to some sources) he had a lasting but secret off-screen romance. Brent began his career as a child, playing small roles in Ireland's Abbey Theater plays. During the Irish Rebellion he participated in subversive activities and had to be smuggled out of the country to Canada where he eventually toured with a stock company for two years before moving on to New York. There he continued to appear with several stock companies, three of which he formed on his own.

Brent found work on Broadway in the late 1920s before starting a film career that spanned two decades. He retired from the big screen in 1953, going on to star as Dean Evans in the television series *Wire Service* (1956–57). His six wives included actresses Ruth Chatterton, with whom he co-starred in *The Rich Are Always with Us* (1932), Constance Worth, and Ann Sheridan, with whom he appeared in *Honeymoon for Three* (1941).

Breslow, Lou Movie director and story writer of over 60 films, sometimes credited as Louis Breslow. Breslow wrote the original story (with Saul Elkins) for *Charlie Chan at the Race Track* (1936). Among the other movies he wrote was the story for *Bedtime for Bonzo* (1951).

Bretherton, Howard P. (February 13, 1896, Tacoma, Washington–April 12, 1969, San Diego, California) Film director and editor of over 100 silent and sound films, sometimes credited as H.P. Bretherton early in his career. He was the director of *The Trap* (1947).

Howard Bretherton started out as a silent movie property man and worked at other lower-level positions for ten years before his directorial debut with *While London Sleeps* (1926). He spent most of the late-silent/early-talkie era at Warner Bros., a studio that favored fast and efficient directors over slow, self-conscious ones. When not calling the camera shots, Bretherton often was reassembling them in the editing room for the benefit of other directors. From 1940 onward, Bretherton was one of Hollywood's busiest "B"-western directors and was one of the first directors of the *Adventures of Superman* (1952) television series.

Brett, Ralph Sinister radio station manager and member of an espionage ring (portrayed by Stanford Jolley in his second of two *Charlie Chan* roles) in *The Scarlet Clue* (1945). Brett, known as Rolf Brot when in Paris years ago, steals radio actress Diane Hall's car for a few hours and murders a foreign agent named Rausch.

Hall's roommate, Gloria Bayne (who is also a radio actress), knows that Brett stole Diane's car and blackmails him into promising her more money and better acting roles. Fearing exposure from Bayne (and knowing that Charlie Chan now suspects that he murdered Rausch after the detective finds a shoe with blood on the heel in his office desk), Brett panics and telephones his unknown espionage ring superior (Mrs. Marsh). Marsh sends him instructions via the teletype in his second-floor office in the Cosmo Radio Center to take the service elevator to the seventh floor. If no one is in the hall, Brett is to go to the tenth floor where he will be aided in making his escape. Mrs. Marsh, secretly looking out the slightly opened door of Room 702, sees Brett get back into the elevator. She throws a hidden control switch that opens a trap door, dropping Brett to the building's basement and killing him instantly.

Brewster Detective Agency Los Angeles agency that employs ex–Scotland Yard policeman Watson King, who is hired by Mrs. Lucy Manderley in *Castle in the Desert* (1942).

Brian, Mary (February 17, 1908, Corsicana, Texas–) Attractive romantic leading lady (real name: Louise Byrdie Dantzler) who appeared in nearly 80 silent and sound films. Brian portrays Yvette Lamartine in *Charlie Chan in Paris* (1935).

One of the best-liked silent movie stars both on and off the screen, Mary Brian came to Hollywood in 1923 by way of a beauty contest. Her first screen role was as Wendy in *Peter Pan* (1924), which resulted in a long-term contract with Paramount Pictures. In 1926 she was chosen by the Western Association of Motion Picture Advertisers as a "WAMPAS Baby Star." Her career lost momentum in the early 1930s, though she briefly rallied with an amusing turn as W.C. Fields' faithful daughter in *The Man on the Flying Trapeze* (1935) and an uncharacteristic appearance as Sally Barnaby, a heartbreaking femme fatale in Henry Fonda's *Spendthrift* (1936).

Mary Brian

Bridge, Alan (February 26, 1891, Philadelphia, Pennsylvania–December 27, 1957) Gravel-voiced American character actor who appeared in almost 150 films, sometimes credited as Al Bridge. He appeared in two *Charlie Chan* films, first as Sheriff Mack in *The Jade Mask* (1945) and then as Capt. Allen in *Shadows Over Chinatown* (1946).

In films from 1931, Alan Bridge was always immediately recognizable thanks to his gravel voice, unkempt mustache, and sour disposition. Bridge spent a lot of time in westerns playing crooked sheriffs and two-bit political hacks. He showed up in so many *Hopalong Cassidy* westerns that he was practically a series regular. From his portrayal of Mr. Hillbeiner in *Christmas in July* (1940) onward, the actor was one of the most prevalent members of Preston Sturges' stock company.

Briggs, Harlan (1880–January 26, 1952, Woodland Hills, California) Stage and screen character actor who appeared in nearly 70 films, often as small-town bigwigs. Briggs portrays the coroner in *Charlie Chan's Murder Cruise* (1940). Perhaps Briggs' most memorable role was as the eminently bribable Doctor Skinner in W.C. Fields' *The Bank Dick* (1940).

Briggs, Steven Ex-con who is convicted of robbing the Lamont Bank (based on his fingerprints being found at the crime scene) in *Dark Alibi* (1946). Briggs died after two months in prison. Briggs, Stanley Gray, and Thomas Harley were each framed in an identical manner. In all three cases no money was recovered, all had a prior prison record, and each man protested his innocence, claiming he was never in the bank that was robbed.

Brill, Eddie Racehorse jockey (portrayed by Frank Coghlan, Jr., in his second of two *Charlie Chan* roles) in *Charlie Chan at the Race Track* (1936). Brill used to ride for

George Chester before Chester left for Australia, and was the winning jockey in the Santa Juanita Handicap two years earlier, but a leg injury from a fall hampered his career.

Because of the publicized threats against Avalanche, none of the jockeys are willing to ride Avalanche in the handicap race. However, Eddie Brill steps up to Chester and offers to ride the horse. Appearing grateful, Chester then promises Brill a bonus of $10,000 to "see that specialist about his leg" if he wins the race. Riding Avalanche, Brill does win the race but the horse stumbles and falls immediately after crossing the finish line from the effects of a tranquilizer dart. However, both Brill and Avalanche are later found to be uninjured.

Brissac, Virginia (June 11, 1883–July, 1979, Hollywood, California) Stern-faced American stage and screen actress who appeared in over 100 films. Brissac portrays the murderess and espionage ring leader, Mrs. Marsh, in *The Scarlet Clue* (1945).

Virginia Brissac was a well-established stage actress in the early part of the twentieth century, and for several seasons she headed a traveling stock company bearing her name. Once Brissac settled down in Hollywood in 1935, she found a niche in authoritative parts, playing a steady stream of schoolteachers, college deans, chaperones, and society matrons.

Bristol, Lady Mary The fiancée (portrayed by Mona Barrie) of Geoffrey Richmond in *Charlie Chan in London* (1934). Fearing that she has important information to give to Chan about the attempt on Chan's life the previous night, Richmond throws some pepper into the eyes of her horse, Hell Cat, during a fox hunt at Richmond's country estate. She and the horse both crash through a railing, falling into a chalk pit. Hell Cat is killed instantly and Lady Mary survives but is unconscious with a concussion.

British Imperial Club Private New York social club where George Kirby and Herbert Fenton are members in *Murder Over New York* (1940). As Kirby's guest, Hugh Drake leaves his briefcase in the club's checkroom. Chan and Kirby find Drake dead in Kirby's library, and a club guest card is found among Drake's effects.

Note: In *Charlie Chan's Chance* (1932), which is the uncredited basis for *Murder Over New York*, the British Imperial Club was called the Cosmopolitan Club.

Bromberg, J. Edward (December 25, 1903, Temesvar, Hungary–December 6, 1951, London, England) Plump, wide-eyed stage and screen actor who appeared in over fifty films and portrays *New York Daily Bulletin* newspaper's managing editor, Murdock, in *Charlie Chan on Broadway* (1937).

Born in Hungary, J. Edward Bromberg came to America with his family while still an infant. He was certain from an early age that he would pursue an acting career, taking odd jobs as a silk salesman, candy maker, and laundry worker to finance his training. He studied with the Moscow Art Theater, then made his American stage bow at age 23 at the Greenwich Village Playhouse. The chubby Bromberg conveyed a perpetual air of ulcerated, middle-aged tension, which allowed him to play characters much older than himself. He worked extensively with the Theatre Guild, coming to Hollywood's attention for his work in the 1934 Pulitzer Prize–winning play *Men in White*.

He portrayed Colonel Ferol in *Under Two Flags* (1936) and began a long association with Twentieth Century–Fox, playing a vast array of foreign villains, blustering buffoons, and the occasional gentle philosopher. When Warner Oland first fell ill, Bromberg had been screen-tested for the Chan role, as was Leo Carrillo, Noah Beery, Sr., and 31 other actors before the role was given to Sidney Toler in 1938. He made a triumphant return to Broadway in 1948 as a Louis Mayer–like movie mogul in Clifford Odets' *The Big Knife*, but the elation would not last.

Accused of being a Communist sympathizer, Bromberg was blacklisted from Hollywood and forced to seek work in England. Though only 47 when he left the U.S., Bromberg looked twenty years older due to the strain of the accusations of the witch-hunters. At age 48, Bromberg died in London in 1951 of what was officially listed as "natural causes," since a broken heart is not officially regarded as a fatal condition.

Bronson, Billie Nightclub dancer (portrayed by Louise Henry in her first of two *Charlie Chan* roles) and ex-girlfriend of Johnny Burke in *Charlie Chan on Broadway* (1937). Bronson was once wanted as a key witness by the grand jury to tell about mob payoffs to the New York police, but Burke helped her escape to Europe to avoid testifying.

Now no longer receiving any money from Burke to live on and nearly broke, Bronson returns to New York and begins to make a lot of people nervous. Prior to landing, however, Bronson hides her diary, which contains information about rackets and New York City politics, in Charlie Chan's luggage—which doesn't get searched by customs agents (as the Police Commissioner has extended Charlie "freedom of the port" and exempted him from having to declare anything).

After getting off the boat, Bronson meets up with reporter Speed Patten in a taxi, promises to later give him an exclusive story that he'll have to print "on asbestos," and agrees to meet him at her hotel at midnight. However, she later telephones Murdock, Patten's managing editor, and asks him if he remembers the deal they spoke of before she skipped town. She says, "Well, we may be able to do business now, but it's going to cost you twice what you offered last time." Murdock is prepared to pay $10,000 for the diary, but before he can meet her in her hotel room at 11:30 P.M. that evening, she has already been murdered by Patten.

Bronson, Frank San Francisco District Attorney (portrayed by Russell Hicks in his last of three *Charlie Chan* roles) in *The Shanghai Chest* (1948). Bronson was the prosecutor in the trial of Tony Pindello, who was framed for murder, tried, found guilty, and executed. However, Bronson now has evidence that Pindello probably was innocent and wrongly executed.

Bronson is the second person murdered by Ed Seward, who makes it appear as part of an alphabet-type serial revenge killing perpetrated by the already dead Tony Pindello, whose fingerprints were found at the murder scene.

Bronson Building The location of the office of Kelso Aviation in *The Chinese Ring* (1947). It is located on Broad Street in Los Angeles.

Brooks, Phyllis (July 18, 1914, Boise, Idaho–August 1, 1995, Cape Neddick, Maine) Attractive blonde actress (real name: Phyllis Steiler) and former model who appeared in over 25 films. In two *Charlie Chan* roles, Brooks portrays Judy Hayes in *Charlie Chan in Honolulu* (1938) and the murderess Vivian Wells in *Charlie Chan in Reno* (1939).

Brot, Rolf Alias Ralph Brett used in Paris years ago in *The Scarlet Clue* (1945).

Brown, Birmingham Charlie Chan's chauffeur (portrayed by Mantan Moreland) in 15 *Charlie Chan* film appearances for Monogram. In the other two Monogram films, Birmingham's role is taken over by his cousin, Chattanooga Brown (portrayed by Willie Best). Like most blacks in movies of the time, Birmingham is a comedic foil and is portrayed as the easily frightened Negro who is even scared of his own shadow.

In the first three *Charlie Chan* Monogram entries, Birmingham is not Charlie Chan's chauffeur but is variously employed as a butler and taxicab driver. Beginning only with *The Jade Mask* (1945) is Birmingham now identified as Chan's chauffeur and sometimes "Second Assistant." Even though the Birmingham role was never completely free of stereotype, by the end of the Chan series in 1949 Monogram recognized Moreland's value to the series by having Charlie Chan refer to Birmingham Brown as either "Number Two assistant" or "my assistant, Birmingham Brown"—not merely "my hired man."

Charlie Chan filmography: *Charlie Chan in the Secret Service* (1944), *The Chinese Cat* (1944), *Black Magic* (1944), *The Jade Mask*

(1945), *The Scarlet Clue* (1945), *The Shanghai Cobra* (1945), *Dark Alibi* (1946), *Shadows Over Chinatown* (1946), *The Trap* (1947), *The Chinese Ring* (1947), *Docks of New Orleans* (1948), *The Shanghai Chest* (1948), *The Golden Eye* (1948), *The Feathered Serpent* (1948), *The Sky Dragon* (1949).

Brown, Charles D. (July 1, 1887, Council Bluffs, Iowa–November 25, 1948, Hollywood, California) American stage and screen character actor who appeared in over 80 films, often in authoritative roles. Brown portrays Reno police chief King in *Charlie Chan in Reno* (1939) and was the newspaper editor in *Mr. Moto's Gamble* (1938), a reworked version of the never-completed *Charlie Chan at the Ringside*.

Brown, Chattanooga Charlie Chan's chauffeur (portrayed by Willie Best) and cousin of Birmingham Brown in *The Red Dragon* (1945) and *Dangerous Money* (1946).

Brown, James S., Jr. Cinematographer for over 80 silent and sound films, including *The Trap* (1947).

Brown, Nicodemus Uncle of Birmingham Brown in *The Scarlet Clue* (1945). When Tommy Chan and Birmingham go to the police station to report a black marketeer, they are handed several books of mug shots. Birmingham comes to one page featuring a mug shot of his uncle, which is numbered 10502, dated September 28, and lists an age of 46, a height of 5'7", and a weight of 152 pounds. Several pages later there is a similar mug shot for Birmingham.

Bruce, Sir Frederic Scotland Yard inspector (portrayed by Gilbert Emery) who is assigned the case of Hilary Galt's murder in *Behind That Curtain* (1929). While in India investigating Galt's death, the Home Office requests that he look into Eve Durand's disappearance.

Bruzlin, Alfred (*–July 3, 1970, Hollywood, California) Sound recording engineer for over 50 films, including four *Charlie Chan* entries at Twentieth Century–Fox: *Charlie Chan's Courage* (1934), *Charlie Chan at the Race Track* (1936), *Dead Men Tell* (1941), and *Charlie Chan in Rio* (1941).

Bryant, Jane Actress who portrays Cole King's variety troupe member Lois in *The Trap* (1947).

Bryar, Paul (1910, New York, New York–) Character actor who appeared in over 70 movies, often cast as a policeman or guard. In two *Charlie Chan* films at Monogram, Bryar appears first as gangster Mike Rogan in *Shadows Over Chinatown* (1946) and later as a police sergeant (unbilled) in *The Chinese Ring* (1947).

B-212 Number of Charlie Chan's stateroom on B Deck aboard the S.S. *Oceanic* while on its voyage from Honolulu to Los Angeles in *Charlie Chan at the Race Track* (1936).

bubonic plague An acute infection in humans and various species of rodents, known as the "Black Death" in 14th-century Europe. It is caused by *Yersinia pestis*, a bacterium transmitted by fleas that have fed on the blood of infected rodents, usually rats. The lymph nodes throughout the infected person's body, especially those in the groin and the thighs, become enlarged and extremely painful. The inflamed lymph nodes, called *buboes*, from which the disease gets its name, become filled with pus, and the disease spreads through the body by way of the infected bloodstream and the lymphatic system. In 60 to 90 percent of untreated cases, death occurs within a few days.

In *Charlie Chan in Panama* (1940), Dr. Rudolph Grosser, a well-known expert on tropical diseases and plagues, is conducting secret experiments on rats, 20 of which have been intentionally infected with bubonic plague. Achmed Halide, above whose tobacco shop Grosser has his makeshift laboratory, knows of these illegal experiments, eventually panics, steals the rats and destroys them. When Jimmy Chan sees the empty cages in Grosser's lab, he erroneously concludes that Grosser is the master saboteur known as Reiner who will use the rats to infect the crews of the ships going through the Panama Canal.

Bungalow Number 9 Charlie Chan's bungalow at the Lazy Y Ranch in *The Golden Eye* (1948).

Bunston, Herbert (April 15, 1873, Surrey, England–February 27, 1935, Los Angeles, California) Stage and screen actor who appeared in nearly 25 films, often in authoritative roles. Bunston portrays Garrick Enderly in *Charlie Chan's Chance* (1932).

As a classically trained British actor, Herbert Bunston began by acting in small parts on-screen and off. Fans will probably remember Bunston as the ineffectual Dr. Seward in Bela Lugosi's *Dracula* (1931). After many years on the British stage, he moved on to Broadway as a very capable actor possessing versatility and a cultured masculinity.

By the late 1930s, Herbert became an older gentlemen in his late fifties and continued both on stage and screen to play authoritative supporting roles, most of which were film versions of classic novels and plays. In 1935 his career was tragically cut short by a heart attack at the age of 61.

Burger, Paul Story writer of *Charlie Chan at the Olympics* (1937).

Burke *see* **Marloff, Ivan**

Burke, James (September 24, 1886, New York, New York–May 28, 1968, Los Angeles, California) American vaudeville and screen character actor who appeared in nearly 150 films and portrays Wilkie, the house detective at the Luani Hotel, in *Charlie Chan's Murder Cruise* (1940). In Columbia's *Ellery Queen* series of the late 1930s and early 1940s, Burke appeared six times as the thick-eared Sgt. Velie who often referred to the scholarly Ellery Queen as "Maestro."

Burke, Johnny Owner (portrayed by Douglas Fowley in his first of three *Charlie Chan* roles) of the Hottentot Club, a New York City nightclub in *Charlie Chan on Broadway* (1937). Burke's current girlfriend is Marie Collins, who is the featured dancer in his club's floor show. His previous girlfriend, Billie Bronson, was wanted as a key witness by the grand jury to tell about mob payoffs to the New York police, but Burke helps her to escape to Europe to avoid testifying.

When Billie returns to New York after a one-year exile, she stops by the club to see Burke. She is later found dead in his office. Charlie Chan gathers the possible suspects in Burke's office at the Hottentot Club for questioning about the death of Billie Bronson, and Burke is considered at the top of the list. On cue from Johnny, his henchman, Louis, turns off the office lights, allowing Burke to escape in the confusion. When finally captured, Burke is asked by Inspector Nelson if he would submit to a paraffin test to prove his innocence. Charlie Chan tells Meeker, Burke's lawyer, what the paraffin test is, and that it is good for up to 72 hours after firing a gun. The police lab technician administers the test on Burke's right hand and the reagent does not turn blue. Consequently, Nelson has to let Burke go. *See also* **paraffin test**.

Burke, Marie The alias of Connie Jackson (portrayed by Elena Verdugo) in *The Sky Dragon* (1949). Burke is a new stewardess on Flight 17 and an accomplice of John Anderson. She drugs the coffee to knock everyone out for Anderson to be able to steal the money shipment aboard. *See also* **Jackson, Connie**.

Burke, P.T. Shady cotton goods trader (portrayed by Dick Elliot) who is employed by All American Cotton Mills in *Dangerous Money* (1946). Burke is part of a gang involved in the sudden appearance of money and artworks stolen from Philippine banks during the Japanese invasion. Burke is also blackmailing Rona Simmonds after he learns that she is traveling under a visa falsified by her fiancé, George Brace. Before Charlie Chan can question Burke about the blackmail scheme, Burke is killed by a knife thrown by Joseph Murdock disguised as Mrs. Whipple.

Burke, Wally A bad gambler (portrayed by Robert Lowery in his first of three *Charlie Chan* roles) who thinks Jeanne Bentley is in love with him in *Charlie Chan in Reno* (1939).

"BURKE SOUGHT IN DIARY DEATH" Newspaper headline from the *New York Daily Star* about the escape of Johnny Burke, a suspect in the death of Billie Bronson who supposedly kept a diary with details about the New York rackets and politics in *Charlie Chan on Broadway* (1937).

Burkett, James S. (1895–October 26, 1970, Palm Springs, California) Producer of all 17 *Charlie Chan* films made at Monogram from 1944 to 1949.

Charlie Chan filmography: *Charlie Chan in the Secret Service* (1944), *The Chinese Cat* (1944), *Black Magic* (1944), *The Jade Mask* (1945), *The Scarlet Clue* (1945), *The Shanghai Cobra* (1945), *The Red Dragon* (1945), *Dark Alibi* (1946), *Shadows Over Chinatown* (1946), *Dangerous Money* (1946), *The Trap* (1947), *The Chinese Ring* (1947), *Docks of New Orleans* (1948), *The Shanghai Chest* (1948), *The Golden Eye* (1948), *The Feathered Serpent* (1948), *The Sky Dragon* (1949).

Burns, Edmund (1892, Philadelphia, Pennsylvania–April 2, 1980, Los Angeles, California) American actor who appeared in nearly 75 silent and sound films, sometimes credited as Eddie Burns, Edward Burns, and Ed Burns. Billed as Edward Burns, he portrays Robert Eden in *The Chinese Parrot* (1927).

Burton, Dr. The Honolulu Police doctor (portrayed by Howard C. Hickman) who gives Charlie Chan his annual physical exam in *Charlie Chan at the Olympics* (1937). After checking Charlie's heart rate, he pronounces Chan physically fit for another year. When Charlie remarks that "If son Lee win 100-meter swimming race, chest expand two inches more," Dr. Burton cautions Charlie that he'd better make sure that it is his chest that expands and not his waistline.

Buttons Ship steward (portrayed by Richard Keene) in *Charlie Chan's Murder Cruise* (1940).

B.V.D. Initials of Bradley, Vorhees & Dey, a 19th-century dry goods manufacturer whose brand name became a synonym for men's underwear. In *Charlie Chan Carries On* (1931), Max Minchin cautions Charlie Chan that he'd better get some "iron underwear—you know, B.V.D.s." Chan then either doesn't know what B.V.D.s are or jokingly plays along when he replies, "Oh, I see—Before Very Dead."

Byron, Walter (June 11, 1899, Leicester, England–March, 1972) British-born leading man (real name: Walter Butler) who appeared in over 40 films. Byron portrays Harry Jennison in *Charlie Chan's Greatest Case* (1933).

C

Cabot, Richard Government engineer (portrayed by Kane Richmond in his last of three *Charlie Chan* roles) and the new superintendent of the Miraflores Power Control Station in *Charlie Chan in Panama* (1940).

Cabot, Sonia Portrayed by Carol Forman in her second of two *Charlie Chan* roles, the fiancée of Professor Henry Farnsworth in *The Feathered Serpent* (1948). Cabot murders Professor Scott with an Aztec sacrificial knife just before he is about to tell Charlie Chan and others details about finding the Aztec Temple of the Sun and his escape from his captors there.

Cabot is involved with Professor Stanley in smuggling Aztec antiquities out of Mexico. Even though she is engaged to Professor Farnsworth, she is unhappy about Stanley's engagement to Joan Farnsworth, her fiancé's sister. Stanley then murders Cabot to keep her from talking about their smuggling activities.

Cady, Jerome (1908–November 8, 1948, Avalon, California) Sometimes credited as Jerry Cady, screenplay writer (with Charles S. Belden) of two *Charlie Chan* films at Twentieth Century–Fox: *Charlie Chan on Broadway* (1937) and *Charlie Chan at Monte Carlo* (1937).

Besides the two *Chan* films, Cady was also the writer of *Mr. Moto's Gamble* (1938), a reworked version of the never-completed *Charlie Chan at the Ringside*, and over 25 others, many of which were mystery and war action films, such as *Guadalcanal Diary* (1943). He was nominated for an Academy Award in the Best Writing (Original Screenplay) category for *Wing and a Prayer* (1944).

Café du Singe Bleu Paris cafe (literally translated as "Cafe of the Blue Monkey") where Nardi performs as a dancer in *Charlie Chan in Paris* (1935). Charlie Chan goes to the café to meet Nardi, who is working undercover for him to investigate Dufresne's financial dealings and his connection to the counterfeiting of bonds issued by the Lamartine Bank.

Chan, Victor Descartes, Yvette Lamartine, Max Corday, and Renee Jacquard arrive at the cafe and watch Nardi's performance, an interpretation of the *dance apache*. The dance ends with her partner tossing Nardi through a prop storefront window, and she lands out of sight of the audience. Before she can stand up and rejoin her dance partner in front of the audience, Nardi is killed by a knife thrown by Henri Latouche, disguised as Marcel Xavier.

Note: There is an error in *Charlie Chan in Paris* when Charlie begs to be excused from an impromptu celebration at Victor Descartes' apartment. Max Corday, a friend of Descartes, then tells all assembled that if Charlie won't join them, then they will join him at "Le Singe Bleu." However, Chan has not previously mentioned the name of the café to Descartes or anyone else at the apartment. Perhaps Corday already knows what Chan's intended moves are.

Cairo, Eve Psychic mind reader (portrayed by Pauline Moore in her last of three *Charlie Chan* roles) in *Charlie Chan at Treasure Island* (1939). Eve is Rhadini's assistant and Pete Lewis' girlfriend. Her mind reading ability helps Charlie Chan identify the mysterious Dr. Zodiac.

Calihan, William A., Jr. Assistant director for three *Charlie Chan* films at Monogram: *Shadows Over Chinatown* (1946), *The Chinese Ring* (1947), and *The Feathered Serpent* (1948). He also served as production manager for *The Trap* (1947).

Callahan, George Mystery writer who wrote the stories (and often the screenplays) for eight *Charlie Chan* films for Monogram. His other credits include *The Shadow Returns* (1946) and *The Babe Ruth Story* (1948).

Charlie Chan filmography: *Charlie Chan in the Secret Service* (1944), *The Chinese Cat* (1944), *Black Magic* (1944), *The Jade Mask* (1945), *The Scarlet Clue* (1945), *The Shanghai Cobra* (1945), *The Red Dragon* (1945), *Dark Alibi* (1946).

camellia Distinctive red or white flower with shiny, dark-green leaves. A camellia is always worn by Belescu in the buttonhole of his lapel in *City in Darkness* (1939).

Cameron, Warden State prison warden (portrayed by Russell Hicks in his second of three *Charlie Chan* roles) in *Dark Alibi* (1946).

The Canarsie Kid Nickname for "Shorty" McCoy (portrayed by Shemp Howard) in *Murder Over New York* (1940). When picked up by the New York police for a lineup, McCoy is masquerading as "The Great Rashid," a Hindu fakir who (the police tell Charlie Chan) makes a living as a panhandler feeding phony religion to suckers.

Candid Camera Night Publicity gimmick at Johnny Burke's Hottentot Club in *Charlie Chan on Broadway* (1937). Camera hounds compete for a free dinner by submitting the best photo entry taken during one of the Hottentot Club's floor shows. "You bring the camera, we supply the subjects," says the sign outside the club.

Cansino, Rita *see* **Hayworth, Rita**

Cantonese Predominant Chinese dialect of southern China which is spoken by Charlie Chan. In *The Chinese Ring* (1947), Chan tries to talk to a mute Chinese boy but is told that the boy only understands a Chinese dialect of northern China, from the same province as Princess Mei Ling. Sergeant Davidson asks Charlie if he also speaks this dialect and Chan tells him that he only speaks Cantonese.

Capitol Night Club Mexico City nightclub where the Countess Irena sings as an entertainer in *The Red Dragon* (1945).

Capt. K The dying message scribbled by Princess Mei Ling on a piece of paper in *The Chinese Ring* (1947). The princess is shot in Charlie Chan's house, and she attempts to write a final message before she dies. Chan eventually determines this clue must refer to either Capt. Kong, the skipper of the *Shanghai Maid*, or Capt. Kelso, the head of Kelso Aviation.

Cardigan, Dr. Macabre psychiatrist (portrayed by George Zucco) in *Charlie Chan in Honolulu* (1938). For a book that he is writing, Cardigan pretends to be deaf so that he can better observe the behavior of the passengers aboard the *Susan B. Jennings* without attracting attention. He first refers to Jimmy Chan as "Mr. Ham," and when corrected, intentionally errs again by calling Jimmy "Mr. Clam."

Jimmy tells his father that Dr. Cardigan is "deaf as a post," but Charlie is suspicious and tests Cardigan by tossing a silver dollar behind Cardigan. When the coin hits the ship's deck, Cardigan immediately turns around and watches it roll away. Chan then remarks to Jimmy and Capt. Johnson that, "When money talks, few are deaf."

In his eerie manner, Cardigan is currently investigating the brains of criminals and in his cabin has apparatus that he claims is keeping alive the brain of the famous Chinese murderer Chang Ho Ping. When Cardigan is asked by Chan to help him set a trap for the murderer, Charlie appears to have carelessly left a gun on Capt. Johnson's desk. Cardigan then picks up the gun and points it toward Charlie, revealing that one of his theories is that detectives as well as murderers invariably make one fatal mistake. Cardigan was annoyed when Charlie exposed his pretended deafness, but (now holding a gun) he tells Chan that he feels better now. Chan disappoints Cardigan a second time, as the gun is not loaded.

Cardosa, Barbara Real name of Helen Ashby, who is Lola Dean's secretary in *Charlie Chan in Rio* (1941). She also is the widow of Manuel Cardozo, who Lola Dean murdered in Honolulu, and plans with her brother-in-law, Alfredo Cardoza, to extract a confession from Dean about the murder. *See also* **Ashby, Helen.**

Note: Ken Hanke in *Charlie Chan at the Movies: History, Filmography, and Criticism* observes that there seems to be confusion as to what her last name is or how it is to be pronounced. In Lola Dean's confession to Marana, she says that she killed Manuel Cardozo. Charlie Chan refers to Marana's real name as Alfredo Cardoza, while Chan identifies Helen Ashby as Barbara Cardosa. *See also* **Ashby, Helen.**

Cardoza, Alfredo The brother (portrayed by Victor Jory) of Manuel Cardozo. Alfredo uses the alias of Alfredo Marana in *Charlie Chan in Rio* (1941). *See also* **Cardosa, Barbara.**

Cardozo, Manuel Barbara Cardosa's husband, who the Honolulu police thought had committed suicide but was actually murdered by Lola Wagner in *Charlie Chan in Rio* (1941). Manuel Cardozo was on a business trip to Honolulu and met Lola Wagner, who fell madly in love with him. When Wagner asked him to divorce his wife and marry her, he refused and Lola killed him. *See also* **Cardosa, Barbara.**

Cardwell, James B. (1921, Camden, New Jersey–February 4, 1954, Hollywood, California) Character actor, sometimes credited as Albert C. Cardwell, who appeared in 20 films. Cardwell portrays private detective Ned Stewart in *The Shanghai Cobra* (1945).

Carewe, Arthur Edmund (December 30, 1884, Trebizond, Armenia–April 23, 1937, Santa Monica, California) Leading man (real name: Jan Fox) in over 40 silent and early sound films. In his last movie role before committing suicide, Carewe portrays Henrietta Lowell's spiritualist advisor, Professor Bowan, in *Charlie Chan's Secret* (1936).

Carey Theatrical Warehouse A storehouse for theater props which is focal point for many of the activities in *Dark Alibi* (1946). Upon his arrest at the Foss Family Hotel, ex-convict Thomas Harley claims to have been locked in the Carey Theatrical Warehouse for four hours. To prove his story, he shows the policemen a typed note from Dave Wyatt, a man Harley knew in prison 20 years ago, asking him to meet him there. The police discount the note, telling Harley that Wyatt has been dead for eight years.

The warehouse is also the location of the second-floor office of Mr. Johnson, an accountant who does the books for the warehouse. When searching the warehouse, Charlie Chan finds large chemical vats that Mr. Johnson uses for photoengraving and forging the fingerprints used to falsely implicate several ex-convicts in bank robberies.

Carioca Casino Rio de Janeiro nightclub where Lola Dean performs as a singer in *Charlie Chan in Rio* (1941). The club gets it name from the Portuguese term *cariocas* given to the inhabitants of Rio de Janeiro.

Carlos, Horace Former Shakespearean actor (portrayed by Leonard Mudie in his first of two *Charlie Chan* roles) who now plays "The Mad Monster" on radio, screen, and television in *The Scarlet Clue* (1945). Charlie Chan accidentally bumps into Carlos in the radio station's hallway, apologizes, and is then introduced to the actor by the station manager, Ralph Brett. In a bit of theatrical showmanship, Carlos brags, "Yes, once the foremost Shakespearean actor of my time, but now—Char. Now I am known only for the mask behind which I hide when I play The Mad Monster on radio, screen, and television. But it *is* still a living."

Carlotta Psychic medium (portrayed by Gloria Roy in her fourth of seven *Charlie Chan* roles) who is the assistant to spiritualist advisor Professor Bowan in *Charlie Chan's Secret* (1936). Bowan and Carlotta conduct séances at Colby House to enable Henrietta Lowell, a devout believer in psychic phenomena, to be in contact with her dead brother Bernard Colby, whose spirit acts as a guide to the world beyond and delivers information about the missing Allen Colby.

When Allen Colby's dead body appears during once of the séances, and Charlie Chan's investigation reveals that much of what transpires at the séance is the result of trickery, Henrietta instructs her lawyer to remove Bowan and Carlotta from her will, denying them a $100,000 endowment they were to receive upon Henrietta's death to continue their psychic research. Also as a result of the trickery, the police now suspect Bowan and Carlotta of murdering Allen Colby.

Carlton Hotel (1) New York hotel stayed at by Charlie Chan, son Lee, and Billie Bronson in *Charlie Chan on Broadway* (1937). Charlie and Lee occupy Room 313; Billie Bronson is in Room 413.

Carlton Hotel (2) Charlie Chan's hotel, staying in Room A-324, in *The Jade Mask* (1945).

Carnival The opera performed by the San Marco Opera Company in *Charlie Chan at the Opera* (1936). *Carnival* was specifically composed for the movie by Oscar Levant, and Gravelle considers the baritone role of Mephisto to be his greatest role.

Caroline Maid for the Manning household in *The Chinese Cat* (1944).

Carper An alias of Cooper in *The Scarlet Clue* (1945). *See also* **Cooper**.

Carré, Ben (December 5, 1883, Paris, France–May 28, 1978, Santa Monica, California) Art director, set decorator, and production designer (real name: Benjamin S. Carré) for nearly 30 silent and sound films. Carré was the art director for *The Black Camel* (1931).

carrier pigeon U.S. Army carrier pigeon, number 13576, which belongs to the Signal Corps, and is entrusted to Jimmy Chan, in *Castle in the Desert* (1942). Charlie Chan tells Jimmy that he prefers a briefer name and names the pigeon Ming Toy, "daughter of happiness." When Jimmy tells Charlie that it is a boy pigeon, Chan responds that Ming Toy is a temporary alias while on the case. While at Manderley's castle estate, the pigeon is poisoned with nightshade.

Carroll, Leo G. (October 25, 1892, Weedon, England–October 16, 1972, Hollywood, California) Distinguished, dry-faced British stage and screen actor (real name: Leo Grattan Carroll) who appeared in over 60 films, often as doctors, judges, or academics. In two *Charlie Chan* films, Carroll portrays the shady locksmith Louis Santelle in *City in Darkness* (1939) and the murderer Jim Eberhart (alias archeologist Professor Gordon) in *Charlie Chan's Murder Cruise* (1940).

Leo G. Carroll was the son of an Irish-born British military officer and intended to follow in his father's footsteps, but his World War I experiences discouraged him from pursuing a military career. On the British stage from the age of sixteen, Carroll settled in the United States in 1924, first appearing in theatrical roles. In films from 1934, Carroll often portrayed shy, self-effacing Britishers who used their humility to hide a larcenous or homicidal streak. He reportedly was Alfred Hitchcock's favorite actor and was seen in half a dozen Hitchcock films, notably as the scheming psychiatrist Dr. Murchison in *Spellbound* (1946) and as the professor in *North by Northwest* (1959).

A method actor before the term was invented, Carroll was known to immerse himself in his roles, frequently confounding strangers by approaching them "in character." On television, Carroll was best known as Cosmo Topper in the ghostly sitcom, *Topper* (1953–55), and as Alexander Waverly on both *The Man from U.N.C.L.E.* (1964) and *The Girl from U.N.C.L.E.* series (1966–68) and their many spin-off movies.

Carter, Ben (August 7, 1912, New York, New York–December 10, 1946, New York, New York) Genial black character actor and comedian (real name: Bennett Lester Carter) who appeared in nearly 30 films. In two *Charlie Chan* films, *The Scarlet Clue* (1945) and *Dark Alibi* (1946), Carter portrays himself.

Ben Carter was a partner with Mantan Moreland in a stage comedy act. The act's "indefinite talk" routines, although not as famous as Abbott and Costello's "Who's On First?" bit, were based on the two having an entire conversation without ever completing a sentence. In *The Scarlet Clue*, the dialogue between Birmingham Brown and Ben Carter would start as follows:

Carter: Ben Carter's the name.
Brown: Benjamin Carter. I haven't seen you since…

Leo G. Carroll (Everett Collection)

Carter: Longer than that. The last time I saw you was…
Brown: Oh, I moved from there. I moved over to…
Carter: How can you live in that neighborhood?

The dialogue would eventually end with Moreland saying something like, "That's why I like to talk with you, 'cause you and me seem to agree with each other, don't we?" In the *Charlie Chan* films, Tommy Chan would be a dumbfounded bystander, not understanding a word of what was said.

In *The Scarlet Clue* (1945), Tommy asks Birmingham, "Who's your friend?" after the conversation ends. Birmingham replies, "He didn't say." In a somewhat similar routine in *Dark Alibi* (1946), Ben Carter is now a convict in prison. At the routine's finish, Tommy asks, "Who was that man?" Birmingham replies, "Oh, he's a fella who used to hang around my house. That's my brother, Ben." Carter died of a strep throat infection at age 34.

Carter, Janet Real name of Hulda Swenson, the Swedish cleaning woman at the Cosmo Radio Center (portrayed by Victoria Faust) in *The Scarlet Clue* (1945). *See also* **Swenson, Hulda.**

Cartwright Inventor of a new remote controlled guidance system for airplanes (portrayed by John Eldredge in his first of four *Charlie Chan* roles) in *Charlie Chan at the Olympics* (1937). Cartright sells a part-interest in his invention, which has strategic military applications, to Mr. Hopkins of the Hopkins Aviation Company, and during a test flight demonstration for the U.S. War Department, Cartwright is in voice radio contact with the test plane.

During the flight, however, the test pilot is attacked and the plane is hijacked. The pilot is later murdered by Miller, an aviation mechanic/henchman, who in turn is murdered by Cartwright as part of an elaborate scheme to sell his invention to an unnamed foreign government represented by Charles Zaraka. Cartwright goes through this plan to steal the device to divert suspicion away from himself, because as the inventor, he could have merely *given* Zaraka the plans.

Cartwright, Peggy Nosy newspaper reporter for the *Morning Herald* (portrayed by Louise Currie) in *The Chinese Ring* (1947). She has a love-hate relationship with police sergeant Bill Davidson and very often the two get in each other's way.

Cartwright, Thomas A member of the jury (portrayed by Edward Coke) who convicted Tony Pindello in *The Shanghai Chest* (1948). Cartwright is the third murder victim of Ed Seward as part of an alphabet-type serial revenge killing by the already dead Tony Pindello, whose fingerprints are found at the murder scene.

Carvero, Inspector Luis Mexico City policeman (portrayed by Fortunio Bonanova) in *The Red Dragon* (1945). Carvero is an old friend of Charlie Chan, with whom he worked four years earlier in Honduras to assist the British government. In Mexico City, Carvero is involved with the investigation of several murders associated with attempts to acquire research papers detailing atomic bomb secrets. Carvero's investigation is complicated by the fact that he is romantically involved with Marguerite Fontan, who is considered one of the suspects.

Cass, Maurice (October 12, 1884, Vilna, Lithuania–June 8, 1954, Hollywood, California) Stage and screen character actor who appeared in over 90 films, typically as a man of gentility. Cass portrays Mr. Arnold, the high-strung stage manager in *Charlie Chan at the Opera* (1936).

With his shock of snow-white hair, Maurice Cass was destined to play stage managers, theatrical impresarios, school principals, and absentminded professors. Cass' theatrical voice provided an amusing contrast to his tiny, bird-like frame.

Castanaro, Henri Portrayed by Emmett Vogan in his fifth of six *Charlie Chan* roles, a business partner of Simon Lafontaine and Theodore Von Scherbe in a syndicate that ships poisonous gas to South America in *Docks of New Orleans* (1948). Castanaro is the second murder victim of Oscar Swendstrom, who uses the same poison gas he had sold to Lafontaine's chemical company for $500.

Castillo, Antonio Alias used by Tony Madero on a fake passport that his wife Marie Dubon had made by Louis Santelle in *City in Darkness* (1939). As a cover, Castillo is supposed to be a coffee planter from Bogotá, Colombia.

***Castle in the Desert* (1942)** The eighteenth *Charlie Chan* film produced by Twentieth Century–Fox Film Corporation.

Source: based on the character "Charlie Chan" created by Earl Derr Biggers. Original Copyright: Twentieth Century–Fox Film Corporation, February 27, 1942; LP11240. Copyright Renewed: January 2, 1970; R475961. PCA Certificate Number: 7821. Production: September 23 to mid–October, 1942. Release Date: February 27, 1942. Sound: Western Electric Mirrophonic Recording. Film: b&w; 6 reels; 5,594 feet. Running Time: 63 minutes.

Producer: Ralph Dietrich. Director: Harry Lachman. Assistant Directors: Hal Herman* and Saul Wurtzel.* Dialogue Director: George A. Wright.* Original Screenplay: John Larkin. Director of Photography: Virgil Miller. Art Direction: Richard Day and Lewis Creber. Film Editor: John Brady. Set Decorations: Thomas Little. Costumes: Herschel. Musical Direction: Emil Newman. Sound: Bernard Freericks and Harry M. Leonard. Production Manager: William Koenig,* Director of Publicity: Harry Brand.*

Cast

Sidney Toler	*as*	Charlie Chan
Arleen Whelan		Brenda Hartford
Richard Derr		Carl Detheridge
Douglass Dumbrille		[Paul] Manderley
Henry Daniell		Watson King [alias for Cesare Borgia]
Edmund MacDonald		Walter Hartford
Sen Yung		Jimmy Chan
Lenita Lane		Lucy Manderley [formerly known as Princess Lucrezia della Borgia]
Ethel Griffies		Madame [Lily] Saturnia
Milton Parsons		[Arthur] Fletcher
Steve Geray		Dr. Retling
Lucien Littlefield		[Professor] Gleason
Eric Wilton*		Wilson
Paul Kruger*		Bodyguard
George Chandler*		Bus driver
Oliver Blake*		Hank Wigley

*Unbilled.

Plot Summary: At a secluded California castle in the Mojave Desert owned by eccentric millionaire Paul Manderley, tragedy strikes when a genealogist guest, Professor Gleason, is poisoned. Fearing that his wife Lucy will be implicated in the poisoning because she is the former Princess Lucrezia della Borgia, Manderley bribes the family physician, Dr. Retling, and family lawyer, Walter Hartford, to take Gleason's body to a hotel in Mojave Wells, the closest town, and make it look as if he died there of a heart attack.

Soon after, Charlie Chan, who is vacationing in San Francisco with his son Jimmy during Jimmy's leave from the Army, receives a note signed by Lucy Manderley asking him to come to the castle. Chan makes the journey, but, upon reaching the castle, finds that Lucy did not send the note. Suspecting that the sender wanted him to be a witness to an upcoming crime, Chan stays. Manderley explains that because he is a medieval scholar studying the life of Cesare Borgia, he wants to live in an atmosphere approximating the fifteenth century. Chan also learns from Dr. Retling that Manderley will lose control of his father's estate if he is involved in any scandal.

Arriving at the same time as Chan is Watson King, a sculptor commissioned to do a bust of Lucy. Soon after, Jimmy also comes to the castle to pass along a threatening letter that came to the hotel after Chan left. Another visitor is Arthur Fletcher, a private detective representing Gleason's family, who is caught prowling on the castle's grounds. Like Gleason, Fletcher falls victim to poison, and Dr. Retling tries to convince Manderley that Lucy is responsible and must be committed to an insane asylum. However, Manderley states only that he will turn over control of the estate to Hartford and leave quietly with his wife.

Chan discusses the situation with Lucy, and she tells him about her stepbrother Cesare, who years ago was acquitted on a charge of poisoning and then killed in the Spanish War. Chan then obtains a confession from Walter Hartford, his wife Brenda, and Dr. Retling that they paid Gleason and Fletcher to pretend to be poisoned so that Manderley would be forced to relinquish the estate. Brenda Hartford also reveals that Cesare is not dead, and that he wrote to her husband a month ago demanding money.

Chan still believes that there is a killer lurking about, and his suspicions are proven correct when Walter Hartford is stabbed to death with an arrow from a crossbow. After explaining that the murderer needed to get rid of Hartford and then Manderley so that Lucy would inherit the estate, Chan reveals that Watson King is both the killer and Lucy's brother, Cesare, having had a facial scar removed so that he would not be recognized.

Notes: *Castle in the Desert* was the last *Charlie Chan* film produced by Twentieth Century–Fox. Toler obtained the rights to the character from Earl Derr Biggers' widow and made 11 more *Charlie Chan* films at Monogram. The Manderley castle set was the same one used in *The Hound of the Baskervilles* (1939).

Catlen Gangster (portrayed by Anthony Warde) in *The Chinese Cat* (1944). With fellow gangsters Gannett, Salos, and the twin brothers Carl and Kurt Karzoff, Catlen is part of a jewelry theft and smuggling ring led by Thomas Manning and Webster Deacon. Catlen murders Webster Deacon by strangling him.

Cauper An alias of Cooper in *The Scarlet Clue* (1945). *See also* **Cooper**.

Cesar The circus gorilla who is initially thought to have murdered circus owner Joe Kinney in *Charlie Chan at the Circus* (1936). Tom Holt, a.k.a. Gangor the snake charmer, purposely releases Cesar from his cage as a diversion while Holt, disguised as a gorilla to look like Cesar, murders Kinney.

Chabing Chinese actress who portrays Princess Mei Ling's maid, Lilly Mae Wong, in *The Chinese Ring* (1947). She also appears (unbilled) as an office receptionist in *The Shanghai Chest* (1948). Her only other known film role was as one of the king's wives in *Anna and the King of Siam* (1946).

Chalmont Building The building from which Mrs. Justine Bonner, under a hypnotic trance, walks off the roof and falls to her death in *Black Magic* (1944). The building is across the street from the Berkeley Building.

Chan, Charlie (陳查禮) Rotund Chinese detective, created by Earl Derr Biggers, who is an inspector with the Honolulu Police Department. Biggers modeled Chan after the real-life Chinese detective, Chang Apana, who lived with his large family in Honolulu on Punchbowl Hill. Apart from Sherlock Holmes, Charlie Chan is the most prolific detective to appear on film.

From the first Chan film, the silent *The House Without a Key* (1925) to the series' finale, *The Sky Dragon* (1949), none of the six actors who played Charlie were Chinese. In the three earliest films, in which Charlie Chan was not even the main character, two actors were Japanese (George Kuwa and Kamiyama Sojin in the two silent films) and one was British (E.L. Park in the first Chan talkie). For the movie series that began its run in 1931, none of the Chan actors was even Oriental. One actor was Swedish (Warner Oland) and two were Americans (Sidney Toler and Roland Winters). Charlie Chan's physical attributes were not typical of most movie detectives, and he often relied on a mixture of brains, good manners, and charm to solve many of his murder cases.

In Biggers' novels, Chan has the rank of a police sergeant, but in the movies he is promoted to the rank of inspector and then lieutenant. Biggers also does very little to describe Chan's physical appearance and mannerisms in his novels. The only real physical description given is in the novel *The*

Chinese Parrot, which describes Chan as a chubby little man who "had round fat cheeks, an ivory skin..." As such, the various actors were left to their own interpretations as to what Chan should look like and how he should behave. With the three actors in the role of Charlie Chan as the film's main character, there evolved three distinct interpretations of Chan's character and his employment.

In the Oland Chans, Charlie is a humble, polite policeman with the Honolulu Police Department, but rarely does he do any actual work for them. Instead, he usually pops up in various locales around the world, such as London, Paris, Egypt, Shanghai, Berlin, New York, Monte Carlo, Reno, Panama, and Rio. The one notable exception is *The Black Camel* (1931), which was filmed entirely on location in Honolulu, although there were other films that would have Charlie start out from Honolulu. In the Fox films made before *Charlie Chan in London* (1934), Charlie is generally left alone to solve the cases, is more energetic in tracking the culprits, and often uses himself as bait in catching the murderer. With the *London* entry, Chan now begins to adopt a more methodical approach by gathering all the suspects that are still alive for the reconstruction of the crime.

When Sidney Toler took over the role after Oland's death, the character became a sharper-tongued, less patient Chan who uses less physical action than Oland did. As a crime solver, Chan is helping the U.S. government as a Secret Service agent, such as in *Charlie Chan in Panama* (1940) where he works undercover to track down an enemy agent known as Reiner. Beginning with *Charlie Chan in the Secret Service* (1944), Charlie now works full-time for the U.S. government fighting enemy spies, which reflected America's participation in World War II.

With Winters' interpretation, Charlie Chan is portrayed as a private detective living in San Francisco, with no mention of his wife or family. Although Winters was the youngest of the Chan actors, he was less physically inclined than either Oland or Toler, but many critics feel that his characterization was closer to Biggers' character in the novels.

Chan, Charlie, Jr. Charlie Chan's Number Two son (portrayed by Layne Tom, Jr., in his first of three *Charlie Chan* roles) in *Charlie Chan at the Olympics* (1937). In this movie, Charlie Jr. is not mentioned by name but only as "Junior" son. When Sen Yung portrays the role of Jimmy Chan after the departure of Keye Luke as Number One son Lee Chan, Jimmy is then referred to as "Number Two son" for the remainder of the Twentieth Century–Fox films.

Chan, Eddie Charlie Chan's Number Four son (portrayed by Edwin Luke, Keye Luke's younger brother) in *The Jade Mask* (1945). Of all Charlie Chan's children, Eddie is the more intellectual, bookworm type. He tells his detective father, "Please father, call me Edward. Eddie is so juvenile." Like all of his siblings, however, Eddie can't resist assisting his father in solving the murder, and conceitedly asks, "What type of murder have we got and how soon do you wish me to produce the murderer?" In one scene Charlie tells Eddie, "My boy, if silence is golden, you are bankrupt."

Chan, Frances One of Charlie Chan's daughters (portrayed by namesake Frances Chan) in *Black Magic* (1944).

Chan, Iris Known as Number Two daughter (portrayed by Marianne Quon) in *Charlie Chan in the Secret Service* (1944).

Chan, Jimmy Starting with *Charlie Chan in Honolulu* (1938), Charlie Chan's Number Two son, sometimes called James Chan. Portrayed by Sen Yung (later billed as Victor Sen Young for the last three Toler films), the character was written into 13 movies, all of which were with Sidney Toler.

Jimmy often tags along with his father on murder cases, but sometimes pops up unexpectedly whenever Charlie Chan comes to town. He occasionally has temporary jobs on freighters, often landing in jail or missing the boat. In *Charlie Chan in Reno* (1939), Jimmy travels to Reno, Nevada, during vacation from classes at University of Southern California to visit his dad after receiving a telegram from him.

Although Jimmy is mentioned as sometimes being in college, errors in continuity do occur. In *Charlie Chan at the Wax Museum* (1940), Jimmy is in law school; in the following picture, *Murder Over New York* (1940), he is a chemistry student, as he was in *Charlie Chan in Reno*.

Like his older brother Lee, the character of Jimmy Chan is an asset to the plots, providing occasional comic relief and serving as the butt of Charlie's jokes. In *Murder Over New York*, for example, Charlie introduces Jimmy to Hugh Drake, an old friend, saying, "This is favorite offspring Jimmy, without whose assistance many cases would have been solved much sooner." Also, like Lee, the exchanges between father and son continued to highlight Charlie's human qualities, despite Toler's less forgiving interpretation of the Charlie Chan character. On the positive side, Jimmy is usually around to provide necessary physical action, which Toler's Chan lacked. Although Jimmy is more bungling and more gullible than Lee, Jimmy nevertheless always has a ready smile and a strong devotion toward his father's welfare.

Charlie Chan filmography—Jimmy Chan: *Charlie Chan in Honolulu* (1938), *Charlie Chan in Reno* (1939),* *Charlie Chan at Treasure Island* (1939),* *Charlie Chan in Panama* (1940), *Charlie Chan's Murder Cruise* (1940), *Charlie Chan at the Wax Museum* (1940), *Murder Over New York* (1940), *Dead Men Tell* (1941), *Charlie Chan in Rio* (1941), *Castle in the Desert* (1942), *Shadows Over Chinatown* (1946), *Dangerous Money* (1946), *The Trap* (1947).

Chan, Lee Charlie Chan's Number One son (portrayed by Keye Luke), undoubtedly the most well-known of Charlie Chan's children. The character is written into ten movies, the first eight of which are with Warner Oland. When Oland died in 1937 and was succeeded by Sidney Toler in the role, Keye Luke left the series and his character was replaced with that of Number Two son Jimmy, portrayed by Sen Yung. After 11 years, Monogram reunited Lee Chan with Charlie for the series' final two movies.

Lee often pops up unexpectedly, whenever Charlie Chan came to town. In some movies Lee actually has a job, often as some kind of purchasing agent or trade representative, and is coincidentally often sent on business to the same location as his honorable father. In *Charlie Chan at the Olympics* (1937), Lee is a member of the U.S. Olympic Team in the 1936 Berlin Olympics, and swims in the 100-meter freestyle race. In *Charlie Chan at Monte Carlo* (1937), Lee is on his way to a Paris art show where one of his paintings is being displayed.

Lee Chan is a definite asset to the films' plots. Often the exchanges between father and Number One son highlight Charlie's human qualities, and Lee is usually around to provide physical action (which Oland's Charlie Chan lacked). Although Lee is bungling, he is not as inept as Benson Fong's portrayal of Number Three son Tommy. With a ready smile, Lee Chan often shows his pleasant side with his strong devotion to his father and concern for his welfare.

When Warner Oland died in 1938 during the filming of what would have been *Charlie Chan at the Ringside*, parts of the movie were salvaged and reworked into *Mr. Moto's Gamble* (1938). In it, Lee Chan becomes an assistant to the Japanese detective Mr. Moto, played by Peter Lorre.

Charlie Chan filmography—Lee Chan: *Charlie Chan in Paris* (1935), *Charlie Chan in Shanghai* (1935), *Charlie Chan at the Race Track* (1936), *Charlie Chan at the Opera* (1936), *Charlie Chan at the Circus* (1936), *Charlie Chan on Broadway* (1937), *Charlie Chan at Monte Carlo* (1937), *Charlie Chan at the Olympics* (1937), *The Feathered Serpent* (1948), *The Sky Dragon* (1949).

Chan, Luke Chinese actor who portrays an unbilled newspaper reporter in *Charlie Chan in Shanghai* (1935) and the sculptor Wu Song in *The Chinese Cat* (1944).

Chan, Tommy The character of Charlie Chan's son Tommy was portrayed at various

**Billed as James Chan.*

times by Layne Tom, Jr., Benson Fong, and Victor Sen Young. When Sidney Toler played Charlie Chan, Tommy is first introduced as Number Five son in *Charlie Chan in Honolulu*, but is later known as "Number Three son" in Toler's Monogram entries, when he is portrayed by Benson Fong.

After Toler died and Roland Winters continued the Chan role for the series' final six movies, Victor Sen Young portrayed Tommy Chan in the first five, and overnight was promoted to "Number Two son" status. This was probably more due to carelessness in the continuity of writing the screenplay rather than for any logical reason. Of the three actors who portrayed Tommy Chan, Benson Fong's was the most bumbling and inept.

Charlie Chan Filmography—
Tommy Chan

Layne Tom, Jr.: *Charlie Chan in Honolulu* (1938).

Benson Fong: *Charlie Chan in the Secret Service* (1944), *The Chinese Cat* (1944), *The Scarlet Clue* (1945), *The Shanghai Cobra* (1945), *The Red Dragon* (1945), *Dark Alibi* (1946).

Victor Sen Young: *The Chinese Ring* (1947), *Docks of New Orleans* (1948), *The Shanghai Chest* (1948), *The Golden Eye* (1948), *The Feathered Serpent* (1948).*

Chan, Willie Charlie Chan's Number Seven son (portrayed by Layne Tom, Jr.) in *Charlie Chan's Murder Cruise* (1940).

The Chan Family One of the features of the *Charlie Chan* series was the inclusion of Charlie's family. The size of the Chan family was always changing from movie to movie. In the original novels by Earl Derr Biggers, Charlie Chan had 11 children.

In *The Black Camel* (1931), there is a scene of Charlie, his wife, and their ten children seated around the breakfast table. Although Charlie in many ways honors tradition, his children are fully Americanized in their behavior, and Charlie finds it hard to understand the new ways. One of the series' best exchanges with his children occurs when one of Charlie's sons presents his less than flattering report card, initiating the following exchange between father, the son, and a daughter:

Charlie: Teacher say you are always at bottom of class. Can't you find better place?
Son: No pop. All the other places are taken.
Charlie: That is no excuse.
Son: Aw, baloney!
Charlie: Baloney?
Daughter: Aw, that's a lot of applesauce. Come on pop. Spill the beans!
Charlie: Baloney, applesauce, beans. One would think you all took lessons in grocery store instead of at school!

One film later, in *Charlie Chan's Chance* (1932), child number 11 is born. Charlie always has a picture of his family in his wallet or near his bed when traveling around the world. In *Charlie Chan in London* (1934), Charlie, his wife, and 10 children are shown in one photograph, while a separate photograph shows the baby (probably child number 11 from *Charlie Chan's Chance*). However, this is at odds with the end of the movie when Charlie says that at home he has 12 children and one wife. In *Charlie Chan's Secret* (1936), Charlie has a picture of himself, his wife, and 11 children. In *Charlie Chan at the Circus* (1936), the entire Chan family of Charlie, his wife, and 12 children are shown together entering a circus tent in the order of increasing height (and probably age), with Charlie last, holding the baby.

In *Charlie Chan in Honolulu* (1938), Charlie and his wife confirm that they have 13 children. Sitting around the dining table are 11 children with Number Two son Jimmy at the head of the table next to Charlie. Keye Luke (a.k.a. Number One son Lee) had left the series when Warner Oland died, but Jimmy remarks that Lee is in art school in New York, and Number One daughter Ling is in the hospital about to give birth to the Chans' first grandchild (a boy). In the same movie, Charlie tells Capt. Johnson that Tommy is Number Five son. Johnson then

**Billed as Victor Sen Yung.*

Some of Charlie Chan's "multitudinous blessings" in a publicity shot from *Charlie Chan's Greatest Case* (Everett Collection).

asks if there are more, and Charlie replies, "Nine more at home." In *Black Magic* (1944), Charlie mentions that he has 14 children.

Several Chinese actresses portray Charlie's "honorable wife" throughout the series, but none were ever credited as such. Even the *American Film Institute Catalog of Motion Pictures Produced in the United States* does not list the names of any unbilled actresses who may have portrayed Mrs. Chan.

Throughout most of the series, many of Chan's children serve as self-appointed assistants, attempting to help their father solve the murder and wrap up the case at hand. Most of the assistants were his sons—Lee, Jimmy, Tommy, Eddie, Willie, and Charlie Jr. In some cases, daughters Frances and Iris are involved.

Chan in Trinidad Title of a screenplay written by John Reinhardt in 1938 which was intended to be a *Charlie Chan* picture. However, Warner Oland died in August of that year and the script was reworked by George Bricker one month later for Twentieth Century–Fox's *Mr. Moto* series. Although the film's working title was *Mr. Moto in Trinidad* (based on the novel *Murder in Trinidad* by John W. Vandercook), the film was released April 7, 1939, as *Mr. Moto in Danger Island.*

Chandler, Eddie (1894, Wilton Junction, Iowa–March 23, 1948, California) Stocky character actor who appeared in over 100 silent and sound films, often as cops and in unbilled roles. Chandler portrays a policeman (unbilled) in *Murder Over New York*

(1940) and Secret Service agent Lewis in *Charlie Chan in the Secret Service* (1944).

Chandler, George (June 30, 1898, Waukegan, Illinois–June 10, 1985, Panorama City, California) Character actor and former vaudevillian who appeared in almost 330 films, usually in sly or comically nervous roles. In four unbilled *Charlie Chan* roles, Chandler portrays a ship's radio operator in *Charlie Chan at the Olympics* (1937), a bus driver in *Castle in the Desert* (1942), a hotel doorman in *The Chinese Cat* (1944), and Joe Nelson, the short-order cook in *The Shanghai Cobra* (1945).

George Chandler entered the University of Illinois after World War I service, paying for his education by playing in an orchestra. He continued moonlighting in the entertainment world in the early 1920s, working as an insurance salesman by day and performing at night. By the end of the decade he was a seasoned vaudevillian, touring in a one-man-band act called "George Chandler, the Musical Nut."

He began making films in 1927, appearing almost exclusively in comedies. Perhaps his best-known appearance of the early 1930s was as W.C. Fields' prodigal son Chester in the two-reeler *The Fatal Glass of Beer* (1932).

In the early 1950s Chandler served for two years as president of the Screen Actors Guild, ruffling the feathers of many prestigious stars and producers with his strongly held political views. From 1958 through 1959 Chandler was featured as Uncle Petrie on the *Lassie* television series, and in 1961 he starred as Ichabod Adams in a CBS sitcom, *Ichabod and Me*, that he helped develop.

Chandler, Tanis Character actress who portrays Mary Conover in *Shadows Over Chinatown* (1946) and Adelaide in *The Trap* (1947).

Chaney, Lon, Jr. (February 10, 1906, Oklahoma City, Oklahoma–July 12, 1973, San Clemente, California) American character actor (real name: Creighton Tull Chaney) who appeared in over 170 films, many of which were in the horror genre. In two *Charlie Chan* roles, Chaney portrays a desk man in *Charlie Chan on Broadway* (1937) and Pierre in *City in Darkness* (1939). In addition, Chaney plays Joey in *Mr. Moto's Gamble* (1938), a reworked version of the never-completed *Charlie Chan at the Ringside*.

Creighton Tull Chaney was the son of actor Lon Chaney and singer Cleva Creighton. He was raised in a strict atmosphere by his father, who refused to allow Creighton to enter show business, instead wanting his son to prepare for a more practical profession. Creighton then worked at menial jobs to support himself without calling upon his father. He was at various times a plumber, a meatcutter's apprentice, a metal worker, and a farm worker. Always, however, there was the desire to follow in his famous father's footsteps. He studied makeup at his father's side, learning many of the techniques that had made his father famous.

It was not until after his father's death in 1930 that Chaney went to work in films at RKO. His first roles were under his real name, but nothing much happened until 1935 when a producer insisted on changing his name to Lon Chaney, Jr., as a marketing ploy. Chaney was uncomfortable with this strategy and always hated the "Jr." suffix, but

Lon Chaney, Jr.

he was also aware that the famous name could help his career, and so kept it. However, Chaney would spend the rest of his life competing with his father's reputation as "The Man of a Thousand Faces."

Up to 1939, most of the parts he played were unmemorable until he was given the role of Lennie, a mentally retarded giant, in the film adaptation of John Steinbeck's *Of Mice and Men*. Chaney's performance was spectacularly touching, and it became one of the two roles for which he would be best remembered. The other came when Universal, in hopes of reviving their horror film franchise (as well as memories of their great silent star Lon Chaney, Sr.), cast Chaney as the tortured Lawrence Talbot in *The Wolf Man* (1941). The highlight of the film was a transformation sequence deliberately evoking memories of Chaney Sr.'s makeup expertise. However, union rules were such that Lon Jr. was not permitted to apply his own wolf man makeup.

Universal would recast Chaney as the Wolf Man in four subsequent films, and also starred him as the Frankenstein monster in *Ghost of Frankenstein* (1942) and as the title character in *Son of Dracula* (1943). Chaney also headlined two "B" horror series, one based on radio's *Inner Sanctum* anthology, the other spun off from the 1932 film *The Mummy*. Never as versatile as his father, Chaney was usually cast in cheap horror productions which traded primarily on his name and those of other fading horror stars. In the late 1960s the now-alcoholic Chaney fell victim to the same throat cancer that had killed his father.

Chapman, Marguerite (March 9, 1918, Chatham, New York–August 31, 1999, Burbank, California) American actress who appeared in nearly 35 films and portrayed (in her first movie role) reporter Mary Bolton in *Charlie Chan at the Wax Museum* (1940).

Note: Some sources list the year of her birth as 1916 or 1920.

Chardo the Great Magician, actor, ventriloquist, and hypnotist in *Black Magic* (1944). While performing in London, his wife Justine runs off with his assistant, William Bonner, and are married. On October 5, 1935, Chardo tries to follow his wife and is injured in an automobile crash. During his hospitalization, the magician has plastic surgery and then assumes the alias of Paul Hamlin as part of his plan to murder both William and Justine Bonner.

Charlie Chan *see* **Chan, Charlie**

Charlie Chan and the Chinese Ring One of two working titles for *The Chinese Ring* (1947) before its release on December 6, 1947. *See also* ***The Chinese Ring* (1947)**.

Charlie Chan at College Title of an unused or unfinished idea for a *Charlie Chan* film from Twentieth Century–Fox.

***Charlie Chan at Monte Carlo* (1937)** The seventh *Charlie Chan* film released by Twentieth Century–Fox Film Corporation.

Source: based on the character "Charlie Chan" created by Earl Derr Biggers. Original Copyright: Twentieth Century–Fox Film Corporation, January 21, 1938; LP8366. Copyright Renewed: December 13, 1965; R375585. PCA Certificate Number: 3797. Production: September 20 to mid–October, 1937. Release Date: December 17, 1937. Sound: Western Electric Mirrophonic Recording. Film: b&w; 8 reels; 6,465 feet. Running Time: 71 minutes.

Associate Producer: John Stone. Director: Eugene Forde. Assistant Director: Saul Wurtzel. Screenplay: Charles Belden and Jerry Cady. Original Story: Robert Ellis and Helen Logan. Photography: Daniel B. Clark. Art Direction: Bernard Herzbrun. Associate: Haldane Douglas. Film Editor: Nick DeMaggio. Costumes: Herschel. Musical Direction: Samuel Kaylin. Sound: Bernard Freericks and Harry M. Leonard.

Cast

Warner Oland	*as*	Charlie Chan
Keye Luke		Lee Chan
Virginia Field		Evelyn Grey
Sidney Blackmer		Victor Karnoff
Harold Huber		[Inspector] Jules Joubert
Kay Linaker		Joan Karnoff
Robert Kent		Gordon Chase

Edward Raquello	Paul Savarin
George Lynn	Albert Rogers
Louis Mercier	Taxi driver
George Davis	Pepite
John Bleifer	Ludwig
Georges Renavent	Renault
Constant Franke,* André Cheron*	Croupiers
Joseph Romantini,* Albert Pollet*	Attaches
Victor Delinsky,* Alphonse Martell,* Louis Lubitch,* Robert Graves,* George Sorel,* Jean Perry*	Gendarmes
Jean De Briac,* Manuel Paris*	Doormen
Eugene Borden*	Hotel clerk
Gennaro Curci,* Antonio Filauri,* John Picorri*	Waiters
Sherry Hall*	Bartender
Marcelle Corday*	Concierge
Leo White*	French butler
Emile Bistagne*	
Art Dupuis*	

Plot Summary: Before Charlie Chan and his son Lee leave Monte Carlo, Lee tries his luck at the casino's roulette wheel but is not successful. There they meet Inspector Jules Joubert, who is the chief of police of Monte Carlo. Chan tells Joubert that they are on their way to Nice airport and then Paris, where a painting by Lee will be exhibited. However, on the road to the Nice airport, their taxi breaks down. Chan and Lee then continue on foot. They see an expensive roadster leave another car and find a dead man in the car.

Upon investigating, Chan and Inspector Joubert learn that the dead man was Renault, a bank messenger on his way to Paris with $1,000,000 in metallurgical bonds. The bonds belonged to financier Victor Karnoff, and were being sent to be sold in Paris. Joubert also discovers that three metallurgical bonds were that day offered for sale at a Monte Carlo bank by Albert Rogers, who is a bartender at the hotel.

Returning to the hotel, Chan recognizes the roadster in front of the hotel, and learns that it belongs to Evelyn Grey, who is a resident there. Joubert and Chan find her with Paul Savarin, Karnoff's bitter rival. Although she admits to stopping by the car on the Nice road, Evelyn says that she fled in fright when she saw Chan and Lee approach. Joubert then learns that Karnoff's chauffeur, Ludwig, who drove Renault, was a paid informant of Savarin and was found dead near the car.

Later that day, Karnoff's wife, Joan, who earlier begged Rogers to give her back the three bonds, admits to Karnoff that she stole them from his room. He gives her until noon the next day to repay him. The next morning, Evelyn promises Gordon Chase, Karnoff's secretary, that she will not see Savarin again. Joubert then learns that Evelyn has been living in luxury with no visible means of income and that Joan pawned jewelry that morning for $25,000, the price of the three bonds. Chan and Joubert go to interrogate Rogers but find him dead in his room with an open valise full of Karnoff's bonds. Joubert then believes that Rogers committed suicide and that the case is closed, but Chan suggests they go to Karnoff's hotel suite.

When they enter Karnoff's suite, they find Joan, Savarin, Gordon Chase, and Evelyn Grey. Confronted with the missing bonds, Joan then confesses that Rogers, whom she married seven years earlier and whom she thought had obtained a divorce, was blackmailing her. She had given him the three bonds but stole them back when she learned of her husband's deal, and had Gordon Chase, her brother, replace them in Karnoff's safe.

Chan concludes that Chase must be the murderer because only he had a key to the valise, and the valise was found open in Rogers' room with no damage to its lock. Gordon then confesses and blames Evelyn, for whom he says he stole from Karnoff months ago to provide her with the finer things in life. When he was in danger of being exposed, he murdered Rogers to place the blame on him. Holding everyone at a distance with his gun, Gordon then escapes through a window, but is run over by a car which he did not see coming. Although making no accusation against them, Joubert insists that Evelyn and Savarin leave Monte Carlo on the next train.

Notes: *Charlie Chan at Monte Carlo* was

**Unbilled.*

Warner Oland's last film. Oland began filming *Charlie Chan at the Ringside* in January 1938, but seven days later Darryl Zanuck scrapped the picture, having finally become fed up with Oland's drinking and absences from the set.

It is interesting to note that the *Monte Carlo* film has Charlie and son Lee on their way to Paris where Lee is exhibiting a painting in an art exhibition. In fact, Keye Luke was an artist prior to starting his acting career.

Charlie Chan at the Arena One of two working titles for *Charlie Chan at the Ringside*, a 1938 movie project that was never completed. *See also* ***Mr. Moto's Gamble.***

***Charlie Chan at the Circus* (1936)** The second *Charlie Chan* film produced by the Twentieth Century–Fox Film Corporation.

Source: based on the character "Charlie Chan" created by Earl Derr Biggers. Original Copyright: Twentieth Century–Fox Film Corporation, March 27, 1936; LP6492 [also January 8, 1937; LP 7043]. Copyright Renewed: December 23, 1963; R328128. PCA Certificate Number: 1978. Production: started January 6, 1936; retakes early February, 1936. Release Date: March 18, 1936. Sound: Western Electric Noiseless Recording. Film: b&w; 7 reels; 6,500 feet. Running Time: 71–72 minutes.

Associate Producer: John Stone. Director: Harry Lachman. Assistant Director: William Eckhardt. Original Screenplay: Robert Ellis and Helen Logan. Photography: Daniel B Clark. Art Direction: Duncan Cramer. Film Editor: Alex Troffey. Costumes: William Lambert. Musical Direction: Samuel Kaylin. Sound: Arthur von Kirbach.

Cast

Warner Oland	*as*	Charlie Chan
Keye Luke		Lee Chan
George Brasno		[Colonel] Tim
Olive Brasno		[Lady] Tiny
Francis Ford		John Gaines
Maxine Reiner		Marie Norman
John McGuire		Hal Blake
Shirley Deane		Louise Norman
Paul Stanton		Joe Kinney
J. Carrol Naish		Tom Holt
Boothe Howard		Dan Farrell
Drue Leyton		Nellie Farrell
Wade Boteler		Lt. Macy
Shia Jung		Su Toy

Plot Summary: Charlie Chan takes his wife and twelve children to the circus owned by kindly John Gaines and his unscrupulous partner, Joe Kinney. Kinney, who had sent Chan free passes to the circus, tells Chan that he has been receiving death threats and wants his advice. As the show goes on, Chan leaves his family to meet Kinney and discuss his problems. When he arrives at Kinney's wagon, Chan, Gaines, and the dancing midgets "Colonel" Tim and Lady Tiny discover that Kinney has been murdered. Since the wagon was locked from the inside, and because of the hairs found on the window sill, the circus performers suspect that Cesar the gorilla had climbed up to the window and strangled Kinney. Chan withholds judgment and turns the case over to Lt. Macy and then leaves with his family to continue their vacation.

Later that night Tiny comes to Chan's hotel room and pleads with Chan to continue the investigation to clear her husband, Mr. Gaines, and the other circus performers who are being held by Lt. Macy for questioning, temporarily closing the circus. Chan goes to the police station and convinces Macy to release all suspects and allow the circus to travel on (accompanied by Chan, son Lee, and Lt. Macy) in hopes that the killer will reveal himself as time passes.

The next day Chan discovers that the business wagon's safe has been broken into and inside is Kinney's insurance policy, naming Marie as the beneficiary, and a marriage certificate stating that Kinney and wardrobe mistress Nellie Farrell were married in Juarez, Mexico, on Declaration Day, May 30th.

Chan, Lee, and Lt. Macy later confront Nellie and her brother Dan. Nellie, after having seen a lawyer, maintains that as Kinney's widow she is entitled to his half of the circus. Marie then replies that Nellie's claim is false and can prove that Kinney could not have been in Juarez on that date. Before she can offer proof of her claim, however, she has to perform her trapeze act. While Marie is on the trapeze, someone shoots her rigging and she falls to the ground. She is alive but seriously injured, and the doctor that was summoned states that she must be operated on immediately.

While the doctor is treating Marie, Chan looks through her scrapbook and discovers that on May 30th Kinney was being held as a witness to a murder in an El Paso casino. Lee then telephones the El Paso police for more information. During this time, as a diversion, someone releases Caesar from his cage. Cesar attempts to kill Marie during the operation but is caught and fatally shot. Chan reveals that it is not the true Caesar who was killed but snake handler Tom Holt, disguised as the ape.

The El Paso police then confirm that Holt was the killer in El Paso, and Chan reasons that Kinney covered up for Holt but was later murdered by Holt when they quarreled over money. Holt then attempted to murder Marie (who is now safely recovering at a hospital) because she could reveal the El Paso incident. Holt is arrested, along with Nellie and Dan, who forged the marriage certificate after Kinney's death. As a reward for his help, Gaines promises Chan and his family lifetime passes to the circus.

Notes: *Charlie Chan at the Circus* was shot on location at the Al G. Barnes Circus winter quarters, and the circus was used as a background for production settings. The film was also the first of five *Charlie Chan* entries directed by Harry Lachman.

Charlie Chan at the Fights One of two working titles for *Charlie Chan at the Ringside*, a 1938 movie project that never saw completion. *See also* ***Mr. Moto's Gamble.***

***Charlie Chan at the Olympics* (1937)** The fifth *Charlie Chan* film produced by Twentieth Century–Fox Film Corporation.

Source: based on the character "Charlie Chan" created by Earl Derr Biggers. Original Copyright: Twentieth Century–Fox Film Corporation, May 21, 1937; LP7170. Copyright Renewed: March 4, 1965; R357017. PCA Certificate Number: 3090. Production: late January to mid–February, 1937. Release Date: May 21, 1937. Sound: Western Electric Mirrophonic Recording. Film: b&w; 7 reels; 6,400 feet. Running Time: 71 minutes.

Associate Producer: John Stone. Director: H. Bruce Humberstone. Assistant Director: Jasper Blystone. Screenplay: Robert Ellis and Helen Logan. Original Story: Paul Burger. Photography: Daniel B. Clark. Art Direction: Albert Hogsett. Associate: Chester Gore. Film Editor: Fred Allen. Costumes: Herschel. Musical Direction: Samuel Kaylin. Sound: E. Clayton Ward and Harry M. Leonard.

Cast

Warner Oland	*as*	Charlie Chan
Katherine DeMille		Yvonne Roland
Pauline Moore		Betty Adams
Allan Lane		Richard Masters
Keye Luke		Lee Chan
C. Henry Gordon		Arthur Hughes
John Eldredge		Cartwright
Layne Tom, Jr.		Charlie Chan, Jr.
Jonathan Hale		[Mr.] Hopkins
Morgan Wallace		Honorable Charles Zaraka
Frederick Vogeding		Captain [Inspector] Strasser
Andrew Tombes		Police Chief Scott
Howard C. Hickman		Dr. Burton
Selmer Jackson*		Navy Commander Wright
Edward Keane*		Col. Webster
Arno Frey*		Carlos
Caroline "Spike" Rankin*		Landlady
O.G. "Dutch" Hendrian*		Miller
Billy Wayne*		Steward
Emmett Vogan*		Ship's officer
George Chandler*		Ship radio operator
Al Kikume*		Police radio operators
William von Brincken*		Guard
Brooks Benedict*		Henchman
Ferdinand Schumann-Heink*		Officer on *Hindenberg*
Hans Fuerberg,* John Peters*		Radio cops
Minerva Urecal*		Maid
Constant Franke*		Attendant
Paul W. Panzer*		Vendor
Virgil B. Nover,* Perry E. Seeley*		Sign language experts
Tom Klune*		Page boy
Ben Hendricks*		Coast Guard officer

**Unbilled.*

Don Brody*	News commentator
Philip Morris,*	
Lee Shumway,*	
Stanley Blystone*	New York cops
Glen Cavender,*	
Walter Bonn*	German policemen
David Horsley*	Edwards
Frank Bruno*	Footman
Theresa Harris*	Olympic athlete
Tony Merlo*	
Louis Natheaux*	
Bill Beggs*	

Plot Summary: A pilot testing a device by which his plane is guided by remote control is hijacked. Chan finds the plane, but the pilot is dead and the device (which could be sold for millions to a foreign power) is gone. Later, he also finds the body of Miller, the pilot's murderer.

Chan, Hopkins (the airplane owner), and Cartwright (the inventor of the device) take the airship *Hindenburg* to Berlin to investigate three people traveling there by ocean liner—Dick Masters, an Olympic pole-vaulter and aviator who did not pilot the plane on the day of its disappearance because of an injured shoulder; Yvonne Roland, who visited Miller's hotel room; and Arthur Hughes, an arms dealer who wanted to buy the device.

In Berlin, Chan finds the remote control device hidden in a box in the luggage of Masters' girlfriend, Betty Adams. As a precaution, Chan then substitutes a German-English dictionary and returns the box to Hopkins. Masters is now suspected in the murder because the box was found in Betty's room, and also from the fact that he was on the boat with Roland. Roland, however, takes the box to Charles Zaraka, a foreign diplomat who discovers the book instead of the device.

When Hughes learns of the switch, Chan's son Lee, an Olympic swimmer, is kidnapped at the Olympic Stadium. Following instructions sent from the kidnapper, Chan is blindfolded and brings the device, which he has had removed and replaced with a transmitter, to an agreed-upon location. He is then taken to Zaraka's estate, where Hopkins is brought in to identify the device. At the same time, Hughes arrives with his henchmen and struggles with Zaraka's men for the device. When the device is knocked loose and hits the floor, it breaks open to reveal a radio transmitter. With their direction-finding equipment, Inspector Strasser's policemen identify the location of the transmitter and then break into Zaraka's house. In the resulting struggles, Hopkins is shot by Cartwright, who earlier murdered Miller and made it appear that Hopkins stole the device.

Notes: *Charlie Chan at the Olympics* contained newsreel footage of the airship *Hindenburg* in which the swastika on the *Hindenburg*'s tail fin was censored/obliterated from the film print. The *Hindenburg* exploded during a violent thunderstorm at Lakehurst on May 6, 1937, before the release of the film on May 21.

In the book *Charlie Chan at the Movies: History, Filmography, and Criticism*, author Ken Hanke notes that Twentieth Century-Fox had a great idea literally blow up in their face. In making the movie, the studio thought that it would be a great publicity notion to send Charlie Chan across the ocean on the *Hindenburg*.

There was also actual film footage from the 1936 Olympic Games, including the 400-meter relay race showcasing American runner Jesse Owens.

***Charlie Chan at the Opera* (1936)** The fourth *Charlie Chan* film produced by Twentieth Century–Fox Film Corporation.

Source: based on the character "Charlie Chan" created by Earl Derr Biggers. Original copyrights (two versions): Twentieth Century–Fox Film Corporation, December 5, 1936; LP7256; and January 8, 1937; LP7043. Copyright Renewed: September 14, 1964; R344722. PCA Certificate Number: 2796. Production: mid–September to mid–October, 1936. Release dates (two versions): December 4, 1936, and January 7, 1937. Sound: Western Electric Noiseless Recording. Film: b&w; 7 reels; 6,175 feet. Running Time: 66 or 68 minutes.

**Unbilled.*

Associate Producer: John Stone. Director: H. Bruce Humberstone. Assistant Director: Sol Michaels. Screenplay: Scott Darling and Charles S. Belden. Story: Bess Meredyth. Photography: Lucien N. Andriot. Art Direction: Duncan Cramer and Lewis Creber. Film Editor: Alex Troffey. Costumes: Herschel. Musical Direction: Samuel Kaylin. Opera "Carnival" by Oscar Levant. Libretto: William Kernell. Orchestration: Charles Maxwell. Sound: George Leverett and Harry M. Leonard.

Cast

Warner Oland	*as*	Charlie Chan
Boris Karloff		Gravelle
Keye Luke		Lee Chan
Charlotte Henry		Mlle. Kitty [Rochelle]
Thomas Beck		Phil Childers
Margaret Irving		Mme. Lilli Rochelle
Gregory Gaye		Enrico Barelli
Nedda Harrington		Mme. Anita Barelli
Frank Conroy		Mr. Whitely
Guy Usher		Inspector Regan
William Demarest		Sergeant Kelly
Maurice Cass		Mr. Arnold
Tom McGuire		Morris
Fred A. Kelsey*		Policeman
Selmer A. Jackson*		Wire-photo technician
Emmett Vogan*		Wire-photo technician
Benson Fong*		Opera extra

Plot Summary: At the Rockland State Sanitarium, Gravelle, an opera-singing amnesiac, regains his memory when he sees a newspaper article about prima donna Lilli Rochelle, and escapes by overpowering a guard. In Los Angeles, Inspector Regan calls Charlie Chan in on the case. As they are in Regan's office discussing Gravelle's escape, Lilli Rochelle, accompanied by her lover and fellow singer, Enrico Barelli, comes in to complain about a threat she received that states she will die that night.

At Regan's suggestion, Chan agrees to go to the opera that night along with Sgt. Kelly to investigate. At the theater that night, Phil Childers and his girlfriend Kitty try to see Mme. Rochelle but are turned away by Kelly just as Regan and Chan arrive and hear Lilli's husband Whitely and Enrico fighting over Lilli. Gravelle appears in the dressing room of Enrico's wife, Anita. She is suddenly terrified because Gravelle was presumed dead in a theater fire years ago. Threatened, she agrees to keep his presence a secret while he carries out his plan of singing Enrico's baritone role of Mephisto in that evening's performance of *Carnival.*

Gravelle then confronts Enrico Barelli, who, along with Lilli, locked Gravelle in the burning theater. Gravelle ties up Barelli, dons a similar costume, and joins Lilli on stage for their duet. When Gravelle begins to sing, Lilli realizes it is Gravelle, not Barelli, beside her and faints after she leaves the stage at the end of the act. As Whitely carries Lilli off to her dressing room, the others rush to Enrico's room only to find that he has been stabbed to death.

While the police search for Gravelle in the opera house, Phil Childers enters Mme. Lilli's room and discovers that she is also dead. Whitely then comes in and has Phil arrested. Chan questions Phil and Kitty and they tell him that Kitty is Lilli's daughter from her previous marriage to Gravelle, and that Lilli refused to acknowledge Kitty to keep her past a secret. The young lovers were there to ask Lilli a final time for her permission to marry, as Kitty is underage. Gravelle, who did not recognize Kitty, is stunned when he overhears the truth.

Later, Childers goes to see Inspector Regan, leaving Kitty alone. Gravelle then enters the room and gently questions Kitty. He even plays the piano for her as he did when she was a child, but she does not remember him and faints from fright. Chan now enters the room and after Gravelle tells him about Lilli and Enrico's attempt to kill him, Chan flatters Gravelle into singing again. As part of his plan, Chan also arranges to have Anita Barelli now sing Lilli's role.

During the duet, which involves Gravelle's character stabbing Anita's character, Anita becomes so scared she screams, causing a police officer to shoot Gravelle. Chan then demonstrates that Gravelle's knife is still well-oiled in its case and could not have been used in the murders of Mme. Rochelle and Barelli. Chan further explains that Anita was

**Unbilled.*

the only one who had access to Enrico and Lilli when they were alone and unconscious, and that she was also the only one who knew Gravelle was there and could therefore frame him. Now confronted with the evidence, Anita confesses that jealousy drove her to kill her husband and his lover. Chan then convinces Kitty to comfort the injured Gravelle, thereby saving his life.

Notes: Several sources have commented that *Charlie Chan at the Opera* has a number of parallels to the silent film, *The Phantom of the Opera* (1925).

The opening credits read: "Warner Oland vs. Boris Karloff" and heavily played upon Karloff's popularity. Although thought by some that Karloff actually sang in the film, baritone Tudor Williams sang Karloff's arias while Zarubi Elmassian sang the soprano parts for both Margaret Irving and Nedda Harrigan.

A news item in the *Motion Picture Daily* noted that *Charlie Chan at the Opera* was banned in Germany for having too many murders. The film also marked the first time that a DeBrie camera, which was lighter and quieter than other models, was used in the United States. In his biography, composer Oscar Levant relates that the words for the opera songs were originally written in English by William Kernell but were then translated into Italian by studio staffers.

***Charlie Chan at the Race Track* (1936)** The third *Charlie Chan* film produced by Twentieth Century–Fox Film Corporation.

Source: based on the character "Charlie Chan" created by Earl Derr Biggers. Original Copyright: Twentieth Century–Fox Film Corporation, August 7, 1936; LP6667. Copyright Renewed: June 16, 1964; R339627. PCA Certificate Number: 2353. Production: May 18 to mid–June, 1936. Release Date: August 7, 1936. Sound: Western Electric Noiseless Recording. Film: b&w; 7 reels; 6,300 feet. Running Time: 70 minutes.

Associate Producer: John Stone. Director: H. Bruce Humberstone. Assistant Director: Aaron Rosenberg. Screenplay: Robert Ellis, Helen Logan, and Edward T. Lowe. Story: Lou Breslow and Saul Elkins. Photography: Harry Jackson. Art Direction: Duncan Cramer. Film Editor: Nick DeMaggio. Costumes: Herschel. Musical Direction: Samuel Kaylin. Sound: Alfred Bruzlin and Harry M. Leonard. Tech Director: Monroe Liebgold.*

Cast

Warner Oland	*as*	Charlie Chan
Keye Luke		Lee Chan
Helen Wood		Alice Fenton
Thomas Beck		Bruce Rogers
Alan Dinehart		George Chester
Gavin Muir		Bagley
Gloria Roy		Catherine Chester
Jonathan Hale		Warren Fenton
G.P. Huntley, Jr.		Denny Barton
George Irving		Major [Gordon] Kent
Frank Coghlan, Jr.		Eddie Brill
Frankie Darro		"Tip" Collins
John Rogers		Mooney
John H. Allen		"Streamline" Jones
Harry Jans		Al Meers
Robert Warwick*		Chan's chief
Sam Flint*		Ship's captain
Selmer Jackson*		[J.L.] Lansing
Ivan "Dusty" Miller*		Wade
Ed Hart,* George Magrill,* David Worth,* James Flavin*		Detectives
Al Kikume*		Hawaiian detective
Boothe Howard*		Ship's doctor
Sidney Bracy*		Ship steward
Jack Mulhall*		Second purser
William Wayne,* Les Sketchley,* Billie Oakley*		Seamen
Eddie Fetherstone,* Charles Williams*		Reporters
Max Wagner*		Joe
Paul Fix*		Lefty
Harlan Tucker,* Sammy Finn,* Wilbur Mack,* Norman Willis,* Jerry Jerome*		Gangsters
Holmes Herbert,* Colin Kenny,* Robert E. Homans*		Judges
Lew Hicks,* Bob Ellsworth*		Policemen
Lucille Miller*		Secretary
James Eagles*		Chick Patten
Bobby Tanzel*		Gilroy
Bruce Mitchell*		Gateman
Clyde McAtee,* Jack Green*		Pinkerton men
Pat O'Malley*		Track official
David Thursby*		Steward
Ray Hanson*		Third officer
Sam Hayes*		Announcer

**Unbilled.*

Plot Summary: Jockey "Tip" Collins, riding Avalanche, the horse in the lead in the Melbourne Sweepstakes, fouls another rider and Avalanche is disqualified. Major Gordon Kent gave Avalanche as a wedding present to George Chester when Chester married his daughter Catherine, and believes that a big gambling ring is behind the foul. Kent sends a telegram to his old friend Charlie Chan instructing him to meet their boat in Honolulu on their way to compete in America. However, Kent dies on the voyage, seemingly from being kicked by Avalanche in his stall.

After the boat docks in Honolulu, Chan goes aboard to investigate and determines from the position and the shape of the bloodstains that the horse could not have kicked Major Kent. Chan also reveals to his chief and the ship's captain that a piece of the ship's winch shoe (the twin of which is missing) could make a shape identical to that of a horseshoe. The chief suggests that Chan travel with the boat to continue the investigation of what they now suspect is a murder.

Chester receives a typed note warning him not to enter Avalanche in the Santa Juanita Handicap. Chan's son Lee, who (against his father's wishes) gets a job on the boat as a cabin boy, determines that the note came from the typewriter of Major Kent's competitor, Warren Fenton. Chan then has Lee secretly distribute notes to the other suspects—Fenton, who offered Chester $20,000 for the horse; Bruce Rogers, Chester's assistant who is in love with Fenton's daughter Alice; Denny Barton, a professional gambler who also loves Alice, but whom she has rebuked; and Chester.

In the meantime, a fire breaks out in the forward hold where Avalanche is kept and Chester claims that this is a warning. In Los Angeles harbor, Chan notices that a monkey, who earlier caused Avalanche to bolt, now causes Fenton's horse, Gallant Lad, to go wild—while Avalanche does not mind the monkey. Chan suspects that the fire was used as a cover so that the horses could be switched, and Fenton's horse could then win the upcoming race with favorable odds. The switch, involving the application of black dye to Gallant Lad, was engineered by Avalanche's trainer, Bagley, working with the gang of gamblers.

On the day of the race Chan has Lee create a diversion so that Chan can enter the stables unnoticed and switch the horses. Bagley, noticing the switch, is arrested as he calls the gambling ring with the information. When the race begins, Al Meers, a track employee who is also part of the gambling ring, replaces a timing device at the track's three-quarter pole with a bogus one fitted with a dart. As the horses approach the pole, Avalanche is in the lead and Meers fires the dart. Although hit, Avalanche wins anyway, but then falls after crossing the finish line. As a crowd surrounds Avalanche, someone then removes the dart. Chan gathers Barton, Bagley, Meers, Chester, and Fenton in the racing association's office. After several accusations, the dart is found in Fenton's pocket and Chester accuses Fenton of wanting to buy Avalanche all along and of murdering Major Kent with the winch shoe because the major would have noticed that the horses had been switched.

Chan then points out that no one other than himself, his chief, the ship's captain and the murderer knew about the winch shoe. Chan says that he suspected Chester all along because Chester, who admits that he suffered gambling losses, did not use his glasses to read the first threatening note he received (which Chester sent to himself to throw off suspicion) but that he *did* use his glasses to read the second note (which Chan sent with Lee's help).

Chan then reveals bloodstains from the dart in the lining of Chester's pocket. Fenton confesses that he knew of the plot to switch horses and tells J.L. Lansing, the racing secretary, that he will remove his horses from the track. Bruce Rogers wins enough money from the race to furnish an apartment for himself and Alice.

Notes: Some scenes for *Charlie Chan at the Race Track* were shot at the Santa Anita Racetrack in Arcadia, California. The film also contained footage of some of the events of that racing season.

Charlie Chan at the Ringside A 1938 movie project that was never completed. The movie, whose working titles were *Charlie Chan at the Arena* and *Charlie Chan at the Fights*, went into production on January 10, 1938, but only seven days later Darryl Zanuck scrapped the picture, having finally become fed up with Warner Oland's drinking and absences from the set. From studio records, $93,820.59 was spent on the filming up to this point.

While filming, Warner Oland and Twentieth Century–Fox had a disagreement and Oland left the set one day and did not return. Eager to see his homeland once more, he sailed to Sweden where he died of bronchial pneumonia on August 6, 1938.

On January 24, 1938, Twentieth Century–Fox salvaged parts of *Charlie Chan at the Ringside* and began reworking it into *Mr. Moto's Gamble* (1938). In this new movie, Lee Chan, long portrayed as Number One son Lee, was again Lee Chan, but now served as an assistant to the Japanese detective Mr. Moto (played by Peter Lorre). *See also* ***Mr. Moto's Gamble.***

***Charlie Chan at the Wax Museum* (1940)** The fourteenth *Charlie Chan* film produced by Twentieth Century–Fox Film Corporation.

Source: based on the character "Charlie Chan" created by Earl Derr Biggers. Original Copyright: Twentieth Century–Fox Film Corporation, September 6, 1940; LP9228. Copyright Renewed: August 22, 1968; R441033. PCA Certificate Number: 6383. Production: began mid–May, 1940. Release Date: September 6, 1940. Sound: RCA High Fidelity Recording. Film: b&w; 5,718 feet. Running Time: 63 minutes.

Associate Producers: Walter Morosco and Ralph Dietrich. Director: Lynn Shores. Associate Director: Jasper Blystone.* Original Screenplay: John Larkin. Director of Photography: Virgil Miller. Art Direction: Richard Day and Lewis Creber. Film Editor: James B. Clark. Set Decorations: Thomas Little. Costumes: Herschel. Musical Direction: Emil Newman. Sound: Bernard Freericks and Harry M. Leonard.

Cast

Sidney Toler	*as*	Charlie Chan
Sen Yung		Jimmy Chan
C. Henry Gordon		Dr. Cream
Marc Lawrence		Steve McBirney
Joan Valerie		Lily Latimer
Marguerite Chapman		Mary Bolton
Ted Osborn		Tom Agnew [alias for Butcher Degan]
Michael Visaroff		Dr. Otto von Brom
Hilda Vaughn		Mrs. Rocke
Charles Wagenheim		Willie Fern
Archie Twitchell		Carter Lane
Edward Marr		Grennock
Joe King		Inspector O'Matthews
Harold Goodwin		Edwards
Charles Trowbridge*		Judge
Emmett Vogan*		Prosecuting Attorney
Stanley Blystone*		Bailiff

Plot Summary: Steve McBirney is convicted of murder (on evidence provided by Charlie Chan) and sentenced to die at Sing Sing Prison. As he is led away after sentencing, he gives a nod to his henchman Grennock, who helps him escape.

Now on the lam, he and Grennock go to Dr. Cream, who was once the country's best facial plastic surgeon and now uses his surgical skills to alter faces of criminals wanted by the law. As a cover for his criminal activities, he runs Dr. Cream's Museum of Crime and is assisted by Lily Latimer. The museum features figures of infamous criminals and is where the weekly *The Crime League* radio broadcasts originate.

While recuperating from facial surgery performed by Dr. Cream, McBirney (bent on revenge against Charlie Chan) coerces the doctor to lure Chan to the museum on the pretense of participating in a crime-solving radio broadcast. Although suspicious of Cream's motives, Chan accepts the invitation to discuss the Rocke case and is unaware that he is to be electrocuted as he sits in one of the museum's chairs. At the last moment Chan changes seats with Dr. Otto von Brom, another crime expert (whose testimony helped convict and execute Joe Rocke for a murder he did not commit), and von Brom is

**Unbilled.*

murdered. The weapon is not electricity, but a poison dart blown by someone hiding within the museum. The occupants of the museum are unable to call the police as the phone is out of order, and Chan knows that the person who leaves to make the call may well be the murderer. Until Chan can summon the police, all suspects are sequestered in the museum.

Acting on an earlier observation by son Jimmy, Chan searches one of the museum's jail cells and discovers a trap door leading to the basement which houses Dr. Cream's secret laboratory and operating room. He sees clues that McBirney had been there and traces von Brom's murder to "Butcher" Degan, McBirney's supposedly dead partner (who also had his face altered by Cream).

After Degan kills McBirney and attempts to murder Chan, Inspector O'Matthews of the police arrives with his men. Chan then unmasks Degan as radio broadcaster Tom Agnew, who killed to keep his criminal identity a secret.

Notes: When *Charlie Chan at the Wax Museum* was to premiere in Honolulu, the theater manager there wrote Sidney Toler and asked if the wax dummy of Charlie Chan used in the movie could be shipped to Honolulu for the premiere. Although Toler had promised it would be done, the studio didn't feel that the costs were worth it and they refused. Since Toler had given his word, he then bought the wax dummy from the studio and had it shipped to Honolulu, keeping his promise.

Charlie Chan at the World's Fair Working title for *Charlie Chan at Treasure Island* (1939) before its release on September 8, 1939. *See also* ***Charlie Chan at Treasure Island* (1939)**.

***Charlie Chan at Treasure Island* (1939)** The tenth *Charlie Chan* film produced by Twentieth Century–Fox Film Corporation.

Working Title: *Charlie Chan at the World's Fair*. Source: based on the character "Charlie Chan" created by Earl Derr Biggers. Original Copyright: Twentieth Century–Fox Film Corporation, September 8, 1939; LP9300. Copyright Renewed: May 29, 1967; R410880. PCA Certificate Number: 5321. Production: April 17 to May 13, 1939. Release Date: September 8, 1939. Sound: RCA High Fidelity Recording. Film: b&w; 8 reels; 6,633 feet. Running Time: 72 or 74 minutes.

Executive Producer: Sol M. Wurtzel.* Associate Producer: Edward Kaufman. Director: Norman Foster. Assistant Director: Charles Hall.* Original Story and Screenplay: John Larkin. Photography: Virgil Miller. Art Direction: Richard Day and Lewis Creber. Film Editor: Norman Colbert. Set Decorations: Thomas Little. Costumes: Herschel. Musical Direction: Samuel Kaylin. Sound: E. Clayton Ward and William H. Anderson.

Cast

Sidney Toler	*as*	Charlie Chan
Cesar Romero		[Fred] Rhadini
Pauline Moore		Eve [Cairo]
Sen Yung		Jimmy Chan
Douglas Fowley		Pete Lewis
June Gale		Myra Rhadini
Douglass Dumbrille		Thomas Gregory [alias for Stewart Salisbury]
Sally Blane		Stella Essex
Billie Seward		Bessie Sibley
Wally Vernon		Elmer Keiner
Donald MacBride		Chief J.J. Kilvaine
Charles Halton		Redley
Trevor Bardette		Abdul
Louis Jean Heydt		Paul Essex
John Elliott*		Doctor

Plot Summary: Charlie Chan is accompanying his son Jimmy on the China Clipper from Hawaii to San Francisco, where Jimmy attends college. Also on the plane is Chan's friend, writer Paul Essex, who has just finished a mystery novel about a fake mystic. Essex is pestered by Thomas Gregory, an insurance actuary, who slyly reads a disturbing radiogram that Paul receives.

As the plane is starting to land, Jimmy discovers Paul dead, an apparent suicide. Chan reads the radiogram, which warns of disaster if Zodiac obligations are ignored. Chan and Jimmy also notice that Essex's

**Unbilled.*

manuscript that he had just completed is missing, along with his briefcase. After the plane lands, Chan tells Paul's wife, Stella, who is waiting for her husband at the airport gate, about the tragedy. Chan thinks that Gregory stole Essex's briefcase and the manuscript, and has Jimmy follow Gregory.

Waiting for a taxi, Chan is kidnapped by two men, who are really plainclothes detectives. They arrive at police headquarters where he is greeted by Deputy Chief J.J. Kilvaine, an old friend, and is introduced to reporter Pete Lewis and magician Fred Rhadini. Rhadini (who operates the "Temple of Magic" theater on Treasure Island) and Pete explain that they are on a crusade to expose fake psychics. Their primary target is Dr. Zodiac, whom they suspect is behind the suicides of three of his clients. Chan believes that Paul Essex is the fourth such suicide, and states that a suicide induced by blackmail is really murder.

Chan, Pete, and Rhadini go to Zodiac's mansion and ask to consult with the heavily-masked spiritualist. While Lewis and Rhadini proclaim Zodiac a fake, Chan cautions that they must be careful because of Zodiac's obvious mental delusions. Later that evening Chan attends a party Rhadini hosts in honor of San Francisco's Golden Gate International Exposition. There he is fascinated by the mind-reading abilities of Eve Cairo, who is Rhadini's assistant and Pete's girlfriend. After the party, Chan, Jimmy, Rhadini, and Pete return to Dr. Zodiac's mansion and find a vault containing file cabinets filled with information with which Zodiac has been blackmailing his clients. One such file had information about Paul Essex, who, as Paul Ellson, was in prison for three years after being convicted of stock swindling.

Chan burns the files and the next day decides to use Zodiac's vanity to trap him by having Rhadini issue a public challenge to Zodiac to subject himself to examination at Rhadini's theater. Zodiac accepts the challenge and comes to the theater, but while Rhadini is levitating Eve during one of his illusions, the man in the Zodiac mask is murdered and revealed to be Abdul, the medium's servant. Kilvaine recognizes Gregory and introduces him to Chan as Stewart Salisbury, an insurance detective investigating the suicides. Together, they help recreate the levitating trick to determine who killed Abdul and how.

When Rhadini performs the levitating again, he is stabbed in the shoulder with a small arrow. Chan then employs Eve's mind-reading ability to help identify the culprit. While he is questioning her, a hand holding a gun appears. The gunman is revealed to be Rhadini who, as the real Dr. Zodiac, had Abdul pose as the psychic to fool the police into believing that he was dead. Chan demonstrates how Rhadini used his magic wand as a blowgun to kill Abdul, and then wounded himself to deflect suspicion.

Notes: Several sources erroneously credit Gerald Mohr as portraying Dr. Zodiac. Neither the on-screen credits nor the *American Film Institute Catalog of Motion Pictures Produced in the United States* list Gerald Mohr for this movie. The Golden Gate International Exposition, held on Treasure Island in San Francisco Bay from February 1939 to October 1940, provided the backdrop for some of the picture's action.

***Charlie Chan Carries On* (novel)** The fifth *Charlie Chan* novel written by Earl Derr Biggers and published in 1930 by Bobbs-Merrill. The novel was serialized in *The Saturday Evening Post* from August 9 to September 13, 1930, and was the basis for both the 1931 film of the same name and the Spanish-language version, *Eran Trece* (1931). The novel was also the basis for *Charlie Chan's Murder Cruise* (1940). *See* photo, page 80.

***Charlie Chan Carries On* (1931)** The second *Charlie Chan* film produced by the Fox Film Corporation.

Source: based on the novel *Charlie Chan Carries On* by Earl Derr Biggers (Bobbs-Merrill, 1930), which was serialized in *The Saturday Evening Post* from August 9 to September 13, 1930. Original Copyright: Fox Film Corporation, February 11, 1931; LP2031. Copyright Renewed: March 7, 1958; R210357. Passed by the National Board of Review. Production: January to late January, 1931.

The cover of an early edition of *Charlie Chan Carries On*, written by Earl Derr Biggers in 1930 (courtesy Don Rogers).

Release Date: April 12, 1931. Film: b&w; 8 reels; 6,200 feet. Running Time: 69 minutes.

Director: Hamilton MacFadden. Assistant Director: Sam Wurtzel. Screenplay and Dialogue: Philip Klein and Barry Conners. Photography: George Schneiderman. Sets: Joseph Wright. Film Editor: Al DeGaetano. Costumes: Sophie Wachner. Sound Engineer: George P. Costello.

Cast

Marguerite Churchill	*as*	Pamela Potter
John Garrick		Mark Kennaway
Warner Oland		Charlie Chan
Warren Hymer		Max Minchin
Marjorie White		Sadie Minchin
C. Henry Gordon		John Ross [alias for Jim Everhard]
William Holden		Patrick Tait
George Brent		Capt. Ronald Keane
Peter Gawthorne		Inspector Duff
John T. Murray		Dr. Lofton
John Swor		Elmer Benbow
Goodee Montgomery		Mrs. Benbow
Jason Robards		Walter Honeywood
Lumsden Hare		Inspector Hanley
Zeffie Tilbury		Mrs. Luce
Betty Francisco		Sybil Conway
Harry Beresford		Kent
John Rogers		Martin
J. Gunnis Davis		Eben
James Farley		

Plot Summary: Inspector Duff of Scotland Yard gets a call about the murder of wealthy Hugo Morris Drake, who is strangled with a suitcase strap while on an around-the-world tour with a party of other Americans. Dr. Lofton, the tour conductor, discovers that the strap came from his bag. Duff interrogates Walter Honeywood, a theatrical manager occupying the room next to Drake's, who hopes to meet his estranged wife, actress Sybil Conway, at San Remo and persuade her to join him on the trip.

Duff then realizes that he cannot hold the twelve remaining tourists because he has no evidence or motive. After they leave for Paris, Duff learns that Honeywood paid a hotel servant not to reveal that he and Drake exchanged rooms the night Drake was killed. That night, as the party stops over in Nice, a gloved hand fires a shot from some bushes and puts the gun in the hand of the deceased Honeywood. When Duff arrives the next day, he learns that Honeywood is dead, apparently a suicide. Duff calls Sybil, who meets him at San Remo and says that the murderer is Jim Everhard, a jewel thief to whom she had been unhappily married. Years earlier, Honeywood and Sybil ran away together, taking two bags of diamonds, and Everhard vowed to kill them both. Sybil agrees to point out the killer, but the figure with the gloved hand shoots and kills her.

During the next part of the trip, Mark Kennaway, the traveling companion of Patrick Tait, an elderly criminal lawyer, becomes fond of Pamela Potter, Drake's granddaughter, who is continuing the trip to help track down the killer. In Hong Kong, Pam and Mark pass a street merchant who calls out Everhard's name as he passes by. When Pam tells the tourist party that Everhard has been spotted, Mark now realizes that she has placed herself in danger. As she sends a telegram to Inspector Duff, a gloved hand fires a gun at her, but Mark pulls her aside in time. Duff travels to Honolulu, the party's next destination. After visiting his friend, Charlie Chan of the Honolulu police, he is shot in the back. Chan prepares to join the party on their voyage to San Francisco and asks his chief to tell the wounded Duff, "Charlie Chan carries on."

In his cabin on the ship, Chan hears movement by his window. Grabbing a gloved hand holding a gun, Chan pulls the glove off, but the murderer escapes. After clues implicate various male members of the party, the ship approaches San Francisco and Chan writes identical letters to the suspects. At a farewell party, Chan explains to the guests that Drake was murdered by mistake, as Everhard really intended to kill Honeywood. Chan says that to save Everhard embarrassment, he has informed him in a note that he will not arrest him until they dock at San Francisco.

The tourists then find the letters Chan left for each of them, and, as part of a trap, Chan fixes a dummy in front of the window of his own room. As he and Kennaway wait in the lifeboat, he turns on a switch rigged to light his room. The murderer enters the room and, after shooting at the dummy, is apprehended by Chan and Kennaway. As the others enter, the murderer is revealed to be John Ross, who expresses regret over killing Drake but not Honeywood or Sybil. He then asks Chan how he knew it was him. Chan reveals that he did not know, but that he wrote the letters to draw the murderer out. Chan then dictates a cable to Duff and, seeing Mark and Pam together, says that they have decided that "two shall be one—more later."

Notes: *Charlie Chan Carries On*, of which no copies are currently known to exist, was the first *Charlie Chan* film to star Warner Oland. The movie was released later the same year in a Spanish-language remake, *Eran Trece*. The film was remade (without acknowledgment) as *Charlie Chan's Murder Cruise* (1940).

**Unbilled.*

Charlie Chan Comes Clean Title of an unused or unfinished idea for a *Charlie Chan* film by Twentieth Century–Fox.

Charlie Chan in Alcatraz One of three working titles for *Dark Alibi* (1946) before its release on May 25, 1946. *See also* ***Dark Alibi*** **(1946).**

Charlie Chan in Black Magic see ***Black Magic*** **(1944)**

Charlie Chan in City in Darkness Working title for *City in Darkness* (1939) before its release on December 1, 1939. *See also* ***City in Darkness*** **(1939).**

Charlie Chan in City in New York Working title for *Murder Over New York* (1940) before its release on December 13, 1940. *See also* ***Murder Over New York*** **(1940).**

Charlie Chan in Egypt **(1935)** The ninth *Charlie Chan* film produced by the Fox Film Corporation.

Source: based on the character "Charlie Chan" created by Earl Derr Biggers. Original Copyright: Fox Film Corporation, June 21, 1935; LP5882. Copyright Renewed: March 18, 1963; R312494. PCA Certificate Number: 905. Production: April, 1935. Release Date: June 21, 1935. Sound: Western Electric Noiseless Recording. Film: b&w; 8 reels; 6,600 feet. Running Time: 72 minutes.

Producer: Edward T. Lowe. Director: Luis King [sic, Louis King]. Original Screenplay: Robert Ellis and Helen Logan. Photography: Daniel B. Clark. Art Direction: Duncan Cramer and Walter Koessler. Editor: Al DeGaetano.* Gowns: Helen Myron. Musical Director: Samuel Kaylin. Sound: Albert Protzman.

Cast

Warner Oland	*as*	Charlie Chan
Pat Paterson		Carol Arnold
Thomas Beck		Tom Evans
Rita Cansino		Nayda
Stepin Fetchit		Snowshoes
Jameson Thomas*		Dr. Anton Racine

Frank Conroy*	Professor John Thurston
Nigel De Brulier*	Edfu Ahmad
James Eagles*	Barry Arnold
Paul Porcasi*	Fuad Soueida
Arthur Stone*	Dragoman
John George*	Ali, gravedigger who dies
Frank Reicher*	Dr. Jaipur
George Irving*	Professor Arnold
Anita Brown*	Snowshoes' friend
John Davidson*	Daoud Atrash, chemist
Gloria Roy*	

Plot Summary: Charlie Chan is sent to Egypt on behalf of the French Archeological Society to investigate Professor Arnold's excavation of Ahmeti's tomb because some of the artifacts discovered in the tomb have been found in other museums. Once there, Chan finds out from the professor's daughter Carol, his son Barry, his brother-in-law, Professor John Thurston, and Tom Evans, who is Arnold's young assistant and Carol's boyfriend, that Arnold has been missing for a month.

Carol is depressed over her father's absence, and Tom sends for Dr. Anton Racine, the family physician. Dr. Racine arrives shortly after Carol hallucinates that she is being threatened by Sekhmet, the Egyptian goddess of vengeance, whose statue was guarding Ahmeti's tomb. Meanwhile, in the basement laboratory, Chan, Thurston, and Evans examine Ahmeti's mummy using an x-ray machine. Chan notices a bullet in the mummy's chest, and they unwrap the mummy and discover the mummy is not Ahmeti but Professor Arnold.

Thurston then admits to Chan that Professor Arnold was a poor businessman and that he sold a few artifacts to pay off money he had borrowed from Dr. Racine. Barry Arnold overhears them discussing his father's death and collapses in hysterics, certain that the tomb's curse will kill the entire family.

Chan decides to investigate the tomb that night with Evans and his helper, Snowshoes. Once inside the tomb they are frightened off by a vision of Sekhmet. The next day Chan goes to Luxor to question Daoud Atrash, the chemist who fills Racine's prescriptions for Carol Arnold. That night when Chan returns to the Arnold house, an autopsy of Professor Arnold is underway and, after the others leave, Chan extracts the bullet from near Arnold's heart. Chan then rejoins the others upstairs and questions Dr. Racine about mapuchari, a drug which causes hallucinations and death and which Chan suspects is being placed in Carol's cigarettes to trigger her attacks.

They are just about to talk to Barry about the secret treasure his father was trying to find when Barry dies while playing his violin. Chan, Evans, and Snowshoes later return to the tomb where they find a secret water passageway. When Evans swims underwater to the next room, which is a storage room for Ahmeti's treasures, he is shot by someone he recognizes. As he falls, he hits a lever that opens a secret door between the rooms, and Chan and Snowshoes take him back to the house.

Unable to locate Dr. Racine, Dr. Jaipur removes the bullet from Evans, which Chan takes as evidence before going to search Barry's room. Examining Barry's violin, Chan finds small fragments of glass inside and deduces that Barry was killed by a tiny vial of deadly gas. In the laboratory, Chan demonstrates to Thurston and Dr. Racine how the violin's vibrations shattered the glass and released the gas. He then tells them it was the hidden treasure room which was the motive for the two murders and the attempt on Tom Evans' life.

Upstairs, Dr. Racine examines Evans, after which Thurston convinces Carol to leave and rest. Now alone with the unconscious Evans, Thurston prepares to stab him with a lancet taken from Dr. Racine's medical bag, but Chan arrives just in time. Chan explains that the bullets recovered from Arnold and Evans came from Thurston's gun, and the police then take Thurston away.

Note: *Charlie Chan in Egypt* is the third in a series of films that has Charlie Chan globetrotting around the world, and provided continuity from the previous film,

**Unbilled.*

Charlie Chan in Paris, by having the French Archeological Society engage Chan to investigate Professor Arnold's excavation of Ahmeti's tomb.

Charlie Chan in Homeland One of two Chinese-language *Charlie Chan* films made in the late 1930s by the Hsin Hwa Chinese motion picture company in Shanghai with Hsu Hsin-Yuan as Charlie Chan. This picture, along with *Charlie Chan in Radio Station*, was never distributed outside mainland China.

***Charlie Chan in Honolulu* (1938)** The eighth *Charlie Chan* film produced by Twentieth Century–Fox Film Corporation.

Source: based on the character "Charlie Chan" created by Earl Derr Biggers. Original Copyright: 20th Century–Fox Film Corporation, January 13, 1939; LP8722. Copyright Renewed: December 8, 1966; R399739. PCA Certificate Number: 4861. Production: October 31 to late November, 1938. Release Date: January 13, 1939. Sound: Western Electric Mirrophonic Recording. Film: b&w; 7 reels; 6,074 feet. Running Time: 67–68 minutes.

Producer: Sol M. Wurtzel.* Associate Producer: John Stone. Director: H. Bruce Humberstone. Assistant Director: Saul Wurtzel.* Original Screenplay: Charles Belden. Photography: Charles Clarke. Art Direction: Richard Day and Haldane Douglas. Film Editor: Nick DeMaggio. Set Decoration: Thomas Little. Costumes: Helen A. Myron. Musical Direction: Samuel Kaylin. Sound: Joseph E. Aiken and William H. Anderson. Casting Director: James Ryan.*

Cast

Sidney Toler	*as*	Charlie Chan
Phyllis Brooks		Judy Hayes
Sen Yung		James Chan
Eddie Collins		Al Hogan
John King		[George] Randolph
Claire Dodd		Mrs. Carol Wayne [alias for Mrs. Elsie Hillman]
George Zucco		Dr. Cardigan
Robert Barrat		Captain Johnson
Marc Lawrence		Johnny McCoy
Richard Lane		[Detective] Joe Arnold [alias for Mike Hannigan]
Layne Tom, Jr.		Tommy Chan
Philip Ahn		Wing Foo
Paul Harvey		Inspector Rawlins
Richard Alexander*		Sailor
James Flavin*		Homicide division cop
Al Kikume*		Policeman

*Unbilled.

Plot Summary: In Honolulu, Charlie Chan is awaiting the arrival of his first grandchild. After he, his wife, and their son-in-law, Wing Foo, rush to the hospital, a call comes in for him to investigate a murder on the freighter *Susan B. Jennings*. Number Two son Jimmy, who wants to become his father's assistant, is persuaded by his little brother Tommy to answer the call himself and prove to their father that he is a good investigator.

Tommy tags along as Jimmy goes to the freighter, which has just arrived from Shanghai. When Jimmy comes aboard, Captain Johnson assumes that Jimmy is Charlie Chan and explains that the murdered man's identity is a mystery and that Judy Hayes was the only eyewitness to the fatal shooting. Jimmy decides to question the rest of the freighter's passengers, who include animal keeper Al Hogan, Mrs. Carol Wayne, psychiatrist Dr. Cardigan, criminal Johnny McCoy, and policeman Joe Arnold (who is taking McCoy back to Shanghai).

Judy Hayes reveals that her employer, a lawyer in Shanghai, instructed her to deliver a package containing $300,000 to a man who would meet her in Honolulu. The man identified himself by a pre-arranged signal, but was shot by an unknown assailant before Judy could give him the money. First mate George Randolph, who has fallen in love with Judy, takes Jimmy to question the bad-tempered crew members.

Having received a telephone call at the hospital from Inspector Rawlins, his superior, Chan hurries to the boat and then questions Carol Wayne, who states that she was on the freighter to rest while her suit for divorce was being heard, and that she recently became a widow anyway. Searching passenger rooms, Chan finds a wrapper for part of the missing money in Dr. Cardigan's compartment and becomes more suspicious of

Judy when she quietly leaves the ship to call her employer about the stolen funds.

Mrs. Wayne reveals that Randolph gave Judy a gun with which to protect herself. Examining it, Chan finds that it is the same caliber as the murder weapon. Judy then protests to Randolph that she is being framed when he questions her about the missing money that he found hidden in her cabin.

Later, Chan and Jimmy find Mrs. Wayne dead in Judy Hayes' cabin, strangled by a scarf tied with a sailor's knot. Chan also reveals that Detective Arnold is actually Mike Hannigan, having recently noticed his picture on wanted posters. Hannigan, while in league with McCoy, murdered the real Detective Arnold after escaping from prison. Chan reveals to the passengers that Carol was really Mrs. Elise Hillman, the dead man's wife, and Judy Hayes states that, although she did not know about Mrs. Hillman, she was delivering the money to the man so that he did not have to declare it in a divorce settlement.

Chan gets assistance from Dr. Cardigan to rig a trap for the killer. It works when the killer attempts to grab the murder weapon and triggers a camera. After Jimmy and Dr. Cardigan develop the photograph, Captain Johnson is revealed as the murderer. Chan then explains that Captain Johnson was after the money, and later killed Mrs. Hillman when she became suspicious. After the case is wrapped up, Chan receives a call from Wing Foo and happily listens as his newborn grandson cries into the phone.

Notes: *Charlie Chan in Honolulu* was the first film in which Sidney Toler appeared as Charlie Chan following the death of Warner Oland. On October 18, 1938, associate producer John Stone chose Toler after seeing him play a Chinese character (Dr. Chang Ling) in the Paramount film, *King of Chinatown* (1939). Toler was the thirty-fifth actor tested for the role, and production began almost two weeks later on October 31.

Charlie Chan in Honolulu was also the first film in which Sen Yung (who later changed his name to Victor Sen Young) played Number Two son, James "Jimmy" Chan. Yung replaced Keye Luke, who had portrayed Lee Chan in eight earlier entries in the series. Luke left the series after Oland's death when he and Twentieth Century–Fox disagreed on his new contract that cut his salary. According to news items, the search for Luke's replacement was "frantic," and led to casting director James Ryan seeking applicants among Los Angeles Chinese university students and Chinatown residents.

Richard Lane was originally signed to play the romantic lead opposite Phyllis Brooks but portrayed Joe Arnold in the film while John King played romantic lead George Randolph.

***Charlie Chan in London* (1934)** The seventh *Charlie Chan* film produced by the Fox Film Corporation.

Source: based on the character "Charlie Chan" created by Earl Derr Biggers. Original Copyright: Fox Film Corporation, September 14, 1934; LP4951. Copyright Renewed: June 25, 1962; R297359. PCA Certificate Number: 171. Production: July 9 to early August, 1934. Release Date: September 12, 1934. Sound: Western Electric Noiseless Recording. Film: b&w; 8 reels; 7,026 feet. Running Time: 77–79 minutes.

Producer: John Stone. Director: Eugene Forde. Assistant Director: Ed O'Fearna.* Original Screenplay: Philip MacDonald. Dialogue: Stuart Anthony* and Lester Cole.* Photography: L.W. O'Connell. Assistant Cameramen: John Schmitz* and Robert Surtees.* Sets: Duncan Cramer. Gowns: Royer. Musical Director: Samuel Kaylin. Sound: E. Clayton Ward. Stunts: Joe Flores,* Clint Sharp,* Walter Nobles,* and Opal Ernie.* Stand-ins: Ann Doran* and Alex Chivra.*

Cast

Warner Oland	*as*	Inspector Charlie Chan
Drue Leyton		Pamela Gray
Raymond Milland		Neil Howard
Mona Barrie		Lady Mary Bristol
Alan Mowbray		Geoffrey Richmond [alias for Paul Frank]

**Unbilled.*

Murray Kinnell	Phillips [alias for Capt. Seeton]
Douglas Walton	Hugh Gray
Walter Johnson	Jerry Gorton
E.E. Clive	Detective Sergeant Thacker
George Barraud	Major Jardine
Madge Bellamy	Mrs. [Becky] Fothergill
David Torrence	Home Secretary [Sir Lionel Bashford]
John Rogers	Lake
Paul England	Bunny Fothergill
Elsa Buchanan	Alice Rooney
Perry Ivins	Kemp
Claude King*	RAF Commandant
Reginald Sheffield*	Flight Commander King
Helena Grant*	Secretary
C. Montague Shaw*	Doctor
Phillis Coghlan*	Nurse
Margaret Mann*	Housemaid
Carlie Taylor,* Doris Stone*	Guests
Arthur Clayton*	Warden

Plot Summary: Pamela Gray goes with Geoffrey Richmond to appeal to Sir Lionel Bashford, the Home Secretary, to intervene and stop the planned hanging of her brother, Paul Gray, in three days. Gray was Richmond's former hunt secretary who was tried and found guilty of the murder of Capt. Hamilton of the Royal Air Force, a guest at Richmond's country home at Redfordshire. After the Home Secretary refuses to help, Kemp (his private secretary) instructs Pamela and her fiancée, Neil Howard, to seek the aid of Inspector Charlie Chan, who had captured a wanted British criminal in Honolulu and brought him back to London.

When Neil, who is Paul's barrister, tells Chan that he believes that Paul is guilty, Pamela overhears the conversation and breaks their engagement. Chan, who wants to help, follows her to Redfordshire, where guests are gathered for a fox hunt.

Chan questions Lake, the stud groom who Chan suspects knows more than he admits. Chan then goes the next morning to question Lake again but is told by Detective Sergeant Thacker that Lake is dead and left a suicide note. Chan then proceeds to reconstruct the crime in his efforts to prove that Paul Gray is not guilty. While investigating in the study, Chan is almost killed by a small missile shot from an air-blown pistol.

The next day during the hunt, Chan goes to the Farnwell Aerodrome where he learns that Capt. Hamilton, an inventor, had developed a scheme for silencing war planes just before he died. Returning to the hunt, Chan learns that Richmond's fiancée, Lady Mary Bristol, who had important evidence for Chan, had met with a near-fatal riding accident because pepper was put on her horse's eyes. After Chan tells the suspected guests that the murderer's fingerprints will be on the missing plans, he tricks Richmond into firing at him with a gun filled with blanks as he seemingly finds the papers. Phillips the butler then identifies himself as Capt. Seeton working undercover for British Intelligence, and he tells Chan that Richmond, who is really Paul Frank, is a spy whom military intelligence has been following for years.

Notes: *Charlie Chan in London* is the first film of the series that was not based on a novel by Charlie Chan's creator, Earl Derr Biggers. It is also the first in a series of films that sends Charlie Chan globetrotting around the world.

*Unbilled.

Charlie Chan in Mexico Working title for *The Red Dragon* (1945) before its release on February 2, 1946. *See also* ***The Red Dragon* (1945)**.

Charlie Chan in New Orleans Working title for *Docks of New Orleans* (1948) before its release on March 21, 1948. *See also* ***Docks of New Orleans* (1948)**.

***Charlie Chan in Panama* (1940)** The twelfth *Charlie Chan* film produced by Twentieth Century–Fox Film Corporation.

Source: based on the character "Charlie Chan" created by Earl Derr Biggers. Original Copyright: Twentieth Century–Fox Film Corporation, March 8, 1940; LP9651. Copyright Renewed: December 12, 1967; R424029. PCA Certificate Number: 5892. Production: began early October, 1939. Release Date:

March 8, 1940. Sound: RCA High Fidelity Recording. Film: b&w; 6,061 feet. Running Time: 67 minutes.

Executive Producer: Sol M. Wurtzel. Director: Norman Foster. Assistant Director: Saul Wurtzel.* Original Screenplay: John Larkin and Lester Ziffren. Photography: Virgil Miller. Art Direction: Richard Day and Chester Gore. Film Editor: Fred Allen. Set Decorations: Thomas Little. Costumes: Helen A. Myron. Musical Direction: Samuel Kaylin. Sound: Joseph E. Aiken and William H. Anderson.

Cast

Sidney Toler *as*	Charlie Chan [alias Fu Yuen]
Jean Rogers	Kathi Lenesch [also as Baroness Kathi von Czardas]
Lionel Atwill	Cliveden Compton
Mary Nash	[Miss] Jennie Finch [alias for Reiner]
Sen Yung	Jimmy Chan
Kane Richmond	Richard Cabot
Chris-Pin Martin	Lt. Montero†
Lionel Royce	Dr. Rudolph Grosser
Helen Ericson	Stewardess
Jack La Rue	[Emil] Manolo
Edwin Stanley	Governor [Col. D.C.] Webster
Donald Douglas	Capt. Lewis
Frank Puglia	Achmed Halide
Addison Richards	[R.J.] Godley
Edward Keane	Dr. Fredericks
Charles Stevens*	Native fisherman, spy
Max Wagner,* Alan Davis*	Soldiers
Charles Sherlock*	Enlisted man
Eddie Acuff*	Suspicious sailor
Harold Goodwin*	Military policeman
Gloria Roy*	Hostess
Lane Chandler*	Officer
Edward Gargan*	Attendant
Philip Morris*	Plainclothesman
Albert Morin*	Hotel clerk
Jimmy Aubrey*	Drunken sailor

Plot Summary: As the U.S. Fleet prepares to navigate the waters of the Panama Canal, Panama City becomes rife with spies. A new group of suspects appears with the arrival of a seaplane bound for Balboa. Among the travelers are British novelist Cliveden Compton, matronly schoolteacher Miss Jennie Finch, sinister scientist Dr. Rudolph Grosser, café proprietor Emil Manolo, singer Kathi Lenesch, cigarette salesman Achmed Halide, government engineer Richard Cabot, and government agent R.J. Godley.

Upon landing, Godley goes to a hat shop owned by Fu Yuen, Charlie Chan's undercover alias. Godley asks Chan's help in unmasking the deadly spy known only as Reiner, who is now thought to be in Panama with a plot to blow up the canal while the U.S. Fleet is passing through it. Just as Godley is about to divulge Reiner's identity while smoking a cigarette, he falls to the ground dead. As Fu Yuen, Chan is arrested on suspicion of murder but is later freed by the governor, who knows Chan's true mission in Panama.

Chan is then left to expose Reiner before the spy can sabotage the canal. One by one, suspects are murdered. The first is Compton, an undercover member of the British Secret Service who comes to Panama on the trail of Reiner but is shot and killed by Manolo, one of Reiner's accomplices. Then Manolo is killed by Reiner. From clues found on Manolo, Chan learns that the canal's Miraflores locks are to be blown up at ten that night. Chan then gathers the suspects at the locks' power plant, forcing Miss Finch to expose herself as Reiner to escape death.

Note: In the movie's credits, Montero is listed as Sgt. Montero, but Miss Jennie Finch calls him Lt. Montero.

***Charlie Chan in Paris* (1935)** The eighth *Charlie Chan* film produced by the Fox Film Corporation.

Source: based on the character "Charlie Chan" created by Earl Derr Biggers. Original Copyright: Fox Film Corporation, January 25, 1935; LP5275. Copyright Renewed: December 7, 1962; R306391. PCA Certificate Number: 507. Production: November 12 to mid–December, 1934. Release Date: January 21, 1935. Sound: Western Electric Noiseless Recording. Film: b&w; 7 reels; 6,413 feet. Running Time: 70 minutes.

Producer: John Stone. Executive Producer: Sol M. Wurtzel.* Director: Lewis Seiler. Assistant Director: Eli Dunn.* Screen-

**Unbilled.* †*Billed as Sgt. Montero.*

play: Edward T. Lowe and Stuart Anthony. Story: Philip MacDonald. Photography: Ernest Palmer. Settings: Duncan Cramer and Albert Hogsett. Gowns: Lillian. Musical Director: Samuel Kaylin. Sound: Eugene Grossman.

Cast

Warner Oland	*as*	Charlie Chan
Mary Brian		Yvette Lamartine
Thomas Beck		Victor Descartes
Erik Rhodes		Max Corday
John Miljan		Albert Dufresne
Murray Kinnell		Henri Latouche
Minor Watson		[Inspector] Renard
John Qualen		Concierge
Keye Luke		Lee Chan
Henry Kolker		Paul Lamartine†
Dorothy Appleby		Nardi
Ruth Peterson		Renee Jacquard
Perry Ivins‡		Bedell
George Davis*		Roberts, butler
Auguste Tollaire*		Concierge
Louis Natheaux*		Reporter
Ed Cecil*		Customs officer
Robert Graves,*		
Harry Cording*		Gendarmes
Marty Faust*		Cab driver
Landers Stevens*		Bank attendant
John Dilson*		Information clerk
Samuel T. Godfrey,*		
Rolfe Sedan*		Cashiers
Moore & Allen*		Apache dancers
Gino Corrado*		Head waiter
Wilfred Lucas*		Doorman
Richard Kipling*		Master of ceremonies
Eddie Vitch*		Sketch artist
Paul McVey*		Detective
Betty Bryson*		
and Fred Wallace*		Apache dance double
Alex Chivra*		
and Gladys Howe*		Stand-ins
Gloria Roy*		

Plot Summary: Charlie Chan arrives in Paris on vacation after solving a noteworthy case in London. On his arrival at the airport he makes an appointment to meet Nardi, a dancer working undercover for him at the Café du Singe Bleu, after her performance that night. But first Chan visits Victor Descartes, whose father is a friend of Chan and is a director of the Lamartine Bank where Victor works as a clerk.

Victor's fiancée, Yvette Lamartine, the bank president's daughter, arrives at Victor's apartment with two friends—Max Corday, an intoxicated sketch artist, and Renee Jacquard. After a few drinks, the group accompanies Chan to the café. As Corday gets out of the car in front of the café, he bumps into a disgruntled man on crutches and wearing dark glasses who then berates him. At the conclusion of Nardi's *dance apache* she is thrown through a prop store-window and lands on some mattresses out of view. Before she can get up, however, Nardi is murdered by a knife thrown by the man on crutches. With her dying breath, Nardi tells Chan to look in her apartment. In Nardi's bedroom Chan finds a diary containing information about Albert Dufresne.

Arriving back at his hotel room, Chan is pleasantly surprised to see his oldest son Lee, who has come to vacation with his father. Chan tells Lee that he is really investigating a case for a London banking house and that his accomplice, Nardi, has been murdered. The next day, when Yvette visits her father at the bank, Dufresne, her father's assistant, threatens to show love letters she once wrote him to Victor unless she visits his apartment.

While Lee waits at the door of the bank, Chan enters the bank and witnesses the office manager, Henri Latouche, and the man on crutches (whom he identifies as Marcel Xavier, a shell-shocked, crippled soldier) escorted out for causing a disturbance. Chan then meets with Lamartine and Dufresne and shows them that some of the bonds issued by the bank are forgeries.

That night, as Lee watches from the street, Yvette visits Dufresne, who is packing and is secretly being watched by Xavier. Just as Dufresne is handing Yvette the old love letters, he is shot in the back by Xavier from the bedroom. Xavier then escapes with the bonds Dufresne had packed, but Lee follows the murderer's taxi. Yvette panics and grabs the gun just as the room is invaded by people from the hallway who heard the shots. When the police arrive, Max and Renee are interrogated by the police. Before she is arrested by Inspector Renard for murder,

**Unbilled.* *†Billed as M. Lamartine.* *‡Billed as Perry Ivans.*

Yvette slips the love letters to Chan, who promises to destroy them.

Lee returns to the hotel and tells his father that Xavier got into a limousine after the taxi ride and that it was the same limousine in which Max Corday and Renee rode when they left the hotel. Chan goes to Corday's apartment and tells him that he suspects that a man named Xavier used Corday's limousine to get rid of his disguise. Corday, thinking that Chan may suspect him, reminds him that it was Xavier who bumped into him outside the car in front of the café. As part of a plan, Chan then leaves. Corday packs the bonds that were in Dufresne's room, but Chan and Lee are waiting outside his apartment door to stop him from leaving. Chan concludes that Corday killed Dufresne, but he still has not found Nardi's murderer.

Lee holds Corday at gun point and Chan goes to the bank where Latouche gives him Xavier's address. Wanting to help, Victor Descartes drives Chan to Xavier's address where they find a secret panel leading to the Paris sewers. Searching further, they find a room with printing and engraving equipment and more forged bonds. Xavier arrives and fires at Chan, but they apprehend him. Chan then removes Xavier's wig, glasses, and mask to reveal that Xavier is Henri Latouche. Inspector Renard and the police arrive with Lee, and Chan explains that Corday and Latouche both used the disguise so that each could have alibis for the other. Dufresne was their accomplice in the bond forgeries and tried to leave town with their money but was murdered by Corday. Chan then tells Inspector Renard that Yvette is his assistant and was sent by him to get important letters from Dufresne. Renard understands, noting that chivalry is not dead, and agrees to release her.

Notes: *Charlie Chan in Paris* provided continuity from the series' previous entry, *Charlie Chan in London*, by having Chan, after finishing the case in London, sent to Paris on behalf of a London bank to investigate bond forgeries. The film is the first in the series in which Keye Luke played the role of Charlie's Number One son, Lee, and is also the first film to have one of Chan's children helping to solve the murder.

Hamilton MacFadden was the original director for *Charlie Chan in Paris* but was replaced by Lewis Seiler after only one week's shooting, and Daniel B. Clark, who was the original cameraman, was replaced by Ernest Palmer. Neither MacFadden nor Clark received on-screen credit. In the film's credits, Henry Kolker's character, Paul Lamartine, is credited only as M. [for Monsieur] Lamartine.

Charlie Chan in Radio Station One of two Chinese-language *Charlie Chan* films made in the late 1930s by the Hsin Hwa motion picture company in Shanghai. This picture, along with *Charlie Chan in Homeland*, was never distributed outside mainland China.

***Charlie Chan in Reno* (1939)** The ninth *Charlie Chan* film produced by Twentieth Century–Fox Film Corporation.

Working Title: *Death Makes a Decree*. Source: based on both the screen story *Death Makes a Decree* by Philip Wylie, and the character "Charlie Chan" created by Earl Derr Biggers. Original Copyright: Twentieth Century–Fox Film Corporation, June 16, 1939; LP9000. Copyright Renewed: December 8, 1966; R339749. PCA Certificate Number: 5160. Production: January 23 to February 24, 1939. Release Date: June 16, 1939. Sound: RCA High Fidelity Recording. Film: b&w; 7 reels; 6,379 feet. Running Time: 70 minutes.

Associate Producer: John Stone. Director: Norman Foster. Assistant Director: Jasper Blystone.* Screenplay: Frances Hyland, Albert Ray, and Robert E. Kent. Original Story: Philip Wylie. Photography: Virgil Miller. Art Direction: Richard Day and David Hall. Film Editor: Fred Allen. Set Decorations: Thomas Little. Costumes: Herschel. Musical Direction: Samuel Kaylin. Sound: Bernard Freericks and William H. Anderson.

**Unbilled.*

Cast

Sidney Toler	*as*	Charlie Chan
Ricardo Cortez		Dr. Ainsley
Phyllis Brooks		Vivian Wells
Slim Summerville		Sheriff [Tombstone] Fletcher
Kane Richmond		Curtis Whitman
Sen Yung		James Chan
Pauline Moore		Mary Whitman
Eddie Collins		Cab driver
Kay Linaker		Mrs. Russell
Louise Henry		Jeanne Bently
Robert Lowery		Wally Burke
Charles D. Brown		Chief of Police King
Iris Wong		Choy Wong
Morgan Conway		George Bently
Hamilton MacFadden		Night clerk
Arthur Rankin*		Bellboy
Fred Kelsey*		Desk Sergeant
Virginia Sale*		Maid
Harry Hayden*		Chemistry professor
Dick Hogan*		College boy in lab
Barbara MacLain*		College girl in lab
Al Kikume*		Honolulu policeman
Ed Stanley*		Chemist
Stanley Blystone*		Policeman
Jack Perry*		Rough drunk
Bob Hale*		
Jim Aubrey*		
Imboden Parrish*		
Hank Mann*		

Plot Summary: Mary Whitman travels to the Hotel Sierra in Reno, Nevada, to establish the necessary residence while she files for divorce from her husband Curtis. After she checks in, she has an unfortunate meeting in the hotel's bar with Curtis' intended wife, a bitchy divorcée named Jeanne Bently. When Jeanne Bently taunts Mary and insults Wally Burke, a former suitor, Mrs. Russell, the owner of the hotel, orders her to leave in the morning for causing the disturbance.

Before she can finish packing her bag, Bently is murdered and Mary is found standing over the body and is arrested for the crime. Her arrest prompts her husband Curtis to ask his old friend Charlie Chan for help. Charlie then accompanies Curtis to Reno where he meets Sheriff "Tombstone" Fletcher, the inept lawman investigating the case. Charlie gets Mary released for lack of evidence.

**Unbilled.*

Charlie visits the murder room, where he finds Dr. Ainsley, who claims that he is looking for the money that Jeanne won on the night of her murder, suggesting that Burke killed her for her winnings. A search of Bently's room by Charlie and his son Jimmy reveals Jeanne's scrapbook with the pages from the years 1935 and 1936 cut out. This causes Chan to consider that a pair of scissors might have been the murder weapon. Searching further, Charlie finds particles of copper and clay on the dead woman's boots which lead him to an abandoned copper mine in a nearby ghost town. There he finds an engineering kit belonging to George Bently, the dead woman's husband, in one of the abandoned buildings. In the dark, Bently escapes but is later captured and accused of murder by Sheriff Fletcher, even though Charlie is unconvinced of his guilt.

Chan examines the murder scene and is intrigued by an acid burn on Mary's sleeve that matches a burn found on the rug in Jeanne's room. Jimmy tells Charlie that nitric acid leaves a nasty burn, and Chan remembers earlier seeing a bottle of nitric acid in Dr. Ainsley's office. Police chief King discovers that Jeanne Bently had written checks to Ainsley and learns from New York that the missing pages in the scrapbook contained newspaper clippings about Jeanne's previous marriage to Mrs. Russell's late husband, Wayne. King also learns that Dr. Ainsley was the attending physician who falsified the death certificate to cover up Wayne's murder by Jeanne.

Before the detectives can question Mrs. Russell, they find her strangled but still alive. Dr. Ainsley is about to administer a hypodermic needle to her, but Jimmy grabs the needle from Ainsley's hand and the syringe is found to contain a poison. Charlie then assembles all the murder suspects and announces that Jeanne had been paying Dr. Ainsley to keep silent about the fact that she murdered Wayne Russell.

Charlie tells them that he found the missing money in Ainsley's room, but before he finishes his explanation, Vivian Wells, the hotel's social director (who is in love with Ainsley), protests his innocence. Charlie then traps Vivian into exposing a burn on her arm, proving that she murdered Jeanne during a struggle for the acid bottle.

Notes: In the Call Bureau Cast Service lists for *Charlie Chan in Reno*, Sheriff Fletcher's name was originally Foster; Mrs. Russell was named Alice Williamson; and Choy Wong was named Sung Li.

***Charlie Chan in Rio* (1941)** The seventeenth *Charlie Chan* film produced by Twentieth Century–Fox Film Corporation.

Source: based on the character "Charlie Chan" created by Earl Derr Biggers. Original Copyright: Twentieth Century–Fox Film Corporation, September 5, 1941; LP10734. Copyright Renewed: April 4, 1969; R458931. PCA Certificate Number: 7370. Production: May 8 to late May, 1941. Release Date: September 5, 1941. Sound: RCA Sound System. Film: b&w; 6 reels; 5,540 feet. Running Time: 60 or 62 minutes.

Executive Producer: Sol M. Wurtzel. Director: Harry Lachman. Assistant Director: William Eckhardt.* Screenplay: Samuel G. Engel and Lester Ziffren. Director of Photography: Joseph P. MacDonald. Art Direction: Richard Day and Lewis H. Creber. Film Editor: Alexander Troffey. Set Decorations: Thomas Little. Costumes: Herschel. Musical Direction: Emil Newman. Music and Lyrics: Mack Gordon and Harry Warren. Sound: Alfred Bruzlin and Harry M. Leonard. Publicity Director: Harry Brand.*

Cast

Sidney Toler	*as*	Charlie Chan
Mary Beth Hughes		Joan Reynolds
Cobina Wright, Jr.		Grace Ellis
Ted North		Clark Denton†
Victor Jory		Alfredo Marana [alias for Alfredo Cardoza]
Harold Huber		Chief [Inspector] Souto
Sen Yung		Jimmy Chan
Richard Derr		Ken Reynolds
Jacqueline Dalya		Lola Dean [alias for Lola Wagner]
Kay Linaker		Helen Ashby [alias for Barbara Cardosa]
Truman Bradley		Paul Wagner
Hamilton MacFadden		Bill Kellogg
Leslie Dennison		Rice
Iris Wong		Lili [Wong]
Eugene Borden		Armando
Ann Codee		Margo

Unbilled. †Billed as Carlos Dantas.

Plot Summary: In Rio de Janeiro, nightclub singer Lola Dean accepts the proposal of Clark Denton and then insists on hosting a celebratory party for their acquaintances—Ken and Joan Reynolds, Grace Ellis, and Bill Kellogg. Clark agrees and Lola then performs her act which is watched by Charlie Chan, his son Jimmy, and the Rio de Janeiro police chief, Inspector Souto, who are there to arrest Lola for the murder of Manuel Cardozo in Honolulu a year and a half ago. Chan persuades Inspector Souto to arrest Lola quietly at her home after she leaves the club with Clark.

Upon the prodding of her secretary, Helen Ashby, Lola visits Alfredo Marana, a noted psychic before she returns home. Once Marana has placed Lola Dean in a semicomatose state with an herbal ingredient (hidden in a cigarette) that is activated by coffee, Marana records her confessing to having killed Manuel Cardozo in Honolulu because she was in love with him and he would not leave his wife for her. Once out of the trance, Marana tells Lola of what she has just revealed. On the way home, Lola persuades Clark to elope that evening with her to the United States, and she begins to pack immediately.

While Helen is telling Lola's guests about the impending elopement, Chan, Jimmy, and Inspector Souto arrive. They go to her room but Lola is found stabbed to death, with a broken brooch lying next to her. Under questioning, Ashby tells Chan about Lola's visit to Marana and about the persistent attentions of a mysterious man named Paul Wagner. Souto has Marana and Wagner brought to the house, and Wagner admits that Lola was his ex-wife and that he came to see her earlier in an attempt to win her back. Upon hearing of her engagement to Clark, however, Wagner left the house.

Marana then plays the record of Lola's session and demonstrates his trance-inducing methods on Jimmy, who doesn't believe that it is possible.

Chan discovers that the pin of the brooch in Lola's room is broken off and deduces that it is now imbedded in the killer's shoe. While Chan and Souto investigate, Jimmy finds the jewelry taken from Lola's room now in the room of Rice, the butler. Jimmy captures Rice trying to escape. When questioned by Charlie and Inspector Souto, Rice admits to stealing the jewels but denies killing Lola. Before he can name who the murderer is, the lights suddenly go out and he is shot dead.

Examination of Helen Ashby's shoe yields the missing brooch pin, but she denies having murdered anyone. Chan then suggests that Marana put her in a trance to make her confess. She drinks some coffee, smokes one of the special cigarettes, and drops into a trance. Under questioning by Chan, Helen maintains that she is innocent. Chan then offers to undergo a similar examination. After smoking the rest of Helen's cigarette and drinking some cold coffee, Chan determines that Marana gave her a cigarette that was not drugged to protect her. Chan then tells all that Marana's real name is Alfredo Cardoza. Marana says that he killed both Lola and Rice to avenge his brother's death. Helen then interrupts her brother-in-law to confess that she committed the murders because she is actually Barbara Cardosa, Manuel's widow. Helen had wanted to take Lola and the recording to the police the next day, but Lola's elopement with Clark could have enabled Lola to escape. Rice saw her with Lola's body and Helen then killed him to keep him quiet.

Notes: *Charlie Chan in Rio* is an uncredited remake of *The Black Camel* (1931). Ted North's character is listed as Carlos Dantas in the film's on-screen credits; but the film's dialogue refers to him as Clark Denton instead.

Charlie Chan in San Francisco Working title for *Charlie Chan's Secret* (1936) before its release on January 10, 1936. *See also* ***Charlie Chan's Secret* (1936).**

***Charlie Chan in Shanghai* (1935)** The tenth *Charlie Chan* film produced by the Fox Film Corporation.

Source: based on the character "Charlie Chan" created by Earl Derr Biggers. Original Copyright: Twentieth Century–Fox Film Corporation, October 11, 1935; LP6053. Copyright Renewed: August 21, 1963; R320839. PCA Certificate Number: 1255. Production: July 11 to August 3, 1935. Release Date: October 11, 1935. Sound: Western Electric Noiseless Recording. Film: b&w; 7 reels; 6,300 feet. Running Time: 70 minutes.

Associate Producer: John Stone. Director: James Tinling. Assistant Director: Aaron

Lobby card for *Charlie Chan in Shanghai* with Russell Hicks and Warner Oland (courtesy Paula McHale).

Rosenberg.* Original Story and Screenplay: Edward T. Lowe, Joseph Hoffman,* Gerard Fairlie, Robert Ellis,* and Helen Logan.* Photography: Barney McGill. Art Direction: Duncan Cramer and Lewis Creber. Film Editor: Nick DeMaggio. Gowns: Alberto Luza. Musical Director: Samuel Kaylin. Sound: Albert Protzman. Stunts: Chic Collins,* Robert Rose,* and Jack Stoney.*

Cast

Warner Oland	*as*	Charlie Chan
Irene Hervey		Diana Woodland
Charles Locher		Philip Nash
Russell Hicks		James Andrews
Keye Luke		Lee Chan
Halliwell Hobbes		Chief of Police [Col. Watkins]
Frederik Vogeding		Ivan Marloff†
Neil Fitzgerald		Dakin
Max Wagner		Taxi driver
Henry Strang*		Chauffeur
Pat O'Malley*		Belden
James B. Leong*		Telephone operator
Jockey Haefeli*		Crook on boat
David Torrence*		Sir Stanley Woodland
Torben Meyer*		French diplomat
Guy Usher*		President, Chamber of Commerce
Moy Ming*		Mr. Sun Wong
Willie Wong,* Pat Somerset,* Phil Tead,* Jimmy Phillips,* Luke Chan,* Jack Chere,* Colin Kenny*		Reporters
Eddie Lee*		Servant
Jehim Wong*		Rikesha boy
Gladden James*		Forrest, Andrew's valet
William Kum*		Porter
Sam Tong,* Walter Wong*		Waiters
Ed Hart,* Russell Hopton*		"G" men
Frank Darien,* Harrison Greene*		Tourists
Regina Rambeau*		

Plot Summary: Before Charlie Chan leaves his boat for his first visit to Shanghai in years, a man stuffs a note in his pocket warning him not to leave the ship. Chan is then greeted at the docks by Sir Stanley Woodland's secretary, Philip Nash, and Sir Stanley's niece, Diana. Also there to meet him is his son Lee, who was sent by his firm to look into the trade situation there.

At a banquet that evening in Chan's honor, Sir Stanley opens a box supposedly containing a special scroll for Chan, but is shot and killed by a gun set to go off from inside the box, which had been in Nash's possession all day. Later that night a man sneaks to the window of Chan's hotel room and, with a silencer on his gun, shoots the figure in Chan's bed and escapes. Chan fortunately had slept on a sofa in his son's room and placed some pillows in the bed to resemble his sleeping form.

The next morning Chan calls for room service, and the switchboard operator telephones Ivan Marloff to inform him that Chan is still alive and that something went wrong the night before. Chan then visits Diana Woodland to offer his condolences, and learns that someone broke into her uncle's library the previous evening and searched through his papers. Chan returns to his hotel room where a man identifying himself as police chief Colonel Watkins' chauffeur gives Chan a note instructing him to accompany the chauffeur. When Chan leaves, Lee receives a telephone call from Col. Watkins, who knows nothing about the note or chauffeur. Realizing it was a trick, Lee tries to follow his father but is subdued by a taxi driver who is part of the gang and is taken to the house where Chan is being interrogated by Marloff, a shadowy figure hidden in darkness. Chan and Lee dupe the gang into believing that the police have followed Lee and, thanks to Lee's vigorous fisticuffs, manage to escape.

Chan then visits the hotel room of James Andrews, who is a secret agent from Washington. They cautiously discuss Sir Stanley, who was a secret agent of the British government and was cooperating with both the opium committee of the League of Nations and with officials in the Chinese government to round up a gang of smugglers who are using Shanghai as a clearinghouse. Noticing in a mirror a gun appearing at the door, Chan ducks and avoids being shot. Nash is then arrested when his fingerprints are found on the gun.

Back in his hotel room, Chan heats the back of a seemingly innocuous letter from Sir Stanley to Andrews marked "important"

**Unbilled. †Billed as Burke.*

and discovers a message written with invisible ink which states that Sir Stanley has made an important discovery concerning Ivan Marloff. Chan first suspects Andrews because Andrews earlier did not seem interested in the letter, but Andrews then arrives and shows Chan that he knows the secret method of communication. Joining forces, Chan and Andrews go to police headquarters. Diana also arrives at the police station, where she slips Nash a gun, enabling them both to escape.

Chan returns to his room to find that Lee has trailed the taxi driver who earlier abducted him to the Versailles Café, a waterfront bar. Andrews calls Chan and says that he has captured one of the gang members and has cracked the case. When Chan arrives at Andrews' room, he watches as Andrews beats a confession out of the chauffeur, who admits that Marloff is at the Versailles Café. Andrews leaves with Chan for the café where, in the meantime, Nash has asked Marloff to put him on a boat for America. Calling Nash's escape from jail a trick arranged by Chan, Marloff punches Nash and tells his men to drop Nash overboard once the boat sails. Upstairs, Chan and Andrews follow the taxi driver into a room where the gang waits.

Searching some boxes, Chan discovers opium packets in a wine bottle. Andrews suggests that Chan go down the ladder first and signal the police to run the boat to the government's dock. However, Chan delays going down the ladder long enough until the police, whom Lee has called, arrive and capture the gang after a shoot-out. Chan then reveals that it was Andrews' valet who attempted to shoot Chan earlier, and that Nash's fingerprints were put on the gun with a stamp pad because the gang felt Nash knew too much about Sir Stanley's investigation.

Andrews then orders that the crooks be removed to his government's boat, but Chan pulls a gun on Andrews and accuses him of being the real leader of the gang. Nash had discovered through Sir Stanley's correspondence that the real James Andrews neither smoked nor drank, yet the man posing as Andrews earlier accepted Chan's offer of scotch and cigarettes. Lee arrives with a wirephoto of Andrews, who was killed three weeks earlier in San Francisco.

Notes: *Charlie Chan in Shanghai* was the last film made prior to the merger between the Fox Film Corporation and Twentieth Century Pictures. However, a few sources claim that this was the series' first film *following* the merger. The opening credits for *Charlie Chan in Shanghai* (released October 11, 1935) name Fox Film Corporation, while the opening credits for *Charlie Chan's Secret* (released only three months later, on January 10, 1936) name Twentieth Century–Fox Film Corporation, making *Secret* the first *Charlie Chan* release after the merger.

Jon Tuska, in his book *The Detective in Hollywood*, relates that when the series' previous film, *Charlie Chan in Egypt* (1935), was released, Warner Oland visited the Orient and was mobbed by fans when his ship docked in Shanghai. The Chinese mayor of Shanghai invited him to a celebration in his honor, attended by many of the important individuals of the city's international quarter. The event was then written into the series' next film.

Charlie Chan in the Murder Chamber One of two working titles for *Black Magic* (1944) before its release on September 9, 1944. *See also* ***Black Magic* (1944).**

***Charlie Chan in the Secret Service* (1944)** The first *Charlie Chan* film by Monogram Pictures Corporation.

Source: based on the character "Charlie Chan" created by Earl Derr Biggers. Original Copyright: Monogram Pictures Corporation, January 8, 1944; LP12543. Copyright Renewed: April 1, 1971; R503820. Production: early September to mid–September, 1943. Release Date: February 14, 1944. Sound: Western Electric Mirrophonic Recording. Film: b&w. Running Time: 65 minutes.

Producers: Philip N. Krasne and James S. Burkett. Director: Phil Rosen. Assistant Director: George Moskov.* Original screenplay:

*Unbilled.

George Callahan. Director of Photography: Ira Morgan. Film Editor: Martin G. Cohn. Set Designing: Dave Milton. Set Decorations: Al Greenwood. Musical Director: Karl Hajos. Sound Recording: Glen Glenn. Production Manager: George Moskov.

Cast

Sidney Toler	*as*	Charlie Chan
Mantan Moreland		Birmingham Brown
Arthur Loft		Jones
Gwen Kenyon		Inez Arranto
Sarah Edwards		Mrs. Hargue
George Lewis		Paul Arranto
Marianne Quon		Iris Chan
Benson Fong		Tommy Chan
Muni Seroff		Peter Laska
Barry Bernard		David Blake
Gene Stutenroth		Luiz Philipe Vega [alias for Philipe von Vegon]
Eddie Chandler		Lewis
Lelah Tyler		Mrs. Winters [alias for Fraulein Manleck]
George Lessey*		Slade
Gene Oliver*		Davison Clark

Plot Summary: George Melton, an inventor developing a secret torpedo to demolish German U-boats, mysteriously dies while opening his closet door. His secret plans disappear, and the U.S. Secret Service summons Charlie Chan to investigate. Two of Chan's children, Tommy and Iris, have come to Washington, D.C., to visit their father and do some sightseeing. He instructs his offspring to wait for him at the hotel while he goes to the Melton house, but the two amateur detectives decide to conduct their own investigation and follow him there.

At the house Chan is greeted by Secret Service agents Jones and Lewis and a roomful of people whom Melton had invited to a cocktail party prior to his death. Chan begins to question the assembled group—Mrs. Winters, a frivolous socialite; her chauffeur, Birmingham Brown; Luiz Vega, a European war refugee now involved in the importation of precious metals; Inez Arranto and her wheelchair-bound brother, Paul; David Blake, a pompous politician; Mrs. Hargue, Melton's housekeeper; and Peter Laska, Vega's valet.

*Unbilled.

Chan discovers a set of forged plans hidden in the right side of the bookcase and deduces that it was unlikely that Melton hid them there because he was left-handed. Afterwards, Chan sends Lewis back to headquarters to retrieve the completed coroner's report on Melton's death. Chan and Mrs. Hargue talk in a room upstairs, and a mysterious figure enters the darkened hallway below and removes a painting, revealing a wall safe hidden behind it. Unable to open the safe, the figure disappears into the darkness. Later, Chan notices that the painting has been moved and discovers the safe, but is also unable to open it.

Proceeding to search Melton's lab, Chan comes across a book about electromagnetic fields written by a scientist named von Vegan. When a shadowy assailant switches off the lights in the lab and begins to shoot at Chan and the others, Tommy hurls an explosive charge at their attacker that sends him scurrying. Chan reassembles everyone in the living room, and Lewis returns with the coroner's report. After scrutinizing the report, Chan calls the group into the hallway to demonstrate how Melton was murdered. Stepping into the closet, Chan pulls the light cord and explains that when Melton pulled the cord, the killer sent a fatal dose of electricity through the light switch in the living room, causing Melton to be electrocuted.

Again reconvening the group in the living room, Chan then accuses Vega of being the celebrated electrical engineer and author, Philipe von Vegon, whose book he found in the laboratory. Chan surmises that Vega, a foreign agent, killed Melton to steal the scientist's plans. As Vega starts to respond, he is shot in the back. Chan begins to question everybody about their acquaintance with Vega. When Lewis, following Chan's instructions, accuses Inez Arranto of Vega's murder and begins to manhandle her, her brother Paul springs from his wheelchair to defend his sister. He then admits that, after recovering from injuries he suffered in an accident, he remained in his wheelchair to test the intentions of his political enemies.

Still hoping to find the secret plans, Chan reassembles the group at the wall safe. After fiddling with the lock, he opens the safe, causing a booby-trapped gun secured inside to fire. Chan then deduces that because Vega was shot in the back while everyone else was standing around the piano to his front, the murder weapon must be attached to the gun display on the wall behind the couch. Chan explains that the gun was fired by a strong electromagnetic field triggered by a switch hidden underneath the piano, and accuses Peter Laska of pulling the switch because he was afraid that Vega would implicate him in Melton's murder. Although protesting his innocence, Laska is arrested by the police and taken away.

Chan then dismisses everyone. Mrs. Winters hurries to leave the room but finds the door blocked by Lewis. Explaining that because she was seated at the piano, Mrs. Winters was the only person who could reach the switch. Chan then accuses her of Vega's murder and finds the secret plans which she had concealed in a plaster statue hidden in her fur coat. After thanking Peter Laska for acting as a decoy in his trap, Chan reveals that Mrs. Winters is the enemy agent known as Manleck. She killed Vega because he was her accomplice in Melton's murder, and she feared he would confess and incriminate her.

Notes: *Charlie Chan in the Secret Service* was the first *Charlie Chan* film that Sidney Toler made at Monogram after Twentieth Century–Fox closed out their series. Toler bought the screen rights to the character from the widow of writer Earl Derr Biggers and continued to star as Charlie Chan in 11 more films for Monogram until his death in 1947, after which time Roland Winters assumed the role. With the Monogram entries, Charlie Chan no longer has ties to the Honolulu police but is now an agent working for the U.S. government, ostensibly in keeping with the United States' involvement in World War II and its fight against espionage by its enemies.

Charlie Chan in the Secret Service was also the first film for Benson Fong, who was brought in as Chan's Number Three son (who is more inept than Lee or Jimmy). Mantan Moreland also made his series debut, but does not function as Chan's chauffeur until three films later in *The Jade Mask* (1945). Finally, the film is the first in the series to feature one of Charlie Chan's daughters, Iris Chan, and marked the first of six films in the series directed by Phil Rosen.

Charlie Chan in Vaudeville An unused 1937 screenplay by Gregory Ratoff for Twentieth Century–Fox in which Charlie Chan is a guest star on a vaudeville bill.

***Charlie Chan on Broadway* (1937)** The sixth *Charlie Chan* film produced by Twentieth Century–Fox Film Corporation.

Source: based on the character "Charlie Chan" created by Earl Derr Biggers. Original Copyright: Twentieth Century–Fox Film Corporation, October 22, 1937; LP7817. Copyright Renewed: September 9, 1965; R367487. PCA Certificate Number: 3570. Production: June 10 to mid–July, 1937. Release Date: September 18, 1937 (New York opening). Sound: Western Electric Mirrophonic Recording. Film: b&w; 7 reels; 6,215 feet. Running Time: 68 minutes.

Associate Producer: John Stone. Director: Eugene Ford. Assistant Director: Samuel Schneider. Screenplay: Charles Belden and Jerry Cady. Original Story: Art Arthur, Robert Ellis, and Helen Logan. Photography: Harry Jackson. Art Direction: Lewis Creber. Film Editor: Alfred DeGaetano. Costumes: Herschel. Music Direction: Samuel Kaylin. Sound: George P. Costello and Harry M. Leonard.

Cast

Warner Oland	*as*	Charlie Chan
Keye Luke		Lee Chan
Joan Marsh		Joan Wendall
J. Edward Bromberg		Murdock
Douglas Fowley		Johnny Burke
Harold Huber		Inspector Nelson
Donald Woods		Speed Patten
Louise Henry		Billie Bronson
Joan Woodbury		Marie Collins
Leon Ames		Buzz Moran
Marc Lawrence		Thomas Mitchell
Tashia Mori		Ling Tse

Charles Williams	Meeker
Eugene Borden	Louie
William Jeffrey*	Coroner
Sidney Fields*	Porter
Norman Ainsley*	Steward
Philip Morris*	Customs officer
George Regas*	Hindu
Sherry Hall,* Creighton Hale,* Allen Fox,* Franklin Parker,* Don Brodie,* Billy Wayne*	Reporters
Allen Wood*	Bellhop
George Guhl*	Smitty
Jack Dougherty,* Harry Strang,* Don Rowan,* Eddie Dunn,* Carl Faulkner,* Lee Shumway,* Harry Burns*	Policemen
Billy O'Brien*	Copyboy
James Blaine*	Detective
Beulah Hutton*	Telephone operator
Harry Depp*	Snapper
Gloria Roy*	Hat check girl
Sam Ash*	Waiter
Blue Washington,* Allan Cavan*	Doormen
Art Miles*	Porter
Henry Otho,* Monte Vandergrift,* Jack Clifford,* James Flavin*	Detectives
Charles Haefeli*	Pickpocket
Victor Adams*	Gangster
Paddy O'Flynn,* Lester Dorr*	Photographers
Edwin Stanley*	Laboratory expert
Robert Middlemass*	Police official

Plot Summary: On an ocean liner approaching New York from Europe, a man named Thomas Mitchell unsuccessfully tries to steal a small package hidden in Billie Bronson's stateroom. Fearful of further attempts, she then hides the package in the room next to hers, which belongs to Charlie Chan and his son Lee. After her arrival at the pier, newspaper reporter Speed Patten slips into a cab with Billie, whom he knows, and she promises to meet him at her hotel at midnight if he will keep quiet about her arrival in New York.

Patten reports the potential story to his editor Murdock, who gets a call from Billie, now demanding twice the amount he was willing to pay one year ago for a certain item. He agrees and sets up a meeting with her that night. Billie then bribes a bellhop for a key to Chan's hotel room. As she tries to enter, Billie is spotted by Lee and she make an excuse about trying to enter the wrong room. She then leaves and is followed by Lee to the Hottentot Club, which is owned by racketeer Johnny Burke. There, local mobster Buzz Moran warns Billie to get out of town before morning, after which she goes to Burke's office.

Meanwhile, Speed Patten arrives at the club with freelance photographer Joan Wendall, and follows Burke to meet Billie in his second-floor office. Inside his office, Billie accuses Burke, her former lover, of giving her the runaround and forcing her to remain in Europe away from the grand jury because of his involvement with Marie Collins, a dancer in the club.

Later that evening, Inspector Nelson gets word at a banquet honoring Charlie Chan that Billie Bronson has been murdered at the Hottentot Club and that Lee Chan is being held as a suspect. After he arrives with Charlie at the club, Nelson orders Lee's release and questions Patten, Burke, Collins, and Wendall. At the crime scene in Burke's office, Chan notices that a napkin placed over a tray is not in the photograph Joan took at the time of the murder. Just then, at Burke's signal, Louie (Burke's henchman) turns out the lights and Burke escapes. When the lights come back on, Chan reveals that the key to his hotel room, which is present in the photograph, is now missing—along with the napkin.

Chan, Lee, and Nelson all return to Chan's hotel room where they now find Thomas Mitchell, the man on the boat who tried to rob Billie Bronson, dead. Marie Collins then enters and faints when she sees her estranged husband. On the floor near the body, Chan finds a crumpled page of the diary which Mitchell was after. Chan and Inspector Nelson then go to Billie Bronson's hotel room and find Murdock there. He explains that he was waiting to buy Billie's diary, which has information on racketeers and their payoffs to the city's politicians.

With Meeker, his lawyer, Burke agrees to go to police headquarters where a paraffin test determines there are no traces of gunpowder on his hands. Chan then reminds

*Unbilled.

Nelson that the napkin may have been used to cover the gun and warns Burke that he is still under investigation. When Burke finds Lee in his office trying to reconstruct the murder, he gives Lee a black eye before throwing him out.

Burke and Marie Collins then try to leave town but are apprehended at the airport. Both are taken back to Burke's office, where Murdock and Moran are also brought. In reconstructing the crime, Chan reveals that Mitchell was trying to get Billie's diary to ruin Burke, who stole his wife. Murdock then shows a page from the diary which says that Patten used his newspaper job as a cover for blackmailing activities. Patten looks at the page and then calls the page a phony, after which Chan accuses him of murder.

Chan explains that he first suspected Patten when his newspaper story mentioned that Billie was shot in the back, a fact known only to the police and the murderer. Chan also reveals that he and Nelson planted the phony diary page to draw Patten out. Chan then states that if Patten knew the page was a forgery, then he must have the original. Now cornered, Patten pulls a gun and confesses that he killed Billie Bronson because she was going to the district attorney with the diary, which would implicate him. He then found Mitchell with the diary and killed him. He is about to shoot Chan when Lee jumps him. In the struggle, Patten is disarmed but Lee gets a second black eye.

***Charlie Chan's Chance* (1932)** The fourth *Charlie Chan* film produced by the Fox Film Corporation.

Source: remake of *Behind That Curtain* (1929), from the novel of the same name written by Earl Derr Biggers in 1928. Original Copyright: Fox Film Corporation, December 29, 1931; LP2752. Copyright Renewed: January 15, 1959; R229219. Production: November 16 to early December, 1931. Release Date: January 24, 1932. Film: b&w; 7 reels; 6,400 or 6,749 feet. Running Time: 71 or 73 minutes.

Director: John Blystone. Assistant Director: Jasper Blystone. Screenplay: Barry Conners and Philip Klein. Photography: Joseph August. Second Camera: Charles Fetters. Assistant Cameramen: Harry Webb and Lou Kunkel. Art Director: Gordon Wiles. Film Editor: Alex Troffey. Costumes: David Cox. Sound Recordist: Albert Protzman. Still Photographer: Alexander Kahle.

Cast

Warner Oland	*as*	Charlie Chan
Alexander Kirkland		John [R.] Douglas
H.B. Warner		Inspector Fife
Marian Nixon		Shirley Marlowe
Linda Watkins		Gloria Garland
James Kirkwood		Inspector Flannery
Ralph Morgan		Barry Kirk
James Todd		Kenneth Dunwood [alias for Alan Raleigh]
Herbert Bunston		Garrick Enderly
James Wang		Kee Lin
Joe Brown		Doctor
Charles McNaughton		Paradise
Edward Peil, Sr.		Li Gung

Plot Summary: Charlie Chan of the Honolulu police and Inspector Fife of Scotland Yard tour the offices of the New York Police Department with Inspector Flannery to study New York police methods. While dining at a Chinese restaurant, Fife receives a phone call informing him that Sir Lionel Grey, a former chief of Scotland Yard, has dropped dead in the Wall Street office of Barry Kirk, which was his base of operations.

All three go to the crime scene and Kirk informs the group that, before his death, Grey was about to solve a big murder case and had invited several guests to a party to be held at Kirk's apartment. Grey had left the party to take a phone call in Kirk's office and then died mysteriously. The doctor assures the group that Grey died of a heart attack, but Chan notices a dead cat in the room and surmises that the same substance killed them both and that Grey was indeed murdered. The assembled guests are questioned and all seem to be hiding something. In Kirk's office, the police discover that the safe has been robbed, a possible motive for the crime, and learn that John Douglas, a chemical manufacturer, had made the last phone call to Grey.

Shirley Marlowe meets with Douglas at a café, and he tells her that Grey demanded to know the whereabouts of Alan Raleigh,

Marlowe's former lover. Grey also threatened to take Shirley back to England as an accessory to murder if Douglas would not provide the information. Douglas then asks Shirley to marry him.

After an interview with one of the assembled guests, Chan is led to Shirley Marlowe, who confesses that she fell in love with Raleigh before she discovered that he had committed the murder which Grey was investigating. When she found out about the murder, she fled, and has been pursued by Scotland Yard ever since. Chan promises to keep her secret and goes to find Li Gung, Raleigh's former houseboy.

Shirley sends a letter to Chan, indicating her plan to tell the police everything. As she prepares to go to the police station, an unidentified man drops a gas bomb in her car in an attempt to poison her, but the bomb kills her chauffeur instead. At the police station Douglas is brought in and denies his acquaintance with Shirley until she tells him that she's confessed everything. He informs the group that he saw a "Chinaman" enter the building with a basket the day he met with Grey.

Chan goes again to Li Gung's home, and the former houseboy tries to kill him with a cleverly designed hidden gun. However, a black cat upsets the setup and the gun shoots and kills Li Gung instead. At the check-in room of the Cosmopolitan Club, Chan discovers Grey's briefcase, which was checked in after the murder. He calls Inspectors Fife and Flannery to watch with him who retrieves it, and the trio are surprised to see Kirk claim the briefcase.

At Kirk's office, the trio, Shirley Marlowe, and members of the original party wait for Kirk. When Kirk arrives, Flannery instructs Kirk to answer the door and pretend to be alone. Dunwood then enters and thanks Kirk for getting his briefcase. Kirk asks Dunwood about when he received his membership card to the club, and it is revealed that Dunwood had not been to the club that day as he had said, but had dropped the case off just after the murder. Shirley Marlowe identifies Dunwood as Alan Raleigh, who grabs Chan's unloaded gun and covers the group. But Chan quickly subdues Raleigh, and he is arrested.

***Charlie Chan's Courage* (1934)** The sixth *Charlie Chan* film produced by the Fox Film Corporation.

Source: *The Chinese Parrot* (1927), from the novel of the same name written by Earl Derr Biggers in 1926. Original Copyright: Fox Film Corporation, July 6, 1934; LP4813. Copyright Renewed: May 7, 1962; R295061. Production: April 23 to late May, 1934. Release Date: July 6, 1934. Technical: b&w; 7 reels; 6,589 feet. Running Time: 70–72 or 74 minutes.

Producer: John Stone. Executive Producer: Winfield R. Sheehan. Directors: George Hadden and Eugene Forde. Assistant Director: Sid Bowen. Screenplay: Seton I. Miller. Photography: Hal Mohr and Arthur Miller. Camera Operator: Joseph La Shelle. Assistant Cameramen: W. Abbott and S. McDonald. Sets: Duncan Cramer. Film Editor: Alex Troffey. Gowns: Royer. Musical Director: Samuel Kaylin. Sound: Alfred Bruzlin. Still Photography: Bill Thomas.

Cast

Warner Oland	*as*	Charlie Chan [alias Ah Kim]
Drue Leyton		Paula Graham
Donald Woods		Bob Crawford
Paul Harvey		J.P. Madden/Jerry Delaney
Murray Kinnell		Martin Thorne
Reginald Mason		Alexander Crawford
Virginia Hammond		Sally Jordan
Si Jenks		Will Holley
Harvey Clark		Professor Gamble
Jerry Jerome		["Shaky" Phil] Maydorf
Jack Carter		Victor Jordan
James Wang		[Louie] Wong
DeWitt C. Jennings		Sergeant Brackett
Francis Ford		Hewitt
Lucille Miller		Stenographer
Mary McLaren		Mother
Gail Kaye		Child
Larry Fisher		Taxi driver
Sam McDaniels		Porter
Carl Stockdale		Station lounger
Lila Chevret, Susan Fleming		Chorus girls
Caryl Lincoln		Leading lady
John David Horsley		Leading man
George Magrill		Heavy
Frank Mills		Prop man
Sherry Hall		Assistant director

James P. Burtis — Eddie Boston
Paul McVey — Director
Wade Boteler — [Capt.] Bliss
Teru Shimada — Jujitsu man

Plot Summary: Mrs. Sally Jordan asks her faithful former houseboy, Charlie Chan, now a detective with the Honolulu police force, to personally transport to Eldorado (a town in California) a pearl necklace that she has sold to millionaire J.P. Madden, as something seems suspicious in the transaction.

Bob Crawford, the son of the jewelry store owner who has set up the deal, precedes Chan to Madden's house to insure that the place is safe. On the train, Bob meets Paula Graham, a film director's assistant traveling to Eldorado to arrange a film shoot on Madden's property. As they approach the ranch by cab, they hear gunshots. Inside the house, Martin Thorne, Madden's secretary, bends over a body in the bedroom. When he answers Paula and Bob's knock, Thorne tells them that Madden is away and urges Crawford to stay, though Bob has revealed that the pearls will arrive the next day by messenger.

Chan arrives the next day, calling himself Ah Kim, and Thorne hires him as the new cook, since the regular cook is away. While snooping around, Chan notices that a revolver from Madden's collection has been removed and recently fired. In Madden's bedroom he finds bullet holes in the wall and blood stains on the carpet, which someone had attempted to conceal. Believing Madden to have been murdered by Thorne, Crawford is amazed when Jerry Delaney, whom he believes to be Madden, shows up.

As Bob Crawford and Chan drive into the garage one night, they find the dead body of the former cook, Louie Wong. The cook's talking parrot, who made comments suggestive of a murder, is then discovered poisoned, which reveals to Chan that both the cook and the bird witnessed something amiss.

Delaney, now disguised as J.P. Madden, demands that the necklace be handed over. Privately, Bob Crawford asks Chan for the goods, but Chan is not yet convinced that everything is as it should be and holds onto Mrs. Jordan's property. Chan and Crawford discover a suitcase in the attic that belongs to Delaney and ascertain that he arrived by train the night before Bob's arrival.

The movie crew finally arrives at the ranch, and when the director asks Paula Graham to investigate an old mine where he wants to shoot a scene, someone jumps out and attacks her. Crawford goes looking for Paula, discovers her at the mine, and struggles with the attacker before finally overpowering him. Paula tells Bob that there is another captive in the mine, J.P. Madden. Soon after, Victor Jordan, Sally Jordan's son, arrives at the Madden ranch and blows the whole investigation by telling Delaney that Crawford should have handed over the pearls days earlier and demanding that Chan, or Ah Kim, deliver the pearls as his mother instructed. Delaney uses his left hand to sign a receipt, and Chan, knowing Madden to be right-handed, quickly grabs the pearls and pulls a gun on him.

Sergeant Brackett arrives. At first he doesn't believe that Ah Kim is really Chan and gives the pearls back to Delaney. Just at that time, the real J.P. Madden enters with a bandaged shoulder and reveals that Delaney, his look-alike, has a history of impersonating him, and accuses Thorne of double-crossing him. The case solved and the pearls safely delivered, Paula, Bob, and Chan travel back to San Francisco.

Note: No copies of *Charlie Chan's Courage* are currently known to exist.

***Charlie Chan's Greatest Case* (1933)** The fifth *Charlie Chan* film produced by the Fox Film Corporation.

Source: remake of *The House Without a Key* (1925), from the novel of the same name written by Earl Derr Biggers in 1925. Original Copyright: Fox Film Corporation, August 29, 1933; LP4105. Copyright Renewed: October 20, 1960; R264439. PCA Certificate Number: 1232-R [August 17, 1935]. Production: began mid–July, 1933. Release Date: September 15, 1933. Film: b&w; 8 reels; 6,200 or 6,749 feet. Running Time: 70–71 minutes.

Producer: Sol M. Wurtzel. Director: Hamilton MacFadden. Assistant Director:

Percy Ikerd. Screenplay: Lester Cole and Marion Orth. Photography: Ernest Palmer. Camera Operator: Don Anderson.* Assistant Camera Operators: Stanley Little* and Robert Mack.* Sets: Duncan Cramer. Editor: Alex Troffey. Gowns: Royer. Musical Director: Samuel Kaylin. Sound: George Leverett. Assistant Sound: W.T. Brent.* Still Photography: Cliff Maupin.*

Cast

Warner Oland	*as*	Charlie Chan
Heather Angel		Carlotta Eagan
Roger Imhof		The Beachcomber
John Warburton		John Quincy Winterslip
Walter Byron		Harry Jennison
Ivan Simpson		T.M. Brade
Virginia Cherrill		Barbara Winterslip
Francis Ford		Captain Hallett
Robert Warwick		Dan Winterslip
Frank McGlynn		Amos Winterslip
Clara Blandick		Minerva Winterslip
Claude E. King		Captain Arthur Temple Cope
William Slack		James Eagan
Gloria Roy		Arlene Compton
Cornelius Keefe		Steve Leatherbee

Plot Summary: Brothers Amos and Dan Winterslip discuss the object of Dan's latest romance, a shady lady named Arlene Compton, of whom the moralistic Amos does not approve. Dan, the family ingrate, throws his brother out of his Honolulu house, and his sister Minerva arrives with the news that cousin John Quincy Winterslip is being sent to Honolulu to bring her back to Boston since, in the family's opinion, she's having too much fun.

Dan sobers when he sees a newspaper item about the arrival on the islands of a T.M. Brade. During a stopover in San Francisco, John Winterslip's uncle Roger gives him a strongbox marked with the initials "TMB" and instructs him to throw it into the Pacific Ocean the next day, as per Dan's orders. As John is about to toss the box into the sea, however, he is tackled by an unidentified man who steals the box. On deck, both Harry Jennison, Dan's lawyer, and Barbara Winterslip, Dan's daughter, are also traveling back to Honolulu. They decide to marry, and telegram her father with the news.

Dan goes to see Arlene Compton to ask that she return an emerald brooch he had given her as a gift. She lies and says that the brooch is at the jeweler's being repaired, and promises to bring it to him later. At Dan's home, Minerva Winterslip sees a prowler and then discovers Dan dead in the den. Captain Hallett at the police station receives the report of the murder and calls detective Charlie Chan. At the crime scene, the doctor reports that Dan Winterslip has been stabbed in the heart and that his arm has been broken. Chan questions Minerva, who remembers only one identifying characteristic of the prowler—a glow-in-the-dark wristwatch with a blurred numeral two. She also tells Chan that she remembers that a James Eagan staying at the Reef & Palm Hotel called repeatedly the day before the murder.

At the hotel, Eagan tries to leave, but Chan reminds him that he had an engagement with Dan Winterslip, which he had canceled. Eagan then admits that Dan insisted on seeing him the night of the murder and that the two met after 11:00 in Dan's garden. Eagan hasn't spoken to Dan in 23 years and refuses to reveal to Chan the nature of their business transaction.

In the meantime, Carlotta Eagan watches the desk of the hotel and Brade, a hotel guest, informs her that he'll be going away for a few days. Dan Winterslip's houseboy, Koahla, enters the hotel with a strongbox for Brade but leaves when he discovers Brade is not there. Seeing Koahla hiding in some bushes on the hotel grounds, John Winterslip attacks him and retrieves the box. John gives this same strongbox, which he had earlier tried to toss into the ocean, to Chan, but they find it empty. Searching further, Chan finds Amos Winterslip's dead body on the grounds of the hotel and apprehends a beachcomber who is wearing the glowing wristwatch Minerva saw on the prowler at her brother's house when he was murdered.

Chan then assembles all the possible suspects at Dan's house, where he plans to reveal the identity of the murderer. When Chan asks Brade about the box, Brade

**Unbilled.*

recounts how Dan Winterslip stole jewels from his father 35 years earlier when Dan was a mate on his father's ship, and that he has scrimped and saved for many years for the chance to reclaim his due. When the emerald brooch, which was found at the crime scene, is produced, both Arlene Compton and Brade claim it. As further evidence, Chan then produces a check for $5,000 which Dan Winterslip had made out to James Eagan. Eagan still refuses to explain his relationship with Dan, and Chan tells Hallett to arrest him.

Carlotta Eagan cries out at the injustice and admits that she had read her father's diary, which told of an incident thirty-five years earlier in which James Eagan, a young bank teller, changed Dan Winterslip's South American gold into Australian currency. Eagan, being the only man alive who could identify Dan Winterslip as the thief of Brade's gold, tried to blackmail him. Koahla then admits that he knew of his master's fear of Brade and so stole the box in San Francisco to blackmail his master. Chan then has Berkeley, another passenger on the boat, brought in, claiming that he is the murderer. Berkeley tries to make a run for it, but he is caught by Jennison, who breaks his arm in the same fashion that Dan's arm was fractured.

Chan then fingers Harry Jennison as the real murderer and reveals that Berkeley was part of Chan's trap. Chan also reveals that Dan's reply to his daughter Barbara's wedding announcement never reached Barbara. Instead of congratulating the couple, the reply contained a warning to Jennison that unless he broke off the engagement, Barbara would be disinherited and the robbery exposed, despite injury to both Jennison and himself. Furthermore, suntan lines on Jennison's wrist revealed that he was the owner of the watch, which he lost in the surf where the beachcomber picked it up following the murder. Confronted with the evidence, Jennison pulls an unloaded gun from Chan's pocket, and Chan has no difficulty subduing him.

**Unbilled.*

Note: This is the last of three *Charlie Chan* films directed by Hamilton MacFadden.

***Charlie Chan's Murder Cruise* (1940)** The thirteenth *Charlie Chan* film produced by Twentieth Century–Fox Film Corporation.

Working Titles: *Charlie Chan's Cruise*, *Chan's Murder Cruise*, *Chan's Cruise*, and *Charlie Chan's Oriental Cruise*. Source: based on the novel *Charlie Chan Carries On* by Earl Derr Biggers (Bobbs-Merrill, 1930). Original Copyright: Twentieth Century–Fox Film Corporation, July 21, 1940; LP9750. Copyright Renewed: April 4, 1968; R432921. PCA Certificate Number: 6084. Production: began late January, 1940. Release Date: July 21, 1940. Sound: Western Electric Sound System. Film: b&w; 6,315 feet. Running Time: 70 or 75 minutes.

Executive Producer: Sol M. Wurtzel. Associate Producer: John Stone. Director: Eugene Forde. Assistant Director: Saul Wurtzel.* Screenplay: Robertson White and Lester Ziffren. Director of Photography: Virgil Miller. Art Direction: Richard Day and Chester Gore. Film Editor: Harry Reynolds. Set Decorations: Thomas Little. Costumes: Helen A. Myron. Musical Direction: Samuel Kaylin. Sound: Joseph E. Aiken and William H. Anderson.

Cast

Sidney Toler	*as*	Charlie Chan
Marjorie Weaver		Paula Drake
Lionel Atwill		Dr. Suderman
Sen Yung		Jimmy Chan
Robert Lowery		Dick Kenyon
Don Beddoe		James Ross
Leo Carroll		Professor Gordon [alias for Jim Eberhardt]
Cora Witherspoon		Susie Watson
Kay Linaker		Mrs. Pendleton
Harlan Briggs		Coroner
Charles Middleton		Mr. [Jeremiah] Walters
Claire DuBrey		Mrs. [Sarah] Walters
Leonard Mudie		Gerald Pendleton
James Burke		Wilkie
Richard Keene		Buttons
Layne Tom, Jr.		Willie Chan
Montague Shaw		Inspector Duff
Walter Miller*		Officer
Harry Strang*		Guard

Plot Summary: Inspector Duff of Scotland Yard visits Charlie Chan in Honolulu to enlist his aid in trapping a strangler who is lurking among ten members of a world cruise being conducted by Dr. Suderman. Before the inspector can divulge his plan, he falls victim to the strangler, and Chan begins his own investigation into the murders.

His first stop is a visit to the members of Dr. Suderman's party, but when he arrives at the hotel he finds that another murder has just been committed. The victim, Mr. Kenyon, is discovered with a bag containing thirty pieces of silver. Chan deduces that the man was killed in the room of fellow passenger Gerald Pendleton and his body dragged into Kenyon's room. In addition to Suderman, the cruise passengers consist of Mr. Kenyon's nephew Dick, Susie Watson, her secretary Paula Drake, playboy James Ross, archeologist Professor Gordon, the very nervous Gerald Pendleton, and the puritanical Mr. and Mrs. Jeremiah Walters.

Because Duff was an old friend and he was murdered in Chan's office, Charlie personally wants to solve the case by traveling with the cruise party as they conclude their voyage to San Francisco. Amid a sea of false clues, Dr. Suderman's party members share an uneventful cruise until Gerald Pendleton is murdered on the night that the ship is to dock. Chan finds the traces of a warning that Pendleton had wired to his wife and concludes that the murderer was absent from the farewell party held at the time of Pendleton's demise. Gathering the pictures taken at the farewell party, Chan develops the negatives, but the killer steals the evidence. As he flees, the murderer is shot and unmasked as James Ross.

However, Chan remains skeptical and, at the coroner's inquest, he produces Mrs. Pendleton, who explains that the killer is her demented, vengeful ex-husband, Jim Eberhardt, a jewelry thief, and that Ross was only his accomplice. Chan then tricks Professor Gordon into trying to kill his ex-wife, thus exposing him as the true murderer.

Note: *Charlie Chan's Murder Cruise* was an uncredited remake of *Charlie Chan Carries On* (1931), which was based on Earl Derr Biggers' 1930 novel of the same name.

***Charlie Chan's Secret* (1936)** The first *Charlie Chan* film produced by Twentieth Century–Fox Film Corporation.

Working Title: *Charlie Chan in San Francisco.* Source: based on the character "Charlie Chan" created by Earl Derr Biggers. Original Copyright: Twentieth Century–Fox Film Corporation, January 10, 1936; LP6049. Copyright Renewed: December 23, 1963; R328114. PCA Certificate Number: 1587. Production: August 26 to September 21, 1935. Release Date: January 10, 1936. Sound: Western Electric Noiseless Recording. Film: b&w; 8 reels; 6,500 feet. Running Time: 71 minutes.

Associate Producer: John Stone. Director: Gordon Wiles. Original Story: Robert Ellis and Helen Logan. Screenplay: Robert Ellis and Helen Logan, in collaboration with Joseph Hoffman. Photography: Rudolph Maté. Art Direction: Duncan Cramer and Albert Hogsett. Film Editor: Nick DeMaggio. Gowns: Helen Myron. Musical Director: Samuel Kaylin. Sound: Al Protzman.

Cast

Warner Oland	*as*	Charlie Chan
Rosina Lawrence		Alice Lowell
Charles Quigley		Dick Williams
Henrietta Crosman		Henrietta Lowell
Edward Trevor		Fred Gage
Astrid Allwyn		Janice Gage
Herbert Mundin		Baxter
Jonathan Hale		Warren T. Phelps
Egon Brecher		Ulrich
Gloria Roy		Carlotta
Ivan Miller		Morton
Arthur Edmund Carewe		Professor Bowan
Jerry Miley*		Allen Colby
William N. Bailey*		Harris
James T. Mack*		Fingerprint man
Landers Stevens*		Coroner
Francis Ford*		Boat captain
Sid Jordan*		Expert marksman
Charles Earnest*		Diver

Plot Summary: During the search for bodies among the wreckage of a boat lost in a storm near Hawaii, Charlie Chan finds the

**Unbilled.*

diary of Allen Colby, heir to his father's fortune, which indicates that he was onboard and that attempts had recently been made on his life. Chan cables Henrietta Lowell, matriarch of the family and sister of Allen's deceased father, that Allen's fate is uncertain. Chan then flies to San Francisco where Mrs. Lowell, a devoted believer in psychic research, schedules a séance.

Chan determines that Allen Colby is not dead and was rescued by a passing ship that didn't have a radio onboard. Upon further investigation, Chan learns that for the seven years that he was out of contact with his family, Colby enlisted in the French foreign legion and later spent time in prison (from which he eventually escaped). Allen returns to Colby House where, upon entering, he is murdered by a thrown dagger.

The séance is conducted by Carlotta, a medium, and attended by Professor Bowan, whom Mrs. Lowell supports financially. Also in attendance are Mrs. Lowell's two daughters, Alice and Janice; Alice's boyfriend, newspaper reporter Dick Williams; Janice's husband, Fred Gage; Ulrich, a disgruntled servant who blames his daughter's suicide seven years earlier on Allen for breaking his engagement with her; and Chan. After the séance begins, Allen's glowing face mysteriously appears in the darkened room. When the lights are turned on, Chan finds that Allen has been murdered.

Chan wants to investigate further and arranges with Mrs. Lowell for him to spend the night in the house (which has many secret panels and passages). Also curious, Mrs. Lowell joins Chan in his search for clues. In the room used for the séances, they find a radio receiver, which Chan explains may account for the music they heard during the séance. Also, Allen Colby's image appeared when a hidden ultraviolet light was directed toward his face, which was covered with quinine sulfate and so glowed when hit with ultraviolet light.

Greatly upset about having been deceived, Mrs. Lowell tells Chan that Professor Bowan knew that if Allen were to return, her patronage would cease. She agrees with Chan's suggestion that she revise her will, and she telephones Warren Phelps, the estate's attorney, informing him of her intention. After seeing a radio transmitter in Ulrich's room, Chan visits Carlotta the next day. She admits using the transmitter but is shocked to learn about the ultraviolet light. When Chan touches the shortwave transmitter coil, Bowan switches on the current, which causes Chan to fall unconscious to the floor. Just then, the police arrive, but Bowan escapes. Inspector Morton arrests Carlotta as Chan is revived.

Later that day, Mrs. Lowell announces to her family that she plans to sign a new will, which her executor Warren T. Phelps will bring at 8:30 that evening. As the church bell rings at 8:30 and Phelps drives up, Mrs. Lowell is shot through the window. Using simple geometry, Chan deduces that the shot was fired from the church's bell tower. Chan and Dick Williams climb to the top of the tower and find a high-powered rifle which had been set to fire at the window when the bell was rung.

Bowan is caught and brought to the Colby house, but he does not confess. Chan then reassembles all those present at the first séance and has Bowan and Carlotta conduct a new séance. Mrs. Lowell's animated image appears. When it starts to speak, a dagger (the twin of the one that killed Allen Colby) is thrown at the image, which cracks the mirror on which it is reflected. The lights are turned on and Chan reveals that Mrs. Lowell is alive and that it was a dummy of her that was shot earlier. Fred Gage accuses Ulrich, and they struggle. Chan, who earlier had put graphite on the knife, reveals the graphite now on Gage's hands and accuses Gage of murdering Allen Colby to cover evidence of forgery in the Lowell accounts. After Gage is led away, charges are dropped against Carlotta and Bowan, who agree to leave town.

Note: *Charlie Chan's Secret* was the first *Charlie Chan* film made after the merger between the Fox Film Corporation and Twentieth Century Pictures. Though some sources claim that the series' previous film, *Charlie Chan in Shanghai* (1935) was the first film following the merger, the opening credits for

Charlie Chan in Shanghai name Fox Film Corporation while the opening credits for *Charlie Chan's Secret* name Twentieth Century–Fox Film Corporation.

Chase, Gordon The scheming and jealous brother (portrayed by Robert Kent) of Joan Karnoff, and secretary to her husband, Victor Karnoff, in *Charlie Chan at Monte Carlo* (1937). Chase commits three murders (for the money from stolen bonds) to continue buying the affection of Evelyn Grey, who is really using him to gain sensitive information (which she passes onto Paul Savarin) about Karnoff's financial dealings. Attempting to escape when Chan uncovers him as the murderer, Chase is accidentally killed by running into the path of an oncoming car.

chemin de fer High-stakes casino game (similar to baccarat) in which Victor Karnoff wins five straight hands from business rival Paul Savarin in *Charlie Chan at Monte Carlo* (1937).

As in the game of baccarat, a chemin de fer table usually has 12 seats (for 11 players and the croupier). The player seated to the right of the croupier is the banker, who determines the amount of the stake. The player to the right has the first chance to bid for the entire stake and in so doing calls *banco*. If the banker wins, the stake is doubled; if not, the position of banker passes to the player on the right.

The object of the game is to obtain cards that total 8 or 9, called "a natural." Picture cards and the ten have no value. The banker deals two cards face down to himself and to the player who has called *banco*. This player may withdraw if the hand is more than 9, or reveal a natural, or ask for another card. Because the rules governing the call for another card are based on the total held, and the banker does not decide whether to draw another card until the opponent's draw card has been seen, the banker has a double advantage.

Sitting together at the chemin de fer table in *Charlie Chan at Monte Carlo* are Karnoff, Savarin (acting as the bank), and Evelyn Grey between them. As the bank, Savarin puts up 50,000 francs. On the first hand, Karnoff keeps his first two cards and dares Savarin to draw into a five hand. Savarin draws a third card and busts and then loses four straight hands to Karnoff. While watching the game, Inspector Jules Joubert tells Charlie Chan, "The money, it is nothing. They play only to give the insult to each other."

Cherbourg French seaport on the English Channel where the ship *Medusa* is docked and is waiting to leave France with a contraband cargo of munitions in *City in Darkness* (1939).

Cherrill, Virginia (April 12, 1908, Carthage, Illinois–November 14, 1996, Santa Barbara, California) Leading lady with a brief career, having appeared in only 15 films. Cherrill portrays Barbara Winterslip in *Charlie Chan's Greatest Case* (1933).

Born on a farm, Virginia Cherrill was discovered by Charlie Chaplin while she was sitting beside him at a boxing match in Los Angeles. He introduced himself at intermission and hired her for her debut as a blind girl in *City Lights* (1931). She met her first husband, Cary Grant, at the premiere of *Blonde Venus* (1933) and stopped working after their marriage that same year. They were divorced two years later.

Cherry One of two possible names chosen by Charlie's son-in-law Wing Foo and Number One daughter Ling if their baby is a girl in *Charlie Chan in Honolulu* (1938). The other name is Lotus.

Chester, Catherine Wife (portrayed by Gloria Roy in her fifth of seven *Charlie Chan* roles) of racehorse owner George Chester in *Charlie Chan at the Race Track* (1936).

Chester, George Murderer and leader of a racetrack gambling ring (portrayed by Alan Dinehart) in *Charlie Chan at the Race Track* (1936). Chester's father-in-law, Major Kent, stubbornly complains that a racetrack gambling ring had paid his jockey, "Tip" Collins (riding Kent's prize racehorse, Avalanche), to intentionally foul another horse during the

Melbourne Sweepstakes, and intends to telegram his old friend Charlie Chan to investigate.

Chester and Kent frequently quarrel over Chester's gambling losses, and an investigation would uncover Chester as the leader of the gambling ring. Before Kent can see Chan in Honolulu, Chester murders his father-in-law with a winch shoe and makes it look like an accident in Avalanche's stall.

When fingered by Chan as Kent's murderer and leader of the gambling ring after Avalanche is struck by a tranquilizer dart during the running of the Santa Juanita Handicap, Chester blunders when he accuses Fenton of murdering Kent with a winch shoe. Chan then remarks that only three people besides himself knew the type of murder weapon—the ship's captain (Capt. Blade), the chief of police, and the murderer.

Chester, Wilbur Radio announcer (portrayed by Reid Kilpatrick) at the Cosmo Radio Center in *The Scarlet Clue* (1945).

Chicago Sun Chicago newspaper which teletypes to the *Los Angeles Bulletin* the details about a fire at an opera house on September 15, 1923, in *Charlie Chan at the Opera* (1936). Charlie Chan also instructs the newspaper to facsimile a photograph of the opera star who supposedly was killed in the fire. When the photograph is received in Los Angeles, Chan recognizes the man as Gravelle, who had recently escaped from the Rockland State Sanitarium.

Childers, Phil Fiancé (portrayed by Thomas Beck in his last of four *Charlie Chan* roles) of Kitty Rochelle in *Charlie Chan at the Opera* (1936). Childers and Kitty go to the opera's opening night performance in Los Angeles to seek permission from Kitty's mother, Mme. Lilli Rochelle, to be married, but they are turned away by Sgt. Kelly.

China Clipper Nickname for the Martin M-130 airplane, which first carried passengers on October 21, 1936. Although at the time it was the largest flying boat ever built, it was both graceful and stylish. The Clipper's central lounge, which was wider than a Pullman club car, was fitted with broad armchairs, and its meal service included china and silverware. The first nine passengers paid $1,438.20 for a round-trip ticket from San Francisco to Manila. It cruised at 150 miles per hour and had a range of 3,200 miles.

Charlie Chan takes the China Clipper from Honolulu to San Francisco in *Charlie Chan's Secret* (1936), *Charlie Chan in Reno* (1939), and *Charlie Chan at Treasure Island* (1939). *See* photo, page 106.

"Chinatown, My Chinatown" Song, whose music was written by Jean Schwartz (with lyrics by William Jerome) in 1906. In *Charlie Chan on Broadway* (1937), the song is played by a New York City police band as a substitute for the Chinese national anthem in honor of Charlie Chan's visit to New York. A police officer suggests this song to Inspector Nelson because no one in the band knows what the Chinese national anthem is.

Chinese boy Mute boy who is befriended by Princess Mei Ling in *The Chinese Ring* (1947). The boy is killed by Mr. Armstrong after he sees Armstrong murdering the princess' maid, Lilly Mae Wong.

***The Chinese Cat* (1944)** The second *Charlie Chan* film produced by Monogram Pictures Corporation.

Alternate Titles: *Charlie Chan in the Chinese Cat* and *Charlie Chan: The Chinese Cat*. Working Title: *Murder in the Fun House*. Source: based on the character "Charlie Chan" created by Earl Derr Biggers. Original Copyright: Monogram Pictures Corporation, April 15, 1944; LP12667. Copyright Renewed: January 7, 1972; R521047. Production: January 11–19, 1944. Release Date: May 20, 1944. Sound: Western Electric Mirrophonic Recording. Film: b&w; 5,824 feet. Running Time: 65 minutes.

Producers: Philip N. Krasne and James S. Burkett. Director: Phil Rosen. Assistant Director: Bobby Ray.* Original Screenplay:

**Unbilled.*

The China Clipper airship flying over the Golden Gate Bridge, with Treasure Island in the upper right (courtesy The Boeing Company).

George Callahan. Director of Photography: Ira Morgan. Art Director: Dave Milton. Film Editors: Fred Allen and Martin Cohn.* Set Decorations: Tommy Thompson. Music Supervision: David Chudnow. Musical Score: Alexander Laszlo. Sound Recording: Tom Lambert. Production Manager: Dick L'Estrange.

Cast

Sidney Toler	*as*	Charlie Chan
Joan Woodbury		Leah Manning
Mantan Moreland		Birmingham Brown
Benson Fong		Tommy Chan
Ian Keith		Dr. Paul Rednick
Cy Kendall		Webster Deacon
Weldon Heyburn		Detective Harvey Dennis
Anthony Warde†		Catlen
John Davidson		Carl Karzoff/Kurt Karzoff
Dewey Robinson		Salos
Stan Jolley		Gannett
Betty Blythe		Mrs. Manning
Jack Norton		Hotel desk clerk
Luke Chan		Wu Song
George Chandler*		Hotel doorman
Sam Flint*		Thomas P. Manning

**Unbilled. †Billed as Anthony Ward.*

Plot Summary: When Thomas Manning, the second husband of a wealthy socialite, is murdered in his locked study, the police are baffled and the district attorney quickly decides to drop the case. Months later, Charlie Chan is passing through town when he is approached by Manning's stepdaughter, Leah, who asks for help in solving the crime.

As Leah talks with Chan in his hotel lobby, a man eavesdrops on their conversation. Leah tells Chan that criminologist Dr. Paul Rednick has recently published a book which names her mother as the murderer and accuses police detective Harvey Dennis of covering up the crime because he is in love with Leah. Intrigued, Chan proceeds to a bookstore and purchases a copy of Rednick's book.

Meanwhile, the man in the hotel lobby hurries to a carnival fun house at the end of a pier, where a gang of jewel thieves is hiding out. Catlen, a member of the gang, reports Chan's activities to twins Carl and Kurt Karzoff. Later, Kurt sneaks out of the hideout to arrange a meeting with Chan. By the time Chan arrives, he finds Kurt dead, a victim of strangulation. Soon after, Dennis is alerted by Leah, arrives, and identifies Kurt as a fence specializing in stolen gems.

Chan invites Dennis to join the investigation, and they both search the fun house and discover several stale loaves of bread with small statues hidden inside. Next, Chan visits Dr. Rednick to discuss his book. Noticing that the criminologist wears gloves, Chan comments that Kurt was killed by a pair of gloved hands, prompting Rednick to explain that he must protect his hands because they were severely burned in a fire. Chan then goes to the Manning house to examine the scene of the murder and there finds a statue identical to the ones hidden in the loaves of bread. While at the house, Chan is confronted by Webster Deacon, Manning's partner, who vehemently objects to the reopening of the Manning murder case. Chan notes that Deacon sports a large diamond on his ring finger.

Chan then visits Wu Song, a well-known Chinese artist who created the statues. When the artist exposes a concealed compartment at the base of the statue, Chan discovers a diamond hidden inside and surmises that it is part of a stolen collection. While at Wu Song's studio, Chan notices the statue of a large cat that is identical to one found in Manning's study. He asks to see Wu Song's sales book, which reveals that the statue was sold to the Sea Tide Art Company located at the pier adjacent to the fun house.

Chan visits Deacon at his office. When Charlie begins to question him about the Sea Tide Art Company, Deacon panics and flees out a back door. Jumping into Birmingham's cab, Chan, Tommy, and Birmingham pursue Deacon to the pier but by the time they arrive, they find Deacon has already been strangled.

At the fun house, Chan is captured by gang members Carl, Catlen, Salos, and Gannett, who demand that Chan produce the diamond. When Tommy and Birmingham arrive at the fun house, the thieves begin to pummel Tommy to coerce Chan into revealing the location of the diamond. Chan convinces the thieves that Birmingham has the jewel.

Detective Dennis then learns that Chan has gone to the fun house and follows him there. After Chan subdues the crooks with a well-aimed spray from a fire extinguisher, Dennis and Leah Manning arrive, and Chan reveals that Manning and Deacon were partners in the diamond theft. Manning then double-crossed the gang, took the diamonds for himself, and Deacon killed him. To prove his supposition, Chan produces the murder weapon with the initials "WD" inscribed on the handle. Chan explains that Deacon killed Kurt after discovering that he was about to betray him. Chan then pulls the murder gloves out of Catlen's pocket and concludes that Catlen killed Deacon to prevent him from leading Chan to the hideout.

***The Chinese Parrot* (novel)** The second *Charlie Chan* novel written by Earl Derr Biggers and published by Bobbs-Merrill in 1926. The novel was serialized in *The Saturday Evening Post* and was the basis for the 1927 silent film of the same name, which was later remade as *Charlie Chan's Courage* (1934). *See* photo, page 108.

***The Chinese Parrot* (1927)**

Source: based on the novel *The Chinese Parrot* by Earl Derr Biggers (Bobbs-Merrill, 1926). Original Copyright: Universal Pictures Corporation, August 24, 1927; LP24331.

Copyright Renewed: June 1, 1955; R150787. Release Date: October 23, 1927. Sound: silent. Film: b&w; 35 mm; 7 reels; 7,304 feet. Running Time: unknown.

Presenter: Carl Laemmle. Director: Paul Leni. Screenplay Adaptation: J. Grubb Alexander. Titles: Walter Anthony. Photography: Ben Kline.

Cast

Marian Nixon	*as*	Sally Phillimore
Florence Turner		Sally Phillimore (older)
Hobart Bosworth		Philip J. Madden/ Jerry Delaney
Edward Burns		Robert Eden
Albert Conti		Martin Thorne
Kamiyama Sojin		Charlie Chan [alias Ah Kim]
J. Fred Esmelton		Alexander Eden
Ed Kennedy		"Shaky" Maydorf
George Kuwa		Louie Wong

Left: **The cover of an early edition of *The Chinese Parrot*, written by Earl Derr Biggers in 1926 (courtesy Don Rogers).** ***Below:*** **Kamiyama Sojin, as Charlie Chan (alias Ah Kim), with Edmund (credited as Edward) Burns in *The Chinese Parrot* (Everett Collection).**

Slim Summerville, Dan Mason	Prospectors
Anna May Wong	Nautch dancer
Etta Lee	Gambling den habitué
Jack Trent	Victor Jordan

Plot Summary: Sally Randall, daughter of a wealthy Hawaiian planter, marries Phillimore, the man of her father's choice, though she has sworn her love to Philip Madden. Tearing from her throat the priceless pearls given her by her father, Madden declares that one day he will buy her at the same price. Twenty years later (and now a widow in financial straits), Sally offers the pearls for sale in San Francisco. Accompanied by her daughter, who is also named Sally, she is astonished to discover Madden bargaining for the pearls, which she has entrusted to Charlie Chan, her former houseboy many years ago and now a police detective. The sale is contingent on her delivery of the jewels to Madden's desert home.

However, Madden is taken prisoner by gangsters and is impersonated by Jerry Delaney, who welcomes Sally and Robert Eden, the jeweler's son. While Chan is secretly undertaking an investigation, the jewels are stolen by various parties, but it develops that a Chinese parrot has witnessed the kidnapping and told him about it.

Notes: No copies of *The Chinese Parrot* are currently known to exist. The film was later remade as *Charlie Chan's Courage* (1934).

***The Chinese Ring* (1947)** The twelfth *Charlie Chan* film produced by Monogram Pictures Corporation.

Alternate Title: *Charlie Chan in the Chinese Ring*. Working Titles: *The Red Hornet* and *Charlie Chan and the Chinese Ring*. Source: remake of *Mr. Wong in Chinatown* (1938). Original Copyright: Monogram Pictures Corporation, November 20, 1947; LP1381. Copyright Renewed: February 26, 1975; R598931. Production: August 21 to mid–September, 1947. Release Date: December 6, 1947. Sound: Western Electric Recording. Film: b&w. Running Time: 67–68 minutes.

Producer: James S. Burkett. Director: William Beaudine. Assistant Director: William Calihan, Jr. Original Screenplay: W. Scott Darling. Photography: William Sickner. Editor: Richard Heermance. Set Dresser: Ray Boltz, Jr.* Musical Director: Edward J. Kay. Recordist: W.C. Smith. Production Supervisor: Glenn Cook. Tech Director: Dave Milton.

Cast

Roland Winters	*as*	Charlie Chan
Warren Douglas		Sergeant Bill Davidson
Mantan Moreland		Birmingham Brown
Louise Currie		Peggy Cartwright
Victor Sen Young		Tommy Chan
Philip Ahn		Captain Kong
Byron Foulger		Mr. Armstrong
Thayer Roberts		Captain James J. Kelso
Jean Wong		Princess Mei Ling
Chabing		Lilly Mae Wong
George L. Spaulding		Dr. Hickey
Paul Bryar*		Sergeant
Thornton Edwards*		Hotel clerk
Lee Tung Foo*		Butler
Richard Wang*		Hamishin
Spencer Chan*		Chinese officer
Jack Mower*		Ballard
Charmienne Harker*		Stenographer

Plot Summary: A Chinese princess arrives in San Francisco by boat, and several weeks later goes to visit Charlie Chan at his home. She gives Chan's butler, Birmingham Brown, a ring with the Chinese characters for "long life and happiness" (壽福, shòu fú) as a means of her introduction. Before she sees Chan, an assailant kills the princess by shooting a poison dart through a window. Her last act before she dies is to write "Capt. K" on a piece of paper but is unable to finish the captain's name. Chan then calls police sergeant Bill Davidson to report the murder. Davidson's friend, reporter Peggy Cartwright, arrives uninvited at Chan's house and identifies the princess as Mei Ling, who came from China a few weeks before on a ship captained by Capt. Kong.

Questioning Kong, Chan learns that the princess came to the United States to purchase warplanes for her brother's army in the Orient from a Captain Kelso, and brought one million dollars with her. However, Kelso has received only half his payment, and Kong is anxious to receive his share of the arms

Unbilled.

sales. With the princess now dead, Kelso and Kong think each other the murderer.

Chan, Davidson, and Peggy then meet Mei Ling's maid, Lilly Mae Wong. They also meet a mute Chinese boy who was befriended by Mei Ling and lives in the basement. Wanting to question the maid again, Chan arrives at the princess' apartment and finds the maid dead. The boy, who is a deaf-mute, tells Chan with hand gestures that he saw a man enter Mei Ling's apartment. Chan visits Mr. Armstrong, the head of the San Francisco branch of the Exchange Specie Bank, who fills Chan in about the princess' banking transactions.

Chan decides to pay Armstrong another visit, this time at his home (which has a high fence and is guarded by attack dogs). After Chan is admitted to the house, Armstrong mentions that he had to put one of his vicious guard dogs to sleep and is ordering a headstone for the grave.

Kong and Kelso are now very anxious to get the rest of their money before their boat sails at midnight. They go to Armstrong's house, kidnap Chan and Armstrong, bind and gag both of them, and drive them to the ship. Birmingham and Tommy together follow the car and are able to free Armstrong and Chan. Meanwhile, Peggy and Sgt. Davidson arrive at the ship. When Kelso sees Peggy, he abducts her. Hearing her screams, Davidson and the police come to her rescue, and Kong and Kelso are arrested.

With everyone assembled together, Chan then explains that it was Armstrong, not Kong or Kelso, who committed the murders. Armstrong stole Mei Ling's money by forging her Chinese signature and then swindled Kelso and Kong out of receiving the balance of their payments. He then killed the maid, as well as the mute Chinese boy, whom he buried instead of his dog.

Note: *The Chinese Ring* is Roland Winters' first film in the role of Charlie Chan, replacing Sidney Toler who died approximately six months earlier.

Chinese slippers Pair of slippers that was once given to Col. John Beetham by the emperor of China for distinguished service in China and is now found on the feet of the murdered body of Hilary Galt in *Behind That Curtain* (1929). Embroidered on the tops of the slippers are Chinese characters whose translation is "Walk softly, go far." After shooting Galt in his office, Eric Durand places the slippers on Galt's feet.

Chivra, Alexander Stand-in for Warner Oland in *Charlie Chan in London* (1934) and *Charlie Chan in Paris* (1935). His job was to fill in for Oland when the crew was adjusting lights or setting up for the next scene.

chlorine water Chemical reagent used by Charlie Chan to determine the presence of quinine in *Charlie Chan's Secret* (1936). *See also* **quinine sulfate**.

Chop Suey A derogatory nickname for Charlie Chan used by Sgt. Kelly in *Charlie*

Warner Oland (*left*) and stand-in Alexander Chivra (Everett Collection).

Chan at the Opera (1936). From the Chinese *tsa-sui* (many pieces), chop suey is a Chinese-American dish consisting of meat and vegetables cooked together in a sauce and served with rice. *See also* **Egg Foo Yung.**

chop suey boogie Name given by Tommy Chan to impromptu boogie-woogie music (with Tommy playing the violin and Birmingham on the piano) in *Docks of New Orleans* (1948).

Chop Suey 108 Walkie-talkie recognition code for Jimmy Chan in *Dangerous Money* (1946). Chattanooga Brown's code is Porkchop 711.

Chudnow, David Film producer, composer, music director, and music supervisor for over 55 films. Chudnow served as music supervisor for *The Chinese Cat* (1944) and music director for *Black Magic* (1944).

Churchill, Marguerite (December 25, 1909, Kansas City, Missouri–) Attractive actress who appeared in over 25 films and portrays Pamela Potter in *Charlie Chan Carries On* (1931).

Marguerite Churchill journeyed from her native Kansas City to New York as a child, where she trained for a theatrical career at Professional Children's School and Theatre Guild Drama School. She was on Broadway before reaching the age of 14. In 1929 she was signed to a Fox Studios contract. Her first film role was as Mary Douglas in *The Valiant* (1929), in which she co-starred with Paul Muni.

Dissatisfied with the sort of roles assigned her at Fox, Churchill returned to Broadway where she appeared in Kaufman and Ferber's *Dinner at Eight* (1933). She gave Hollywood a second chance in 1935, but, except for her portrayal of Janet Blake in *Dracula's Daughter* (1936), most of her film roles were largely forgettable. She left films again in 1936 to spend more time with her husband, cowboy star George O'Brien. After the breakup of their marriage in 1948, Churchill made one final screen appearance as Barbara Madison in RKO's *Bunco Squad* (1950).

Marguerite Churchill

Citizen's State Bank Bank that Thomas Harley is supposed to have robbed (murdering one of its bank guards) in *Dark Alibi* (1946). The bank was the third to be robbed in two years, all in an identical manner, and no money has been recovered. Harley, an ex-convict, is framed by an elaborate scheme whereby his forged fingerprints were left at the crime scene.

***City in Darkness* (1939)** The eleventh *Charlie Chan* film produced by Twentieth Century–Fox Film Corporation.

Working Title: *Charlie Chan in City in Darkness*. Source: based on an unproduced play by Gina Kaus and Ladislaus Fodor and the character "Charlie Chan" created by Earl Derr Biggers. Original Copyright: Twentieth Century–Fox Film Corporation, December 1,

1939; LP9341. Copyright Renewed: September 7, 1967; R417120. PCA Certificate Number: 5531. Production: began July 6, 1939. Release Date: December 1, 1939. Sound: RCA High Fidelity Recording. Film: b&w; 8 reels; 6,686 feet. Running Time: 69 minutes.

Executive Producer: Sol M. Wurtzel.* Associate Producer: John Stone. Director: Herbert I. Leeds. Assistant Director: Charles Hall.* Screenplay: Robert Ellis and Helen Logan. Director of Photography: Virgil Miller. Art Direction: Richard Day and Lewis Creber. Film Editor: Harry Reynolds. Set Decorations: Thomas Little. Costumes: Herschel. Musical Direction: Samuel Kaylin. Sound: Joseph E. Aiken and William H. Anderson.

Cast

Sidney Toler	*as*	Charlie Chan
Lynn Bari		Marie Dubon
Richard Clarke		Tony Madero
Harold Huber		Marcel
Pedro de Córdoba		Antoine
Dorothy Tree		Charlotte Ronnell
C. Henry Gordon		[Romaine], Prefect of police
Douglass Dumbrille		Petroff
Noel Madison		Belescu
Leo G. Carroll		Louis Santelle
Lon Chaney, Jr.		Pierre
Louis Mercier		["Gentleman"] Max
George Davis		Alex
Barbara Leonard		Lola
Adrienne d'Ambricourt		Landlady
Frederick Vogeding		Captain
Alphonse Martell*		Gendarme
Eugene Borden*		Gendarme
Gino Corrado*		Café owner
Rolfe Sedan*		Hotel manager
Ann Codee*		Complainant at police station

Plot Summary: In the fall of 1938, the great powers of Europe struggle to halt the encroaching war by convening at a conference in Munich. As the peace of Europe hangs in the balance, Charlie Chan is drawn into the conflict when Petroff, a foreign agent, is murdered during a Paris blackout.

As Chan's investigation progresses, he narrows the suspect list to Tony Madero, a man whom Petroff had framed for forgery because he had objected to Petroff's unwelcome attentions to his wife, Marie Dubon; Alex, Max, and Lola, three burglars who had broken into Petroff's house on the night of the murder; Belescu, Petroff's business partner; Louis Santelle, a locksmith in the business of forging passports; and Antoine, Petroff's French butler.

Chan discovers that Petroff died while dictating a telegram about obtaining clearance papers for a special cargo, and he begins to suspect that Petroff was a foreign agent dealing in munitions. Chan then traces Petroff and Belescu to Charlotte Ronnell, the leader of a spy ring that was shipping munitions to the enemy. After a high-speed chase, Charlotte and the boat captain board a chartered plane but die in a fiery crash. Antoine then admits that he killed Petroff to protect France, and is told by Romaine that he will be awarded the Croix de Guerre (Cross of War) for his bravery.

Clark, Daniel B. (April 28, 1890–December 14, 1961) Cinematographer and special effects photographer for over 60 movies, about half of which were silent films when he was often credited as either Dan Clark or Daniel Clark. Clark was the cinematographer for six *Charlie Chan* films with Twentieth Century–Fox and also was the original cameraman for *Charlie Chan in Paris* (1935), but did not receive on-screen credit.

During the 1943 Academy Awards, he was presented with the Scientific and Engineering Award (Class II-Plaque) for the development of a lens calibration system and the application of this system to exposure control in cinematography.

Charlie Chan filmography: *The Black Camel* (1931), *Charlie Chan in Egypt* (1935), *Charlie Chan at the Circus* (1936), *Charlie Chan at Monte Carlo* (1937), *Charlie Chan at the Olympics* (1937), *Charlie Chan at the Wax Museum* (1940).

Clark, Harvey (1886, Boston, Massachusetts–July 19, 1938, Hollywood, California) Versatile American stage and screen actor

**Unbilled.*

who appeared in nearly 125 silent and sound films, sometimes credited as Harvey Clarke. Clark portrays Professor Gamble, an alias for Henry Maydorf, in *Charlie Chan's Courage* (1934).

Vaudeville performer Harvey Clark entered films in 1916 with the New York Picture Company and proved versatile enough to portray everything from greasy western gamblers to huffy British lords. Laurel and Hardy fans will remember Clark as the long-suffering tailor in *Putting Pants on Philip* (1927). In the talkies, he was generally seen as pop-eyed, befuddled characters, with the spectacular exception of his "maniacal killer" turn as a janitor in *A Shriek in the Night* (1933).

Clarke, Charles Galloway (May 19, 1899, Potter Valley, California–July 1, 1983, Beverly Hills, California) Cinematographer for over 100 films, including *Charlie Chan in Honolulu* (1938) and *Dead Men Tell* (1941); nominated for four Academy Awards in the Best Cinematography category: *Moontide* (1942), *Hello, Frisco, Hello* (1943), *Green Grass of Wyoming* (1948), *Sand* (1949). Clarke received a Technical Achievement Award (Class III-Citation) in 1944, and in 1980 was awarded its Medal of Commendation in appreciation for outstanding service and dedication in upholding the high standards of The Academy of Motion Picture Arts and Sciences.

Clarke, Richard Character actor who appeared in nearly 20 films and portrays Tony Madero in *City in Darkness* (1939).

Clementine Member of Cole King's variety troupe (portrayed by Rita Quigley) who finds Marcia's body, a silk cord wrapped around her neck, washed up on the beach in *The Trap* (1947).

Clive, E.E. (August 28, 1879, Monmouthshire, Wales–June 6, 1940, North Hollywood, California) British character actor (real name: Edward E. Clive) who played a succession of sour-faced but often amiable butlers, policemen, burgermeisters, and statesmen in over 80 films. Clive portrays Detective Sgt. Thacker in *Charlie Chan in London* (1934).

Born in Wales, E.E. Clive studied for a medical career before switching to acting at age 22. Touring the provinces for a decade, Clive became an expert at virtually every sort of regional dialect in the British Isles. He moved to the U.S. in 1912 where, after working on the Orpheum vaudeville circuit, he set up his own stock company in Boston. By the 1920s his company was operating in Hollywood. Among his repertory players were such up-and-comers as Rosalind Russell.

He made his film debut as a rural police officer in *The Invisible Man* (1933) and then spent the next seven years showing up in bit roles as burgermeisters, butlers, reporters, aristocrats, shopkeepers, and cabbies. Though he seldom settled down for long in any one characterization, Clive was a semi-regular as Tenny the Butler in Paramount's *Bulldog Drummond* series.

"Clue!" Kashimo's frequent expletive to Charlie Chan in *The Black Camel* (1931). When Chan asks, "Clue? Which case?" Kashimo replies, "No case, just clue." Frustrated by the annoying interruptions of his overzealous and inept assistant, Charlie tells Kashimo to "spend more time hunting for nothing to do!"

Cobb, Edmund (June 23, 1892, Albuquerque, New Mexico–August 15, 1974, Woodland Hills, California) Veteran American character actor who appeared in over 275 silent and sound films, often cast as a lawman or gangster. Cobb portrays an unnamed miner in Driscoll's gang in *The Golden Eye* (1948).

Cocos Islands Also known as the Keeling Islands, located in the east Indian Ocean about 2,300 miles west of Darwin, Australia, and about 1,600 miles south of Yangon (Rangoon), Myanmar (Burma). Discovered in 1609 by the British explorer William Keeling and settled in 1826, the islands since 1955 have been administered by Australia, which assumed total sovereignty in 1978. On April 6,

1984, the Cocos Islanders voted for full integration with Australia with full rights as Australian citizens. Most islanders are descendants of Malays taken there to farm coconuts. The island's main importance is as a weather station in the Indian Ocean.

In *Dead Men Tell* (1941), Cocos Island is the location of the reported $60 million in buried treasure as drawn on a map by Black Hook, the pirate grandfather of Miss Patience Nodbury. Also, Captain Kane explains to Charlie Chan that many years ago he went on a treasure hunt to Cocos Island with his partner, but that the man left him there to die.

Codee, Ann (1890, Belgium–May 18, 1961, Hollywood, California) Stage and screen actress who appeared in 65 films, including two *Charlie Chan* entries. Codee portrays the woman complainant at the police station in *City in Darkness* (1939) and Margo, the servant-cook for Lola Dean in *Charlie Chan in Rio* (1941).

Ann Codee toured American vaudeville in the teens and twenties in a comedy act with her husband, American-born Frank Orth. The team made its film debut in 1929, appearing in a series of multilingual movie shorts. Thereafter, both Codee and Orth flourished as character actors. Codee was seen in dozens of films as florists, music teachers, landladies, governesses, and grandmothers. She played a variety of ethnic types, from the very French Mme. Poullard in *Jezebel* (1938) to the Teutonic Tante Berthe in *The Mummy's Curse* (1961).

Coffin, Tristram (1910–March 26, 1990) American character actor who appeared in over 90 films, sometimes credited as Tristam Coffin and Tris Coffin. In two *Charlie Chan* roles, Coffin portrays Scott Pearson in *Dangerous Money* (1946) and lawyer Ed Seward in *The Shanghai Chest* (1948).

The namesake nephew of American journalist Tris Coffin, actor Tristram Coffin set his stage career in motion at age 14. By 1939, the tall, silver-mustached Coffin was well on his way to becoming one of the screen's most prolific character actors. Generally cast as crooked lawyers, shifty business executives, and gang bosses in "B" pictures, Coffin projected a pleasanter image in "A" films, where he often played soft-spoken doctors and educators.

Tristram Coffin

Even busier on television than in films, he was virtually a regular guest villain on the *Superman* series (1952–57) and appeared as Captain Ryning of the Arizona Rangers in the weekly syndicated western, *26 Men* (1957–58).

Coghlan, Frank, Jr. (March 16, 1917, New Haven, Connecticut–) Diminutive-sized actor who appeared in over 80 silent and sound films, sometimes credited as Frank Coghlan or Junior Coghlan. In two *Charlie Chan* roles, Coghlan portrays the jockey Eddie Brill in *Charlie Chan at the Race Track* (1936) and the British Imperial Club hatcheck attendant, Gilroy (unbilled), in *Murder Over New York* (1940).

Born in Connecticut and raised in Los Angeles, Frank Coghlan began appearing in films at age three. His meager income helped to pay his father's way through chiropractic school. Though his mother was reluctant to allow her son to appear before the cameras, young Frank took to performing with ease. Placed under contract to Cecil B. DeMille, who considered the boy "the perfect example of a homeless waif," Coghlan became a popular juvenile performer. Billed as Junior Coghlan, he appeared prominently in such major silent films as *The Yankee Clipper* (1926), *Let 'Er Go Gallegher* (1927), and *Slide, Kelly, Slide* (1927).

During the early talkie era, Coghlan co-starred with fellow child actor Leon Janney in *Penrod and Sam* (1930), and played James Cagney as a boy in *Public Enemy* (1931). As a freelancer, Coghlan appeared in several serials, including *The Adventures of Captain Marvel* (1941), in which he was top-billed as the Captain's youthful alter ego Billy Batson. He also showed up in many bit roles, usually playing a Western Union messenger boy.

With the onslaught of World War II, Coghlan began his 23-year Navy career as an aviator. He rose to the rank of commander, and from 1952 through 1954 was in charge of the movie section of the Pentagon's Office of Information, acting as liaison and technical advisor for such films as *The Caine Mutiny* (1954) and *Bridges of Toko-Ri* (1955). He was later in charge of the Navy's Hollywood office, coordinating official naval cooperation for films like *In Harm's Way* (1964) and television series like *Hennessey*. After retiring from the Navy, Coghlan worked in public relations for the Los Angeles Zoo and the Port of Los Angeles.

Cohn, Martin G. (c. 1896–November 19, 1953, Hollywood, California) Film editor of nearly 50 films, including *Charlie Chan in the Secret Service* (1944) and (unbilled) *The Chinese Cat* (1944).

Colbert, Norman Film editor for *Charlie Chan at Treasure Island* (1939).

Colby, Allen Heir (portrayed by Jerry Miley) to the Colby family estate of his father Bernard Colby in *Charlie Chan's Secret* (1936). Allen and his father had a disagreement about his father's psychic beliefs, which Allen didn't share and left home.

Seven years earlier, Allen Colby was on the S.S. *Nestor*, a ship that was caught in a storm and sunk off the coast of Hawaii. His was not one of the two bodies recovered from the wreckage by divers, nor was he among those rescued in the lifeboats. With Allen the only passenger unaccounted for, Charlie Chan is hired by the Colby family to determine whether or not Colby is actually dead, so that the status of the Colby estate can be settled.

Chan then hypothesizes that Colby is probably still alive, having perhaps been rescued by a passing ship that didn't have a radio onboard. Upon further investigation, Chan learns that for the seven years that he was out of contact with his family, Colby enlisted in the French foreign legion and later spent time imprisoned by the Riffs (Berber tribesmen in Morocco). He eventually escapes and returns to Colby House in San Francisco but is murdered by Fred Gage, a cousin by marriage, before he can meet with his relatives to explain his disappearance and claim his inheritance. With Colby now dead, the estate would pass to Henrietta, who for the last seven years has been siphoning off large amounts of the estate money to spend on psychic research. Now she would not have to account for how the money was spent.

Colby, Bernard The father of Allen Colby and brother of Henrietta Lowell in *Charlie Chan's Secret* (1936). Like his sister, Bernard also believed in psychic phenomena and rebuilt Colby House with its many secret passages and rooms. At Colby House, spiritualist advisor Professor Bowan performs séances using his assistant Carlotta as the medium to contact Bernard as a guide to the world beyond.

Colby House Eerie estate house built by Bernard Colby in *Charlie Chan's Secret* (1936). The entire compound consists of vast grounds surrounded by stone walls, the main house, and a caretaker's cottage. As a believer in psychic phenomena, Colby rebuilt the original house to include many secret passages and rooms. At Colby House, spiritualist advisor Professor Bowan performs séances with his assistant Carlotta as a medium to contact Bernard as a guide to the world beyond. It is in the main house that the long-missing Allen Colby is murdered with a knife thrown by Fred Gage.

Cole, Lester (June 19, 1904, New York, New York–August 15, 1985, San Francisco, California) Screenwriter of over 30 films who co-wrote both the screenplay for *Charlie Chan's Greatest Case* (1933) and the dialogue (unbilled) for *Charlie Chan in London* (1934).

Lester Cole was the son of Polish immigrants and began writing and directing plays at age 16 after he dropped out of high school. During the 1920s and 1930s he worked as an actor on stage and screen before embarking on his screenwriting career. While in Hollywood he was a union activist and became a co-founder of the Screen Writers Guild in 1933.

Cole will be best remembered in cinema history as a member of the original "Hollywood Ten," one of the first people in the film industry to be blacklisted by the studios after standing up to the House Un-American Activities Committee in 1947. He was blackballed for challenging the committee's right to interrogate him about his political beliefs. He then served one year in prison, leaving behind an unfinished script that was later completed by John Steinbeck for Kazan's *Viva Zapata!* (1952). Following his release from prison he worked a series of odd jobs. In 1961 he went to London, but eventually returned to the States where he began collaborating on screenplays under the assumed names of Gerald L.C. Copley, Lewis Copley, and J. Redmond Prior. He also taught screenwriting at the University of California, Berkeley.

Collins, Eddie (January 30, 1883–September 1, 1940, Arcadia, California) Short vaudeville comic (real name: Edward Bernard Collins) who appeared in 20 films in two years before suffering a fatal heart attack. In two *Charlie Chan* roles, Collins portrays animal keeper Al Hogan in *Charlie Chan in Honolulu* (1938) and the taxicab driver in *Charlie Chan in Reno* (1939).

Collins, Marie Estranged wife (portrayed by Joan Woodbury in her first of two *Charlie Chan* roles) of Thomas Mitchell in *Charlie Chan on Broadway* (1937). Collins is a headline dancer in a floor show at Johnny Burke's Hottentot Club. Although married to Mitchell, she is Burke's current girlfriend and was once friends with Burke's previous girlfriend, Billie Bronson.

Collins, "Tip" Jockey (portrayed by Frankie Darro) who rides Avalanche to apparent victory in the Melbourne (Australia) Sweepstakes in *Charlie Chan at the Race Track* (1936). However, Collins intentionally fouls Stardust during the race on orders from Bagley, who is the horse's trainer and is part of a racetrack gambling ring. Avalanche is then disqualified and Collins is barred from further racing for two years. After the race, Collins expects his payoff of $5,000, but Bagley pays him only $2,000 in race tickets to be cashed in, saying that this has to be split too many ways.

Collins travels to America. When at the Santa Juanita racetrack, Collins notices that there is something strange about Gallant Lad. The horse has been switched with Avalanche, and both horses look nearly the same (thanks to some coloring dye applied to Gallant Lad). Collins confronts Bagley and is told the whole story about the fixed race to come. As a favor, the gambling ring lets Collins in on the action to convince him that they still appreciate him for throwing the race back in Melbourne. Bagley asks "Lefty," one of the ring's henchmen, to drive Collins back home. Later, Collins' body is fished out of the Pacific Ocean at Santa Monica by the police.

Colonel Tim Midget (42 inches tall) circus entertainer (portrayed by George Brasno) in *Charlie Chan at the Circus* (1936). His wife, Lady Tiny (40 inches tall), is portrayed by his real-life younger sister, Olive Brasno, who together form a sideshow dancing act in the Kinney & Gaines Combined Circus. Charlie

Chan, his wife, and their 12 children are introduced to Tim and Tiny by circus owner Joe Kinney. Tim asks Chan if he would like a cigar. Politely refusing the offer, Charlie in turn offers peppermint sticks to the midgets, after which Tiny then asks Chan for his autograph.

Compañia de Aqua Pura Sign on truck driven by Manolo (as Ramon Gonzales) delivering nitroglycerin disguised as bottled water to the office watercooler of the Miraflores Power Control Station in *Charlie Chan in Panama* (1940).

Compton, Arlene Shady lady (portrayed by Gloria Roy in her first of seven *Charlie Chan* roles) who is the object of Dan Winterslip's latest romance in *Charlie Chan's Greatest Case* (1933).

Compton, Cliveden Undercover member of the British Secret Service (portrayed by Lionel Atwill in his first of two *Charlie Chan* roles) posing as a novelist in *Charlie Chan in Panama* (1940). Compton comes to Panama on the trail of Reiner, but is shot and killed by Manolo, one of Reiner's accomplices.

Compton, Joyce (January 27, 1907, Lexington, Kentucky–October 13, 1997, Los Angeles, California) Good-looking blonde actress (real name: Eleanor Hunt) who appeared in over 135 silent and sound films, often cast in "dumb blonde" roles. Compton portrays dancer-stripper Emily Evans in *Dark Alibi* (1946).

Because Joyce Compton was born into a traveling family, she received her schooling bit by bit in classrooms from Texas to Toronto. In the company of her parents, Compton made the Hollywood casting-office rounds in the mid–1920s, finally landing her first role in *What Fools Men* (1925). When talkies came, she cornered the market in squeaky-voiced dumb blondes, often applying her natural Southern accent for full comic effect. She worked frequently in two-reel comedies with such comedians as Clark and McCullough, Walter Catlett, and Charley Chase. Compton's feature appearances were confined to supporting roles as waitresses, good-time girls, and ditzy Southern belles. Occasionally a big part would come her way and she'd make the most of it.

Her best role of the 1930s was probably that of nightclub singer Dixie Belle Lee in *The Awful Truth* (1937), whose "Gone with the Wind" striptease number is later hilariously imitated by the film's star, Irene Dunne. Retiring from the screen in 1961, Compton worked from time to time as a private nurse, preferring to spend her spare hours painting and designing clothes.

Confucius (551–479 B.C.) Chinese philosopher and teacher born in the feudal state of Lu, now Shandong province. Confucius' original name was *Kung Chiu*, but he was later known in Chinese as *Kung Fu-tse* (孔夫子), whom Western scholars call Confucius. Many of Confucius' sayings were compiled in *The Analects*, two of which comprise what is commonly referred to as the Golden Rule: "Do not do to others what you would not like yourself" and "Do unto others what you wish to do unto yourself." On occasion, Charlie Chan would cite wisdom attributed to Confucius, such as "Confucius say no man is poor who have worthy son" (*Charlie Chan at the Race Track* [1936]). *See also* **aphorisms**.

Conners, Barry Screenwriter of nearly 20 films, including three *Charlie Chan* entries: *Charlie Chan Carries On* (1931), *The Black Camel* (1931), and *Charlie Chan's Chance* (1932).

Conover, Mary Former escort working for the Bay City Escort Bureau (portrayed by Tanis Chandler in her first of two *Charlie Chan* roles) in *Shadows Over Chinatown* (1946). Her grandmother and boyfriend, Joe Thompson, both fear that she is missing or dead, and travel to San Francisco to find her.

Charlie Chan recognizes her working as a waitress (using the alias of Mary McCoy) in the coffee shop of the Mayfair Hotel, where he is staying. Mary leaves the escort bureau after being annoyed and frightened by henchman Mike Roberts' suggestions that she could become a wealthy widow after a former employee had also become a widow and disappeared.

Conover, Mrs. Elderly grandmother of Mary Conover in *Shadows Over Chinatown* (1946). Portrayed by Mary Gordon in her second of two *Charlie Chan* roles, Mrs. Conover travels by bus to San Francisco with her friend Kate Johnson to find her missing granddaughter, Mary Conover, and fears that she may have been killed as part of a series of "torso" murders. After viewing the body of the latest murder victim, Charlie Chan assures Mrs. Conover that it was not her granddaughter because the victim had an appendectomy scar, which Mrs. Conover's granddaughter never had.

Conroy, Frank (October 14, 1890, Derby, England–February 24, 1964, Paramus, New Jersey) British-born stage and screen actor who appeared in over 70 films. In two *Charlie Chan* roles, Conroy portrays Professor John Thurston in *Charlie Chan in Egypt* (1935) and Mr. Whitely in *Charlie Chan at the Opera* (1936).

Conti, Albert (January 29, 1887, Trieste, Austria [now Italy]–January 18, 1967, Hollywood, California) Actor (real name: Albert de Conti Cadassamare) who appeared in nearly 85 silent and sound films and portrays Martin Thorne in *The Chinese Parrot* (1927).

Albert Conti was a career soldier in the Austrian army who came to America after the close of World War I. Like many impoverished post-war Europeans, Conti was obliged to take a series of manual labor jobs. While working in the California oil fields, Conti answered an open call placed by director Erich von Stroheim, who was in search of an Austrian military officer to act as technical advisor for his upcoming film, *Merry Go Round* (1922).

He later was able to secure dignified character roles in several silent and sound films. His credits ranged from Josef von Sternberg's *Morocco* (1930), as Colonel Quinnovieres, to portraying the Honorable Winchester Squirtz in Laurel and Hardy's *Slipping Wives* (1926). Even though he made his last film in 1942 (*My Gal Sal*), Albert Conti remained in the industry as an employee of the MGM wardrobe department, where he worked until his retirement in 1962.

Continental Hotel Rio de Janeiro hotel that is the residence of psychic Alfredo Marana (an alias used by Alfredo Cardoza) and Paul Wagner (the ex-husband of Lola Dean) in *Charlie Chan in Rio* (1941).

Conway, Morgan (March 16, 1900, Newark, New Jersey–November 16, 1981, Livingston, New Jersey) Character actor who appeared in nearly 30 films and who portrays George Bently in *Charlie Chan in Reno* (1939). While under contract to RKO, Conway was assigned to star in *Dick Tracy, Detective* (1945) as the second actor to play Chester Gould's comic-strip detective. Conway was also one of the founding members of the Screen Actors Guild.

Conway, Sybil Former actress (portrayed by Betty Francisco) who was once married to jewel thief Jim Everhard in *Charlie Chan Carries On* (1931). She runs away with Walter Honeywood (and two bags of diamonds that had been stolen by Everhard) and is later murdered by Everhard.

Note: The character Sybil Conway loosely parallels that of Mrs. Pendleton in *Charlie Chan's Murder Cruise* (1940).

Cook, Glenn N. Production manager for seven *Charlie Chan* films at Monogram: *The Shanghai Cobra* (1945), *The Red Dragon* (1945), *Dark Alibi* (1946), *Shadows Over Chinatown* (1946), *Dangerous Money* (1946), *The Chinese Ring* (1947), and *Docks of New Orleans* (1948).

Cooper Gangster (portrayed by Crane Whitley) and old accomplice of Ralph Brett (when the two worked together in Paris years ago) in *The Scarlet Clue* (1945). Cooper is on the other end of the telephone in Room 211 in the Algard Building whenever Brett dials Harding 2535 to speak to his unknown superior in the espionage ring. Charlie Chan finds out the location, and when Cooper opens the door, Chan recognizes Cooper as someone he arrested six years ago in Singapore who had used the names of Carper and Cauper as aliases.

Cooper, Lt. TR-4 bomber test pilot for the Metropolitan Aircraft Company (portrayed by Alan Davis [unbilled]) in *Murder Over New York* (1940).

Cooper, Melville (October 15, 1896, Birmingham, England–March 29, 1973, Woodland Hills, California) British comedy actor of stage and screen who appeared in over 60 films, often as pompous, upper-class society types or confidence tricksters. Cooper portrays Herbert Fenton in *Murder Over New York* (1940).

In 1934 Cooper settled in the U.S. after making an excellent impression as Leporello in the Alexander Korda–produced film *The Private Life of Don Juan* (1934). Among Cooper's most famous screen portrayals were the High Sheriff of Nottingham in *The Adventures of Robin Hood* (1938), the amorous Reverend Collins in *Pride and Prejudice* (1940), and the rude wedding-rehearsal supervisor, Mr. Tringle, in *Father of the Bride* (1950).

coquina bark An ingredient mixed in the special cigarettes smoked by André Pereaux in *Docks of New Orleans* (1948). Charlie Chan notes that cigarette ash on the floorboard of Simon Lafontaine's stolen car contains coquina bark. Charlie later confirms that this same ingredient comes from Pereaux's cigarettes when Charlie bums a smoke from Pereaux, lights it, and notices the mild flavor.

Coquina is derived from the Spanish word meaning "cockle" or "shellfish," and is a form of limestone composed of fragments of fossil debris which are easily broken. Soft and highly porous, coquina is found in varying tones of white. Deposits found in Florida have been used as roadbed material and masonry stone for homes.

Corday, Max Artist (portrayed by Erik Rhodes) who is the leader of a bond counterfeiting ring in *Charlie Chan in Paris* (1935). Corday and confederate Henri Latouche take turns masquerading as a fictitious person known as Marcel Xavier, a crippled beggar, to provide each other with perfect alibis.

Charlie Chan questions Corday about his car being used by Marcel Xavier, and Charlie comments that the car is utilized as a place for removing a disguise and that Xavier really doesn't exist. When Charlie infers that Corday is Xavier, Corday unemotionally reminds Chan that he was sitting with Chan at the table at Le Singe Bleu when Nardi was killed. Charlie agrees and leaves. With son Lee, he then waits outside Corday's apartment door in the hallway and captures Corday trying to escape with two million francs. Chan matches a broken wax bank-seal, found in Dufresne's apartment, with the corresponding piece among the money envelopes. Chan then concludes that Corday murdered Dufresne but couldn't also have murdered Nardi.

Corpus Delicti One of two working titles for *Shadows Over Chinatown* (1946) before its release on July 27, 1946. *See also* ***Shadows Over Chinatown* (1946)**.

Cortez, Ricardo (September 19, 1899, Vienna, Austria–April 28, 1977, New York, New York) Handsome, suave actor (real name: Jacob Krantz) who appeared in almost 100 silent and sound films. In two *Charlie Chan* roles, Cortez portrays Dr. Ainsley in *Charlie Chan in Reno* (1939) and George Kirby in *Murder Over New York* (1940).

Born in Austria, Jacob emigrated with his family to New York where he worked a number of jobs while he trained as an actor. When he arrived in Hollywood in 1922 to work in movies, the Valentino era was at its peak. Although the producers liked the darkly handsome Krantz, they felt that neither his name nor his Jewish heritage would do for publicity purposes. Thus he became the Latin lover Ricardo Cortez from Spain.

Starting with small parts, the tall, dark Cortez was being groomed by Paramount to be the successor to Rudolph Valentino, but Cortez would never be viewed, or consider

Ricardo Cortez

himself, as the equal to the late Valentino (who died in 1926). Though a popular star, Cortez was caught in a number of run-of-the-mill romantic movies which depended more on his looks than on the script. Cortez would be the only actor to ever have his name billed above Greta Garbo's, appearing (as Don Rafael Brull) in her first American movie, *The Torrent* (1926).

Cortez made the transition to sound movies in 1929, and he played Sam Spade in the 1931 version of *The Maltese Falcon* (a.k.a. *Dangerous Female*). In many of the "B" movies that followed, Cortez shed his Valentino image to play wisecracking urban types, and was often cast as a smirking womanizer. He even portrayed Perry Mason in *The Case of the Black Cat* (1936). When he retired from the screen, Cortez returned to Wall Street, where he had started as a runner decades before. Only this time he returned as a member of one of Wall Street's top brokerage firms and lived a comfortable life until his death in 1977.

Cosgrove Petty pickpocket (portrayed by Jack Norton in his last of three *Charlie Chan* roles) in *Shadows Over Chinatown* (1946). Chan notices that Cosgrove had lifted the wallet of a lawyer and the watch and gun of private detective Jeff Hay while on a bus bound for San Francisco. Chan then convinces Cosgrove to return the stolen items in the same manner in exchange for Charlie's silence about the matter.

Near the movie's end, Cosgrove repays Chan's earlier favor by participating in a trap laid by Chan, picking the gun from Jeff Hay's coat and removing all but one bullet from the gun. After shooting Cosgrove in the shoulder with a single shot to avoid capture, Hay is then captured by Chan when he is told that there are no bullets left in his gun.

Cosmo Radio Center Office building, whose radio station's studios are on the second floor, in *The Scarlet Clue* (1945). Room 702, the office of radio announcer Wilbur Chester, is where Mrs. Marsh throws a hidden control switch that opens the trap door of the building's service elevator. Room 703 is an office where Mrs. Marsh uses a teletype to send messages to Ralph Brett. There is also a radio transmitter Mrs. Marsh uses to break gas pellets that murder Gloria Bayne and Willie Rand. The offices for the radio station and the Hamilton Laboratory are on the tenth floor. *See also* **Hamilton Laboratory**.

Cosmopolitan Club (1) San Francisco venue where Col. John Beetham is to lecture about his explorations in the Persian Desert in *Behind That Curtain* (1929).

Cosmopolitan Club (2) New York private club where Sir Lionel Grey's briefcase was checked in after his murder in *Charlie Chan's Chance* (1932). Charlie Chan discovers Grey's briefcase there and calls Inspectors Fife and Flannery over to watch and see who retrieves it. The culprit is Barry Kirk.

Note: The Cosmopolitan Club loosely parallels that of the British Imperial Club in *Murder Over New York* (1940).

Costello, Don (1901–October 24, 1945, Hollywood, California) American character actor who appeared in over 30 films. Costello portrays enemy agent Charles Masack in *The Red Dragon* (1945).

Costello, George P. Sound recordist for *Behind That Curtain* (1929) and *Charlie Chan on Broadway* (1937).

Courtney Arms New York apartment building on East 67th Street where George Kirby lives in *Murder Over New York* (1940).

CR 1000 Telephone number for Ned Stewart's Apex Detective Agency in *The Shanghai Cobra* (1945).

Cramer, Duncan Art director and production designer for over 40 films, including ten *Charlie Chan* films with Twentieth Century-Fox: *Charlie Chan's Greatest Case* (1933), *Charlie Chan's Courage* (1934), *Charlie Chan in London* (1934), *Charlie Chan in Paris* (1935), *Charlie Chan in Egypt* (1935), *Charlie Chan in Shanghai* (1935), *Charlie Chan's Secret* (1936), *Charlie Chan at the Circus* (1936), *Charlie Chan at the Race Track* (1936), and *Charlie Chan at the Opera* (1936).

Crawford, Alexander San Francisco jeweler (portrayed by Reginald Mason) who arranges the sale of the Phillimore pearl necklace to wealthy financier J.P. Madden in *Charlie Chan's Courage* (1934).

Note: In *The Chinese Parrot* (1927), of which *Charlie Chan's Courage* (1934) is a remake, the San Francisco jeweler is named Alexander Eden.

Crawford, Bob The son (portrayed by Donald Woods in his first of two *Charlie Chan* roles) of a San Francisco jeweler in *Charlie Chan's Courage* (1934). On behalf of his father, Crawford travels to J.P. Madden's California ranch to assist in the transfer of the Phillimore pearl necklace to its new owner.

Note: In *The Chinese Parrot* (1927), of which *Charlie Chan's Courage* (1934) is a remake, the jeweler's son is named Robert Eden.

Cream, Dr. Once the country's best facial surgeon (portrayed by C. Henry Gordon in his last of five *Charlie Chan* roles), Dr. Cream now uses his surgical skills to alter faces of criminals wanted by the law in *Charlie Chan at the Wax Museum* (1940). As a cover for his criminal activities, he runs Dr. Cream's Museum of Crime, assisted by Lily Latimer.

When convicted murderer Steve McBirney escapes from a New York courthouse, he and his bodyguard, Grennock, eventually make their way to the museum. As part of his plan to get revenge on Chan, McBirney has Dr. Cream perform plastic surgery on his face so no policeman (nor Charlie Chan) will be able to recognize him. Dr. Cream also at one time changed the appearance of McBirney's enemy, "Butcher" Degan, who is still alive after McBirney thought he had killed him.

Creber, Lewis H. (c. 1902–December 1, 1966, Hollywood, California) Art director for nine *Charlie Chan* films with Twentieth Century–Fox: *Charlie Chan in Shanghai* (1935), *Charlie Chan at the Opera* (1936), *Charlie Chan on Broadway* (1937), *Charlie Chan at Treasure Island* (1939), *Murder Over New York* (1940), *Charlie Chan at the Wax Museum* (1940), *Dead Men Tell* (1941), *Charlie Chan in Rio* (1941), and *Castle in the Desert* (1942).

Crehan, Joseph (July 12, 1883, Baltimore, Maryland–April 15, 1966, Hollywood, California) American character actor (real name: Charles Wilson) who appeared in over 250 films, often as a sheriff or cop. In two *Charlie Chan* roles, Crehan portrays Inspector Matthews in *Black Magic* (1944) and cruise ship skipper Captain Black in *Dangerous Money* (1946).

The Crime League Weekly radio show run by Dr. Cream in *Charlie Chan at the Wax Museum* (1940). From Dr. Cream's Museum of Crime, the show each week has a famous detective try to unravel an old unsolved crime. It is hosted by Tom Agnew, who is really "Butcher" Degan, a murderer whose face had been surgically altered by Dr. Cream years ago.

This week's show is the thirteenth, which is hastily changed from a presentation of the "Bradley Case" to the "Joe Rocke Case."

Doctor Cream, newspaper reporter Mary Bolton, and Number Two son Jimmy Chan persuade Charlie to go on the radio program that night to throw some light on the Joe Rocke Case, which is Charlie's famous unsolved crime. Chan always believed that Joe Rocke was framed by "Butcher" Degan while criminologist Dr. Otto von Brom helped convict Rocke on his scientific evidence.

At first Charlie wants no part of the show, but he is forced into appearing after son Jimmy accepts a challenge from von Brom made in front of his law school classmates on behalf of his father. Chan eventually accepts the challenge, saying, "Will imitate woman and change mind." Chan later tells police Inspector O'Matthews that the radio challenge may solve more than the Rocke case tonight.

Croix de Guerre (Cross of War) French Republic honor awarded to members of the French armed forces, regardless of rank, who are commended for outstanding bravery or ability in dispatches by a high ranking officer. The decoration consists of a bronze cross with crossed swords, hilts down. The center medallion shows a female head surrounded with the inscription *République Française*. The ribbon used during World War II (from 1939 to 1945) is green with a wide stripe of red on each edge and three narrow vertical red stripes in the center.

In *City in Darkness* (1939) the awarding of the Croix de Guerre is mentioned twice. Marcel, after realizing that a spy ring is about to be broken up, says that they will get the Croix de Guerre, "with palms." The second time the Croix de Guerre is mentioned is when Antoine is told by Romaine, the Paris prefect of police, that, although he killed his employer, Petroff, who was shipping munitions to be used against France, a general will award him the Croix de Guerre and kiss him on both cheeks as a hero.

Note: In order to receive palms with the Croix de Guerre, the recipient must have previously received the award.

Crosman, Henrietta (September 2, 1861, Wheeling, West Virginia–October 31, 1944, Pelham Manor, New York) Former leading stage and film actress who appeared in over 20 silent and sound films, usually in grande dame roles. Crosman portrays Henrietta Lowell in *Charlie Chan's Secret* (1936).

"La Cucaracha" Popular Mexican folk song which Tommy has learned to sing and play on the guitar in less than one week in *The Feathered Serpent* (1948). However, Tommy sings so badly off-key that brother Lee grimaces in pain. Tommy then asks his father, "Don't you think I've improved, Pop?" Charlie responds with, "Man who improve house before building solid foundation apt to run in very much trouble."

cuckoo clock Wall clock in Nardi's apartment in *Charlie Chan in Paris* (1935). Chan searches Nardi's apartment, and when he hears the cuckoo clock chime, guesses correctly that the hidden information about Albert Dufresne is behind the clock. Written by Nardi, the note says: "Tonight, met with Albert Dufresne, of the Lamartine Bank, to a gambling house in Montparnasse. He lost ten thousand francs and is obviously spending beyond his income."

Cummings, Irving (October 9, 1888, New York, New York–April 18, 1959, Los Angeles, California) Stage and screen actor, director, producer, and writer of silent and sound films. Cummings was the director for *Behind That Curtain* (1929).

Irving Cummings began acting in films in 1909 and appeared in over 50 movies, including such notables as Cecil B. DeMille's *Don't Change Your Husband* (1919) and the comedy *The Saphead* with Buster Keaton. In the early 1920s Cummings switched to directing and guided numerous silent dramas and action films. In the 1930s and 1940s he showed a special flair for musicals, directing performers such as Shirley Temple (*Curly Top* [1935], *Poor Little Rich Girl* [1936], *Little Miss Broadway* [1938], *Just Around the Corner* [1938]), Alice Faye (*Hollywood Cavalcade* [1939], *Lillian Russell* [1940], *That Night in Rio* [1941]), and Betty Grable (*Down Argentine Way* [1940], *Springtime in the Rockies* [1942], *Sweet Rosie O'Grady* [1943], *The Dolly*

Sisters [1945]). Cummings' other notable talkies include the Cisco Kid western, *In Old Arizona* (1929), which he co-directed with Raoul Walsh (and for which he received an Academy Award nomination in the "Best Director" category), the Irving Berlin musical *Louisiana Purchase* (1941) starring Bob Hope, and the Paul Dresser biography *My Gal Sal* (1942) with Rita Hayworth.

Currie, Louise American actress who portrays the nosy newspaper reporter Peggy Cartwright in *The Chinese Ring* (1947).

Currier, Richard C. Film editor, sometimes credited as Dick Currier, of over 80 silent and sound films, including six *Charlie Chan* entries: *The Jade Mask* (1945),* *The Scarlet Clue* (1945), *Dark Alibi* (1946), *Shadows Over Chinatown* (1946), *Dangerous Money* (1946), and *The Trap* (1947).

Curtis, Bob Character actor who portrays Watkins, an airplane pilot who helps Charlie Chan with the reconstruction of the crime, in *The Sky Dragon* (1949). Curtis is perhaps best recognized as Father Bob on the television series *Falcon Crest* (1985 to 1990).

Czechoslovakia A Central European state uniting the Czech and Slovak peoples that existed after World War I (from 1918 to 1939) and again from 1945 to 1993, with Prague as its capital. It was bounded by Germany, Poland, Hungary, Austria, and Ukraine. As a result of the widespread fall of Communism in Eastern Europe in the late 1980s, the Czech and Slovak regions agreed to separate peacefully, and on December 31, 1992, the Czechoslovak federation ceased to exist.

Czechoslovakia is mentioned in two *Charlie Chan* films. In *Charlie Chan in Panama* (1940), Czechoslovakia is the country from which Kathi Lenesch, a.k.a. Baroness Kathi von Czardas, escapes. She now lives in fear of a secret-police agent named Reiner who had both her father and brother executed. In *The Red Dragon* (1945), Charlie Chan notes that it was Marguerite Fontan's uncle, Joseph Fontan, who, in Czechoslovakia, discovered a previously unknown 95th element and formula for the atomic bomb and died preventing the Nazis from using his discovery.

**Unbilled.*

D

D249 Major Kent's cabin number on the S.S. *Oceanic* in *Charlie Chan at the Race Track* (1936).

The Daily Record Newspaper for which Mary Bolton works as a reporter in *Charlie Chan at the Wax Museum* (1940).

Dakin The secretary (portrayed by Neil Fitzgerald) to Shanghai police commissioner Col. Watkins in *Charlie Chan in Shanghai* (1935).

Dale, Virginia (1918, Charlotte, North Carolina–October 3, 1994, Burbank, California) American dancer and character actress (real name: Virginia Paxton) who appeared in over 20 films. Dale portrays Simon Lafontaine's niece, René, in *Docks of New Orleans* (1948).

d'Ambricourt, Adrienne (1888, France–December 6, 1957, Hollywood, California) French character actress who appeared in over 50 films and portrays the landlady of the Hotel de Voyageurs in *City in Darkness* (1939).

dance apache A semiacrobatic, violent dance duet which originated in the Parisian underworld and was popular in both vaudeville and burlesque shows. Chan, Victor Descartes, Yvette Lamartine, Max Corday, and Renee Jacquard arrive at the Café du Singe Bleu to watch Nardi's performance, an interpretation of the *dance apache*, in *Charlie Chan in Paris* (1935). The dance ends when Nardi's partner tosses her through a prop store-front window, with her landing out of sight of the audience.

***Dangerous Money* (1946)** The tenth *Charlie Chan* film produced by Monogram Pictures Corporation.

Alternate Title: *Charlie Chan in Dangerous Money*. Working Title: *Hot Money*. Source: based on the character "Charlie Chan" created by Earl Derr Biggers. Original Copyright: Monogram Pictures Corporation, September 29, 1946; LP6561. Copyright Renewed: April 5, 1974; R574061. PCA Certificate Number: 11824. Production: mid– to late June, 1946. Release Date: October 12, 1946. Sound: Western Electric Mirrophonic Recording. Film: b&w. Running Time: 66 minutes.

Producer: James S. Burkett. Director: Terry O. Morse. Assistant Director: Wesley Barry. Screenplay: Miriam Kissinger. Director of Photography: William Sickner. Technical Director: Dave Milton. Supervising Film Editor: Richard Currier. Editor: William Austin. Musical Director: Edward J. Kay. Recordist: Tom Lambert. Makeup: Harry Ross. Production Manager: Glenn Cook.

Cast

Sidney Toler	*as*	Charlie Chan
Gloria Warren		Rona Simmonds
Victor Sen Young		Jimmy Chan
Rick Vallin		Tao Erickson
Joseph Crehan		Captain Black
Willie Best		Chattanooga Brown
John Harmon		Freddie Kirk
Bruce Edwards		Harold Mayfair
Dick Elliott		P.T. Burke
Joe Allen, Jr.		George Brace
Amira Moustafa		Laura Erickson
Tristram Coffin		Scott Pearson
Alan Douglas		Mrs. Whipple [alias for Joseph Murdock]
Selmer Jackson		Ship's doctor
Dudley Dickerson		Big Ben
Rito Punay		Pete
Elaine Lange		Cynthia Martin
Emmett Vogan		Professor Dick Martin
Leslie Dennison		Reverend Whipple [alias for Theodore M. Lane]
Jerry Groves*		Polynesian native
Kit Carson*		Seaman
Mavis Russell*		Kirk's assistant
Don McCracken*		Junior officer

Plot Summary: On a foggy night onboard a ship bound for Samoa and Australia, undercover U.S. Treasury agent Scott Pearson tells Charlie Chan that he is being sent to Samoa to investigate the sudden appearance of money and artworks stolen from Philippine banks during the Japanese invasion. Later, while the passengers gather in the salon for a ceremony to celebrate the crossing of the equator, Pearson is killed by a knife thrown into his back.

The captain tells Chan that Pearson's portfolio is in his office safe. It mentions a man named Lane but does not identify him. Later, Chan questions the ship's passengers, who include Freddie Kirk, an exhibition knife-thrower; P.T. Burke, a trader in cotton goods; Professor Dick Martin, an ichthyologist, and his wife Cynthia; Tao Erickson, a half–Polynesian who owns a restaurant on Samoa; Tao's Polynesian wife, Laura; missionaries Rev. and Mrs. Whipple; and Rona Simmonds, an English tourist in love with the ship's purser, George Brace.

After he dismisses most of the passengers, Chan speaks privately to Rona Simmonds and George Brace and asks them to identify a man named Lane, but Brace insists that they have nothing to reveal. Chan's son Jimmy checks the knife used to kill Pearson for fingerprints, but finds none. Chan then learns that Burke and Kirk are blackmailing Rona because she is traveling on an improper visa.

The ship docks in Samoa, giving Chan only 24 hours to solve the murder before he must leave for Australia. Chan receives a telegram which explains that Rona's father was an Australian who was stranded during the war in Manila with valuable art objects, and Rona is now trying to discover their whereabouts. Chan finds out that Rona is traveling under papers that were falsified by Brace, and this is the reason Burke is blackmailing her.

Chan then wants to question Burke, but Burke is killed by a thrown knife before he can reveal anything. Meanwhile, Jimmy and Chattanooga Brown stumble upon money hidden in Professor Martin's fish museum near the Ericksons' restaurant. Kirk then is

**Unbilled.*

also killed with a thrown knife, and the remaining suspects converge on the fish museum. Chan learns that Reverend Whipple is the leader of a gang (including the Ericksons, Burke, and Kirk) which planned to sell the stolen artworks. The Whipples are revealed to be Theodore Lane and his valet, Joseph Murdock, who is dressed as a woman.

Daniell, Henry (March 5, 1894, London, England–October 31, 1963, Santa Monica, California) Cold-eyed stage and screen character actor (real name: Charles Henry Daniel) who appeared in over 65 films, often as a villain. Daniell portrays Watson King, an alias for Cesare Borgia, in *Castle in the Desert* (1942).

An actor since the age of 18, Henry Daniell worked in London until coming to America in an Ethel Barrymore play. He co-starred with Ruth Gordon in the 1929 Broadway production of *Serena Blandish*, for which he won critical plaudits in the role of Lord Iver Cream. He made his movie debut in *Jealousy* (1929), which co-starred another stage legend, Jeanne Eagels. With his haughty demeanor and near-satanic features, Henry Daniell was the perfect screen "gentleman villain," exemplified by his role as Baron de Varville in *Camille* (1940). However, he was less at home in action roles, and refused to participate in the climactic dueling scene in *The Sea Hawk* (1940), requiring Errol Flynn to duel with a none-too-convincing stunt double.

Daniell appeared in three of the Basil Rathbone–Nigel Bruce *Sherlock Holmes* films made at Universal in the 1940s, even playing the infamous Professor Moriarty in *The Woman in Green* (1945). Though seldom in pure horror films, Daniell excelled in the leading role of Dr. Wolfe "Toddy" MacFarlane in *The Body Snatcher* (1945). While portraying Prince Gregor of Transylvania in *My Fair Lady* (1964), Daniell died suddenly. Although his few completed scenes remained in the film, his name was removed from the cast credits.

Daniels, Rick Press agent (portrayed by Larry J. Burke) for Cole King in *The Trap* (1947). To deflect embarrassing publicity away from Cole King, Daniels suggests that they try to make Lois' death appear to be an accidental drowning.

Daniels, Steve Press agent and passenger on the *Suva Star* (portrayed by Robert Weldon) in *Dead Men Tell* (1941). Daniels helps Miss Nodbury arrange the trip to Cocos Island for the treasure hunt.

Dansiger, Sgt. New Orleans policeman (portrayed by George J. Lewis in his second of three *Charlie Chan* movies) in *Docks of New Orleans* (1948). Dansiger's commanding officer is Capt. Pete McNalley.

Dantas, Carlos *see* **Denton, Clark**

Danvers, Mr. Loud-mouthed traveling salesman (portrayed by Ray Walter) who sells protection supplies for banks, such as tear gas and burglar alarms, in *Dark Alibi* (1946). Danvers is one of several boarders living at the Foss Family Hotel, and is a confederate of a bank robbery gang who cases the banks before the robberies. Fearing that Charlie Chan is getting close to solving the burglaries, Danvers murders Mr. Johnson, another gang member who forges the fingerprints, and hides his body inside a suit of armor at the Carey Theatrical Warehouse.

***Dark Alibi* (1946)** The eighth *Charlie Chan* film produced by Monogram Pictures Corporation.

Alternate Title: *Charlie Chan in Dark Alibi*. Working Titles: *Fatal Fingerprints*, *Fatal Fingertips*, and *Charlie Chan in Alcatraz*. Source: based on the character "Charlie Chan" created by Earl Derr Biggers. Original Copyright: Monogram Pictures Corporation, March 26, 1946; LP1841. Copyright Renewed: October 25, 1973; R561680. PCA Certificate Number: 11408. Production: began mid–December, 1945. Release Date: May 25, 1946. Sound: Western Electric Mirrophonic Recording. Film: b&w. Running Time: 60–61 minutes.

Producer: James S. Burkett. Director: Phil Karlson. Assistant Director: Theodore Joos.

Original Screenplay: George Callahan. Photography: William Sickner. Second Camera: Al Niclin.* Special Effects: Larry Glickman* and Mario Castegnaro.* Technical Director: Dave Milton. Supervising Film Editor: Richard Currier. Editor: Ace Herman. Set Dresser: Max Pittman.* Musical Director: Edward J. Kay. Recordist: Tom Lambert. Re-recording and Effects Mixing: Joseph I. Kane.* Music Mixing: William H. Wilmarth.* Production Manager: Glenn Cook.

Cast

Sidney Toler	*as*	Charlie Chan
Mantan Moreland		Birmingham Brown
Ben Carter		Ben Carter
Benson Fong		Tommy Chan
Teala Loring		June Harley
George Holmes		Hugh Kenzie
Joyce Compton		Emily Evans
John Eldredge		Anthony R. Morgan
Russell Hicks		Warden Cameron
Tim Ryan		Foggy
Janet Shaw		Miss Petrie
Edward Earle		Thomas Harley
Ray Walker		Mr. Danvers
Milton Parsons		Mr. Johnson
Edna Holland		Mrs. Foss
Anthony Warde		Jimmy Slade
George Eldredge		Brand
Meyer Grace		Doorman
William Ruhl*		Mr. Thompson
Frank Marlowe*		Barker

Plot Summary: When ex-convict Thomas Harley arrives at the Foss Family Hotel (a boarding house where he lives with his daughter June) he is arrested for robbing a bank and killing a bank guard. However, Harley claims that he was summoned to the Carey Theatrical Warehouse by a note from his former cellmate, Dave Wyatt, and subsequently was locked inside. The police do not believe his alibi because Wyatt has been dead for eight years. After fingerprints found at the scene are identified as belonging to Harley, he is convicted and sentenced to death.

Determined to prove her father innocent, June contacts detective Charlie Chan, who agrees that the case against her father is suspect. Together with June's boyfriend, prison guard Hugh Kenzie, Chan questions Mrs. Foss, the boardinghouse landlady who is an amateur social worker and often rents to ex-convicts. Chan discovers that the note purporting to be from Wyatt was written on Foss' typewriter. Chan then questions the other boarders—Miss Petrie, who works for a small salary at a social foundation; Mr. Johnson, a bookkeeper for The Carey Theatrical company; Mr. Danvers, a salesman of bank alarm systems; and Emily Evans, a showgirl whose costume was found in the warehouse. Both Mr. Danvers and Emily Evans had traveled to other cities immediately before banks in those locations were robbed.

The next day, Chan, his son Tommy, and his chauffeur Birmingham Brown, drive to the prison where an unknown assailant shoots at them on the road. Chan now becomes convinced that the fingerprints found at the scene were forged. After studying the police reports, Chan discovers that although a different man was convicted for each of the previous robberies, each man had been jailed in the same prison, and the method used was identical in each case.

Miss Petrie is revealed to be the wife of Jimmy Slade, a convict trustee, who is employed in the fingerprint bureau of the prison. When Petrie disappears, Chan, Birmingham, and Tommy hurry to the warehouse. There they locate Johnson, and later see Miss Petrie killed by a truck outside the warehouse. When Chan returns to the prison and discovers that the fingerprint cards have been tampered with, Slade overhears Chan and is wounded while trying to escape. After stating that he will not take the rap, Slade dies when a gun he uses is plugged up and explodes.

Chan then takes prints of all the boarders at the boardinghouse and finds Mr. Johnson's fingerprints on one of the prison cards. Chan returns to the warehouse and uncovers the equipment necessary for forging fingerprints in the truck that killed Petrie. Danvers then tries to kill Chan, as he did Johnson, to stop him from talking.

After Harley is freed by the new-found

**Unbilled.*

evidence, Chan explains that Slade sent the prints to Mr. Johnson, who copied them for Danvers, who then carried out the robberies. He adds that Kenzie is the leader of the gang, and when Harley had opposed his marriage to June, the guard framed him.

Note: Although the Call Bureau Cast Service lists Minerva Urecal as Mrs. Foss, production information in the Academy of Motion Picture Arts and Sciences (AMPAS) library states that she was replaced by Edna Holland, who is listed in the on-screen credits.

Darling, W. Scott (May 28, 1898, Toronto, Ontario, Canada–October 29, 1951, Santa Monica, California) Screenwriter, sometimes credited as Scott Darling, who wrote over 50 films. Darling penned the screenplay for five *Charlie Chan* entries: *Charlie Chan at the Opera* (1936), *The Chinese Ring* (1947), *The Shanghai Chest* (1948), *Docks of New Orleans* (1948), and *The Golden Eye* (1948).

Darling, William S. (September 14, 1882, Sandorház, Hungary–September 15, 1964, Laguna Beach, California) Production designer, art director, and set decorator (real name: Wilhelm Sandorházi) for over 55 silent and sound films. Darling was in charge of the settings and decorations for *Behind That Curtain* (1929).

William S. Darling got his start in Hollywood in 1920 and began working with Twentieth Century–Fox around 1933. It was with Fox that he received seven Academy Award nominations, winning three:

Art Direction

**Cavalcade* (1933)
Lloyd's of London (1936)
Wee Willie Wilkie (1937)
The Rains Came (1939)

Art Direction–Interior Decoration (Black-and-White)

**The Song of Bernadette* (1943)
The Keys of the Kingdom (1944)
**Anna and the King of Siam* (1946)

**Academy Award winner.*

Darro, Frankie (December 22, 1918, Chicago, Illinois–December 25, 1976, Huntington Beach, California) Small, tough-looking stage and screen character actor (real name: Frank Johnson) who appeared in over 115 silent and sound films, sometimes credited as Frankie Darrow. Darro portrays jockey "Tip" Collins in *Charlie Chan at the Race Track* (1936).

The son of circus performers, the diminutive Frankie Darro began appearing in films as a juvenile player in 1924, co-starring with western star Tom Tyler in several silents at FBO in the mid–1920s. He was also cast in leading roles, such as Mickey Grogan in *Little Mickey Grogan* (1927) and as Buddy in *The Circus Kid* (1928). During the 1930s, Darro showed up in numerous bit and supporting roles, often playing juvenile delinquents.

He was given star billing at such minor-league studios as Ambassador and Monogram, co-starring with black comedian Mantan Moreland at Monogram in an enjoyable series of action programmers (in which he was often cast as a jockey because of his stature). In the late 1940s Darro was a frequent stunt double for such pint-sized actors as Leo Gorcey.

dates (fictitious) The following dates are mentioned in the *Charlie Chan* film series:

September 15, 1923: Chicago opera house fire when Gravelle was intentionally locked in his dressing room and left to die in *Charlie Chan at the Opera* (1936).

May 30, 1935: Nellie Farrell claims she and Joe Kinney were married in Juarez, Mexico, in *Charlie Chan at the Circus* (1936).

October 5, 1935: Chardo the Great is injured in an automobile crash in *Black Magic* (1944).

September 2, 1936: Accidental death of Major Kent in *Charlie Chan at the Race Track* (1936).

September 28, 1939: Notice ordered by the Paris police to prepare residents for possible air raids by German bombers in *City in Darkness* (1939).

Davidson, Ed Associate (portrayed by Lyle Latell in his second of two *Charlie Chan* roles) of John Anderson in *The Sky Dragon* (1949). Davidson and Anderson are both traveling on Flight 17 to San Francisco, during which the money shipment is stolen en route and Davidson and the guard, Ben Edwards, are found dead.

Davidson, John W. (December 25, 1886, New York, New York–January 15, 1968, Los Angeles, California) American character actor who appeared in over 90 silent and sound films, sometimes credited as Jack Davidson. In two *Charlie Chan* roles, Davidson portrays the pharmacist Dauod (David) Atrash in *Charlie Chan in Egypt* (1935) and played the dual role of the twins Carl and Kurt Karzoff in *The Chinese Cat* (1944).

Though a native New Yorker, John Davidson seemed most at home playing sinister Middle Easterners or Europeans. For example, he was cast as the sheik in Priscilla Dean's version of *Under Two Flags* (1922) and (with Rudolph Valentino) as Cardinal Richelieu in *Monsieur Beaucaire* (1924). In the talkies, he was seen in roles ranging from bit-part concierges to criminal masterminds.

Davidson, Sgt. Bill Policeman (portrayed by Warren Douglas) in *The Chinese Ring* (1947) who has a love-hate relationship with nosy newspaper reporter Peggy Cartwright. Davidson is called in to investigate the murder of Princess Mei Ling at Charlie Chan's house.

Davis, Alan (1902–December 4, 1943, Los Angeles, California) Actor who portrays a soldier (unbilled) in *Charlie Chan in Panama* (1940) and TR-4 test pilot Lt. Cooper (unbilled) in *Murder Over New York* (1940).

Davis, Eddie Assistant director for four *Charlie Chan* films at Monogram: *The Jade Mask* (1945), *The Scarlet Clue* (1945),* *The Shanghai Cobra* (1945),* and *The Red Dragon* (1945).

**Unbilled.*

Davis, George (November 7, 1889, Amsterdam, The Netherlands–April 19, 1965, Woodland Hills, California) Vaudeville and character actor who appeared in almost 100 silent and sound films. In three *Charlie Chan* roles, Davis portrays Roberts the butler in *Charlie Chan in Paris* (1937); Pepite, the Monte Carlo policeman who arrests Charlie Chan and Lee, in *Charlie Chan at Monte Carlo* (1937); and Alex, the "sloppy fellow" thief in *City in Darkness* (1939).

Davis, Inspector Harry Homicide squad chief of the 12th Precinct (portrayed by Walter Fenner) in *The Shanghai Cobra* (1945). Davis is an old friend of Charlie Chan, the two having walked the same beat together in Honolulu. When Samuel Black becomes the third employee of the Sixth National Bank to be murdered with cobra venom, Davis sends a telegram to Chan requesting his help, since Chan is the only person known to be familiar with this murder method (from a similar case eight years ago in Shanghai).

Dawson Police lab technician (portrayed by Edward Earle in his first of two *Charlie Chan* roles) in *Black Magic* (1944). Dawson's chemical tests confirm that William Bonner was killed using a bullet made from frozen blood, and that the drug manasterol was on Mrs. Justine Bonner's coat when she walked off the roof of the Chalmont Building and fell to her death. As a precaution, Charlie Chan obtains antidote pills for manasterol from Dawson, but Dawson warns Chan he is not exactly sure how quickly the antidote will take effect.

Day, Richard (May 9, 1896, Victoria, British Columbia, Canada–May 1972, California) Award-winning art director and production designer for nearly 165 films, including ten *Charlie Chan* movies at Twentieth Century–Fox.

Richard Day first gained industry notice as one of the most trusted associates of director Erich von Stroheim. After successfully translating Stroheim's designs into on-set reality in *Blind Husbands* (1919), Day remained as the director's principal set decorator throughout the 1920s. Working in collaboration during the early-talkie years, Day went solo as a production designer in 1930, then latched onto the Samuel Goldwyn studios. Richard Day's final assignment was *Tora! Tora! Tora!* (1970), a painstakingly accurate restaging of the Pearl Harbor attack, for which Twentieth Century–Fox spent more money than the Japanese had on the original attack in 1941.

In his career, Day received 20 Academy Award nominations, winning seven of them:

Art Direction

Whoopee! (1930)
Arrowsmith (1931)
The Affairs of Cellini (1934)
**The Dark Angel* (1935)
**Dodsworth* (1936)
Dead End (1937)
The Goldwyn Follies (1938)

Art Direction (Color)

Down Argentine Way (1940)

Art Direction (Black-and-White)

Lillian Russell (1940)

Art Direction–Interior Decoration (Color)

Blood and Sand (1941)
**My Gal Sal* (1942)
Joan of Arc (1948)
Hans Christian Andersen (1952)
The Greatest Story Ever Told (1965)

Art Direction–Interior Decoration (Black-and-White)

**How Green Was My Valley* (1941)
**This Above All* (1942)
The Razor's Edge (1946)
**A Streetcar Named Desire* (1951)
**On the Waterfront* (1954)

Art Direction–Set Decoration

Tora! Tora! Tora! (1970)

Charlie Chan filmography: *Charlie Chan in Honolulu* (1938), *Charlie Chan in Reno* (1939), *Charlie Chan at Treasure Island* (1939), *Charlie Chan in Panama* (1940), *Charlie Chan's Murder Cruise* (1940), *Charlie Chan at the Wax Museum* (1940), *Murder Over New York* (1940), *Dead Men Tell* (1941), *Charlie Chan in Rio* (1941), and *Castle in the Desert* (1942).

**Academy Award winner.*

Deacon, Webster Realtor and gem smuggler (portrayed by Cy Kendall) in *The Chinese Cat* (1944). Deacon is a business partner of Thomas Manning in the Manning-Deacon Realty Company, and both were somehow involved in the theft of the Kalinor diamond collection in Chicago a year earlier. However, Manning double-crosses Deacon and takes the largest diamond for himself, for which he is shot and killed by Deacon.

Deacon learns that Leah Manning has asked Charlie Chan to reopen the investigation of her stepfather's murder, and tries (unsuccessfully) to persuade Leah and her mother to drop the inquiry, telling Chan that a halt will keep his business from being ruined by more bad publicity.

When Chan later questions Deacon in his real estate office, Chan asks Deacon about the Sea Tide Art Company that bought Chinese figurines in which stolen diamonds are hidden. Deacon claims that he no longer owns that company and can get the papers from the next room to prove it. Instead, he flees from his office building and leads Chan on a car chase to the Shore End Pier and the Sea Tide Art Company. Arriving at the pier, Chan finds Deacon dead, having been murdered by Catlen.

Note: The newspaper headline of the story of Deacon's death incorrectly gives his first name as George instead of Webster.

dead canary Charlie Chan, George Kirby, and Jimmy Chan find Hugh Drake dead in Kirby's library in *Murder Over New York* (1940). When searching the room further, Chan notices that the canary in the birdcage is also dead. "Canary, unlike faithful dog," says Chan, "do not die for sympathy." On the floor below the birdcage Chan retrieves some glass fragments which contain a chemical that Jimmy, having had chemistry in college, says is a new poison gas called tetrogene.

"A dead horse isn't worth $20,000" Warning message in a note Lee Chan secretly places in the coat pocket of Warren Fenton in *Charlie Chan at the Race Track* (1936). Fenton earlier offers $20,000 to George Chester to buy and retire Avalanche from racing. Charlie Chan has son Lee secretly distribute different warning messages to Fenton, Bruce Rogers, George Chester, and Denny Barton as part of a plan to identify the leader of a racetrack gambling ring.

Dead Man's Canyon Location of an abandoned Nevada ghost town where Charlie Chan goes to look for some clues in *Charlie Chan in Reno* (1939).

***Dead Men Tell* (1941)** The sixteenth *Charlie Chan* film produced by Twentieth Century Fox–Film Corporation.

Source: based on the character "Charlie Chan" created by Earl Derr Biggers. Original Copyright: Twentieth Century Fox–Film Corporation, March 28, 1941; LP10391. Copyright Renewed: December 17, 1968; R451271. PCA Certificate Number: 6981. Production: mid–December, 1940 to mid–January, 1941. Release Date: March 28, 1941. Film: b&w; 6 reels; 5,383 or 5,441 feet. Running Time: 60–61 minutes.

Associate Producers: Walter Morosco and Ralph Dietrich. Director: Harry Lachman. Assistant Director: Saul Wurtzel.* Original Screenplay: John Larkin. Director of Photography: Charles Clarke. Art Direction: Richard Day and Lewis Creber. Film Editor: Harry Reynolds. Set Decorations: Thomas Little. Costumes: Herschel. Musical Director: Emil Newman.* Sound: Alfred Bruzlin and Harry M. Leonard. Publicity Director: Harry Brand.*

Cast

Sidney Toler	*as*	Charlie Chan
Sheila Ryan		Kate Ransome
Robert Weldon		Steve Daniels
Sen Yung		Jimmy Chan
Don Douglas		Jed Thomasson
Katharine Aldridge		Laura Thursday
Paul McGrath		Charles Thursday
George Reeves		Bill Lydig
Truman Bradley		Captain Kane
Ethel Griffies		Miss [Patience] Nodbury
Lenita Lane		Dr. Anne Bonney
Milton Parsons		Gene LaFarge
Stanley Andrews		Inspector Vessey
Lee Tung Foo*		Wu Mei
Ralph Dunn,* Lee Phelps*		Detectives
Pat Flaherty*		Policeman
Tim Ryan*		Red Eye
Jimmy Aubrey*		English sailor
John Wallace*		Peg Leg
Charles Tannen*		Sailor

**Unbilled.*

Plot Summary: On the night before the *Suva Star* is to leave for Cocos Island on a treasure hunt, Captain Kane discusses the journey's sponsor, Miss Patience Nodbury, with press agent Steve Daniels, who helped arrange the trip. Just then Charlie Chan arrives to look for his son Jimmy, who has stowed away in search of adventure.

Miss Nodbury explains to Chan that she tore the treasure map, drawn by her pirate ancestor Matthew "Black Hook" Nodbury, into four pieces and mailed three of them to other passengers. She also tells Chan that the ghost of Black Hook, who has a peg leg and a hook, appears to each of the Nodburys as they are about to die.

Shortly after Miss Nodbury retires to her stateroom, she hears the tap of Black Hook's peg leg and the scratching of his hook on her door. The elderly woman opens the door, sees her ancestor, and dies of a heart attack, after which the pirate takes her piece of the map. Meanwhile, the ship's passengers arrive and all claim that they received a mysterious message from Steve. The passengers include: Bill Lydig, a journalist about whom Chan is curious because he thought Lydig was dead; rare-coin dealer Jed Thomasson; typist Kate Ransome; and newlyweds Charles and Laura Thursday.

Kate discovers Miss Nodbury's body, after which Chan finds part of the Black Hook disguise that someone wore to frighten the elderly woman to death. When Chan sends Jimmy ashore to telephone the police, Jimmy overhears a suspicious conversation between Dr. Anne Bonney, a psychoanalyst, and her patient, Gene LaFarge, who are also passengers on the *Suva Star*. Under questioning by Chan, LaFarge admits that he saw Miss Nodbury's corpse, but denies that he killed her.

Laura Thursday and Jed Thomasson give their pieces of the map to Chan for safekeeping, after which Jimmy finds the rest of the disguise and a piece of the map in Steve Daniels' room. Daniels protests that he is being framed, and it is discovered that the two map pieces Chan was given are now stolen. The group then finds Kate, who had fainted after reading in a magazine that Lydig is really an escaped murderer from Alcatraz. Before Lydig can be questioned, however, he is found dead of suffocation in the ship's diving bell below deck.

Chan then goes ashore and finds Captain Kane, who reveals that he has not met any of his passengers yet. When Chan questions the captain about his strange behavior, Kane explains that he went on a treasure hunt many years ago to Cocos Island with his partner, but that the man left him there to die. Believing that his former partner would not now be able to resist returning to the island, Kane arranged the journey so that he could find and kill the man.

After Chan calls the police, Inspector Vessey arrives and arrests Daniels because of the circumstantial evidence against him. Chan, who has the map piece found in Daniels' room, now uses himself as bait to trap the real killer. As Chan waits, Black Hook stalks him. Secretly watching, Jimmy's signal alerts his father, and Chan captures the mysterious pirate—who is Thomasson in disguise. Kane confirms that Thomasson is his former partner. Thomasson admits to killing Miss Nodbury and Lydig, who had stolen the map pieces from Chan's pocket.

Note: Jean Rogers, who portrays Kathi Lenesch in *Charlie Chan in Panama* (1940), was originally cast as Laura Thursday in *Dead Men Tell* but was replaced after shooting began by Katharine Aldridge when Rogers became ill with the flu.

Dean, Lola Rio de Janeiro nightclub singer (portrayed by Jacqueline Dalya) whose real name is Lola Wagner in *Charlie Chan in Rio* (1941). A little more than a year ago, when in Honolulu, Manuel Cardozo was on a business trip and met Lola Wagner, who fell madly in love with him. When Wagner asked Cardozo to divorce his wife and marry her, he refused, and Lola killed him.

Helen Ashby, Dean's secretary, is really Cardozo's widow, Barbara Cardosa. She and her brother-in-law, Alfredo Cardoza (alias Alfredo Marana), set up a plan to get Dean to confess to the murder during a drug-induced trance. When Marana tells her of her confession, Dean persuades her fiancé, Clark Denton, to elope that evening on a late night flight to the States. At the same time, Charlie Chan is in Rio to arrest her for Cardozo's murder (with the assistance of Rio police chief Souto). When they go to Lola Dean's house to arrest her, they find that she has been stabbed to death.

Note: The character Lola Dean loosely parallels that of Shelah Fane in *The Black Camel* (1931).

Deane, Shirley (1912–1983) Character actress who appeared in 20 films and portrays trapeze artist Marie Norman in *Charlie Chan at the Circus* (1936).

Death Makes a Decree Story written by Philip Wylie which is the basis for *Charlie Chan in Reno* (1939). *Death Makes a Decree* was also the film's working title before its release on June 16, 1939.

De Brulier, Nigel (July 8, 1878, Bristol, England–January 30, 1948, Los Angeles, California) Character actor who appeared in over 90 silent and sound films and portrays the Egyptian servant Edfu Ahmad in *Charlie Chan in Egypt* (1935).

de Córdoba, Pedro (September 28, 1881, New York, New York–September 17, 1950, Sunland, California) Lean and often sinister-looking stage and screen character actor who appeared in over 100 silent and sound films. He portrays Petroff's butler, Antoine, in *City in Darkness* (1939).

DeGaetano, Alfred (c. 1894–May 2, 1958, Hollywood, California) Film editor of over 25 films, who also edited five *Charlie Chan* movies for Fox and Twentieth Century–Fox: *Behind That Curtain* (1929), *Charlie Chan Carries On* (1931), *The Black Camel* (1931), *Charlie Chan in Egypt* (1935),* and *Charlie Chan on Broadway* (1937).

Degan, "Butcher" Gangster (portrayed by Ted Osborn) who was thought to have been killed by Steve McBirney but is now posing as Tom Agnew in *Charlie Chan at the Wax Museum* (1940). Criminals Degan and McBirney were once partners in an honest business venture with Joe Rocke, but Degan hated Rocke and framed him for a murder that Rocke didn't commit to get control of the business.

As revenge for Rocke's execution, McBirney shoots a man whom he thinks to be Degan. Chicago police retrieve what they thought was Degan's faceless body from Lake Michigan, it having been in the water for three months with 13 bullets in it. With everyone thinking that he was now dead, Degan goes to Dr. Cream to have his face changed, and now poses as Ted Agnew.

During the *Crime League* broadcast concerning the Rocke Case, criminologist Dr. von Brom, whose scientific evidence was used to convict Joe Rocke, now realizes that he was wrong and says he will reveal the real solution to the Joe Rocke case. Before he can do so, von Brom is killed with a poison-tipped bamboo dart, a clue that convinces Charlie Chan that "Butcher" Degan is still alive. Since Dr. Cream says that he does not know Degan, no one else knows what he now looks like. Degan eventually finds Steve McBirney alone in one of the museum rooms and stabs him in the back with a knife.

Delaney, Jerry Actor who is hired to impersonate the wealthy financier P.J. Madden. In *The Chinese Parrot* (1927), Delaney and Madden are both portrayed by Hobart Bosworth. In *Charlie Chan's Courage* (1934), a remake of *The Chinese Parrot*, the dual role is played by Paul Harvey.

In both films, Delaney, Martin Thorne, "Shaky" Phil Maydorf, and Henry Maydorf (alias Thaddeus Gamble) are all part of a scheme to steal the Phillimore pearl necklace by having Delaney impersonate Madden, who has bought the necklace and is awaiting its delivery.

Delevanti, Cyril (February 23, 1887, England–December 13, 1975, Hollywood California) British-born stage and screen character actor who appeared in almost 40 films. In two *Charlie Chan* roles, Delevanti portrays Mr. Harper's butler, Roth, in *The Jade Mask* (1945) and Larkin (unbilled) in *The Shanghai Cobra* (1945). Delevanti also made frequent television appearances on *Gunsmoke*, *The Twilight Zone*, *Perry Mason*, and *You Are There*.

Dell, Claudia (January 10, 1909, San Antonio, Texas–1977) Actress and former Ziegfeld Girl who appeared in over 30 films. Dell portrays Vera Starkey in *Black Magic* (1944).

DeMaggio, Nick Film Editor for over 30 movies, including five *Charlie Chan* films with Twentieth Century–Fox and *Mr. Moto's Gamble* (1938), a reworked version of the never-completed *Charlie Chan at the Ringside*.

Charlie Chan filmography: *Charlie Chan in Shanghai* (1935), *Charlie Chan's Secret* (1936), *Charlie Chan at the Race Track* (1936), *Charlie Chan at Monte Carlo* (1937), and *Charlie Chan in Honolulu* (1938).

Demarest, William (February 27, 1892, St. Paul, Minnesota–December 28, 1983, Palm Springs, California) American character actor who appeared in over 140 films. Demarest portrays Sgt. Kelly in *Charlie Chan at the Opera* (1936).

Famed for his ratchety voice and cold-fish stare, William Demarest began his stage career at age 13, holding down a variety of colorful jobs, including being a professional boxer during the off-season. After years working in carnivals, as a vaudeville headliner, and on the Broadway stage, Demarest

**Unbilled.*

William Demarest

signed with Warner Bros. in 1926. While at Paramount in the 1940s, Demarest was a special favorite of writer-director Preston Sturges, who cast Demarest in virtually all his films.

In 1947 Demarest was nominated for an Academy Award in the Best Supporting Actor category for his role as Steve Martin in *The Jolson Story* (1946). Demarest continued appearing in films until 1975, whenever his increasingly heavy television schedule would allow. He is perhaps best remembered as uncle Charley O'Casey in the television series *My Three Sons* (1966–72).

DeMille, Katherine (June 29, 1911, Vancouver, British Columbia, Canada–April 27, 1995)

Attractive actress (real name: Katherine Lester) who appeared in almost 30 films. DeMille portrays the Mata Hari–type spy Yvonne Roland in *Charlie Chan at the Olympics* (1937).

Orphaned when nine years old, Katherine was adopted by director Cecil B. DeMille. Early in her acting career she occasionally received reviews in which critics noted the strong determination of her looks and bearing, traits which the critics suggested she obviously "inherited" from her famous film director father. First appearing before the cameras in her father's *Madam Satan* (1930), Katherine also managed to do quite well for herself in those films without her father's influence. She was most often cast in supporting roles, usually playing disgruntled cast-off lovers or exotic villainesses. One of her best screen scenes was a knock-down, drag-out fight with Barbara Stanwyck in *Banjo on My Knee* (1936), where DeMille portrays Leota Long. From 1936 to 1963 DeMille was married to actor Anthony Quinn, with whom she co-starred as Sarah Eagle in *Black Gold* (1947). Katherine DeMille died at age 83 from Alzheimer's disease.

Dennis, Detective Harvey San Francisco policeman (portrayed by Weldon Heyburn) who originally investigated the murder of Thomas Manning in *The Chinese Cat* (1944). Once a detective lieutenant, Dennis has been demoted to an ordinary member of the homicide squad after it was alleged in a book written by noted criminologist Dr. Rednick that Dennis fell in love with Manning's stepdaughter, Leah, and then concealed evidence.

When Charlie Chan and Dennis first meet, Chan mentions that he knew Dennis' father, a San Francisco police captain. Chan tells Dennis how he solved the case of the Manning murder so that Dennis will get credit for it and perhaps become a police lieutenant again, even "maybe captain."

Dennison, Leslie Actor who appeared in over 40 films, sometimes credited as Leslie Denison early in his career. In three *Charlie Chan* roles, Dennison portrays Rice the butler (as Leslie Denison) in *Charlie Chan in Rio* (1941), Reverend Whipple in *Dangerous Money* (1946), and Professor Henry Farnsworth in *The Feathered Serpent* (1948).

Denton, Clark B. Lola Dean's fiancé (portrayed by Ted North) in *Charlie Chan in Rio* (1941). Denton used to be the boyfriend of Grace Ellis.

Note: The film's on-screen credits list Ted

North's character incorrectly as Carlos Dantas. Furthermore, the character Clark Denton loosely parallels that of Alan Jaynes in *The Black Camel* (1931).

Depp, Harry (February 22, 1883, Missouri–March 31, 1957, Hollywood, California) Character actor who appeared in over 40 silent and sound films. In three *Charlie Chan* roles, Depp portrays Snapper (unbilled) in *Charlie Chan on Broadway* (1937), Charles Edwards in *Black Magic* (1944), and veterinarian Dr. Denby (unbilled) in *Shadows Over Chinatown* (1946).

Derr, Richard (1918, Norristown, Pennsylvania–May 8,1992, Santa Monica, California) American leading man who appeared in almost 30 films, including two *Charlie Chan* entries. Derr portrays Ken Reynolds in *Charlie Chan in Rio* (1941) and historian Carl Detheridge in *Castle in the Desert* (1942).

Descartes, Victor Bank teller at the Lamartine Bank (portrayed by Thomas Beck in his first of four *Charlie Chan* roles) in *Charlie Chan in Paris* (1935). Descartes is engaged to Yvette Lamartine, whose father owns the bank. Descartes' father, who is an old friend of Charlie Chan, is a director of the Lamartine Bank.

"The desert gives, and the desert takes" Words of philosophic consolation spoken by Col. Beetham's Sudanese servant (portrayed by Boris Karloff in his first of two *Charlie Chan* roles) to his master in *Behind That Curtain* (1929). Beetham is to give a lecture that evening about the Persian Desert and mentions that his heart is not in it, saying "The desert is too full of memories."

Detheridge, Carl Professor of medieval history (portrayed by Richard Derr in his second of two *Charlie Chan* roles) in *Castle in the Desert* (1942). An old acquaintance of Charlie Chan, Detheridge is head of the European History Department at Manderley College and is currently a house guest at Paul Manderley's castle estate to research some old books in Manderley's personal library.

De Velasco, Mercedes Actress who portrays Eric Durand's Indian servant and mistress, Nunah, in *Behind That Curtain* (1929).

Devereaux, Helen Actress who portrays radio actress Diane Hall in *The Scarlet Clue* (1945).

Devlin, Joe (1899–October 1, 1973, Burbank, California) Bald, prominently chinned stage and screen character actor who appeared in nearly 50 films, usually as two-bit crooks and sarcastic tradesmen. Devlin portrays a gangster named Taylor in *The Shanghai Cobra* (1945). Because of his uncanny resemblance to Benito Mussolini, Devlin received a number of "cameos" during the war years, as well as full-fledged Mussolini imitations in two Hal Roach films—*The Devil with Hitler* (1942) and *That Nazty Nuisance* (1943). In 1950 Joe Devlin was cast as Sam Catchem in the *Dick Tracy* television series based on Chester Gould's comic-strip cop.

deWitt, Jacqueline Character actress who appeared in over 30 films and portrays Justine Bonner in *Black Magic* (1944).

Diablo Mountains Location of the lost Aztec Temple of the Sun near the Mexican village of San Pablo in *The Feathered Serpent* (1948).

Dickerson, Dudley (1906–September 23, 1968) Black actor who appeared in 45 films and portrays Big Ben in *Dangerous Money* (1946).

Diego Aztec Indian impersonator (portrayed by Jay Silverheels) in *The Feathered Serpent* (1948). Diego is part of a smuggling operation headed by Professor John Stanley, and is shot by Pedro Lopez before Diego can kill Charlie Chan by throwing a knife.

Dietrich, Ralph Movie editor and producer of over 30 films. He served as producer or associate producer on three *Charlie Chan* films: *Charlie Chan at the Wax Museum* (1940), *Dead Men Tell* (1941),* and *Castle in the Desert* (1942).

**Associate producer.*

Dinehart, Alan (October 3, 1889, Missoula, Montana–July 17, 1944, Hollywood, California) Brawny, round-faced stage and screen character actor who appeared in over 80 films and portrays the murderer George Chester in *Charlie Chan at the Race Track* (1936).

Alan Dinehart liked to bill himself as Hollywood's most versatile villain. He appeared in dozens of bad guy roles, most often in the "B" pictures of Twentieth Century–Fox. He was most often seen as a shifty businessman or respectability seeking racketeer, and showed up with equal frequency as either the much-hated victim or "surprise" killer in murder mysteries.

distributor cap Automotive part missing from the Manderley Castle car, stranding all guests at the castle in *Castle in the Desert* (1942). It is removed by Watson King, who hides it in a clay bust he is sculpting of Lucy Manderley.

"DIVORCEE QUESTIONED IN RENO SLAYING" Newspaper headline of the *San Francisco Daily Dispatch* about Mary Whitman as a suspect in the murder of Jeanne Bently in *Charlie Chan in Reno* (1939).

Dixon, Ralph H. (c. 1897–May 1, 1948, Hollywood, California) Film editor for *Shadows Over Chinatown* (1946).

"Do not challenge the supernatural unless you are prepared to visit your ancestors" Warning message in a note given to Charlie Chan in *Charlie Chan at Treasure Island* (1939). Chan tells son Jimmy that the ancient proverb is badly misquoted and should read, "Do not challenge the supernatural unless armed with sword of truth."

***Docks of New Orleans* (1948)** The thirteenth *Charlie Chan* film produced by Monogram Pictures Corporation.

Alternate Title: *Charlie Chan in Docks of New Orleans*. Working Title: *Charlie Chan in New Orleans*. Source: Remake of Monogram's *Mr. Wong, Detective* (1938). Original Copyright: Monogram Pictures Corporation, March 21, 1948; LP16101. Copyright Renewed: August 5, 1975; R610850. PCA Certificate Number: 12895. Production: November 17 to November 25, 1947. Release Date: March 21, 1948. Sound: Western Electric Recording. Film: b&w; 7 reels; 5,802 feet. Running Time: 64 minutes.

Producer: James S. Burkett. Director: Derwin Abrahams. Assistant Director: Theodore Joos. Original Screenplay: W. Scott Darling. Photography: William Sickner. Camera Operator: John Martin.* Stills: Jim Fullerton.* Supervising Film Editor: Otho Lovering. Editor: Ace Herman. Set Decoration: Ken Schwartz.* Musical Director: Edward J. Kay. Recordist: Tom Lambert. Hair Stylist: Lela Chambers.* Production Supervisor: Glenn Cook. Technical Director: Dave Milton. Screenplay Supervisor: Mary Chaffee.* Grip: George Booker.*

Cast

Roland Winters	*as*	Charlie Chan
Virginia Dale		René
Mantan Moreland		Birmingham Brown
John Gallaudet		Capt. Pete McNalley
Victor Sen Young		Tommy Chan
Carol Forman		Nita Aguirre
Douglas Fowley		Grock
Harry Hayden		Dr. Oscar Swendstrom
Howard Negley		André Pereaux
Stanley Andrews		Theodore Von Scherbe
Emmett Vogan		Henri Castanaro
Boyd Irwin		Simon Lafontaine
Rory Mallinson		Mr. Thompson
George J. Lewis		Sergeant Dansiger
Diane Fauntelle*		Mrs. Swendstrom
Ferris Taylor*		Dr. Dooble, coroner
Haywood Jones*		Mobile Jones
Eric Wilton*		Butler
Forrest Matthews*		Detective
Wally Walker*		Chauffeur
Larry Steers*		Doctor
Paul Conrad*		Man from D.A.'s office
Frank Stephens*		Sergeant
Fred Miller*		Armed guard
Charlie Jordan*		Fingerprint expert

Plot Summary: Simon Lafontaine, head of the Lafontaine Chemical Company, goes to meet with Charlie Chan, as he thinks that he has an enemy who is having him followed everywhere he goes. The trouble started

**Unbilled.*

when he entered into a partnership with two foreigners, Henri Castanaro and Theodore Von Scherbe, to ship a cargo of poisonous gas to South America. After Chan agrees to investigate further at Lafontaine's office, and Lafontaine is about to leave Chan's house, Lafontaine discovers that his chauffeur has been beaten up and his car stolen, confirming that he is in danger.

The next morning at his office, Lafontaine's secretary, René (who is also his niece), tells him that his new partners are waiting to speak with him. Castanaro and Von Scherbe are concerned about the possibility of one of them dying suddenly, and have added a clause to their agreement. In the event of the death of any of the principals, his share will revert to the survivors. After Lafontaine reluctantly signs the new agreement, Oscar Swendstrom, who had sold the formula for the poisonous gas to Lafontaine's company for $500, shows up at the office with a gun and claims that Lafontaine stole his formula for the chemical. René phones police captain Pete McNalley to have Swendstrom arrested, but when McNalley and his assistant, Dansiger, arrive, they find Lafontaine dead in his office.

Charlie Chan then shows up to keep his appointment, and the police tell him that they think Lafontaine may have died from a heart attack. Chan investigates and finds a shattered tube in the office radio, and the police take Swendstrom in for questioning. Meanwhile, son Tommy Chan and chauffeur Birmingham Brown locate Lafontaine's car in a Bourbon Street garage. Chan looks it over and finds some cigarette ash containing traces of coquina bark for flavoring.

Chan discovers later that a certain sound frequency will cause the glass in radio tubes to shatter. Chan then visits Castanaro. While he is there, André Pereaux and Nita Aguirre, who have an interest in diverting the chemical shipment for their own use, arrive. Pereaux offers Chan one of his specially made cigarettes, and Chan detects in it the same coquina bark he found in Lafontaine's car.

A letter is delivered to Castanaro, which prompts him to phone McNalley to report that he is in great danger. However, by the time the police arrive, Castanaro is dead under circumstances similar to Lafontaine's death. Chan investigates Pereaux and finds that he has been booted out of at least three armies, has used various aliases (Fernand, Citron, Boronoff, and Grumbauer), and is apparently after the formula. Swendstrom finally tells McNalley that Von Scherbe is the murderer, who is then also found murdered.

All of the suspects are invited to Chan's house. Pereaux and Aguirre, along with their henchman Grock, then demand information from Chan about the Lafontaine deal and the formula. In response, Chan tells them that a radio tube he is holding contains a deadly poison gas. He then plays a recording of a soprano singing a note which is of a pitch high enough to shatter the glass. When the glass shatters Chan tells everyone that there is now gas in the room. Tommy and Birmingham break into the room, but discover that there was no poison gas in the tube. Capt. McNalley and his men arrive and arrest Pereaux, Grock, and Aguirre. Chan then explains that it was Swendstrom who had used the gas in the tubes to kill his former business partner and who had also carried out the subsequent murders. Swendstrom's wife was in on the crimes, as it was her singing voice on the radio programs that triggered the shattering of the tubes.

Dr. Cream's Museum of Crime New York tourist stop run by Dr. Cream featuring wax dummy exhibits of famous criminals and detectives in *Charlie Chan at the Wax Museum* (1940). The museum originates *The Crime League* weekly radio show hosted by Dr. Cream whereby a famous detective tries to unravel an old unsolved crime. However, the museum is actually a cover for Dr. Cream's unlawful sideline of using his surgical skills to change the faces of criminals wanted by the law.

Dodd, Claire (December 29, 1908, Des Moines, Iowa–November 23, 1973, Beverly Hills, California) Pert, second-lead actress (real name: Dorothy Anne Dodd) who appeared in nearly 60 films. Dodd portrays Elsie Hillman, alias Mrs. Carol Wayne, in *Charlie Chan in Honolulu* (1938).

Although born in Des Moines (when her mother was there on a trip), Claire Dodd preferred to claim that she was born in Little Rock, Arkansas, where she was raised, as Des Moines did not appeal to her. Her father was a doctor who abandoned both her and her mother before Dodd was ten years old. Her mother suffered from tuberculosis, and Dorothy was forced to support both of them. At the age of 15, she went to New York, lied about her age, and joined the Ziegfeld Follies, where she was eventually discovered by Darryl F. Zanuck. He brought her to Hollywood and shepherded her throughout most of her career.

In films, Dodd often played a scheming seductress, and could not be cast as a "dumb blond" because of her cerebral nature and demeanor. Dodd projected a different, down-to-earth image when cast as Perry Mason's secretary, Della Street, in *The Case of the Curious Bride* (1935) and *The Case of the Velvet Claws* (1936). In the latter episode Della marries Mason (who is portrayed by Warren William).

"Don't enter Avalanche in the Santa Juanita Handicap—A Dead Horse can't win a race" Warning message in a note given to George Chester by the ship's purser onboard the S.S. *Oceanic* in *Charlie Chan at the Race Track* (1936). Chester has written the note to himself to divert Charlie Chan's suspicion of him as the murderer of Major Kent and the leader of a racetrack gambling ring.

Charlie notices that Chester doesn't require his glasses to read the note but *does* need glasses to read the note's very legible time stamp (6:04 P.M.). Chan later reasons that Chester wrote the note to himself and does not need glasses because the contents are already known. Another clue on the note was that it was written on a typewriter which has a clogged "e," and the letter "r" is raised slightly above the line. A search of cabin rooms by Charlie's son Lee, working as a ship's steward, reveals that a typewriter having the same characteristics is in Warren Fenton's stateroom.

Doran, Ann (July 28, 1911, Amarillo, Texas–) American character actress who appeared in nearly 170 films and was a stand-in actress in *Charlie Chan in London* (1934).

Ann Doran was approximately ten years old when she appeared in her first film, Douglas Fairbanks' *Robin Hood* (1922). After attending USC and UCLA, she returned to films in teenaged roles at Educational Studios but was her busiest at Columbia Pictures in the 1930s and 1940s. There she had supporting roles and bits in features, including several Frank Capra productions, and leading roles in two-reel comedies starring the likes of Charley Chase and Andy Clyde.

Doran freelanced in Hollywood for nearly five decades, playing everything from the sob-sister reporter Miss Rogers (to whom Bob Hope tells his life story) in *My Favorite Brunette* (1947) to the seemingly benign leader of an outlaw gang in a 1956 *Lone Ranger* television episode. Her most famous film portrayal was as James Dean's mother in *Rebel Without a Cause* (1955).

Doran was given ample opportunity to exhibit her versatility on television, with multiple appearances on *Perry Mason*, *Bewitched*, and *Emergency*. She also had co-starring roles on the television series *National Velvet* (1960; as Martha Brown), *Longstreet* (1971; as Mrs. Kingston), and *Shirley* (1979; as Charlotte McHenry).

Dorn, Walter Murdered secretary (portrayed by Donald D. Taylor) of Alfred Wyans in *The Red Dragon* (1945). Before he dies, Dorn (who is an undercover agent for the United States and an old friend of Charlie Chan) types the cryptic letters TH E$M OST.

Dorr, Lester (May 8, 1893, Massachusetts–August 25, 1980, Los Angeles, California) General purpose actor (real name: Harry Lester Dorr) who appeared in over 90 films. In two unbilled *Charlie Chan* roles, Dorr portrays a photographer in *Charlie Chan on Broadway* (1937) and Michael Strong,

Mr. Harper's mute chauffeur and handyman, in *The Jade Mask* (1945).

Douglas, Alan Actor who portrays Mrs. Whipple (an alias for Joseph Murdock) in *Dangerous Money* (1946).

Douglas, Donald (August 24, 1905, Kinleyside, Scotland–December 31, 1945, Los Angeles, California) Soft-spoken stage and screen actor and opera performer who appeared in over 80 films. In two *Charlie Chan* roles, Douglas portrays Capt. Lewis in *Charlie Chan in Panama* (1940) and Jed Thomasson in *Dead Men Tell* (1941).

Though occasionally a villain, the Scottish-born Douglas was usually cast in bland good-guy roles, such as Randall, the dull detective at odds with Dick Powell's Philip Marlowe in *Murder My Sweet* (1944). One of his few leading roles was the title character in Columbia's *Deadwood Dick* (1940).

Douglas was given more of a chance to shine on radio. In the 1943 Mutual network mystery anthology *Black Castle*, Douglas played all the parts, including the announcer.

Donald Douglas died suddenly at the age of 40, not long after completing work on *Gilda* (1946), in which he played Thomas Langford.

Douglas, Haldane Art director and production designer for over 20 movies, including *Charlie Chan at Monte Carlo* (1937) and *Charlie Chan in Honolulu* (1938). Douglas was also the art director for *Mr. Moto's Gamble* (1938), a reworked version of the never-completed *Charlie Chan at the Ringside*. In 1944 Douglas shared an Academy Award nomination with Hans Dreier in the Best Art Direction (Color) category for his work on *For Whom the Bell Tolls* (1943).

Douglas, John A chemical manufacturer (portrayed by Alexander Kirkland) who is under suspicion of Sir Lionel Grey's murder and who wants to marry Shirley Marlowe in *Charlie Chan's Chance* (1932).

Note: The character John Douglas loosely parallels that of David Elliot in *Murder Over New York* (1940).

Douglas, Warren (July 29, 1911, Minneapolis, Minnesota–) American actor and writer who portrays police sergeant Bill Davidson in *The Chinese Ring* (1947). He received the New York Critics Award three times for his acting in *It Happened in Springfield*, *Devil Boats*, and *Mountain Fighters*.

Douglas wrote television scripts for such shows as *Bat Masterson*, *Cheyenne*, *Gunsmoke*, *The High Chaparral*, *Laramie*, *McCloud*, *77 Sunset Strip*, and *This Is Your Life*.

Douglas 1101 Telephone number of San Francisco's Cosmopolitan Club in *Behind That Curtain* (1929). Eve Durand tries to telephone Col. Beetham, who will be giving a lecture that evening about the Persian Desert at the club, to warn him that her estranged husband Eric is after him.

DPE Initials on the business card of David Blake, which stand for Department of Political Economy, in *Charlie Chan in the Secret Service* (1944). Charlie Chan asks what the initials stand for and Blake lectures Chan, "If you read the newspapers, you'd know more about me." Chan then retorts, "I know what columnist say in morning paper: What David Blake does not know about political economics would fill many books."

dragoman In the Middle East, a term used for an interpreter or professional guide. In *Charlie Chan in Egypt* (1935), Arthur Stone portrays an unnamed, enterprising con man/guide who appears to be second to no one in sniffing out what can be done for money. He tells Snowshoes that he has located the tomb of Snowshoes' great, great, great, great, etc., grandpappy, for which Snowshoes had paid him money.

Drake, Hugh An old friend of Charlie Chan (portrayed by Frederick Worlock) who once worked for Scotland Yard but is now working for British Military Intelligence in *Murder Over New York* (1940).

Drake and Chan are unexpectedly seated across from each other on an airplane flight to New York. Drake tells Chan that he is currently on the trail of Paul Narvo, who he thinks is the leader of an aviation sabotage ring that murdered an official of the British Air Ministry three years ago and is now working in the U.S. Since Narvo is believed to have substantially changed his appearance and voice as a result of a car accident, Drake says he has been following Narvo's estranged wife, herself on the run from Narvo, around the world—Shanghai, Bombay, Copenhagen, the Orient, San Francisco—and he now believes she is in New York. Smiling, Charlie remarks, "Needle can be found when correct thread located."

When he arrives in New York, Drake stays as the guest of friend George Kirby, who hosts a small party for him that evening. Charlie and Jimmy come to see Drake in Kirby's library later, and they find him dead. At first Kirby says it must have been from a heart attack, but Charlie figures Drake was poisoned by a new gas called tetrogene. All of the papers Drake had with him about Paul Narvo's identity are in a briefcase which was left by Drake at the British Imperial Club's checkroom.

Note: The character Hugh Drake loosely parallels that of Sir Lionel Grey in *Charlie Chan's Chance* (1932).

Drake, Hugo Morris Murdered passenger on an around-the-world tour organized by Dr. Lofton in *Charlie Chan Carries On* (1931). Drake is strangled by Jim Everhard in a London hotel with a suitcase strap belonging to Dr. Lofton. Because Walter Honeywood had earlier changed hotel rooms with Drake, Everhard mistakenly murders Drake.

Drake, Oliver (c. 1903, Boise, Idaho–August 5, 1991, Las Vegas, Nevada) Screenwriter, director, producer, composer, and editor of over 120 films, many of which were westerns. Sometimes credited as C.O. Drake, he wrote the story and the screenplay for *The Feathered Serpent* (1948), *The Riders of the Whistling Skull* (1937—from which *The Feathered Serpent* was remade), and *The Sky Dragon* (1949).

Drake, Paula Portrayed by Marjorie Weaver in her first of two *Charlie Chan* roles, the fiancée of Dick Kenyon and secretary of Susie Watson in *Charlie Chan's Murder Cruise* (1940).

Driscoll, Mr. The manager of the Golden Eye Mine (portrayed by Ralph Dunn in his third of three *Charlie Chan* roles) in *The Golden Eye* (1948). Driscoll works for Talbot Bartlett (posing as a local assayer) and helps run the gold smuggling operation at the mine without the knowledge of the mine's owner, Mr. Manning, or his daughter Evelyn. Fearing that Driscoll would be captured and reveal details about the gold smuggling, Bartlett shoots and kills Driscoll under the pretext of stopping him from getting away from Chan and Lt. Ruark.

Driscoll, Mrs. Margaret The wife (portrayed by Lois Austin in her third of three *Charlie Chan* roles) of Driscoll, the manager of the Golden Eye Mine, in *The Golden Eye* (1948). After the mine's owner, Mr. Manning, is killed, Mrs. Driscoll takes Manning's place in the sickbed as a sedated, almost lifeless body whose head is entirely covered with bandages to hide her identity.

Dubon, Marie The wife (portrayed by Lynn Bari) of Tony Madero in *City in Darkness* (1939). Anxious to get her husband out of France, Dubon purchases a ticket on a boat bound for Panama from Louis Santelle for 15,000 francs. She later goes to Santelle's locksmith shop to pay him for a fake passport that will let her brother travel as Antonio Castillo. She starts to pay Santelle the 10,000 francs he quoted to her earlier, but he now wants 50,000 francs. Not having that much money with her, Dubon says that she will return later.

DuBrey, Claire (August 31, 1892, New York, New York–August 1, 1993, Woodland Hills, California) Character actress (real name: Clara Gates) who appeared in 100 silent and sound films, sometimes credited as Claire Dubrey. DuBrey portrays Mrs. Sarah Walters in *Charlie Chan's Murder Cruise* (1940).

The lengthy screen career of actress Claire DuBrey began as early as 1917. Alternating between leading roles and choice character parts, DuBrey appeared in such major productions as *The Sea Hawk* (1924). When talkies came in, she could be seen in dozens of minor roles as waitresses, nurses, landladies, and American Indians. She also played three of the least fortunate wives in screen history—the raving Bertha Rochester in *Jane Eyre* (1934), Mrs. Bob "Dirty Little Coward" Ford in *Jesse James* (1939), and Emma Smith, widow of slain Mormon leader Joseph Smith, in *Brigham Young, Frontiersman* (1940). A busy television performer, DuBrey was a regular during the 1953-54 season of *The Ray Bolger Show*. Retiring in 1958 at the age of 76, Claire DuBrey died in 1993, a month shy of her 101st birthday.

"The Duchess" Nickname for George Melton's housekeeper, Mrs. Hargue, in *Charlie Chan in the Secret Service* (1944).

Duff, Inspector (1) Scotland Yard inspector (portrayed by Peter Gawthorne in his second of two *Charlie Chan* roles) in *Charlie Chan Carries On* (1931). Duff is an old friend of Charlie Chan and is on the trail of a jewel smuggler and murderer named Jim Everhard.

Duff investigates the death of wealthy Hugo Morris Drake in a London hotel room and, while visiting Chan in Honolulu, is shot in the back but is not killed. Chan tells his superior that when Inspector Duff awakes, to tell him that, "Charlie Chan carries on," as he joins the tour moving on to San Francisco.

Duff, Inspector (2) Scotland Yard inspector (portrayed by C. Montague Shaw in his last of three *Charlie Chan* roles) in *Charlie Chan's Murder Cruise* (1940).

Duff is traveling incognito simply as British manufacturer John Duff on an around-the-world cruise in search of a deadly strangler named Jim Eberhardt. When the cruise ship stops in Honolulu on its last leg to San Francisco, Duff visits Charlie Chan and tells him of his latest case, requesting his assistance in a plan to flush out the strangler. When Chan leaves his office to ask permission from his superior, Duff, standing by the office window, is strangled by Eberhardt, who is disguised as a bearded beggar. Chan returns to find Duff unconscious on the floor. Though alive, Duff later dies at the hospital.

Dufresne, Albert Ex-boyfriend (portrayed by John Miljan) of Yvette Lamartine and the assistant to bank president Paul Lamartine in *Charlie Chan in Paris* (1935). Dufresne is a confederate of Max Corday and Henri Latouche in a scheme to counterfeit bonds issued by the Lamartine Bank.

Prior to his arrival in Paris, Charlie Chan has Nardi, a dancer working undercover for him, investigate Dufresne's financial dealings to see if he has any connection to counterfeit bonds issued by the Lamartine Bank. Nardi writes in a diary that Dufresne lost 10,000 francs at a gambling house in Montparnasse and is spending beyond his income.

Charlie Chan meets with Paul Lamartine and tells him about bank bonds that are counterfeits but have Lamartine's genuine signature. When Chan shows Lamartine and Albert Dufresne one of the bogus bonds, Dufresne remarks that the counterfeit bonds were probably slipped in with genuine ones when Lamartine was signing them. Dufresne now panics and fears that he will be discovered as part of the counterfeiting scheme. He starts packing a suitcase containing two million francs received from the sale of the bogus bonds and prepares to flee to Switzerland on a midnight plane.

While he's packing, Yvette Lamartine comes to Dufresne's apartment to retrieve some "silly old love letters" she had once written to him. When Dufresne is just about to give them to her (just to get rid of her so he can leave for Switzerland), he is shot in the back from the bedroom by Max Corday (disguised as the crippled beggar, Marcel Xavier). However, it is Yvette Lamartine who is arrested for Dufresne's murder.

Dumbrille, Douglass (October 13, 1889, Hamilton, Ontario, Canada–April 2, 1974, Woodland Hills, California) Canadian-born character actor of nearly 250 films,

Douglass Dumbrille

often cast as a smooth, suave villain or a comedic foil. In three *Charlie Chan* roles, Dumbrille portrays Petroff in *City in Darkness* (1939), insurance investigator Stuart Salisbury (alias Thomas Gregory) in *Charlie Chan at Treasure Island* (1939), and the reclusive historian Paul Manderley in *Castle in the Desert* (1942).

Born in Canada, Douglass Dumbrille did most of his stage work in the United States, breaking into films as Alisandroe in *His Woman* (1931). He bounced between supporting parts and unbilled bits in the early 1930s, where his sleek brand of skullduggery fit right in with the gangsters, shysters, and political phonies prevalent in movies at the time. Also superb in modern dress roles, Dumbrille excelled at costume villainy, and his pompous demeanor made him an ideal foil for such comedians as the Marx Brothers (with whom he appeared twice) and Abbott and Costello (who included Dumbrille in four different films). Sometimes Dumbrille's reputation helped him to convincingly portray red-herring suspects in murder mysteries.

In real life he was a gentle man whose diabolical features were softened by a pair of spectacles. Dumbrille mellowed his image as he grew older, often playing bemused officials and judges who couldn't make head nor tails of Gracie Allen's thought patterns on television's *The Burns and Allen Show*. After his first wife died, Dumbrille married Patricia Mowbray, the daughter of his close friend Alan Mowbray, who portrays the murderer Geoffrey Richmond in *Charlie Chan in London* (1934).

Duncan, Charles Civil engineer who committed suicide by shooting himself in *Black Magic* (1944). One year earlier, William and Justine Bonner obtain some information from Duncan's company and sell it to a competitor, which ruins Duncan and his reputation and prompts his suicide. His daughter Norma attends the Bonners' séances to get information proving her father's innocence.

Duncan, Norma Real name of Nancy Woods (portrayed by Helen Beverley) in *Black Magic* (1944). Her father, Charles Duncan, committed suicide one year earlier because of the information stolen by William and Justine Bonner from her father's company which ruined him. Using the name of Nancy Woods, Norma attends the Bonners' séances to get information to prove her father's innocence. When William Bonner is murdered during the séance, Sgt. Matthews thinks that Norma Duncan has a very strong motive for killing Bonner.

Dunn, Eli Assistant director (unbilled) for *Charlie Chan in Paris* (1935).

Dunn, Ralph (1902–February 19, 1968) Character actor who appeared in 100 films, three of them *Charlie Chan* entries. Dunn portrays unbilled policemen in both *Murder Over New York* (1940) and *Dead Men Tell* (1941), and Golden Eye Mine manager Mr. Driscoll in *The Golden Eye* (1948).

Dunn, Violet Actress who portrays Shelah Fane's maid, Anna, in *The Black Camel* (1931).

Dunwood, Kenneth Alias for Alan Raleigh (portrayed by James Todd) in *Charlie Chan's Chance* (1932). *See also* **Raleigh, Alan**.

Note: The character Kenneth Dunwood loosely parallels that of Keith Jeffrey (an alias for Paul Narvo) in *Murder Over New York* (1940).

Durand, Eric Greedy fortune hunter (portrayed by Philip Strange) who marries Eve Mannering, the niece of Sir George Mannering, against his wishes in *Behind That Curtain* (1929). Durand also murders Hilary Galt, a lawyer hired by Mannering to collect information about Durand's checkered past.

Alf Pornick, a night porter at Galt's building, sees Durand leaving Galt's office after the murder and starts blackmailing him. To escape Pornick, Durand and Eve move to India, where he squanders his wife's money. He also loses interest in Eve in favor of liquor and takes his female servant Nunah as his mistress. After the money runs out, Eve leaves him, and Durand eventually returns to London and murders Pornick. Durand is revealed to be the murderer and is killed evading the law.

E

8251 Prisoner number of convict Jimmy Slade in *Dark Alibi* (1946). Slade, a convicted forger, is a trustee employed in the state prison's fingerprint bureau file room.

8:00 P.M. Time of the first hobby horse race, the final night's cruise activity planned by Dr. Suderman in *Charlie Chan's Murder Cruise* (1940). Starting at 8:00 P.M., there would be races every 15 minutes on the quarter hour.

8:20 P.M. Time that Willie Fern, the dimwitted night watchman for Dr. Cream's Crime Museum, is to throw the switch on an electrical panel in *Charlie Chan at the Wax Museum* (1940). Steve McBirney's bodyguard, Grennock, convinces Willie that he is a prison warden and asks Willie to execute the wax dummy seated in the museum's own electric chair as part of a plan to murder Charlie Chan under the guise of a practical joke gone wrong.

8:30 P.M. Time that a church bell rings and Henrietta Lowell is shot through her study room window in *Charlie Chan's Secret* (1936). The rifle is mounted in a clock tower that was cleverly rigged to fire at Mrs. Lowell's window when the clock bell rang at 8:30 P.M.

11:30 P.M. Time that Billie Bronson tells Murdock to meet her in her hotel room so that he can buy a diary in *Charlie Chan on Broadway* (1937).

Eagan, Carlotta The daughter (portrayed by Heather Angel) of James Eagan in *Charlie Chan's Greatest Case* (1933).

Eagan, James Blackmailer (portrayed by William Slack) in *Charlie Chan's Greatest Case* (1933). As a young bank teller 35 years ago, Eagan changed the gold Dan Winterslip stole into Australian currency. Being the only man alive who could identify Dan Winterslip as the thief of Brade's gold, Eagan blackmails him and receives a check for $5,000.

Eagles, James C. Character actor who appeared in over 30 films. In two *Charlie Chan* roles, Eagles portrays Barry Arnold in *Charlie Chan in Egypt* (1935) and Chick Patten (unbilled) in *Charlie Chan at the Race Track* (1936).

Earle, Edward (July 16, 1882, Toronto, Ontario, Canada–December 15, 1972, Woodland Hills, California) Character actor who appeared in over 150 silent and sound films, sometimes as Edward Earl and Edward C. Earle. In two *Charlie Chan* roles, Earle portrays Dawson, the police lab technician, in *Black Magic* (1944) and Thomas Harley in *Dark Alibi* (1946).

Edward Earle had toured in vaudeville and stock before entering movies in 1915. The blonde, muscular Earle soon began playing romantic leads in films like *Ranson's Folly* (1915), *The Gates of Eden* (1916), and *East Lynne* (1920). In the 1920s he could be seen supporting such stars as George Arliss in *The*

Man Who Played God (1922) and Lillian Gish in *The Wind* (1928).

In talkies Earle became a character player, often with unbilled roles in everything from prestige pictures like *Magnificent Obsession* (1935; in which he portrayed Mr. Miller) to "B" pictures such as Laurel and Hardy's *The Dancing Masters* (1943) and *Nothing But Trouble* (1945). In *Beware of Blondie* (1950) Earle played Dagwood Bumstead's boss, Mr. Dithers, but his back was turned to the camera and his voice was dubbed by the *Blondie* series' former Mr. Dithers, Jonathan Hale (who appeared in three *Charlie Chan* films himself).

Easter egg Charlie Chan is trying to make an Easter egg with an "elusive Easter Rabbit" in the Honolulu police department's crime laboratory for his Number One grandchild in *Charlie Chan in Reno* (1939). *See also* **Number One grandchild**.

Eberhardt, Jim Jewelry thief, smuggler, and former husband of Mrs. Pendleton in *Charlie Chan's Murder Cruise* (1940). Eberhardt tries to force his wife to use her profession as an actress to smuggle jewelry, but she betrays him to the police instead, and he swears that he will have his revenge. Five years earlier, he escaped from prison and was captured to finish out his sentence. Eberhardt is released from prison just before Dr. Suderman's cruise starts.

Posing as Professor Gordon, an archeologist, Eberhardt joins Dr. Suderman's cruise in his plan to get revenge on those who helped send him to prison. On the cruise's first night out of New York, Eberhardt strangles a judge (possibly the one who sentenced him to prison). The only clue was a request by the judge for a list of the members of Dr. Suderman's cruise. In turn, Eberhardt strangles Inspector Duff in Charlie Chan's office, Mr. Kenyon in his hotel room, and Gerald Pendleton in his cabin room.

When Charlie Chan is about to determine the identity of the elusive strangler, Eberhardt forces Frederick Ross, a small-time fence and accomplice, to wear the disguise of a bearded beggar and steal incriminating photographic negatives from Chan. After hitting Chan over the head and trying to escape capture, Ross is shot to death at close range in the ship's hold by Eberhardt.

Note: The character Jim Eberhardt loosely parallels that of Jim Everhard in *Charlie Chan Carries On* (1931).

Eckhardt, William G. (c. 1909–May 25, 1977, Vista, California) Assistant director for three *Charlie Chan* films at Twentieth Century–Fox: *Charlie Chan at the Circus* (1936), *Murder Over New York* (1940),* and *Charlie Chan in Rio* (1941).*

Eden, Alexander (Alec) San Francisco jeweler (portrayed by Fred Esmelton) who arranged the sale of the Phillimore pearl necklace to wealthy financier P.J. Madden in *The Chinese Parrot* (1927).

Eden, Robert The son (portrayed by Edmund [credited as Edward] Burns) of a San Francisco jeweler who travels to P.J. Madden's California ranch to assist in the transfer of the Phillimore pearl necklace to its new owner in *The Chinese Parrot* (1927).

Edwards (1) Substitute test pilot (portrayed by an unbilled David Horsley) in *Charlie Chan at the Olympics* (1937). Prior to a test flight demonstrating a new remote controlled guidance system invention in Honolulu, Masters, the original test pilot, injures his shoulder. Edwards then fills in at the last minute as a substitute, but is attacked during the test flight by Miller, a mechanic of the Hopkins Aviation Company who stows away and then hijacks the plane with the valuable guidance system. Edwards' dead body is later found in a lagoon by Charlie Chan while on a fishing outing with "junior" son Charlie Chan, Jr.

Edwards (2) Radio engineer for the weekly *Crime League* broadcasts (portrayed by Harold Goodwin in his second of two *Charlie Chan*

**Unbilled.*

roles) in *Charlie Chan at the Wax Museum* (1940).

Edwards, Ben Courier (portrayed by Steve Pendleton) in *The Sky Dragon* (1949). Edwards is employed by John Anderson, an insurance investigator, to guard a shipment of $250,000 being transported by airplane.

During the flight, everyone is knocked out by a drug put in the coffee by stewardess Marie Burke, an accomplice of Anderson. When Lee Chan awakes, he finds Edwards dead near the plane's cockpit and the money shipment missing.

Edwards, Bruce Actor who appeared in 30 films and portrays Professor Martin's assistant, Harold Mayfair, in *Dangerous Money* (1946).

Edwards, Charles Manufacturer of magic supplies (portrayed by Harry Depp in his second of three *Charlie Chan* roles) whose office is in Room 726 of the Berkeley Building) in *Black Magic* (1944). Edwards is at the Bonner's séance to talk to his dead wife, Gertrude, who always calls him "Mr. Edwards."

Edwards, Gertrude Charles Edwards' deceased wife, with whom phony psychic William Bonner is in contact during a séance in *Black Magic* (1944). During the séance, the ghostlike apparition of Mrs. Edwards is a disguise worn by Vera Starkey, an assistant of the Bonners.

Edwards, Sara (1892–January 7, 1965, Hollywood, California) Stage and screen character actress of over 60 films who portrays Mrs. Hargue, nicknamed "The Duchess," in *Charlie Chan in the Secret Service* (1944).

In many of her roles, Edwards portrays the kindly grandmother, overbearing widow, hardy pioneer wife, ill-tempered teacher, or strict governess. She occasionally played unbilled peripheral roles, such as a wardrobe woman in *The Great Ziegfeld* (1936) and a doctor's wife in *Shadow of a Doubt* (1942). Edwards also enjoyed larger assignments, playing "The Colonel" in Hal Roach's *Dudes Are Pretty People* (1942) and Mrs. Hatch in Frank Capra's *It's a Wonderful Life* (1946).

effendi From the Turkish *efendi*, a Middle-Eastern title of respect meaning "sir" or "master." The term is used in *Charlie Chan in Egypt* (1935) by both the dragoman and Edfu Ahmad.

Egg Foo Yung A derogatory nickname for Charlie Chan used by Sgt. Kelly in *Charlie Chan at the Opera* (1936). *See also* **Chop Suey.**

E.H. to R.H. Inscription inside a wedding ring that is given to Judy Hayes by E. Hillman aboard the *Susan B. Jennings* as a receipt for a package containing $300,000 in cash in *Charlie Chan in Honolulu* (1938). When searching the cabin of Mrs. Carol Wayne, Charlie Chan and son Jimmy find a bracelet with the same initials. They conclude that the murdered man was the estranged husband of Carol Wayne whose passport identifies her as Elsie Hillman.

Eilers, Sally (December 11, 1908, New York, New York–January 5, 1978, Woodland Hills, California) Soft-spoken, popular leading lady (real name: Dorothea Sally Eilers) who appeared in over 60 late silent and early sound films. Eilers portrays Julie O'Neil in *The Black Camel* (1931) and in 1928 was chosen by the Western Association of Motion Picture Advertisers as a "WAMPAS Baby Star."

Eldorado Times Small-town newspaper whose editor is Will Holley in *Charlie Chan's Courage* (1934).

Eldredge, George Character actor who appeared in over 70 films and had roles in four *Charlie Chan* films at Monogram. He portrays Chief Brannigan in *Shadows Over Chinatown* (1946), Brand in *Dark Alibi* (1946), policeman Pat Finley in *The Shanghai Chest* (1948), and the policeman Stacy (unbilled) in *The Sky Dragon* (1949).

Eldredge, John (August 30, 1904, San Francisco, California–September 23, 1961,

John Eldredge

Laguna Beach, California) American character actor who appeared in over 80 films, sometimes credited as John Eldridge. In three *Charlie Chan* roles, Eldredge portrays Cartwright the inventor in *Charlie Chan at the Olympics* (1937), public defender Anthony R. Morgan in *Dark Alibi* (1946), and Apex Insurance and Bonding Company president William French (as John Eldridge) in *The Sky Dragon* (1949). Eldredge has the distinction of being only one of six actors who appeared with three different actors playing Chan.

Elkins, Saul Movie producer and story writer of over 10 films. Elkins wrote the original story (with Lou Breslow) that was the basis for *Charlie Chan at the Race Track* (1936).

Elliot, David Chemical engineer and owner of a chemical research company (portrayed by Robert Lowery in his second of three *Charlie Chan* roles) in *Murder Over New York* (1940). Elliot is a friend of Patricia West, Paul Narvo's estranged wife. As the last person to see Hugh Drake alive, Elliot is considered by Inspector Vance a prime suspect in Drake's murder. Because of his chemical business, Elliot was experimenting with tetrogene (the same gas that killed Hugh Drake) as the basis for a new powerful explosive.

Note: The character David Elliot loosely parallels that of John Douglas in *Charlie Chan's Chance* (1932).

Elliot, Dick (April 30, 1886, Massachusetts–December 22, 1961, Burbank, California) Short, fat-bellied character actor (real name: Richard Damon Elliott) of stage and screen who appeared in 100 films, usually cast as a blowhard or windbag. Elliot portrays cotton trader P.T. Burke in *Dangerous Money* (1946), and is perhaps best known as Mayor Pike on *The Andy Griffith Show* (1960–68) television series.

Elliott, John (July 5, 1876, Pella, Iowa–December 12, 1956, Los Angeles, California) Stage and screen character actor who appeared in nearly 150 silent and sound films, sometimes credited as John Elliot, John H. Elliot, or John H. Elliott. Elliott portrays the doctor who treats Fred Rhadini for a knife wound and shock in *Charlie Chan at Treasure Island* (1939).

Although John Elliott's deep, booming voice was ideal for talkies, he remained busy in bits and character roles until his final appearance as Homer Lynch in *Perils of the Wilderness* (1956). John Elliot is best known to audiences for his unbilled opening-scene performance as "The Exhausted Ruler" in Laurel and Hardy's *Sons of the Desert* (1933).

Ellis, Grace The former girlfriend (portrayed by Cobina Wright) of Clark Denton in *Charlie Chan in Rio* (1941).

Ellis, Robert Reel (June 27, 1892, Brooklyn, New York–December 29, 1974, Santa Monica, California) Stage and screen actor of over 100 silent and sound films, and also a story and screenplay writer of over 45 movies. Ellis teamed up with Helen Logan, his third wife, and wrote the story and/or screenplay for nine *Charlie Chan* films at Twentieth Century–Fox: *Charlie Chan in Egypt* (1935), *Charlie Chan in Shanghai*

(1935),* *Charlie Chan's Secret* (1936), *Charlie Chan at the Circus* (1936), *Charlie Chan at the Race Track* (1936), *Charlie Chan on Broadway* (1937), *Charlie Chan at Monte Carlo* (1937), *Charlie Chan at the Olympics* (1937), and *City in Darkness* (1939).

Ellson, Paul Real name of Paul Essex, who was in prison for three years for a stock swindle scheme, in *Charlie Chan at Treasure Island* (1939). Dr. Zodiac finds out Paul Essex's real identity and secret past and blackmails him. *See also* **Essex, Paul.**

emerald ring Jeweled ring taken off the dead Shelah Fane's finger by Jimmy Bradshaw at the insistence of Julie O'Neil in *The Black Camel* (1931). On the inside of the ring's band is inscribed Denny Mayo's name, the dead actor with whom Shelah had a love affair three years ago. Julie feels this would be embarrassing if it were publicly known.

Emery, Gilbert Screenwriter and character actor of stage and screen (real name: Gilbert Emery Bensley Pottle) who appeared in over 80 films, often playing distinguished or aristocratic types. Emery portrays Scotland Yard inspector Sir Frederic Bruce in *Behind That Curtain* (1929).

Although born in New York, Gilbert Emery was raised in England and succeeded as a stage actor, director, and playwright on both sides of the Atlantic in the teens and twenties. Emery made his American movie debut (and his talkie debut as well) in *Behind That Curtain.* Briefly parting company with Hollywood in 1932 and 1933 to concentrate on stage work, he returned to films on a permanent basis in 1934.

His better-known roles include the pipe-smoking police inspector, Sir Basil Humphrey, in *Dracula's Daughter* (1936); Mae West's business manager in *Goin' to Town* (1937); Thomas Jefferson in *The Remarkable Andrew* (1942); and the self-effacing Mr. Cliveden-Banks in *Between Two Worlds* (1944). As a screenwriter, he worked on such films as *Cuban Love Song* (1931), *Mata Hari* (1931), and *Gallant Lady* (1933).

*Unbilled.

Engel, Samuel G. (December 29, 1904, Woodridge, New York–April 7, 1984, California) Producer and screenplay writer of over 35 films. With Lester Ziffren, Engel wrote the screenplay for *Charlie Chan in Rio* (1941).

After majoring in chemistry and pharmacology at the University of Tennessee, Samuel Engel signed on as an assistant director at Warner Bros. in 1933. Three years later he was invited by Darryl F. Zanuck to join the producers staff at Twentieth Century–Fox. Following Navy and OSS service in World War II, Engel returned to Fox where he rapidly re-established himself as the producer and co-writer of *My Darling Clementine* (1946). He stayed with Fox until 1962, four years before his retirement. Engel had been on the Motion Picture Academy Board from 1950 to 1951, and served as its vice president from 1952 to 1958, and again from 1959 to 1960. He was also president of the Producers Guild of America from 1955 to 1958.

England, Paul (1894–November 21, 1968, Devonshire, England) Writer and actor who portrays the often inebriated Bunny Fothergill in *Charlie Chan in London* (1934).

***Eran Trece* (1931)** Translated as "There Were Thirteen," the Spanish-language version of *Charlie Chan Carries On* (1931). It was made by Fox Film Corporation, with Spanish dialogue by José López Rubio. Release Date: December 4, 1931.

Cast

Manuel Arbó	*as*	Charlie Chan
Juan Torena		Dick Kennaway
Ana María Custodio		Elena Potter
Rafael [Luis] Calvo		[Inspector] Duff
Raúl Roulien		Max Minchin
Blanca [de] Castejón		Peggy Minchin
Miguel Ligero		Frank Benbow
Carmen Rodríguez		Señora Rockwell
Julio Villarreal		Doctor Lofton
José Nieto		Capitán Kin

Carlos Díaz de Mendoza	Walter Decker
Lia Torá	Sybil Conway
Martin Garralaga	John Ross
Antonio Vidal	Paul Nielson
Ralph Navarro	Inspector Gardner
Amelia Santee*	Señora Benbow

See also ***Charlie Chan Carries On*** **(1931)**.

Erickson, Laura The Polynesian wife (portrayed by Amira Moustafa) of trader Tao Erickson in *Dangerous Money* (1946). Both Ericksons are part of a gang that plans to sell artworks stolen from Philippine banks during the Japanese invasion.

Erickson, Tao Half-Swedish, half-Polynesian trader (portrayed by Rick Vallin) who is returning to Pago Pago, Samoa, from Honolulu on a buying trip in *Dangerous Money* (1946). With his wife Laura, they run the Mango Inn Boarding House on Samoa and are part of a gang that plans to sell artworks stolen from Philippine banks during the Japanese invasion.

Ericson, Helen Actress who portrays the unnamed stewardess aboard the seaplane bound for Balboa in *Charlie Chan in Panama* (1940).

"ESCAPED KILLER STILL AT LARGE" Newspaper headline of *The Daily Mercury* about the escape of convicted murderer Steve McBirney from a New York courthouse in *Charlie Chan at the Wax Museum* (1940).

Esmelton, Fred (June 22, 1872, Melbourne, Australia–October 23, 1933) Character actor who appeared in 25 silent and early sound films, sometimes credited as Frederick Esmelton or Frederic Esmelton. Esmelton portrays San Francisco jeweler Alexander "Alec" Eden in *The Chinese Parrot* (1927).

Essex, Paul Alias of Paul Ellson (portrayed by Louis Jean Heydt) a mystery novelist and an old friend of Charlie Chan in *Charlie Chan at Treasure Island* (1939). After spending a month in Honolulu to relax and finish writing *The Secret of the Pigmy Arrow*, a mystery novel about a fake mystic, Essex (along with Charlie Chan and Number Two son Jimmy) is flying to San Francisco on the China Clipper.

During the flight, Paul receives a disturbing radiogram which reads, "Sign of Scorpio indicates disaster if Zodiac obligations ignored." As Paul Ellson, he was in prison for three years after being convicted of stock swindling, a secret known by Dr. Zodiac, whose message now threatens blackmail. When the plane is about to land, Jimmy and Charlie find Essex dead, having committed suicide using poison, and his briefcase containing the completed manuscript of the mystery novel has been taken by Thomas Gregory.

Essex, Stella Wife (portrayed by Sally Blane) of Paul Essex in *Charlie Chan at Treasure Island* (1939). Stella is waiting at the San Francisco airport with her uncle, Mr. Redley, to welcome Paul home, but instead is met by Charlie Chan who gives her the bad news that Paul died on the plane.

Evans, Emily Over-the-hill dancer-stripper (portrayed by Joyce Compton) who is one of several boarders living at the Foss Family Hotel in *Dark Alibi* (1946).

Evans, Professor Paul The fiancé (portrayed by Nils Asther) of Joan Farnsworth in *The Feathered Serpent* (1948). Evans is a member of the archeological expedition headed by Professor Henry Farnsworth. When Sonia Cabot is murdered in camp by Professor Stanley, Evans is taken away to the police because he was found kneeling beside her body while holding a knife.

Evans, Tom Egyptologist and archeologist (portrayed by Thomas Beck in his second of four *Charlie Chan* roles) in *Charlie Chan in Egypt* (1935). Evans is engaged to Carol Arnold and is part of the Luxor-based archeological expedition headed by Professor Arnold.

*Unbilled.

After Professor Arnold's body is discovered in Ahmeti's mummy case, Evans assists Charlie Chan in unraveling the mysteries of ancient Egypt, investigating Professor Arnold's murder as well as several other strange events that have occurred recently. When Evans, Chan, and Snowshoes finally discover the hidden treasure room inside Ahmeti's tomb, Evans is shot by Professor Thurston while wearing a headmask of the goddess Sekhmet as a disguise. Although he is shot twice, the bullets are quickly removed by Dr. Jaipur.

Evanson, Edith (1899–November 29, 1980) American character actress who appeared in over 40 films and portrays Louise Harper in *The Jade Mask* (1945).

Evelyn Tommy Chan's girlfriend. In *The Red Dragon* (1945), Charlie Chan observes Tommy's interest in Iris Wong, a pretty Chinese artist. Chan then threatens to tell Tommy's girlfriend Evelyn about Iris but stops and wants to make a deal when Tommy returns the blackmail threat by hinting that he will tell Charlie's wife how he was dancing the rhumba with Iris. Chan concludes, "There is an old saying. Mother know best, but in this case perhaps it best mother know nothing whatsoever. I make deal."

"Evening Is Nigh" Title of the tune that Gravelle plays on the piano to his estranged grown-up daughter Kitty Rochelle in *Charlie Chan at the Opera* (1936). Gravelle asks her if she remembers him playing it for her when she was little but she doesn't remember. It was written a year earlier for the Shirley Temple picture, *Our Little Girl* (1935).

Everhard, Jim Jewel thief, alias John Ross (portrayed by C. Henry Gordon in his first of five *Charlie Chan* roles) in *Charlie Chan Carries On* (1931). Everhard was once married to Sybil Conway, but she and Walter Honeywood ran away together with two bags of stolen diamonds. In London, he mistakenly kills Hugo Morris Drake, with whom Honeywood had earlier changed hotel rooms, and murders both Walter Honeywood and Sybil Conway in revenge.

Note: The character Jim Everhard loosely parallels that of Jim Eberhardt in *Charlie Chan's Murder Cruise* (1940).

Exchange Specie Bank of Peiping The bank into whose San Francisco branch Princess Mei Ling deposits $1 million in travelers checks in *The Chinese Ring* (1947). The bank's president, Mr. Armstrong, murders the princess and embezzles some of the funds by forging the princess' Chinese signature.

"Eye of Alla Mata, The" The introductory title given to Dr. Zodiac before he enters his mansion's séance room to meet Charlie Chan, Pete Lewis, and Fred Rhadini (disguised as Professor Bixby) in *Charlie Chan at Treasure Island* (1939).

F

50¢ (1) Amount Charlie Chan places on Avalanche to win the Melbourne Sweepstakes race in *Charlie Chan at the Race Track* (1936). Not normally a betting man, Charlie relents when son Lee tells him that he should place a bet for "old times sake," as Avalanche's owner is Chan's old friend, Major Kent.

Charlie says, "Will become reckless gambler for sake of old friend. Will bet tail of shirt 50¢ on shnozznalola" (i.e., nose). Although Avalanche crosses the finish line first, he fouls another horse and is disqualified. Upon losing his 50-cent bet, Chan philosophically says to Lee, "Shirt tail now bob tail."

50¢ (2) Price of a room as painted on a lantern outside the Mojave Wells Hotel in *Castle in the Desert* (1942). However, the hotel's owner, Hank, quotes a price of $2.00 a day without breakfast to Jimmy Chan.

$4.90 Taxi fare Charlie Chan owes for a ride in Birmingham Brown's cab in *The Chinese Cat* (1944). In the cab, Birmingham remembers that he first (and last) met Chan in Washington, D.C. (in *Charlie Chan in the Secret Service* [1944]), and there were "two or three murders." Chan tells Birmingham that son Tommy is also in town from University of California. When Chan gets out of the cab in front of the Hotel Francis, Birmingham mentions, "One Chan at a time is enough. No more murders for me!" and quickly drives off before Chan can pay the fare.

5L-18R-21L-0R Combination to Dr. Zodiac's vault where file cabinets containing blackmail information are stored in *Charlie Chan at Treasure Island* (1939).

53 Code number for U.S. government agent James Andrews, who is investigating opium smuggling, in *Charlie Chan in Shanghai* (1935). *See also* **Andrews, James.**

402 Arcade Building Office address of lawyer Frederick Garner in *Charlie Chan at the Circus* (1936). After the death of circus owner Joe Kinney, Kinney's ex-girlfriend, Nellie Farrell, visits Garner with Kinney's forged signature on a bogus marriage certificate in a scheme with her brother Dan Farrell to take over half ownership of the circus.

457N Number of the secret assignment file for the opium smuggling operation being investigated by British secret agent Sir Stanley Woodland and U.S. government agent James Andrews in *Charlie Chan in Shanghai* (1935).

$500 Amount paid by Simon Lafontaine to Oscar Swendstrom for the formula of a poison gas that he develops in *Docks of New Orleans* (1948).

£500 Amount owed by Eric Durand as blackmail payment to Alf Pornick in *Behind That Curtain* (1929). Pornick sends a letter to Eve, Eric's wife, in India and asks why the money hasn't been sent. The letter also asks Eve to wonder why Eric wanted to leave England so quickly the day after Hilary Galt's murder.

$1,500 (1) Amount Wally Burke receives after sending a telegram home that he is broke from gambling and needs money to pay his hotel bill in *Charlie Chan in Reno* (1939).

$1,500 (2) Amount of each of two checks written by Jeanne Bently to Dr. Ainsley as blackmail payments in *Charlie Chan in Reno* (1939). Three years earlier, Jeanne Bently murdered her husband, Wayne Russell, and Dr. Ainsley was the attending physician who falsified the death certificate to indicate that the man died from a heart attack.

$5,000 (1) Amount of a check Dan Winterslip had made out to James Eagan as a blackmail payment in *Charlie Chan's Greatest Case* (1933). Eagan is the only man alive who can identify Dan Winterslip as the thief of Brade's gold 35 years ago.

$5,000 (2) Amount Jeanne Bently tells her estranged husband, George Bently, she needs (but does not tell him why) in *Charlie Chan in Reno* (1939). On the day before her murder, Mrs. Bently travels to a ghost town near Dead Man's Canyon to meet her husband. Charlie Chan deduces that Dr. Ainsley is blackmailing her.

15,000 feet Altitude to which Lt. Cooper takes the TR-4 bomber on a test flight before descending into a dive in *Murder Over New York* (1940).

15,000 francs The price of a boat ticket to Panama that Marie Dubon purchases from Louis Santelle in *City in Darkness* (1939). The ticket was originally offered for sale to Charlie Chan, but the ever-polite Chan, seeing that Dubon needs the ticket more than he does, allows her to buy it instead.

$50,000 Amount of the death benefit of Joe Kinney's life insurance policy (with Kinney's ex-girlfriend, Nellie Farrell, as the beneficiary) in *Charlie Chan at the Circus* (1936).

50,000 francs Amount Louis Santelle now demands from Marie Dubon for his making a forged passport for her husband Tony Madero in *City in Darkness* (1939). Dubon starts to pay Santelle the 10,000 francs he quoted earlier, but Santelle now wants 50,000 francs. Not having that much money, she says that she will return later.

58367 1946-dated Louisiana license plate number on the car belonging to Simon Lafontaine in *Docks of New Orleans* (1948).

Fairlie, Gerard Screenwriter for *Charlie Chan in Shanghai* (1935).

Fane, Shelah Movie actress (portrayed by Dorothy Revier) who is in Honolulu making a movie in *The Black Camel* (1931). Three years ago she murdered a well-known fellow actor, Denny Mayo, with whom she was madly in love (even though he was married). Shelah is in turn murdered by Mayo's widow.

Note: The character Shelah Fane loosely parallels that of Lola Dean in *Charlie Chan in Rio* (1941).

Farnsworth, Joan The sister (portrayed by Beverly Jons) of Professor Henry Farnsworth and the fiancée of Professor John Stanley in *The Feathered Serpent* (1948).

Farnsworth, Professor Henry Old friend of Charlie Chan (portrayed by Leslie Dennison in his last of three *Charlie Chan* roles) in *The Feathered Serpent* (1948). Farnsworth, an acknowledged expert on Aztec civilizations, is held captive and tortured by Professor Stanley and his gang, forcing him to decipher some hieroglyphics that would reveal the location of an ancient treasure.

Farnum, Francis Actor who portrays Mike, the ticket taker for the Kinney & Gaines Combined Circus, in *Charlie Chan at the Circus* (1936).

Farnwell Aerodrome RAF airbase where Capt. Hamilton was stationed in *Charlie Chan in London* (1934). There, Chan learns that Hamilton was somewhat of a loner, and his only apparent friend, Flight Commander King, says that Hamilton was working on a method to silence war planes before he was murdered.

Farrar, Vincent J. Cinematographer for three *Charlie Chan* films. Farrar was also involved in filming many of the *Blondie* films of the late 1940s.

Charlie Chan filmography: *Behind That Curtain* (1929), *The Shanghai Cobra* (1945), *The Red Dragon* (1945).

Farrell, Dan Assistant animal trainer for the Kinney & Gaines Combined Circus (portrayed by Boothe Howard in his first of two *Charlie Chan* roles) in *Charlie Chan at the Circus* (1936). With the death of the circus' half-owner, Joe Kinney, Farrell and his sister Nellie Farrell forge Kinney's signature on a bogus marriage certificate (to "prove" that Nellie and Kinney had been married) in a scheme to take half-ownership of the circus.

Farrell, Nellie The circus wardrobe mistress (portrayed by Drue Leyton in her last of three *Charlie Chan* roles) and ex-girlfriend of Joe Kinney in *Charlie Chan at the Circus* (1936). With the death of the circus' half-owner, Kinney, Farrell and her brother Dan Farrell forge Kinney's signature on a bogus marriage certificate. They then claim that Nellie and Kinney had been secretly married and she is now half-owner of the circus.

Fat, Wong San Francisco curio shop owner (portrayed by an unbilled Lee Tung Foo in his last of three *Charlie Chan* roles) in *The Golden Eye* (1948).

Fatal Fingerprints One of three working titles for *Dark Alibi* (1946) before its release on May 25, 1946. *See also* ***Dark Alibi* (1946).**

Fatal Fingertips One of three working titles for *Dark Alibi* (1946) before its release on May 25, 1946. *See also* ***Dark Alibi* (1946).**

Faust, Victoria Actress who portrays Swedish cleaning woman Hulda Swenson in *The Scarlet Clue* (1945).

"FEAR SABOTAGE IN CRASH OF BOMBER" Newspaper headline of *The Daily Globe* about the crash of the TR-3 bomber in *Murder Over New York* (1940).

***The Feathered Serpent* (1948)** The sixteenth *Charlie Chan* film produced by Monogram Pictures Corporation.

Alternate Title: *Charlie Chan in the Feathered Serpent.* Source: remake of *The Riders of the Whistling Skull* (1937). Original Copyright: Monogram Pictures Corporation, January 9, 1948; LP2171. Copyright Renewed: June 21, 1977; R635320. Production: late September to early October, 1948. Release Date: January 9, 1948. Sound: Western Electric Recording. Film: b&w. Running Time: 60 minutes.

Producer: James S. Burkett. Director: William Beaudine. Assistant Director: William Calihan. Story and Screenplay: Oliver Drake. Additional Dialogue: Hal Collins.* Photography: William A. Sickner. Camera Operator: John Manin.* Stills: Eddie Jones.* Gaffer: Lloyd Garnell.* Special Effects: Ray Mercer. Technical Director: David Milton. Supervising Film Editor: Otho Lovering. Editor: Ace Herman. Set Decoration: Ray Boltz.* Musical Director: Edward J. Kay. Recordist: Tom Lambert. Makeup: Webb Overlander.* Production Manager: Allen K. Wood. Screenplay Supervisor: Ilona Vas.* Grip: Harry Lewis.*

Cast

Roland Winters	*as*	Charlie Chan
Keye Luke		Lee Chan
Mantan Moreland		Birmingham Brown
Victor Sen Yung		Tommy Chan
Carol Forman		Sonia Cabot
Robert Livingston		John Stanley
Nils Asther		Professor Paul Evans
Beverly Jons		Joan Farnsworth
Martin Garralaga		Pedro
George J. Lewis		Capt. Juan Gonzalez
Leslie Dennison		Professor Henry Farnsworth
Jay Silverheels*		Diego
Charles Stevens*		Manuel
Fred Cordova*		Filippe
Erville Alderson*		Professor Scott
Juan Duval*		Dr. Castelar
Frank Leyva*		José

**Unbilled.*

Plot Summary: In San Pablo, Mexico, an expedition prepares to look for archeology Professors Scott and Farnsworth, who have been searching for the lost Aztec Temple of the Sun but have been missing for months. Charlie Chan is traveling with his two sons, Lee and Tommy, and chauffeur Birmingham Brown toward Mexico City on vacation. On the way to San Pablo, they find Prof. Scott delirious, and he collapses. They bring Scott into town and locate the rest of the expedition party. After treatment by a doctor, Scott explains that after he and Farnsworth found the temple, they were held hostage and forced to unearth a fortune in jade and gold. Before Scott can name his captor, however, he is stabbed to death with an Aztec sacrificial knife.

Chan decides that they should form a search party and start where they found Prof. Scott. The search party includes Farnsworth's sister, Joan, who is also his heir; her fiancé, archeologist John Stanley; Farnsworth's fiancée, Sonia Cabot; and archeologist Paul Evans. Before the expedition starts, Chan discusses the case with Captain Gonzalez.

Chan and his sons join the expedition, and they make camp at the foot of the Diablo mountains. There they search for a stone containing ancient hieroglyphics that Scott said will lead them to the secret entrance of the temple. While on night watch, Birmingham sees an Indian named Manuel leaving the camp, and both Chan and Lee follow him. Meanwhile, Prof. Stanley sneaks out of the camp and enters the secret temple, where he is holding Farnsworth hostage to unearth the tomb of an ancient king that contains a fortune in antiques.

Stanley orders his henchman Diego to kill Chan, but Diego is shot by Pedro, the camp cook, who turns out to be a member of the Mexican secret service and was following Charlie. Chan removes Diego's wig and reveals that he is not an Aztec but an American wearing a disguise to cast suspicion on the Aztec Indians. Stanley threatens to kill Joan and Sonia if Farnsworth does not cooperate, but during the night Sonia is killed at the camp with Paul Evans' knife.

Needing to search the mountain area again, two search parties go out. Lee, Tommy, and Birmingham form one group and find the rock containing hieroglyphic directions to the temple, but they do not know how to enter it. Wanting to rest, Birmingham inadvertently sits on the rock that opens the temple's secret entrance and is then quickly pulled inside by Stanley's henchmen. Both Lee and Tommy now think Birmingham has disappeared.

In the other search team, Prof. Stanley forces Joan and their Mexican guide, Filippe, into the temple, where Manuel shoots Filippe. Chan and his sons finally realize that the rock, which is marked by a symbol of a feathered serpent, is the temple's entrance, and they enter with Pedro. They knock out Stanley and overpower the rest of the gang. Chan explains that Sonia murdered Prof. Scott and was involved with Stanley in smuggling Aztec antiquities out of Mexico. Even though she is engaged to Prof. Farnsworth, Sonia was unhappy about Stanley's engagement to Joan Farnsworth, her fiancé's sister. Stanley then murdered Sonia to keep her from talking about their smuggling activities.

Note: *The Feathered Serpent* is the only film in which Victor Sen Yung and Keye Luke appear together as Charlie Chan's sons. It had been nearly 11 years since Keye Luke had last appeared as Number One son Lee Chan in *Charlie Chan in Monte Carlo* (1937).

Fenner, Walter (1881–1947) Character actor who appeared in over 15 films and portrays Inspector Harry Davis in *The Shanghai Cobra* (1945). Because he bore a strong resemblance to Walt Disney, Fenner was cast in an unbilled role as Walt Disney's double in *Once Upon a Time* (1944).

Fenton, Alice The daughter (portrayed by Helen Wood) of Warren Fenton in *Charlie Chan at the Race Track* (1936). She is engaged to Bruce Rogers.

Fenton, Herbert Oxford school chum (portrayed by Melville Cooper) of Hugh Drake in *Murder Over New York* (1940). Fenton is a confederate of Paul Narvo (alias Keith Jeffrey) in an aviation sabotage ring.

As part of a plan to uncover Narvo's true identity, Charlie Chan arranges for a test flight of the TR-4 bomber. Fenton gets two aircraft mechanics to hide a glass pellet containing tetrogene inside the aircraft that will break when the plane goes into a test dive and kill the pilots, the same method they used to cause the TR-3 test bomber to crash. Suspecting a new attempt to sabotage the TR-4, Chan searches the plane prior to the test flight and replaces the deadly gas with a pellet of a harmless gas.

Chan assembles all the suspects at the airport and invites them to take a look at the inside of the bomber before its test flight. Suddenly, all are locked inside and the bomber takes off. After reaching its peak altitude, the pilot is instructed to perform a test dive. Not wanting to die, Fenton catches what he thinks is the real pellet of tetrogene before it can hit the floor and break. When the plane lands, Fenton then throws the glass pellet to the floor and quickly exits from the plane but is promptly captured by Inspector Vance. Under further questioning by Charlie Chan, Fenton fears he will be killed if he reveals Narvo's true identity.

Fenton, Warren Racehorse owner (portrayed by Jonathan Hale, Jr., in his second of three *Charlie Chan* roles) of Gallant Lad in *Charlie Chan at the Race Track* (1936). His daughter, Alice Fenton, is engaged to Bruce Rogers, the secretary of rival racehorse owner George Chester.

During the ocean voyage from Australia to California, a racetrack gambling ring switches Fenton's horse with Avalanche, which is owned by Chester. With some coloring dye, the two horses look almost identical, but Fenton is not fooled. Knowing that the real Avalanche is the better horse of the two and that Gallant Lad is virtually unknown in America, Fenton lets the switch remain. Because Gallant Lad is now a "ringer," Fenton figures he can win a lot of money by betting on an unknown long shot. Just before the race, however, Charlie Chan realizes that the horses were switched and reverses the pair so that they will be running under their true names.

Fern, Willie Dimwitted night watchman for Dr. Cream's Crime Museum (portrayed by Charles Wagenheim) in *Charlie Chan at the Wax Museum* (1940). To pass the time, Willie sometimes talks to the wax dummies, especially to that of his friend, Joe Rocke, a man who was hanged ten years earlier for a crime that he didn't commit.

Steve McBirney's bodyguard, Grennock, convinces Willie that he is a prison warden and asks Willie to execute the wax dummy seated in the museum's electric chair as part of a plan to murder Charlie Chan under the guise of a practical joke gone wrong. At 8:20 P.M. Willie is to throw the switch on an electrical panel that normally controls the power to the museum, but is now wired to a chair where McBirney and Dr. Cream hope Chan will be sitting during the radio broadcast.

Fernand One of several aliases of André Pereaux in *Docks of New Orleans* (1948). As Fernand, he, Grock, and Nita Aguirre (herself masquerading as a Countess and Fernand's cousin) together confront Chan at gunpoint to find out what Chan knows about them and their activities. From information received from U.S. government files, Chan recognizes Fernand as Pereaux and asks him if he wishes to be referred to as Citron, Boronoff, or Grumbauer, other aliases he has used (having been booted out of at least three armies).

Fetchit, Stepin (May 30, 1902, Key West, Florida–November 19, 1985, Woodland Hills, California) Black comic actor (real name: Lincoln Theodore Monroe Andrew Perry) who appeared in over 40 silent and sound films, often cast in roles that today might be perceived as racist stereotypes. Fetchit portrays "Snowshoes" in *Charlie Chan in Egypt* (1935).

Lincoln Perry left his home in 1914 to pursue a show-business career. He first joined the Royal American Shows plantation revues, adopting the stage name "Stepin Fetchit" (taken from a racehorse on which he had won money). He went on to spend several years on the vaudeville circuit, and in the late 1920s arrived in Hollywood where he made an immediate impact. By the time he appeared as Gummy in *Hearts in Dixie* (1929), Fetchit was being hailed by some as one of the greatest screen comedians.

Stepin Fetchit would always be cast as a lazy, inarticulate, and easily frightened Negro.

In the more politically correct 1990s, Fetchit's screen persona of the lazy, inarticulate, and easily frightened Negro would be considered extremely racist and offensive by many. In the 1930s, however, audiences found him hysterically funny, and he was the most celebrated black comic actor in Hollywood. He made few films after 1940 and drifted into obscurity before resurfacing in the late 1960s as a member of boxer Muhammad Ali's entourage. Later on, Fetchit was the litigant in a suit against CBS, whom he felt had negatively represented him in a 1968 television documentary.

Field, Virginia (November 4, 1917, London, England–January 2, 1992, Palm Desert, California) British-born blonde actress (real name: Margaret Cynthia Field) who appeared in over 40 films, sometimes credited

Virginia Field

as Katherine Burke. Field portrays the seductive former model Evelyn Grey in *Charlie Chan at Monte Carlo* (1937).

Fife, Inspector Scotland Yard inspector (portrayed by H.B. Warner) who tours the offices of the New York Police Department with Charlie Chan and Inspector Flannery to study New York police methods in *Charlie Chan's Chance* (1932).

Filippe One of two undercover Mexican secret police agents (portrayed, unbilled, by Fred Cordova) under the command of Pedro Lopez in *The Feathered Serpent* (1948). Lopez, José, and Filippe together investigate the smuggling of Aztec antiquities out of Mexico and the disappearance of Professor Henry Farnsworth. When captured by Professor Stanley and his men while attempting to arrest Stanley, Filippe is shot and killed by Stanley's henchman, Manuel. *See also* **José**.

Finch, Jennie The alias used by the master spy and saboteur known as Reiner (portrayed by Mary Nash), who poses as a middle-aged Chicago schoolteacher in *Charlie Chan in Panama* (1940). Supposedly having taught algebra and geometry for 18 years, Miss Finch tells Cliveden Compton that she is now traveling to see some of the world. *See also* **Reiner**.

First Assistant (1) Nickname Charlie Chan uses for his Number Three son Tommy in *The Scarlet Clue* (1945). Birmingham Brown is Number Two assistant. *See also* **Chan, Tommy**.

First Assistant (2) Title given to Jimmy Chan by Chattanooga Brown in *Dangerous Money* (1946). Brown refers to himself as Charlie Chan's "Second Assistant."

Fitzgerald, Neil (1891, Ireland–June 15, 1982) Character actor who portrays Dakin, the secretary to Shanghai police commissioner Col. Watkins, in *Charlie Chan in Shanghai* (1935).

Fix, Paul (March 13, 1901, Dobbs Ferry, New York–October 14, 1983) Steely-eyed American general purpose actor (real name: Paul Fix Morrison) who appeared in over 200

Paul Fix (Everett Collection)

films, often as sheriffs, ranchers, or doctors. Fix portrays the gangster "Lefty" (unbilled) in *Charlie Chan at the Race Track* (1936) and has a similar gangster role (also unbilled) in *Mr. Moto's Gamble* (1938), a reworked version of the never-completed *Charlie Chan at the Ringside.*

The son of a brewery owner, Paul Fix went the vaudeville and stock-company route before settling in Hollywood in 1926. During the 1930s and 1940s he was most closely associated with westerns, essaying many a villainous role at various "B"-picture mills. In the mid–1930s Fix befriended young John Wayne, and helped coach the star-to-be in the whys and wherefores of effective screen acting. Fix ended up appearing in 27 films with Wayne, among them *Pittsburgh* (1942), *The Fighting Seabees* (1943), *Tall in the Saddle* (1944), *Back to Bataan* (1945), *Red River* (1948), and *The High and the Mighty* (1954).

Fix was busy in television during the 1950s and often found himself softening his bad-guy image to portray crusty old gents with golden hearts. His most familiar role was as the honest but often ineffectual sheriff, Micah Torrance, on the television series *The Rifleman.* Although also cast in television westerns such as *Gunsmoke*, Fix also portrayed District Attorney Hale in four television episodes of *Perry Mason.*

Flannery, Inspector New York policeman (portrayed by James Kirkwood) who is called in to investigate the murder of former Scotland Yard chief Sir Lionel Grey in *Charlie Chan's Chance* (1932).

Note: The character Inspector Flannery loosely parallels that of Inspector Vance in *Murder Over New York* (1940).

Flavin, James (May 14, 1906, Portland, Maine–April 23, 1976, Los Angeles, California) Irish-American stage and screen character actor of nearly 200 films (often cast as a policeman) who appeared in four *Charlie Chan* films. Flavin portrays a police detective (unbilled) in *Charlie Chan at the Race Track* (1936), a policeman (unbilled) in *Charlie Chan on Broadway* (1937), a homicide division cop (unbilled) in *Charlie Chan in Honolulu* (1938), and H.R. Jarvis in *The Shanghai Cobra* (1945).

Fletcher, Arthur Private detective (portrayed by Milton Parsons in his second of four *Charlie Chan* roles) hired by Professor Gleason's family who apparently dies from poison of tagara weed in a drink given him by Lucy Manderley in *Castle in the Desert* (1942). Fletcher is one of two persons hired by Dr. Retling, Brenda Hartford, and Walter Hartford to pretend having been poisoned by Lucy to convince her wealthy husband that Lucy is insane.

Fletcher, Sheriff "Tombstone" Acid-tongued, rustic country sheriff (portrayed by Slim Summerville in his second of two *Charlie Chan* roles) in *Charlie Chan in Reno* (1939). Fletcher is assigned to investigate the murder of Jeanne Bently and is not too keen on Charlie Chan, an outsider, meddling in his investigation.

When Fletcher questions Charlie Chan's wisdom of releasing Wally Burke from custody, Chan replies, "If want wild bird to sing—do not put him in cage." Unlike Sgt. Thacker, who is told the same aphorism in *Charlie Chan in London* (1934), Fletcher has a ready reply of, "Maybe he won't sing, but leastwise he won't take off either," to which Chan politely smiles.

Note: In the Call Bureau Cast Service lists, Sheriff Fletcher's name was originally Foster.

Fletcher, Walter President of the Sixth National Bank (portrayed by Roy Gordon) in *The Shanghai Cobra* (1945). Like Jan Van Horn, who Charlie Chan arrested eight years ago in Shanghai but who later escaped, Fletcher also has dark black hair with an unusual white streak, and was in Shanghai from 1936 to 1937 with the International Bank Company.

Flight 17—Gate A Flight number and arrival gate of the airplane bound for San Francisco in *The Sky Dragon* (1949). While in flight, a shipment of $250,000 is stolen and

Ben Edwards (the courier guard) is murdered while everyone, including Charlie Chan and son Lee, are in a drugged sleep.

Flint, Sam (October 19, 1882, Gwinett County, Georgia–October 24, 1980, Woodland Hills, California) Stage and screen actor who appeared in over 100 films. He portrays (all unbilled) the ship's captain in *Charlie Chan at the Race Track* (1936), Thomas P. Manning in *The Chinese Cat* (1944), and Dr. Groves in *The Golden Eye* (1948). Flint has the distinction of being only one of six actors who appeared opposite three different actors playing Chan.

Silver-haired and authoritative, and distinguished by an executive-style mustache, Flint entered films in the early 1930s after a long stage career. Though his movie roles were usually confined to one or two scenes per picture, Flint was always instantly recognizable in his characterizations of businessmen, bankers, chairmen of the board, politicians, publishers, fathers of the bride, and doctors. In addition to his feature film work, Flint appeared in short subjects featuring the *Our Gang* troupe, Abbott and Costello, and The Three Stooges. On television, Flint appeared frequently in episodes of *Adventures of Wild Bill Hickok* and *Zane Grey Theater*.

Flynn, Capt. Policeman (portrayed by Robert E. Homans in his last of three *Charlie Chan* roles) of the 12th Precinct in *The Scarlet Clue* (1945). Flynn is an old friend of Charlie Chan and is asked to keep an eye on Rausch, a foreign agent trying to steal radar secrets from the U.S. government.

Fodor, Ladislas Writer, sometimes credited as Ladislao Fodor, Ladislaus Fodor, or Laszlo Fodor. With Gina Kaus, Fodor wrote a play that served as the basis for the film *City in Darkness* (1939).

Foggy Convict (portrayed by Tim Ryan in his second of five *Charlie Chan* roles) who is sent to jail by Charlie Chan in *Dark Alibi* (1946).

Fong, Benson (October 10, 1916, Sacramento, California–August 1, 1987, Los Angeles, California) Chinese-American actor who portrays Charlie Chan's Number Three son, Tommy Chan, in six films at Monogram. Besides his role as Tommy Chan, Fong, years earlier, portrayed (uncredited) a Chinese soldier in *Charlie Chan at the Opera* (1936).

Except for a few brief bit parts in the late 1930s, Benson Fong's acting career began during World War II, a time when Asian actors were in demand for Chinese and Japanese characters in Hollywood's war movies. Besides the *Charlie Chan* series, Fong appeared in nearly 45 other films, including an uncredited role in *Thirty Seconds Over Tokyo* (1944), as the patriarch Wang Chi-Yang in *Flower Drum Song* (1961), as Dr. Schneider in *Our Man Flint* (1965), and as "The Old One" in *Kung Fu: The Movie* (1986). Fong also frequently appeared in television series such as *Perry Mason*, *Family Affair*, *Kung Fu*, *Mission: Impossible*, and *It Takes a Thief*. On the advice of his friend Gregory Peck, Fong added to his acting income by becoming a successful restaurateur in Southern California before his death from a stroke.

Benson Fong in *China Sky* (1944) (Everett Collection).

Benson Fong in a post–*Charlie Chan* series role as Wang Chi-Yang in the 1961 version of *Flower Drum Song* (Everett Collection).

Charlie Chan filmography (as Tommy Chan): *Charlie Chan in the Secret Service* (1944), *The Chinese Cat* (1944), *The Shanghai Cobra* (1945), *The Scarlet Clue* (1945), *The Red Dragon* (1945), and *Dark Alibi* (1946).

Fontan, Joseph The uncle of Marguerite Fontan in *The Red Dragon* (1945). Charlie Chan reveals that it was Marguerite Fontan's uncle in Czechoslovakia who discovered the 95th element and formula for the atomic bomb, and died preventing the Nazis from using his discovery. In actuality, the discovery of the 95th element (americium) is credited to a team of American scientists led by Glenn T. Seaborg. *See also* **95th element**; **Seaborg, Glenn T.**

Fontan, Marguerite Attractive tourist (portrayed by Carol Hughes in her first of two *Charlie Chan* roles) in *The Red Dragon* (1945). Fontan has been living in Mexico City for the past three years (since the death of her father) and is romantically involved with Inspector Carvero. Fontan has strong personal reasons for desiring possession of Alfred Wyans' secret research papers, since it was her uncle, Joseph Fontan, who in Czechoslovakia discovered the 95th element and formula for the atomic bomb, and who died preventing the Nazis from using his discovery.

Foo, Lee Tung (1874–1966) Chinese actor who appeared in almost 30 films, including three *Charlie Chan* entries. Foo portrays (unbilled) the ship's cook, Wu Mei, in *Dead Men Tell* (1941), Mr. Armstrong's butler in *The Chinese Ring* (1947), and curio shop owner Wong Fat in *The Golden Eye* (1948).

Foo, Wing Charlie Chan's son-in-law (portrayed by Philip Ahn in his first of two *Charlie Chan* roles). Foo is the husband of Chan's Number One daughter Ling in *Charlie Chan in Honolulu* (1938). As an expectant father, Wing Foo repeatedly telephones Chan from the hospital maternity ward about the status of the impending arrival of Charlie's first grandchild, a boy.

Ford, Francis (August 15, 1882, Portland, Maine–September 5, 1953, Los Angeles, California) Film director, writer, and producer (real name: Francis O'Fearna) of over 40 silent films, and a character actor in over 140 silent and sound films. Ford was the elder brother of movie directors John Ford (real name: Sean Aloysius O'Fearna) and Edward O'Fearna. Brother Edward worked (unbilled) as the assistant director on *Charlie Chan in London* (1934).

Francis Ford had acted in his own films and those of other directors, but turned to acting exclusively around 1928, often providing convincing portrayals of men of authority, as well as those that were sometimes ruthless. Ford appeared in four *Charlie Chan* roles: as Captain Hallett in *Charlie Chan's Greatest Case* (1933), Hewitt in *Charlie Chan's Courage* (1934), the boat captain (unbilled) in *Charlie Chan's Secret* (1936), and circus owner Mr. Gaines in *Charlie Chan at the Circus* (1936).

Forde, Eugene J. (November 8, 1898, Providence, Rhode Island–1986, California) Juvenile actor and director of almost 40 films, including five *Charlie Chan* entries at Twentieth Century–Fox.

Eugene Forde made his debut at the age of five and later appeared in plays with notables such as William S. Hart, Mary Pickford, and Blanche Sweet. In several silent films with the American Film Company, Forde played the juvenile lead. He quit acting at age 9 to return to school. After a short stint as a bank clerk, Forde returned to the movie industry as a script clerk with Fox and was directing shorts by 1926.

Following the merger between Fox and Twentieth Century in 1935, Forde moved up to directing "B" pictures such as *Berlin Correspondent* (1942) and several entries of both the *Charlie Chan* and *Michael Shayne* detective series. He remained at Twentieth Century–Fox for the rest of his career and retired when Sol M. Wurtzel shut down the "B"-pictures division in 1947.

Charlie Chan filmography: *Charlie Chan's Courage* (1934), *Charlie Chan in London* (1934), *Charlie Chan on Broadway* (1937), *Charlie Chan at Monte Carlo* (1937), and *Charlie Chan's Murder Cruise* (1940).

Forman, Carol (1919–July 8, 1997, Burbank, California) Buxom brunette actress who appeared in over 20 films and specialized in exotic villainy. In two *Charlie Chan* roles, Forman portrays spy Nita Aguirre in *Docks of New Orleans* (1948) and murderess Sonia Cabot in *The Feathered Serpent* (1948).

Forrest Valet to the impostor posing as U.S. government agent James Andrews in *Charlie Chan in Shanghai* (1935). Portrayed by Gladden James (unbilled), he is part of the opium smuggling operation in Shanghai along with his "master" (who had killed the real James Andrews in San Francisco several weeks earlier). Forrest tries to shoot Charlie Chan in Andrews' hotel room.

Foss Family Hotel Boarding house run by Mrs. Foss in *Dark Alibi* (1946). Its residents are June Harley, Thomas Harley, Emily Evans, Miss Petrie, Mr. Johnson, and Mr. Danvers.

Foss, Mrs. Amateur social worker (portrayed by Edna Holland in her first of two *Charlie Chan* roles) who runs the Foss Family Hotel in *Dark Alibi* (1946). Mrs. Foss sometimes takes in lodgers who are ex-convicts, hoping to rehabilitate them.

Note: Although the Call Bureau Cast Service lists Minerva Urecal as Mrs. Foss, production information in the Academy of Motion Picture Arts and Sciences (AMPAS) library states that she was replaced by Edna Holland, who is listed in the on-screen credits.

Foster, Norman (December 13, 1900, Richmond, Indiana–July 7, 1976, Santa Monica, Los Angeles, California) Screenwriter and director (real name: Norman Hoeffer) of over 50 films, and an actor who appeared in nearly 45 films. Foster directed three *Charlie Chan* movies.

Norman Foster became a stage actor in 1926 and by the end of the decade was acting in films. He switched to directing in 1936 and helmed six of the eight *Mr. Moto* mysteries starring Peter Lorre. In 1942 he completed Orson Welles' thriller, *Journey Into Fear*. Of his work from the next 25 years, Foster is most fondly remembered for the westerns *Rachel and the Stranger* (1948) and *Navajo* (1952), and the crime thriller *Woman on the Run* (1950). He was first married to actress Claudette Colbert in 1928, whom he divorced in 1935, and then was married to Sally Blane, who portrayed Stella Essex in *Charlie Chan at Treasure Island* (1939).

Charlie Chan filmography: *Charlie Chan in Reno* (1939), *Charlie Chan at Treasure Island* (1939), and *Charlie Chan in Panama* (1940).

Fothergill, Becky Wife (portrayed by Madge Bellamy) of Bunny Fothergill, and houseguest of Geoffrey Richmond at the time of the "Midnight Stable Murder," in *Charlie Chan in London* (1934).

Fothergill, Bunny The often inebriated houseguest (portrayed by Paul England) of Geoffrey Richmond in *Charlie Chan in London* (1934).

Byron Foulger

Foulger, Byron (August 27, 1899, Ogden, Utah–April 4, 1970, Hollywood, California) Veteran actor who appeared in over 200 films, often cast as the worried, bespectacled clerk. Foulger portrays Mr. Armstrong, the bank president of the San Francisco branch of the Exchange Specie Bank of Peiping, in *The Golden Ring* (1947).

Byron Foulger's bespectacled, tremble-chinned, moon-shaped face was one of the most familiar ever on the screen. A graduate of the University of Utah, Foulger developed a taste for performing in community theater, making his Broadway debut in the 1920s. Foulger then toured with Moroni Olsen's stock company, which led him to the famed Pasadena Playhouse as both actor and director.

In films from 1936, Foulger usually played whining milksops, weak-willed sycophants, hypocritical sales clerks, shifty political appointees, and the occasional unsuspected murderer. In addition to his film work, Foulger built up quite a gallery of portrayals on television. Most noted were his role as Mr. Timberlake in *Dennis the Menace* (1959) and the recurring role of engineer Wendell Gibbs on the popular sitcom *Petticoat Junction* (1963–70).

The Four Star Murder Case Title of an unused story written in 1942 for a potential *Charlie Chan* film at Twentieth Century–Fox. As mentioned by William K. Everson in *The Detective on Film*, the story deals with a jewel robbery and a series of murders in a mansion in upstate New York. Philo Vance is a guest at the mansion when the murders begin, and when he is unable to solve the case, celebrated detectives Charlie Chan, Mr. Moto, and Michael Shayne are called in to assist.

Fowley, Douglas (May 30, 1911, New York, New York–May 21, 1998, Woodland Hills, California) American character actor (real name: Daniel Vincent Fowley) who appeared in over 210 films, often as a gangster. Fowley, sometimes credited as Douglas Victor Fowley, appeared in three *Charlie Chan* films, and has the distinction of being only one of six actors who appeared with three different actors playing Chan. Fowley portrays nightclub owner Johnny Burke in *Charlie Chan on Broadway* (1937), reporter Peter Lewis in *Charlie Chan at Treasure Island* (1939), and the shady gangster Grock in *Docks of New Orleans* (1948). In addition, Fowley portrays Nick Crowder in *Mr. Moto's Gamble* (1938), a reworked version of the never-completed *Charlie Chan at the Ringside*.

Douglas Fowley

Born and raised in the Greenwich Village section of New York, Douglas Fowley did his first acting while attending St. Francis Xavier Military Academy. A stage actor and nightclub singer-dancer during the regular theatrical seasons, Fowley took such jobs as athletic coach and shipping clerk during summer layoffs. He made his first film, *The Mad Game*, in 1933. Thanks to his somewhat forbidding facial features, Fowley was usually cast as a gangster. On television, Fowley made sporadic appearances as Doc Holiday in the weekly series *The Life and Legend of Wyatt Earp* (1955–61).

Fox Film Corporation American production and distribution company (started by William Fox) which made the first nine *Charlie Chan* films starring Warner Oland, although Fox originally intended to make only four *Charlie Chan* movies. Fox acquired the rights to *The House Without a Key* (1925), which provided the basis for *Charlie Chan's Greatest Case* (1933). The rights to *The Chinese Parrot* (1927) was acquired from Universal as the basis for *Charlie Chan's Courage* (1934). Warner Oland was supposed to be paid $10,000 a picture, but the popular response to *Charlie Chan Carries On* (1931) prompted him to ask for $12,500 for *The Black Camel* (1931) and $20,000 for *Charlie Chan's Chance* (1932). Oland, however, was kept at $12,500 for the remaining eight pictures made by Fox.

In May 1935, after filming *Charlie Chan in Shanghai*, Fox merged with Joseph Schenck's Twentieth Century Pictures to form the Twentieth Century–Fox Film Corporation, and this new company continued to make 18 more movies in the series until 1942, after which Monogram took over the series in 1944. *See also* **Fox, William; Twentieth Century–Fox Film Corporation.**

Charlie Chan Fox filmography: *Behind That Curtain* (1929), *Charlie Chan Carries On* (1931), *The Black Camel* (1931), *Charlie Chan's Chance* (1932), *Charlie Chan's Greatest Case* (1933), *Charlie Chan's Courage* (1934), *Charlie Chan in London* (1934), *Charlie Chan in Paris* (1935), *Charlie Chan in Egypt* (1935), and *Charlie Chan in Shanghai* (1935).

Fox, William (January 1, 1879, Tulchva, Hungary–May 8, 1952, New York, New York) Hungarian-born filmmaker and industry visionary (real name: Wilhelm Fried, a.k.a. William Fried) who founded the Fox Film Corporation, which later merged with Twentieth Century Pictures to form the Twentieth Century–Fox Film Corporation.

William Fox was the oldest child of a large family of immigrants. Growing up on New York's Lower East Side, Fox held down a series of jobs before setting up his own business in 1900, the Knickerbocker Cloth Examining and Shrinking Company. When his profits reached $50,000, Fox sold the company in 1904 to realize even more capital. Two years later he bought a failing Brooklyn nickelodeon from British film pioneer J. Stuart Blackton. As the new owner of an empty house, Fox hired a coin manipulator and a barker to entice patrons into the dark 146-seat theater and bolstered business by hiring live acts to entertain the audience between movies.

In time, more nickelodeons were opened and he became a successful film exhibitor. He then set up his own film exchange, the Greater New York Rental Company, in defiance of the monopolistic Motion Pictures Patent Company. He earned the respect of his fellow exchange executives by winning a long legal battle against the Motion Pictures Patent Company that ended the film trust and allowed him to start his own production company in 1913.

Fox entered the production end of the business with Box Office Attractions in 1913 and eventually merged his theatrical, exchange, and studio operations into the Fox Film Corporation, which opened for business in 1914. Banking on the popularity of his biggest stars (which included Theda Bara and Tom Mix), Fox maintained one of the most successful and prolific studios in Hollywood. He also accumulated a theater chain numbering 1,000 movie houses by 1927. His bread-and-butter product, directed by such dependables as John Ford and Frank Borzage, enabled Fox to engage such "artistic" directors as F.W. Murnau, who wouldn't bring in much at the box office but could be counted upon for the prestige items that won awards and gained critical adulation. In 1927 Joseph P. Kennedy arranged a series of lectures at the Harvard Graduate School of Business by representatives of all the big film companies. Marcus Loew and William Fox, two immigrants who had never finished grammar school, were among those included.

In 1927 Fox acquired the American patent rights to the Movietone sound-on-film process developed by a Swiss firm, which was far superior to the competing sound-on-disc Vitaphone—a move which enabled his studio to make a smooth transition to talkies. In 1929 Fox received an Academy Award nomination in the Best Picture, Production category for *Seventh Heaven* (1927).

Fox also pioneered the wide-screen film format with such productions as *The Big Trail* (1930), but this innovation was not as successful as Movietone. Ever-expanding his empire, Fox acquired a controlling interest in Gaumont-British. When he tried to purchase MGM, however, he overextended his credit. In dire financial straits thanks to the 1929 Wall Street crash, Fox came under attack from many of those in Hollywood who resented his megalomania. A federal antitrust investigation, coupled with the financial mismanagement of certain studio executives, resulted in Fox's ouster in 1930 from the company which bore his name.

In 1936, a year after his old studio merged with Twentieth Century, William Fox declared bankruptcy. During the subsequent legal proceedings, Fox tried to bribe a judge and was sentenced to a year in prison in 1941. Paroled in 1943, he tried to set up his own production firm, but no backer was interested in bankrolling a Hollywood pariah. Although secure from his many patent holdings, the industry for which he had been so visionary was now closed to him. No industry representative came to eulogize him at his funeral in 1952.

Francisco, Betty (September 26, 1900, Little Rock, Arkansas–November 25, 1950, El Cerrito, California) Character actress (real name: Elizabeth Bartman) who appeared in nearly 50 silent and early sound movies. Francisco portrays Sybil Conway in *Charlie Chan Carries On* (1931).

Frank, Paul Geoffrey Richmond's real name in *Charlie Chan in London* (1934). *See also* **Richmond, Geoffrey.**

Franklin, Lena The maid (portrayed by Louise Franklin) to follies dancer Wanda LaFern in *The Sky Dragon* (1949).

Franklin, Louise Black actress who portrays an unbilled maid in *Shadows Over Chinatown* (1946) and Lena Franklin, the maid of follies dancer Wanda LaFern, in *The Sky Dragon* (1949).

Fredericks, Dr. Military doctor (portrayed by Edward Keane in his second of two *Charlie Chan* roles) who performed the autopsy on R.J. Godley in *Charlie Chan in Panama* (1940).

Freericks, Bernard Sound director of four *Charlie Chan* films at Twentieth Century–Fox. In addition, Freericks directed sound for nearly 40 other movies, including *Mr. Moto's Gamble* (1938; a reworked version of the never-completed *Charlie Chan at the Ringside*), *A Tree Grows in Brooklyn* (1945), *The Robe* (1953), *The Sun Also Rises* (1957), *Cleopatra* (1963), *Hush … Hush, Sweet Charlotte* (1964), *The Sound of Music* (1965), and *M*A*S*H* (1970).

Charlie Chan filmography: *Charlie Chan at Monte Carlo* (1937), *Charlie Chan in Reno* (1939), *Charlie Chan at the Wax Museum* (1940), and *Castle in the Desert* (1942).

French, William E. President of the Apex Insurance and Bonding Company (portrayed by John Eldredge [billed as John Eldridge] in his last of three *Charlie Chan* roles) in *The Sky Dragon* (1949). French's company had insured the shipment of the $250,000 that is stolen during an airplane flight to San Francisco. However, French and his insurance investigator, John Anderson, are partners in a scheme that has Anderson stealing the money during the flight.

When the plane lands and the police arrive to check everyone, Anderson, who is known to Lt. Ruark, departs the plane with the money hidden in the lining of his overcoat folded over his arm. He exchanges coats with French before they both come inside the plane to get the details of the missing money shipment. French is never searched because he wasn't on the plane when the money was stolen. French is probably the shadowy figure who knocks Jonathon Tibbetts unconscious in the garage of the Orange Blossom Manor wedding chapel and sets the garage afire to destroy all photographic evidence of the wedding between Connie Jackson and Andrew Barrett.

frozen bullet Ingenious bullet made from frozen blood, used by Paul Hamlin (an alias of Chardo the Great) to kill William Bonner during a séance in *Black Magic* (1944). The "bullet" is fired from a spring-loaded gun disguised as a cigar case designed by Hamlin and insulated to keep the bullet from melting prior to its use.

Frye, Dwight (February 22, 1899, Salina, Kansas–November 7, 1943, Holly, California) Small, squirmy, crazy-eyed character actor (real name: Dwight Iliff Fry) who was the originator of several characterizations in the horror film genre. Frye portrays Jessop the butler in *The Black Camel* (1931).

Dwight Frye appeared as the real estate agent-cum-madman Renfield in Tod Browning's *Dracula* (1931) and as Fritz, the sadistic hunchbacked lab assistant, in James Whale's *Frankenstein* (1931). From then on, Frye seemed to be typecast, and often played lunatics or spies in over 60 films, most of which were horror movies. He occasionally returned to the stage in comedies, musicals, and thrillers, such as a stage version of *Dracula.*

Dwight Frye (Everett Collection)

In the early 1940s he worked nights between films and local theater productions as a tool designer for the Lockheed Aircraft Company. An uncanny physical resemblance to the then–Secretary of War Newton D. Baker led to Frye being signed for a substantial role in an upcoming film called *Wilson*, based on the life of U.S. President Woodrow Wilson. However, Frye died of a heart attack on a bus a few days later.

Fu, Princess Ming Lo Central character of a Chinese children's lullaby sung by Charlie Chan in *Charlie Chan in Shanghai* (1935). After playing a game of leap frog on the deck of an ocean liner sailing to Shanghai, a young Chinese girl asks Chan if he would sing the song about Princess Ming Lo Fu.

Although there are several films where Chan dances—*The Red Dragon* (1945) and *Dangerous Money* (1946)—this film is the only time in the entire series that Charlie Chan actually sings. Lyrics are: "Long the journey on the way, but his heart was gay,/ For was he not the Prince both strong and brave,/ But the Princess fair to save./ And he slew the mighty dragon, even cut off his seven heads,/ And in his cave he found the Princess bound to her lowly bed./ Then came they both back to the land of the mighty Emperor Fu Manchu,/ To claim his reward, the dainty hand of lovely Ming Lo Fu."

Fuller, John C. Film editor of nearly 25 films, including *The Jade Mask* (1945).

Fyfe, Robert The actor and ex-husband (portrayed by Victor Varconi) of Shelah Fane in *The Black Camel* (1931). Fyfe is in Honolulu appearing in a play. Because he still has strong feelings for his ex-wife, he sends her flowers and a message for her to call him at the Royal Theater.

Note: The character Robert Fyfe loosely parallels that of Paul Wagner in Charlie Chan in Rio (1941).

G

Gage, Fred The scheming husband (portrayed by Edward Trevor) of Janice Gage in *Charlie Chan's Secret* (1936). Fred Gage murders Allen Colby to prevent Colby from claiming his father's estate (when Allen suddenly returns after an absence of seven years) and to cover forgery in the Colby estate accounts.

If Allen Colby were not dead, the Colby family, Gage, and Warren Phelps (the family lawyer) would now have to account to Colby for all the money that they have spent and misappropriated over the years from Bernard Colby's estate. Gage also tries to murder his mother-in-law, using a rifle mounted in a clock tower that was cleverly rigged to fire at Mrs. Lowell's study window when the clock bell rang at 8:30 P.M.

Gage, Janice Portrayed by Astrid Allwyn, one of two daughters of Henrietta Lowell, and the wife of murderer Fred Gage in *Charlie Chan's Secret* (1936).

Gaines, John Half-owner of a circus (portrayed by Francis Ford in his last of four *Charlie Chan* roles) in *Charlie Chan at the Circus* (1936). Because Gaines needs money to keep the circus afloat, Joe Kinney loans Gaines money in return for a half-interest in the circus.

Gale, June (*, San Francisco, California–November 13, 1996, Los Angeles, California) Stage and screen actress of nearly 25 films, and who portrays the jealous Myra Rhadini in *Charlie Chan at Treasure Island* (1939).

Beginning her career as a dancer, June Gale was part of the dancing Gale Quadruplets, which were actually two sets of twins. The act was popular in vaudeville during the 1920s and made it to Broadway. Gale moved to Los Angeles at age 19 and soon signed with Fox Studios. While touring in a production of *Stage Door*, she met pianist-humorist Oscar Levant (who composed the opera *Carnival* for *Charlie Chan at the Opera* [1936]), married him in 1939, and they remained together until Levant's death in 1972.

During the early 1950s Gale became well-known for her devotion to Levant as she helped him recover from a heart attack and a subsequent addiction to prescription drugs. In 1956 Levant and Gale co-hosted *The Oscar Levant Show* on television in Los Angeles. They were quite popular until they had an on-air disagreement. Gale then received her own show on the same station.

Gallant Lad Racehorse owned by Warren Fenton in *Charlie Chan at the Race Track* (1936). When Fenton purchased the horse, he had to take a mischievous monkey mascot, Lollipop, as part of the deal.

While in the stable area onboard the S.S. *Oceanic*, Charlie Chan notices that Lollipop excites Avalanche when he jumps on the horse's back but has no effect on Gallant Lad. After a small fire that is purposely started on the ship as a distraction, the gambling ring switches the horses. Chan notices that something is wrong when Gallant Lad now acts up when Lollipop is nearby, while Avalanche is calm.

Gallaudet, John (1903, Philadelphia, Pennsylvania–) American character actor who

John Gallaudet

appeared in over 80 movies and two *Charlie Chan* films at Monogram. Gallaudet portrays murderer Jeff Hay in *Shadows Over Chinatown* (1946) and Capt. McNalley in *Docks of New Orleans* (1948).

The son of an Episcopal priest, John Gallaudet began his professional acting career after graduating from Williams College. He appeared on both Broadway and in stock opposite actors ranging from Fred Astaire to Helen Hayes. The slight, thinnish-haired Gallaudet spent several years in the 1930s playing everything from kindhearted doctors to serpent-like crooks. Active in films until the 1950s, Gallaudet was well known and highly regarded throughout the film community for his off-camera vocation as a champion golfer.

Gamble, Professor Thaddeus An alias for "Shaky" Phil Maydorf's brother, Henry Maydorf (who is portrayed by Harvey Clark) in *Charlie Chan's Courage* (1934). Posing as a nature scientist, Gamble, Jerry Delaney, Martin Thorne, and brother "Shaky" Phil are all part of a scheme to steal the Phillimore pearl necklace by having Delaney impersonate the real Madden, who has bought the pearls and is awaiting their delivery.

Note: In Earl Derr Biggers' novel *The Chinese Parrot*, which serves as the basis for *Charlie Chan's Courage* (1934), Professor Gamble and Henry Maydorf are mentioned, but the film credits of *The Chinese Parrot* (1927) in the *American Film Institute Catalog of Motion Pictures Produced in the United States* do not list either character.

Gangor Stage name for circus snake charmer Tom Holt (portrayed by J. Carrol Naish) in *Charlie Chan at the Circus* (1936). *See also* **Holt, Tom**.

Gannett Sinister gangster (portrayed by Stanford [credited as Stan] Jolley in his first of two *Charlie Chan* roles) in *The Chinese Cat* (1944). With fellow gangsters Catlen, Salos, and the twin brothers Carl and Kurt Karzoff, Gannett is part of a jewelry theft and smuggling ring led by Thomas Manning and Webster Deacon.

Garner, Frederick Unseen lawyer visited by Nellie Farrell in *Charlie Chan at the Circus* (1936). In his office in Room 402 in the Arcade Building, Farrell seeks Garner's legal opinion as to her rights in the estate of circus owner Joe Kinney, using Kinney's forged signature on a bogus marriage certificate to take over one-half ownership of the circus.

Garralaga, Martin (1894–June 12, 1981, Woodland Hills, California) Actor (real name: Martin Goralaag) who appeared in over 90 films and portrays the guitar-playing troubadour, Pedro Francisco Lopez, in *The Feathered Serpent* (1948). Garralaga also had a role as John Ross in *Eran Trece* (1931), the Spanish-language remake of *Charlie Chan Carries On* (1931).

Although he was from a mixture of European and Scandinavian ancestry, Garralaga was most effectively cast in Latin American roles. Many of his screen appearances were unbilled, but in 1944 he was awarded co-starring status in a series of *Cisco Kid* westerns produced at Monogram. Duncan Renaldo starred as Cisco, with Garralaga as his comic sidekick Pancho. In 1946 Monogram producer Scott R. Dunlap realigned the *Cisco Kid* series whereby Renaldo remained in the lead but Garralaga's character name changed from picture to picture (and he sometimes even showed up as the villain). Eventually, Garralaga was replaced altogether by Leo Carrillo, who revived the Pancho character. Outside of his many roles in westerns, Garralaga could be seen in many wartime films with foreign settings; he even portrayed a headwaiter in *Casablanca* (1942).

Garrick, John (August 31, 1902, Brighton, England–) British-born stage and screen actor (real name: Reginald Doudy) who appeared in nearly 30 films, usually in the "other man" roles. Garrick portrays Mark Kennaway in *Charlie Chan Carries On* (1931).

Gawthorne, Peter (1884, Queen's County, Ireland–March 17, 1962, London, England) Pompous-looking British stage and screen actor who appeared in almost 60 films, often seen in authoritative military or police roles.

In two *Charlie Chan* roles, Gawthorne portrays an unnamed Scotland Yard inspector in *Behind That Curtain* (1929) and Inspector Duff in *Charlie Chan Carries On* (1931).

Gaye, Gregory (October 10, 1900, St. Petersburg, Russia–1993, California) Character actor, sometimes credited as Gregory Gay, who appeared in over 60 films, often playing aristocrats and Europeans. He portrays the baritone Enrico Barelli in *Charlie Chan at the Opera* (1936), who is murdered by his wife Anita.

Russian-born Gregory Gaye came to the U.S. after the 1917 revolution. He flourished in films of the 1930s, playing a variety of ethnic types. Besides his lone *Charlie Chan* film, Gaye had unbilled roles as an exiled Russian nobleman, Count Brekenski, in *Tovarich* (1937), an indignant German banker in *Casablanca* (1942), and a Latin named Ravez in the 1945 *Sherlock Holmes* film, *Pursuit to Algiers* (1946).

Gayety Theatre San Francisco theater where the follies show, "A Night in Paris" (starring Wanda LaFern), is playing in *The Sky Dragon* (1949).

"Gentleman" Max Jewelry thief (portrayed by Louis Mercier in his second of two *Charlie Chan* roles) who is referred to as "the fastidious one" in *City in Darkness* (1939). Max and Alex break into Petroff's house and wait in the cellar for Petroff to go to bed before attempting to rob the house. While waiting, they find a bottle of cognac (Napoleon brandy) and drink it. Unlike his uncouth partner, who drinks directly from the bottle and spills brandy on himself, Max uses a glass.

George, John (January 21, 1898, Syria–August 25, 1968, Los Angeles, California) Character actor who appeared in almost 30 silent and sound films. George portrays Ali, the head digger who dies when Ahmeti's tomb is opened in *Charlie Chan in Egypt* (1935). George also had an unbilled role in *City in Darkness* (1939).

Gerald, Helen Actress who portrays Ruby, a member of Cole King's variety troupe, in *The Trap* (1947).

Geray, Steven (November 10, 1904, Uzhored, Czechoslovakia [later Uzhgorod, USSR/Ukraine]–December 26, 1973, Hollywood, California) Stage and screen character actor (real name: Stefan Gyergyay) who appeared in nearly 90 films, sometimes billed as Stefan Gyergay. Geray portrays Dr. Retling in *Castle in the Desert* (1942).

Czech actor Steven Geray was for many years a member in good standing of the Hungarian National Theater. He launched his English-speaking film career in Britain in the role of Steve Sarel in *Dance Band* (1935) and then moved to the U.S. in 1941. His roles ranged from sinister to sympathetic, from "A" productions like *Gilda* (1946), as the bartender Uncle Pio, to potboilers like *El Paso* (1949). He flourished during the war years, attracting critical praise for his portrayal of Dirk Stroeve in *The Moon and Sixpence* (1942), and enjoyed top billing portraying Henri Cassin in *So Dark the Night* (1946).

Many of Geray's film appearances in the 1950s were unbilled, and when he *was* given screen credit, it was usually as *Steve* Geray. Geray's busy career in film and television continued into the 1960s, when he appeared in such television series as *Perry Mason*, *The Untouchables*, and *I Dream of Jeannie*.

Gertie Captain Kane's talking parrot in *Dead Men Tell* (1941). Having learned phrases by hearing Captain Kane speak them, two phrases often repeated by Gertie are: "You die as you left me to die" and "Help, let me out of here."

Girard 3232 Telephone number of Hilary Galt's office in *Behind That Curtain* (1929).

"Give My Regards to Broadway" Song, whose lyrics and music were written by George M. Cohan in 1904, that is used as the title song for *Charlie Chan on Broadway* (1937).

Gleason, Professor Genealogist (portrayed by Lucien Littlefield) who apparently dies from poison of tagara weed in a drink given him by Lucy Manderley in *Castle in the Desert* (1942). Paul Manderley bribes Dr. Retling and Walter Hartford to quietly take Gleason's body to the Mojave Wells Hotel in the town closest to the castle and make it look as if he died there of a heart attack.

Gleason is one of two persons hired by Dr. Retling and the Hartfords (Brenda and Walter) to pretend having been poisoned by Lucy. It's part of a scheme to convince her wealthy husband that Lucy is insane, and to turn the control of a $20 million estate over to Walter Hartford via power of attorney and leave quietly with his wife.

Glenn, Glen Sound recording engineer for nearly 70 films, including *Charlie Chan in the Secret Service* (1944).

The Globe San Francisco newspaper for which Dick Williams works as a reporter in *Charlie Chan's Secret* (1936).

Godfrey, Inspector Government agent (portrayed by Henry Hall) who is an acquaintance of Charlie Chan in *The Jade Mask* (1945). When Mr. Harper is murdered, he tells Chan that the government wants him on the case and that Harper's house is out of Godfrey's jurisdiction.

Godley, R.J. American diplomat (portrayed by Addison Richards in his first of two *Charlie Chan* roles) in *Charlie Chan in Panama* (1940). Responding to undercover investigations by Charlie Chan revealing that the U.S. Navy's Pacific Fleet may be sabotaged when it passes through the canal, Godley comes to Panama. Godley suspects that the plot's mastermind, an enemy agent known as Reiner, is now in Panama. Before Godley can tell Chan anything, however, he is killed by smoking a poisoned cigarette.

***The Golden Eye* (1948)** The fifteenth *Charlie Chan* film produced by Monogram Pictures Corporation.

Alternate Titles: *Charlie Chan in the Golden Eye* and *Charlie Chan and the Golden Eye*. Working Title: *The Mystery of the Golden Eye*. Source: based on the character "Charlie Chan" created by Earl Derr Biggers. Original Copyright: Monogram Pictures Corporation, August 22, 1948; LP1857. Copyright Renewed: October 2, 1975; R615165. PCA Certificate Number: 13185. Production: mid–April to late April, 1948. Release Date: August 29, 1948. Sound: Western Electric Recording. Film: b&w; 6,224 feet. Running Time: 69 minutes.

Producer: James S. Burkett. Director: William Beaudine. Assistant Director: Wesley Barry. Original Screenplay: W. Scott Darling. Photography: William Sickner. Camera Operator: John Martin.* Stills: Al St. Hilaire.* Art Director: Dave Milton. Supervising Film Editor: Otho Lovering. Editor: Ace Herman. Set Decoration: Raymond Boltz, Jr.* Musical Director: Edward J. Kay. Recordist: Franklin Hansen. Sound: John Kean.* Makeup: Webb Overlander.* Hair Stylist: Lela Chambers.* Production Supervisor: Allen K. Wood. Screenplay Supervisor: Jules Levy.* Grip: Grant Tucker.*

Cast

Roland Winters	*as*	Charlie Chan
Wanda McKay		Evelyn Manning
Mantan Moreland		Birmingham Brown
Victor Sen Young		Tommy Chan
Bruce Kellogg		Talbot Bartlett
Tim Ryan		Lt. Mike Ruark
Evelyn Brent		Sister Teresa
Ralph Dunn		Mr. Driscoll
Lois Austin		Mrs. Margaret Driscoll
Forrest Taylor		Manning
Lee "Lasses" White		Pete
Lee Tung Foo*		Wong Fat
Michael Gaddis*		Pursuer
Sam Flint*		Dr. Groves
Geraldine Cobb*		Girl in riding clothes
Mary Ann Hawkins,* Aileen Babs Cox*		Bathing girls
Edmund Cobb,* John Merton*		Miners
Jack Gargan*		Voice from darkness

Plot Summary: In San Francisco's Chinatown, Arizona mine owner Manning, fearing that someone is trying to kill him, seeks help from Charlie Chan. Manning suggests that

**Unbilled.*

Chan pose as a tourist and check into the Lazy Y Dude Ranch near his Golden Eye mine. Chan's son Tommy and chauffeur Birmingham Brown accompany Chan to the ranch in Arizona. When they arrive, Chan encounters San Francisco policeman Lt. Mike Ruark working undercover for the government, posing as playboy Vince O'Brien.

After Chan admits that their cases may be related, Lt. Ruark tells Chan that Manning has just fallen down a mine shaft and has a possible skull fracture. Ruark also informs Chan that after many years of low output, the Golden Eye Mine has recently become one of the richest in the country. Chan goes to the Manning home posing as a dealer in Oriental curios and meets Manning's daughter Evelyn, mine superintendent Driscoll, his wife, and local gold assayer Talbot Bartlett. Chan sees Manning, who is unconscious, his head completely swathed in bandages. Because of his condition, the doctor recommends that Manning receive around-the-clock nursing care.

When back at the ranch, Chan runs into Bartlett, who had earlier recognized Charlie as the famous Chinese detective and reminded Chan that he played first base on Number One son Lee's high school baseball team. Bartlett tells Chan that he is assaying some of the gold coming from the Golden Eye Mine. Evelyn, who is unaware of the mine's recent increase in productivity, tells Bartlett that the nurse, Sister Teresa (whom Driscoll has hired from the nearby mission), is strange and uncommunicative.

Pete, an old-time prospector, has gained access to one of the mine's passages through a trap door in his shack at Hay Canyon. He brings a sample of ore for assaying and Bartlett tells him it is worthless but knows it came from the mine. Chan then arranges for Pete to take him into the mine through the trapdoor, but when Chan, Tommy, and Birmingham show up, Pete is not there. However, they find the trap door, enter the mine, and eventually find Pete's body in one of the mine's passages.

When they meet later, Lt. Ruark tells Chan that he has learned that Driscoll has a criminal record, and Chan discovers that Manning's nurse is a fake. Chan also discovers that Driscoll has been smuggling gold from Mexico (where the price is much lower) and passing it off at a much higher value in Arizona. Consequently, Driscoll wants Manning and everyone else out of the way so that his operation can continue.

When Chan, Tommy, and Birmingham return to the mine, Chan finds another dead body—but with a bandaged head. It is Manning. They all return to the Manning house, and when Chan begins to remove the bandages from the patient's head, Sister Teresa rushes in, gun drawn, just as Chan reveals the patient to be Mrs. Driscoll. Chan has to tell Evelyn that her father is dead and was found in the mine. Driscoll then enters the room and draws his gun, but Tommy outsmarts him and tells his father that he has received a phone call from the Mexican police informing him that they have stopped the next shipment of gold at the border. Driscoll tries to escape but is shot dead by Bartlett, who Chan captures and reveals to be the brains behind the entire operation.

Note: Copyright records list George L. Spaulding as Dr. Groves, but the role was played by Sam Flint.

Golden Eye Mine Arizona gold mine owned by Mr. Manning in *The Golden Eye* (1948). Lt. Ruark, working undercover as playboy Vince O'Brien, is investigating the mine's sudden large output of gold after years of low returns.

The large gold output from the mine is due to a smuggling scheme headed by the mine's manager, Mr. Driscoll, and is unknown to Mr. Manning or his daughter Evelyn. Gold is mined in Mexico, where it is worth $7 an ounce, and is then smuggled to the Golden Eye in the U.S., where it is now worth $35 an ounce.

Gonzales, Capt. Head of the Mexican border patrol who is a friend of Lt. Ruark in *The Golden Eye* (1948). When Charlie Chan and Lt. Ruark uncover the details of a gold smuggling operation in Mexico with ties to the Golden Eye Mine in Arizona, Ruark telephones Capt. Gonzales to be on the lookout for Driscoll's men crossing the border with smuggled gold.

Gonzales, Ramon Alias used by Panama cabaret owner Emil Manolo, a confederate of Reiner in *Charlie Chan in Panama* (1940). Manolo disguises himself as a worker and delivers nitroglycerin (disguised as bottled water) to the Miraflores Power Control Station. There he activates a timer connected to a bomb that is set to explode at 10 o'clock. When Manolo is killed by Reiner (a.k.a. Miss Jennie Finch), Charlie Chan finds a power station pass for Ramon Gonzales.

Gonzalez, Capt. Juan The police chief of San Pablo (portrayed by George J. Lewis in his last of three *Charlie Chan* roles) in *The Feathered Serpent* (1948). Gonzalez is in charge of investigating the murder of Professor Scott.

Goodwin, Harold R. (December 1, 1902, Peoria, Illinois–July 12, 1987) Character actor who appeared in almost 120 silent and sound films. In two *Charlie Chan* roles, Goodwin portrays a military policeman (unbilled) in *Charlie Chan in Panama* (1940) and the radio engineer, Edwards, in *Charlie Chan at the Wax Museum* (1940).

Harold Goodwin started performing as a child in Los Angeles community theater and appeared in his first film, *The Little Orphan*, in 1915. Though initially cast as underfed waifs, Goodwin matured into an athletic leading man, working in roles of varying size and importance at Fox, Universal, and other studios during the 1920s. He became a close pal and baseball buddy of comedian Buster Keaton while playing Jeff, a B.M.O.C. villain, in Keaton's film, *College* (1927).

Even when Goodwin dropped into small character roles in the 1930s, Keaton saw to it that Goodwin was cast in substantial secondary parts in Buster's Educational Studios two-reelers of the 1930s. In between acting assignments, Goodwin worked as a dialogue director. When a British actor named Harold Goodwin rose to prominence in the 1940s and 1950s, the American Harold Goodwin then changed the spelling of his first name to Herold to avoid confusion.

C. Henry Gordon

Gordon, C. Henry (June 17, 1883, New York, New York–December 3, 1940, Los Angeles, California) American stage and screen actor (real name: Henry Racke) who appeared in almost 70 films. Gordon has roles in five *Charlie Chan* films produced by Fox and Twentieth Century–Fox, most of them villainous. Gordon portrays John Ross (an alias for Jim Everhard) in *Charlie Chan Carries On* (1931); Van Horn in *The Black Camel* (1931); Arthur Hughes in *Charlie Chan at the Olympics* (1937); Romaine, the prefect of police, in *City in Darkness* (1939); and Dr. Cream in *Charlie Chan at the Wax Museum* (1940).

Gordon, Dick Actor who portrays phony psychic William Bonner in *Black Magic* (1944).

Gordon, Mary (May 16, 1882, Glasgow, Scotland–August 23, 1963, Pasadena, California) Short, plump, kind-faced character actress (real name: Mary Gilmour) who appeared in almost 170 silent and sound films. In two *Charlie Chan* roles, Gordon portrays Mrs. MacMasters in *The Black Camel* (1931) and Mrs. Conover in *Shadows Over Chinatown* (1946). Gordon is best remembered for

Mary Gordon

her top-knotted silver hair, dangling earrings, and her role as Mrs. Hudson, the housekeeper at 221B Baker Street, opposite Basil Rathbone in both the *Sherlock Holmes* films of the 1930s and 1940s.

Gordon, Professor Bogus archeologist and alias used by Jim Eberhardt (portrayed by Leo G. Carroll in his second of two *Charlie Chan* roles) in *Charlie Chan's Murder Cruise* (1940).

Charlie Chan observes Gordon and Dick Kenyon playing mah-jongg with only two persons. Gordon tells Chan that the two-player game is an American innovation and had undergone many changes since it was introduced during the Han Dynasty, which Gordon claims was the "Golden Era of southern China." However, Chan knows better and strongly suspects that Gordon is a fraud, telling son Jimmy at the film's conclusion that China's "Golden Era" was during the Shang Dynasty in northern China. *See also* **Eberhardt, Jim.**

Note: The character of Professor Gordon loosely parallels that of John Ross in *Charlie Chan Carries On* (1931).

Gordon, Roy (1895–October 12, 1978, Los Angeles, California) Character actor and drama coach who appeared in nearly 70 films, often as a college dean, banker, or military officer. Gordon portrays bank president Walter Fletcher in *The Shanghai Cobra* (1945).

Gore, Chester Art director associate for *Charlie Chan at the Olympics* (1937) and art director (with Richard Day) for both *Charlie Chan in Panama* (1940) and *Charlie Chan's Murder Cruise* (1940).

Gorton, Jerry American house guest (portrayed by Walter Johnson) of Geoffrey Richmond at the time of the "Midnight Stable Murder" in *Charlie Chan in London* (1934). Gorton is romantically attracted to Lady Mary Bristol even though she is engaged to marry Geoffrey Richmond.

Grady, Inspector Fictitious name given by Ralph Brett to the information operator when he requests the address of telephone number Harding 2535 in *The Scarlet Clue* (1945). Brett always dials this number to contact his unknown espionage ring superior. The operator tells Brett that the location of the telephone is in Room 211 of the Algard Building.

Graham, Stella Wife (portrayed by Dorothy Granger in her first of two *Charlie Chan* appearances) of Lloyd Archer in *The Jade Mask* (1945). When in vaudeville with her husband, Graham was a strong woman and master puppeteer. Mr. Harper, an absent-minded and paranoid inventor, had Graham assist him with puppets for an idea he had of developing a toy robot for children. Graham helps her husband, who murders five people, to make some of the murdered people appear when Graham and Archer need alibis. However, Archer tries to kill his wife by telling her how to gain entrance to Harper's secret room but *not* telling her that the desk is a death trap when opened.

Grail, Mr. The shady undertaker of the AAA Funeral Parlor (portrayed by Milton Parsons in his last of four *Charlie Chan* roles) in *The Shanghai Chest* (1948). Being paid by the surviving brother, Joseph Pindello, Grail secretly reburies the body of Tony Pindello (who was executed for murder and buried in a San Francisco city cemetery). Joseph Pindello himself was in prison at the time of his brother's death six months earlier and was unable to give him a proper burial.

Granger, Dorothy (November 21, 1914, New London, Ohio–January 4, 1995, Los Angeles, California) Actress who appeared in almost 90 films, and a charter member of the Screen Actors Guild when it was founded in 1933. In two *Charlie Chan* roles, Granger portrays Stella Graham in *The Jade Mask* (1945) and Joan Mercer in *Shadows Over Chinatown* (1946).

A beauty contest winner at age 13, Dorothy Granger went on to perform in vaudeville with her large and talented family. Granger made her first film appearance in *Words and Music* in 1929, and the following year landed a contract with comedy producer Hal Roach, working with such masters as Harry Langdon, Laurel and Hardy, and Charlie Chase.

During her long association with two-reelers, she appeared with the likes of W.C. Fields (in *The Dentist*, 1932), The Three Stooges (in *Punch Drunks*, 1934), Walter Catlett, Edgar Kennedy, and Hugh Herbert among others. Granger is perhaps most fondly remembered for her appearances in RKO's long-running Leon Errol short-subject series (1935–51) in which she was usually cast as Errol's highly suspicious wife.

She retired from films in 1963 and kept busy by helping her husband manage a successful Los Angeles upholstery store. Dorothy Granger made her last public appearance in 1993 at the Screen Actors Guild's fiftieth anniversary celebration.

granny knot Style of knot tied like a square knot but with its ends crossed the wrong way. George "Doc" Brandt observes that a silk cord from a bathrobe tied in a granny knot was used to strangle and kill Cole King's girlfriend, Marcia, in *The Trap* (1947).

Granville Insurance Company Insurance company for which Stuart Salisbury, alias Thomas Gregory, works as a private investigator in *Charlie Chan at Treasure Island* (1939). Salisbury is investigating three recent suicides and Paul Essex's death because they were all clients of the mystic Dr. Zodiac.

Gravelle Opera star (portrayed by Boris Karloff) who suffers from amnesia for years after being intentionally locked in a dressing room during a Chicago opera house fire in *Charlie Chan at the Opera* (1936). For years he is a patient at the Rockland State Sanitarium, often playing the piano and singing opera. Gravelle is unaware of his identity until he sees a picture of his wife, Mme. Lilli Rochelle, in a newspaper story about an upcoming opera performance in Los Angeles. He then escapes from the hospital by tying up an attendant and putting on his uniform.

Traveling to Los Angeles and evading police, he enters the opera house and confronts baritone Enrico Barelli, who had helped Mme. Rochelle lock him in the dressing room during the fire years ago. Realizing that the opera to be performed is *Carnival*, which Gravelle considers his greatest triumph, he ties up Barelli, takes his costume, and appears in the role of Mephisto. For the remainder of the film, Gravelle evades the police while being suspected of the murders of Enrico Barelli and Mme. Rochelle. He also finally sees his long-lost daughter, who doesn't recognize him.

When Gravelle tries to help his daughter remember him by playing a song on the piano he always played for her as a child, she faints. Charlie Chan discovers both Gravelle and his daughter, and convinces him to perform his aria one more time as a trap to catch the real murderer, Mme. Barelli.

Gray, Pamela Portrayed by Drue Leyton in her second of three *Charlie Chan* roles, the sister of condemned murderer Paul Gray in *Charlie Chan in London* (1934). She and her fiancé Neil Howard plead with Charlie Chan to help prove that her brother (who is sentenced to hang in three days) did not kill Capt. Hamilton.

Gray, Paul The brother (portrayed by Douglas Walton) of Pamela Gray in *Charlie Chan in London* (1934). Paul is convicted of murdering

Capt. Hamilton and is sentenced to hang. At the time of the murder, Paul was Geoffrey Richmond's hunt secretary. He is later freed when Charlie Chan exposes Geoffrey Richmond as the real murderer.

Gray, Stanley Ex-convict who is convicted of robbing the Rodin Bank (based on his fingerprints being found at the crime scene) but who contends that he was never in that bank, in *Dark Alibi* (1946). After his conviction, Gray died in the prison's psycho ward. Gray, Steven Briggs, and Thomas Harley were each framed in an identical manner—no money was recovered, all three had a prior prison record, and each man protested his innocence, claiming he was never in the bank that was robbed.

"Great happiness follows great pain" Translation of the Chinese message on a card in *Charlie Chan at Treasure Island* (1939). As a test of Eve Cairo's mind reading ability, Charlie Chan hands Fred Rhadini (a.k.a. The Great Rhadini) a card with Chinese writing and asks if Eve can read Rhadini's mind. Not being able to read Chinese, Rhadini then asks Charlie to concentrate on the English translation, and Eve is then able to read the Chinese message.

The Great Rashid Phony Hindu fakir (portrayed by Shemp Howard) who is rounded up along with other "Ali Baba" look-alikes by the New York police in *Murder Over New York* (1940). At the police lineup, the fakir calls himself the "Grand Lama of the Sacred Cult of Psychic Believers," but he is really "Shorty" McCoy, also known as "Canarsie Kid," who (the police tell Charlie Chan) makes a living as a panhandler by feeding suckers phony religion.

Green, Harriet Woman (portrayed by Geraldine Wall) who has an affair with William Bonner and is being blackmailed by him in *Black Magic* (1944).

Greenwood, Al Set director for *Charlie Chan in the Secret Service* (1944) and *Black Magic* (1944).

Gregory, Thomas Alias of Stuart Salisbury, who poses as an insurance actuary in *Charlie Chan at Treasure Island* (1939). *See also* **Salisbury, Stuart**.

Grennock Steve McBirney's bodyguard (portrayed by Edward Marr) who helps McBirney escape from the courthouse in *Charlie Chan at the Wax Museum* (1940). Grennock convinces the crime museum's night watchman, Willie Fern, that he is a prison warden and directs Willie to execute the wax dummy seated in the museum's electric chair exhibit as part of a plan to murder Charlie Chan.

Grey, Evelyn The seductive 24-year-old London-born former model (portrayed by Virginia Field) in *Charlie Chan at Monte Carlo* (1937). As noted by Inspector Jules Joubert, Grey is a former mannequin whose lavish lifestyle is supported by an invisible income. She makes Gordon Chase think she is attracted to him but only uses him to gain sensitive information about his employer's financial dealings, which she passes on to Paul Savarin.

Grey, Sir Lionel Former chief of Scotland Yard who has mysteriously dropped dead in the Wall Street office of Barry Kirk in *Charlie Chan's Chance* (1932). At his office, Kirk informs Charlie Chan that, before his death, Grey was about to solve a big murder case and had invited several guests to a party to be held at Kirk's apartment.

Grey had left the party to take a phone call in Kirk's office and then died mysteriously. The doctor assures the group that Grey died of a heart attack, but Chan notices a dead cat in the room and surmises that the same substance killed them both and that Grey was indeed murdered.

Note: The character Sir Lionel Grey loosely parallels that of Hugh Drake in *Murder Over New York* (1940).

Griffies, Ethel (April 26, 1878, Sheffield, Yorkshire, England–September 9, 1975, London, England) Stage and screen actress (real name: Ethel Woods) who appeared in over 60 films. In two *Charlie Chan* roles, Griffies portrays Patience Nodbury in *Dead Men Tell* (1941) and Mme. Saturnia (a.k.a. Lily) in *Castle in the Desert* (1942).

Daughter of actor-manager Samuel Rupert Woods and actress Lillie Roberts, Ethyl Griffies began her own stage career at the age of three. She made her first Broadway appearance in *Havoc* (1924) at the age of 46. She made her movie debut by repeating her stage role of Adela Heythord in *Old English* (1930). Habitually cast as a crotchety old lady with the proverbial heart of gold, Griffies alternated between bits and prominently featured roles for the next 35 years. Her larger parts included Grace Poole in both the 1935 and 1944 versions of *Jane Eyre*, and the abusive matron, Mrs. Bundy, in Hitchcock's *The Birds* (1963).

On occasion, Griffies would leave film work to concentrate on the stage. She made her last Broadway appearance in 1967, at which time she was England's oldest working actress. Presumably at the invitation of fellow Briton Arthur Treacher, Ethel Griffies was a frequent guest on television's *Merv Griffin Show* in the late 1960s and never failed to bring down the house with her wickedly witty comments on her 80 years in show business.

Grock Shady gangster (portrayed by Douglas Fowley in his last of three *Charlie Chan* roles) in *Docks of New Orleans* (1948).

On orders of Pereaux, Grock attempts to kidnap Simon Lafontaine in front of Charlie Chan's house after Lafontaine seeks Chan's help. Grock poses as Lafontaine's driver, but when Tommy and Birmingham find the real driver unconscious in the alley next to Chan's house, Grock speeds away (without Lafontaine) before he can be caught.

Grosser, Dr. Rudolph Viennese scientist (portrayed by Lionel Royce) who is an expert on tropical diseases and plagues in *Charlie Chan in Panama* (1940). In Panama City, Grosser is conducting secret experiments on rats, 20 of which have been intentionally infected with bubonic plague. Achmed Halide, above whose tobacco shop Grosser has his makeshift laboratory, knows of these illegal experiments, eventually panics, steals the rats, and destroys them.

Grossman, Eugene Sound engineer for *Charlie Chan in Paris* (1935).

Gung, Li Alan Raleigh's former houseboy (portrayed by Edward Peil, Sr.) in *Charlie Chan's Chance* (1932). When Charlie Chan goes a second time to Li Gung's home, Gung tries to kill him with a cleverly designed hidden gun. But a black cat upsets the setup and the gun shoots and kills Gung instead.

Note: The character Li Gung loosely parallels that of Ramullah in *Murder Over New York* (1940).

H

Hajos, Karl Music director and composer for over 25 films. He served as music director for *Charlie Chan in the Secret Service* (1944). Hajos was nominated for two Academy Awards in the Best Music, Scoring of a Dramatic or Comedy Picture category for *Summer Storm* (1944) and *The Man Who Walked Alone* (1945).

Hale, Jonathan, Jr. (March 21, 1891, Ontario, Canada–February 28, 1966, Woodland Hills California) Actor (real name: Jonathan Hatley) who appeared in over 190 films, including three *Charlie Chan* entries. Hale portrays estate lawyer Warren T. Phelps in *Charlie Chan's Secret* (1936), racehorse owner Warren Fenton in *Charlie Chan at the Race Track* (1936), and Hopkins in *Charlie Chan at the Olympics* (1937). Hale's most noticed film role was probably that of Dagwood Bumstead's boss, J.C. Dithers, in 16 *Blondie* films that were made between 1938 and 1946.

Halide, Achmed An Egyptian (portrayed by Frank Puglia) who owns a tobacco shop across the street from Fu Yuen (an alias employed by Charlie Chan) in *Charlie Chan in Panama* (1940). Besides selling tobacco, he also sells information about the comings and goings of foreign agents to the undercover British agent Cliveden Compton.

Hall, Charles Assistant director (unbilled) for both *Charlie Chan at Treasure Island* (1939) and *City in Darkness* (1939).

Hall, David Art director for *Charlie Chan in Reno* (1939).

Hall, Diane Radio actress (portrayed by Helen Devereaux) whose car was stolen for a few hours by station manager Ralph Brett in *The Scarlet Clue* (1945). Diane Hall and her roommate, Gloria Bayne, are both radio actresses at the Cosmo Radio Center.

Hall, Henry Character actor who appeared in almost 90 films and portrays Police Inspector Godfrey in *The Jade Mask* (1945).

Hall, Jon (February 23, 1913, Fresno, California–December 13, 1979) Athletic American actor (real name: Charles Hall Loeher) who appeared in almost 50 films, sometimes credited as Lloyd Crane or Charles Locher. Hall portrays Philip Nash (credited as Charles Locher) in *Charlie Chan in Shanghai* (1935).

Jon Hall is perhaps most recognized for his role as Dr. Tom Reynolds (a.k.a. "Ramar") in the *Ramar of the Jungle* television series from 1952 to 1954. He retired from films to run a photography business as an accomplished manufacturer of photographic equipment, making an excellent living renting out his underwater cameras to various Hollywood producers. To end the weakness and suffering he experienced due to cancer of the bladder, he committed suicide by shooting himself.

Jon Hall was billed as Charles Locher early in his career.

Hallett, Captain Honolulu policeman (portrayed by Francis Ford in his first of four *Charlie Chan* roles) in *Charlie Chan's Greatest Case* (1933). At the police station, Capt. Hallett receives the report of Dan Winterslip's murder and calls Charlie Chan at home to investigate.

Halton, Charles (March 16, 1876, Washington D.C.–April 16, 1959, Los Angeles, California) Stage and screen character actor who appeared in nearly 140 silent and sound films. Halton portrays Stella Essex's uncle, Mr. Redley, in *Charlie Chan at Treasure Island* (1939).

American actor Charles Halton was forced to quit school at age 14 to help support his family. When his boss learned that the young Halton was interested in the arts, he financed the boy's training at the New York Academy of Dramatic Arts. For the next three decades, Halton appeared in every aspect of "live" performing. Once in Hollywood, his rimless spectacles and snapping-turtle features enabled him to play innumerable "nemesis" roles, such as a grasping attorney, a rent-increasing landlord, or a dictatorial office manager.

Halton was also capable of portraying believable human beings—with the help of the right director, like Ernst Lubitsch, who cast Halton as Dobosh, the long-suffered Polish stage manager, in *To Be or Not to Be* (1942). Alfred Hitchcock also elicited a similar portrayal from Halton, casting him as Mr. Deever, the small-town court clerk who reveals that Robert Montgomery and Carole Lombard are not legally married, in *Mr. and Mrs. Smith* (1941). After completing his last film in 1956, Halton retired and died three years later of hepatitis.

Hamilton, Capt. Air force pilot, stationed at the Farnwell Aerodrome, who was supposedly murdered by Paul Gray in the stables at Geoffrey Richmond's country house in *Charlie Chan in London* (1934). Hamilton had become interested in fox hunting and was invited by Richmond to his country house for the weekend. He was reported to be a loner who liked to tinker and invent things, and was murdered by Richmond when Richmond stole the plans for Hamilton's invention of a method for silencing war planes.

Hamilton, John R. (January 16, 1887, Shippensburg, Pennsylvania–October 15, 1958, Glendale, California) Chubby stage and screen character actor who appeared in over 200 films and worked in Broadway and touring theatrical companies for many years prior to his 1930 film debut. Hamilton portrays the unbilled San Francisco–bound lawyer, Mr. Pronnet, in *Shadows Over Chinatown* (1946). Hamilton also portrays Philip Benton in *Mr. Moto's Gamble* (1938), a reworked version of the never-completed *Charlie Chan at the Ringside*.

Hamilton is perhaps best known for his role of Perry White, editor of the *Daily Planet*, in the television series *Adventures of Superman* (1952–57) and a number of movies made from the *Superman* series.

Hamilton Laboratory Research laboratory located on the tenth floor of the Cosmo Radio Center building in *The Scarlet Clue* (1945). The laboratory is engaged in secret radar and radio work for the U.S. government, and their inventions and use of radar allow fighter planes to hunt down enemy planes at night without seeing them. Because an enemy espionage ring has been trying to steal the radar secrets from the laboratory, Charlie Chan has an undercover government investigator pose as a cleaning woman to keep a watch on who comes and goes from the laboratory.

Hamlin, Paul Alias used by Chardo the Great (portrayed by Frank Jaquet) in *Black Magic* (1944). For reasons not explained in the movie, Hamlin is being blackmailed by William Bonner, who is unaware of Hamlin's true identity. *See also* **Chardo the Great**.

Hammond, Virginia (1893–April 6, 1972, Washington, D.C.) Actress who appeared in over 30 silent and sound films and portrays Mrs. Jordan in *Charlie Chan's Courage* (1934).

Han Dynasty Chinese dynasty which ruled southern China (202 B.C.–A.D. 220) and brought the Chinese empire to a peak of power, wealth, and cultural significance. Two of the great Chinese inventions, paper and porcelain, date from Han times. Even today, the ethnic Chinese call themselves Han to distinguish themselves from the Manchus and other minorities in China.

In *Charlie Chan's Murder Cruise* (1940), phony archeologist Professor Gordon tells Charlie Chan that the game of mah-jongg has undergone many changes since it was introduced during the Han Dynasty, which Gordon claims was the "Golden Era of southern China." Chan then remarks that he was under the impression that mah-jongg was from an earlier dynasty.

At the movie's conclusion, Chan gives Number two son Jimmy a history lesson about his ancient ancestors, stating that the "Golden Era" was during the Shang Dynasty of north China. This corrects information that Professor Gordon told Chan earlier. *See also* **mah-jongg; Shang Dynasty**.

Hannah, Habib Police representative of the Persian government (portrayed by Jamiel Hasson) who accompanies Sir Frederic Bruce to see Col. John Beetham in *Behind That Curtain* (1929).

Hannigan, Mike Gangster (portrayed by Richard Lane) who is wanted by the San Francisco police for murder and poses as Detective Arnold in *Charlie Chan in Honolulu* (1938). Hannigan has murdered the real Detective Arnold in Shanghai, where his body was pulled from the Yangtze River. Now posing as Arnold, Hannigan is on the *Susan B. Jennings* with fellow murderer Johnny

McCoy under the guise of extraditing McCoy to the United States. However, Charlie Chan has already recognized Hannigan from police wanted posters received from San Francisco and knows he is an impostor.

Harding 2535 Telephone number Ralph Brett asks the information operator the address for in *The Scarlet Clue* (1945). On the telephone, Brett poses as fictitious police inspector Grady from Precinct Station 27 to inquire the location of the number he always dials to contact his unknown espionage-ring superior. The operator tells Brett that the location of the telephone is Room 211 of the Algard Building.

Hare, Lumsden (April 27, 1875, Cashel, Ireland–August 28, 1964, Hollywood, California) Character actor who appeared in over 110 silent and sound films, sometimes credited as F. Lumsden Hare or Francis Lumsden Hare. He portrays Inspector Hanley in *Charlie Chan Carries On* (1931).

"HARLEY DENIES GUILT" Newspaper headline of the *Star Dispatch* about the trial of Thomas Harley in *Dark Alibi* (1946). Harley is convicted of bank robbery and the murder of a bank guard at the Citizen's State Bank but protests his innocence, claiming he was never in the bank.

Harley, June A boarder (portrayed by Teala Loring) at the Foss Family Hotel (along with her father, ex-convict Thomas Harley) in *Dark Alibi* (1946). June spends most of the movie trying to help Charlie Chan prove her father innocent of bank robbery and murder. After her father is shown to be innocent, both June and public defender Anthony R. Morgan tell Charlie Chan that they plan to be married.

Harley, Thomas Father of June Harley and an ex-convict (portrayed by Edward Earle in his second of two *Charlie Chan* roles) in *Dark Alibi* (1946). Harley, who has lived at the Foss Family Hotel for 15 years, is convicted and sentenced to die for robbing the Citizen's State Bank and murdering a bank guard. However, he was framed by an elaborate scheme whereby his forged fingerprints were left at the crime scene.

Upon his arrest at the Foss Family Hotel, Harley claims to have been locked in the Carey Theatrical Warehouse for four hours. To prove his story, he shows the policemen a typed note from Dave Wyatt, a man Harley knew in prison 20 years ago, asking to meet him there. The police discount the note, telling Harley that Wyatt has been dead for eight years. Uncovering the method by which Harley's fingerprints were forged and left at the crime scene, Charlie Chan saves Harley just hours before he is to be executed.

Harmon, John Bald, hook-nosed character actor of screen and television who appeared in 75 films, often as shifty-eyed gangsters, rural law enforcement officials, or henpecked husbands. Harmon portrays knife thrower/entertainer Freddie Kirk, who Charlie Chan refers to as the "little showman," in *Dangerous Money* (1946). Besides films, Harmon made multiple appearances on various television series, such as *The Big Valley* (9), *Perry Mason* (8), *The Twilight Zone* (2), *Wanted: Dead or Alive* (3), *Star Trek* (2), *The Untouchables* (4), and *Wagon Train* (2), among others.

Harper, Louise Mr. Harper's sister (portrayed by Edith Evanson) who is forced to wear the uniform of a housekeeper in *The Jade Mask* (1945).

Harper, Mr. Absent-minded and paranoid inventor (portrayed by Frank Reicher in his second of two *Charlie Chan* roles) in *The Jade Mask* (1945). Harper doesn't trust his relatives or his servants, and has developed a gas process that hardens wood to the toughness and durability of metal in two hours, which is of interest to the U.S. government. Harper is murdered by stepson Lloyd Archer in his gas lab with a poison dart.

Harrigan, Nedda (1899–April 1, 1989, New York, New York) Actress who portrays Mme.

Anita Barelli in *Charlie Chan at the Opera* (1936).

Harris San Francisco policeman (portrayed by William Bailey) in *Charlie Chan's Secret* (1936). Harris' commanding officer is Inspector Morton.

Harris, Bradford Vice president of the Sixth National Bank (portrayed by Arthur Loft in his second of two *Charlie Chan* roles) in *The Shanghai Cobra* (1945). The name Harris is actually an alias used by Special Agent Hume, the leader of a gang who plans to steal radium belonging to the U.S. government that is stored in a vault in his bank. Using cobra venom as his weapon, Harris murders three bank employees and Larkin, an undercover policeman. *See also* **Hume, Special Agent.**

Hartford, Brenda The wife (portrayed by Arleen Whelan) of Manderley lawyer Walter Hartford in *Castle in the Desert* (1942).

Hartford, Walter Paul Manderley's lawyer and Brenda Hartford's husband (portrayed by Edmund MacDonald) in *Castle in the Desert* (1942). Hartford and Dr. Retling hire both Professor Gleason and Arthur Fletcher to pretend to have been poisoned by Manderley's wife, Lucy, in order to convince Manderley that Lucy is insane and that Manderley should sign the control of a $20 million estate over to Walter via power of attorney.

To get Charlie Chan to be a witness to the upcoming (apparent) poisonings at the Manderley Castle, Hartford sends Chan a fake note from Lucy Manderley requesting Chan to come to the castle. Hartford is murdered by Watson King to keep Hartford from telling Chan that Cesare Borgia (alias Watson King) is still alive.

Harvey, Paul (September 10, 1884, Illinois–December 14, 1955, Hollywood, California) Stage and screen character actor who appeared in almost 170 films, often as a hot-tempered executive or kindly father. In two *Charlie Chan* roles, Harvey portrays millionaire J.P. Madden in *Charlie Chan's Courage* (1934) and Honolulu police inspector Rawlins in *Charlie Chan in Honolulu* (1938).

Paul Harvey had appeared in a variety of character roles, ranging from the Sheik Mulhulla in *Kid Millions* (1934) to the gangster Crawford in *Alibi Ike* (1935) before settling into his particular niche as one of filmdom's favorite blowhard executives.

Hasson, Jamiel Actor, sometimes credited as Jamiel Hassen, who portrays Habib Hanna in *Behind That Curtain* (1929).

Hatchet in the Head Horror/thriller movie seen by Tommy Chan and Birmingham Brown in *The Shanghai Chest* (1948). While walking home from the movie, the pair see a figure crawling through the open window of a house across the street, and they try to catch what they think is a burglar. The unknown person turns out to be Frank Bronson, the district attorney, whose wife is out of town and who has forgotten his house keys. Both Tommy and Birmingham then find themselves in jail until Charlie Chan can explain the mix-up to Bronson, an old friend of his.

Hay, Jeff Alias used by Craig Winfield (portrayed by John Gallaudet in his first of two *Charlie Chan* roles) in *Shadows Over Chinatown* (1946). As Winfield, he was the former manager of the Bon Ton Burlesque Company, but now poses as private detective Jeff Hay and runs the Bay City Escort Bureau as a cover for insurance fraud.

The escort bureau has some of their escorts marry wealthy older men who then mysteriously die on their honeymoons. The beneficiaries then disappear after the death benefits are paid. Hay murders Grace Gortner Pendleton, a former girlfriend at the Bon Ton Burlesque Company who also had worked for the escort bureau and become caught up in the murder-insurance payment scheme. Hay next murders Mrs. Conover's friend, Kate Johnson, in Mary Conover's apartment, having mistaken Johnson for Mary. He then murders his accomplice, Mike Roberts, before Roberts can be captured and tell the police about the insurance fraud scheme.

Hayden, Harry (1882, Oklahoma Territory–July 24, 1955, West Los Angeles, California) Bespectacled, thick-set character actor of stage and screen who appeared in over 160 films. In two *Charlie Chan* roles, Hayden portrays Jimmy Chan's USC chemistry professor (unbilled) in *Charlie Chan in Reno* (1939) and inventor Oscar Swendstrom in *Docks of New Orleans* (1948).

As a slight, grey-templed, bespectacled American actor, Harry Hayden was cast to best advantage as small-town store proprietors, city attorneys, and minor bureaucrats. Dividing his time between stage and screen work since 1936, Hayden became one of the busiest members of Central Casting, appearing in everything from pictures like *Mr. Smith Goes to Washington* (1939) to the RKO two-reelers of Leon Errol and Edgar Kennedy. Among his better known unbilled assignments are horn factory owner Mr. Sharp in Laurel and Hardy's *Saps at Sea* (1940) and Farley Granger's harrumphing boss (who brusquely announces that there'll be no Christmas bonus) in O. Henry's *Full House* (1951).

Rita Hayworth (née Cansino) as a relative unknown in *Charlie Chan in Egypt*.

Hayden's final role was that of next-door neighbor Harry on the 1954-55 season of television's *The Stu Erwin Show* (a.k.a. *The Trouble with Father*). From the mid–1930s until his death in 1955, Harry Hayden and his actress wife Lela Bliss ran Beverly Hills' Bliss-Hayden Miniature Theater, where several Hollywood aspirants were given an opportunity to learn their craft before live audiences. Most noted among the theater's alumni were Jon Hall, Veronica Lake, Doris Day, Craig Stevens, Debbie Reynolds, and Marilyn Monroe.

Hayes, Judy A secretary (portrayed by Phyllis Brooks in her first of two *Charlie Chan* roles) who is instructed to deliver a package containing $300,000 in *Charlie Chan in Honolulu* (1938). Hayes is told by her boss, Shanghai lawyer John Emery, to board the freighter *Susan B. Jennings* in Shanghai en route to San Francisco. Hays is to give the money to a man that will board the ship near Honolulu and give her a ring as a receipt, but he is killed before he gets the money. Hayes then puts the money in an attaché case in a trunk in her cabin. The money soon goes missing, having been stolen by Capt. Johnson who hides the attaché case in one of the ship's lifeboats (later to be discovered by Johnny McCoy).

Hayworth, Rita (October 17, 1918, Brooklyn, New York–May 14, 1987, New York, New York) Known as "The Love Goddess," popular American song and dance actress (real name: Margarita Carmen Cansino) who appeared in over 60 films. Very early in her career, Hayworth (credited as Rita Cansino) portrays the Egyptian maid Nayda in *Charlie Chan in Egypt* (1935).

Rita Hayworth was the daughter of Spanish dancer Eduardo Cansino and Ziegfeld Follies showgirl Volga Haworth. Trained as a dancer from early childhood, she joined the family dancing act at age 12. She was spotted three years later by Fox studio head Winfield Sheehan, leading to her first studio contract and film debut at age 16 in *Dante's*

Inferno (1935), which, in addition to a few other films in the 1930s, billed her under her real name and utilized her real hair color (black).

Her Fox contract was dropped after five small roles, but expert, exploitative promotion by first husband Edward Judson soon won Rita a new contract at Columbia, where studio head Harry Cohn changed her name to Hayworth, approved raising her hairline by electrolysis, and had her hair dyed auburn. After a number of minor roles, Columbia lent her to Warner Bros. for her first big success—as Virginia Brush in *The Strawberry Blonde* (1941). Her splendid dancing, as Sheila Winthrop, with Fred Astaire in *You'll Never Get Rich* (1941) made her a star.

In person, Rita was shy, quiet, and unassuming. Only when the cameras rolled did she turn on the explosive sexual charisma that, with *Gilda* (1946), made her a superstar. To Rita, though, domestic bliss was a more important, if elusive, goal. After marriages to Judson and Orson Welles, she became involved in a heated romance with the already married Aly Khan, son of the Moslem leader, and they married in 1949. Following their divorce in 1951, she was married to singer Dick Haymes from 1953 to 1955, and then for three years to James Hill, producer of her film, *Separate Tables* (1958).

Rita Hayworth at the peak of her fame.

Her career had slowed down in the 1950s and virtually came to a stop in the 1960s, when rumors of erratic and supposedly drunken behavior began to circulate. In reality, she was suffering from the first symptoms of Alzheimer's disease, which went undiagnosed until 1980. Almost helpless by 1981, she would be cared for by her daughter, Princess Yasmin Khan, until her death.

Hell Cat Excitable mare owned by Lady Mary Bristol in *Charlie Chan in London* (1934). The horse "cuts up" when any stranger is near, but is easily controlled by Lake, the stud groom. Fearing that Lady Mary has important information to give to Charlie Chan about the attempt on Chan's life the night before, Geoffrey Richmond throws some pepper into the eyes of Hell Cat as Mary rides the horse during a fox hunt at Richmond's country estate. Both she and the horse crash through a railing and fall into a chalk pit. Hell Cat is killed instantly but Lady Mary survives and is unconscious with a concussion.

Henri Nineteen-year-old son of Antoine in *City in Darkness* (1939).

Henry, Charlotte V. (March 3, 1915, Brooklyn, New York–April 11, 1980, San Diego, California) American juvenile actress in the 1930s who portrays Kitty Rochelle in *Charlie Chan at the Opera* (1936).

Henry, Louise Character actress who appeared in 15 films. In two *Charlie Chan* roles, Louise Henry portrays Billie Bronson in *Charlie Chan on Broadway* (1937) and Jeanne Bently in *Charlie Chan in Reno* (1939).

Herman, Ace Film editor of over 20 films, including nine *Charlie Chan* films at Monogram: *The Shanghai Cobra* (1945), *The Red Dragon* (1945), *Dark Alibi* (1946), *The Trap* (1947), *Docks of New Orleans* (1948), *The Shanghai Chest* (1948), *The Golden Eye* (1948),

The Feathered Serpent (1948), and *The Sky Dragon* (1949).*

Herman, Hal Assistant director for *Castle in the Desert* (1942).

Herschel Costume designer, costumer, and wardrobe supervisor (full name: Herschel McCoy) for over 25 movies. He was associated with 13 *Charlie Chan* films at Twentieth Century–Fox.

Herschel McCoy was nominated for two Academy Awards. He was nominated for an Oscar in the Best Costume Design (Color) category for *Quo Vadis* (1951) and shared the Oscar nomination with Helen Rose in the Best Costume Design (Black-and-White) category for the movie *Dream Wife* (1953).

Charlie Chan filmography: *Charlie Chan at the Race Track* (1936), *Charlie Chan at the Opera* (1936), *Charlie Chan at the Olympics* (1937), *Charlie Chan on Broadway* (1937), *Charlie Chan at Monte Carlo* (1937), *Charlie Chan in Reno* (1939), *Charlie Chan at Treasure Island* (1939), *City of Darkness* (1939), *Charlie Chan at the Wax Museum* (1940), *Murder Over New York* (1940), *Charlie Chan's Murder Cruise* (1940), *Charlie Chan in Rio* (1941), and *Castle in the Desert* (1942).

Hervey, Irene (July 11, 1910, Los Angeles, California–December 20, 1998, Los Angeles, California) Blonde, American leading lady (real name: Irene Herwick) who appeared in over 40 films, and who portrays Diana Woodland in *Charlie Chan in Shanghai* (1935). Besides movies, she also frequently appeared on television, and her appearance on *My Three Sons* earned her an Emmy Award in 1969. Hervey was married to singer Allen Jones from 1936 until 1957, and they had one child, singer-entertainer Jack Jones.

Herzbrun, Bernard Art director and production designer of over 150 films. Herzbrun was the art director for *Charlie Chan in Monte Carlo* (1937) and *Mr. Moto's Gamble* (1938), a reworked version of the never-completed *Charlie Chan at the Ringside*. He shared an Academy Award nomination in the Best Art Direction category with Boris Leven for *Alexander's Ragtime Band* (1938).

Heyburn, Weldon (1904–May 18, 1951, Hollywood, California) Dimpled-chin actor who appeared in over 40 films. He portrays Detective Harvey Dennis in *The Chinese Cat* (1944).

Heydt, Louis Jean (April 17, 1905, Montclair, New Jersey–January 29, 1960, Boston, Massachusetts) Stage and screen character actor who appeared in nearly 90 films and portrays novelist Paul Essex in *Charlie Chan at Treasure Island* (1939).

Louis Heydt was educated at Worcester Academy and Dartmouth College. He intended to go into journalism and briefly worked as a reporter for the *New York World* before opting for a stage career. Among his Broadway appearances was the lead in Preston Sturges' *Strictly Dishonorable*, establishing a long working relationship with Sturges that would extend to the latter's film productions of *The Great McGinty* (1940) and *The Great Moment* (1942).

Heydt's film characters often seemed destined to be killed off before the fourth reel, either because they were hiding something or because they'd just stumbled upon important information that could prove damaging to the villains. His character committed suicide in the first three minutes of *Charlie Chan at Treasure Island* (1939) and, as Joe Brody, was shot full of holes just before revealing an important plot point to Humphrey Bogart in *The Big Sleep* (1946).

Heydt's many other assignments include the hungry soldier in *Gone with the Wind* (1939), Mentor Graham in *Abe Lincoln in Illinois* (1940), a frustrated general practitioner in *Tortilla Flat* (1941), and a squadron leader in *Gung Ho* (1943). Heydt was also familiar as Bobby Blake's stepfather in the MGM *Our Gang* shorts *Dad for a Day* (1939) and *All About Hash* (1940).

Hickman, Howard C. (February 9, 1880, Columbia, Missouri–December 31, 1949,

**Unbilled.*

Los Angeles, California) Stage and screen actor who appeared in 115 silent and sound films. Hickman portrays Dr. Burton, the Honolulu police doctor who gives Charlie Chan his annual physical exam, in *Charlie Chan at the Olympics* (1937).

Hicks, Russell (June 4, 1895, Baltimore, Maryland–June 1, 1957, Hollywood, California) Stage and screen character actor (real name: Edward Russell Hicks) who appeared in over 200 films, usually as executive types. In three *Charlie Chan* roles, Hicks portrays James Andrews in *Charlie Chan in Shanghai* (1935), prison warden Cameron in *Dark Alibi* (1946), and District Attorney Frank Bronson in *The Shanghai Chest* (1948). Hicks has the distinction of being only one of six actors who appeared with three different actors playing Chan.

Although trained in prep school for a career as a businessman, Russell Hicks decided to pursue a theatrical career over the protests of his family. As an actor, Hicks came full circle, spending the bulk of his career playing businessmen. Hicks' earliest recorded Hollywood job occurred in 1920 when he was hired as an assistant casting director for Famous Players (later Paramount). Making his stage debut in *It Pays to Smile*, Hicks acted in stock companies and on Broadway before his official film debut in *Happiness Ahead* (1934).

Russell Hicks

The tall, authoritative-looking Hicks frequently used his dignified persona to throw the audience off guard when playing crooked or villainous roles. He portrayed the glib confidence man J. Frothingham Waterbury in W.C. Fields' *The Bank Dick* (1940), and more than once he was cast as the surprise killer in murder mysteries.

hieroglyphics Pictorial symbols used in the earliest known writing systems. Each hieroglyph is recognizable as the whole or part of some object or objects, such as living creatures; vegetation; astronomical, geographical, and similar phenomena; or buildings and artifacts.

A number of hieroglyphic scripts have been discovered. The earliest (c. 3100–2700 B.C.) appeared in Mesopotamia, Romania, Iran, and Egypt. The Maya of Central America used hieroglyphics from the first to the eighth century, as did the Aztecs in Mexico from the twelfth to the sixteenth century.

In *The Feathered Serpent* (1948), Aztec hieroglyphics are chiseled in a rock at the base of the cliff at the foot of the Diablo Mountains. Tommy Chan sees that one of the hieroglyphs is a feathered serpent with its head pointed down, a clue to the secret entrance to the lost Aztec Temple of the Sun. While held prisoner by Professor John Stanley, Professor Henry Farnsworth is forced to decipher hieroglyphs that will locate the entrance to a king's tomb in the temple and its vast treasure.

Hillman, Elsie Real name of Mrs. Carol Wayne (portrayed by Claire Dodd) in *Charlie Chan in Honolulu* (1938). *See also* **Wayne, Mrs. Carol.**

Hillman, R. Estranged husband of Elsie Hillman (alias Mrs. Carol Wayne) in *Charlie Chan in Honolulu* (1938). In the process of getting a divorce from his wife, Hillman comes up with a plan for Shanghai lawyer John Emery to get $300,000 out of China and avoid a property settlement. Emery has his secretary, Judy Hayes, travel from Shanghai to San Francisco on the freighter *Susan B. Jennings* with a package containing $300,000.

When the ship nears Honolulu, Hillman comes aboard the boat. As he is about to give Hayes a wedding ring as a receipt for the package, Hillman is shot dead by Capt. Johnson. At first there is no clue as to Hillman's identification. However, Charlie Chan notices that the deceased man was married by the mark left on the ring finger of his left hand where a wedding ring is typically worn.

Hindenburg Rigid airship (originally designated as the L.Z. 129) built by the firm of Luftschiffbau Zeppelin in Friedrichshafen, Germany. Completed and tested in 1936, the *Hindenburg* was the world's first transatlantic commercial airliner. The airship was 804 feet long, had a maximum diameter of 135 feet, and was kept aloft by hydrogen gas in 16 cells. Four 1,050-horsepower Daimler-Benz diesel engines provided a top speed of 82 miles per hour.

In May of 1936, the *Hindenburg* inaugurated the first scheduled air service across the North Atlantic, flying between Frankfurt am Main, Germany, and Lakehurst, New Jersey. It accommodated more than 70 passengers and had a dining room, a library and lounge with a grand piano, a cocktail lounge, and promenades with large windows. The flight to the United States took 60 hours, while the return trip to Europe took 50 hours.

While maneuvering to land during a violent thunderstorm at Lakehurst on May 6, 1937, the airship's hydrogen supply was ignited and the *Hindenburg* was destroyed by the resulting fire. Thirty-five of the passengers and crew died, along with one member of the ground crew. Claims and speculation that the *Hindenburg* was a victim of sabotage have never been supported by evidence. The destruction of the *Hindenburg* marked the end of the use of airships in world air commerce.

In *Charlie Chan at the Olympics* (1937), Charlie Chan tells police Chief Scott, "Take Zeppelin *Hindenburg* from Lakehurst, New Jersey, across Atlantic Ocean to Friedrichshafen—sixty-one hours." In the book *Charlie Chan at the Movies: History, Filmography, and Criticism*, author Ken Hanke notes that Twentieth Century–Fox had a great idea literally blow up in their face. When making the movie, the studio thought that it would generate wonderful publicity to have Charlie Chan cross the ocean on the *Hindenburg*, but the airship tragically blew up on docking in New Jersey a little less than three weeks before the film's release on May 23, 1937.

Note: The swastikas on the *Hindenburg's* tail fins were censored/obliterated from the newsreel footage used in the movie.

Hip Sing tong The name of a San Francisco–based Chinese tong in *The Chinese Ring* (1947). Tommy Chan finds out from Lee Chin, a fraternity brother whose grandfather is head of the Hip Sing tong, that warplanes are to be shipped to the Orient on the *Shanghai Maid*.

A tong is a community or fraternal organization of Chinese in the United States. The first tongs were founded in the 1850s and functioned as secret societies for immigrants, primarily those from the Guangzhou (Canton) region. The term "tong" is derived from the Chinese word for "hall" or "reception room." In such meeting places, family elders and village officials in China traditionally gathered to make decisions and set community policies. The word could also mean "court of justice."

When the Chinese first arrived in North America, they discovered that their new environment was harsh, with many economic, political, and social restrictions. To aid and protect themselves, many Chinese banded together in communal groups based on former village structures and ties. In time, competition between the various tongs resulted in much-publicized violence.

Hobbes, Halliwell (November 16, 1877, Stratford-on-Avon, England–February 20, 1962, Santa Monica, California) British-born stage and screen character actor (real name: Herbert Halliwell Hobbes) who appeared in over 100 films. Hobbs portrays Shanghai police commissioner Col. Watkins in *Charlie Chan in Shanghai* (1935).

hobby horse races Final night's cruise activity planned by Dr. Suderman (with Charlie Chan as the judge) in *Charlie Chan's Murder Cruise* (1940). Starting at 8:00 P.M., there would be races every 15 minutes on the quarter hour. The first race is won by Slippery Sam, who is ridden by Frederick Ross and owned by Susie Watson. During the races, Chan discovers that Gerald Pendleton has been murdered in his cabin. Based on the time that a telegram was sent by someone in Pendleton's cabin, Chan concludes that the murder occurred during the fifth race.

Hodgson, Leyland (1892, London, England–March 16, 1949, Hollywood, California) British stage and screen character actor who appeared in over 60 films, sometimes credited as Layland Hodgson or Leland Hodgson. Hodgson portrays Boggs the butler in *Murder Over New York* (1940).

At the age of six, Leyland Hodgson launched his theatrical career. From 1915 to 1919 he toured the English Far East colonies with the Bandmann Opera Company, and then retraced most of this tour as head of his own stock company. A star of the Australian stage from 1920 to 1929, Hodgson moved to Hollywood, where he appeared in his first film as Lt. Winfried in *The Case of Sergeant Grischa* (1930). Largely confined to minor roles in films, Hodgson enjoyed some prominence as a regular in Universal's *Sherlock Holmes* films of the 1940s. Otherwise, he contented himself with bits as butlers, military officers, hotel clerks, reporters, and chauffeurs until his retirement in 1948.

Hoffman, Joseph (1909, New York, New York–May 16, 1997, Los Angeles, California) Screenwriter of over 50 films who collaborated with Robert Ellis and Helen Logan in writing the screenplay for *Charlie Chan's Secret* (1936).

Hogan, Al Animal keeper on the *Susan B. Jennings* (portrayed by Eddie Collins in his first of two *Charlie Chan* roles) in *Charlie Chan in Honolulu* (1938). Hogan has a tame lion named Oscar for a pet and is in charge of all the animals that are being sent to a zoo in San Francisco.

Hogsett, Albert Art director for over 20 films, including three *Charlie Chan* entries: *Charlie Chan in Paris* (1935), *Charlie Chan's Secret* (1936), and *Charlie Chan at the Olympics* (1937).

Holden, William (1872–March 3, 1932) Character actor who appeared in late silent and early sound films, not to be confused with the leading man, William Holden, of later films. Holden portrays Patrick Tait in *Charlie Chan Carries On* (1931).

Holland, Edna Character actress who appeared in over 30 films, including two *Charlie Chan* entries. Holland portrays Mrs. Foss in *Dark Alibi* (1946) and (unbilled) the demanding old-woman airplane passenger in *The Sky Dragon* (1949).

Holley, Will Editor of the *Eldorado Times* (portrayed by Si Jenks) in *Charlie Chan's Courage* (1934).

Note: In Earl Derr Biggers' novel *The Chinese Parrot*, which serves as the basis for *Charlie Chan's Courage* (1934), Will Holley is mentioned, but the film credits for *The Chinese Parrot* (1927) in the *American Film Institute Catalog of Motion Pictures Produced in the United States* do not list this character.

Holmes, George (1918–February 19, 1985) Character actor who portrays prison guard Hugh Kenzie in *Dark Alibi* (1946).

Holt, Tom Gangor the snake charmer in the Kinney & Gaines Combined Circus (portrayed by J. Carrol Naish) in *Charlie Chan at the Circus* (1936). Before he was with Joe Kinney's circus, Holt and Kinney were caught cheating at cards one night in a casino in El Paso, Texas, and Holt killed the sheriff while trying to escape. Given a job in the circus by Kinney, Holt begins to send Kinney unsigned, threatening letters in a quarrel over gambling money. Fearing that he would be turned over to the police, Holt kills Kinney by breaking his neck with his strong hands.

When Charlie Chan investigates Kinney's murder, Holt lets a poisonous cobra loose in Charlie's sleeping quarters on the circus train in an attempt to kill him. Holt also tries to kill trapeze performer Louise Norman after she claims she can prove that Kinney could not have been married to Nellie Farrell in Juarez, Mexico on May 30, 1935. Fearing that she would expose him as the killer of an El Paso sheriff, Holt shoots one of the trapeze ropes while Norman is performing her circus act, causing her fall to the ground, alive but unconscious. In a last, desperate attempt to finish the job (since Norman is still alive), Holt releases Cesar the gorilla as a diversion and puts on a gorilla suit. Before he can shoot Louise Norman during what was a trap staged as an emergency operation, Holt is himself shot and killed.

Homans, Robert Emmett (November 8, 1874, Malden, Massachusetts–July 28, 1947, Los Angeles) Grim-faced American character actor of stage and film who appeared in almost 200 silent and sound films, often as judges and lawmen. In three *Charlie Chan* roles, Homans portrays the Chief of Police (unbilled) in *The Black Camel* (1931), a racetrack judge (unbilled) in *Charlie Chan at the Race Track* (1936), and Capt. Flynn in *The Scarlet Clue* (1945).

Robert E. Homans

Honeywood, Walter Theatrical manager (portrayed by Jason Robards, Sr.) who occupied the hotel room next to Hugo Morris Drake in *Charlie Chan Carries On* (1931). Honeywood runs away with Everhard's wife, Sybil Conway, taking with them two bags of Everhard's stolen diamonds, but both are later murdered by Everhard.

Hoopii, Sol, Jr. (1902, Honolulu, Hawaii–November 16, 1953, Seattle, Washington) Hawaiian musician (real name: Solomon Hoopii Kaaiai) who was known as the "King of the Hawaiian Guitar." He both wrote and played the song, *I Have a Thought in My Heart for You* in *The Black Camel* (1931). This was the only film in the *Charlie Chan* series he was credited for, although he probably also appeared in *Dangerous Money* (1946).

Hopkins, Mr. Owner of the Hopkins Aviation Company (portrayed by Jonathan Hale, Jr.) in *Charlie Chan at the Olympics* (1937). Hopkins acquires a part interest in a militarily strategic remote guidance system for airplanes which is later stolen during a test flight. When the invention is found by Charlie Chan in Berlin, Hopkins wants to personally take responsibility for the device's safe return to the United States.

When alone with his partner, Cartwright, in a Berlin hotel, Hopkins is kidnapped by enemy agents working for Charles Zaraka and Cartwright. Chan is brought to Zaraka's residence with an imitation remote control box that contains a hidden homing pigeon–type transmitter to be traded as the ransom for Chan's son Lee, who had been kidnapped. Hopkins is then brought in to check if the control box is genuine. Seeing that the control box is a fake, and realizing that Chan has something to do with it, Hopkins tells Zaraka that it is genuine at the risk of his own life.

Horn, Van Hollywood actor friend (portrayed by C. Henry Gordon in his second of five *Charlie Chan* roles) of Shelah Fane in *The Black Camel* (1931).

"horsefeathers" Frequent expletive used by Sheriff "Tombstone" Fletcher in *Charlie Chan in Reno* (1939).

Hoshelle, Marjorie Actress who played enemy agent–singer Countess Irena in *The Red Dragon* (1945).

"HOT DIARY HITS SECOND VICTIM" Newspaper headline of the *New York Gazette* about the murder of Thomas Mitchell, the estranged husband of Marie Collins, in *Charlie Chan on Broadway* (1937). Mitchell's death is thought to be connected to the death of Billie Bronson, who kept a diary with details about the rackets and politics.

Hotel de Voyageurs Paris hotel hiding place of Marie Dubon's husband, Tony Madero, in *City in Darkness* (1939).

Hotel Francis Charlie Chan's hotel in San Francisco (where he stays in Room 538) in *The Chinese Cat* (1944). The desk clerk is portrayed by Jack Norton in his first of three *Charlie Chan* roles.

Hotel Imperial In *Charlie Chan at Monte Carlo* (1937), the residence of Evelyn Grey and Paul Savarin. Albert Rogers works at the hotel's bar as a bartender.

Hotel Mazarin Charlie Chan's Paris hotel (where he stays in Room 502) in *Charlie Chan in Paris* (1935).

Hotel Miramar Mexico City hotel residence of Alfred Wyans where his secretary, Walter Dorn, was murdered in *The Red Dragon* (1945).

Hotel Regale Monte Carlo hotel residence of bartender Albert Rogers (where he is murdered) in *Charlie Chan at Monte Carlo* (1945).

Hotel San Pablo Cliveden Compton's Panama City hotel in *Charlie Chan in Panama* (1940). Compton is staying in Room 35, which is next door to Emil Manolo's room.

Hotel Sierra Reno, Nevada, hotel and casino run by Mrs. Russell that caters to those filing for a Nevada divorce in *Charlie Chan in Reno* (1939). Mary Whitman arrives at the hotel to establish residence for the requisite six weeks waiting period prior to obtaining a divorce from her estranged husband, Curtis. Jeanne Bently, a New York socialite who is also getting a divorce and is staying at the hotel across the hall from Mary, plans to marry Mary's husband once the divorce is final.

Later that evening, after Mary's arrival at the hotel, Jeanne Bently is murdered in her room and Mary Whitman is found standing over the body. After Mary is accused of the murder, Charlie Chan wants to stay in Room 105, the murdered woman's room, while working on the case, telling Mrs. Russell, "When searching for needle in haystack, haystack only sensible location."

Hotel Versailles Belescu's Paris hotel residence in *City in Darkness* (1939).

hotels Charlie Chan was usually everywhere but at home in Honolulu, and often stayed in hotels during his travels. Some hotels were simply locations for banquets he attended or the residence of other characters throughout the series. *See* table, page opposite.

Hot Money Working title for *Dangerous Money* (1946) before its release on October 12, 1946. *See also* ***Dangerous Money* (1946)**.

Hottentot Club New York nightclub owned by Johnny Burke in *Charlie Chan on Broadway* (1937). After Billie Bronson returns to New York, she visits the club to see her ex-boyfriend Burke and runs into a local mobster named Buzz Moran, who warns her to leave town.

When Lee Chan follows his father and Inspector Nelson to the club, Lee is told by the doorman that the rules don't allow anyone to go in without a "lady friend." Not discouraged, Lee sneaks in via a second-floor side window and is soon arrested on suspicion of Billie Bronson's murder.

***The House Without a Key* (novel)** The first *Charlie Chan* novel written by Earl Derr

Hotels

Hotel	City	Movie
Adelphi Hotel	San Francisco	*Charlie Chan's Murder Cruise* (1940)
Astor Hotel	New York	*Charlie Chan on Broadway* (1937)
Carlton Hotel	New York	*Charlie Chan on Broadway* (1937)
Carlton Hotel	unknown	*The Jade Mask* (1945)
Continental Hotel	Rio de Janeiro	*Charlie Chan in Rio* (1941)
Foss Family Hotel	unknown	*Dark Alibi* (1946)
Hotel de Voyageurs	Paris	*City in Darkness* (1939)
Hotel Francis	San Francisco	*The Chinese Cat* (1944)
Hotel Imperial	Monte Carlo	*Charlie Chan at Monte Carlo* (1937)
Hotel Mazarin	Paris	*Charlie Chan in Paris* (1935)
Hotel Miramar	Mexico City	*The Red Dragon* (1945)
Hotel Regale	Monte Carlo	*Charlie Chan at Monte Carlo* (1937)
Hotel San Pablo	Panama City	*Charlie Chan in Panama* (1940)
Hotel Sierra	Reno	*Charlie Chan in Reno* (1939)
Hotel Versailles	Paris	*City in Darkness* (1939)
Imperial Hawaiian Hotel	Honolulu	*Charlie Chan's Murder Cruise* (1940)
Larchmont Hotel	unknown	*Dark Alibi* (1946)
Luani Hotel	Honolulu	*Charlie Chan's Murder Cruise* (1940)
Mango Inn Boarding House	Pago Pago	*Dangerous Money* (1946)
Mayfair Hotel	San Francisco	*Shadows Over Chinatown* (1946)
Mojave Wells Hotel	Mojave Wells	*Castle in the Desert* (1942)
Palace Hotel	Teheran	*Behind That Curtain* (1929)
Palace Hotel	San Francisco	*The Chinese Ring* (1947)
Reef & Palm Hotel	Honolulu	*Charlie Chan's Greatest Case* (1933)
Royal Hawaiian Hotel	Honolulu	*Charlie Chan at the Olympics* (1937)
St. Francis Hotel	San Francisco	*Charlie Chan at Treasure Island* (1939)
Savoy Hotel	London	*Behind That Curtain* (1929)
Shattuck Hotel	unknown	*Black Magic* (1944)
Tropic Hotel	Honolulu	*Charlie Chan at the Olympics* (1937)

The cover of an early edition of *The House Without a Key*, written by Earl Derr Biggers in 1925 (Courtesy Don Rogers.)

Biggers and published by Bobbs-Merrill in 1925. The novel was serialized in the *Saturday Evening Post* from January 24 to March 25, 1925, and was the basis for the 1925 silent film of the same name. It was later remade as *Charlie Chan's Greatest Case* (1933).

***The House Without a Key* (1925)**

Source: based on the novel *The House Without a Key* by Earl Derr Biggers (Bobbs-Merrill, 1925), which was serialized in the *Saturday Evening Post* from January 24 to March 25, 1925. Original Copyright: Pathé Exchange, Inc.

Chapter Titles (Original Copyright/Registration Number): 1. "The Spite Fence" (October 1, 1926/LP23322); 2. "The Mystery Box" (October 1, 1926/LP23349); 3. "The Missing Numeral" (October 8, 1926/LP23350); 4. "Suspicion" (December 2, 1926/LP23397); 5. "The Death Buoy" (December 5, 1926/LP23398); 6. "Sinister Shadows" (December 14, 1926/

Walter Miller and Allene Ray surround villain Frank Lackteen while George Kuwa (as Charlie Chan) looks on in *The House Without a Key*, written by Earl Derr Biggers in 1925 (Everett Collection).

LP23446); 7. "The Mystery Man" (December 18, 1926/LP23447); 8. "The Spotted Menace" (December 24, 1926/LP23471); 9. "The Wrist Watch" (December 27, 1926/LP23472); 10. "The Culprit" (December 29, 1926/LP23480).

Copyright Renewed: not renewed. Release Date: same as copyright dates. Sound: silent. Film: b&w; all 2 reels each except Chapter One ("The Spite Fence") which is three reels.

Director: Spencer G. Bennett. Screenplay: Frank Leon Smith.

Cast

George Kuwa	*as*	Charlie Chan
William Bailey		
John Webb Dillon		
Frank Lackteen		
Walter Miller		
Allene Ray		
Natalie Warfield		
Charles West		

Notes: No copies of *The House Without a Key* are currently known to exist. The film was later remade as *Charlie Chan's Greatest Case* (1933).

How to Disappear: Vanishment Made Easy Title of a magic book given to Birmingham Brown by the Bonners' soon-to-be ex-butler, Mr. Johnson, in *Black Magic* (1944). Johnson tells Birmingham that the book is "guaranteed to make you go from where you is to ain't where you was, in a flash" when you snap your fingers and say the magic word "abracadabra."

Howard, Boothe (1889–October 4, 1936, Los Angeles, California) Actor who portrays the assistant circus animal trainer Dan Farrell in *Charlie Chan at the Circus* (1936) and the ship's doctor (unbilled) in *Charlie Chan at the Race Track* (1936).

Howard, Neil British barrister (portrayed by Ray Milland) who is engaged to Pamela

Gray in *Charlie Chan in London* (1934). As a lawyer, he unsuccessfully defended Pamela's brother Paul at his trial but confesses privately to Chan that he thought Paul was guilty of murdering Capt. Hamilton. Pamela overhears his confession and breaks off the engagement, taking off her engagement ring and throwing it to the ground. Howard spends the rest of the film helping Chan find the real murderer.

Howard, Samuel "Shemp" (March 17, 1895, Brooklyn, New York–November 23, 1955, Hollywood, California) Stage and screen comedy actor (real name: Samuel Horwitz) who appeared in over 130 films as part of The Three Stooges. Howard portrays "Shorty" McCoy, a.k.a. "The Canarsie Kid," posing as a Hindu fakir in *Murder Over New York* (1940).

Comedian Shemp Howard was the oldest of five sons of a Lithuanian immigrant couple and was a prankish kid who used humor to obscure the fact that he lived in mortal fear of practically everything from automobiles to oceans. Following the lead of his younger brother Moe, Shemp went into vaudeville with a blackface act. In 1922 Shemp and Moe were hired as stooges for comedian Ted Healy in an act billed as "Ted Healy and His Stooges." Three years later Larry Fine joined the act that had graduated from vaudeville to Broadway. Healy liked his stooges to look as ridiculous as possible and insisted that they each adopt an eccentric hairstyle. Shemp chose to part his hair down the middle and slick it into place with Vaseline, a style he'd retain for the rest of his career.

Shemp Howard, who was best known as one of The Three Stooges.

In 1932 Shemp left the act and was featured in dozens of Vitaphone two-reel comedies. In 1940 he signed a contract with Universal pictures, appearing in such films as *Hellzapoppin'* (1941), *Pittsburgh* (1942), and *Ali Baba and the 40 Thieves* (1944). Shemp was invariably hilarious in these films, but too hilarious for the tastes of such comedians as W.C. Fields and Lou Costello, who insisted that many of Shemp's best bits be left on the cutting room floor.

While headlining his own series of Columbia two-reelers in 1946, Shemp was asked by brother Moe and Larry Fine to rejoin their old act, which by now had gained fame as The Three Stooges. Shemp was to replace his kid brother Jerome ("Curly") Howard (who had suffered a stroke), and he would be the new patsy and target of Moe's physical assaults. Shemp remained with The Three Stooges through 1955. At age 60, Howard died of a sudden heart attack in the back seat of a car on the way home from watching a boxing match.

Howe, Gladys One of two stand-ins in *Charlie Chan in Paris* (1935).

Hsin Hwa Chinese motion picture company in Shanghai which made two Chinese-language *Charlie Chan* films in the late 1930s—*Charlie Chan in Homeland* and *Charlie Chan in Radio Station*—with Hsu Hsin-Yuan as Charlie Chan. Neither was distributed outside mainland China.

Hsu Hsin-Yuan Chinese actor who portrays Charlie Chan in the Chinese-language films *Charlie Chan in Homeland* and *Charlie Chan in Radio Station*. These were made by the Hsin Hwa Motion Picture Company in

Harold Huber

Shanghai in the late 1930s and were never distributed outside mainland China.

Huber, Harold (1910, New York, New York–September 26, 1959, New York, New York) Mustachioed American character actor of stage, screen, and radio (as well as a producer and former lawyer—a graduate of Columbia Law School) who appeared in almost 80 films, including four *Charlie Chan* roles, all as policemen. Huber portrays Inspector Nelson in *Charlie Chan on Broadway* (1937), Inspector Jules Joubert in *Charlie Chan at Monte Carlo* (1937), Marcel in *City in Darkness* (1939), and Chief Souto in *Charlie Chan in Rio* (1941). Besides these films, Huber portrays police Lt. Riggs in *Mr. Moto's Gamble* (1938), a reworked version of the never-completed *Charlie Chan at the Ringside*.

Hughes, Arthur Shady war profiteer (portrayed by C. Henry Gordon in his third of five *Charlie Chan* roles) in *Charlie Chan at the Olympics* (1937). Hughes is in Honolulu trying to acquire (by whatever means possible) a revolutionary remote controlled guidance system being developed and tested by the Hopkins Aviation Company. At the same time, he is trying to prevent Charles Zaraka and his country from getting the invention.

When Charlie Chan is a guest of Charles Zaraka and Yvonne Roland, seated in Box 22 of the Olympic Stadium during the games' opening ceremonies, Hughes is seated across the stadium with an expert lip-reader to find out what is being said between Chan, Zaraka, and Roland.

Hughes, Carol (1915, Chicago, Illinois–) American character actress who appeared in over 40 films and portrays Marguerite Fontan in *The Red Dragon* (1945).

Hughes, Mary Beth (November 13, 1919, Alton, Illinois–August 27, 1995) Attractive, hard-boiled blonde actress who appeared in nearly 50 films. Hughes portrays the jealous Joan Reynolds in *Charlie Chan in Rio* (1941).

Mary Beth Hughes seldom rose above starlet or second-echelon star status, even though she worked steadily and enjoyed a loyal fan following during her career. Encouraged to pursue a theatrical career by her grandmother, herself a one-time actress, Hughes went from stage to films in 1938. From 1940 through 1943, Hughes was part of the "B"-picture crew at Twentieth Century–Fox, playing both good and bad girls in the popular *Michael Shayne* series with Lloyd Nolan in addition to the usual "other woman" roles, such as Caroline in *Orchestra Wives* (1942).

While her film career never really went anywhere, Hughes remained in the public eye through her many cheesecake photos in movie magazines of the era. In the mid–1950s, Hughes gave up films in favor of work as a nightclub singer and musician, and as a television actress. She was often cast as nagging wife Clara Appleby on television's *The Red Skelton Show*, possibly because she was one of the few actresses whom Skelton couldn't break up laughing.

Humberstone, H. Bruce (November 18, 1902, Buffalo, New York–October 11, 1984, Woodland Hills, California) American film director (nicknamed "Lucky") who directed nearly 50 silents and talkies, including four *Charlie Chan* films with Twentieth Century–Fox.

H. Bruce Humberstone was a juvenile actor and script clerk during his first few years in Hollywood. He also worked in a number of other capacities (such as grip, prop man, or production assistant) on several silent westerns of the 1920s. It was during this time he earned the nickname "Lucky" for reasons that he'd keep changing from interview to interview later in life.

After serving time as an assistant director, Humberstone was given his first solo directing assignment with *Strangers of the Evening* (1932). Exhibiting no discernible style of his own, Humberstone was able to shift from comedy to drama to melodrama with ease. During his long stay at Twentieth Century–Fox, he directed several of the *Charlie Chan* films, where he hit upon the dubious technique of keeping star Warner Oland drunk so that Oland would deliver his lines in the slow, hesitant cadence necessary for the Chan role. Humberstone often employed electronic gadgets in his Chan films, such as electronic timing heads with photoelectric cells, sending of pictures over the telephone using facsimile, and remote control guidance systems for airplanes.

Humberstone's best work of the '40s include several Fox Technicolor musicals, the shadow-laden mystery *I Wake Up Screaming* (1941), and Danny Kaye's *Wonder Man* (1945). In the 1950s Humberstone switched his attentions to television, finding a few spare moments to direct some of the *Tarzan* programmers.

Charlie Chan filmography: *Charlie Chan at the Race Track* (1936), *Charlie Chan at the Opera* (1936), *Charlie Chan at the Olympics* (1937), and *Charlie Chan in Honolulu* (1938).

Humbolt County California county where Connie Jackson and Andy Barrett were married eight years earlier in *The Sky Dragon* (1949). The marriage was performed by Justice of the Peace Jonathon Tibbetts at the Orange Blossom Manor on July 21, 1941.

Hume, Special Agent The man who signed the receipt for the transport of the prisoner Jan Van Horn from Shanghai to Singapore for trial in *The Shanghai Cobra* (1945).

Charlie Chan recounts to police inspector Harry Davis that Hume was the only man who never fully believed that Van Horn robbed the bank in Shanghai and was also the man who collected the only evidence against Van Horn (which was destroyed in a Japanese bombing raid on Shanghai eight years earlier). After Van Horn escaped from a boat's launch in Shanghai, Hume also disappeared, later assuming the alias of Bradford Harris. *See also* **Harris, Bradford.**

Huntley, G.P. Character actor who appeared in over 25 films, sometimes credited as G.P. Huntley, Jr., or George P. Huntley. Huntley portrays professional gambler Denny Barton in *Charlie Chan at the Race Track* (1936).

Hutchinson, Max Sound engineer for *Black Magic* (1944).

Hyland, Frances (April 25, 1927, Saskatchewan, Canada–) Actress and screenwriter of nearly 45 films, including *Charlie Chan in Reno* (1939).

Hymer, Warren (February 25, 1906, New York, New York–March 25, 1948, Los Angeles, California) Stage and screen character actor who appeared in over 100 films, often as gangsters or dumbwitted characters. Hymer portrays gangster Max Minchin in *Charlie Chan Carries On* (1931).

Though he appeared to be illiterate, the not-so-handsome Warren Hymer was actually the son of two affluent stage performers, John B. Hymer and Elsie Hunt. Far from being an illiterate, he was a graduate of Yale University and a moderately successful Broadway stage actor before coming to Hollywood in 1928. Because of his rough-hewn facial features and his ability to feign incredible stupidity, Hymer was much in demand for gangster roles.

So popular was Hymer during the early-talkie period that he shared co-starring status with Spencer Tracy in two films, and, as Dannemora Dan, was billed over Humphrey Bogart in *Up the River* (1930). Unfortunately, Hymer's love of acting took second place to his love of liquor, and things went from bad to worse as Hymer's condition deteriorated. At one point, he began filming a scene, opened his mouth to speak, and collapsed cold on the floor.

Producers were willing to overlook this in view of Hymer's talent, but Hymer also had an uncontrollable temper. The axe fell on the day that Hymer, arguing with Columbia Pictures head Harry Cohn, punctuated his tirade by urinating on Cohn's desk. After that, Hymer was virtually blackballed from Hollywood and resurfaced from time to time for an unbilled bit or a barely coherent supporting role. Warren Hymer died in 1948 at the age of 42, not having worked in two years.

Hytten, Olaf (1888, Scotland–March 11, 1955, Los Angeles, California) Scottish-born character actor who appeared in over 110 silent and sound films. Hytten portrays Judge Armstrong's butler, Bates, in *The Shanghai Chest* (1948).

I

"I hear you are a man of many friends" First phrase of recognition code exchange between Godley and Charlie Chan in *Charlie Chan in Panama* (1940). Posing as Fu Yuen, Chan responds with, "Thousand friends too few." Godley, an American agent, then asks, "Do you have enemies?" to which Chan concludes with, "One enemy one too many."

"If you wish news of your son, be in your same seat in the Olympic Stadium alone and unguarded" Warning note to Charlie Chan attached to a rock thrown through a glass window in *Charlie Chan at the Olympics* (1937). Charlie's son Lee, a member of the U.S. Olympic Team, is kidnapped in Berlin outside the Olympic Stadium and held as barter for the new remote controlled airplane guidance system which Charlie has. The seat in the Olympic Stadium is in Box 22 in an area reserved for the diplomatic corps. *See also* **22**.

Ikerd, Percy Assistant director for *Charlie Chan's Greatest Case* (1933). Ikerd received an Academy Award nomination in 1934 in the Best Assistant Director category.

Imhof, Roger (August 15, 1875–April 15, 1958, Hollywood, California) Character actor who appeared in 35 films and portrays the unnamed beachcomber in *Charlie Chan's Greatest Case* (1933).

Imperial Hawaiian Hotel Honolulu hotel from which Gerald Pendleton claims he will obtain a room quieter than the one he currently has in the Luani Hotel in *Charlie Chan's Murder Cruise* (1940).

Ingram, Jack (November 15, 1902, Illinois–February 20, 1969, Canoga Park, California) Character actor (real name: John Samuel Ingram) who appeared in over 175 films, often as a villain. Ingram portrays murderer Lloyd Archer in *The Jade Mask* (1945).

Writing about serial villains in the early 1970s, film historian William K. Everson favorably compared the talents of such performers as Lionel Atwill and Eduardo Cianelli to the "listless and thoughtless reading of lines" of Jack Ingram. Perhaps this assessment was a bit unfair, but it is considered by many that Ingram was seldom any better than adequate in his many movie bad-guy appearances. In films since the mid–1930s, Ingram, a muscle-bound, stubble-bearded brute of a man, was often cast as a cattle rustler or gangster's henchman.

Irena, Countess Enemy agent (portrayed by Marjorie Hoshelle) who is secretly the wife of Charles Masack (also an enemy agent) in *The Red Dragon* (1945). Countess Irena works as a nightclub singer at the Capitol Night Club and sings the song *My Heart Is Yours*. She is murdered by Joseph Brandish just before she can tell Charlie Chan that Brandish is the one who killed Chan's friend, Walter Dorn, and Alfred Wyans.

iron maiden Ancient spiked torture device onboard the *Suva Star* in *Dead Men Tell* (1941). Kate Ransome faints after seeing in a magazine the picture of an escaped murderer who's posing as fellow passenger Bill Lydig. Lydig then puts her inside the iron maiden in the ship's hold. The iron maiden is also shown (but not mentioned) in Dr. Cream's Crime Museum in *Charlie Chan at the Wax Museum* (1940).

Irving, George H. (1874, New York, New York–September 11, 1961, Hollywood, California) Veteran American stage and screen character actor, often in roles as a middle-aged businessman, in over 140 silent and sound films after a career as a film director of over 25 silents. Irving portrays archeologist Professor Arnold in *Charlie Chan in Egypt* (1935) and racehorse owner Major Gordon Kent in *Charlie Chan at the Race Track* (1936).

Irving, Margaret (1897–1988) Actress who portrays Mme. Lilli Rochelle in *Charlie Chan at the Opera* (1936).

Irwin, Boyd (March 12, 1880, Brighton, England–January 22, 1957, Woodland Hills, California) British-born stage and screen character actor who appeared in over 50 silent and sound films. Irwin portrays Simon Lafontaine in *Docks of New Orleans* (1948).

"ISLAND WOMAN HELD ON MURDER CHARGE" Newspaper headline of the *Honolulu Daily Journal* reporting the arrest of Mary Whitman for the murder of Jeanne Bently in *Charlie Chan in Reno* (1939).

"It's all Chinese to me!" Phrase spoken in two Charlie Chan films. In *Charlie Chan in Rio* (1941), Charlie Chan and son Jimmy are talking to each other in Chinese about the murder victim. Bill Kellogg asks Lili Wong what they are saying but she pleads ignorance and explains that she was raised in an American orphanage in San Francisco and doesn't speak or understand Chinese. In *Charlie Chan in the Secret Service* (1942), Number Two daughter Iris and Number Three son Tommy get into an argument, and Charlie this time, surprisingly, is unaware of the meaning when he is asked by Birmingham.

"It's dangerous to know too much about other people's business" Warning message in a note dropped at the feet of Bruce Rogers in *Charlie Chan at the Race Track* (1936). Charlie Chan has son Lee secretly distribute different warning messages to Rogers, Warren Fenton, George Chester, and Denny Barton as part of a plan to identify the leader of a racetrack gambling ring.

Ivins, Perry (1895–1963) British-born actor who appeared in over 30 films and had roles in two *Charlie Chan* movies. Ivins portrays Mr. Kemp, the private secretary to Home Secretary Sir Lionel Bashford, in *Charlie Chan in London* (1934) and Bedell, the secretary to Albert Dufresne, in *Charlie Chan in Paris* (1935).

J

Jackson, Connie Marie Burke's real name in *The Sky Dragon* (1949). She is Wanda LaFern's younger sister; together they were billed as the LaFern Sisters in a follies act.

Eight years earlier, Jackson had married Andrew Barrett. Together with her sister and husband, the three are involved in a confidence scheme at a crooked airline operation, but Connie made off with $60,000 that was never recovered. Now on the run from her husband and sister, she changes her name to Marie Burke and becomes an airline stewardess. Insurance investigator John Anderson, who helped send her husband to prison, then takes her as a partner in his criminal activities. Marie drugs the coffee during Flight 17 so that Anderson can steal a $250,000 cash shipment.

Charlie Chan later reconstructs the events during a flight on the same airplane. Jackson, as Marie Burke, soon panics, starts to draw a gun from her handbag, and is quickly shot and killed by Anderson under the pretense of defending himself and the others aboard the plane. In reality, Anderson kills her before she can expose him as the one who stole the money shipment and murdered Edwards, Blake, and Davidson.

Jackson, Harry (1896–August 3, 1953, Hollywood, California) Cinematographer for over 50 films, including two *Charlie Chan* movies at Twentieth Century–Fox—*Charlie Chan at the Race Track* (1936) and *Charlie Chan on Broadway* (1937). In 1948 Jackson was nominated for an Academy Award in the Best Cinematography (Color) category for *Mother Wore Tights* (1947).

Jackson, Selmer A. (May 7, 1888, Lake Mills, Iowa–March 30, 1971, Burbank, California) Silver-haired character actor who appeared in over 210 films, sometimes credited as Selmar Jackson. In four *Charlie Chan* roles, Jackson portrays J.L. Lansing (unbilled) in *Charlie Chan at the Race Track* (1936), a wire-photo technician (unbilled) in *Charlie Chan at the Opera* (1936), U.S. Navy Commander Wright (unbilled) in *Charlie Chan at the Olympics* (1937), and the S.S. *Newcastle* ship's doctor in *Dangerous Money* (1946).

Selmer Jackson first stepped before the cameras in the silent film *Supreme Passion* (1921). Both silver-haired and silver-tongued, Jackson so closely resembled such dignified character players as Samuel S. Hinds and Henry O'Neill that at times it was hard to tell which actor was which, especially when all three showed up in the same picture. During World War II Jackson spent most of his time in uniform as naval and military officers.

Jacquard, Renee Social companion (portrayed by Ruth Peterson) of Max Corday in *Charlie Chan in Paris* (1935).

***The Jade Mask* (1945)** The fourth *Charlie Chan* film produced by Monogram Pictures Corporation.

Alternate Title: *Charlie Chan in the Jade Mask.* Working Title: *Mystery Mansion.* Source: based on the character "Charlie Chan" created by Earl Derr Biggers. Original Copyright: Monogram Pictures Corporation, November 22, 1944; LP13002. Copyright Renewed: July 20, 1972; R533124. Production: September, 1944. Release Date: January 26, 1945. Sound: Western Electric Recording. Film: b&w. Running Time: 64 or 69 minutes.

Producer: James S. Burkett. Director: Phil Rosen. Assistant Director: Eddie Davis. Original Screenplay: George Callahan. Director of Photography: Harry Neumann. Editors: John C. Fuller and Dick Currier.* Set Decorations: Vin Taylor. Musical Director: Edward J. Kay. Music Score: Dave Torbett. Sound Recording: Tom Lambert. Production Manager: Wm. Strohbach. Technical Director: Dave Milton.

Cast

Sidney Toler	*as*	Charlie Chan
Mantan Moreland		Birmingham Brown
Edwin Luke		Eddie Chan
Hardie Albright		Walter Meeker
Frank Reicher		Mr. Harper
Janet Warren		Jean Kent
Cyril Delevanti		Roth
Alan Bridge		Sheriff Mack
Ralph Lewis		Officer Jim Kimball
Dorothy Granger		Stella Graham
Edith Evanson		Louise Harper
Joe Whitehead		Dr. Samuel R. Peabody
Henry Hall		Inspector Godfrey
Jack Ingram		Lloyd Archer, also disguised as Walter Meeker
Danny Desmond		Bellboy
Lester Dorr*		Michael Strong, chauffeur

Plot Summary: Disguised as a policeman, a murderer breaks into the mansion of a scientist named Harper, kills him, and disposes of his body. Charlie Chan, now working as a government agent, is called to the case by police inspector Godfrey, who informs him that the scientist was working for the government to create a formula whereby wood could be made as strong as metal.

At the scientist's mansion, Chan and Godfrey (with the help of Sheriff Mack) question the Harper household—Louise Harper, his sister; Jean Kent, his orphaned niece; his butler Roth; Michael Strong, his mute chauffeur and handyman; and his assistants Walter Meeker and Stella Graham. Chan quickly learns that all of them hated Harper, whose cruelty went so far as to force his relatives to work for him as servants. Meanwhile, Eddie, Chan's fourth son, and Birmingham Brown,

**Unbilled.*

his chauffeur, arrive at the Harper estate, having been thrown out of their hotel.

Chan concludes that Harper was murdered inside the scientist's gas chamber, and Meeker tells him that all of Harper's work will be rendered useless unless Chan can find the scientist's secret formula. After Dr. Samuel R. Peabody, the local coroner, declares that Harper died of natural causes, Chan and Sheriff Mack visit Dr. Peabody and, after closer inspection, discover a poisonous dart inside the dead scientist's mouth.

Chan learns that Jim Kimball, a missing local policeman, was having a secret romance with Jean Kent, but she insists that he was not the officer seen in the mansion at the time of Harper's disappearance. Roth the butler is then killed soon after he promises to tell Chan the name of the murderer. After examining the dead butler's quarters, Chan determines that Roth was killed in his room, despite the fact that both Eddie and Birmingham saw the butler walking downstairs shortly before his death. Lloyd Archer, Harper's stepson, then arrives at the estate, claiming that Harper's secret gas formula was stolen from his birth father.

That night, Chan is nearly killed by a poisoned dart while searching for clues. The next morning, Louise discovers her brother's secret hiding place, but the vault can only be opened by Harper's voice speaking a coded message. Realizing that someone inside is being gassed, Chan, after several attempts, finally opens the vault by playing a Dictaphone recording of Harper that contains the correct sequence of words. Unconscious, Jean Kent is then removed from the vault, but she later insists that she was not attempting to steal her uncle's formula.

Michael is killed after he writes Eddie a note claiming to know who the murderer is. Officer Kimball's dead body is then discovered in the gas chamber by Birmingham, and Chan announces that all the murder victims were killed by an air gun hidden inside a ventriloquist's dummy. Furthermore, although dead, Roth appeared to walk with the aid of puppeteer's strings. Knowing that Stella is a master puppeteer, Chan names her as the murderer's accomplice.

Chan then states that the life mask broken during Michael's murder was of Meeker. The laboratory assistant attempts to escape but is immediately captured. Chan then pulls a rubber mask from Meeker's face to show that Meeker is really Archer. The dead body of the real Meeker is later found in the basement, and when Chan convinces Stella Graham to tell all, she states that Archer, a vaudevillian quick-change artist and impersonator, is actually her husband.

Notes: *The Jade Mask* was the first film in the Monogram series that Mantan Moreland's character of Birmingham Brown is specifically identified as Charlie Chan's chauffeur. In the first three Monogram films of the series, Birmingham was either a taxi driver or someone's butler. Many sources have mistakenly credited Edwin Luke, the younger brother of Keye Luke, as Tommy Chan instead of Eddie Chan.

Jaipur, Dr. Fez-wearing Luxor physician (portrayed by Frank Reicher in his first of two *Charlie Chan* roles) in *Charlie Chan in Egypt* (1935). When Tom Evans is shot in Ahmeti's tomb by Professor Thurston, Dr. Jaipur is called in to perform emergency surgery to remove the bullets, since Dr. Racine, the family doctor, is not readily available.

Jans, Harry (1899–February 4, 1962, Hollywood, California) Character actor who portrays the gangster Al Meers in *Charlie Chan at the Race Track* (1936).

Jaquet, Frank (March 16, 1885, Wisconsin–May 11, 1958, Los Angeles, California) Short, fat, jut-jawed character actor (real name: Frank Garnier Jaquet) who appeared in nearly 45 films, often as pompous windbags or slimy villains. Jaquet portrays the murderer Paul Hamlin in *Black Magic* (1944).

Jardine, Major An RAF officer (portrayed by George Barraud) who is Geoffrey Richmond's hunt secretary in *Charlie Chan in London* (1934). Jardine becomes the hunt secretary after Paul Gray is convicted of Hamilton's murder and sentenced to be hanged.

Jarvis, H.R. Chemical engineer (portrayed by James Flavin in his last of four *Charlie Chan* roles) in *The Shanghai Cobra* (1945). When in Shanghai, Jarvis is on the launch from which Jan Van Horn escapes, and has some of the jewels Van Horn was accused of stealing.

Now in America, Jarvis takes an office on the second floor of the Sixth National Bank Building as part of a plan to steal a U.S. government radium stockpile stored in the building's bank vault. Falsely identifying himself as Jan Van Horn, Jarvis puts a juke box in Joe's Coffee Shop which is used to murder three people with cobra venom when they press the coin return button. Under orders from Bradford Harris, the gang's leader, Jarvis develops a rocket loaded with explosives, intending to blow a hole in the storage vault of the bank.

Jaynes, Alan Would-be fiancé (portrayed by William Post, Jr.) of Shelah Fane in *The Black Camel* (1931). Jaynes asks Shelah Fane to marry him and leave with him on a boat that evening. However, she holds off his request because she has to discuss this with Tarneverro, a psychic.

Note: The character of Alan Jaynes parallels that of Clark Denton in *Charlie Chan in Rio* (1941).

Jeffrey, Keith Alias used by Paul Narvo (portrayed by John Sutton), who is a stockbroker for George Kirby and Ralph Percy in *Murder Over New York* (1940). *See also* **Narvo, Paul.**

Note: The film's credits list Jeffrey's first name as Richard, but he is never called that in the film. Furthermore, the character Keith Jeffrey loosely parallels that of Kenneth Dunwood (the alias used by Alan Raleigh) in *Charlie Chan's Chance* (1932).

Jenkins Policeman (portrayed by Charles Jordan in his third of five *Charlie Chan* roles) in *Shadows Over Chinatown* (1946). Jenkins' commanding officer is Capt. Allen.

Jenks, Si (September 23, 1876, Pennsylvania–January 6, 1970, Woodland Hills, California) Former circus performer and stage and screen actor (real name: Howard Jenkins) who appeared in nearly 90 films. In Westerns, he was always cast as a grizzled, toothless old codger. Jenks portrays newspaper editor Will Holley in *Charlie Chan's Courage* (1934).

Jennings, DeWitt C. (June 21, 1879, Cameron, Missouri–March 1, 1937, Hollywood, California) Stage and screen actor who appeared in nearly 130 silent and sound films, usually as gruff police captains or baffled suburban fathers. Jennings portrays Constable Brackett in *Charlie Chan's Courage* (1934).

Jennison, Harry Dan Winterslip's lawyer (portrayed by Walter Byron) who wants to marry Winterslip's daughter, Barbara, in *Charlie Chan's Greatest Case* (1933). Both Jennison and Barbara are traveling back to Honolulu by boat, and Barbara telegrams her father with the news. Instead of congratulating the couple, Winterslip's reply warns Jennison that unless he breaks off the engagement, Barbara will be disinherited. In time, Jennison murders both Amos and Dan Winterslip.

Jerome, Jerry Character actor who appeared in over 30 films. Jerome portrays "Shaky" Phil Maydorf in *Charlie Chan's Courage* (1934) and a detective (unbilled) in *Charlie Chan at the Race Track* (1936).

Jessop The butler (portrayed by Dwight Frye) in *The Black Camel* (1931). Jessop is strongly attracted to Anna, a maid, and thinks she shares the same affection towards him, declaring to her, "There isn't anything in the world I wouldn't do to help you." To protect Anna, who has murdered Shelah Fane, Jessop kills Smith, the beachcomber, and attempts to murder Charlie Chan.

Joe's Coffee Shop Coffee shop located at 1410 Dexter Street (around the corner from the Sixth National Bank) in *The Shanghai Cobra* (1945). Joe, the shop's owner, is portrayed by George Chandler in his last of four *Charlie Chan* roles. Because of its proximity to the bank, the bank's employees are the coffee shop's best customers. In the coffee shop is a juke box that is used to murder three people with cobra venom when they press the coin return button.

Johnson, Capt. Skipper (portrayed by Robert Barrat) of the freighter *Susan B. Jennings* in *Charlie Chan in Honolulu* (1938). Johnson murders a man named Hillman, who is the estranged husband of one his ship's passengers.

Hillman comes aboard the boat when it is near Honolulu to receive a package containing $300,000, which only Johnson and Mrs. Carol Wayne (an alias of Elsie Hillman) know is being held by Judy Hayes. Johnson later strangles Wayne in Judy Hayes' cabin with a scarf tied with a sailor's knot. The sailor's knot is the clue that points Charlie Chan towards Capt. Johnson as Wayne's murderer.

Johnson, Dr. The S.S. *Oceanic* ship's doctor who examines the dead body of Major Kent in *Charlie Chan at the Race Track* (1936).

Johnson, Kate Friend (portrayed by Myra McKinney) of Mrs. Conover in *Shadows Over Chinatown* (1946). Kate accompanies Mrs. Conover to San Francisco to find Conover's missing granddaughter. Kate is later murdered in Conover's apartment by Jeff Hay, who mistakes her for Mary Conover.

Johnson, Mr. (1) Butler for the phony psychics William and Justine Bonner who is more than eager to give Birmingham Brown his job in *Black Magic* (1944). Johnson explains to Birmingham that a séance is nothing more than a "group of people who sit around the table in the dark and hold hands." Birmingham then naively asks, "Do that make 'em happy to hold hands?" to which Johnson replies with a straight face, "Sort of raises their spirits some."

Before Mr. Johnson steps out the kitchen door, he gives the gullible Birmingham a magic book whose title is *How to Disappear: Vanishment Made Easy*. When Birmingham asks if it works, Johnson, who can't wait to leave, snaps his fingers and says "abracadabra" and exits.

Johnson, Mr. (2) Shady public accountant and confederate in a bank robbery gang (portrayed by Milton Parsons in his third of four *Charlie Chan* roles) in *Dark Alibi* (1946). Mr. Johnson is one of several boarders living at the Foss Family Hotel, and makes photoengravings of fingerprints on rubber gloves as part of an elaborate scheme whereby the forged fingerprints are left at a crime scene to falsely implicate ex-convicts. When Charlie Chan begins to unravel the complex scheme of how the fingerprints were forged, Mr. Danvers, another gang member, kills Johnson and hides his body inside a suit of armor at the Carey Theatrical Warehouse.

Johnson, Walter Character actor who portrays Jerry Gorton in *Charlie Chan in London* (1934).

Johnston, Clint Writer of the screenplay (with Oliver Drake) for *The Sky Dragon* (1949). In 1967 Johnson was nominated (with Don Peters) for an Academy Award in the Best Writing (Story and Screenplay—written directly for the screen) category for *The Naked Prey* (1966).

Jolley, I. Stanford (October 24, 1900–December 7, 1978, Woodland Hills, California) Scrawny, pencil-mustachioed supporting stage and screen actor who appeared in almost 140 films, sometimes credited as Stan Jolley or Stanford Jolley. In two *Charlie Chan* roles, Jolly portrays gangsters Gannett (credited as Stan Jolley) in *The Chinese Cat* (1944) and Ralph Brett (unbilled) in *The Scarlet Clue* (1945).

Western fans were more familiar with Stanford Jolley's scores of appearances as crooked gamblers, vacillating sheriffs, cattle rustlers, and suspicious bartenders. Jolley first began showing up as a posse member in films around 1937. On television westerns, Jolley was frequently seen in episodes of *Gunsmoke*, *The Big Valley*, *Wagon Train*, and *Adventures of Wild Bill Hickok*.

Jones Secret Service agent in charge (portrayed by Arthur Loft) nicknamed "Jonesy" in *Charlie Chan in the Secret Service* (1944). Jones is one of two Secret Service agents assigned by the president as bodyguards to George Melton. Jones is an old friend of Charlie Chan and hasn't worked on a case with Chan in ten years. When Jones asks Charlie about his wife and seven children, Charlie corrects him, saying, "Only there are seven more. Everything grow rapidly in Hawaii."

Jones, "Mobile" The attendant at the Bourbon Street Garage (portrayed by Haywood Jones) who is holding the stolen car of Simon Lafontaine in *Docks of New Orleans* (1948). "Mobile" is a friend of Birmingham (and to whom Birmingham owes money). When they meet at the garage, the two go into an abridged version of Mantan Moreland's (playing Birmingham) well-known "indefinite talk" comedy routine.

Jones, "Streamline" Warren Fenton's stable boy (portrayed by John Henry Allen) in *Charlie Chan at the Race Track* (1936). When Major Kent is murdered aboard the S.S. *Oceanic* on its voyage from Australia to America, it is "Streamline" who finds Kent's body in the stable area in the ship's forward hold.

Jons, Beverly Actress who portrays Joan Farnsworth in *The Feathered Serpent* (1948).

Jordan, Charles Character actor who appeared in over 40 films and five *Charlie Chan* roles. Jordan portrays Tom Starkey in *Black Magic* (1944), Nelson (unbilled) in *The Scarlet Clue* (1945), Jenkins (unbilled) in *Shadows Over Chinatown* (1946), a police fingerprint expert (unbilled) in *Docks of New Orleans* (1948), and the Gayety Theatre stage manager (unbilled) in *The Sky Dragon* (1949).

Jordan, Victor Son of Sally (Phillimore) Jordan. In *The Chinese Parrot* (1927) he is portrayed by Jack Trent; in *Charlie Chan's Courage* (1934) he is portrayed by Jack Carter. In both films Jordan arrives at the Madden ranch and blows the whole murder investigation by telling Jerry Delaney (who is impersonating Madden) that Bob should have handed over the pearls days earlier and demanding that Chan (using the alias Ah Kim) deliver the pearls as his mother instructed.

Jory, Victor (November 23, 1902, Dawson City, Yukon Territory, Alaska–February 11, 1982, Santa Monica, California) Handsome actor who appeared in over 100 films. Jory portrays the psychic Alfredo Marana in *Charlie Chan in Rio* (1941).

Victor Jory attended the University of California for only one year before he joined the Coast Guard, where he distinguished himself as a champion in several contact sports. Sharp-featured, muscular, and possessed of a rich theatrical voice, Jory made his New York stage debut in 1929, and one year later he co-starred in the original Broadway production of *Berkeley Square*.

Inaugurating his film career as a young officer in *Renegades* (1930), Jory spent the next five decades in roles ranging from romantic leads to villains. Highlights in his screen career include a sinister but strangely beautiful performance as Oberon in *A Midsummer Night's Dream* (1935); the vicious Injun Joe in *The Adventures of Tom Sawyer* (1938); carpetbagger Jonas Wilkerson in *Gone with the Wind* (1939); Texas patriot William Travis in *Man of Conquest* (1940); the crippled patriarch Jeb Torrance in *The Fugitive Kind* (1959); the close-mouthed father of Helen Keller (Captain Keller) in *The Miracle Worker* (1962); and the ancient South American Indian chief in *Papillon* (1973).

In 1940 Jory starred in the Columbia serial *The Shadow* (1940), portraying the dual role of the mind-clouding shadow and his alter ego, Lamont Cranston. An occasional theatrical director and playwright, Jory wrote the Broadway production *Five Who Were Mad*. On television Jory starred as detective Lt. Howard Finucane in the popular syndicated detective series *Manhunt* (1959–61) and guested on dozens of other programs.

José One of two undercover Mexican secret police agents (portrayed by an unbilled Frank

Leyva) who are under the command of Pedro Lopez in *The Feathered Serpent* (1948). Lopez, Filippe, and José together investigate the smuggling of Aztec antiquities out of Mexico and the disappearance of Professor Henry Farnsworth. *See also* **Filippe.**

Josephine Attractive maid (portrayed by Mildred Boyd) of Marguerite Fontan in *The Red Dragon* (1945). Chattanooga Brown is attracted to her when he first sees her in the hallway of the hotel. When told that her name is Josephine, Chattanooga responds with, "No wonder I feel like Napoleon."

Joubert, Inspector Jules Chief of police of Monte Carlo (portrayed by Harold Huber in his second of four *Charlie Chan* roles) in *Charlie Chan at Monte Carlo* (1937). After Joubert introduces himself to Charlie and Lee at the casino, Lee then attempts to impress Joubert with his limited knowledge of French, to which Joubert replies, "That is French, no?"

July 21, 1941 Date of the marriage of Connie Jackson and Andy Barrett, performed by Jonathon Tibbetts at the Orange Blossom Manor, in *The Sky Dragon* (1949).

Jung, Shia Actress who portrays circus contortionist Su Toy, dubbed "The Human Knot," in *Charlie Chan at the Circus* (1936).

K

Kalinor Diamonds Collection of diamonds stolen in Chicago one year earlier in *The Chinese Cat* (1944). After their theft, the diamonds are hidden in secret compartments inside Chinese figurine sculptures that are bought from artist Wu Song by Webster Deacon's Sea Tide Art Co. The largest of the diamonds is hidden in a statue of a black cat, which normally rests on Thomas Manning's desk in his house. Manning double-crosses his partner, Webster Deacon, taking the diamond for himself, and is killed by Deacon.

kanaka Hawaiian word for "man," but it is also used to refer to a native Hawaiian or any South Sea Islander. In *Dangerous Money* (1946), P.T. Burke uses the term "kanaka" when telling Charlie Chan who could have thrown the knife that killed undercover U.S. Treasury agent Scott Pearson.

Kane, Captain Captain of the *Suva Star* (portrayed by Truman Bradley in his second of two *Charlie Chan* roles) in *Dead Men Tell* (1941). Kane explains to Charlie Chan that many years ago he went on a treasure hunt to Cocos Island with his partner, but that the man left him there to die. Believing that his former partner, now known as Jed Thomasson, would not be able to resist returning to the island, Kane arranges the journey for Miss Nodbury's treasure hunt so that he can find and kill the man.

Karloff, Boris (November 23, 1887, London, England–February 2, 1969, Sussex, England) The long-reigning king of Hollywood horror films, Karloff was a stage and screen actor (real name: William Henry Pratt) who appeared in 170 silent and sound films, sometimes billed simply as "Karloff." In two

Boris Karloff, the king of Hollywood horror, even appeared in two *Charlie Chan* films.

Charlie Chan roles, Karloff portrays Col. Beetham's Sudanese servant in *Behind That Curtain* (1929) and opera singer Gravelle in *Charlie Chan at the Opera* (1936).

Born in South London, Boris Karloff was the youngest of nine children and was educated at London University in preparation for a career as a diplomat. However, in 1909 he immigrated to Canada to accept a job on a farm and, while living in Ontario, began pursuing acting, joining a touring company and adopting the stage name Boris Karloff. His first role was as an elderly man in a production of Molnar's *The Devil*, and for the next decade Karloff toiled in obscurity, traveling across North America in a variety of theatrical troupes.

Karloff's first sound-era role (unbilled) was as Abdoul in *The Unholy Night* (1929, a.k.a. *The Green Ghost*). His role as Ned Galloway in Columbia's *The Criminal Code* (1931) became his first significant hit, and soon Karloff was an in-demand character actor. Meanwhile, at Universal, plans were underway to adapt the Mary Shelley classic, *Frankenstein*, in the wake of the studio's Bela Lugosi hit, *Dracula* (1931). Lugosi, however, rejected the role of the monster, opting instead to attach his name to a project titled *Quasimodo*, which ultimately went unproduced. Karloff, billed only as "?" in the opening credits (though named in the cast list at film's end), then replaced Lugosi as Dr. Frankenstein's monster in *Frankenstein* (1931). With the aid of the studio's makeup and special effects unit, he entered into his definitive role, becoming an overnight superstar.

Touted as the natural successor to Lon Chaney, Karloff was then signed by Universal to a seven-year contract and portrayed Morgan, a deaf-mute killer in *The Old Dark House* (1932), followed by the dual role of Imhotep and Ardath Bey in *The Mummy* (1932). When on loan to MGM, Karloff portrayed the evil Dr. Fu Manchu in *The Mask of Fu Manchu* (1932), but on his return to Universal, the studio reneged on their promised salary hike, and he walked out.

Karloff then traveled back to England, where he portrayed Professor Morlant in *The Ghoul* (1933) before coming back to Hollywood to appear in John Ford's *The Lost Patrol* (1934). After making amends with Universal, he co-starred with Lugosi as Hjalmar Poelzig in *The Black Cat* (1934), the first of several pairings for the two actors. In 1935 Karloff played The Monster in the sequel *Bride of Frankenstein*.

Karloff spent the remainder of the 1930s continuing to work at an incredible pace, and like many of his fellow horror movie actors, the quality of his films would taper off dramatically. Finally, in 1941 he began a three-year theatrical run in *Arsenic and Old Lace* before returning to Hollywood to star as Dr. Hohne in the "A" production, *The Climax*. By the mid–1950s, Karloff was a familiar presence on television, and hosted his own series from 1956 to 1958.

Karlson, Phil (July 2, 1908, Chicago, Illinois–August 25, 1975, West Los Angeles, California) Film director (real name: Philip N. Karlstein) of over 50 films, including *The Shanghai Cobra* (1945) and *Dark Alibi* (1946).

Phil Karlson was the son of popular Irish actress Lillian O'Brien, and studied painting at Chicago's Art Institute. At his father's behest, Karlson went on to study law at California's Loyola Marymount College before obtaining his first movie job as a Universal Studios propman. He worked his way up the ladder as a cutter, editor, and short-subjects director. He graduated to feature-film directing at the Columbia Pictures "B" unit, and then turned out several low-budget thrillers at Monogram. Karlson also directed Marilyn Monroe's first starring picture, *Ladies of the Chorus* (1949).

In 1959 he directed the two-part pilot for *The Untouchables* television series, which was later released theatrically as *The Scarface Mob* (1962). Karlson also directed the Dean Martin *Matt Helm* spy spoofs of the 1960s. Karlson regained his cult following with the action-packed surprise hit, *Walking Tall* (1973), which made him a millionaire many times over thanks to his farsighted financial investment in the project.

Karnoff, Joan The wife of financier Victor Karnoff in *Charlie Chan at Monte Carlo* (1937).

Portrayed by Kay Linaker in her first of four *Charlie Chan* roles, Joan is blackmailed by her supposed former husband, Albert Rogers. Mrs. Karnoff removes three bonds worth $25,000 from her husband's safe to pay off Rogers, from whom she never really was divorced.

Karnoff, Victor The ruthless financier (portrayed by Sidney Blackmer) in *Charlie Chan at Monte Carlo* (1937). Karnoff wins a high stakes chemin de fer game against business rival Paul Savarin.

Karzoff, Carl and Kurt Eccentric twin brothers who specialize in stolen gems (both portrayed by John Davidson in his second of two *Charlie Chan* roles) in *The Chinese Cat* (1944). With fellow gangsters Gannett, Catlen, and Salos, Carl and Kurt are part of a jewelry theft and smuggling ring led by Thomas Manning and Webster Deacon. When it becomes known that Charlie Chan is reopening the investigation of Thomas Manning's murder, Kurt becomes nervous and telephones Chan to arrange a meeting. However, he is strangled by Deacon before Chan arrives.

Kashimo Charlie Chan's overzealous but inept Japanese policeman assistant (portrayed by Otto Yamaoka) in *The Black Camel* (1931). Unlike Charlie's children, who as comic foils often try to assist their father in solving murders in later films, Kashimo often bears the brunt of Chan's insults.

Kaufman, Edward Producer of *Charlie Chan at Treasure Island* (1939).

Kaus, Gina Writer, sometimes credited as Gina Kauss, who wrote a play (with Ladislas Fodor) that served as the basis for the film *City in Darkness* (1939).

Kay, Edward J. Music director, composer, and producer of over 130 films. Kay was the music director for 12 *Charlie Chan* films at Monogram, and was nominated for five Academy Awards:

Best Music (Scoring of
a Dramatic Picture)

King of the Zombies (1941)

Best Music (Scoring of a Dramatic
or Comedy Picture)

Klondike Fury (1942)
G.I. Honeymoon (1945)

Best Music (Scoring of
a Musical Picture)

Lady, Let's Dance (1944)
Sunbonnet Sue (1945)

Charlie Chan filmography: *The Jade Mask* (1945), *The Scarlet Clue* (1945), *The Shanghai Cobra* (1945), *The Red Dragon* (1945), *Dark Alibi* (1946), *Shadows Over Chinatown* (1946), *Dangerous Money* (1946), *The Trap* (1947), *The Chinese Ring* (1947), *The Shanghai Chest* (1948), *The Golden Eye* (1948), and *The Sky Dragon* (1949).

Kaylin, Samuel Musical director and composer for over 125 movies, including 18 *Charlie Chan* films with Twentieth Century–Fox and *Mr. Moto's Gamble* (1938), a reworked version of the never-completed *Charlie Chan at the Ringside*.

Charlie Chan filmography: *Charlie Chan's Greatest Case* (1933), *Charlie Chan's Courage* (1934), *Charlie Chan in London* (1934), *Charlie Chan in Paris* (1935), *Charlie Chan in Egypt* (1935), *Charlie Chan in Shanghai* (1935), *Charlie Chan's Secret* (1936), *Charlie Chan at the Opera* (1936), *Charlie Chan at the Circus* (1936), *Charlie Chan at the Race Track* (1936), *Charlie Chan at the Olympics* (1937), *Charlie Chan on Broadway* (1937), *Charlie Chan at Monte Carlo* (1937), *Charlie Chan in Honolulu* (1938), *Charlie Chan in Reno* (1939), *Charlie Chan at Treasure Island* (1939), *Charlie Chan in Panama* (1940), and *Charlie Chan's Murder Cruise* (1940).

Keane, Capt. Ronald Ship captain (portrayed by George Brent) of the boat taken by Charlie Chan from Honolulu to San Francisco on the trail of Jim Everhard in *Charlie Chan Carries On* (1931).

Keane, Edward (May 28, 1884, New York, New York–October 12, 1959, California) Character actor who appeared in over 120 films, mostly in roles requiring tuxedos and military uniforms. In two *Charlie Chan* roles, Keane portrays Col. Webster (unbilled) in *Charlie Chan at the Olympics* (1937) and the military doctor, Dr. Fredericks, in *Charlie Chan in Panama* (1940).

Keane, Robert E. (March 4, 1885–July 2, 1981, Hollywood, California) Stage and screen actor who was often effectively cast as confidence men, shady attorneys, and mystery murderers. Keane portrays Alfred Wyans in *The Red Dragon* (1945).

Robert Keane is perhaps best remembered by Laurel and Hardy fans for his roles in three of the team's Twentieth Century–Fox films of the 1940s, playing con artists in two of them—*A-Haunting We Will Go* (1942) and *Jitterbugs* (1943). In the early 1950s, Keane played Captain Brackett in the national touring company of Rodgers and Hammerstein's *South Pacific*.

Kearney, Mr. Faceless manager of the Bay City Escort Bureau in *Shadows Over Chinatown* (1946). Although he is never seen, it is thought that Mr. Kearney is actually Jeff Hay.

Keefe, Cornelius (July 13, 1900, Boston, Massachusetts–December 11, 1972, Los Angeles, California) Actor who appeared in nearly 45 silent and sound films, sometimes credited as Connie Keefe and Cornelius O'Keefe. Keefe portrays Steve Leatherbee in *Charlie Chan's Greatest Case* (1933).

Keene, Richard (September 16, 1890, Philadelphia, Pennsylvania–March 11, 1971) Character actor of nearly 20 films who portrays Buttons, the ship steward, in *Charlie Chan's Murder Cruise* (1940).

Keiner, Elmer An assistant in Rhadini's magic act (portrayed by Wally Vernon) who provides some measure of comedic relief in *Charlie Chan at Treasure Island* (1939).

Keith, Ian (February 27, 1899, Boston, Massachusetts–March 26, 1960, New York, New York) Tall Broadway and movie actor (real name: Keith Ross) who appeared in almost 80 silent and sound films. Keith portrays criminologist and author Dr. Paul Rednick in *The Chinese Cat* (1944).

Tall, handsome, golden-throated leading man Ian Keith became a Broadway favorite in the 1920s and also pursued a sporadic silent film career, appearing opposite Gloria Swanson and Lon Chaney, Sr. A natural for talkies, Keith appeared in early films as Bill Thorpe in Raoul Walsh's *The Big Trail* (1930) and John Wilkes Booth in D.W. Griffith's *Abraham Lincoln* (1930). A favorite of Cecil B. DeMille, Keith stole the show as the cultured, soft-spoken Saladin in *The Crusades* (1935).

A rambunctious night life and an inclination towards elbow-bending reduced Keith's stature in Hollywood, and by the mid–1940s he was occasionally obliged to appear in low-budget films such as the Bowery Boys' *Mr. Hex* (1946). Keith's final screen appearance was a cameo as Rameses I in DeMille's *The Ten Commandments* (1956).

Kellogg, Bill Escort (portrayed by Hamilton MacFadden in his last of three *Charlie Chan* roles) of Grace Ellis in *Charlie Chan in Rio* (1941).

Kellogg, Bruce Character actor, sometimes credited as William Kellogg, who portrays Joe Thompson (alias Jack Tilford) in *Shadows Over Chinatown* (1946) and Talbot Bartlett in *The Golden Eye* (1948).

Kelly, Sgt. Rude, short-tempered Los Angeles policeman (portrayed by William Demarest) in *Charlie Chan at the Opera* (1936). When told by his commanding officer, Inspector Regan, that Charlie Chan has been brought in on the case of the escaped maniac Gravelle, Kelly is peeved that "Chop Suey" is now involved. Regan then reminds Kelly that he could learn some manners from the Chinese.

Kelsey, Fred A. (August 20, 1884, Sandusky, Ohio–September 2, 1961, Hollywood, California) American character actor who appeared in over 130 silent and sound films, often as a policeman. In two unbilled *Charlie Chan* roles, Kelsey portrays policemen in both *Charlie Chan at the Opera* (1936) and *Charlie Chan in Reno* (1939).

Kelso, Capt. James J. Unscrupulous, shady smuggler portrayed by Thayer Roberts, in *The Chinese Ring* (1947). As the head of the phony Kelso Aviation Company, Kelso is the partner of Capt. Kong in scheme to smuggle war airplanes to a Chinese warlord in the Orient on the *Shanghai Maid*.

Kelso Aviation Company Phony Los Angeles–based company headed by Capt. Kelso, in *The Chinese Ring* (1947).

Kemp, Mr. Private secretary to Home Secretary Sir Lionel Bashford in *Charlie Chan in London* (1934). Portrayed by Perry Ivins in his first of two *Charlie Chan* roles, Kemp telephones Pamela Gray, suggesting that she should try to persuade Charlie Chan to help prove that her brother is innocent of murder.

Kendall, Cy (March 10, 1898, St. Louis, Missouri–July 22, 1953, Woodland Hills, California) Heavy-set stage and screen character actor (real name: Cyrus W. Kendall) who appeared in over 90 films, often as a cigar-chewing, shady type. Kendall portrays Webster Deacon in *The Chinese Cat* (1944).

Cy Kendall was eight years old when he made his acting debut at the fabled Pasadena Playhouse. As an adult, the portly Kendall became a charter member of the Playhouse's Eighteen Actors Inc., acting in and/or directing over 100 theatrical productions. In films from 1936, he was usually typecast as an abrasive, cigar-chomping detective, gangster, or machine politician. Kendall showed up in roles both large and small in feature films, and was prominently cast in several of MGM's *Crime Does Not Pay* short subjects.

Typical Kendall assignments of the 1940s included Jumbo Madigan in *Alias Boston Blackie* (1941) and "Honest" John Travers in *Outlaw Trail* (1944). Remaining active into the early years of live television, Kendall appeared in several guest spots on the 1949 quiz show and anthology, *Armchair Detective*, and co-starred with Robert Bice, Spencer Chan, and Herb Ellis on the Hollywood-based ABC weekly series, *Mysteries of Chinatown* (1949–50).

Kennaway, Mark Traveling companion (portrayed by John Garrick) to Patrick Tait on Dr. Lofton's tour in *Charlie Chan Carries On* (1931). While on the ship, he becomes fond of Hugo Drake's granddaughter, Pamela Potter, and they plan to marry.

Kennedy, Edgar (April 26, 1890, Monterey, California–November 9, 1948, Woodland Hills, California) American comic actor who appeared in nearly 215 silent and sound films, sometimes credited as E. Livingston Kennedy and Ed Kennedy. Kennedy portrays "Shaky" Phil Maydorf in *The Chinese Parrot* (1927).

Acknowledged as the master of the "slow burn" when antagonized, and the brother of actor Tom Kennedy, Edgar Kennedy left home in his teens with the urge to see the world. He worked a number of manual labor jobs and sang in touring musical shows before returning to his native California in 1912 to break into the infant movie industry. Hired by Mack Sennett in 1914, Kennedy played countless roles in the *Keystone Kops* comedies. He would later claim to be one of the original Keystone Kops, but his specialty during this period was portraying mustache-twirling villains. By the early 1920s, Kennedy's screen image had mellowed, and he most often played detectives or middle-aged husbands.

He joined Hal Roach Studios in 1928 where he did some of his best early work, co-starring with Laurel and Hardy, Charlie Chase, and appearing in the *Our Gang* comedies. He also directed two-reelers under the stage name E. Livingston Kennedy. However, Kennedy was dropped from the Roach payroll in a 1930 economy drive, but he'd already made a satisfactory talkie debut even though he'd had to lower his voice to his more familiar gravely growl after it was discovered that his natural voice sounded high-pitched and effeminate. During his Roach

Studio stay, Kennedy developed his patented "slow burn," wherein he'd confront a bad situation or personal humiliation by glowering at the camera, pausing, then slowly rubbing his hand over his face.

In 1931 Kennedy was hired by RKO studios to star in a series of two-reelers, unofficially titled *Mr. Average Man.* These films, precursors to the many television sitcoms of the 1950s, cast Kennedy as head of a maddening household consisting of his dizzy wife (usually Florence Lake, sister of Arthur "Dagwood" Lake), a nagging mother-in-law, and a lazy brother-in-law. Kennedy made six of these shorts per year for the next 17 years, taking time out to contribute memorable supporting role performances to several film classics, playing the lemonade vendor in *Duck Soup* (1933), the sheriff in *San Francisco* (1936), Pop Randall in *A Star Is Born* (1937), and a police captain in *Anchors Aweigh* (1944).

Some of Kennedy's most rewarding movie assignments came late in his career, such as Jake the poetic bartender in Harold Lloyd's *Sin of Harold Diddlebock* (1946) and the classical music–loving private detective, Sweeney, in *Unfaithfully Yours* (1948), both directed by Preston Sturges. On November 9, 1948, shortly after completing his 103rd *Average Man* two-reeler (and 36 hours before a Hollywood testimonial dinner was to be held in his honor), Kennedy died of throat cancer. His last film appearance, as Doris Day's long-suffering father in *Romance on the High Seas* (1948), was released posthumously.

Kent, Jean Niece (portrayed by Janet Warren in her first of two *Charlie Chan* roles) of Mr. Harper who's made to function as a housemaid in *The Jade Mask* (1945).

Kent, Major Gordon Horse race sportsman (portrayed by George Irving in his second of two *Charlie Chan* roles) in *Charlie Chan at the Race Track* (1936). Kent is the original owner of a racehorse named Avalanche, but turns the horse over to his son-in-law, George Chester, as a wedding present.

In Australia Kent had entered Avalanche in the Melbourne Handicap, and when Avalanche's jockey, "Tip" Collins, fouled another horse, Avalanche was disqualified. Kent strongly feels that a racetrack gambling ring paid Collins to throw the race and vows to get to the bottom of it by sending his old friend Charlie Chan a telegram.

Before Charlie can meet Kent when the S.S. *Oceanic* stops in Honolulu en route to Los Angeles, Kent is killed in Avalanche's stall in the ship's forward hold during the voyage. His death is at first thought to be an accident, Avalanche having kicked Kent in the head, but Chan quickly proves that the pattern of blood stains in the horse's stall is a poor attempt at a cover-up for murder. Chester and Kent frequently quarreled over Chester's gambling losses, and any investigation would have uncovered Chester as the leader of the gambling ring.

Kent, Robert (December 3, 1908, Hartford, Connecticut–May 4, 1955) Handsome stage and screen actor (real name: Douglas Blackley, Jr.) who appeared in almost 40 films. Kent portrays Victor Karnoff's secretary and brother-in-law, Gordon Chase, in *Charlie Chan at Monte Carlo* (1937).

Before becoming a star of action movies, Robert Kent was an amateur boxer and adolescent lead in theatrical productions. In the mid–1930s he appeared frequently in Hollywood "B" movies as a hard-fighting leading man, and frequently played opposite Rochelle Hudson. Kent was married to (and divorced from) Astrid Allywn, who portrays Janice Gage in *Charlie Chan's Secret* (1936).

Kent, Robert E. Producer and screenwriter for almost 80 films. Kent was one of the screenwriters for *Charlie Chan in Reno* (1939).

Kenyon, Dick Lawyer (portrayed by Robert Lowery in his second of three *Charlie Chan* roles) who is engaged to Paula Drake in *Charlie Chan's Murder Cruise* (1940). Dick and his uncle are members of Dr. Suderman's cruise, and Dick is initially suspected of his uncle's murder since he was overheard by Mrs. Walters having a loud disagreement with his uncle about his intended marriage to Paula Drake.

Kenyon, Gwen Character actress who appeared in almost 20 films and portrays Inez Arranto in *Charlie Chan in the Secret Service* (1944).

Kenyon, Mr. Retired businessman who, along with his nephew Dick, is a member of Dr. Suderman's cruise in *Charlie Chan's Murder Cruise* (1940). Mr. Kenyon, having earlier changed hotel rooms with Gerald Pendleton (the intended victim) is mistakenly strangled with a leather strap from Dr. Suderman's suitcase by Jim Eberhardt, and a pouch of 30 dimes is placed in his hands. *See also* **thirty pieces of silver.**

Kenzie, Hugh State prison guard (portrayed by George Holmes) who is the leader of a bank robbery gang in *Dark Alibi* (1946). Kenzie wants to marry June Harley, but the marriage is opposed by her father.

Kenzie gets Jimmy Slade, a convicted forger and prisoner trustee who works in the prison's fingerprint bureau file room, to remove fingerprint cards of previous inmates at the prison, which are then smuggled out by Kenzie to be forged by Mr. Johnson at the Carey Theatrical Warehouse. When Charlie Chan suspects Slade of being part of the bank robbery and forgery scheme, Kenzie gives Slade a gun for protection, but the gun barrel is purposely plugged by Kenzie. Cornered in the prison bailing shed, Slade tries to shoot Chan, but Slade is killed when his gun explodes.

Kernell, William Writer and composer who composed the libretto for the opera *Carnival* in *Charlie Chan at the Opera* (1936).

Kerrigan, Joseph M. (December 16, 1884, Dublin, Ireland–April 29, 1964, Hollywood, California) Irish-born film director and stage and screen character actor who appeared in almost 80 silent and sound films. Kerrigan portrays Tarneverro's friend, Thomas MacMasters, in *The Black Camel* (1931).

Kibbee, Milton (1896–April 21, 1970, Simi Valley, California) Character actor who appeared in almost 150 films, often in bit roles as desk clerks, reporters, and waiters, and was the younger brother of prominent stage and screen character actor Guy Kibbee. Kibbee portrays Herbert Sinclair, the henpecked assistant (unbilled) of Mrs. Marsh, in *The Scarlet Clue* (1945).

Kikume, Al (1893, Hawaii–March 27, 1972, Hollywood, California) Character actor, often cast as a Pacific island native, who appeared in over 25 films, and had unbilled roles in four *Charlie Chan* films. Kikume portrays the plainclothes policeman in a white suit in *Charlie Chan at the Race Track* (1936), a uniformed officer at the police station desk microphone in *Charlie Chan at the Olympics* (1937), a police officer on the gang plank of the *Susan B. Jennings* in *Charlie Chan in Honolulu* (1938), and a Honolulu policeman in *Charlie Chan in Reno* (1939). He is perhaps best known for the role of Chief Mehevi, Dorothy Lamour's father, in *The Hurricane* (1937).

Kilpatrick, Reid Actor who portrays radio announcer Wilbur Chester at the Cosmo Radio Center in *The Scarlet Clue* (1945).

Kilvaine, Deputy Chief J.J. San Francisco policeman (portrayed by Donald MacBride in his first of two *Charlie Chan* roles) and an old friend of Charlie Chan in *Charlie Chan at Treasure Island* (1939). Kilvaine is investigating three recent suicides, all of whom were clients of the mystic, Dr. Zodiac.

Kim, Ah Alias used by Charlie Chan while posing as a cook-houseboy in both *The Chinese Parrot* (1927) and its remake, *Charlie Chan's Courage* (1934). Because Chan feels suspicious about the terms for the delivery of the Phillimore pearl necklace to the Madden ranch instead of New York, as was originally agreed upon, Chan is entrusted by Sally (Phillimore) Jordan, a former employer, to personally deliver the necklace. In *The Chinese Parrot* Chan travels to the Madden ranch with Robert Eden; in *Charlie Chan's Courage* his companion is Bob Crawford.

Kimball, Officer Jim Police officer (portrayed by Ralph Lewis) who is murdered by Lloyd

Archer in *The Jade Mask* (1945). Kimball goes to the Harper house to see Jean Kent (with whom he appears to have a romantic relationship) but is instead murdered by Archer, who then impersonates Kimball to gain entrance to the house.

King, Chief Reno police chief (portrayed by Charles D. Brown) who is an old friend of Charlie Chan in *Charlie Chan in Reno* (1939).

King, Claude Ewart (January 15, 1879, Northampton, England–September 18, 1941, Los Angeles, California) British-born actor who appeared in over 50 films, often playing British aristocrats or military officers, and who was a founding member of the Screen Actors Guild. Appearing in three *Charlie Chan* films at Fox, King portrays Sir George Mannering in *Behind That Curtain* (1929), Capt. Arthur Temple Cope in *Charlie Chan's Greatest Case* (1933), and the RAF commandant (unbilled) in *Charlie Chan in London* (1934).

King, Cole Leader of a variety troupe (portrayed by Howard Negley in his first of two *Charlie Chan* roles) in *The Trap* (1947). His ex-wife, Mrs. Thorn, deserted him by running away with a dancer, and when she wants to return to him, he humiliates her by offering her a job as his wardrobe mistress. She then kills Lois and Marcia and frames King to ruin him and make him suffer.

King, Flight Commander A friend (portrayed by Reginald Sheffield) of Capt. Hamilton at the Farnwell Aerodrome in *Charlie Chan in London* (1934).

King, Joe (February 9, 1883, Austin, Texas–April 11, 1951, Woodland Hills, California) American stage and screen character actor who appeared in almost 100 silent and sound films, often as a policeman. King portrays New York Police Inspector O'Matthews in *Charlie Chan at the Wax Museum* (1940).

King, John "Dusty" (July 11, 1909, Cincinnati, Ohio–November 11, 1987, California) Actor (real name: Miller McLeod Everson) who appeared in 25 films, generally westerns, and who is the younger brother of Western actor Bob Livingston, who himself portrays Professor John Stanley in *The Feathered Serpent* (1948). John King plays George Randolph, the chief officer on the *Susan B. Jennings*, in *Charlie Chan in Honolulu* (1938).

King, Louis (June 28, 1898, Christiansburg, Virginia–September 7, 1962, Hollywood, California) Character actor and film director of nearly 85 silent and sound films, sometimes credited as L.H. King or Lewis King. Credited as Luis King, he was the director of *Charlie Chan in Egypt* (1935).

The younger brother of film director Henry King, Louis King entered movies in 1919 as a character actor. Specializing in villains and blusterers, King alternated his billing between Louis King and Lewis King throughout the silent era. In 1927 he followed his brother's lead by becoming a film director, churning out several westerns and melodramas at FBO Studios, which later became RKO. Most of his talkies were strictly "B" pictures, such as the *Bulldog Drummond* series which he directed for Paramount in the 1930s.

King was finally afforded larger budgets at Twentieth Century–Fox during the 1940s and was able to turn out *My Friend Flicka* sequels—*Thunderhead: Son of Flicka* (1945) and *Green Grass of Wyoming* (1948).

King, Watson Alias used by Cesare Borgia (portrayed by Henry Daniell), who is the younger stepbrother of Lucy Manderley (a.k.a. Lucrezia della Borgia), in *Castle in the Desert* (1942). Watson King arrives at the Manderley Castle, having been commissioned to complete a bust of Lucy Manderley. He also secretly removes the distributor cap from the Manderley Castle's car, stranding the Manderleys, Charlie Chan, and their house guests.

King tells Chan that he was formerly with Scotland Yard and is currently employed by the Brewster Detective Agency in Los Angeles. Although long thought to have been killed in the Spanish War, King really comes to the castle to kill Paul Manderley so that his stepsister would inherit the estate. King stabs Walter Hartford to death with an arrow from a crossbow to keep Hartford from telling Chan that Cesare Borgia is still alive, having had a prominent facial scar removed so that he would not be recognized.

Kinnell, Murray (1888, England–August 11, 1954, Santa Barbara, California) Character actor who appeared in almost 50 films and had roles in four *Charlie Chan* films with Fox. Kinnell portrays the beachcomber, Smith, in *The Black Camel* (1931); Martin Thorne in *Charlie Chan's Courage* (1934); Phillips the butler in *Charlie Chan in London* (1934); and Henri Latouche in *Charlie Chan in Paris* (1935).

Murray Kinnell

Kinney, Joe Half-owner of the Kinney & Gaines Combined Circus (portrayed by Paul Stanton) and fiancé of Marie Norman who is easily disliked by everyone in *Charlie Chan at the Circus* (1936). Because the circus' owner, John Gaines, needed money to keep the circus afloat, Kinney loans Gaines money in return for a half-interest in the circus.

Prior to getting involved in the circus business, Kinney and Tom Holt were caught cheating at cards at an El Paso, Texas casino on May 30, 1935 (Decoration Day, now Memorial Day). Holt killed the sheriff while trying to escape and Kinney was held as a witness. In a quarrel over gambling money after being given a job in the circus by Kinney, Holt begins to send Kinney unsigned, threatening letters. Learning that Charlie Chan is in town with his wife and 12 children on a vacation to the mainland, Kinney sends Charlie 14 free passes to the circus. His ulterior motive is to ask Chan to look at the threatening letters and offer whatever advice he can. Before Charlie can meet Kinney at the business wagon during the circus performance, Holt, fearing that he will be found out and turned over to the police, kills Kinney with his strong hands by breaking Kinney's neck.

Kinney & Gaines Combined Circus Circus owned by Joe Kinney and John Gaines in *Charlie Chan at the Circus* (1936). Because Gaines needs money to keep the circus afloat, Kinney loans Gaines the money in return for a half-interest in the circus.

Kirby, George President of the Metropolitan Aircraft Company (portrayed by Ricardo Cortez) and a friend of Hugh Drake in *Murder Over New York* (1940). When Drake arrives in New York to track down Paul Narvo, Kirby puts him up at his apartment as his guest and lets him use his library as an office. Kirby's aircraft company is developing a new bomber that has been sabotaged once already by a sabotage ring headed by Paul Narvo, who murders both Drake and Kirby with tetrogene.

Note: The character George Kirby loosely parallels that of Barry Kirk in *Charlie Chan's Chance* (1932).

Kirk, Barry Wall Street stockbroker (portrayed by Ralph Morgan) in whose office Sir Lionel Grey was murdered in *Charlie Chan's Chance* (1932).

Note: The character Barry Kirk loosely parallels that of George Kirby in *Murder Over New York* (1940).

Kirk, Freddie Knife-thrower entertainer (portrayed by John Harmon) who is referred to as "little showman" by Charlie Chan in *Dangerous Money* (1946). Kirk is part of a gang which plans to sell artworks stolen from Philippine banks during the Japanese invasion. He is killed by a knife thrown by Joseph Murdock, dressed as a woman (Mrs. Whipple).

Kirkland, Alexander (September 15, 1908, Mexico City, Mexico–) Leading man of stage and screen who portrays John Douglas in *Charlie Chan's Chance* (1932).

Alexander Kirkland was born in Mexico City to U.S. citizens and began his career in theater, coming to film in the 1930s. He returned to the stage to act, direct, and produce in the 1940s, and appeared only sporadically in films. With the advent of television, he began writing for live broadcasts. Kirkland left the industry in the 1950s to work as an art dealer. Kirkland's third wife was burlesque dancer Gypsy Rose Lee.

Kirkwood, James (February 22, 1875, Grand Rapids, Michigan–August 24, 1963, Woodland Hills, California) Silent film director of nearly 35 films and an actor who appeared in almost 120 silent and sound films. Kirkwood portrays New York Police Inspector Flannery in *Charlie Chan's Chance* (1932).

James Kirkwood opened up his film career at the Biograph studios in 1909 and closed it out with 1962's *The Ugly American*. He occasionally interrupted his acting career for a spot of directing (in 1912 alone, he directed nine pictures featuring Mary Pickford). Lacking the drive and organizational skills to excel as a director, Kirkwood willingly switched back to full-time acting by 1918. His silent film acting credits include D.W. Griffith's *Home Sweet Home* (1914) and W.C. Fields' *That Royale Girl* (1925).

His talkie roles frequently found Kirkwood on the wrong side of the law, as in the Tom Mix western, *My Pal the King* (1932). Kirkwood's third wife was actress Lila Lee, and their son was James Kirkwood, Jr., coauthor of the Broadway long-runner, *A Chorus Line*.

Kissinger, Miriam Screenwriter for *Dangerous Money* (1946) and *The Trap* (1947).

Klein, Philip (c. 1889–June 8, 1935, Hollywood, California) Screenplay writer of over 35 silent and sound films, and the writer of the screenplay and dialogue for three *Charlie Chan* films.

Philip Klein joined the Fox writing staff in 1926 and went on to work with John Ford on *Four Sons* (1928) and *Hangman's House* (1928). In the talkie era, he scripted three of the early *Charlie Chan* entries, the musical *Stand Up and Cheer* (1934), and the Spencer Tracy melodrama *Dante's Inferno* (1935). He was evidently downsized when Fox merged with Twentieth Century in 1935. Philip Klein's last screen credit was *Pier 13*, a remake of his comedy-drama *Me and My Gal* (1932).

Charlie Chan filmography: *Charlie Chan Carries On* (1931), *The Black Camel* (1931), and *Charlie Chan's Chance* (1932).

Kline, Benjamin H. (July 11, 1894, Birmingham, Alabama–January 7, 1974, Hollywood, California) Cinematographer for nearly 175 silent and sound films, sometimes credited as Ben H. Kline, Benjamin Kline, Bennie Kline, or Ben Kline. He was the cinematographer for *The Chinese Parrot* (1927).

Koenig, William Production manager for *Castle in the Desert* (1942).

Koessler, Walter Art director for *Charlie Chan in Egypt* (1935).

Kolker, Henry (November 13, 1870, Quincy, Illinois–July 15, 1947, California) Stage and film actor who appeared in nearly 160 silent and sound films, often as lawyers and heavy fathers. He also directed 14 silent films. Kolker portrays Paul Lamartine in *Charlie Chan in Paris* (1935).

Being heavy-set, heavy-eyebrowed, heavily-mustached, and icily forbidding, actor Henry Kolker was a reliable screen menace for over 30 years. After nearly a quarter century on stage, Kolker portrayed John Stoddard in his first film, *The Bigger Man* (1915). From there, Kolker was generally cast as unpleasant corporate types, but could also portray positive characters, such as that of Friar Laurence in *Romeo and Juliet* (1936). Perhaps one of Kolker's largest and most representative roles was that of Edward Seton, the "old money" father of Katharine Hepburn, in *Holiday* (1938).

Note: The screen credits for *Charlie Chan in Paris* (1935) credit Henry Kolker as M. [probably for "Monsieur"] Lamartine.

Kong, Capt. Skipper of the *Shanghai Maid* (portrayed by Philip Ahn) in *The Chinese Ring* (1947). Kong is the partner of Capt. Kelso in a scheme to smuggle warplanes to a Chinese warlord in the Orient.

Krasne, Philip N. Producer of nearly 20 films, including (with James S. Burkett) the first three *Charlie Chan* films at Monogram: *Charlie Chan in the Secret Service* (1944), *The Chinese Cat* (1944), and *Black Magic* (1944).

Kruger, Paul (July 25, 1895, Eau Claire, Wisconsin–November 6, 1960) Character actor (real name: Henry Paul Kreuger) who appeared in almost 30 silent and sound films, sometimes credited as Paul Kreuger. In two unbilled *Charlie Chan* roles, Kruger portrays a guard in *Murder Over New York* (1940) and Paul Manderley's bodyguard in *Castle in the Desert* (1942).

Kuwa, George K. (April 7, 1885, Japan–October 13, 1931) Japanese stage and screen actor who appeared in over 30 silent and sound films, often as a Chinese character. Kuwa was the first to portray the character of Charlie Chan (in the 1925 silent film, *The House Without a Key*). Oddly enough, Kuwa also appeared in the second *Charlie Chan* film, *The Chinese Parrot* (1927), but as Louie Wong, a caretaker who is murdered, while another Japanese actor, Kamiyama Sojin, played Chan.

L

Lachman, Harry (June 29, 1886, La Salle, Illinois–March 19, 1975, Beverly Hills, California) Film director of 35 films who directed five *Charlie Chan* films at Twentieth Century–Fox. A onetime magazine illustrator, Harry Lachman became one of the leading European post-impressionist painters in the teens and twenties.

George Kuwa (Courtesy John Hunt)

At age 42, Harry Lachman put aside his oils to become a film director in England and came to Hollywood when signed by the Fox Studios in 1933. Lachman's most impressive American directorial projects included the elaborate Spencer Tracy film, *Dante's Inferno* (1935) and Laurel and Hardy's *Our Relations* (1936), both made in collaboration with Rudolph Maté, Lachman's favorite cinematographer. In 1943, Lachman returned to painting.

Charlie Chan filmography: *Charlie Chan at the Circus* (1936), *Murder Over New York* (1940), *Dead Men Tell* (1941), *Charlie Chan in Rio* (1941), and *Castle in the Desert* (1942).

Lady Tiny Midget (40" tall) circus entertainer (portrayed by Olive Brasno) in *Charlie Chan at the Circus* (1936). Her husband,

Colonel Tim (42" tall), is portrayed by her real life older brother, George Brasno. In the film they form a sideshow dancing act at the Kinney & Gaines Combined Circus.

Laemmle, Carl (January 17, 1867, Laupheim, Germany–September 24, 1939, Los Angeles, California) Film studio owner and producer of over 230 silent and sound films, sometimes credited as Carl Laemmle, Sr. Considered the father of the great Hollywood star system, Laemmle was the presenter for the silent film, *The Chinese Parrot* (1927).

Carl Laemmle, the founder of Universal Studios, was born to a middle-class Jewish family, the tenth of 13 children, in Laupheim, Germany. By age 13 he had become a bookkeeper, and four years later he was an office manager. In search of new opportunities, he moved to the U.S. at age 17 and began working as a courier for a New York drugstore in 1884. After holding down several odd jobs in Chicago, Laemmle settled in Oshkosh, Wisconsin, where he became the manager of a clothing store. A salary dispute led Laemmle to quit, and he returned to Chicago with hopes of acquiring a store of his own, but bought a nickelodeon instead.

Soon Laemmle had also established a film distribution business that became one of the largest in America. In 1909 he produced his first picture, a 15-minute version of Longfellow's *Hiawatha*. By this time Laemmle had become a leader of the "Independents," those producers and distributors who defied the would-be monopolists of Edison's Patents Company. By the late teens, Laemmle's company, Universal, was the country's leading film producer.

A small, portly, and eccentric man, it wasn't long before Laemmle was labeled "Uncle Carl" by his innumerable employees, whom he treated like family. During this time, Laemmle helped such studio giants as Irving Thalberg and Harry Cohn get their start. When his son Carl Laemmle, Jr., turned 21, Carl Sr. turned over the company to him, a mistake that nearly ruined the studio, for the younger Laemmle proved to be too extravagant to be able to successfully lead the company through the Depression. Thanks to his son's mismanagement, the elder Laemmle ended up selling the once-great studio for a mere $5 million. He died four years later, just as Universal was beginning to once again rise to its former greatness.

LaFarge, Gene Neurotic passenger (portrayed by Milton Parsons in his first of four *Charlie Chan* roles) from New Orleans on the *Suva Star* for the Cocos Island treasure hunt in *Dead Men Tell* (1941). As Dr. Bonney's patient, LaFarge suffers from anxiety neurosis, and avoids facing unpleasant situations by running away from problems.

Miss Nodbury fears that someone is trying to steal her treasure map, so she tears it into four pieces, sending LaFarge one of the pieces. When LaFarge fears that he may be murdered for his part of the map, he puts it into the coat pocket of a suit belonging to Steve Daniels.

LaFern, Wanda Follies star (portrayed by Iris Adrian) in *The Sky Dragon* (1949). She is the sister of Connie Jackson (alias Marie Burke) who once appeared with Wanda in a follies sister act. Years ago, with her sister and brother-in-law Andrew Barrett, Wanda hatched a confidence scheme, but Connie made off with $60,000 that was never recovered. In San Francisco, LaFern stars in the twice nightly follies show, *A Night in Paris*, at the Gayety Theatre.

Lafontaine, Simon The head of the Lafontaine Chemical Company (portrayed by Boyd Irwin) in *Docks of New Orleans* (1948). Lafontaine has entered into a business syndicate with Theodore Von Scherbe and Henri Castanaro, which he now regrets. He seeks Charlie Chan's assistance because of threats he has received (and the fact that he's being followed) since the syndicate was formed. After being threatened with a gun in his office by Oscar Swendstrom (from whom Lafontaine bought the formula for a poison gas for $500), Lafontaine is ingeniously murdered by Swendstrom using the poisonous gas, becoming the first of three such victims.

Lafontaine Chemical Company Chemical company owned by Simon Lafontaine in *Docks of New Orleans* (1948). The company is shipping a cargo of poisonous gas to South America on the *Presidente.*

Lake Stud groom (portrayed by John Rogers in his third of four *Charlie Chan* roles) for Geoffrey Richmond in *Charlie Chan in London* (1934). Lake is murdered by Richmond (in what is made to look like an attempted suicide) to silence him from telling what he knows of Capt. Hamilton's murder.

Lakehurst, New Jersey United States location used by the *Hindenburg* Zeppelin for its trips to and from Frankfurt am Main, Germany. While maneuvering to land during a violent thunderstorm on May 6, 1937, the airship's hydrogen was ignited and the *Hindenburg* was destroyed by the resulting fire. Thirty-five of the passengers and crew died, along with one member of the ground crew. In *Charlie Chan at the Olympics* (1937), Charlie Chan tells police chief Scott, "Take Zeppelin *Hindenburg* from Lakehurst, New Jersey, across Atlantic Ocean to Friedrichshafen—sixty-one hours." *See also* **Hindenburg.**

Lamartine, Paul President of the Lamartine Bank (portrayed by Henry Kolker) in *Charlie Chan in Paris* (1935). His daughter, Yvette Lamartine, is engaged to Victor Descartes, a teller at the bank.

With the assistance of Victor Descartes, Charlie Chan meets with Lamartine and tells him about some bank bonds that are counterfeits but have Lamartine's genuine signature. Showing Lamartine and his assistant, Albert Dufresne, one of the bogus bonds, Dufresne remarks that the counterfeit bonds were probably slipped in with genuine ones when Lamartine was signing them.

Note: In the film's credits, Paul Lamartine is credited as M. Lamartine.

Lamartine, Yvette Daughter (portrayed by Mary Brian) of bank president Paul Lamartine, and fiancée of Victor Descartes, in *Charlie Chan in Paris* (1935). Before her engagement to Descartes, Yvette was the girlfriend of Albert Dufresne, her father's assistant at the bank. When Dufresne asks if Descartes knows of their previous relationship, Yvette says that she told Descartes that it was harmless. Dufresne warns that Descartes may not think so if he reads the love letters Yvette had written Dufresne, which he kept.

Later that evening, Yvette goes to Dufresne's apartment to retrieve the "silly old love letters" she had once written to him. When Dufresne is just about to give them to her, he is shot in the back from the bedroom by Max Corday (disguised as the crippled beggar Marcel Xavier). Corday then throws the gun into the room near the body. In the confusion that follows, Yvette carelessly picks up the gun and attempts to escape from those who had rushed into the apartment after hearing the gunshot. However, she is captured by a policeman before she can leave the room and is arrested for Dufresne's murder.

Lamartine Bank (Banque Lamartine) Paris bank, founded in 1882, whose president is Paul Lamartine in *Charlie Chan in Paris* (1935). Charlie Chan comes to Paris on behalf of London investors to investigate the counterfeiting of bonds issued by the bank.

Lambert, Tom Sound engineer for 12 *Charlie Chan* films at Monogram: *The Chinese Cat* (1944), *The Jade Mask* (1945), *The Scarlet Clue* (1945), *The Shanghai Cobra* (1945), *The Red Dragon* (1945), *Dark Alibi* (1946), *Shadows Over Chinatown* (1946), *Dangerous Money* (1946), *The Trap* (1947), *Docks of New Orleans* (1948), *The Feathered Serpent* (1948), and *The Sky Dragon* (1949).

Lambert, William Costume designer, sometimes credited simply as Lambert, for *Charlie Chan at the Circus* (1936).

Lamont Bank Bank that Steven Briggs is convicted of robbing in *Dark Alibi* (1946). Briggs, an ex-convict, is framed by an elaborate scheme whereby his forged fingerprints are left at the crime scene. *See also* **Briggs, Steven.**

Lane, Allan "Rocky" (September 22, 1904, Mishawaka, Indiana–October 27, 1973,

Woodland Hills, California) Stage and screen actor (real name: Harry Albershart) who appeared in over 80 films, and portrays the U.S. Olympic pole vaulter (and boyfriend of Betty Adams) Richard Masters in *Charlie Chan at the Olympics* (1937).

Allan Lane was a professional football player and a model before working on the stage in the late 1920s. His film debut was in *Not Quite Decent* (1929), where he played the lead as Jerry Connor. In 1930 he worked with Robert Montgomery in *Love in the Rough* (1930) at MGM. After that, his career quickly failed as he ended 1932 out of the movies. When he came back four years later, Lane would play small roles at a number of studios, including RKO and Warner Bros.

In 1940 he signed on with Republic and starred as Sergeant King in serials such as *King of the Royal Mounted* (1940) and *King of the Mounties* (1942). Even with these serials, his output was slim until he hit the westerns in 1944 as Jack Adams in *Silver City Kid*. He found his calling playing the good-guy cowboy, but it would take another two years before he was cast as Red Ryder. In 1948 Lane would add the nickname "Rocky" and become the cowboy star Allan "Rocky" Lane, who was never far from his stallion Black Jack.

But as quickly as the fame came, it disappeared when the "B"-movie western reign ended. With his movie career over, Lane headed for television. It could have been a fitting end, but when the show *Mr. Ed* was on television from 1961 to 1966, Lane was the off-camera voice of Mr. Ed, the talking horse.

Lane, Carter Attorney (portrayed by Archie Twitchell) for Mrs. Joe Rocke in *Charlie Chan at the Wax Museum* (1940). Lane arrives at the crime museum trying to stop the weekly *Crime League* broadcast (this one about the "Rocke Case") in the interest of his client. Dr. Cream refuses, saying, "We are well within our rights." Lane then threatens, "A suit for damages will determine that."

Lane, Lenita Actress who appeared in two *Charlie Chan* films. Lane portrays Doctor Anne Bonney in *Dead Men Tell* (1941) and Lucy Manderley in *Castle in the Desert* (1942).

Lane, Richard (May 28, 1899, Rice Lake, Wisconsin–September 5, 1982, Newport Beach, California) American supporting player who appeared in over 130 films, often as a reporter, tough cop, or exasperated executive. Lane portrays gangster Mike Hannigan, alias Detective Joe Arnold, in *Charlie Chan in Honolulu* (1938).

Richard Lane was singing and dancing in vaudeville by the time he reached his thirteenth birthday. He appeared with Al Jolson in the late–1920s musical *Big Boy*, and was a headliner with George White's Scandals when he was signed to an RKO movie contract in 1937. There, Lane developed his standard characterization of a fast-talking sharpster, which secured him a recurring role on Al Pearce's popular radio program.

He played a variety of detectives, con artists, and traveling salesmen throughout the 1940s. He was also featured in several comedies by Abbott and Costello and Laurel and Hardy during the decade, and co-starred as Inspector Farraday in the *Boston Blackie* series. Teamed with comic actor Gus Shilling, Lane appeared in 11 Columbia two-reel comedies.

A television pioneer, Lane worked at Los Angeles' KTLA-TV as a newsman, sportscaster, and used-car pitchman. For over twenty years he was the mile-a-minute commentator for KTLA's nationally syndicated wrestling and roller derby matches.

Lane, Theodore M. Real name of Rev. Whipple (portrayed by Leslie Dennison in his second of three *Charlie Chan* roles) in *Dangerous Money* (1946). Lane is the leader of a gang which includes Tao and Laura Erickson, P.T. Burke, and Freddie Kirk, and they plan to sell artworks stolen from banks during the Japanese invasion.

Scott Pearson, an undercover U.S. Treasury agent, is murdered by Lane while going to Samoa to investigate the sudden appearance of money and artworks stolen from Philippine banks during the Japanese invasion. In papers he kept in the office safe of

Capt. Black, Pearson mentions a man named Lane but does not identify him. *See also* **Rev. Whipple.**

Lange, Elaine Actress who portrays Cynthia Martin, the wife of Professor Dick Martin, in *Dangerous Money* (1946).

Lansing, J.L. Secretary of the Santa Juanita Racing Association in *Charlie Chan at the Race Track* (1936).

Larchmont Hotel Charlie Chan's hotel in *Dark Alibi* (1946).

Larkin Policeman (portrayed by Cyril Delevanti in his second of two *Charlie Chan* roles) who works undercover for Inspector Harry Davis as a janitor at the Sixth National Bank in *The Shanghai Cobra* (1945). Like three other bank employees who are murdered, Larkin is killed with cobra venom by Bradford Harris.

Larkin, John Screenwriter for five *Charlie Chan* films at Twentieth Century–Fox: *Charlie Chan at Treasure Island* (1939), *Charlie Chan in Panama* (1940), *Charlie Chan at the Wax Museum* (1940), *Dead Men Tell* (1941), and *Castle in the Desert* (1942).

La Rue, Jack (May 3, 1903, New York, New York–January 11, 1984, Santa Monica, California) Stage and screen character actor (real name: Gaspere Biondolillo) who appeared in nearly 120 films and is often mistaken for Humphrey Bogart by casual fans. La Rue portrayed Emil Manolo in *Charlie Chan in Panama* (1940).

After stage work in New York, Jack La Rue appeared in films, usually as hoodlums. He decided to shift gears and try romantic leading roles, but this image disappeared after the Mayfair Studios budget film, T*he Fighting Rookie* (1934), and it was back to gangsters and thugs, with a few exceptions like his sympathetic role as Thad Terrill in *A Gentleman from Dixie* (1941).

By the 1940s La Rue had spent most of his movie savings and was compelled to seek out any work available. Things improved a bit when La Rue moved to England in the late 1940s to play American villains in British pictures. His most memorable appearance during this period was as Slim Grissom in the notorious *No Orchids for Miss Blandish* (1948), a virtual reprisal of his part in *The Story of Temple Drake* (1933).

Laska, Peter Servant (portrayed by Muni Seroff) of Paul Arranto in *Charlie Chan in the Secret Service* (1944). Charlie Chan falsely accuses Laska of von Vegon's murder as part of a plan to identify the real killer.

Laszlo, Alexander Music composer for over 15 films, including *The Chinese Cat* (1944) and *Black Magic* (1944).

Latell, Lyle (April 9, 1904, Elma, Iowa–October 24, 1967, Hollywood, California) Character actor (real name: Lyle Zeiem) who appeared in over 30 films. In two *Charlie Chan* roles, Latell portrays an unnamed police clerk in *Shadows Over Chinatown* (1946) and Ed Davidson (unbilled) in *The Sky Dragon* (1949).

Latimer, Lily Dr. Cream's icy blonde assistant (portrayed by Joan Valerie in her first of two *Charlie Chan* roles) in *Charlie Chan at the Wax Museum* (1940). Steve McBirney plans to kill Charlie Chan by wiring up his own version of an electric chair at Dr. Cream's crime museum. However, Lily secretly cuts the electric wires to the chair using one of the museum exhibit's pliers but cuts her finger, whose unusual wound is noticed by Chan with suspicion. Chan concludes that Lily did not want a murder that might expose the museum's profitable plastic surgery sideline.

Latouche, Henri Office manager of the Lamartine bank (portrayed by Murray Kinnell in his last of four *Charlie Chan* roles) in *Charlie Chan in Paris* (1935). With Max Corday as a confederate, both take turns masquerading as a fictitious crippled beggar known as Marcel Xavier to provide each other with perfect alibis. When at the Café du Singe Bleu, Latouche is disguised as

Xavier and murders Charlie Chan's undercover agent, Nardi, while Charlie is sitting at a table with Corday.

lavaliere An ornament or piece of jewelry hanging from a chain that is worn around the neck. At George Kirby's apartment in *Murder Over New York* (1940), Charlie Chan notices that a lavaliere worn by actress June Preston has a pearl missing from it. When searching Kirby's library desk for clues about the murder of Hugh Drake, Chan finds the missing pearl in the inkwell, concluding that Miss Preston must have been in the room earlier and seen Drake alive.

Lawrence, Marc (February 17, 1910, New York, New York–) Swarthy, pock-marked actor (real name: Max Goldsmith) who often portrayed gangster types throughout his long career in over 130 films. In three *Charlie Chan* roles, Lawrence portrays Thomas Mitchell in *Charlie Chan on Broadway* (1937), gangster Johnnie McCoy in *Charlie Chan in Honolulu* (1938), and convicted murderer Steve McBirney in *Charlie Chan at the Wax Museum* (1940).

After attending City College of New York, Marc Lawrence studied acting with Eva Le Gallienne. When first signed for films by Columbia in 1932, Lawrence's scarred face and growly voice made him well-suited for gangster parts, though he generally displayed an intelligence far higher than the average goon or gunman. Lawrence was not always confined to villainous city-dweller roles, and had successful roles as Pete, a mountaineer in *Shepherd of the Hills* (1942), and as Farnley, a saddle tramp in *The Ox-Bow Incident* (1943). By his own account, Lawrence's favorite role was that of Corio in *Captain from Castille* (1947).

Marc Lawrence

During the House Un-American Activities Committee investigations of the 1950s, Lawrence reluctantly offered testimony implicating several of his co-workers as alleged communist sympathizers. This experience virtually destroyed his American career and left him embittered and defensive. He was then forced to seek out work in Europe, where he'd emerge in the early 1960s as a director of crime films and spaghetti westerns. During this period, Lawrence appeared in two of the James Bond 007 films—as a goon in *Diamonds Are Forever* (1971) and as the hitman Rodney in *The Man with the Golden Gun* (1974).

Back in the U.S. in the 1980s, Lawrence made several television appearances and was typecast again as gangster Vinnie "The Cannon" DiMotti in *The Big Easy* (1987) and as Kloppman in *Newsies* (1992). He portrayed one of the biggest real-life gangsters when he played Carlo Gambino in the television film *Gotti* (1996).

Lawrence, Rosina (December 30, 1912, Westboro, Ontario, Canada–June 23, 1997, New York, New York) Attractive Canadian-born dancer and singer, who was an actress in 30 silent and sound films. Lawrence portrayed Alice Lowell in *Charlie Chan's Secret* (1936).

In 1934 Rosina Lawrence appeared on the same Mexican dinner club bill with The Dancing Cansinos—which included Margarita Cansino, later known as Rita Hayworth. Shortly after, the two women were chosen as two of the "Four Debutante Stars of 1936." Lawrence also appeared in comedies, such as *Bored of Education* (1936; as

Miss Lawrence), a number of *Our Gang* shorts, and several comedies by Laurel and Hardy (including playing Mrs. Chase in *On the Wrong Trek* [1936]). She married in 1939 and thereupon retired from the screen.

Lazy Y Ranch Arizona dude ranch in *The Golden Eye* (1948). The ranch is located about a half mile from Mr. Manning's ranch and the Golden Eye Mine. Manning asks Charlie Chan to investigate recent attacks on his life and suggests Chan stay as a vacationing guest at the Lazy Y rather than at Manning's own ranch in order to avoid arousing suspicion.

leather shoelaces Shoelaces that are used to strangle Gerald Pendleton in *Charlie Chan's Murder Cruise* (1940). Charlie Chan asks son Jimmy (who has been pressed into service as a cabin boy and shoe-shiner as his punishment for being caught as a stowaway) which passengers have shoes with leather laces. Jimmy says that he can't remember, to which Charlie replies, "Better a father lose his son than a detective his memory." Moments later, Professor Gordon tells Chan that his shoes were returned from being shined earlier that morning without their leather shoelaces.

Lefty Gambling ring gangster (portrayed by Paul Fix) in *Charlie Chan at the Race Track* (1936). Bagley requests Lefty to drive jockey "Tip" Collins back home after convincing Collins that he will "take care" of him by telling him that he can be part of the gambling operation. Later, Collins' body is fished out of the Pacific Ocean at Santa Monica by the police.

Lenesch, Kathi Czechoslovakian refugee (portrayed by Jean Rogers) who is forced by Emil Manolo to be a singer at his cabaret in *Charlie Chan in Panama* (1940). Manolo orders Lenesch to get friendly with Richard Cabot, a government engineer, and find out all she can about him. Charlie Chan learns that she is really Baroness Kathi von Czardas, and that her brother and father were executed by Reiner of the secret police, who she still fears and who Chan believes is now in Panama.

Leni, Paul (July 8, 1885, Stuttgart, Germany–September 3, 1929, Hollywood, California) Production designer, art director, and film director of nearly 20 silent films, including *The Chinese Parrot* (1927).

A native of Berlin, Paul Leni became an avant-garde painter at age 15 and then began working as a theater set designer, serving such prominent directors as Max Reinhardt. Around 1914 he became an art director for and was a key figure in German expressionist cinema, making his greatest contributions with *Hintertreppe* (1921; a.k.a. *Backstairs*) and *Das Wachsfigurenkabinett* (1923; a.k.a. *Waxworks*), both of which were most notable for their spooky ambiance and innovative techniques. For the bulk of his films, Leni not only directed, he also functioned as the art director.

In 1927 Leni moved to Hollywood and accepted Carl Laemmle's invitation to become a director at Universal. There, Leni made a distinguished directorial debut with *The Cat and the Canary* (1927), a classic Gothic haunted house film that greatly influenced Universal's later classic horror series. Leni proved to be a master at creating nightmarish suspense through allusion, and has had untold influence on subsequent American thrillers. Unfortunately, Leni was only to make three more such films before dying of blood poisoning in 1929.

Leonard, Barbara Actress who portrays Lola, the lookout accomplice for burglars Alex and "Gentleman" Max, in *City in Darkness* (1939).

Leonard, Harry M. Sound engineer and director of almost 90 films, including ten *Charlie Chan* entries at Twentieth Century–Fox. Leonard was nominated (with Fred Sersen, Sol Halprin, and Roger Heman) for an Academy Award in the Best Special Effects category for *Captain Eddie* (1945).

Charlie Chan filmography: *Charlie Chan at the Opera* (1936), *Charlie Chan at the Race Track* (1936), *Charlie Chan at the Olympics*

(1937), *Charlie Chan on Broadway* (1937), *Charlie Chan at Monte Carlo* (1937), *Charlie Chan at the Wax Museum* (1940), *Murder Over New York* (1940), *Dead Men Tell* (1941), *Charlie Chan in Rio* (1941), and *Castle in the Desert* (1942).

Lessey, George Actor who portrays (unbilled) Charlie Chan's Secret Service boss, Mr. Slade, in *Charlie Chan in the Secret Service* (1944).

L'Estrange, Richard (December 27, 1889, Asheville, North Carolina–November 19, 1963, Burbank, California) Actor, director, and production manager (real name: Gunther Von Strensch) of nearly 25 films, sometimes credited as Dick L'Estrange, Dick La Strange, Dick Le Strange, or Richard Le Strange. L'Estrange was the production manager for both *The Chinese Cat* (1944) and *Black Magic* (1944) at Monogram.

Leung Probable name for the Chans' Number One grandchild. In *Charlie Chan in Honolulu* (1938), son-in-law Wing Foo tells Charlie Chan that he and his wife, Number One daughter Ling, have decided that if the baby is a boy, the name will be Leung; otherwise, Lotus or Cherry if it is a girl. At the conclusion of the film, Wing Foo tells Charlie that the baby is a boy.

Levant, Oscar (December 27, 1906, Pittsburgh, Pennsylvania–August 14, 1972, Beverly Hills, California) American actor, pianist, and composer possessing a bizarre wit that he applied to movies, radio, and television. Levant composed the opera *Carnival* in *Charlie Chan at the Opera* (1936). In 1939 Levant married actress June Gale, who portrays the jealous Myra Rhadini in *Charlie Chan at Treasure Island* (1939).

Leverett, George (c. 1883–March 20, 1968, Hemet, California) Sound recordist for *Charlie Chan's Greatest Case* (1933) and *Charlie Chan at the Opera* (1936). In 1943 Leverett shared an Academy Award nomination with Fred Sersen and Roger Heman in the Best Special Effects category for *The Black Swan* (1942).

Levien, Sonya (c. 1889, Russia–March 19, 1960, Hollywood, California) Movie screenwriter of nearly 60 films who, with Clarke Silvernail, wrote the screenplay for *Behind That Curtain* (1929).

A U.S. citizen from childhood, Russian-born Sonya Levien had been a lawyer, magazine editor, and fiction writer before concentrating on screenwriting in the early 1920s. Most often employed by Fox Studios in the first decade of the talkies, Levien wrote or co-wrote the scripts of several Will Rogers films. Her script for Rogers' *State Fair* (1933) not only earned her an Oscar nomination (shared with Paul Green) in the Best Writing, Adaptation category, but served as the model for the movie's 1945 and 1962 remakes.

While at Fox, Levien worked extensively on the films of Janet Gaynor. In addition, she worked on the adaptation of Molnar's *Liliom* (1930) and John Ford's first Technicolor film, *Drums Along the Mohawk* (1939). Her efforts at other studios included RKO's *Hunchback of Notre Dame* (1939) and Warner Bros.' Gershwin biography, *Rhapsody in Blue* (1945). From 1941, Levien could usually be found at MGM, where she won an Academy Award (shared with William Ludwig) in the Best Writing, Story and Screenplay category for *Interrupted Melody* (1955).

Lewis One of two Secret Service agents (portrayed by Eddie Chandler in his second of two *Charlie Chan* roles) in *Charlie Chan in the Secret Service* (1944). Lewis is assigned as a bodyguard for inventor George Melton.

Lewis, Capt. U.S. Army military intelligence officer stationed at the Panama Canal Zone (portrayed by Donald Douglas in his first of two *Charlie Chan* roles) in *Charlie Chan in Panama* (1940).

Lewis, George J. (December 10, 1903, Mexico–) Character actor who appeared in over 160 films, including three *Charlie Chan* entries. Lewis portrays Paul Arranto in *Char-*

lie Chan in the Secret Service (1944), police Sgt. Dansiger in *Docks of New Orleans* (1948), and San Pedro police chief Capt. Juan Gonzalez in *The Feathered Serpent* (1948).

Born in Mexico, George Lewis gained prominence in the mid–1920s as an athletic all–American boy in Universal's popular *Collegiates* two-reeler series. Sporting a mustache in many of his talkie appearances, Lewis played a steady stream of society villains, weaklings, "other men," and cads at both Republic Studios and the Columbia short-subjects unit. Lewis also portrayed Don Alejandro de la Vega, the father of Don Diego, in the Disney television series *Zorro* (1957–59).

Lewis, Pete *San Francisco Union Telegraph* reporter (portrayed by Douglas Fowley in his second of three *Charlie Chan* roles) in *Charlie Chan at Treasure Island* (1939). Lewis is an old friend of Charlie Chan and is engaged to Eve Cairo, a psychic mind reader. Lewis tells Charlie Chan that he, his newspaper, and Rhadini (who operates a magic theater on Treasure Island), are on a crusade to expose fake psychics in the San Francisco area, with Dr. Zodiac as their primary target.

Lewis, Ralph (1872, Englewood, Illinois–December 4, 1937, Los Angeles, California) American stage and screen actor of silent and sound films who portrays police officer Jim Kimball in *The Jade Mask* (1945). Ralph Lewis was 64 years old when he was accidentally struck and killed by a car reportedly driven by producer Jack Warner's chauffeur.

Leyton, Drue (1903, Somers, Wisconsin–February 8, 1997, Corona del Mar, California) American actress (real name: Dorothy Elizabeth Blackman) who portrays Paula Graham in *Charlie Chan's Courage* (1934), Pamela Gray in *Charlie Chan in London* (1934), and Nellie Farrell in *Charlie Chan at the Circus* (1936).

Drue Leyton became an actress after her marriage to a Los Angeles architect failed, appearing in *Green Grow the Lilacs* on Broadway. Later acting in Europe, Leyton broadcasted for the Voice of America from Paris, earning condemnation from the Nazis. After the United States entered the war, she escaped from a German prisoner of war camp and became active in the French resistance. Over three years, Leyton helped 42 downed American, Canadian, and British fliers escape occupied France, and hid others in her home until the liberation. She wrote of her wartime experiences in the book *The House Near Paris*, which was published in 1946. Leyton was honored for her exploits by the French, American, British, and Canadian governments.

Drue Leyton

lie detector In *The Black Camel* (1931), Van Horn tells Charlie Chan that Charlie needs a lie detector, a device to tell when a person is lying. Chan responds by saying, "Oh, you mean a wife. I have one!"

Liebgold, Monroe Technical director (unbilled) for *Charlie Chan at the Race Track* (1936).

Lily *see* **Saturnia, Mme.**

Kay Linaker

Linaker, Kay Actress, sometimes credited as Kate Phillips, who appeared in almost 45 films and had roles in four *Charlie Chan* entries at Twentieth Century–Fox. Linaker portrays Joan Karnoff in *Charlie Chan at Monte Carlo* (1937), Mrs. Russell in *Charlie Chan in Reno* (1939), Mrs. Pendleton in *Charlie Chan's Murder Cruise* (1940), and Helen Ashby in *Charlie Chan in Rio* (1941).

Ling Charlie Chan's Number One daughter, portrayed by Florence Ung (uncredited), who is married to Wing Foo, in *Charlie Chan in Honolulu* (1938).

Ling, Iris Chinese artist (portrayed by Jean Wong in her first of two *Charlie Chan* roles) who uses Red Dragon Chinese Ink in *The Red Dragon* (1945).

Ling, Princess Mei Chinese princess (portrayed by Jean Wong in her second of two *Charlie Chan* roles) who is murdered by a poison dart at Charlie Chan's house in *The Chinese Ring* (1947). Before she dies, her last act is to scribble the message "Capt. K" on a piece of paper as a clue. The Princess is in San Francisco to buy airplanes for her warlord brother, Field Marshal Chun Sze.

Link, John F., Sr. Film editor for *Black Magic* (1944). Link was nominated for an Academy Award (shared with Sherman Todd) in the Best Film Editing category for the movie *For Whom the Bell Tolls* (1943).

Little, Thomas K. Award-winning production designer and set decorator for almost 220 films, including ten *Charlie Chan* entries at Twentieth Century–Fox. In his career, Little received 21 Academy Award nominations, winning six of them.

Art Direction–Interior Decoration (Black-and-White)

How Green Was My Valley (1941)
This Above All (1942)
The Song of Bernadette (1943)
Laura (1944)
The Keys of the Kingdom (1944)
Anna and the King of Siam (1946)
The Razor's Edge (1946)
The Foxes of Harrow (1947)
Come to the Stable (1949)
All About Eve (1950)
Fourteen Hours (1951)
The House on Telegraph Hill (1951)
Viva Zapata! (1952)

Art Direction–Interior Decoration (Color)

Blood and Sand (1941)
My Gal Sal (1942)
The Gang's All Here (1943)
Wilson (1944)
Leave Her to Heaven (1945)
David and Bathsheba (1951)
On the Riviera (1951)
The Snows of Kilimanjaro (1952)

Charlie Chan filmography: *Charlie Chan in Honolulu* (1938), *Charlie Chan in Reno* (1939), *Charlie Chan at Treasure Island* (1939), *Charlie Chan in Panama* (1940), *Charlie Chan's Murder Cruise* (1940), *Charlie Chan at the Wax Museum* (1940), *Murder Over New York* (1940), *Dead Men Tell* (1941), *Charlie Chan in Rio* (1941), and *Castle in the Desert* (1942).

"little showman" Nickname given to Freddie Kirk, a knife-thrower entertainer, by Charlie Chan in *Dangerous Money* (1946). *See also* **Kirk, Freddie**.

Littlefield, Lucien (August 16, 1895, San Antonio, Texas–June 4, 1960, Hollywood, California) Versatile stage and screen character actor who appeared in over 225 silent and sound films. Littlefield portrays Professor Gleason in *Castle in the Desert* (1942).

Lucien Littlefield attended a military academy before making his first stage appearance at the age of 17 and his first film in 1913. Short and balding even in his teens, Littlefield began impersonating old men before he was eligible to vote. He played Kentucky Rose, the grizzled sidekick of William S. Hart in *Tumbleweeds* (1925), and three years later he portrayed Pa Johnson, the sore-footed father of Mary Pickford in *My Best Girl* (1928). His most memorable silent role was as the threatening Doctor Patterson in *The Cat and the Canary* (1927).

When talkies arrived, Littlefield starred in his own Vitaphone short subjects series, *The Potters*, and played roles both large and small in a number of feature films. He was the veterinarian Dr. Horace Meddick in Laurel and Hardy's *Sons of the Desert* (1934), office manager Mr. Peabody in W.C. Fields' *The Man on the Flying Trapeze* (1935), the snobbish Charles Belknap-Jackson in *Ruggles of Red Gap* (1935), and Cpl. Lucken in *Whistling in Dixie* (1942).

Livingston, Robert (December 9, 1904, Quincy, Illinois–March 7, 1988, Tarzana, California) Actor (real name: Robert Randall) who appeared in over 70 films, many of them westerns. Livingston portrays archeologist Professor John Stanley in *The Feathered Serpent* (1948), which is a remake of *The Riders of the Whistling Skull* (1937)—in which Livingston also starred, this time as Stony Brooke.

Robert Livingston began his professional life as a reporter for the *Los Angeles Daily News*. When he did a story on the Pasadena Playhouse, he became interested in acting, and was soon performing on stage and in film shorts. In his mid-twenties he was doing bit parts for Universal and Fox and went from there to romantic roles with MGM and on to Republic. By 1934 he had become an actor in feature films, and in 1936 he began a long stretch as the cowboy star Stony Brooke in the *Three Mesquiteers* series of westerns, going on to play the character 29 times.

Livingston played other cowboy roles, such as Zorro in *The Bold Caballero* (1939) and the Lone Ranger in *The Lone Ranger Rides Again* (1939) and was the co-star, with Al "Fuzzy" St. John, in the *Lone Rider* Series (1941–43). Livingston finished up his career in a number of character parts in Gene Autry and Roy Rogers movies.

Locher, Charles *see* **Hall, Jon**

Loeffer, Louis Film editor, sometimes credited as Louis Löffler, for nearly 75 films, including *Murder Over New York* (1940). Loeffer was twice nominated for Academy Awards in the Best Film Editing category—for *Anatomy of a Murder* (1959) and *The Cardinal* (1963).

Loft, Arthur (May 25, 1897, Colorado–January 1, 1947, Los Angeles, California) American stage and screen supporting actor who appeared in nearly 140 films, usually cast as pushy types. In two *Charlie Chan* roles, Loft portrays Secret Service agent "Jonesy" Jones in *Charlie Chan in the Secret Service* (1944) and murderer Bradford Harris in *The Shanghai Cobra* (1945).

Lofton, Dr. Organizer and conductor of an around-the-world tour (portrayed by John T. Murray) in *Charlie Chan Carries On* (1931).

Note: The character Dr. Lofton loosely parallels that of Dr. Suderman in *Charlie Chan's Murder Cruise* (1940).

Logan, Helen Story and screenplay writer of over 40 movies. Logan teamed up with husband Robert Ellis to write the story and/or screenplay for nine *Charlie Chan* films with Twentieth Century–Fox.

Charlie Chan filmography: *Charlie Chan in Egypt* (1935), *Charlie Chan in Shanghai*

(1935),* *Charlie Chan's Secret* (1936), *Charlie Chan at the Race Track* (1936), *Charlie Chan at the Circus* (1936), *Charlie Chan at the Olympics* (1937), *Charlie Chan on Broadway* (1937), *Charlie Chan at Monte Carlo* (1937), and *City in Darkness* (1939).

Lois Member of Cole King's variety troupe (portrayed by Jayne Bryant) in *The Trap* (1947). King's girlfriend, Marcia, forces Lois to steal several incriminating letters from Adelaide's trunk by threatening to tell King that Lois is under eighteen. Lois is later found strangled with a silk cord from King's bathrobe, having been murdered by Mrs. Thorn.

Lola The lookout accomplice (portrayed by Barbara Leonard) for burglars Alex and "Gentleman" Max in *City in Darkness* (1939). Lola stands guard while Alex and Max break into Petroff's house and wait in the cellar for Petroff to go to bed before attempting to rob the house.

Lollipop Mascot monkey (attired in a white sailor's suit with circular hat) for the racehorse Gallant Lad in *Charlie Chan at the Race Track* (1936). When Fenton purchased the horse, he tells Charlie Chan that had to take Lollipop as part of the deal.

While in the stable area onboard the S.S. *Oceanic*, Charlie notices that Lollipop excites Avalanche when he jumps on the horse's back, but does not bother Gallant Lad. After a small fire that was purposely started on the ship by the gambling ring as a distraction so that they could switch the horses, Chan notices that something is strange when Gallant Lad now acts up when Lollipop is nearby but Avalanche is calm.

"long life and happiness" Translation of the two Chinese characters (壽福, shòu fú) on the ring of Princess Mei Ling in *The Chinese Ring* (1947).

Lopez, Pedro Francisco Undercover Mexican secret policeman (portrayed by Martin Garralaga) in *The Feathered Serpent* (1948). Lopez uses the cover of a guitar-playing troubadour who offers his services to the Farnsworth archeological expedition as a cook as a ruse to investigate the smuggling of Aztec antiquities out of Mexico and the disappearance of Professor Henry Farnsworth.

Loring, Teala (1927, Denver, Colorado–) Actress who portrays June Harley in *Dark Alibi* (1946).

Lorraine The woman (portrayed by Janet Warren in her second of two *Charlie Chan* roles) who is the voice in the jukebox located in Joe's Coffee Shop in *The Shanghai Cobra* (1945). As an accomplice of H.R. Jarvis and Bradford Harris, Lorraine remotely operates the musical jukebox from a hidden room in Jarvis' office on the second floor of the Sixth National Bank Building, which is located around the corner from the coffee shop. Lorraine can talk to the jukebox customers using a microphone and speaker, and also can see the customers with a television camera.

Lorre, Peter (June 26, 1904, Rózsahegy [Rosenberg, now Rízomberok, Slovakia], Hungary–March 23, 1964) Gnome-like, wide-eyed actor (real name: Ladislav Löwenstein, a.k.a. Laszlo Löwenstein) who appeared in over 80 films. With the possible exception of Edward G. Robinson, no actor has so often been the target of impressionists as the incomparable Hungarian-born Peter Lorre.

Peter Lorre was born in Hungary to Alois and Elvira Lorre and was educated in elementary and secondary schools in Vienna, Austria. He ran away from home when he was 17 and joined an improvised theater, working as a bank clerk during down periods. For most of his first seven years as a professional actor, Lorre employed his familiar repertoire of wide eyes, toothy grin, and nasal voice to invoke laughs rather than shudders. He performed in Switzerland and

*Unbilled.

Peter Lorre (*left*) clowns around with Boris Karloff while visiting during filming of *Charlie Chan at the Opera*.

Austria before settling in Germany. In fact, he was appearing in a stage comedy at the same time that he was filming his breakthrough picture, the Fritz Lang–directed *M* (1931; a.k.a. *Mörder unter uns*), in which he portrayed Hans Beckert, a psychopathic child killer. It was Lorre's image from *M* that was unwittingly used on the German poster for the anti–Semitic propaganda film, *The Eternal Jew* (1940), as an example of a typical Jew.

When Hitler rose to power in 1933, Lorre fled to Paris and then to London, where he appeared in his first English-language picture, Hitchcock's *The Man Who Knew Too Much* (1934). Since Lorre only spoke Hungarian and German, he had to learn his English language lines phonetically for the Hitchcock film. He picked up English fairly rapidly and by 1935 he was well equipped both vocally and psychologically to take on Hollywood. On the strength of *M*, Lorre was at first cast in roles calling for varying degrees of madness, such as the love-obsessed surgeon Dr. Gogol in *Mad Love* (1935) and Raskolnikov, the existentialist killer in *Crime and Punishment* (1935).

Signed to a Twentieth Century–Fox contract in 1936, Lorre asked for and received a chance to play a good guy for a change. From 1937 to 1939, he starred in eight installments of the Mr. Moto series, playing an ever-polite Japanese detective. When Warner Oland died in 1938 during the filming of what would have been *Charlie Chan at the Ringside*, parts of this movie were salvaged and reworked into *Mr. Moto's Gamble* (1938), the third Mr. Moto entry of the series. In it, Lee Chan is an assistant to the Japanese detective Mr. Moto.

While under contract to Warner Bros., Lorre played effeminate thief Joel Cairo in *The Maltese Falcon* (1941), launching an unofficial series of films in which Lorre was teamed with his "Falcon" co-star Sidney Greenstreet (playing Ugarte) in *Casablanca* (1942) and seven other movies during the early 1940s. During this period, Lorre's co-workers either adored or reviled him for his wicked sense of humor and bizarre on-set behavior. As far as Warners' director Jean Negulesco was concerned, Lorre was the finest actor in Hollywood, and Negulesco fought bitterly with the studio brass for permission to cast Lorre as the sympathetic leading man, Cornelius Latimer Leyden, in *The Mask of Dimitrios* (1944), in which the diminutive actor gave one of his finest and subtlest performances.

In 1951 Lorre briefly returned to Germany, where he directed and starred in the post-war psychological drama *Der Verlorene* ("*The Lost One*" [1951]). After that, somewhat heavier, he played in a string of not-so-stellar efforts—with one notable exception. Lorre portrayed Skeeter the clown in *The Big Circus* (1959). In the 1960s he made frequent appearances on live television anthologies (such as *Climax*), guested on comedy and variety shows, and continued to appear in character parts in films.

He remained a popular commodity, especially after co-starring with the likes of Vincent Price, Boris Karloff, and Basil Rathbone in a pair of tongue-in-cheek Edgar Allan Poe adaptations—*Tales of Terror* (1962) and *The Raven* (1963). Lorre's last movie was as Morgan Heywood, a director of comedy films, in Jerry Lewis' *The Patsy* (1964). Having been separated from his third wife, Annemarie Brenning, since October, 1962, a divorce hearing had been scheduled for March 23, 1964, the same day Lorre died from a heart attack.

Los Angeles California city which was the location for *Charlie Chan at the Opera* (1936).

Los Angeles Bulletin Newspaper which receives teletyped details from the *Chicago Sun* about a fire at an opera house on September 15, 1923, in *Charlie Chan at the Opera* (1936). Charlie Chan also instructs the newspaper to facsimile a photograph of the opera star who was thought to have been killed in the fire. When received in Los Angeles, Chan recognizes the man as Gravelle, who has recently escaped from the Rockland State Sanitarium.

Lotus One of two possible names chosen by Charlie's son-in-law, Wing Foo, and Number One daughter Ling if their baby is a girl in *Charlie Chan in Honolulu* (1938). The other name is Cherry.

Lotus Garden Café Chinese restaurant meeting place for Charlie Chan, Paula Webb (alias Pauline Webster), and Ned Stewart in *The Shanghai Cobra* (1945). Paula reads the newspaper story that Ned Stewart has been arrested for the murder of Samuel Black and then telephones Chan to meet her at the restaurant at 7:30, where she gives Chan information that clears Ned Stewart of the murder charge.

Louis Henchman (portrayed by Eugene Borden in his first of three *Charlie Chan* appearances) of Johnny Burke in *Charlie Chan on Broadway* (1937). When Charlie Chan gathers suspects for questioning about the death of Burke's ex-girlfriend, Billie Bronson, in Burke's office at the Hottentot Club, it is Louis who, on Burke's cue, turns off the office lights, allowing Burke to escape in the confusion.

Lovering, Otho Film director and editor for over 60 movies, sometimes credited as Otto Levering or Otto Lovering. Lovering was the film editor for *Docks of New Orleans* (1948) and *The Shanghai Chest* (1948) and the supervising editor for *The Golden Eye* (1948), *The Feathered Serpent* (1948), and *The Sky Dragon* (1949). In 1940 he was nominated (with Dorothy Spencer) for an Academy Award in the Best Film Editing category for *Stagecoach* (1939).

Lowe, Edward T., Jr. (June 29, 1890, Nashville, Tennessee–April 17, 1973, Los Angeles, California) Film producer and screenplay writer of more than 50 films. Lowe was the producer of *Charlie Chan in Egypt* (1935) and wrote the screenplays for *Charlie Chan in*

Paris (1935), *Charlie Chan in Shanghai* (1935), and *Charlie Chan at the Race Track* (1936).

Lowell, Alice One of two daughters (portrayed by Rosina Lawrence) of Henrietta Lowell in *Charlie Chan's Secret* (1936). Alice is engaged to newspaper reporter Dick Williams.

Lowell, Henrietta The matriarchal head of the Colby family (portrayed by Henrietta Crosman) who is a devout believer in psychic phenomena in *Charlie Chan's Secret* (1936). Lowell and her two daughters, Alice Lowell and Janice Gage, would stand to benefit from the estate of her late brother, Bernard Colby, if her nephew Allen were declared dead.

Lowery, Robert (October 17, 1914, Kansas City, Missouri–December 26, 1971, Hollywood, California) American leading man (real name: Robert Lowery Hanks) of the 1940s who appeared in over 80 films. In three *Charlie Chan* roles, Lowery portrays Wally Burke in *Charlie Chan in Reno* (1939), David Elliot in *Murder Over New York* (1940), and Dick Kenyon in *Charlie Chan's Murder Cruise* (1940).

Robert Lowery came to Hollywood on the strength of his talent as a band vocalist. He was signed to a movie contract in 1937 by Twentieth Century–Fox, but from 1942 onward he freelanced, starring in a few low-budget films at Universal and Monogram. In 1949 he portrayed the dual role of Bruce Wayne and Batman in the Columbia serial *Batman and Robin*. On television, Robert Lowery co-starred as Big Jim Champion on the kiddie series *Circus Boy* (1956–57) and played the smooth-talking villain, Buss Courtney, on the Anne Sheridan sitcom *Pistols and Petticoats* (1966–67).

Luana The native Hawaiian girlfriend (portrayed by Rita Rozelle) of Smith in *The Black Camel* (1931).

Luani Hotel Honolulu hotel where Dr. Suderman's cruise members are staying in *Charlie Chan's Murder Cruise* (1940). Mr. Kenyon, one of the cruise members, is found strangled in Room 342.

Lucifer Mrs. Henrietta Lowell's mischievous black cat in *Charlie Chan's Secret* (1936).

Ludwig Victor Karnoff's chauffeur (portrayed by John Bleifer) in *Charlie Chan at Monte Carlo* (1937). Ludwig is paid by Paul Savarin to tip him off by telephone when Karnoff will be shipping $1 million in bonds to Paris for sale, a move that would financially hurt Savarin. Ludwig is then murdered (along with Renault, the bank messenger) by Gordon Chase.

Lugosi, Bela (October 20, 1882, Lugos, Hungary–August 16, 1956, Los Angeles, California) Hungarian-born stage and screen actor (real name: Béla Ferenc Dezs Blaskó) with chilling eyes and voice (sometimes credited as Arisztid Olt early in his career). Lugosi appeared in over 100 films, and he portrays the fortune teller, Tarneverro, in *The Black Camel* (1931).

Bela Lugosi as Dracula, the role that made him famous.

Bela Lugosi began his stage career in 1901 as a distinguished stage actor in his native Hungary, and started appearing in films during World War I. Lugosi fled to Germany in 1919 as a result of left-wing political activity in organizing an actors union in Hungary. In 1921 he immigrated to the U.S. and made a living as a character actor, shooting to fame when he played Count Dracula in the legendary 1927 Broadway stage adaptation of Bram Stoker's novel. It ran for three years and was subsequently filmed by Tod Browning in 1931, establishing Lugosi as one of the screen's greatest personifications of pure evil. Lugosi was at his best when he played Dracula, but had good performances opposite other horror icons such as Boris Karloff (in *The Black Cat* [1934], *The Invisible Ray* [1936], and *Son of Frankenstein* [1939]) and Lon Chaney, Jr. (in *The Wolf Man* [1941]).

Because of his notable heavy accent and a face that became synonymous with terror, Lugosi had difficulty finding work other than in horror films. Sadly, his reputation rapidly declined, as did his personal life (with his failing marriage and addiction to morphine). He was only too happy to accept any part offered, and ended up playing pathetic parodies of his greatest role, such as in *Abbott and Costello Meet Frankenstein* (1948). He ended his career working for the worst director of all time, Edward D. Wood, Jr. Lugosi died of a heart attack while anticipating his next abysmal Ed Wood project and was buried in his Dracula cape.

Luke, Edwin The younger brother of Keye Luke (Number One son Lee Chan) who portrayed Number Four son Eddie Chan in *The Jade Mask* (1945).

Luke, Keye (June 18, 1904, Canton, China–January 12, 1991, Whittier, California) China-born actor who portrays Lee Chan, Charlie Chan's Number One son, in 10 films.

Keye Luke immigrated to the U.S. at an early age and grew up in Seattle, where he graduated from Franklin High School and then went to the University of Southern California. During World War II he returned to college to learn Mandarin Chinese for the Marines.

Keye Luke, who played Number One son Lee Chan (Everett Collection).

He was a talented artist and entered the film industry as a billboard designer and caricaturist. Luke became a performer by accident when an MGM producer needed a Chinese actor with educated diction to play a supporting role in the 1934 Greta Garbo film, *The Painted Veil*, which coincidentally featured Charlie Chan's Warner Oland, whom Luke would join one year later in the *Charlie Chan* series.

His first appearance as Lee Chan was in *Charlie Chan in Paris* (1935), even though Fox Film Corporation had already made six previous *Charlie Chan* films with Warner Oland. He continued the role as Lee in seven more films with Oland. During the filming of *Charlie Chan at the Ringside* in 1938, however, Oland unexpectedly left the set and eventually went to Sweden, where he died. Twentieth Century–Fox salvaged much of this uncompleted project and reworked it as *Mr. Moto's Gamble* (1938), with Luke still playing the part of Lee Chan, but now as an assistant to the Japanese detective, Mr. Moto.

When Oland died and the series continued with Sidney Toler, Keye Luke resented

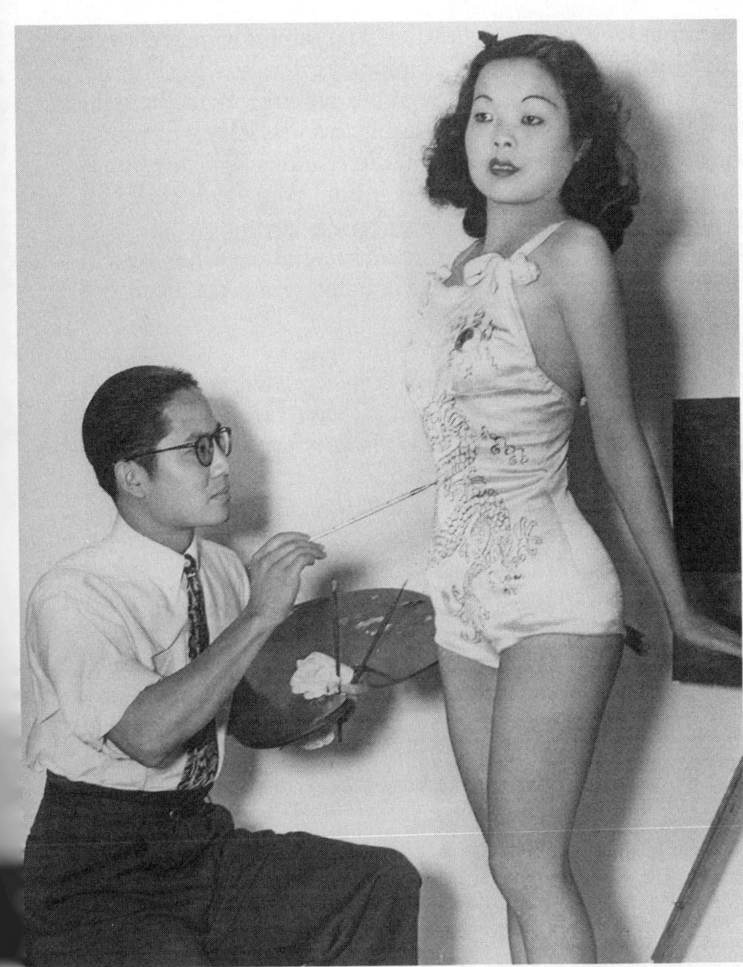

Inspired by the film *The Good Earth* (1937), Keye Luke shows off his artistic talent as he paints Oriental designs on a silk bathing suit worn by Suzanna Kim (Everett Collection).

the cut in pay required by the studio. In addition, Sol Wurtzel once commented to Luke, "With this team, there's one smart one and one dumb one. You're the dumb one." Consequently, Luke lost interest and left the series. His role was then replaced with the character of Jimmy Chan (portrayed by Sen Yung (later renamed Victor Sen Young). After 10 years, Luke returned to the series for the last two movies with Roland Winters at Monogram. Although he was never in a *Charlie Chan* film with Warner Oland's successor, Sidney Toler, Keye Luke and Toler did appear together in *Adventures of Smilin' Jack* (1943), in which Toler played General Kai Ling and Luke played Captain Wing.

By 1940 there were three Oriental detectives in films—Charlie Chan, Mr. Moto, and Mr. Wong. Each series continued the industry practice of casting a non–Oriental as the lead detective. However, after Boris Karloff had appeared as James Lee Wong in five *Mr. Wong* films at Monogram, Keye Luke was chosen for the role of Mr. Wong in *Phantom of Chinatown* (1940). This marked the first time an Oriental actor was cast in the lead role of an Oriental detective. Unfortunately, Luke was mismatched in the part and no further films were made.

In nearly 60 years Luke made more than 100 films. As a contract player in the studio era, Keye Luke had to appear in many minor movies, but he excelled in supporting roles in major films that included *Oil for the Lamps of China* (1935), *The Good Earth* (1937), *Across the Pacific* (1942), *Dragon Seed* (1944), and *Love Is a Many Splendored Thing* (1955). Luke played the loyal Kato in *The Green Hornet* film serials and a dedicated intern in the *Dr. Kildare* films of the 1940s. On Broadway in 1958, he played the patriarch of a Chinese-American family in Richard Rodgers and Oscar Hammerstein's second musical, *Flower Drum Song*.

Besides movies and Broadway, Luke appeared on many television series, such as *Perry Mason*, *Gunsmoke*, *The A-Team*, *Miami Vice*, *MacGyver*, *Harry-O*, *Night Court*, *Cannon*, *Remington Steele*, *Magnum P.I.*, *It Takes a Thief*, *I Spy*, and *Star Trek*. He was also the voice of Charlie Chan on the Saturday morning cartoon show, *Charlie Chan and the Chan Clan* in the 1970s. However, he attained his greatest popularity as Master Po, a blind, gentle, but masterly instructor in Asian philosophy and martial arts, in *Kung Fu*, which ran from 1972 to 1975.

When not acting, Luke was a technical adviser on films with Chinese themes and was a founder of the Screen Actors Guild. In 1986 he won the first Lifetime Achievement Award bestowed by the Association of Asian/Pacific American Artists, and just before his death from a stroke at the age of 86 he was honored with a sidewalk star on the Hollywood Hall of Fame.

Charlie Chan Filmography—As Lee Chan: *Charlie Chan in Paris* (1935), *Charlie Chan in Shanghai* (1935), *Charlie Chan at the Circus* (1936), *Charlie Chan at the Race Track* (1936), *Charlie Chan at the Opera* (1936), *Charlie Chan at the Olympics* (1936), *Charlie Chan on Broadway* (1937), *Charlie Chan at Monte Carlo* (1937), *The Feathered Serpent* (1948), and *The Sky Dragon* (1949).

Luxor A city in upper Egypt at the site of ancient Thebes. Located south of Cairo on the Nile River, it was the capital of ancient Egypt during the 11th dynasty (2133–1991 B.C.) and during the New Kingdom (1575–1085 B.C.). To the ancient Egyptians, Luxor was known as *Waset* or *No*, meaning "the city." The Greeks called it Thebes, which was probably derived from *Tape*, a name of the great temple of Karnak, which is near the city. The name "Luxor" comes from the Arabic *al-uqSuur*, meaning "the palaces." In *Charlie Chan in Egypt* (1935), the location of Professor Arnold's archeological expedition camp is just outside of Luxor.

Luza, Alberto Sometimes credited as Albert Luzi, costume designer of gowns for *Charlie Chan in Shanghai* (1935).

Lydig, Bill The alias of an unnamed murderer who escapes from San Quentin Prison and poses as a newspaper reporter for the *St. Louis Sun Herald*, taking passage on the *Suva Star* for the Cocos Island treasure hunt, in *Dead Men Tell* (1941).

When Lydig is introduced to Charlie Chan, Chan remarks that he was under the impression that Bill Lydig had died six months earlier. The impostor then corrects Chan by claiming that it was his brother, Phil Lydig, also a reporter. Kate Ransome faints after seeing in a magazine a picture of an escaped murderer and recognizing him as fellow passenger Bill Lydig. Lydig then puts her inside the iron maiden in the ship's hold. Before Lydig can be questioned, however, he is found dead of suffocation in the diving bell below deck.

Lynn, George Veteran character actor, sometimes credited as Peter George Lynn, who appeared in 45 films. Lynn portrays the blackmailing bartender Albert Rogers in *Charlie Chan at Monte Carlo* (1937).

M

M 2756, M 2757, and M 2758 Serial numbers of three 250,000-franc Ateliers Metallurgiques bonds (each worth $25,000) that are missing from Victor Karnoff's safe in *Charlie Chan at Monte Carlo* (1937).

McBirney, Steve Convicted murderer (portrayed by Marc Lawrence in his last of three *Charlie Chan* appearances) in *Charlie Chan at the Wax Museum* (1940). Charlie Chan helps convict McBirney for murder, and the judge sentences him to death at Sing Sing Prison during the week of December 9. McBirney then tells the judge, "Thanks. I won't have to do any Christmas shopping."

McBirney, Joe Rocke, and "Butcher" Degan were once partners in an honest business venture, but Degan didn't like Rocke and framed him for a murder he didn't commit in order to acquire the business. As revenge for Rocke's execution, McBirney shoots a man whom he thinks is Degan.

Charlie Chan helps convict McBirney for a different murder. McBirney escapes from the courthouse with help from his bodyguard Grennock. He eventually seeks Dr. Cream to change his face through plastic surgery and hatches a plan to get revenge on Charlie Chan. Degan, whose face has also been surgically changed, eventually finds Steve

McBirney alone in one of the museum rooms and stabs him in the back with a knife.

MacBride, Donald (June 23, 1894, Brooklyn, New York–June 21, 1957, Los Angeles, California) Stage and screen comedian and character actor who appeared in over 80 silent and sound films, often as explosive editors and dumb policemen. In two *Charlie Chan* roles, MacBride portrays San Francisco Police Chief J.J. Kilvaine in *Charlie Chan at Treasure Island* (1939) and New York Police Inspector Vance in *Murder Over New York* (1940).

McCoy, Herschel *see* **Herschel**

McCoy, Johnny Gangster (portrayed by Marc Lawrence in his second of three *Charlie Chan* roles) who is supposedly being returned to the United States from Shanghai by Mike Hannigan, a murderer posing as Detective Arnold, in *Charlie Chan in Honolulu* (1938). McCoy escapes from jail in the States while awaiting sentencing for murder and flees to Shanghai. Hannigan (posing as Detective Arnold) remarks that McCoy is returning to a sentence of 110 years, with time off for good behavior. Both McCoy and Hannigan are trying to secretly reenter the United States.

McCoy, Mary Alias used by Mary Conover in *Shadows Over Chinatown* (1946). *See also* **Conover, Mary.**

McCoy, "Shorty" Panhandler known as "The Canarsie Kid" (portrayed by Shemp Howard) in *Murder Over New York* (1940). When picked up by the New York police for a lineup, McCoy masquerades as "The Great Rashid," a Hindu fakir who (the police tell Charlie Chan) makes a living feeding suckers phony religion.

MacDonald, Edmund (c. 1911–1951, Los Angeles, California) American character actor who appeared in nearly 40 films, usually cast as plainclothes detectives or minor gangsters. MacDonald portrays scheming lawyer Walter Hartford in *Castle in the Desert* (1942).

MacDonald, Joseph Cinematographer for over 60 films, whose first film was *Charlie Chan in Rio* (1941). MacDonald was nominated three times for Academy Awards: Best Cinematography (Black-and-White)—*The Young Lions* (1958); Best Cinematography (Color)—*Pepe* (1960), and *The Sand Pebbles* (1966).

MacDonald, Philip (1900, Scotland–December 10, 1980, Woodland Hills, California) Screenplay writer for *Charlie Chan in London* (1934) and *Charlie Chan in Paris* (1935).

MacFadden, Hamilton (April 26, 1901, Chelsea, Massachusetts–*) American film director, actor, and writer of "B" pictures who sometimes acted in the films he directed. He directed three *Charlie Chan* films and, as an actor, also appeared in three Chan films. MacFadden portrays a movie director (unbilled) in *The Black Camel* (1931), a hotel night clerk in *Charlie Chan in Reno* (1939), and Bill Kellogg in *Charlie Chan in Rio* (1941).

Hamilton MacFadden attended Harvard Law School before entering the world of the theater. At first an actor, MacFadden decided that stage directing was his forte and remained in this line of work until brought to Hollywood by Fox Studios in 1929. For the first few years of the 1930s, it seemed as though every major Fox production was directed by either MacFadden or his fellow contractee David Butler.

It was MacFadden who launched Fox's *Charlie Chan* series with *Charlie Chan Carries On* and *The Black Camel* in 1931. He also was put in charge of Fox's Depression-busting musical, *Stand Up and Cheer* (1934), which was an artistic fiasco except for the presence of Shirley Temple in her first important role. However, MacFadden was eased out of Fox when the studio merged with Darryl F. Zanuck's Twentieth Century Productions in 1935. The merger probably was the reason why MacFadden, who was the original director for *Charlie Chan in Paris* (1935), was replaced by Lewis Seiler after only one week's production. By the end of the 1930s, Hamilton MacFadden had returned to acting in supporting and minor roles. Ironically, he was cast as a suspect in *Charlie Chan in Rio* (1941), an uncredited remake of MacFadden's own *The Black Camel* (1931).

Charlie Chan filmography—As Director: *Charlie Chan Carries On* (1931), *The Black Camel* (1931), and *Charlie Chan's Greatest Case* (1933).

McGill, Barney "Chick" (c. 1891–January 11, 1942, Los Angeles, California) Cameraman, sometimes credited as Bernard McGill or Chick McGill, of over 70 silent and sound films, including *Charlie Chan in Shanghai* (1935). In 1932 McGill was nominated for an Academy Award in the Best Cinematography category for *Svengali* (1931).

McGlynn, Frank, Sr. (1867, San Francisco, California–May 17, 1951, Newburgh, New York) Gaunt-looking American character actor who appeared in nearly 60 silent and sound films and was best remembered for his many portrayals of President Abraham Lincoln. McGlynn portrays Amos Winterslip in *Charlie Chan's Greatest Case* (1933).

McGrath, Paul (April 11, 1904, Chicago, Illinois–April 13, 1978, London, England) Stage and screen actor who portrays movie actor Charles Parks (alias Charles Thursday) in *Dead Men Tell* (1941).

McGraw, Sgt. Policeman (portrayed by Charles Sherlock) in *The Scarlet Clue* (1945). McGraw's commanding officer is Capt. Flynn.

McGuire, John (1911–1980) Character actor who appeared in over 30 films and portrays the head animal trainer, Hal Blake, in *Charlie Chan at the Circus* (1936).

McGuire, Thomas (September 1, 1873, England–May 6, 1954, Hollywood, California) Character actor (real name: Thomas Maguire) who appeared in over 40 silent and sound films and portrays Morris in *Charlie Chan at the Opera* (1936).

Mack, James T. (1870, Chicago, Illinois–August 12, 1948, Hollywood, California) Character actor who appeared in 20 silent and sound films. Mack portrays a police fingerprint technician (unbilled) in *Charlie Chan's Secret* (1936).

Mack, Louis Ex-convict whose forged fingerprints are placed on the pocketbook of Miss Petrie in *Dark Alibi* (1946). Upon further examination, a police fingerprint technician finds that Mr. Johnson's fingerprints are on Mack's fingerprint card from the state prison, which helps explain how fingerprints of ex-convicts were forged.

Mack, Sheriff Policeman (portrayed by Alan Bridge in his first of two *Charlie Chan* roles) in *The Jade Mask* (1945). Mack is called in to investigate the murder of Mr. Harper.

McKay, Wanda (1916, Portland, Oregon–April 11, 1996) Attractive brunette character actress (real name: Dorothy McKay) who appeared in over 25 films. McKay portrays Evelyn Manning in *The Golden Eye* (1948). Ten years earlier, in 1938, she was voted the title of Miss American Aviation.

Mackintosh, Louise (1865–November 1, 1933, Beverly Hills, California) Actress who portrays the housekeeper in *The Black Camel* (1931).

MacMasters, Mrs. Australian friend (portrayed by Mary Gordon in her first of two *Charlie Chan* roles) of Tarneverro in *The Black Camel* (1931). She reveals to Chan that Tarneverro's real name is Arthur Mayo and that he bears a striking resemblance to his murdered brother.

MacMasters, Thomas Australian friend (portrayed by Joseph M. Kerrigan) of Tarneverro in *The Black Camel* (1931).

McNalley, Capt. Pete New Orleans policeman (portrayed by John Gallaudet in his second of two *Charlie Chan* roles) in *Docks of New Orleans* (1948). McNalley is romantically involved with Lafontaine's niece, René.

McWhorter, Frank Sound recordist for *The Shanghai Chest* (1948).

Macy, Lt. Policeman (portrayed by Wade Boteler in his second of two *Charlie Chan* roles) in *Charlie Chan at the Circus* (1936). When circus owner Joe Kinney is murdered, Lt. Macy is called in to investigate.

Madden, J.P. *see* **Madden, Philip J.**

Madden, Philip J. Wealthy financier (portrayed by Hobart Bosworth) whose obsession is to purchase the Phillimore pearl necklace in *The Chinese Parrot* (1927). Many years ago Madden had admired Sally Randall, the daughter of a wealthy Hawaiian planter, but she married a man named Phillimore, the man of her father's choice who had given her a priceless pearl necklace. Rejected, Madden then vows that he will someday humiliate her and buy the pearl necklace.

Many years later, when Sally Phillimore (now Sally Jordan—a widow in financial straits) offers the pearls for sale in San Francisco, Madden immediately buys them, having recognized their owner. Before the delivery of the necklace is made, Madden is kidnapped by his long-time secretary, Martin Thorne, as part of a scheme to have Jerry Delaney impersonate Madden and steal the necklace.

Note: In *Charlie Chan's Courage* (1934), a remake of *The Chinese Parrot*, Madden is referred to as J.P. Madden and is portrayed by Paul Harvey in his first of three *Charlie Chan* roles.

Madero, Tony Husband of Marie Dubon, and the former secretary of Petroff, in *City in Darkness* (1939). Madero objects to the attention being paid to his wife by Petroff and threatens to expose Petroff's undercover deals with foreign governments if he doesn't stop. Instead, Petroff fires Madero and files false embezzlement charges against him with the police. Now on the run from the police, Madero secretly stays at the Hotel de Voyageurs while his wife tries to get a boat ticket out of the country and a false passport (under the alias of Antonio Castillo, a Bogotá coffee planter) from Louis Santelle.

When Madero is checking out of the hotel, Charlie Chan sees Madero's fake passport identifying him as Antonio Castillo from Bogotá. Sensing that the Castillo identity is a phony, Chan remarks that he had once been in Bogotá and liked the view of the river from the mountain. He then asks Castillo the name of the river, to which Castillo replies, "The Colombia River." Chan then exposes Castillo as a fraud since Bogotá is an inland city and has no river.

Madison, Noel (1898, New York, New York–January 6, 1975, Fort Lauderdale, Florida) Stage and character film actor (real name: Nowell Nathaniel Moscovitch) who appeared in over 65 films, often as gangsters and low-lifes in films and as highly sophisticated characters on stage. Madison portrays Belescu in *City in Darkness* (1939).

The son of famed Yiddish actor Maurice Moscovitch, Noel Madison was educated at the University of Lausanne in Switzerland, in Paris, and in Loudoun House in London. At first he was billed as Nat Madison, and he established his reputation on Broadway as an actor and director. In films from 1930, he was usually cast as a smooth-talking gangster. During World War II, Madison's unique facial features permitted him to play both German and Japanese bad guys. In 1943 he left films and returned full-time to the theater, where he was active both as an actor and as a director.

"MADMAN ELUDES DRAGNET" Newspaper headline of the *Los Angeles Telegraph* about Gravelle's escape from the Rockland State Sanitarium in *Charlie Chan at the Opera* (1936).

Maestro Nickname for Cole King in *The Trap* (1947).

mah-jongg American adaptation of the 19th-century Chinese game of *ma jiang* (or *ma* *chiang*), similar to rummy. Although there are many stories citing the game's origins, the most logical theory suggests that the game has been developed from various Chinese games. The introduction to the western world is thought to have begun with two brothers named White who, in the early 1900s, introduced mah-jongg to the English speaking clubs of Shanghai, where it quickly gained popularity among the foreign residents.

Importation of mah-jongg tiles began with Joseph P. Babcock, who at that time was the Soochow representative of the Standard Oil Company. Babcock had simplified the game's scoring and is credited with starting the practice of putting English numerals on the tiles. In September of 1920, Mr. Babcock patented the game and put his rules into print.

It is played by four persons in the traditional Chinese version. Mah-jongg consists of 144 tiles, 108 of which are suit tiles. The suits are bamboos, circles, and characters, each of which has 36 tiles numbered 1 through 9, with four tiles of each numeral. There are also 28 honor tiles—four each of the four winds (marked E, S, W, and N for the compass directions) and four each of the three dragons (red, green, and white)—and eight bonus tiles, four each of flowers and seasons. Each player begins with 13 tiles, except the player designated "East," who has 14. The players draw from a square with walls that are 18 tiles long and 2 tiles high. Play opens with East discarding a tile and proceeds as each player in turn either takes a discarded tile or draws one from the wall. A player wins with a complete hand of four sets plus a pair.

In *Charlie Chan's Murder Cruise* (1940), Charlie Chan observes Dick Kenyon and Professor Gordon playing mah-jongg with only two persons. Gordon tells Chan that the two-player game is an American innovation and that mah-jongg has undergone many changes since it was introduced during the Han Dynasty, which Gordon claims was the "Golden Era of southern China" (of which he has made quite a study). However, Chan remarks that he was under the impression that mah-jongg was from an earlier dynasty.

At the movie's conclusion, Chan gives Number Two son Jimmy a history lesson about his ancient ancestors, stating that China's "Golden Era" was during the Shang Dynasty of north China. This corrects information Professor Gordon, a bogus archeologist, told Chan earlier (that the "Golden Era" was during the Han Dynasty).

Major 4782 Charlie Chan's home telephone number in *The Chinese Ring* (1947).

Mallinson, Rory (October 10, 1903–March 26, 1976) Character actor (real name: Charles Joseph Mallinson) who appeared in almost 40 films. Mallinson portrays Mr. Thompson, Simon Lafontaine's office manager, in *Docks of New Orleans* (1948).

"manager please" Opening code words Ralph Brett speaks to reach the unknown leader of an espionage ring. To contact the unknown leader, Brett dials telephone number Harding 2535, tells the person on the other end (an old accomplice named Cooper), "manager please." Cooper than asks, "Who's calling?" whereupon Brett responds with "Brett" and is then switched to the mysterious leader (who communicates with Brett only via teletype).

manasterol Derivative of a fictitious powerful shock drug that leaves a person with no physical or mental resistance so that the person can be easily hypnotized. In *Black Magic* (1944), Paul Hamlin gives manasterol to both Norma Duncan (alias Nancy Woods) and Justine Bonner, who, under his hypnotic suggestion, walks off the roof of the Chalmont Building to her death.

Charlie Chan is attacked when searching Room 722 in the Berkeley Building, the same room in front of whose door he found Mrs. Bonner's glove prior to her walking off the roof of a building while in a hypnotic trance. When Chan awakes, he is restrained in a chair in a darkened room and is about to be hypnotized by an unknown voice (Hamlin). Chan says that he needs to take some medicine for his heart, a ruse so that he can take an antidote pill for the hypnotic drug manasterol, which is in the drinking water.

The Mandarin's Secret One of two working titles for *Shadows Over Chinatown* (1946) before its release on July 27, 1946. *See also* ***Shadows Over Chinatown* (1946)**.

Manderley, Lucy Married name of Princess Lucrezia della Borgia (portrayed by Lenita Lane in her second of two *Charlie Chan* roles) in *Castle in the Desert* (1942). Lucy is married to Paul Manderley and lives in a 16th-century–style castle built in the Mojave Desert.

Because Lucy is a descendant of the infamous Borgia family (known for poisoning their victims), Dr. Retling and Brenda and Walter Hartford hire Professor Gleason and Arthur Fletcher to imitate being poisoned by Lucy in a plan to convince Paul Manderley that Lucy is insane, turn the control of a $20 million estate over to Walter Hartford via power of attorney, and leave quietly with his wife. Lucy tells Charlie Chan that she once had a younger stepbrother, Cesare, who was reportedly killed many years ago in the Spanish War (though Mme. Saturnia says is still alive).

Manderley, Paul Wealthy recluse and historian (portrayed by Douglass Dumbrille in his last of three *Charlie Chan* roles) in *Castle in the Desert* (1942). For his research for writing a book on Cesare Borgia, Manderley wants to understand the minds of men living 400 years ago, even putting up with its inconveniences by living in a castle without electricity or telephone. To provide an alibi for his being a recluse, Manderley wears a scarf mask intended to cover up a non-existent, unsightly scar on one side of his face.

Manderley is the sole administrator of a $20 million estate, the control of which he loses if he is involved in any sort of scandal. Because it is known that Manderley's wife, Lucy, is a descendant of the infamous Borgia family (known for poisoning their victims), Dr. Retling and Brenda and Walter Hartford hire Professor Gleason and Arthur Fletcher to imitate being poisoned by Lucy in a plan to convince Manderley that Lucy is insane, turn the control of the estate over to Walter Hartford via power of attorney, and leave quietly with his wife.

Manderley Castle Secluded Mojave Desert castle home of Paul Manderley, the main location setting for *Castle in the Desert* (1942). As an historian, Manderley builds the castle with no telephone or electricity to better study the minds of men 400 years ago, putting up with its inconveniences and living there with his wife. The castle has its own apothecary, dungeon, torture room, library collection of rare books, and chapel.

Mango Inn Boarding House Samoan restaurant, general store, and hotel owned by Tao Erickson in *Dangerous Money* (1946).

"MANIAC OVERPOWERS GUARD, ESCAPES" Newspaper headline of the *Los Angeles Chronicle* about Gravelle's escape from the Rockland State Sanitarium in *Charlie Chan at the Opera* (1936).

Manleck German master spy, alias Mrs. Winters (portrayed by Lelah Tyler), who murders confederate Philipe von Vegon, alias Luiz Vega, when she fears he will talk about his murdering George Melton in *Charlie Chan in the Secret Service* (1944).

Mann, Margaret (April 4, 1868, Aberdeen, Scotland–February 4, 1941, Los Angeles, California) Character actress who appeared in nearly 30 silent and sound films. Mann portrays the terrified housemaid who thinks that all foreigners, especially Orientals, are murderers in *Charlie Chan in London* (1934).

Reportedly born into a poverty-stricken family, Margaret Mann was widowed early on and forced to take whatever jobs she could to keep her family fed. In the talkies, she was generally consigned to bit roles as maids, nursing-home residents, and comforting mothers. Margaret Mann holds a special place in the hearts of *Our Gang* fans for her portrayal of the frail-looking but iron-willed granny in the 1931 two-reelers *Helping Grandma* and *Fly My Kite*.

Mannering, Eve Niece of Sir George Mannering (portrayed by Lois Moran) who secretly marries greedy fortune hunter Eric Durand against her uncle's wishes in *Behind That Curtain* (1929). While in India, Eve discovers that her husband murdered Hilary Galt and is everything her uncle had warned her about.

Mannering, Sir George Wealthy Englishman (portrayed by Claude King in his first of three *Charlie Chan* roles) in *Behind That Curtain* (1929). Suspicious of his niece's fiancé, Eric Durand, Mannering hires lawyer Hilary Galt to investigate Durand's past, which is that of a scheming fortune hunter. He tells his niece, Eve Mannering, of his findings, but she refuses to believe him. When Mannering gives her an ultimatum, Eve and Durand inform him that they were married the night before. Heartbroken, Mannering demands that the couple leave his house and never see him again.

Manning, Evelyn The daughter (portrayed by Wanda McKay) of Mr. Manning in *The Golden Eye* (1948).

Manning, Leah Thomas Manning's stepdaughter (portrayed by Joan Woodbury in her second of two *Charlie Chan* roles) in *The Chinese Cat* (1944). Leah is in love with Detective Harvey Dennis, who is the police inspector assigned to solve the murder of her stepfather.

Manning, Mr. Arizona rancher and owner of the Golden Eye Mine (portrayed by Forrest Taylor) in *The Golden Eye* (1948). Manning seeks the assistance of Charlie Chan after there are several attempts to kill him.

Before Chan can visit Manning at his ranch, Manning has had a serious "accident" when he falls from a ladder in the mine. He is now critically ill with head injuries and is required by the doctor to be heavily sedated (and is unable to talk to anyone). Manning is later killed by Driscoll to insure that he will not recover from his injuries, and to hopefully keep Chan from learning more about the gold smuggling at the mine.

With the help of a woman masquerading as Sister Teresa (a supposed nun who is a nurse but who is really part of the smuggling operation), Mrs. Driscoll then takes Manning's place in the sickbed as a sedated, almost lifeless body whose head is entirely covered with bandages to hide her identity.

Manning, Mrs. Wealthy socialite (portrayed by Betty Blythe) whose second husband is Thomas Manning in *The Chinese Cat* (1944).

Manning, Thomas P. Realtor and chess expert (portrayed by Sam Flint [unbilled] in his second of two *Charlie Chan* roles) in *The Chinese Cat* (1944). Manning is a business partner of Deacon in the Manning-Deacon Realty Company, and both were involved in the theft of the Kalinor diamond collection in Chicago a year earlier.

However, Manning double-crosses Deacon and steals the largest diamond for himself, for which he is shot and killed by Deacon while in a locked room in Manning's house. No gun is found, however, and the police never solve the case. Offering a clue to his killer's identity, the dying Manning, seated at a chessboard, clears the board of all the pieces except a lone black bishop; both the bishop and deacon are church officers.

Manning-Deacon Realty Company Real estate company owned by Thomas Manning and Webster Deacon in *The Chinese Cat* (1944).

Manolo, Emil Owner of Manolo's Cabaret (portrayed by Jack La Rue) who is a confederate of master saboteur Reiner in *Charlie Chan in Panama* (1940). Manolo poisons American agent Godley and kills undercover British agent Cliveden Compton. To carry out his superior's plan to sabotage the U.S. fleet as it passes through the Panama Canal, Manolo disguises himself as Ramon Gonzales to place nitroglycerin (disguised as bottled water for the plant's watercooler) inside the Miraflores Power Control Station. Once inside, he sets a time bomb to blow up the station and the canal. He is later shot and killed by Miss Finch, who is really Reiner.

Manuel Villainous henchman (portrayed by Charles Stevens in his second of two *Charlie Chan* roles) in *The Feathered Serpent* (1948).

Manuel is part of a smuggling operation headed by Professor Stanley and is hired to be part of an archeological expedition to keep an eye on Charlie Chan, who is investigating the death of Professor Scott and the disappearance of Professor Farnsworth. Manuel shoots and kills Filippe, an undercover Mexican secret police agent, when Filippe tries to arrest Stanley.

mapuchari One of many alternative names and forms of cannabis (hashish; marijuana). In *Charlie Chan in Egypt* (1935), Charlie Chan notices that cigarettes smoked by Carol Arnold contain the drug mapuchari. When asked about the effects of mapuchari, Dr. Racine tells Chan that by taking the drug, one loses all sense of time and reality, and suffers from false convictions and hallucinations—which are the symptoms currently experienced by Miss Arnold. Although the cigarettes are supplied by her servant, Edfu Ahmad, it is Carol's uncle, Professor Thurston, who actually tampers with the cigarettes to drug her.

Marana, Alfredo Indian mystic (portrayed by Victor Jory) who is really Alfredo Cardoza in *Charlie Chan in Rio* (1941). His brother, Manuel Cardozo, was murdered in Honolulu a year earlier by Lola Dean, and Marana finally tracks her down in Rio de Janeiro.

As a mystic, Marana puts Lola Dean in a semi-comatose, hypnotic state by having her drink some coffee and smoke a special cigarette. Marana then cryptically tells Dean, "Now let's go from the sublime to the infinite. Let's peek around the corner of infinity and see what we shall see." Upon questioning Dean, Marana gets Lola to admit that she once killed a man, Manuel Cardozo, when he wouldn't divorce his own wife and marry her, all of which he is recording as evidence.

Note: The character Alfredo Marana loosely parallels that of Tarneverro in *The Black Camel* (1931).

Marcel The bumbling secretary (portrayed by Harold Huber in his third of four *Charlie Chan* roles) to Paris prefect of police J. Romaine in *City in Darkness* (1939). He calls Romaine "Papa" because Romaine is his godfather. Marcel's real father is the police chief of Bucharest, Romania, who sent Marcel to Paris to learn French police methods.

Marcia Bitchy star of Cole King's variety troupe (portrayed by Rita Quigley), who is also King's girlfriend, in *The Trap* (1947). When Adelaide criticizes Marcia about her attitude, Marcia threatens to reveal that Adelaide is secretly married to physician George Brandt, hinting that she knows Brandt's real identity.

Marcia then forces Lois to steal several incriminating letters from Adelaide's trunk by threatening to tell King that Lois is under eighteen. Marcia is later found washed up on the beach, having been strangled with a silk cord by Mrs. Thorn.

Margo Lola Dean's servant-cook (portrayed by Ann Codee) in *Charlie Chan in Rio* (1941).

Market Street Location of the San Francisco branch of the Exchange Specie Bank of Peiping in *The Chinese Ring* (1947).

Marloff, Ivan Sinister gangster (portrayed by Frederick Vogeding in his first of three *Charlie Chan* roles) in *Charlie Chan in Shanghai* (1935). Marloff is part of an opium smuggling operation in Shanghai that kidnaps Charlie Chan to find out what Chan knows.

Note: The character of Ivan Marloff is incorrectly credited as Burke in the on-screen credits.

Marlowe, Shirley The former lover of murderer Alan Raleigh (portrayed by Marian Nixon in her second of two *Charlie Chan* roles) who is asked by John Douglas to marry her in *Charlie Chan's Chance* (1932).

Note: The character Shirley Marlowe

loosely parallels that of Patricia West (Mrs. Paul Narvo) in *Murder Over New York* (1940).

Marr, Edward Character actor who portrays Steve McBirney's bodyguard Grennock, in *Charlie Chan at the Wax Museum* (1940). In addition, Marr portrays Sammy in *Mr. Moto's Gamble* (1938), a reworked version of the never-completed *Charlie Chan at the Ringside*.

Marsh, Joan (July 10, 1913, Porterville, California–) Attractive platinum blonde actress (real name: Nancy Ann Rosher) who appeared in over 40 silent and sound films. Marsh portrays freelance photographer Joan Wendall in *Charlie Chan on Broadway* (1937).

Joan Marsh was the daughter of cinematographer Charles Rosher and was on stage virtually from infancy (as Nancy Ann Rosher). Changing her name to Dorothy Rosher, she played bit roles in the movies from 1915 and began the adult phase of her career in 1930 as Joan Marsh. The least tiring of her talkie roles was the "poster girl" over whom Lew Ayres and his fellow soldiers fantasize in the Oscar-winning *All Quiet on the Western Front* (1930).

During the 1930s she played a variety of buoyant characters, notably W.C. Fields' daughter, Pauline Bisbee, in *You're Telling Me* (1934) and photographer Joan Wendall in *Charlie Chan on Broadway* (1939). She also showed up as Elaine in Clark Gable's *Les Blondes* troupe in *Idiot's Delight* (1939) and as carnival girl "Dimples" in Bob Hope and Bing Crosby's *Road to Zanzibar* (1941).

After portraying Janet Blake in the Republic serial *Secret Service in Darkest Africa* (1942) and playing the nominal female lead in three low-budget *East-Side Kids* comedies, Marsh retired from show business to open a profitable stationery company called Paper Unlimited. She was once married to Charles S. Belden, a screenplay writer of four *Charlie Chan* films and *Mr. Moto's Gamble* (1938), a reworked version of the never-completed *Charlie Chan at the Ringside*.

Marsh, Mrs. Leader of an espionage ring (portrayed by Virginia Brissac) in *The Scarlet Clue* (1945). As her cover, Mrs. Marsh is a bossy, rude, and demanding sponsor of a radio program aired at the Cosmo Radio Center. Marsh's office is Room 703 at the radio station, three floors below the Hamilton Laboratory, whose radar secrets she is trying to steal.

Marsh uses Ralph Brett and Cooper as confederates in the spy ring, both of whom are ignorant of their superior's real identity. To contact the unknown leader, Brett dials telephone number Harding 2535 and tells the person on the other end (Cooper), "manager please." When asked by Cooper, "Who's calling?" he responds with "Brett," and is then switched to the mysterious leader (who answers Brett via teletype).

Through Brett, Mrs. Marsh is aware of everything that is going on. Before Gloria Bayne can tell Charlie Chan anything about Rausch's murderer (who Chan mentions is the same person who stole Diane Hall's car), Bayne is killed by Mrs. Marsh after inhaling gas from a radio actuated gas pellet inside a radio studio stage microphone and then smoking a cigarette, the combination producing a deadly poison.

Brett panics after Chan suspects him of murdering Rausch, and telephones his unknown espionage ring superior. Marsh sends him instructions on the teletype to take the service elevator to the seventh floor. If no one is in the hall, Brett is to go to the tenth floor and is told that he will get away. Mrs. Marsh, secretly looking out the slightly opened door of Room 702, sees Brett get back into the elevator. She then throws a hidden control switch which opens a trap door, dropping Brett to the building's basement, killing him instantly. In an attempt to flee from Chan, Mrs. Marsh is killed in her own trap when she takes the service elevator, unaware that the control switch has already activated the trap door.

Marshall, Jane Airline stewardess on Flight 17 (portrayed by Noel Neill) in *The Sky Dragon* (1949). She is engaged to pilot Tim Norton.

Marston, Joel (1922–) Actor who appeared in over 15 films and portrays co-pilot Don Blake in *The Sky Dragon* (1949).

Martin, Chris-Pin (November 19, 1893, Tucson, Arizona–June 27, 1953, Los Angeles, California) Roly-poly Yaqui Indian comic actor (real name: Yabel Ponciana Chris-Pin Martin Piaz) who appeared in over 70 films (sometimes credited as Chris King Martin) often as a lazy, dull-witted Hispanic comic foil. Martin portrays Panamanian policeman Lt. Montero in *Charlie Chan in Panama* (1940).

Born in the Arizona Territory to Mexican parents, Chris-Pin Martin developed a reputation as a comic at an early age. During his heyday in the 1930s and 1940s, Martin perpetuated the stereotype of a lazy, dull-witted Hispanic in many *Cisco Kid* films as the sidekick Pancho (sometimes named Gorditor) to such screen Ciscos as Warner Baxter, Cesar Romero, Gilbert Roland, and Duncan Renaldo.

Martin, Cynthia The wife (portrayed by Elaine Lange) of Professor Martin, who seems to spend more time with her husband's assistant, Harold Mayfair, than her husband, in *Dangerous Money* (1946).

Martin, Professor Dick Absent-minded ichthyologist (portrayed by Emmett Vogan in his third of five *Charlie Chan* roles) in *Dangerous Money* (1946). Six years earlier, Martin established an ichthyological museum in Samoa, but his work was interrupted by World War II and he vowed to return. With the war over, he now returns to Samoa with his wife, Cynthia, and his assistant, Harold Mayfair, and is shocked to find out that his museum is being used by a gang to hide money and artwork stolen from Philippine banks during the Japanese invasion.

Martinelli, Arthur (c. 1882–September 7, 1967, Hollywood, California) Cinematographer for over 50 films, including *Black Magic* (1944).

Masack, Charles Enemy agent (for defeated Nazis) posing as an importer, who is trying to acquire secret research papers that have information about the discovery of a 95th element in *The Red Dragon* (1945). Portrayed by Don Costello, Masack is secretly married to the Countess Irena, who is also an enemy agent.

Mason, Dan (1853–July 6, 1929) Stage and screen actor (real name: Dan Grassman) who appeared in over 26 silent films and portrays an unnamed prospector in *The Chinese Parrot* (1927).

Mason, Reginald (June 27, 1875, San Francisco, California–July 10, 1962, Hermosa Beach, California) Actor who portrays Alexander Crawford in *Charlie Chan's Courage* (1934).

Masters, Richard (Dick) Pole vaulter for the U.S. Olympic Team (portrayed by Allan Lane) in *Charlie Chan at the Olympics* (1937). Masters works as a test pilot for the Hopkins Aviation Company, which is developing a new remote controlled guidance system for airplanes. Prior to a test flight in Honolulu to demonstrate the new invention (which has strategic military applications for the U.S. War Department), Masters, the official test pilot, injures his shoulder and is replaced by Edwards at the last minute. Masters' girlfriend is Betty Adams, who is also on the U.S. Olympic Team and is jealous of the scheming Yvonne Roland (who directs her charms at Masters to get information about the remote controlled guidance system).

During the Olympics, a movie scene shows Masters pole vaulting 14'2", and Betty Adams tells another team member that "Dick can do better than that." However, the official results for the 1936 Berlin Olympics reveal that the gold medal winner was Earle Meadows (USA) with an Olympic record vault of 14'3¼"; Shuheu Nishida of Japan came in second with 13'11¼". As each country was limited to three entries in each event, the other two Americans in the pole vault were William Sefton (fourth place at 13'11¼") and William Graber (fifth place at 13'7¼").

Maté, Rudolph (January 21, 1898, Cracow, Poland–October 26, 1964, Hollywood, California) Cinematographer (real name: Rudolph Matheh) of 40 films, and later a director of almost 30 films. Maté was the cameraman for *Charlie Chan's Secret* (1936). For each year from 1941 to 1945, Maté was nominated for an Academy Award, but never won in the following categories: Best Cinematography (Black-and-White): *Foreign Correspondent* (1940), *That Hamilton Woman* (1941), *The Pride of the Yankees* (1942), and *Sahara* (1943); Best Cinematography (Color): *Cover Girl* (1944).

Matthews, Sgt. Police sergeant (portrayed by Joseph Crehan in his first of two *Charlie Chan* roles) in *Black Magic* (1944). When phony psychic William Bonner is murdered during a séance, Sgt. Matthews is called in to investigate.

Maxey, Paul (March 15, 1908, Wheaton, Illinois–June 3, 1963, Pasadena, California) Heavy-set American character actor who appeared in over 35 films. Maxey portrays insurance investigator and multiple murderer John Anderson in *The Sky Dragon* (1949).

Maxwell, Charles Music orchestrator for *Charlie Chan at the Opera* (1936).

May 30, 1935 Date (Decoration Day, now called Memorial Day) on which Nellie Farrell claims she and Joe Kinney were secretly married in Juarez, Mexico, in *Charlie Chan at the Circus* (1936). Despite Nellie's claim, Marie Norman, who is Kinney's fiancée, claims she has proof (a newspaper clipping) that Kinney could not have been in Juarez on that date, since both Kinney and Tom Holt were caught cheating at cards at an El Paso, Texas, casino, and Holt killed the Sheriff. *See also* **Ace Casino**.

Maydorf, Henry The brother (portrayed by Harvey Clark) of "Shaky" Phil Maydorf who poses as Professor Gamble in *Charlie Chan's Courage* (1934). *See also* **Gamble, Professor Thaddeus**.

Maydorf, "Shaky" Phil New York gangster (portrayed by Edgar Kennedy) who murders Louie Wong in *The Chinese Parrot* (1927). Martin Thorne, Jerry Delaney, and "Shaky" Phil Maydorf are all part of a scheme to steal the Phillimore pearl necklace by having Delaney impersonate Madden.

Mayfair, Harold Professor Martin's assistant (portrayed by Bruce Edwards), who seems to spend more time with Professor Marin's wife, Cynthia, than does her husband, in *Dangerous Money* (1946).

Mayfair Hotel San Francisco hotel patronized by Charlie Chan, Mrs. Conover, and her friend Kate Johnson in *Shadows Over Chinatown* (1946). Today, there really is a Mayfair Hotel in San Francisco, which is located at 625 Polk Street.

Mayo, Arthur Real name of Tarneverro, who was the brother of the murdered actor Denny Mayo, in *The Black Camel* (1931).

Mayo, Denny Film actor romantically involved with Shelah Fane (although he is already married) in *The Black Camel* (1931). In a fit of anger, Fane kills Mayo, and the murder remains unsolved for three years, even though both his widow and brother try to gather evidence.

Medusa Cargo ship, docked at Cherbourg, which is set to smuggle a contraband cargo of munitions to France's enemies in *City in Darkness* (1939).

Meeker The lawyer (portrayed by Charles Williams in his second of two *Charlie Chan* roles) for Hottentot Club owner Johnny Burke in *Charlie Chan on Broadway* (1937). When Burke agrees to take a paraffin test, Meeker asks what the test is. Charlie Chan explains that the test determines if there is any gunpowder residue on the hand of anyone who recently fired a gun, to which Meeker replies, "That's silly. He washes his hands, you know." *See* **paraffin test.**

Meeker, George (March 5, 1904–1984, Carpenteria, California) Character actor who appeared in over 100 films and portrays Edmond Slade in *The Red Dragon* (1945).

Meeker, Walter Mr. Harper's laboratory assistant (portrayed by Hardie Albright) in *The Jade Mask* (1945). Lloyd Archer murders Meeker with a poison dart and then impersonates him to give him alibis when he kills two more people.

Meers, Al Technician who works at the Santa Juanita racetrack (portrayed by Harry Jans) in *Charlie Chan at the Race Track* (1936). Professional gambler Denny Barton has Meers explain to Charlie Chan that timing heads are located every quarter of a mile around the track and are used to electronically time the race. Meers also shows how a picture is taken of the horses crossing the finish line.

Meers is part of a racetrack gambling ring that is betting on Gallant Lad (actually Avalanche, as the faster horse has been switched with Gallant Lad) to win the Santa Juanita Handicap race. To help make sure that the bogus Gallant Lad wins, Meers plans to use a special timing head that has a tranquilizer dart and is set to fire at any horse that is in front of Gallant Lad at the three-quarter mile pole.

Meeting at Midnight Reissue title for *Black Magic* (1944). *See also* ***Black Magic*** **(1944)**.

Mehra, Lal Chand Actor who portrays Paul Narvo's servant, Ramullah (alias Aga Singh), in *Murder Over New York* (1940).

Mei, Wu *Suva Star* cook (portrayed by Lee Tung Foo [unbilled] in his first of three *Charlie Chan* roles) who plays the eerie sounding ocarina in *Dead Men Tell* (1941).

Melbourne Cup Australian horse race in which Avalanche, the number 4 horse (ridden by jockey "Tip" Collins), crosses the finish line first in *Charlie Chan at the Race Track* (1936). However, Collins is paid to intentionally foul Stardust during the race on orders of Avalanche's trainer, Bagley, who is part of a racetrack gambling ring. Because of the foul, Avalanche is then disqualified from the race, and Stardust, as the second-place finisher, is declared the winner. The track stewards feel that Collins should have been able to prevent Avalanche from pulling wide, and Collins is barred from further racing for two years.

Melton, George Inventor of a new torpedo the U.S. Navy believes will help destroy German U-boats in *Charlie Chan in the Secret Service* (1944). Because of the importance of the invention to the United States, the president of the United States assigns Secret Service agents Jones and Lewis as bodyguards. However, Melton is electrocuted by von Vegon when Melton pulls the light chain to turn on a closet light, and von Vegon takes the secret torpedo plans from Melton's coat pocket.

Mercer, Joan Hostess of the Bay City Escort Bureau (portrayed by Dorothy Granger in her second of two *Charlie Chan* roles) in *Shadows Over Chinatown* (1946). When she discovers that Mary Conover is part of a trap set by the police, Mercer dresses up in Mary's clothes and top coat to escape from the police.

Mercer, Ray F. Property master and creator of special effects for over 60 films, including *The Feathered Serpent* (1948) and *The Sky Dragon* (1949).

Mercier, Louis (March 7, 1901, Algiers, Algeria–*) French actor who appeared in over 40 films and had roles in two *Charlie Chan* entries. Mercier portrays the hard luck taxi driver in *Charlie Chan at Monte Carlo* (1937) and "Gentleman" Max in *City in Darkness* (1939).

Meredyth, Bess (1890, Buffalo, New York–July 13, 1969, Woodland Hills, California) Story writer (real name: Helen MacGlashan) for *Charlie Chan at the Opera* (1936). Bess Meredyth was one of the 36 founders of the Academy of Motion Picture Arts and Sciences (AMPAS) and was twice nominated for an Academy Award in the Best Writing, Achievement category for *A Woman of Affairs* (1928) and *Wonder of Women* (1929).

Mexico City Capital city of Mexico, which is the location setting for *The Red Dragon* (1945).

Michaels, Sol Assistant director for *Charlie Chan at the Opera* (1936).

Middleton, Charles B. (October 3, 1879, Elizabethtown, Kentucky–April 22, 1949, Los Angeles, California) Tall, hatchet-faced, stern-speaking, stage and screen character actor who appeared in nearly 150 films, often as stern judges, cruel orphanage officials, backwater sheriffs or small-town bigots. Middleton portrays the puritanical Jeremiah Walters in *Charlie Chan's Murder Cruise* (1940).

Beginning his career in circuses and carnivals in the South, Charles Middleton worked in vaudeville and stock companies before his 1927 entry into films. Of all his roles, Middleton was perhaps best known as Ming the Merciless, the evil and satanic ruler of the planet Mongo, in four *Flash Gordon* films from 1936 to 1940. Outside of his extensive work in serials and westerns, Middleton was used to best advantage in the films of Laurel and Hardy and Will Rogers. In a far less villainous vein, Middleton was cast as Abe Lincoln's father, Tom Lincoln, in *Abe Lincoln in Illinois* (1940). Middleton also played Lincoln himself on several occasions and, in *Stand-In* (1937), was hilariously cast (though unbilled) as an unsuccessful actor who dresses like Lincoln in hopes of landing a movie role.

"MIDNIGHT STABLE MURDER LATEST!" Newspaper headline of the *London Planet* in *Charlie Chan in London* (1934).

Miley, Jerry Character actor who appeared in 15 silent and sound films and portrays Allen Colby in *Charlie Chan's Secret* (1936).

Miljan, Thomas (November 9, 1892, Lead City, South Dakota–January 24, 1960, Hollywood, California) Handsome actor who appeared in over 160 silent and sound films, often cast as the suave villain. Miljan portrays Albert Dufresne in *Charlie Chan in Paris* (1935).

An actor since the age of 15, John Miljan entered films in 1923. Miljan was handsome enough for leading roles but realized early on that he'd have a longer screen career as a villain. He made his talkie debut in the promotional trailer for *The Jazz Singer* (1927), inviting the audience to see the upcoming production of the first talkie film. While he continued playing bad guys in the sound era, he was just as often seen as military officers and police inspectors. His slender frame and authoritative air enabled him to play such roles as General Custer in DeMille's *The Plainsman* (1936) and a character based on General Wainwright in *Back to Bataan* (1945).

Milland, Ray (January 3, 1908, Neath, Glamorganshire, Wales–March 10, 1986, Torrance, California) Leading man (real name: Reginald Alfred Truscott-Jones) and film director with a ready smile. Having appeared in over 140 films, Milland got his stage name from the flat area of land called the mill lands on the banks of the river that Neath stands upon. Milland portrays the lawyer Neil Howard in *Charlie Chan in London* (1934). He also appeared many times on television, most

Ray Milland (Everett Collection)

notably in several episodes of *Columbo* and as Jennifer Hart's father in *Hart to Hart*.

In 1946 Milland won both a Golden Globe award in the Best Motion Picture Actor category and an Academy Award for Best Actor for his portrayal of Don Birhnam in *The Lost Weekend* (1945).

Miller, E. Airplane mechanic for the Hopkins Aviation Company who is a henchman for a spy ring in *Charlie Chan at the Olympics* (1937). Miller stows away on the plane that is to make a test flight demonstrating a new remote controlled guidance system in Honolulu. During the flight, Miller attacks the test pilot, Edwards, and then hijacks the plane with the valuable guidance system. After the missing plane and Edwards' dead body are found, Charlie Chan (suspecting Miller) and the aviation company's owner search Miller's room at the Tropic Hotel, finding Miller dead in one of the closets, having been murdered by Cartwright.

Miller, Ivan "Dusty" Character actor who appeared in almost 30 films, often seen as a policeman. In two *Charlie Chan* roles, Miller portrays San Francisco Police Inspector Morton in *Charlie Chan's Secret* (1936) and the gangster Wade (unbilled) in *Charlie Chan at the Race Track* (1936).

Miller, Virgil (1887–October 5, 1974, Hollywood, California) Cinematographer for over 85 films, including eight *Charlie Chan* entries at Twentieth Century–Fox. In 1953 Miller was nominated for an Academy Award in the Best Cinematography (Black-and-White) category for *Navajo* (1952).

Charlie Chan filmography: *Charlie Chan at Treasure Island* (1939), *City in Darkness* (1939), *Charlie Chan in Reno* (1939), *Charlie Chan in Panama* (1940), *Charlie Chan's Murder Cruise* (1940), *Charlie Chan at the Wax Museum* (1940), *Murder Over New York* (1940), and *Castle in the Desert* (1942).

Milton, David Art director, set designer, and production designer for over 130 films. At Monogram, Milton was the art director for seven Charlie Chan films and was also the technical director for 11 films in the series.

Charlie Chan filmography—as art director: *Charlie Chan in the Secret Service* (1944), *The Chinese Cat* (1944), *Black Magic* (1944), *The Shanghai Cobra* (1945),* *Shadows Over Chinatown* (1946), *Docks of New Orleans* (1948), and *The Shanghai Chest* (1948).

Charlie Chan filmography—as technical director: *The Jade Mask* (1945), *The Scarlet Clue* (1945), *The Red Dragon* (1945), *Dark Alibi* (1946), *Shadows Over Chinatown* (1946), *Dangerous Money* (1946), *The Trap* (1947), *The Chinese Ring* (1947), *The Golden Eye* (1948), *The Feathered Serpent* (1948), and *The Sky Dragon* (1949).

Minchin, Max Gangster (portrayed by Walter Hymer) who, with his wife, are members of Dr. Lofton's world tour in *Charlie Chan Carries On* (1931).

Minchin, Sadie The wife (portrayed by Marjorie White in her first of two *Charlie Chan* roles) of Max Minchin in *Charlie Chan Carries On* (1931). Both are members of Dr. Lofton's world tour.

Miraflores locks One of three pairs of Panama Canal locks. Located between the Pedro Miguel locks and the Pacific Ocean, they raise or lower ships from one level to another depending on the tide of the Pacific Ocean. In *Charlie Chan in Panama* (1940), Charlie Chan learns that the Miraflores locks are to be blown up at ten that night while U.S. naval ships are passing through the canal.

"MISSING DIARY ROCKS UNDERWORLD" Newspaper headline of the *New York Daily Bulletin* about the escape of Johnny Burke, a suspect in the death of Billie Bronson, in *Charlie Chan on Broadway* (1937). Bronson supposedly kept a diary with details about the rackets and politicians

Mr. Moto *see* **Moto, Mr.**

**Unbilled.*

***Mr. Moto's Gamble* (1938)** A film by Twentieth Century–Fox Corporation whose working title was *Mr. Moto at the Ringside*. It is the third film (in a series of eight) in which Peter Lorre portrays Japanese detective Kentaro Moto.

The movie's original screenplay, written by Charles Belden and Jerome Cady, was intended for the 1938 film *Charlie Chan at Ringside*, which was never completed. *Ringside* went into production on January 10, 1938, but only seven days later Darryl Zanuck scrapped the picture, having finally been fed up with Warner Oland's drinking and absences from the set. While filming this movie, Oland and Twentieth Century–Fox had a disagreement and Oland left the set one day and never returned. From studio records, $93,820.59 was spent on the production up to this point.

On January 24, 1938, Twentieth Century–Fox salvaged parts of *Charlie Chan at Ringside* and continued the production, now as part of the *Mr. Moto* series. The studio reworked it into *Mr. Moto's Gamble* (1938), with all but two of the original *Ringside* cast. Warner Oland and his Charlie Chan character was replaced by Peter Lorre as Mr. Moto, and Paul Hurst was replaced by Harold Huber as Lt. Riggs. The film was released on March 25, 1938.

Records of correspondence from Sol M. Wurtzel revealed that $46,341.10 was saved by converting the original film to the *Mr. Moto* series, and he suggested that the amount of $39,979.49 be billed to Warner Oland. It

Keye Luke, Harold Huber, and Peter Lorre in *Mr. Moto's Gamble*, parts of which were salvaged from an unfinished *Charlie Chan at the Ringside* (Everett Collection).

is not known if this was actually done, as Oland, eager to see his homeland once more, sailed to Sweden where he died of bronchial pneumonia on August 6, 1938.

Producer: Sol M. Wurtzel.* Associate Producer: John Stone. Director: James Tinling. Dialogue Direction: Harvey G. Parry,* Arthur Berthelet,* and Lionel Bevans.* Assistant Director: Jasper Blystone* and Charles Faye.* Original Screenplay: Charles Belden and Jerry Cady. Photography: Lucien Andriot. Camera Operator: Edward Fitzgerald.* First Assistant Cameraman: Roger Sherman.* Second Assistant Cameraman: Edward Collins.* Gaffer: Jack McAvoy.* Art Direction: Bernard Herzbrun and Haldane Douglas. Film Editor: Nick DeMaggio. Assistant Cutter: Jack Lebowitz.* Costumes: Helen A. Myron. Wardrobe Girl: Gladys Isaacson.* Wardrobe Man: Jack Adams.* Musical Direction: Samuel Kaylin. Sound: Bernard A. Freericks and William H. Anderson. Assistant Sound: Joe Mazzoletti.* Boom Man: Harry Roberts.* Cableman: Fred Casey.* Makeup: Webster Phillips.* Production Manager: Ed Ebele.* Unit Manager: Ben Wurtzel.* Script Clerk: Stanley Scheuer.* Grip: Hank Gersen.* Assistant Grip: Jimmie Reemer.* Props: Don Greenwood.* Assistant Props: Stanley Detlie* and Aaron Wolf.* Best Boy: Kenneth McDonald.* Still Photography: John Jenkins.*

Cast

Peter Lorre	*as*	Mr. Moto
Keye Luke		Lee Chan
Dick Baldwin		Bill Steele
Lynn Bari		Penny Kendall
Douglas Fowley		Nick Crowder
Jayne Regan		Linda Benton
Harold Huber		Lt. Riggs
Maxie Rosenbloom		[Horace "Knockout"] Wellington
John Hamilton		Philip Benton
George E. Stone		[Jerry] Connors
Bernard Nedell		Clipper McCoy
Charles Williams		Gabby Marden
Ward Bond		Biff Moran
Cliff Clark		McGuire
Edward Marr		Sammy
Lon Chaney, Jr.		Joey
Pierre Watkin		District Attorney
Charles D. Brown		Editor
Paul Fix		Gangster
Dick Dickinson*		Knock-down timer
Fred Kelsey*		Mahoney
Ralph Dunn,* David Newell,* Frank McGlynn, Jr.*		Detectives
George Magrill,* Bob Ryan,* Eddie Hart,* James Blaine,* Harry Strang,* Stanley Blystone,* Lee Shumway,* Dick Rush,* Adrian Morris,* Max Wagner*		Policemen
Jack Stoney*		Kid Grant
Edwin Stanley,* Landers Stevens*		Doctors
Frank Fanning*		Turnkey
Allen Mathews*		Handler
Lester Dorr,* Allen Fox,* Franklin Parker,* Dick French		Reporters
Emmett Vogan*		Fingerprint man
Edward Earle*		Medical examiner
Gladden James*		Cashier
Sherry Hall*		Ticket taker
Matty Roubert*		Elevator boy
William E. Coe*		Timekeeper
Bob Perry,* George Blake,* Larry McGrath*		Referees
Gary Breckner*		Announcer
Dan Toby*		Fight announcer
Joe Gray,* Tommy Herman,* Pete De Grasse		Fighters
Stanley Mack,* Jack Gargan*		Ushers
Syd Saylor*		Hotel clerk
Don Brodie*		Ticket seller
Arthur Gardner*		Elevator boy
Irving Bacon*		Sheriff
Olin Howland*		Deputy sheriff
Matty Fain,* Harrison Greene,* Wilbur Mack,* Dick Elliott		Gamblers
George Chandler*		Man in fight crowd
Gloria Roy*		
Chester Clute*		Boxing detective

Plot Summary: At the end of one of Mr. Moto's classes in criminology, student Lee Chan, the eldest son of Charlie Chan, notices that his watch has been stolen. Horace "Knockout" Wellington, another student, confesses that he is the culprit and reveals that he cannot help taking things that attract his eye and later cannot remember where he took the objects.

Moto invites Lee to accompany him and Lt. Riggs to a boxing match between Bill Steele and Frankie Stanton that will decide who will fight world champion Biff Moran eight weeks later. Before the fight, gambler

**Unbilled.*

Nick Crowder bets $10,000 with bookie Clipper McCoy that Stanton will not last until the fifth round. Because he has already taken similar bets from gamblers in six other cities, Clipper warns Stanton's manager, Jerry Connors, that Stanton better not throw the fight.

Riggs, Moto, and Lee sit with Philip Benton, whose company owns the arena, and Benton's snooty daughter Linda, who is interested in Bill Steele (even though he likes sports reporter Penny Kendall). After Stanton's eye is cut, the referee threatens to stop the fight. Connors applies collodion to close the wound, and in the next round Steele knocks Stanton out. When the doctor pronounces Stanton dead, Moto recovers a dried bit of collodion. Connors throws the collodion bottle he used out a window and gives Moto another bottle to examine. Benton, who earlier told Riggs that he never bets, then calls Clipper, who has lost $130,000 on the fight, to say that he will send a check for $10,000 to cover his bet.

The poison that killed Stanton is subsequently found on Steele's gloves. He is charged with manslaughter and suspended by the boxing commission. Although Penny convinces her editor to put up the bond money, she finds Steele leaving jail with Linda Benton, who has already paid with a check from her father. Moto finds that Wellington has taken his overcoat and left one he earlier took from the arena, which has a stain on the inside that matches the stain found on Bill's glove.

Meanwhile, at Moran's training camp, Benton and press agent Gabby Marden overhear Clipper accuse Crowder of placing bets in other cities to keep the odds up at the fight. As Gabby goes to call Riggs with the information, someone takes a shot at him. Riggs and Moto find that the owner of the overcoat, John Howard, has died from the same poison that killed Stanton. Moto, believing that Howard was a fall guy, convinces the boxing commission to lift its suspension of Bill Steele and promises to have the murderer arrested at ringside the night of Steele's fight with Moran.

At the vacant arena a mysterious figure places a gun attached to a clock under the ring and aims it at the seat Mr. Moto will be occupying during the fight. Before the fight, Penny kisses Bill and wishes him well and then berates Linda for only caring for a winner. With the gun pointed at him, Moto watches his suspects as the fight proceeds. He then invites Linda to sit in his seat. After Steele knocks out Moran, Moto announces that he will shortly produce Stanton's murderer. Despite Benton's attempt to get his daughter away, Moto insists that Linda remain in the seat. Benton then rushes to the ring and disconnects the gun before it fires.

Moto explains that he searched the arena before the fight because he knew that the murderer would try to kill him to keep him from revealing his identity. Finding the gun, Moto then removed the bullets from the gun. Benton then takes the elevator to his office where Clipper shoots and kills him for arranging the bets on Stanton from the other cities. The police then capture Clipper as Lee Chan and Wellington arrive, and the murder weapon is found to be a water gun filled with poison.

Back in his classroom, Mr. Moto explains why he suspected Benton and, as he goes to leave, discovers his watch is missing. Wellington returns it, and Moto reveals that he now has Wellington's wallet, which, it turns out, Wellington stole from Lee.

Mr. Wong *see* **Wong, Mr.**

***Mr. Wong, Detective* (1938)** Film by Monogram Pictures Corporation, released on October 5, 1938. In this first in a series of six movies, Boris Karloff portrays San Francisco–based Chinese detective James Lee Wong. The movie's original screenplay, written by Houston Branch, was later reworked by Monogram and W. Scott Darling as the *Charlie Chan* film *Docks of New Orleans* (1948).

***Mr. Wong in Chinatown* (1939)** Film by Monogram Pictures Corporation starring Boris Karloff as the Chinese detective James Lee Wong, released on July 18, 1939, as the third entry in the series. The movie's original screenplay, written by W. Scott Darling, was later reworked by Monogram as the *Charlie Chan* film *The Chinese Ring* (1947).

Mitchell, Thomas Shady, estranged husband (portrayed by Marc Lawrence in his first of three *Charlie Chan* roles) of Marie Collins who searches for Billie Bronson's diary (containing details about the rackets and politicians) in *Charlie Chan on Broadway* (1937). While on the same ship as Billie returning to New York from Europe, Mitchell traps Bronson in the bathroom of her stateroom with a chair wedged under the doorknob. Before she realizes that the door won't open, Mitchell searches her room for the diary but finds nothing.

Mitchell wants the diary to embarrass nightclub owner Johnny Burke, who stole his wife Marie. Upon arriving in New York, and thinking that she still has the diary or knows where it is, he follows Bronson to the Carlton Hotel but is later stabbed to death by Speed Patten in Chan's hotel room.

Mojave Wells Hotel California hotel in the Mojave Desert in *Castle in the Desert* (1942). Paul Manderley bribes Dr. Retling and Walter Hartford to quietly take Gleason's body to the Mojave Wells Hotel in the town closest to the castle and make it look as if he died there of a heart attack.

Monogram Pictures Corporation A subsidiary of Allied Artists Corporation known for producing "B" movies. From 1944 to 1949 Monogram continued the filming of the final 17 *Charlie Chan* movies two years after its run with Twentieth Century–Fox had ended. Compared with Twentieth Century–Fox, the Monogram efforts were clearly shoestring affairs, costing about $75,000 per film (compared to the $250,000 to $275,000 spent by Twentieth Century–Fox). Smaller budgets meant fewer sets, reworked scripts, and virtually every other cost-cutting measure Monogram was famous for.

Prior to filming its *Charlie Chan* movies, Monogram introduced its own Oriental detective with *Mr. Wong, Detective* (1938), starring Boris Karloff, to compete with Twentieth Century–Fox's Japanese detective, Mr. Moto, played by Peter Lorre. As with Charlie Chan and Mr. Moto, the *Mr. Wong* series, in its first five films, continued the industry practice of casting the lead Oriental detective with an actor who was not Chinese—or even Oriental for that matter. The one lone exception was the final *Mr. Wong* entry, *Phantom of Chinatown* (1940), in which Keye Luke was mismatched in the lead role of James Lee Wong that Karloff developed in the previous five films of the series.

Charlie Chan filmography: *Charlie Chan in the Secret Service* (1944), *The Chinese Cat* (1944), *Black Magic* (1944), *The Jade Mask* (1945), *The Scarlet Clue* (1945), *The Shanghai Cobra* (1945), *The Red Dragon* (1945), *Dark Alibi* (1946), *Shadows Over Chinatown* (1946), *Dangerous Money* (1946), *The Trap* (1947), *The Chinese Ring* (1947), *Docks of New Orleans* (1948), *The Shanghai Chest* (1948), *The Golden Eye* (1948), *The Feathered Serpent* (1948), and *The Sky Dragon* (1949).

Monte Carlo The resort town in the Principality of Monaco which is approximately nine miles west of Nice, France, on the Côte d'Azur overlooking the French Riviera and the Mediterranean Sea. The city is the setting for *Charlie Chan at Monte Carlo* (1937).

Montero, Sgt. Panamanian policeman (portrayed by Chris-Pin Martin) in *Charlie Chan in Panama* (1940). He arrests Charlie Chan (as Fu Yuen) for the murder of R.J. Godley, and is an unwilling escort of Miss Finch.

Note: In the movie's credits, Montero is listed as Sgt. Montero but Miss Jennie Finch calls him Lt. Montero.

Montgomery, Goodee (1906–June 5, 1978, Hollywood, California) Actress who portrays Mrs. Benbow in *Charlie Chan Carries On* (1931).

Montparnasse Artistic quarter of Paris, France, on the left bank of the Seine River. In *Charlie Chan in Paris* (1935), Nardi writes in her diary that Dufresne lost 10,000 francs at a gambling house in Montparnasse and spends beyond his income.

Mooney Ship steward on the S.S. *Oceanic* (portrayed by John Rogers in his last of four *Charlie Chan* roles) in *Charlie Chan at the Race Track* (1936).

Moore, Mary Actress who portrays Rita (unbilled), the female confederate of H.R. Jarvis, who tends the counter of a laundry that hides a hidden entrance to the sewer system leading to the Sixth National Bank in *The Shanghai Cobra* (1945).

Moore, Pauline (June 17, 1914, Philadelphia, Pennsylvania–) Attractive actress who appeared in nearly 25 films, including three *Charlie Chan* entries. Moore portrays Betty Adams in *Charlie Chan at the Olympics* (1937), Mary Whitman in *Charlie Chan in Reno* (1939), and psychic mind reader Eve Cairo in *Charlie Chan at Treasure Island* (1939).

After a handful of bit roles, including one as an unbilled bridesmaid in *Frankenstein* (1931), Pauline Moore landed a Twentieth Century–Fox contract in 1937. Her career shifted into gear when she played alongside Loretta Young and Marjorie Weaver as Elizabeth Charters in the "looking for rich husbands" film *Three Blind Mice* (1938). She went on to choice roles like Ann Rutledge in *Young Mr. Lincoln* (1939), Lady Constance de Winter in *The Three Musketeers* (1939), and, best of all, psychic Eve Cairo in *Charlie Chan at Treasure Island* (1939). For reasons best known only to Darryl F. Zanuck, Fox summarily dropped Moore from their payroll in 1940, and she spent the next year playing cowgirls in such less-than-impressive efforts as *King of the Texas Rangers* (1941) and *Double Cross* (1941).

Pauline Moore and Alan "Rocky" Lane, who both appeared in *Charlie Chan at the Olympics*.

Moran, Buzz New York mobster (portrayed by Leon Ames) in *Charlie Chan on Broadway* (1937).

Moran, Lois (March 1, 1908, Pittsburgh, Pennsylvania–July 13, 1990, Sedona, Arizona) American stage and screen actress who appeared in over 30 silent and sound films. Moran portrays Eve Mannering in *Behind That Curtain* (1929).

Before making her Hollywood film debut as Laurel in *Stella Dallas* (1925), Lois Moran had been a dancer with the Paris National Opera and had already appeared in a few French films. Despite the potential she exhibited in *Stella Dallas*, Moran's career never took hold, and her movies were only of average quality. She left films in 1931 and began appearing on Broadway. Moran eventually left Broadway when she married a business executive and became a dance and drama instructor at Stanford University during the 1950s. She also appeared on television as May "Mom" Herrick in the *Waterfront* (1954) series.

Moreland, Mantan (September 3, 1902, Monroe, Louisiana–September 28, 1973, Hollywood, California) Chubby black actor and comedian who appeared in over 85 films, often as a frightened chauffeur. Moreland portrays Birmingham Brown in 15 of the 17 *Charlie Chan* films made at Monogram.

Appropriately nicknamed "Google Eyes" by his childhood friends, Mantan Moreland joined a carnival at the age of 14 and a

Comedian Mantan Moreland, shown here in the post–Chan movie *Rock 'n' Roll Revue* (1955), appeared in 15 *Charlie Chan* entries as Birmingham Brown (Everett Collection).

medicine show a year later—both times he was dragged home by juvenile authorities. Most of Moreland's early adult years were spent on the "Chitlin Circuit," the nickname given by performers to all-black vaudeville. After a decade of professional ups and downs, Moreland teamed with several comics, notably Ben Carter, in an act based on the "indefinite talk" routine of Flournoy and Miller wherein each teammate would start a sentence only to be interrupted by the other teammate ("Say, have you seen...?" "I saw him yesterday. He was at..." "I thought they closed that place down!").

Moreland began appearing in films in 1936, usually in the minor porter, waiter, servant, and bootblack roles then reserved for black actors. Because of his comedy, Moreland began getting better parts in a late–1930s series of comedy adventures produced at Monogram. Co-starring white actor Frankie Darro, the series' screen friendship between Moreland and Darro was rare for films of this period.

Monogram had strong movie distribution in the South and other areas having large black audiences. For this reason Monogram decided to cast Moreland as Birmingham Brown in its *Charlie Chan* series as the easily frightened Negro. (The variations Moreland wrought upon the line, "Feets, do your duty," were astonishing and hilarious when he was frightened.) In the first three Monogram Chans—*Charlie Chan in the Secret Service* (1944), *The Chinese Cat* (1944), and *Black Magic* (1944)—Moreland did not portray Charlie Chan's chauffeur, the role he is most remembered for.

Even though the Birmingham Brown role was never completely free of stereotype, Monogram did recognize Moreland's value to the series by the end of the Chan films in 1949 by having Charlie Chan refer to the Birmingham Brown character as either "Number Two assistant" or "my assistant, Birmingham Brown"—not merely "my hired man." Always popular with black audiences, Moreland was frequently given top billing in the advertising of the Chan films by Harlem theater owners, and he also starred in a series of crude but undeniably entertaining comedies filmed by Toddy Studios for all-black theaters.

Changing racial attitudes in the 1950s and 1960s lessened Moreland's ability to work in films, and in the wake of the civil rights movement a frightened black man was no longer considered amusing, even by Moreland's fans. Virtually broke, Moreland suffered a severe stroke in the early 1960s and it looked as though his career was ended. However, things improved for Moreland with a bit part as a messenger in the horror picture *Spider Baby* (1964) and a pair of prominent cameos in *Enter Laughing* (1968) and *The Comic* (1969), both directed by Carl Reiner.

With more and more blacks being hired for television and films in the late 1960s, Moreland was again in demand. He worked on such television sitcoms as *Love, American Style* and *The Bill Cosby Show*, and even revived his "indefinite talk" routine for a gasoline commercial. He also enjoyed a solid film role as a race-conscious counterman in *Watermelon Man* (1970). In his last years, Mantan Moreland was an honored guest at the meetings of the international Laurel and Hardy fan club "The Sons of the Desert," thanks to his brief but amusing appearance in the team's comedy *A-Haunting We Will Go* (1942).

Charlie Chan filmography: *Charlie Chan in the Secret Service* (1944), *The Chinese Cat* (1944), *Black Magic* (1944), *The Jade Mask* (1945), *The Scarlet Clue* (1945), *The Shanghai Cobra* (1945), *Dark Alibi* (1946), *Shadows Over Chinatown* (1946), *The Trap* (1947), *The Chinese Ring* (1947), *Docks of New Orleans* (1948), *The Shanghai Chest* (1948), *The Golden Eye* (1948), *The Feathered Serpent* (1948), *The Sky Dragon* (1949).

Morgan Gangster (portrayed by Gene Roth [credited as Gene Stutenroth] in his second of two *Charlie Chan* roles) in *The Shanghai Cobra* (1945). Morgan is involved with Bradford Harris, H.R. Jarvis, and Taylor in a plan to steal radium belonging to the U.S. government from the vault at the Sixth National Bank.

Morgan, Anthony R. City public defender (portrayed by John Eldredge in his second of three *Charlie Chan* roles) in *Dark Alibi* (1946). Morgan is an old friend of Charlie Chan who defends Thomas Harley at his trial. Having been framed, Harley is convicted of bank robbery and murder. After Harley is shown to be innocent, Harley's daughter June and Morgan tell Chan that they plan to be married.

Morgan, Ira H. (1889–April 10, 1959, San Rafael, California) Cinematographer for 100 silent and sound films, including *Charlie Chan in the Secret Service* (1944) and *The Chinese Cat* (1944).

Morgan, Ralph (July 6, 1882, New York, New York–June 11, 1956, New York, New York) American stage and screen character actor (real name: Raphael Kuhner Wuppermann) who appeared in nearly 100 films, often as a smooth villain. Morgan portrays Barry Kirk in *Charlie Chan's Chance* (1932).

Ralph Morgan graduated from Columbia University with a law degree but opted for the vocation of journeyman actor. So successful was Morgan in stock and Broadway that his younger brother Frank was encouraged to give the theater a try, and became even more famous than Ralph. Ralph made his film bow in 1931, playing leading roles such as Charlie Marsden in *Strange Interlude* (1932) and Czar Nicholas II in *Rasputin and the Empress* (1932) before settling into secondary character parts.

It was Morgan's distinction to play "surprise" killers in more murder mysteries than virtually any other actor in Hollywood. Among Morgan's off-camera interests were politics and labor relations. He was one of the founders and charter members of the Screen Actors Guild. Ralph Morgan was the father of Claudia Morgan, an actress best known for her portrayal of Nora Charles on the *Thin Man* radio series. At the Academy Awards in 1940, Morgan was given an honorary award by The Academy of Motion Picture Arts and Sciences acknowledging the outstanding services to the industry during the past year of the Motion Picture Relief Fund and its progressive leadership.

Mori, Tashia (January 1, 1913, Kyoto, Japan–) Actress who portrays Chinese girl Ling Tse, who sells cigarettes, film, and flash bulbs, in *Charlie Chan on Broadway* (1937).

Morosco, Walter (1899, San Francisco, California–December 30, 1948, Coronado, California) Associate producer for *Charlie Chan at the Wax Museum* (1940) and producer for *Dead Men Tell* (1941).

Morse, Terry O. Director, editor, and producer of almost 60 films, sometimes credited as Terrell Morse or Terrill Morse. He was the film editor for *Shadows Over Chinatown* (1946) and *Dangerous Money* (1946).

Morton, Inspector San Francisco policeman (portrayed by Ivan Miller in his first of two *Charlie Chan* roles) in *Charlie Chan's Secret* (1936). Morton is in charge of investigating the murder of Allen Colby.

Moskov, George Assistant director (unbilled) and production manager for *Charlie Chan in the Secret Service* (1944).

Moto, Mr. Mild-mannered Japanese detective who was the basis for a series of eight movies (1937–39) produced by Twentieth Century–Fox (from the stories of novelist John P. Marquand). Peter Lorre portrays Kentaro Moto, who was quite unlike Charlie Chan in that he was a master of disguises and physically more active, often using jujitsu.

Many of the actors and crew members who were associated with the *Charlie Chan*

Peter Lorre, *Mr. Moto* novelist John P. Marquand, and director Norman Foster. *Inset:* Peter Lorre as the mysterious Mr. Moto.

series at Twentieth Century–Fox were also involved with the *Mr. Moto* films. Most notable of the actors and actresses were Thomas Beck, Harold Huber, Erik Rhodes, Virginia Field, Murray Kinnell, and Lionel Atwill.

Even Keye Luke, who had already appeared as Number One son Lee Chan in eight films with Warner Oland, reprised his role as Lee Chan in *Mr. Moto's Gamble* (1938), much of which was salvaged from *Charlie Chan at the Ringside*, a 1938 movie project that was never completed.

Mr. Moto filmography: *Think Fast, Mr. Moto* (1937), *Thank You, Mr. Moto* (1937), *Mysterious Mr. Moto* (1938), *Mr. Moto Takes a Chance* (1938), *Mr. Moto's Gamble* (1938), *Mr. Moto's Last Warning* (1939), *Mr. Moto Takes a Vacation* (1939), and *Mr. Moto in Danger Island* (1939).

Moustafa, Amira Actress who portrays Laura Erickson in *Dangerous Money* (1946).

movie remakes Hollywood movie studios were well-known for squeezing virtually every drop of value from a literary property. Remakes generally underwent a change in title but kept the basic story plot. Variations were often achieved by changing the locale, character names, and even the sexes of the characters. Films from the *Charlie Chan* series were no exception. *See* table, below.

Mowbray, Alan (August 18, 1896, London, England–March 25, 1969, Hollywood, California) Arrogant-mannered British stage and screen character actor who appeared in nearly 150 films, often as a butler or pompous emissary. Mowbray portrays murderer Geoffrey Richmond in *Charlie Chan in London* (1934).

Born to a non-theatrical British family, Alan Mowbray climbed relatively quickly to Broadway and London stardom, spending several seasons on the road with the Theatre Guild. His favorite stage parts were those conceived by Bernard Shaw and Noel Coward. Turning to films in the early talkie era, Mowbray received good notices for his portrayal of George Washington in *Alexander Hamilton* (1931).

Mowbray has the distinction of appearing with three of the screen's Sherlock Holmes—Clive Brook (*Sherlock Holmes* [1932]), Reginald Owen (*A Study in Scarlet* [1933], in which Mowbray played Lestrade), and Basil Rathbone (*Terror by Night* [1946]). Mowbray appeared as alcoholic ham actors in John Ford's *My Darling Clementine* (1946) and *Wagonmaster* (1950). He was also a founding member of the Screen Actors Guild.

Mudge, Madge Member of Cole King's variety troupe (portrayed by Margaret Brayton) in *The Trap* (1947).

Mudie, Leonard (April 11, 1883, England–April 14, 1965, Hollywood, California) British stage and screen character actor (real name: Leonard Mudie Cheetham) who appeared in over 80 films. Mudie portrays actor

Movie Remakes

Original Film	Remake
The House Without a Key (1925)	*Charlie Chan's Greatest Case* (1933)
The Chinese Parrot (1927)	*Charlie Chan's Courage* (1934)
Behind That Curtain (1929)	*Charlie Chan's Chance* (1932)
Charlie Chan Carries On (1931)	*Eran Trece* (1931, Spanish language)
	Charlie Chan's Murder Cruise (1940)
The Black Camel (1931)	*Charlie Chan in Rio* (1940)
Charlie Chan at the Ringside (1938, never completed)	*Mr. Moto's Gamble* (1938)
The Riders of the Whistling Skull (1937)	*The Feathered Serpent* (1948)
Mr. Wong, Detective (1938)	*Docks of New Orleans* (1948)
Mr. Wong in Chinatown (1939)	*The Chinese Ring* (1947)

Horace Carlos (unbilled) in *The Scarlet Clue* (1945).

The gaunt, rich-voiced Leonard Mudie made his stage bow in 1908 with the Gaiety Theater in Manchester, England, and first appeared on the New York stage in 1914. In movies, Mudie's notable roles included Dr. Pearson in *The Mummy* (1932), Porthinos in *Cleopatra* (1934), Maitland in *Mary of Scotland* (1936), and De Bourenne in *Anthony Adverse* (1936). Mudie was a semi-regular as Commissioner Andy Barnes in seven *Bomba* pictures from 1951 to 1955.

Muir, Gavin (September 8, 1909, Chicago, Illinois–May 24, 1972, Ft. Lauderdale, Florida) Stage and screen character actor (real name: Gaven Muir), educated in England, who appeared in 40 films and customarily affected a British-style accent in his portrayals of effete, shifty types. Muir portrays the horse trainer, Bagley, in *Charlie Chan at the Race Track* (1936).

Mulhall, Jack (October 7, 1887, Wappingers Falls, New York–June 1, 1979, Woodland Hills, California) Character actor who appeared in more than 200 silent and sound films. Mulhall portrays a ship's purser (unbilled) aboard the S.S. *Oceanic* in *Charlie Chan at the Race Track* (1936).

multiple appearances The character Charlie Chan is the only character that appears in every movie in the series. However, many faces showed up from time to time, often in different roles. Most were usually contract actors and actresses who often went unbilled. Only six actors—John Eldredge, Sam Flint, Douglas Fowley, Russell Hicks, C. Montague Shaw, and Emmett Vogan—have the distinction of having appeared with three different Chan actors. Apart from those who had recurring roles in the series, Gloria Roy had the most appearances (seven), followed by Emmett Vogan (six).

The following is a listing of those actors and actresses who have been identified as having appeared in three or more *Charlie Chan* films (using the on-screen credits from the films themselves and information from both the *American Film Institute Catalog of Motion Pictures Produced in the United States* and the Call Bureau Cast Service lists for unbilled roles). There are over 80 actors and actresses who appeared in only two films in the series.

22 appearances: Sidney Toler; ***18 appearances:*** Victor Sen Young; ***16 appearances:*** Warner Oland; ***15 appearances:*** Mantan Moreland; ***10 appearances:*** Keye Luke; ***7 appearances:*** Benson Fong, Gloria Roy; ***6 appearances:*** Emmett Vogan, Roland Winters; ***5 appearances:*** C. Henry Gordon, Charles Jordan, Tim Ryan; ***4 appearances:*** Thomas Beck, Stanley Blystone, Eugene Borden, George Chandler, George Eldredge, James Flavin, Francis Ford, Harold Huber, Selmer A. Jackson, Al Kikume, Murray Kinnell, Kay Linaker, Milton Parsons, John Rogers; ***3 appearances:*** Lois Austin, Willie Best, George Davis, Leslie Dennison, Harry Depp, Douglass Dumbrille, Ralph Dunn, John Eldredge, Sam Flint, Lee Tung Foo, Douglas Fowley, Jonathan Hale, Jr., Russell Hicks, Robert E. Homans, Claude King, Marc Lawrence, George J. Lewis, Drue Leyton, Robert Lowery, Hamilton MacFadden, Jack Norton, Lee Phelps, Kane Richmond, William Ruhl, C. Montague Shaw, Edwin Stanley, Harry Strang, Layne Tom, Jr., Frederick Vogeding, Max Wagner.

mummy An embalmed body dating from ancient Egyptian times. The word is derived through Arabic from the Persian *mumiai*, meaning "pitch" or "asphalt." This was presumably because Egyptian mummies of the late period were often coated with a layer of black resin resembling pitch. The ancient Egyptians placed great emphasis on the preservation of the human body after death because they believed that the spirit of the deceased returned to it when visiting the tomb.

In *Charlie Chan in Egypt* (1935), the tomb and the mummy of Ahmeti, an Egyptian High Priest of the 21st Dynasty, are discovered by Professors Arnold and John Thurston. After Thurston discovers the secret location of the treasure inside the tomb, he kills Professor Arnold, places Ahmeti's necklace around Arnold's neck, wraps the body like a mummy, and seals the body in Ahmeti's mummy case.

Mundin, Herbert (August 21, 1898, Lancashire, England–March 4, 1939, Van Nuys, California) British stage and screen character actor who portrays Henrietta Lowell's cowardly butler, Baxter, in *Charlie Chan's Secret* (1936).

Born into a Lancashire farming family, Herbert Mundin served in the first World War as a wireless operator. After the war's end, Mundin joined a traveling troupe of British music hall performers. Though only in his early twenties, Mundin was always cast in older character parts on stage due to his bulbous nose and short, penguin-like frame. On Broadway from 1928, Mundin signed a contract with Fox studios in 1931 and then appeared as Albert Miggles in *Chandu the Magician* (1932) and as Alfred Bridges in *Cavalcade* (1933).

Mundin's popularity at this period was such that, when it was decided that the Fox production *Sherlock Holmes* (1932) needed some comedy relief, Mundin was hastily fitted in as a cockney pubkeeper, being billed ahead of that film's Doctor Watson. Two of Mundin's better roles were in a classical vein. He was Barkis in *David Copperfield* (1934) and Much the Miller's Son in *Adventures of Robin Hood* (1938). Shortly after completing his role as Layton the Butler in *Society Lawyer*, Herbert Mundin was killed in a car accident in Van Nuys, California.

Munich Conference The Munich Conference was held September 29–30, 1938, and was attended by Neville Chamberlain (England), Edouard Daladier (France), Adolf Hitler (Germany), and Benito Mussolini (Italy). There, Britain and France acceded to Hitler's demand for immediate German occupation of the predominantly German-speaking Sudetenland region in western Czechoslovakia.

The conference created an international commission to demarcate the area and provided for plebiscites in some parts of the Sudetenland to give residents a choice of Czech or German nationality. The plebiscites were never held, however. Chamberlain prematurely stated that the agreement had secured "peace in our time," but Winston Churchill insisted that the surrender to the Nazi government was a "total and unmitigated defeat." The Munich Conference became the primary symbol of the West's appeasement of Germany in the years before the outbreak of World War II.

City of Darkness (1939), which was made a year after the actual Munich Conference, finds Charlie Chan on vacation in Paris on the eve of the Munich Conference, and the city is blacked out because of expected German air raids.

Murder by Alphabet Working title for *The Shanghai Chest* (1948) before its release on July 11, 1948. *See also* ***The Shanghai Chest* (1948)**.

Murder by Madame Novel written by noted criminologist Dr. Rednick in *The Chinese Cat* (1944). The book is an account of Thomas Manning's murder and accuses Leah Manning's mother, Mrs. Manning, of the crime. The book also implies that the police inspector on the case, Detective Lt. Harvey Dennis, fell in love with Leah and concealed evidence. Charlie Chan tells Dr. Rednick that the book explains everything so easily—except what happened to the murder gun. Rednick replies that if his book is wrong, then the murder can't be solved.

Murder Chamber One of two working titles for *Black Magic* (1944) before its release on September 9, 1944. *See also* ***Black Magic* (1944)**.

murderers (*See* table, opposite) There cannot be a *Charlie Chan* mystery without a murder. In some of the films there is more than one murderer, and a single murderer sometimes kills more than one person. The methods the murderers use for killing their victims ranged from the mundane to the ingenious. Their victims were either poisoned, shot, stabbed, strangled, garroted, slugged,

Murderers

Movie	Murderer	Victim(s)
The Chinese Parrot	"Shaky" Phil Maydorf	Louie Wong
Behind That Curtain	Eric Durand	Hilary Galt, Alf Pornick
Charlie Chan Carries On	Jim Everhard/John Ross	Hugo Morris Drake, Walter Honeywood, Sybil Conway
The Black Camel	Anna	Shelah Fane
	Jessop	Smith
Charlie Chan's Chance	James Dunwood/Alan Raleigh	Sir Lionel Grey
Charlie Chan's Greatest Case	Harry Jennison	Amos Winterslip, Dan Winterslip
Charlie Chan's Courage	unknown	Louie Wong
Charlie Chan in London	Geoffrey Richmond	Capt. Hamilton, Lake
Charlie Chan in Paris	Henri Latouche/Marcel Xavier	Nardi
	Max Corday/Marcel Xavier	Albert Dufresne
Charlie Chan in Egypt	Professor John Thurston	Professor Arnold, Barry Arnold
Charlie Chan in Shanghai	James Andrews (impostor)	James Andrews (real)
Charlie Chan's Secret	Fred Gage	Allen Colby
Charlie Chan at the Circus	Tom Holt	Joe Kinney
Charlie Chan at the Race Track	George Chester	Major Gordon Kent
	Lefty	"Tip" Collins
Charlie Chan at the Opera	Anita Barelli	Lilli Rochelle, Enrico Barelli
Charlie Chan at the Olympics	Miller	Edwards
	Cartwright	Miller
Charlie Chan on Broadway	Speed Patten	Billie Bronson, Thomas Mitchell
Charlie Chan at Monte Carlo	Gordon Chase	Renault, Ludwig, taxi driver
Charlie Chan in Honolulu	Capt. Johnson	Elsie Hillman/Carol Wayne
Charlie Chan in Reno	Jeanne Bently	Wayne Russell
	Vivian Wells	Jeanne Bently
Charlie Chan at Treasure Island	Fred Rhadini	Abdul the Turk
City in Darkness	Antoine	Petroff
	Charlotte Ronnell	Belescu
Charlie Chan in Panama	Emil Manolo	R.J. Godley, Cliveden Compton
	Jennie Finch (alias of Reiner)	Manolo
Charlie Chan's Murder Cruise	Professor Gordon	Inspector Duff, Mr. Kenyon, Gerald Pendleton, Frederick Ross
Charlie Chan at the Wax Museum	"Butcher" Degan/Tom Agnew	Joe Rocke, Dr. Otto von Brom, Steve McBirney
Murder Over New York	Keith Jeffrey/Paul Narvo	Hugh Drake, Ramullah, George Kirby
Dead Men Tell	Jed Thomasson	Miss Nodbury, Bill Lydig
Charlie Chan in Rio	Lola Dean	Manuel Cardoza
	Helen Ashby	Lola Dean
Castle in the Desert	Cesare Borgia/Watson King	Walter Hartford
Charlie Chan in the Secret Service	Philipe von Vegon/Luiz Vega	George Melton
	Mrs. Winters	Philipe von Vegon/Luiz Vega
The Chinese Cat	Webster Deacon	Tom Manning, Kurt Karzoff
	Catlin	Webster Deacon
Black Magic	Paul Hamlin/Chardo the Great	William Bonner, Justine Bonner
The Jade Mask	Lloyd Archer	Officer Kimball, Mr. Harper, Walter Meeker, Roth, Michael Strong
The Scarlet Clue	Mrs. Marsh	Gloria Bayne, Ralph Brett, Willie Rand
	Ralph Brett	Rausch
The Shanghai Cobra	Bradford Harris/Hume	Samuel Black, Larkin

[table continued]

Movie	Murderer	Victim(s)
The Red Dragon	Joseph Brandish	Walter Dorn, Countess Irena, Alfred Wyans
Dark Alibi	Mr. Danvers	Mr. Johnson
Shadows Over Chinatown	Jeff Hay	Grace Gortner, Kate Johnson, Mike Roberts
Dangerous Money	Joseph Murdock/Mrs. Whipple	Scott Pearson, P.T. Burke, Freddie Kirk
The Trap	Mrs. Thorn	Lois, Marcia
The Chinese Ring	Mr. Anderson	Princess Mei Ling, Lilly Mae Wong, little Chinese boy
Docks of New Orleans	Oscar and Mrs. Swendstrom	Simon Lafontaine, Henri Castanaro, Theodore Von Scherbe
The Shanghai Chest	Ed Seward	Judge Armstrong, Frank Bronson, Thomas Cartwright
The Golden Eye	Talbot Bartlett	Driscoll
The Feathered Serpent	Sonia Cabot	Professor Scott
	John Stanley	Sonia Cabot
	Manuel	Felipe
The Sky Dragon	John Anderson	Ben Edwards, Ed Davidson, Don Blake, Connie Jackson, Andrew Barrett

frightened to cause a fatal heart attack, suffocated, electrocuted, gassed, or hanged.

Of all the murderers throughout the series, both Lloyd Archer (*The Jade Mask*) and John Anderson (*The Sky Dragon*) share the dubious honor of being the most prolific, each killing five. Professor Gordon (*Charlie Chan's Murder Cruise*) murders four, while there were 12 murderers who each kill three persons.

Often Charlie Chan would reveal the murderer's identity by uttering the classic line, "You are murderer!" In some cases, the murderer uses an alias to hide his or her real identity.

Murder in Malibu Beach Working title for *The Trap* (1947) before its release on November 30, 1946. *See also* ***The Trap* (1946).**

Murder in the Air Working title for *The Sky Dragon* (1949) before its release on May 1, 1949. *See also* ***The Sky Dragon* (1949)**

Murder in the Fun House Working title for *The Chinese Cat* (1944) before its release on May 20, 1944. *See also* ***The Chinese Cat* (1944).**

***Murder Over New York* (1940)** The fifteenth *Charlie Chan* film produced by Twentieth Century–Fox Film Corporation.

Working Title: *Charlie Chan in New York*. Source: based on the character "Charlie Chan" created by Earl Derr Biggers. Original Copyright: Twentieth Century–Fox Film Corporation, December 13, 1940; LP10207. Copyright Renewed: August 22, 1968; R441041. PCA Certificate Number: 6517. Production: began mid–July, 1940. Release Date: December 13, 1940. Sound: RCA Sound System. Film: b&w. Running Time: 65 minutes.

Executive Producer: Sol M. Wurtzel. Director: Harry Lachman. Assistant Director: William Eckhardt.* Original Screenplay: Lester Ziffren. Director of Photography: Virgil Miller. Art Direction: Richard Day and Lewis Creber. Film Editor: Louis Loeffler. Set Decorations: Thomas Little. Costumes: Herschel. Musical Direction: Emil Newman. Sound: Joseph E. Aiken and Harry M. Leonard.

**Unbilled.*

Cast

	as
Sidney Toler	Charlie Chan
Marjorie Weaver	Patricia West†
Robert Lowery	David Elliot
Ricardo Cortez	George Kirby
Donald MacBride	Inspector Vance
Melville Cooper	Herbert Fenton
Joan Valerie	June Preston
Kane Richmond	Ralph Percy
Sen Yung	Jimmy Chan
John Sutton	Keith Jeffrey‡ [alias for Paul Narvo]
Leyland Hodgson	[Robert] Boggs
Clarence Muse	Butler
Frederick Worlock	Hugh Drake
Lal Chand Mehra	Ramullah
Dorothy Dearing*	Mrs. Percy
Catherine Craig*	Stewardess
Lee Phelps*	First policeman
Stanley Blystone*	Fingerprint expert
Ralph Dunn*	Second policeman
Shirley Warde*	Mrs. Felton
George Walcott*	First mechanic
Paul Kruger*	Guard
Alan Davis*	Lt. Cooper, pilot
Carl Faulkner,* Jimmie Dundee,* Eddie Chandler,* Frank Fanning*	Policemen
Shemp Howard*	"Shorty" McCoy, a.k.a. The Canarsie Kid
Trevor Bardette*	Hindu businessman
Frank Coghlan, Jr.*	Gilroy
Bud Geary*	Second mechanic

Plot Summary: While on a plane en route to a police convention in New York, Charlie Chan meets his old friend, Hugh Drake, a former inspector with Scotland Yard who is now a British intelligence officer. Drake tells Chan that he is on the trail of Paul Narvo, a spy who has been sabotaging U.S.-built bombers bound for England. At the airport in New York, Drake is met by his host, aircraft tycoon George Kirby, who invites Chan to a party he is giving for Drake that evening.

Later that evening, Chan and son Jimmy arrive at Kirby's party only to find Drake murdered by a poison gas pellet. Aided by Inspector Vance, Chan interrogates the guests—Herbert Fenton, Drake's old school friend; actress June Preston; stockbroker Keith Jeffrey; Ralph Percy, an aircraft designer; and Kirby's butler, Boggs. Learning little from the guests, Chan then tracks down Narvo's ex-wife, Patricia West, who explains that she fled from her husband and his sinister servant, Ramullah, in London upon learning that he was a spy.

Chan also questions David Elliot, a chemist who visited Drake on the night of his death. After Chan's search for Ramullah ends in the servant's death, and Kirby is found poisoned, Chan assembles all the suspects on a test flight of the TR-4 bomber that is to be sabotaged by poison gas pellets. As the bomber descends to the level that will cause the pellets to fall to the floor and break, Fenton grabs the hidden pellets, revealing himself to be involved in the plot. When the plane lands safely, Chan announces that Fenton is too old to be Narvo and then cleverly tricks the real Paul Narvo, Keith Jeffrey, into exposing himself as the spy.

Notes: The credits for *Murder Over New York* list Marjorie Weaver as portraying Patricia Shaw, but nowhere in the film is she mentioned as such (and the mailbox of her rooming house lists her as Patricia West). When Charlie Chan and Inspector Vance search through Hugh Drake's briefcase, they see a Scotland Yard Criminal Identification Bureau report that gives Mrs. Paul Narvo's maiden name as Miriam Shaw, with aliases of Lucy Millard, Dorothy Cochran, and Patricia West.

Although many sources, including the *American Film Institute Catalog of Motion Pictures Produced in the United States*, cite that *Charlie Chan's Chance* (1932) is in part based on (or is a remake of) *Behind That Curtain* (1929), the plot for *Murder Over New York* more closely follows that of *Charlie Chan's Chance*.

Murdock Managing editor of the *New York Daily Bulletin* (portrayed by J. Edward Bromberg) in *Charlie Chan on Broadway* (1937). Billie Bronson telephones Murdock and asks him if he remembers the deal they spoke of before she skipped town last year. She tells him, "Well, we may be able to do business now, but it's going to cost you twice what

**Unbilled. †Billed as Patricia Shaw. ‡Billed as Richard Jeffrey.*

you offered last time." Murdock is prepared to pay $10,000 for the diary but wants to read it first. Before he can meet her in her hotel room at 11:30 P.M. that evening, Bronson is murdered by Patten, who takes the diary.

Murdock, Joseph Theodore Lane's handyman and valet (portrayed by Alan Douglas) who murders Scott Pearson, P.T. Burke, and Freddie Kirk in *Dangerous Money* (1946). Murdock dresses as a woman, posing as the wife of Rev. Whipple, who is really Lane. Together they lead a gang planning to sell artworks stolen from Philippine banks during the Japanese invasion.

Murphy Arms Company Sponsor of *The Crime League* radio broadcast in *Charlie Chan at the Wax Museum* (1940).

Murray, John T. (August 28, 1886, Australia–February 12, 1957, Woodland Hills, California) Character actor who appeared in nearly 50 silent and sound films and portrays Dr. Lofton in *Charlie Chan Carries On* (1931).

Muse, Clarence (October 7, 1889, Baltimore, Maryland–October 13, 1979, Perris, California) Black stage and screen character actor who appeared in nearly 110 films and portrays one of George Kirby's two butlers in *Murder Over New York* (1940).

Even though he held a law degree from Pennsylvania State University's Dickinson School of Law, Clarence Muse opted for a show business career. He appeared as an opera singer, minstrel show performer, vaudeville and Broadway actor, and also composed songs and wrote plays and sketches. His Hollywood film assignments generally confined him to stereotypes as butlers, doormen, and porters, though Muse was usually able to rise above the shuffling, "yassuh, boss" characterizations required of virtually all black actors of the time. Muse also wrote the songs and co-wrote the story for the Bobby Breen musical *Way Down South* (1938).

In 1955 Muse was a regular on the weekly television version of *Casablanca*, playing Sam the pianist, a role he had very nearly gotten in the 1942 film version with Humphrey Bogart. Though he was an outspoken advocate for better and more equitable treatment of black performers, Muse was a staunch supporter of the *Amos 'n' Andy* television series, pointing out that, despite the leading characters being what today would be considered by many as racist stereotypes, the series did allow black actors to play doctors, bankers, judges, professors, and other parts generally denied them in "white" shows. In 1973 Clarence Muse was inducted into the Black Filmmakers Hall of Fame and remained active in films until the year of his death, when he was featured as Snoe in *The Black Stallion* (1979).

"My boy, if silence is golden, you are bankrupt" Phrase spoken by Charlie Chan to the talkative Number Four son Eddie in *The Jade Mask* (1945).

"My Heart Is Yours" Song (composer unknown) sung by Countess Irena at Mexico City's Capitol Night Club during her performance in *The Red Dragon* (1945).

Myron, Helen A. Costume designer of gowns for five *Charlie Chan* films at Twentieth Century–Fox. Myron also was the costume designer for *Mr. Moto's Gamble* (1938), a reworked version of the never-completed *Charlie Chan at the Ringside*.

Charlie Chan filmography: *Charlie Chan in Egypt* (1935), *Charlie Chan's Secret* (1936), *Charlie Chan in Honolulu* (1938), *Charlie Chan in Panama* (1940), *Charlie Chan's Murder Cruise* (1940).

Mystery Mansion Working title for *The Jade Mask* (1945) before its release on January 26, 1945. *See also* ***The Jade Mask* (1945).**

The Mystery of the Golden Eye Working title for *The Golden Eye* (1948) before its release on August 29, 1948. *See also* ***The Golden Eye* (1948).**

"MYSTERY PLANE VANISHED" Newspaper headline of the *Honolulu Citizen* about the missing remote controlled test plane in *Charlie Chan at the Olympics* (1937).

N

9B2 X54 License plate number of Diane Hall's car which she reports stolen in *The Scarlet Clue* (1945). The car is stolen from the radio station parking lot for a few hours by Ralph Brett and is used as a getaway car after Brett murders a foreign agent named Rausch. After reporting the car stolen to the police and then eating dinner, Diane Hall sees that her car has been mysteriously returned to the parking lot.

95th element In *The Red Dragon* (1945), the "95th element" is not mentioned by its chemical name by Charlie Chan when speaking to Inspector Carvero. Chan states that during the invention of the atomic bomb, two new elements, plutonium and neptunium, were found. Alfred Wyans' stolen research papers were said to contain an unknown 95th element. According to the periodic table, this represents the element americium.

Chan later reveals that it was Marguerite Fontan's uncle, Joseph Fontan, who discovered the 95th element and formula for the atomic bomb in Czechoslovakia and died preventing the Nazis from using his discovery. However, the actual discovery of the 95th element (americium) was made by a team of American scientists led by Glenn T. Seaborg. *See also* **americium**; **Seaborg, Glenn T.**

1935 and 1936 Pages removed from Mrs. Bently's publicity scrapbook, covering the years 1935 and 1936, in *Charlie Chan in Reno* (1939). From information Chief King receives from New York newspaper files, Jeanne Bently in 1935 was married to Wayne Russell, Mrs. Russell's ex-husband. In 1936 Wayne Russell died suddenly, and the attending physician was Dr. Ainsley. Charlie Chan later learns that Dr. Ainsley falsified the death certificate to indicate that Russell died from a heart attack, when he was really murdered by his wife.

1936 Olympic Games The eleventh modern Olympic Games, held in Berlin, Germany, during the early reign of Adolf Hitler. The games were held from August 1 to August 16, 1936, and were part of Hitler's propaganda plan to showcase the supremacy of the Aryan race in all aspects, including sports. The 1936 games would long be remembered as the one in which American Jesse Owens, a black man, would win four gold medals, toppling Hitler's claim of Aryan sport superiority.

The 1936 Olympic Games in Berlin is the location setting for *Charlie Chan at the Olympics* (1937), which, of all things, has Number One son Lee as a member of the U.S. team as a swimmer in the 100-meter freestyle event. In particular, the film shows participation in three events—the men's 400-meter relay, pole vault, and men's 100-meter freestyle swimming. Of these, only the 4 × 100–meter relay was consistent with the true facts.

Men's 4 × 100–Meter Relay. For the men's 4 × 100–meter relay (referred to as the 400-meter relay in 1936), the movie shows historical footage of the race. For the Americans, the race had Jesse Owens running the leadoff leg, followed by Ralph Metcalfe, Foy Draper, and Frank Wykoff. The Americans won the race in a world record time of 39.8 seconds that would last for 20 years.

The 4 × 100–meter relay was the focus of one of the 1936 games' uglier incidents and caused great embarrassment to the United States. Prior to the games, it had been assumed that the relay team would be composed of Sam Stoller, Marty Glickman, Frank Wykoff, and Foy Draper. On August 5, three days before the qualifying heats, Jesse Owens won his third gold medal in the 200-meter dash. When asked if Owens would be added to the 4 × 100–meter relay team, coach Lawrence Robertson answered: "Owens has had enough glory and collected enough gold medals and oak trees to last him a while. We want to give the other boys a chance to enjoy the *cérémonie protocolaire*. Marty Glickman, Sam Stoller, and Frank Wykoff are assured places on the relay team. The fourth choice rests between Foy Draper and Ralph Metcalfe."

Two days later, however, Robertson announced that Owens would probably replace Glickman. Then on the morning of the qualifying heats, the U.S. team coaches informed both Glickman and Stoller they were being dropped from the team and replaced by Owens and Metcalfe. The ugly embarrassment was that both Glickman and Stoller were the only Jews on the U.S. track team. They returned home as the only members of the team who didn't compete. Despite his earlier statements, Robertson's excuse was that he was concerned about the speed of the Dutch and German teams and naturally wanted to field the fastest four runners.

With Owens running the leadoff leg, followed by Metcalfe, Draper, and Wykoff, the Americans easily won the race in world record time by 15 yards, followed in order by Italy, Germany, Argentina, and Canada (Holland was disqualified). Running the anchor leg, Frank Wykoff won his third straight relay gold medal (1928, 1932, 1936), setting a world record each time.

Pole vault. A scene shows Richard Maters pole vaulting 14'2", and Betty Adams tells another team member that "Dick can do better than that." The official results reveal that the gold medal winner was Earle Meadows (USA) with an Olympic record vault of 14'-3¼"; Shuheu Nishida of Japan was second with 13'11¼"; and Sueo Oe of Japan was third with 13'11¼". As each country was limited to three entries in each event, the other two Americans in the pole vault were William Sefton (fourth place at 13'11¼") and William Graber (fifth place at 13'7¼").

After it had been determined that Meadows had won and Sefton had placed fourth, the two Japanese athletes, Nishida and Oe, refused to vault off for the silver and bronze medals. Instead, they drew lots to decide the final order, with Nishida drawing second and Oe third. When the two arrived home in Japan, they took their medals to a jeweler and had them cut lengthwise in half and fused back together so that both men had a medal that was half silver and half bronze.

Men's 100-Meter Freestyle. In the movie's final scene, Lee Chan is shown swimming in the 100-meter freestyle (Lane 3) and winning. The official Olympic results give the following order of finish of the actual event:

1. Ferenc Csík (Hungary)	57.6 seconds
2. Masanori Yusa (Japan)	57.9 seconds
3. Shigeo Arai (Japan)	58.0 seconds
4. Masaharu Taguchi (Japan)	58.1 seconds
5. Helmut Fischer (Germany)	59.3 seconds
6. Peter Fick (USA)	59.7 seconds
7. Arthur Lindegren (USA)	59.9 seconds

It appeared that after the first round the race would be between Peter Fick (then the world record holder at 56.4 seconds) and the three Japanese swimmers. In the final, while the Americans and the Japanese raced against each other, Ferenc Csík, a 23-year-old Hungarian medical student, sneaked up on the outside lane and won the gold medal. Dr. Csík later died during an air raid in 1945 while administering first aid to a wounded man.

9325 Calendar year Lee Chan gives as the current Chinese year to justify his lucky number hunch of 25 (red) as his bet on the casino's roulette wheel in *Charlie Chan at Monte Carlo* (1937). Actually, for the year 1937 the Chinese year according to an ancient cyclical dating method is 4634.

Nobody knows for sure, but the Chinese calendar is supposed to have been started by Ta Nao in 2697 B.C. The Chinese calendar is measured in lunar years, and one complete cycle finishes every 60 years. There are ten celestial stems and 12 terrestrial branches that give 120 different combinations over two cycles. Lunar months in the Chinese calendar have either 29 or 30 days. As such, every third year an extra month is put into the calendar. For the year that *Charlie Chan at Monte Carlo* was made (1937), this corresponds to the 14th year in the 77th cycle, making the Chinese year 4634.

9506 Mug shot number for the convicted murderer who escaped from San Quentin Prison and now poses as newspaper reporter Bill Lydig in *Dead Men Tell* (1941).

95066 Police identification number shown in passport photograph of Baroness Kathi von Czardas (a.k.a. Kathi Lenesch) in *Charlie Chan in Panama* (1940).

Nagel, Anne (September 30, 1912, Boston, Massachusetts–July 6, 1966, Hollywood, California) Brunette stage and screen actress (real name: Anne Dolan) who appeared in over 60 films and portrays Cole King's scheming girlfriend, Marcia, in *The Trap* (1947).

Anne Nagel made her film debut at age 21 in an unbilled role in *I Loved You Wednesday* (1933). She signed a contract with Warner Bros., appearing as everything from western ingenues to murder suspects. In 1935 she married another Warners' contract player, leading man Ross Alexander, but after his sudden suicide in 1937, Nagel was quietly dropped by Warners and was then optioned by Universal.

Nagel was at her busiest in the early 1940s when she appeared in numerous Universal serials, such as *Don Winslow of the Navy* (1940), and horror films, such as *Man Made Monster* (1940). She was cast as Madame Gorgeous, the circus aerialist mother of Gloria Jean, in W.C. Fields' *Never Give a Sucker an Even Break* (1941), but nearly her entire part, including a spectacular death scene, ended up on the cutting room floor. Leaving Universal in 1943, Nagel freelanced at such minor operations as PRC and Republic.

Naish, J. Carrol (January 21, 1897, New York, New York–January 24, 1973, La Jolla, California) American stage and screen actor (real name: Joseph Patrick Carrol Naish) who appeared in almost 160 films and portrays murderer Tom Holt in *Charlie Chan at the Circus* (1936).

J. Carrol Naish (Everett Collection)

Though descended from a highly respected family of Irish politicians and civil servants, J. Carrol Naish played every sort of nationality *except* Irish during his long career. Naish joined the Navy at age 16 and spent the next decade traveling all over the world, absorbing the languages, dialects, and customs of several nations. Drifting from job to job while stranded in California, Naish began picking up extra work in Hollywood films. The acting bug took hold and Naish made his stage debut in a 1926 touring company of *The Shanghai Gesture*. Within five years he was a well-established member of the theatrical community.

Naish thrived during the early days of talking pictures thanks to his expertise in a limitless variety of foreign dialects. At various times he was seen as Chinese, Japanese, a Frenchman, a South Seas Islander, Portuguese, an Italian, a German, and an American Indian (playing Sitting Bull in the 1954 film of the same name). Many of his assignments were villainous in nature, and he was a gangster boss in virtually every Paramount "B" picture of the late 1930s.

Naish continued to flourish on radio and television, at one point playing both a priest and a rabbi on the same anthology series. He starred in both the radio and television versions of the melting-pot sitcom *Life with Luigi* and portrayed Charlie Chan in 39 episodes of *The New Adventures of Charlie Chan* (1957).

Naish was twice nominated for Academy Awards in the Best Supporting Actor category. In 1944 he received a nomination for his role as the Italian POW, Giuseppe, in *Sahara* (1943). In 1946 he was nominated for his role as an indigent Mexican father of a deceased war hero in *A Medal for Benny* (1945), for which he won a Golden Globe.

Napata Ancient Nubian city in present-day Sudan. Napata is situated north of the Sudanese capitol of Khartoum in the Upper

Nubia region between the Third and Fourth Cataracts of the Nile River. The city was the capital city of the Kingdom of Kush from approximately the 9th to the 4th century B.C.

In *Charlie Chan in Egypt* (1935), Professor Thurston tells Charlie Chan that Professor Arnold, after discovering the Ahmeti tomb, had found evidence of a royal burial ground at Napata on the Upper Nile and went there to investigate. It was from Napata that Thurston claims he had received his last letter from Arnold.

Nardi Undercover agent (portrayed by Dorothy Appleby) for Charlie Chan who performs as a dancer at the Café du Singe Bleu in *Charlie Chan in Paris* (1935). Chan plans to go to the cafe to meet Nardi, who has information on Albert Dufresne's financial dealings and connection to the counterfeiting of bonds issued by the Lamartine Bank.

Chan, Victor Descartes, Yvette Lamartine, Max Corday, and Renee Jacquard arrive at the cafe and watch Nardi's performance, an interpretation of the *dance apache*. The dance ends with Nardi's partner tossing her through a prop store front window, where she lands out of sight of the audience. Before she can stand up and rejoin her dance partner, Nardi sees Marcel Xavier (Henri Latouche) and screams before he throws a knife at her. When Chan reaches her, Nardi tells Charlie before she dies, "Look in apartment. It…," but it is not clear what Charlie is to find.

Chan then searches Nardi's apartment, and when he hears the cuckoo clock chime, guesses correctly that the hidden information is behind the clock. Written by Nardi, the note says: "Tonight, met with Albert Dufresne, of the Lamartine Bank, to a gambling house in Montparnasse. He lost ten thousand francs and is obviously spending beyond his income."

Narvo, Mrs. Paul The estranged wife (portrayed by Marjorie Weaver) of sabotage ring leader Paul Narvo in *Murder Over New York* (1940). When Charlie Chan and Inspector Vance search through Hugh Drake's briefcase, they see a Scotland Yard Criminal Identification Bureau report that gives Mrs. Paul Narvo's maiden name as Miriam Shaw, with aliases of Lucy Millard, Dorothy Cochran, and Patricia West. *See also* **West, Patricia.**

Narvo, Paul Alias Keith Jeffrey, leader of aviation sabotage ring (portrayed by John Sutton) in *Murder Over New York* (1940). Inspector Drake is on the trail of Narvo, who he thinks murdered an official of the British Air Ministry three years ago and is now in the U.S. Narvo is believed to have substantially changed his appearance and voice as a result of a car accident. In New York, Narvo poses as a stockbroker and murders Drake and George Kirby using a new poisonous gas called tetrogene.

Note: In *Charlie Chan's Chance* (1932), which is the (uncredited) basis for *Murder Over New York*, the character of Alan Raleigh (an alias used by Kenneth Dunwood) parallels that of Paul Narvo.

Nash, Mary (August 15, 1885, Troy, New York–December 3, 1976, Brentwood, California) Stage and screen character actress (real name: Mary Ryan) who appeared in over 20 films. Nash portrays Jennie Finch (a.k.a. master saboteur Reiner) in *Charlie Chan in Panama* (1940).

After a brief stab at films in 1913, Mary Nash returned to the stage where she remained until settling in Hollywood permanently in 1934. In films until 1946, Nash was often cast as seemingly mild-mannered women who turned vicious when challenged, such as her role as Mrs. Fresnel in *College Scandal* (1936) or as Jennie Finch in *Charlie Chan in Panama* (1940). As the hateful Fraulein Rottenmeier in *Heidi* (1937), Nash proved so effective she was rehired to portray Amanda Minchin in *The Little Princess* (1939). Mary Nash's most sympathetic role was as the long-suffering wife of blustering capitalist J.B. Ball in *Easy Living* (1937).

Nash, Philip Portrayed by Jon Hall (credited as Charles Locher), the secretary to Sir Stanley Woodland in *Charlie Chan in*

Shanghai (1935). Nash has custody of a booby-trapped presentation box containing a small gun that kills Woodland at a dinner honoring the arrival in Shanghai of Charlie Chan.

Because his thumbprint (with its telltale scar) is on the gun that was used in an attempt to murder Chan, Nash is taken away by the police on suspicion of Woodland's murder. Charlie and the police then set in motion a plan to find out who is involved in the opium smuggling ring by having Diana Woodland help Nash "escape" from the police station.

Nayda Female servant of the Arnold household (portrayed by Rita Cansino [later Rita Hayworth]) in *Charlie Chan in Egypt* (1935).

NC-203R Identification number of the single-propeller test airplane flown by Edwards and hijacked by Miller in *Charlie Chan at the Olympics* (1937). While on a fishing outing with his detective father, Number Two son Charlie Jr. finds the plane that had disappeared during the test flight.

NC 16001 Identification number of the American Airlines plane carrying Hugh Drake and Charlie Chan to New York in *Murder Over New York* (1940). The plane is flying Trip Number 19, which is scheduled to depart at 10:15 A.M. from Gate 3 and make stops in Phoenix, Dallas, Nashville, Washington, D.C., and New York. Charlie is attending a police convention while Drake is on the trail of Paul Narvo, the leader of an aviation sabotage ring.

ND Initials of a monogram on the purse of Nancy Woods, whose real name is Norma Duncan, in *Black Magic* (1944).

Negley, Howard General purpose character actor who appeared in over 40 films, often in nameless bit parts as police captains, politicians, and reporters. In two *Charlie Chan* roles, Negley portrays variety troupe leader Cole King in *The Trap* (1947) and spy André Pereaux in *Docks of New Orleans* (1948).

Neill, Noel (1920, Minneapolis, Minnesota–) Baby-faced American actress who appeared in over 55 movies and portrays airline stewardess Jane Marshall in *The Sky Dragon* (1949). Neill is perhaps best known in the role of the second Lois Lane (78 episodes), a newspaper reporter for the *Daily Planet*, in the television series *Adventures of Superman* (1953–57) and a number of movies made from the *Superman* series.

Nelson, Inspector Fast-talking New York policeman (portrayed by Harold Huber in his first of four *Charlie Chan* roles) in *Charlie Chan on Broadway* (1937). For some reason he is always asking someone for either a cigarette or a match.

Nelson, Joe Short order cook (portrayed by George Chandler [unbilled] in his last of four *Charlie Chan* roles) in *The Shanghai Cobra* (1945).

neptunium A radioactive, silvery metal and chemical element whose symbol is Np, the 93rd element in the periodic table. The name is derived from the planet Neptune. Neptunium is mentioned by Charlie Chan to Inspector Carvero in *The Red Dragon* (1945) as one of the elements discovered during the development of the atomic bomb. The element was first synthesized in 1940 at the University of California–Berkeley by E.M. McMillan and P. Abelson using a cyclotron to bombard uranium with neutrons. *See also* **95th element.**

Neumann, Harry C. (February 11, 1891–January 14, 1971, Hollywood, California) Cinematographer for over 220 films, including *The Jade Mask* (1945).

New Orleans Louisiana city that is the location setting for *Docks of New Orleans* (1948). Charlie Chan lives there with Number Two son Tommy and chauffeur Birmingham for reasons that are never explained in the film.

New York City Location setting for *Charlie Chan's Chance* (1932), *Charlie Chan on*

Broadway (1937), *Charlie Chan at the Wax Museum* (1940), *Murder Over New York* (1940), and *The Shanghai Cobra* (1945).

New York Daily Bulletin New York newspaper in *Charlie Chan on Broadway* (1937). Murdock is its managing editor and Speed Patten is its ace reporter.

"NEW YORK SOCIALITE MURDERED" Newspaper headline of the *Reno Courier* about the murder of Jeanne Bently in *Charlie Chan in Reno* (1939).

Newman, Emil Music director for almost 60 films, including the last five *Charlie Chan* movies made at Twentieth Century–Fox. In 1942 Newman received an Academy Award nomination in the Best Music (Scoring of a Musical Picture) category for *Sun Valley Serenade* (1941).

Charlie Chan filmography: *Charlie Chan at the Wax Museum* (1940), *Murder Over New York* (1940), *Dead Men Tell* (1941),* *Charlie Chan in Rio* (1941), and *Castle in the Desert* (1942).

Newman, Samuel Writer of the original story and screenplay (with W. Scott Darling) of *The Shanghai Chest* (1948).

newspapers The following newspapers are mentioned or shown in the *Charlie Chan* film series.

Newspaper	Movie
Chicago Sun	*Charlie Chan at the Opera* (1936)
The Daily Globe	*Murder Over New York* (1940)
Daily Mercury	*Charlie Chan at the Wax Museum* (1940)
Eldorado Times	*Charlie Chan's Courage* (1934)
The Globe	*Charlie Chan's Secret* (1936)
Honolulu Citizen	*Charlie Chan at the Olympics* (1937)
Honolulu Daily Courier	*Charlie Chan at the Olympics* (1937)
Honolulu Daily Journal	*Charlie Chan in Reno* (1939)
Honolulu Post Dispatch	*Charlie Chan at the Olympics* (1937)
Honolulu Standard	*Charlie Chan at the Race Track* (1936)
London Daily Post	*Charlie Chan in London* (1934)
London Gazette	*Charlie Chan in London* (1934)
London Planet	*Charlie Chan in London* (1934)
Los Angeles Bulletin	*Charlie Chan at the Opera* (1936)
Los Angeles Chronicle	*Charlie Chan at the Opera* (1936)
Los Angeles Star	*Charlie Chan at the Opera* (1936)
Los Angeles Telegraph	*Charlie Chan at the Opera* (1936)
Morning Herald	*The Chinese Ring* (1947)
New York Dispatch	*The Shanghai Cobra* (1945)
Reno Courier	*Charlie Chan in Reno* (1939)
St. Louis Sun Herald	*Dead Men Tell* (1941)
San Francisco Daily Dispatch	*Charlie Chan in Reno* (1939)
San Francisco Union Telegraph	*Charlie Chan at Treasure Island* (1939)
Star Dispatch	*The Chinese Cat* (1944), *Dark Alibi* (1946)

Nice (1) Southeastern French Riviera resort where Water Honeywood is shot and killed by Jim Everhard in *Charlie Chan Carries On* (1931).

Nice (2) The city stayed at by Charlie Chan and Number One son Lee while briefly visiting Monte Carlo before traveling to Paris in *Charlie Chan at Monte Carlo* (1937).

"A Night in Paris" Name of the follies show (starring Wanda LaFern) at the Gayety Theatre in *The Sky Dragon* (1949). Searching in the newspaper as to where Wanda LaFern is performing, Lee Chan and Birmingham Brown come across the show's advertisement: "Sam Gordon Presents Wanda LaFern in 'A Night in Paris.' Gayety Theatre. Two shows nightly."

nightshade Common name for the botanical family *Solanaceae*, consisting of more than 2,000 species of herbs, shrubs, and small trees. Poisonous alkaloids are present in many of

*Unbilled.

these species, including the common potato, which is perfectly safe to eat if cooked. The common, or black, nightshade is native to Europe but is now widespread elsewhere.

Although the common nightshade is often reported to be a poisonous plant, it is sometimes cooked as a pot herb, and its ripe (not green) berries are sometimes made into pies or preserves. The related deadly nightshade, or belladonna (*Atropa belladonna*), is cultivated for medicinal purposes as the source of the drug atropine.

In *Castle in the Desert* (1942), Charlie Chan observes that nightshade was used to kill Jimmy Chan's carrier pigeon, dubbed "Ming Toy," and that a search of the Manderley castle's apothecary shows that a large amount of nightshade is missing from a bottle. Watson King, who is really Cesare Borgia, puts some of the missing nightshade in a decanter of wine, intending to poison Paul Manderley.

nitroglycerin Highly unstable and toxic pale yellow oil, also known as glyceryl trinitrate, which was first made in 1846 by Ascario Sobrero. Alfred Nobel's first attempts in 1863 to utilize its explosive power were unsuccessful because the extremely unstable nature of the substance precluded its safe transport, storage, and employment. But in 1864 Nobel produced solid preparations by mixing nitroglycerin with porous substances such as kieselguhr, thus allowing the explosive to be employed as a safe, stable, blasting agent called dynamite. In medicine, nitroglycerin is used as a vasodilator to reduce arterial tension, especially for the treatment of heart diseases such as angina pectoris. It is also used for relaxing spasms of the biliary tract, the ureters, and respiratory system.

In *Charlie Chan in Panama* (1940), Charlie Chan and son Jimmy discover some cans found in Achmed Halide's crypt in the old Panama Cemetery. With a quick taste test, Charlie determines that it is nitroglycerin. Miss Finch gives herself away as Reiner when she suggests to Chan and Capt. Lewis that they use nitroglycerin to "blast their way out" of the locked crypt, even though Chan never mentioned the name of the explosive.

Nixon, Marian (October 20, 1904, Superior, Wisconsin–February 13, 1983, Los Angeles, California) Actress (real name: Marion Nixon) who appeared in nearly 70 silent and sound films and portrayed the young Sally Phillimore in *The Chinese Parrot* (1927) and Shirley Marlowe in *Charlie Chan's Chance* (1932).

A vaudeville chorus dancer in her early teens, actress Marian Nixon entered films in 1922. Two years later she was chosen by the Western Association of Motion Picture Advertisers as a "WAMPAS Baby Star." After serving an apprenticeship as a western ingenue, she was given leading-lady assignments opposite such popular male stars as Raymond Griffith, Reginald Denny, John Barrymore, Richard Barthelmess, and Al Jolson.

Nixon made a successful transition to talkies, but her peaches-and-cream screen image, exemplified by her appearance as the title character in *Rebecca of Sunnybrook Farm* (1932), was growing out of fashion. In 1934 she tried in vain to change her image with the Grace Allen–type, scatterbrain role of Arabella in *We're Rich Again* (1934). While the film wasn't a howling success, it turned out to be beneficial to Nixon—she married the film's director, William Seiter, a marriage that lasted until Seiter's death in 1964.

"NO TRACE OF MISSING PLANE" Newspaper headline of the *Honolulu Daily Courier* about the missing remote controlled test plane in *Charlie Chan at the Olympics* (1937).

Nodbury, Matthew "Black Hook" *see* **Black Hook**

Nodbury, Miss Patience Elderly woman (portrayed by Ethel Griffies in her first of two *Charlie Chan* roles) who is the sponsor and instigator of a treasure hunt to Cocos Island in *Dead Men Tell* (1941). Nodbury has a map supposedly drawn by her pirate grandfather, Matthew "Black Hook" Nodbury, showing the location of a $60 million treasure buried on Cocos Island.

Miss Nodbury fears that someone is trying to steal her treasure map, so she tears it into four pieces, keeping one piece and secretly sending the other three to Gene LaFarge, Laura Thursday, and Jed Thomasson. Nodbury tells Charlie Chan that Black Hook had a peg leg and a hook, and recounts the legend of how the ghost of Black Hook appears to each of the Nodburys as they are about to die. When she retires to her cabin, Jed Thomasson masquerades as Black Hook and, knowing that she has a weak heart, scares her, causing her to die from a heart attack. He then takes her portion of the map.

Norman, Louise Portrayed by Shirley Deane, circus trapeze performer (with her sister Marie Norman) in *Charlie Chan at the Circus* (1936). Tom Holt tries to kill Louise after she claims she can prove that Joe Kinney could not have been married to Nellie Farrell in Juarez, Mexico, on May 30, 1935.

Fearing that she will expose him as the killer of an El Paso sheriff, Holt shoots one of the trapeze ropes while Louise is performing her circus act, causing her to fall to the ground. In a last, desperate attempt to finish the job (she is still alive), Holt releases Cesar the gorilla as a diversion and puts on a gorilla costume. Before he can try to shoot Louise during a (staged) emergency operation, Holt is himself shot and killed.

Norman, Marie Portrayed by Maxine Reiner, circus trapeze performer (with her sister Louise Norman) in *Charlie Chan at the Circus* (1936). She is engaged to Joe Kinney, one of the circus' owners.

Norton, Jack (September 2, 1889, Brooklyn, New York–October 15, 1958, Saranac Lake, New York) Pencil-mustachioed character actor (real name: Mortimer J. Naughton) who appeared in over 80 films, perennially as an amiable, well-dressed drunk with a sour expression. In three *Charlie Chan* roles, Norton portrays the Hotel Francis desk clerk in *The Chinese Cat* (1944), radio actor Willie Rand in *The Scarlet Clue* (1945), and Cosgrove the pickpocket in *Shadows Over Chinatown* (1946).

A confirmed teetotaler, Jack Norton nonetheless earned cinematic immortality for his innumerable film appearances as a comic drunk. A veteran vaudevillian, Norton entered films in 1934, often playing stone-cold sober characters. In one Leon Errol two-reeler, *One Too Many* (1934), he was a stern night court judge sentencing Errol on a charge of public inebriation.

From *Cockeyed Cavaliers* (1934) onward, the Jack Norton that audiences loved began staggering his way from one film to another. It seemed that no film could have a scene in a nightclub or saloon without Norton, three sheets to the wind and in top hat and tails, leaning precariously against the bar. To perfect his act, Norton would follow genuine drunks for several city blocks, memorizing each nuance of movement.

To avoid becoming too involved in his roles, the actor drank only ginger ale and bicarbonate of soda. Though his appearances as a drunk could fill a book, Norton could occasionally be seen sober, notably in *You Belong to Me* (1940), *The Fleet's In* (1941), and Harold Lloyd's *Sin of Harold Diddlebock* (1946).

Retiring from films in 1948 due to illness, Norton occasionally appeared on live television in the early 1950s. Jack Norton's final appearance would have been in a 1955 episode of Jackie Gleason's *The Honeymooners*, but age and infirmity had so overwhelmed him that he was literally written out of the show as it was being filmed. However, Jackie Gleason saw to it that Norton was fully paid for the performance he was ready, willing, but unable to give.

Norton, Tim Airplane pilot (portrayed by Milburn Stone) who is helping Lee Chan study for his commercial pilot's license in *The Sky Dragon* (1949). While piloting Flight 17 to San Francisco, Norton and all the other flight's crew and passengers are drugged asleep by stewardess Marie Burke while a shipment of $250,000 is stolen and its in-flight courier guard is murdered by insurance investigator John Anderson.

novels Earl Derr Biggers wrote six *Charlie Chan* novels, five of which were the basis for *Charlie Chan* films and subsequent remakes. Only his 1932 novel, *Keeper of the Keys*, failed to be turned into a movie. *See* table, page 261.

Novels

Novel	Original Film	Film Remake
The House Without a Key (1925)	*The House Without a Key* (1925)	*Charlie Chan's Greatest Case* (1933)
The Chinese Parrot (1926)	*The Chinese Parrot* (1927)	*Charlie Chan's Courage* (1934)
Behind That Curtain (1928)	*Behind That Curtain* (1929)	*Charlie Chan's Chance* (1932)
The Black Camel (1929)	*The Black Camel* (1931)	*Charlie Chan in Rio* (1941)
Charlie Chan Carries On (1930)	*Charlie Chan Carries On* (1931)	*Eran Trece* (1931, Spanish)
		Charlie Chan's Murder Cruise (1940)

Number Five son Nickname for Tommy Chan (portrayed by Layne Tom, Jr.) in *Charlie Chan in Honolulu* (1938). *See also* **Chan, Tommy**.

Number Four son Nickname for Eddie Chan (portrayed by Keye Luke's brother, Edwin Luke) in *The Jade Mask* (1945). *See also* **Chan, Eddie**.

Number One daughter Nickname for Charlie Chan's daughter Ling, who is married to Wing Foo, in *Charlie Chan in Honolulu* (1938).

Number One grandchild Charlie Chan tries to make an Easter egg for his Number One grandchild in *Charlie Chan in Reno* (1939). The Chans' only grandchild, a boy which was to be named Leung, is born at the conclusion of the series' previous entry, *Charlie Chan in Honolulu* (1938), to Number One daughter Ling and her husband Wing Foo. *See also* **Easter egg**.

Number One son Nickname for Charlie Chan's oldest child, Lee Chan, who is portrayed by Keye Luke. *See also* **Chan, Lee**.

Number Seven son Nickname for Willie Chan (portrayed by Layne Tom, Jr.) in *Charlie Chan's Murder Cruise* (1940).

Number Three assistant Nickname for Birmingham Brown (portrayed by Mantan Moreland), Charlie Chan's chauffeur, in *The Chinese Ring* (1947). It is not clear why Birmingham is now Number Three when he is Number Two assistant seven films earlier in *The Scarlet Clue* (1945). *See also* **Brown, Birmingham**.

Number Three son Nickname for Tommy Chan (portrayed by Benson Fong in six *Charlie Chan* movies). However, when later portrayed by Victor Sen Young, Tommy Chan is mysteriously promoted to Number Two son status, starting with *The Chinese Ring* (1947). *See also* **Chan, Tommy.**

Number Two assistant In *The Scarlet Clue* (1945), Birmingham Brown is referred to as Charlie Chan's Number Two assistant.

Number Two daughter Nickname for Charlie Chan's daughter, Iris Chan (portrayed by Marianne Quon), in *Charlie Chan in the Secret Service* (1944).

Number Two son Charlie Chan, Jr. (portrayed by Layne Tom, Jr.), in *Charlie Chan at the Olympics* (1937), is the first to be referred to as the Number Two son. When Sen Yung portrays the role of Jimmy Chan (sometimes listed as James Chan) in 13 films after the departure of Keye Luke as Number One son Lee, Jimmy Chan is referred to as "Number Two son" for the remainder of the Twentieth Century–Fox films. In the Monogram films, however, Tommy Chan, once again the number three son, is mysteriously upgraded to Number Two status. *See also* **Chan, Jimmy**.

Nunah Eric Durand's Indian servant and mistress (portrayed by Mercedes De Velasco) in *Behind That Curtain* (1929).

O

$100 (1) The amount of money Robert Fyfe gives to the artist Smith to keep quiet about what he overheard Shelah Fane tell Fyfe in *The Black Camel* (1931). Fyfe gives Smith $100 and promises to pay $200 more.

$100 (2) The amount of money that Murdock agrees to pay freelance photographer Joan Wendall for a picture of Billie Bronson she took that day in *Charlie Chan on Broadway* (1937).

125th Street and 8th Avenue Harlem street corner Birmingham tells himself he wishes he were back at when brothers Tommy and Lee Chan leave him alone to examine nearby Aztec hieroglyphics in *The Feathered Serpent* (1948). Apparently Birmingham feels that he would be safer in Harlem than in the woods looking for Aztec ruins after two people have already been murdered.

191 Golden Gate Avenue San Francisco address of the residence of Thomas Cartwright, a member of the jury who convicted Tony Pindello, in *The Shanghai Chest* (1948).

1055 Harley Street Rooming house address of Paula Webb (alias Pauline Webster) in *The Shanghai Cobra* (1945).

1313 Telephone number of Shelah Fane's actor ex-husband Robert Fyfe at the Royal Theater in *The Black Camel* (1931).

1410 Dexter Street New York City street address of Joe's Coffee Shop in *The Shanghai Cobra* (1945).

1714 Howard Street San Francisco street address of George Bently in *Charlie Chan in Reno* (1939). Charlie Chan finds a mining engineer's kit that belongs to Bently in an abandoned ghost town near Reno. Inside the kit is a copy of an order Bently placed with the Golden Gate Co., a wholesale drug firm, for the following chemicals:

3/6	Nitric Acid	$ 3.50
3/9	Sulphuric Acid	2.75
3/9	Ammonia	1.50
3/9	Glacial Acetic	4.25
3/6	Hydrochloric Acid	3.75
		$15.75

10502 Mug shot number for Birmingham Brown's uncle, Nicodemus Brown, in *The Scarlet Clue* (1945). When Tommy Chan and Birmingham go to the police station to report a black marketeer, they are handed several books of mug shots. On one page Birmingham sees a mug shot of his uncle, dated September 28 and listing an age of 46, a height of 5'7", and a weight of 152 pounds.

10896 Mug shot number for Birmingham Brown in *The Scarlet Clue* (1945). When Tommy Chan and Birmingham go to the police station to report a black marketeer, they are handed several books of mug shots. On one page Birmingham sees a mug shot of his uncle, Nicodemus Brown. Several pages later there is a similar one for Birmingham, dated July 1 and listing an age of 38, a height of 5'5", and a weight of 158 pounds.

13576 Identification number assigned to a carrier pigeon that belongs to the U.S. Army's Signal Corps in *Castle in the Desert* (1942). *See also* **carrier pigeon; Toy, Ming**.

15380 Telephone number of police commissioner Col. Watkins in *Charlie Chan in Shanghai* (1935).

$100,000 Amount of money that Henrietta Lowell's will indicates is to be given to spiritualists Professor Bowan and his assistant Carlotta upon Lowell's death as an endowment to continue psychic research in *Charlie Chan's Secret* (1936). When Charlie Chan exposes the trickery involved in the duo's séances, Henrietta Lowell instructs the family lawyer, Warren Phelps, to write the two psychics out of her will.

100,000 francs Payment paid to Belescu for clearance papers in *City in Darkness* (1939). The shipment of contraband munitions on the *Medusa* is to be declared as a cargo of fruit.

$1 million The amount of travelers checks deposited by Princess Mei Ling in her account at the San Francisco branch of the

Exchange Specie Bank of Peiping in *The Chinese Ring* (1947).

O'Brien, Vince Alias used by Lt. Mike Ruark, who goes undercover as an inebriated San Francisco playboy while staying at the Lazy Y Ranch, in *The Golden Eye* (1948). Charlie Chan is at the same ranch but investigating recent attacks on Mr. Manning's life, while Lt. Ruark is investigating the sudden production of gold from Manning's Golden Eye Mine, making it one of the richest in the country after years of low output.

ocarina From the Italian diminutive *oca*, meaning "goose," a small simple wind instrument that produces soft, hollow tones. It is shaped like a sweet potato and is usually made of terra cotta with finger holes and a mouthpiece. In *Dead Men Tell* (1941), *Suva Star* cook Wu Mei plays the ocarina, whose eerie sounding music Jimmy Chan refers to as "ghost music."

O'Connell, L. William Cinematographer of over 100 films, including *Charlie Chan in London* (1934).

O'Fearna, Edward (c. 1890–January 15, 1969, Los Angeles, California) Assistant director for more than 15 films, sometimes credited as Edward Feeney. O'Fearna was the assistant director (unbilled) for *Charlie Chan in London* (1934) and was the brother of director John Ford (real name: Sean Aloysius O'Fearna) and actor Francis Ford (real name: Francis O'Fearna), who himself had roles in four *Charlie Chan* films.

Oland, Warner (October 3, 1879, Nyby, Sweden–August 6, 1938, Stockholm, Sweden) Warner Oland is perhaps the best-known and best-liked of the actors who portrayed Charlie Chan. He was born Johan Värner Ölund to shopkeeper Jonas Ölund and Maria Johanna Forsberg in the small village of Nyby in Bjurholm parish in the county of Vasterbotten, Sweden.

Known as "Jack" to his friends, Warner Oland and his parents immigrated to the United States on October 15, 1892, when he was 13 years old. Educated in Boston, Oland received his dramatic training at Dr. Curry's Acting School. His first acting experience was in the Shakespearean theater, where he was also proficient in set design. He also appeared in a Sarah Bernhardt theater troupe and went on to put on his own plays.

Warner Oland prior to his *Charlie Chan* days.

However, this venture failed and he went to Hollywood where he broke into silent film work in 1915 with Theda Bara in the film *Sin* (1915), playing an Italian gangster named Pietro. In time he became a successful character actor, having changed his name to Warner Oland. Now as Oland, he appeared in over 35 silent pictures before playing Al Jolson's father, a Jewish cantor, in *The Jazz Singer* (1927), the movies' first talking picture.

Although born to Swedish and Russian parents, a previous Mongol presence in Sweden provided Oland with uncanny but natural features that suited the portrayals of Orientals when a mustache and beard were added. Unlike the future character of Charlie Chan, who represented law and order, Oland initially portrayed Oriental villains, such as Wu Fang in *The Lightning Raider*

(1919), Li Hsun in *Mandarin Gold* (1919), and Dr. Fu Manchu in a trio of films—*The Mysterious Dr. Fu Manchu* (1929), *The Return of Dr. Fu Manchu* (1930), and *Daughter of the Dragon* (1931). With his Oriental features and experience playing Oriental roles, Oland was the obvious selection to portray Charlie Chan. In the 16 films made by Fox and its successor, Twentieth Century–Fox, it was the character of Charlie Chan that brought Warner Oland international fame.

As a true Renaissance man of culture, Oland was a scholar of philosophy, classical music, and art. He also practiced Chinese calligraphy with Keye Luke. Besides these interests, Oland spoke several languages and was a translator of the Swedish works of August Strindberg into English.

Warner Oland was supposed to be paid $10,000 a picture in the *Charlie Chan* series. However, the popular response to his first film, *Charlie Chan Carries On* (1931), prompted him to ask for $12,500 for *The Black Camel* (1931) and $20,000 for *Charlie Chan's Chance* (1932). Oland was kept at $12,500 for the remaining eight pictures made by Fox. When the Fox and Twentieth Century studios merged in 1935, Oland was also paid $12,500 for *Charlie Chan's Secret* (1936). Starting with *Charlie Chan at the Circus* (1936), he was paid $20,000 for the next three films, and when his option was picked up again, Oland received $30,000 for each of his last three movies.

While filming the Chan series, Oland appeared in other films, usually as an Oriental. Most notable among these were: *Shanghai Express* (1932), as Henry Chang, with Marlene Dietrich; *The Painted Veil* (1934), as General Yu, with Greta Garbo; and *Werewolf of London* (1935), as Dr. Yogami. In all, Oland appeared in over 75 films.

Very often in public, Oland would talk in the stilted speech pattern and employ mannerisms that were associated with his Charlie Chan characterization. He would quote sayings that he used in the films and often referred to himself as "humble father," giving many the impression that he actually thought he *was* Charlie Chan. Unlike the Charlie Chan character, who neither smoked nor drank liquor, Oland did both. Oland's alcoholic binges on and off the set were legendary and often created problems for directors and wreaked havoc with shooting schedules, besides ruining his health and his marriage to Edith, to whom he had been married since 1907. Despite the studio hiring a private nurse to see to it that Oland didn't drink, he would find inventive means to obtain his liquor.

Oland had now separated from his wife, and his health deteriorated to a point that it was reported that it affected his mind. He would fumble over his lines, often requiring a dozen or more takes just to get one line correct. The filming of what would have been *Charlie Chan at the Ringside* went into production on January 10, 1938, but Oland was found far from Hollywood, somewhat deranged and unable to tell who he was. Oland's problems were such that he had unexpectedly walked off the set several times during the first week of production. On January 17 he walked out again, and Darryl Zanuck, having finally become fed up with the actor's drinking and absences from the set, scrapped the picture and put Oland on suspension. According to studio records, $93,820.59 was spent on the filming of *Charlie Chan at the Ringside* up to this point, and records of correspondence from Sol M. Wurtzel revealed that $46,341.10 was saved by converting the *Ringside* film into *Mr. Moto's Gamble* as the third entry in the Peter Lorre *Mr. Moto* series. Wurtzel also suggested that the amount of $39,979.49 be billed to Warner Oland, but it is not known if this was actually done.

During his suspension, Oland was hospitalized in February for a month, reportedly for a nervous breakdown. After his release in March, he and Zanuck settled their differences and Oland even signed a new contract to make three more *Charlie Chan* films for the 1938-39 season. Oland had talked of visiting Europe once again and, with talk of a possible reconciliation between Warner and Edith, Zanuck thought it would be a good idea for Oland to take that ocean voyage before resuming production on the new films. However, the reconciliation never went any further, and, eager to see his homeland once more, Oland sailed for Sweden. There he died of bronchial pneumonia in his mother's bed on August 6, 1938, at age 58.

Charlie Chan filmography: *Charlie Chan Carries On* (1931), *The Black Camel* (1931), *Charlie Chan's Chance* (1932), *Charlie Chan's Greatest Case* (1933), *Charlie Chan's Courage* (1934), *Charlie Chan in London* (1934), *Charlie Chan in Paris* (1935), *Charlie Chan in Egypt* (1935), *Charlie Chan in Shanghai* (1935), *Charlie Chan's Secret* (1936), *Charlie Chan at the Circus* (1936), *Charlie Chan at the Race Track* (1936), *Charlie Chan at the Opera* (1936), *Charlie Chan at the Olympics* (1937), *Charlie Chan on Broadway* (1937), and *Charlie Chan at Monte Carlo* (1937).

O'Malley, Pat (September 3, 1890, Forest City, Pennsylvania–May 21, 1966, Van Nuys, California) Irish-American character actor who appeared in almost 150 silent and sound films. In two unbilled *Charlie Chan* roles, O'Malley portrays Belden in *Charlie Chan in Shanghai* (1935) and a track official in *Charlie Chan at the Race Track* (1936).

O'Matthews, Inspector New York policeman (portrayed by Joe King) in *Charlie Chan at the Wax Museum* (1940).

"On the night of September 28..." Notice posted by the Paris police to prepare residents for possible air raids by German bombers in *City in Darkness* (1939). The complete notice reads: "On the night of September 28, the City of Paris will be in darkness as a precaution against air raids. Do not allow light to penetrate through windows or doors. Negligence will be met with punishment and fines. By order of J. Romaine, Prefect of Police."

O'Neil, Julie Shelah Fane's ward (portrayed by Sally Eilers) in *The Black Camel* (1931). Shelah Fane became her guardian when Julie's parents died.

Orange Blossom Manor Name of the wedding chapel in Humbolt County, California, where Connie Jackson married Andrew Barrett in *The Sky Dragon* (1949). The wedding chapel is run by Jonathon Tibbetts, a Justice of the Peace, who performed the ceremony on June 21, 1941.

Ordinances 106, 109, and 214A Ordinances for which Jimmy Chan is arrested (in addition to being thought nuts) while in a police lineup in *Charlie Chan in Reno* (1939). Jimmy attends college at USC and borrows a car from a friend during the spring break to go to Reno and help his father solve the murder of Jeanne Bently. However, along the way Jimmy picks up two highway thieves who rob him of the car, his clothes, and money.

Orth, Marion American screenwriter of nearly 50 silent and sound films, including *Charlie Chan's Greatest Case* (1933).

Osborn, Ted Character actor, sometimes credited as Ted Osborne, who portrayed reporter Tom Agnew (an alias for "Butcher" Degan) in *Charlie Chan at the Wax Museum* (1940).

Oscar Al Hogan's tame, pet lion, whose growl is worse than his bite, in *Charlie Chan in Honolulu* (1938). Along with other animals, Oscar is being transported on the *Susan B. Jennings* to a zoo in San Francisco.

O'Shaughnessy, Frankie Evening shift checkroom attendant at the British Imperial Club (portrayed by Frank Coghlan, Jr. [unbilled], in his second of two *Charlie Chan* roles) in *Murder Over New York* (1940). After he sees a picture of Hugh Drake in the newspaper with a story reporting that Drake had been murdered, O'Shaughnessy tells police inspector Vance that there is a briefcase in the cloakroom at the club that belongs to Drake which Vance and Charlie Chan have been looking for.

Ouija A board game in which two players ask questions of and receive answers from a seemingly supernatural source. The board, which has the letters of the alphabet and the numbers zero through nine printed on it, is placed across the knees of the players. Players then lightly rest their fingertips on the message indicator, a three-legged, heart-shaped device with a clear viewfinder. One player poses a question, and the message indicator is then supposed to move to appropriate numbers or letters, spelling out an answer. Originally called "Ouija Talking Board," the game was developed in the late 1890s by William Fuld and is now distributed by Parker Bros.

In *Charlie Chan's Secret* (1936), Henrietta Lowell uses a Ouija board with a reluctant Baxter, her butler, to find information about her missing nephew, Allen Colby. In succession, Lowell spells the letters "D-E-A-D" and concludes that there is no doubt that Allen is dead.

Owens, Jesse (September 12, 1913, Danville, Alabama–March 31, 1980, Tucson, Arizona)

Jesse Owens winning the 100-meter race for one of his record four gold medals at the 1936 Olympics in Berlin (Courtesy The Jesse Owens Foundation).

Black American track star (real name: James Cleveland Owens) who will be best remembered both for his performance in the 1936 Olympic Games in Berlin and for achieving probably the finest one-day performance ever in track history. In *Charlie Chan at the Olympics* (1937), there is actual footage of Owens helping the U.S. team win the 4 × 100–meter relay.

On May 25, 1935, at the Big Ten championships at Ann Arbor, Michigan, Jesse Owens broke five world records and equaled a sixth in the space of 45 minutes. At 3:15 P.M. he won the 100-yard dash by five yards in 9.4 seconds to tie the world record. At 3:25, on his only jump of the day, he set a new long-jump record of 26'8¼" (8.13 m) which then stood for 25 years. At 3:45 P.M. he won by ten yards in the 220-yard dash with a clocking of 20.3 seconds, bettering the current mark by three-tenths of a second and at the same time was given credit for breaking the world record in the shorter 200-meter dash. At 4:00 P.M. he won the 220-yard hurdles in 22.6 seconds (becoming the first to beat 23 seconds). He was also given credit for breaking the world record for the 200-meter hurdles in the same race.

In the 1936 Olympic Games, Owens won four gold medals in the 100-meter (10.3 seconds) and 200-meter dashes (Olympic record of 20.7 seconds) and the long jump (Olympic record of 26'5½") and was on the winning 4 × 100-meter relay team. *Charlie Chan at the Olympics* shows the actual 4 × 100-meter relay race which had Jesse Owens running the leadoff leg, followed by Ralph Metcalfe, Foy Draper, and Frank Wykoff. The Americans won the race by 15 yards over the Italians in a world record time of 39.8 seconds, which would last for 20 years.

Nazi propaganda had portrayed Blacks and Jews as inferior to the blue-eyed, blond-haired Aryans, and Hitler taunted the Americans for relying on "black auxiliaries." A famous myth relates how Hitler snubbed Owens by refusing to meet him after Owens had won the 100-meter dash (Hitler had personally congratulated three previous gold medal winners). However, Owens *was* snubbed several times before and after the Olympics.

The Amateur Athletic Union (A.A.U.) twice bypassed him for the Sullivan Award, which is given to the best U.S. amateur athlete of the year. In 1935, when he set the six world records in the space of 45 minutes, the award was given to Lawson Little, a golfer. In 1936, the year of his four Olympic gold medals, the award went to Glenn Morris, the Olympic decathlon champion. Owens was also snubbed by U.S. President Franklin Delano Roosevelt, who not only failed to invite Owens to the White House but never even sent him a letter of congratulations. Owens died of lung cancer after 35 years of a pack-a-day cigarette habit. *See also* **1936 Olympic Games.**

P

Palace Hotel (1) Sir Frederic Bruce's Teheran hotel in *Behind That Curtain* (1929).

Palace Hotel (2) Capt. Kong's San Francisco hotel in *The Chinese Ring* (1947).

Palmer, Ernest G. (1885–February 22, 1978, Pacific Palisades, California) Cinematographer of over 150 silent and sound films, including *Charlie Chan's Greatest Case* (1933) and *Charlie Chan in Paris* (1935).

Ernest Palmer spent many years at Fox Studios on both sides of the company's 1935 merger with Twentieth Century Pictures. In the early 1930s, Palmer helped found the American Society of Cinematographers and received four Academy Award nominations, winning one Oscar.

Best Cinematography

Street Angel (1928)
Four Devils (1928)

Best Cinematography (Color)

**Blood and Sand* (1941)
Broken Arrow (1950)

Note: Daniel Clark was the original cameraman for *Charlie Chan in Paris* (1935) but did not receive on-screen credit.

Panama Location setting for *Charlie Chan in Panama* (1940).

**Academy Award winner.*

Panama Canal Completed in 1914, man-made waterway across the Isthmus of Panama that connects the Atlantic and Pacific Oceans. The passage through the waterway, taking seven to eight hours, shortens the trip from New York to San Francisco by more than 5,200 miles. At the time of its opening, the canal was universally acknowledged as the greatest engineering feat of the modern age, and it is still so regarded by many. The total length of the canal is 50.72 miles, from Cristobal at Limón Bay on the north canal Atlantic Ocean side to the Bay of Panama at Balboa on the south canal Pacific Ocean side. Traveling through three pairs of locks (Gatun, Pedro Miguel, and Miraflores), a ship actually leaves the canal (on the Pacific side) 27 miles east of where it enters it at Limón Bay.

In *Charlie Chan in Panama* (1940), Charlie Chan investigates rumors that the Panama Canal will be a target of sabotage, masterminded by a spy known as Reiner.

Panama Canal Zone Until 1979, a U.S. government reservation that ran through the middle of the Republic of Panama, from the Atlantic to the Pacific Ocean, extending for five miles on either side of the Panama Canal. The governor of the Canal Zone was appointed by the U.S. president, and U.S. Army, Air Force, and Navy personnel were stationed there with other employees of the Panama Canal Company and their dependents.

In *Charlie Chan in Panama* (1940), Col. D.C. Webster is the governor of the Panama Canal Zone, which is the target of sabotage by a master spy known as Reiner.

Panama hat Stylish and comfortable hat that is handwoven from fine toquilla straw made out of palm leaves grown in the Ecuadorian province of Manabi. Although its name would imply otherwise, the true Panama hat is a product unique to Ecuador, which began producing the Panama hat as early as 1630 (but didn't actively export the product until the early 1800s).

The hats were sold in Panamanian ports,

Charlie Chan wore a variety of hat styles: black, white, round without brim, and Panamas.

resulting in travelers and merchants associating the fine quality and workmanship with the country of Panama. Workers on the Panama Canal found them to be durable headwear and comfortable under the tropical sun. When President Teddy Roosevelt visited during the construction of the canal, he returned to the United States wearing one of these hats. The press dubbed it the "Panama hat," and it has been known as that ever since.

The Panama hat is one of several styles of hats worn by Charlie Chan. In *Charlie Chan in Panama* (1940), Chan poses as Fu Yuen, a shopkeeper who sells Panama hats, while Number Two son Jimmy sports a Fedora-style hat. The style with the distinctive center ridge on the crown sometimes worn by Chan (when played by George Kuwa and Sidney Toler) is known as the "Optimo."

paper dolls Trademark habit of Steve McBirney who, during his trial, cuts out paper doll silhouettes from folded paper in *Charlie Chan at the Wax Museum* (1940). When Charlie Chan uncovers Dr. Cream's secret laboratory in the basement of Cream's crime museum, Charlie notices folded paper dolls that have been left on the desk, which means that Steve McBirney was in the office earlier and had intercepted a telephone call intended for the police.

paraffin test Forensic chemical test used to determine whether an individual has fired a firearm, and was once of great significance in the investigation of both homicides and suicides. The paraffin test is also known as the dermal nitrate, or diphenylamine test, and was introduced in the United States in 1933 by Teodoro Gonzalez of the Criminal Identification Laboratory at Mexico City police headquarters.

Melted paraffin is brushed over the "shooting" hand of the suspect until a thin coat is obtained. The glove can be built up in layers by using thin sheets of fabric until it is about ⅛-inch thick. After cooling, the cast is removed and treated with diphenylamine reagent used to detect nitrates and nitrites that originate from gunpowder which may be deposited on the skin after firing a weapon. The diphenylamine reagent is prepared by adding 10 cubic centimeters of concentrated sulfuric acid to 2 milliliters of distilled water. To this is added 0.05 grams of diphenylamine. The reagent is dropped on the paraffin with a pipette. Dark blue specks appearing on the inner surface of the cast indicate a positive reaction.

Theoretically, the diphenylamine reagent is used to test for the presence of nitrates, which are contained in the residue of gunpowder blown back on the hand in discharging a firearm. Although this test often (but not invariably) gives positive results on the hands of individuals who fired weapons, it also gives positive results on the hands of individuals who had *not* fired weapons due to the widespread distribution of nitrates and nitrites in our environment in fertilizers, tobacco, urine, kitchen matches, and cosmetics. The paraffin test is, in fact, nonspecific and is of no scientific use today.

In *Charlie Chan on Broadway* (1937), Hottentot Club owner Johnny Burke is suspected of murdering former girlfriend Billie Bronson. When captured, Burke is asked by Inspector Nelson if he would submit to a paraffin test to prove his innocence. Charlie Chan tells Meeker, Burke's lawyer, what the paraffin test is and that it is good for up to 72 hours after firing a gun. The police lab technician administers the test on Burke's right hand, but the reagent does not turn blue.

Paris French capital city which is the location setting for *Charlie Chan in Paris* (1935) and *City of Darkness* (1939).

Park, E.L. British actor who portrays the screen's first *talking* Charlie Chan (as the minor character of a San Francisco policeman who assists Scotland Yard's Sir Frederic Bruce) in *Behind That Curtain* (1929).

Parks, Charles Movie star posing as Charles Thursday in *Dead Men Tell* (1941). *See also* **Thursday, Charles.**

Parks, Eddie Character actor who portrays Jonathon Tibbetts, the Justice of the Peace and owner of the Orange Blossom Manor, in *The Sky Dragon* (1949).

Parsons, Milton (May 19, 1907, Gloucester, Massachusetts–May 15, 1980, Los Angeles,

Gilbert Emery (left) and E.L. Park, the screen's third Charlie Chan, in *Behind That Curtain*.

California) Gloomy-looking American character actor who appeared in over 60 films, often as an undertaker. In four *Charlie Chan* roles, Parsons portrays Gene LaFarge in *Dead Men Tell* (1941), private investigator Arthur Fletcher in *Castle in the Desert* (1942), Mr. Johnson the accountant in *Dark Alibi* (1946), and Mr. Grail the undertaker in *The Shanghai Chest* (1948).

Bald, cadaverous, hollow-eyed, doom-voiced actor Milton Parsons began appearing in films in the late 1930s. In an era when being typecast in Hollywood assured an actor a steady paycheck, Parsons fattened his bank account by playing dozens of undertakers and morticians. He was also an effective psychotic type, most notably as John Channing in *The Hidden Hand* (1942). Parsons entered the film noir hall of fame by playing the tiny role of the jury foreman in *They Won't Believe Me* (1947). The film's unforgettable final image was a screen-filling close-up of Parsons, gloomily intoning an all-too-late "Not Guilty."

Paterson, Pat (April 7, 1911, Bradford, England–August 24, 1978, Phoenix, Arizona) British-born leading lady who portrays Carol Arnold in *Charlie Chan in Egypt* (1935). Paterson gave up her short film career to marry actor Charles Boyer.

Patten, Speed Newspaper reporter for the *New York Daily Bulletin* and double murderer (portrayed by Donald Woods in his second of two *Charlie Chan* roles) in *Charlie Chan on Broadway* (1937). Patten murders Billie Bronson, who was once wanted as a key witness by a New York grand jury investigating what she knew about the rackets and politics, and who skipped town. Patten also murders Thomas Mitchell, a shady character who is looking for Billie Bronson's diary.

Charlie Chan, in reading Patten's newspaper stories, is curious as to how Patten knows several unpublished facts about the murders. In particular, Patten writes in one account that Billie Bronson was shot in the back—which only the murderer could know since the body was found face up. Chan plants a fake page from Billie Bronson's missing diary, about which Patten foolishly remarks, "The page is a forgery. Even the paper it's written on..." Here Chan interrupts and says, "To know forgery, must have original. You are murderer."

"PAUL GRAY GUILTY" Newspaper headline of the *London Daily Post* in *Charlie Chan in London* (1934).

"PAUL GRAY MUST HANG!" Newspaper headline of the *London Gazette* in *Charlie Chan in London* (1934).

PC M22 23 California license plate number of the taxi that takes Jimmy Chan and Mme. Saturnia near the Manderley Castle in *Castle in the Desert* (1942).

Peabody, Dr. Samuel R. County coroner (portrayed by Joe Whitehead in his first of two *Charlie Chan* roles) who performs the autopsy on Mr. Harper in *The Jade Mask* (1945). At Charlie Chan's request, Dr. Peabody discovers that a poison dart, imbedded in Harper's throat, is the murder weapon.

Peabody, Mr. The representative of the owners of the S.S. *Oceanic* in *Charlie Chan in Honolulu* (1938). Because Charlie Chan is investigating a murder onboard the ship, the ship is unable to take on or unload its cargo and leave port. Peabody threatens Inspector Rawlins that the owners will sue the city if the boat is held up further.

Pearson, Scott Undercover agent of the U.S. Treasury Department (portrayed by Tristram Coffin in his first of two *Charlie Chan* roles) in *Dangerous Money* (1946). Pearson is sent to Samoa to investigate the sudden appearance of money and artworks stolen from Philippine banks during the Japanese invasion. After two unsuccessful attempts on his life, Pearson is killed by a knife thrown by Joseph Murdock (disguised as Mrs. Whipple) before he can tell Charlie Chan anything. Pearson left papers on the case in the office safe of Capt. Black. The papers mention a man named Lane but does not identify him.

Peil, Edward, Sr. (January 18, 1882, Racine, Wisconsin–December 29, 1958, Hollywood, California) Character actor (real name: Charles Edward Peil) who appeared in nearly 170 silent and sound films and portrays Li Gung in *Charlie Chan's Chance* (1932).

Note: Peil's last name was very often misspelled in credits, and he was often credited as: Edward Peel, Edward J. Peel, Ed Peil, Sr., Edward J. Peil, Edward Peil, Ed Peil, Edward Pell, Ed Piel, Sr., E.J. Piel, Edward J. Piel, Edward Piel, or Ed Piel.

Pendleton, Gerald Nervous, paranoid passenger of Dr. Suderman's cruise (portrayed by Leonard Mudie in his first of two *Charlie Chan* roles) in *Charlie Chan's Murder Cruise* (1940). Pendleton changes rooms in the Luani Hotel with Mr. Kenyon since Kenyon's room is quieter. Although Pendleton is the intended victim, Mr. Kenyon is mistakenly strangled by Jim Eberhardt with a leather strap from Dr. Suderman's suitcase, and a pouch of 30 silver dimes is placed in Kenyon's hands. Frightened, Pendleton tells Charlie Chan that he needs a quiet room and is moving to the Imperial Hawaiian Hotel.

When Pendleton sees a second bag of 30 dimes dropped through the door vent of his cabin room, Pendleton tells Chan that his wife once received a similar bag five years earlier. He had no idea of its meaning then but now considers it a warning of death—his. Charlie later learns that Pendleton's wife was once married to a jewelry thief and smuggler named Jim Eberhardt, whom she turned in to the police, and that Eberhardt swore he would get revenge. During the cruise, Pendleton is found dead in his cabin, having been strangled with a leather shoelace by Eberhardt.

A search of Pendleton's cabin by Chan yields a radiogram sent to his wife which reads, "We are in danger. Do not come to San Francisco. Love Gerald." However, Jimmy notices that the message was raised from the sheet of paper underneath the original, and no original copy was found. Chan then requests from the radio room the text of the radiogram that was sent by the murderer: "All is well. Meet me Adelphi Hotel San Francisco. Love Gerald."

Pendleton, Grace Gortner Missing 30-year-old widow of Homer B. Pendleton (who dies on his honeymoon and is thought to be one of the "torso" murder victims) in *Shadows Over Chinatown* (1946). Before she was married, Grace Pendleton once worked as a chorus girl for the Bon Ton Burlesque Company and was romantically attracted to its manager, Craig Winfield, who years later poses as Jeff Hay, a private detective.

Pendleton, Mrs. Former wife (portrayed by Kay Linaker in her third of four *Charlie Chan* roles) of Jim Eberhardt and widow of Gerald Pendleton in *Charlie Chan's Murder Cruise* (1940). Eberhardt, a jewelry thief, tries to force his wife to use her profession as an actress to smuggle stolen jewelry, but she turns him in instead to the police and he swears that he will have his revenge. Five years earlier, Mrs. Pendleton once received a bag of 30 dimes which frightened her because she knew its meaning.

Note: The character Mrs. Pendleton loosely parallels that of Sybil Conway in *Charlie Chan Carries On* (1931).

Pendleton, Steve Character actor who appeared in almost 60 films, sometimes credited as Gaylord Steve Pendleton and Gaylord Pendleton. Pendleton portrays courier guard Ben Edwards in *The Sky Dragon* (1949).

Pentonville Prison London jail where Paul Gray is imprisoned and awaiting execution in *Charlie Chan in London* (1934).

Percy, Ralph Chief designer for the Metropolitan Aircraft Company (portrayed by Kane Richmond in his second of three *Charlie Chan* roles) in *Murder Over New York* (1940).

Pereaux, André Foreign spy (portrayed by Howard Negley in his second of two *Charlie Chan* roles) in *Docks of New Orleans* (1948). Pereaux heads an espionage team consisting of Grock and Nita Aguirre that tries to prevent Simon Lafontaine and his syndicate partners from shipping a cargo of poisonous gas to an opposition party in Pereaux's country in South America. When Pereaux is unable to stop the ship from sailing, he tries to forcibly get the secret formula from Lafontaine. From police files Charlie Chan learns that Pereaux had been booted out of at least three armies and has been known to use the aliases Fernand, Citron, Boronoff, and Grumbauer.

Pete (1) Ship steward on the S.S. *Newcastle* (portrayed by Rito Punay) who gets information for P.T. Burke from the purser's safe about the falsification of Rona Simmonds' visa in *Dangerous Money* (1946). When he demands his payment from Burke, Burke stalls and threatens Pete to keep quiet or else. Pete elects to jump overboard and attempts a four- to five-mile swim to the nearest island.

Pete (2) A local prospector (portrayed by Lee White) who discovers some fresh gold ore in the Golden Eye Mine in *The Golden Eye* (1948). Through a trap door in his shack at the bottom of Hay Canyon, Pete finds one of the mine's passages. However, he is soon killed by Talbot Bartlett to keep him from talking to Charlie Chan about the gold that is now supposedly being produced at the mine.

Peters, Ralph (c. 1902–June 5, 1959, Hollywood, California) Moon-faced American character actor who appeared in almost 80 films, many of them westerns. Peters portrays Officer Rafferty in *Black Magic* (1944).

Peterson, Ruth Actress who portrays Renee Jacquard in *Charlie Chan in Paris* (1935).

Petrie, Miss Wife (portrayed by Janet Shaw in her second of two *Charlie Chan* roles) of convicted forger Jimmy Slade in *Dark Alibi* (1946). As one of several boarders living at the Foss Family Hotel, Miss Petrie is a typist of dubious abilities and works afternoons for a social agency, yet Charlie Chan notices that she wears expensive clothes. She is run down by a truck and killed outside the Carey Theatrical Warehouse.

Petroff Shady businessman and war profiteer (portrayed by Douglass Dumbrille in his first of three *Charlie Chan* roles) in *City in Darkness* (1939). Petroff collaborates with enemy agent Charlotte Ronnell in a plan to smuggle contraband munitions out of France aboard the *Medusa*. He has Belescu arrange the details for a commission of 100,000 francs for clearance papers that will declare the cargo as fruit.

That night Petroff's butler, Antoine, returns to Petroff's house from seeing his son Henri off to the army and overhears Petroff making plans to sell ammunition to France's enemies with forged clearance papers. Antoine takes the papers from Petroff's desk and then struggles with Petroff, killing him with a gunshot.

Phelps, Lee (1894–March 19, 1953, Culver City, California) Stage and screen character actor who appeared in over 160 films. In three unbilled *Charlie Chan* roles, Phelps portrays policemen in both *Murder Over New York* (1940) and *Dead Men Tell* (1941), and the police detective at airport Gate A in *The Sky Dragon* (1949).

Lee Phelps was a longtime resident of Culver City, California, the home of several film studios, including MGM and Hal Roach. Whenever the call went out for street extras, Phelps was always available. His Irish face and shiny pate can be easily spotted in such silent two-reelers as *Laurel and Hardy*'s film *Putting Pants on Philip* (1927). Phelps was active in films from 1921 through 1953, often in anonymous bit or atmosphere parts, usually playing a cop or a delivery man.

Phelps had appeared in two famous films of the early 1930s. He portrayed (unbilled) Steve, the cowering speakeasy owner slapped around by Jimmy Cagney in *The Public Enemy* (1931) and Larry, the waterfront waiter to whom Greta Garbo delivers her first talking-picture line ("Gif me a viskey, baby") in *Anna Christie* (1930).

Phelps, Warren T. Colby family lawyer and estate administrator (portrayed by Jonathan Hale, Jr., in his first of three *Charlie Chan* roles) in *Charlie Chan's Secret* (1936). Charlie

Chan discovers that Phelps recently had large losses in the stock market and would be financially hurt if Allen Colby is alive and Phelps could no longer be the paid administrator of Bernard Colby's estate.

Phillimore, Mrs. Sally The daughter (portrayed by Florence Turner) of a wealthy Hawaiian planter in *The Chinese Parrot* (1927). When she marries a man named Phillimore, her father gives her a priceless pearl necklace. Many years later, as the now widowed and financially strained Sally Jordan, she is forced to sell the necklace, which is eagerly bought by wealthy financier, P.J. Madden. In *Charlie Chan's Courage* (1934; a remake of *The Chinese Parrot*), the credits list the character as Mrs. Jordan, who is portrayed by Virginia Hammond.

Phillimore, Sally The daughter (portrayed by Marian Nixon in her first of two *Charlie Chan* roles) of Sally Phillimore in *The Chinese Parrot* (1927).

Phillips Geoffrey Richmond's butler (portrayed by Murray Kinnell in his third of four *Charlie Chan* roles) in *Charlie Chan in London* (1934). Phillips is the undercover alias for Capt. Seeton of British military intelligence who has been investigating Richmond for several years for stealing military secrets.

pier 52 New Orleans dock location of the *Presidente*, a steamer bound for South America, in *Docks of New Orleans* (1948). *See also* ***Presidente.***

pier 56 San Francisco dock location of Capt. Kong's ship, the *Shanghai Maid*, in *The Chinese Ring* (1947). *See also* ***Shanghai Maid.***

pier 178-210 New York dock location for the boat on which Charlie Chan and son Lee arrive from Europe in *Charlie Chan on Broadway* (1937).

Pierre The assistant (portrayed by Lon Chaney, Jr., in his second of two *Charlie Chan* appearances) to shady locksmith Louis Santelle in *City in Darkness* (1939). Charlie Chan visits Santelle's shop and notices that he has lots of equipment and supplies that could be used for purposes other than locksmithing. Pierre strangles Chan with a rope, rendering him unconscious, and then ties Chan up in a chair.

pigmy arrow The murder weapon in Paul Essex's novel *The Secret of the Pigmy Arrow* in *Charlie Chan at Treasure Island* (1939). Elmer Keiner tells Charlie Chan that the Temple of Magic has a pigmy bow and arrow with the statue of a Batwa tribe pigmy in the lobby, but the weapon is now missing.

Pindello, Joseph Safecracker (portrayed by Philip Van Zandt) and the brother of Tony Pindello in *The Shanghai Chest* (1948). Joseph himself was in prison when his brother Tony was executed in San Quentin's gas chamber. He escapes from prison six months later and, wanting to give his brother a proper burial, pays Mr. Grail, a shady undertaker, to have his brother's body secretly removed from a San Francisco city cemetery and reinterred elsewhere.

At the movie's conclusion, Pindello agrees to help Charlie Chan in a plan to extract the necessary confession from Ed Seward, the real murderer of three people and Tony Pindello's partner in the insurance swindles.

Pindello, Tony A criminal who was unsuccessfully defended by lawyer Ed Seward in a murder case that was tried before Judge Wesley Armstrong and prosecuted by District Attorney Frank Bronson in *The Shanghai Chest* (1948).

Seward and Tony Pindello were once partners in an insurance swindle. However, Seward becomes greedy and frames Pindello for murder. Pindello is found guilty and executed in San Quentin's gas chamber. When new evidence surfaces that might prove Tony Pindello was innocent, Seward then embarks on a plan to forge Pindello's fingerprints and successively murder Judge Armstrong, Frank Bronson, and Thomas Cartwright. Seward leaves Pindello's fingerprints at each murder scene, giving the uncanny impression that a man who died six months earlier is now responsible for three murders.

Place de Lafayette Albert Dufresne's apartment in *Charlie Chan in Paris* (1935). Yvette Lamartine goes to see Dufresne to retrieve some "silly old love letters" she had once written to him. When Dufresne is just about to give them to her, he is shot in the back by Max Corday (who's posing as the crippled beggar Marcel Xavier).

plutonium A radioactive, silvery metal that becomes yellowish when exposed to air. Its chemical symbol is Pu, and it is the 94th element in the periodic table. The name is derived from the planet Pluto. Plutonium is mentioned by Charlie Chan to Inspector Carvero as one of the elements discovered during the development of the atomic bomb in *The Red Dragon* (1945).

In 1940 Glenn T. Seaborg and his associates at the University of California–Berkeley created a plutonium isotope by bombarding uranium with deuterons in a cyclotron. Plutonium is very important because it is used as a fuel in nuclear fission (breeder) reactors and in nuclear weapons, such as the atomic bomb. Because the element is specifically absorbed by bone marrow in humans, and because it emits alpha particles at a high rate, plutonium is a highly dangerous radiological poison. For this reason, the possibility of plutonium contamination of water near nuclear power plants has caused public concern. *See also* **95th element**; **Seaborg, Glenn T.**

poison dart Murder weapon fired from a European air rifle used by Mr. Armstrong to kill Princess Mei Ling and her maid Lilly Mae Wong in *The Chinese Ring* (1947). It is also the murder weapon (made of bamboo) propelled from a hollow goose quill toothpick used by "Butcher" Degan in *Charlie Chan in the Wax Museum* (1940).

police With very few exceptions, there is always a local police officer assigned to the case Charlie Chan happens to be involved in. In most situations they are portrayed as being incompetent individuals, comedic foils, or resentful of an outsider. Apart from the two silent films, there are three entries in the series that have no outside policeman—*Castle in the Desert* (1942), *Dark Alibi* (1946), and *Dangerous Money* (1946).

Movie	**Police Officer(s)**
Behind That Curtain	Sir Frederic Bruce, Habib Hanna
Charlie Chan Carries On	Inspector Duff, Inspector Hanley
The Black Camel	unnamed Police Chief, Kashimo
Charlie Chan's Chance	Inspector Flannery, Inspector Fife
Charlie Chan's Greatest Case	Capt. Hallett
Charlie Chan's Courage	Constable Brackett, Capt. Bliss
Charlie Chan in London	Detective Sergeant Thacker
Charlie Chan in Paris	Inspector Renard
Charlie Chan in Egypt	Fuad Soueida
Charlie Chan in Shanghai	Col. Watkins
Charlie Chan's Secret	Inspector Morton
Charlie Chan at the Circus	Lt. Macy
Charlie Chan at the Race Track	unnamed Police Chief
Charlie Chan at the Opera	Inspector Regan, Sergeant Kelly
Charlie Chan at the Olympics	Chief Scott, Inspector Strasser
Charlie Chan on Broadway	Inspector Nelson
Charlie Chan in Monte Carlo	Inspector Jules Joubert
Charlie Chan in Honolulu	Inspector Rawlins
Charlie Chan in Reno	Chief King, Sheriff "Tombstone" Fletcher
Charlie Chan at Treasure Island	Deputy Chief J.J. Kilvaine
City in Darkness	J. Romaine, Marcel
Charlie Chan in Panama	Sergeant Montero
Charlie Chan's Murder Cruise	Inspector Duff, Wilkie
Charlie Chan at the Wax Museum	Inspector O'Matthews
Murder Over New York	Inspector Vance
Dead Men Tell	Inspector Vessey
Charlie Chan in Rio	Chief Souto
Charlie Chan in the Secret Service	Mr. Slade, Jones, Lewis, Sergeant Billings
The Chinese Cat	Detective Harvey Dennis
Murder at Midnight	Sergeant Matthews, Officer Rafferty
The Jade Mask	Inspector Godfrey, Sheriff Mack
The Scarlet Clue	Capt. Flynn, Sergeant McGraw

Movie	Police Officer(s)
The Shanghai Cobra	Inspector Harry Davis
The Red Dragon	Inspector Luis Carvero
Shadows Over Chinatown	Chief Brannigan, Capt. Allen, Jenkins
The Trap	Sergeant Reynolds
The Chinese Ring	Sergeant Bill Davidson
Docks of New Orleans	Capt. Pete McNalley, Sergeant Dansiger
The Shanghai Chest	Lt. Mike Ruark, Pat Finley
The Golden Eye	Lt. Mike Ruark
The Feathered Serpent	Capt. Juan Gonzalez, Pedro Lopez
The Sky Dragon	Lt. Mike Ruark, Stacey

Porcasi, Paul (1880, Palermo, Sicily–August 8, 1946, Hollywood, California) Bull-necked and wax-mustached stage and screen character actor who appeared in over 110 films and was noted for his portrayals of tough, cigar-puffing men of authority. Porcasi portrays Luxor police official Fuad Soueida in *Charlie Chan in Egypt* (1935).

A former opera singer in his native Sicily, Paul Porcasi made his screen bow in *Fall of the Romanoffs* (1917). He flourished in the talkie era, playing innumerable speakeasy owners, impresarios, chefs, and restaurateurs. The nationalities of his screen characters ranged from Italian to French to Greek to Spanish. Most often, however, he played Greeks with such monikers as Papapopolous.

Porcasi's best-remembered roles include Nick the Greek in *Broadway* (1929), obsequious garment merchant Hassan in *Devil in the Deep* (1932), stern border guard Gonzalez in Eddie Cantor's *The Kid from Spain* (1932), and the apple vendor in *King Kong* (1933). Porcasi also starred in the first three-strip Technicolor short subject, *La Cucaracha* (1934), wherein his face turned a deep crimson after he ingested one too many hot chili peppers.

Porkchop 711 Walkie-talkie recognition code for Chattanooga Brown in *Dangerous Money* (1946). Jimmy Chan's code is Chop Suey 108.

Pornick, Alf Cockney night porter at the Galt Building (portrayed by John Rogers in his first of four *Charlie Chan* roles) in *Behind That Curtain* (1929). One evening Pornick hears a gunshot from Hilary Galt's office and sees Eric Durand leaving the office after murdering Galt. When questioned by Sir Frederic Bruce of Scotland Yard, Pornick says that he did not see or hear anything. Pornick then blackmails Durand, who ultimately squanders his wife's wealth to pay Pornick. In return, Pornick openly flaunts his newly found affluence. When Durand's wife's money runs out, she leaves him. Durand then returns to London and murders Pornick.

portside Nickname for one who is left-handed. In *Charlie Chan in the Secret Service* (1944), Chan notices a Yale baseball team picture of George Melton with an inscription that addresses Melton as "portside."

Post, William, Jr. Actor who portrays Shelah Fane's would-be fiancé Alan Jaynes in *The Black Camel* (1931).

Potter, Pamela Granddaughter (portrayed by Marguerite Churchill) of the murdered Hugo Morris Drake in *Charlie Chan Carries On* (1931). She continues on Dr. Lofton's world tour to help track down the killer, and at the movie's end she and Mark Kennaway tell Charlie Chan of their plans to marry.

Powers, Phyllis Judge Wesley Armstrong's secretary (portrayed by Deannie Best) in *The Shanghai Chest* (1948).

Prentiss U.S. Embassy official (portrayed by Charles Trowbridge) in *The Red Dragon* (1945). Prentiss is warned by Walter Dorn about the attempted theft of his employer's research papers concerning an atomic bomb. Dorn demands that Prentiss request that Charlie Chan, a friend of Dorn's, come to Mexico City to investigate repeated attempts to steal Wyans' papers.

President Pierce The ship Charlie Chan sails on from Honolulu to San Francisco in *The Chinese Parrot* (1927).

Presidente A steamer docked at pier 52 and bound for South America carrying a cargo of poisonous gas manufactured by the Lafontaine Chemical Company in *Docks of New Orleans* (1948).

Preston, June Blonde actress (portrayed by Joan Valerie in her second of two *Charlie Chan* roles) in *Murder Over New York* (1940). Preston attends a party for Hugh Drake at the apartment of George Kirby before Drake is murdered.

When questioning all persons who are at the party, Charlie Chan notices that a lavaliere worn by Preston has a pearl missing from it. At first she tells Chan that she doesn't know where she may have lost it. Searching Kirby's library desk for clues about Drake's murder, Chan finds the missing pearl in the inkwell and concludes that Miss Preston must have been in the room earlier and seen Drake alive.

Chan goes to June Preston's apartment at the Roxbury House to return the pearl, which fits perfectly in the lavaliere. When confronted with information about where Chan found the pearl, Preston tells Chan that Drake was inquiring about a girl named Patricia West, who played in a show with her in London five years ago.

Princess Ming Lo Fu *see* **Fu, Princess Ming Lo.**

Priscilla Sheriff Fletcher's cat in *Charlie Chan in Reno* (1939).

"PRIVATE DETECTIVE HELD FOR MURDER" Newspaper headline of the *New York Dispatch* about the arrest of Ned Stewart for the murder of bank guard Samuel Black in *The Shanghai Cobra* (1945). The arrest and newspaper story is part of Charlie Chan's plan to find Pauline Webster who has disappeared after Black's murder.

Protzman, Albert Sound engineer for four *Charlie Chan* films: *Charlie Chan's Chance* (1932), *Charlie Chan in Egypt* (1935), *Charlie Chan in Shanghai* (1935), and *Charlie Chan's Secret* (1936).

pseudologia fantastica Name of psychological disease Charlie Chan characterizes Dr. Zodiac (a man of great ego) as suffering from in *Charlie Chan at Treasure Island* (1939). Quoting from the book *History of Psychiatry* by Kahne, Chan explains that pathological liars and swindlers suffer from exaggerated fantasy, unleashed vanity, and ambition which robs them of the caution known to saner men.

Puglia, Frank (March 9, 1892, Sicily, Italy–October 25, 1975, South Pasadena, California) Opera performer and stage and screen character actor who appeared in over 120 silent and sound films, often in roles of Middle Eastern ethnic types. Puglia portrays Achmed Halide in *Charlie Chan in Panama* (1940).

Frank Puglia started his career with a traveling operetta company at age 13. He and his family moved to the U.S. in 1907, where he worked in a laundry until he hooked up with an Italian-language theatrical troupe based in New York. In 1921 Puglia was appearing as Pierre Frochard in a revival of *The Two Orphans* when he was spotted by film director D.W. Griffith. Griffith hired him to repeat his role for Griffith's film version of the play, retitled *Orphans of the Storm*. For the rest of his long film career, Puglia portrayed a wide variety of ethnic supporting parts, playing priests, musicians, diplomats, and street peddlers.

In 1942's *Casablanca* Puglia had a memorable bit as a Moroccan rug merchant who automatically marks down his prices to any friend of Rick Blaine (Humphrey Bogart). Frank Puglia also played a larger but less likable role as Cassim, the treacherous slave to sultan Kurt Katch in *Ali Baba and the Forty Thieves* (1944). When the film was remade as *Sword of Ali Baba* in 1965, so much stock footage from the 1944 film was utilized that Puglia was hired to reprise his original part.

Punay, Rito Actor who portrayed Pete, the ship steward who jumps overboard, in *Dangerous Money* (1946).

Punchy Cellmate of Foggy in *Dark Alibi* (1946).

putrefied Word used by Mrs. Winters to explain to Charlie Chan why she didn't run into the hallway when Inez Arranto screamed (after seeing George Melton's body) in *Charlie Chan in the Secret Service* (1944). Mrs. Winters says, "At first I couldn't move. I was simply putrefied." Charlie questions if she really meant to use the word putrefied, thinking she really meant to say "petrified" instead.

Q

Quigley, Charles (February 12, 1906, New Britain, Connecticut–1964, Los Angeles, California) Stage and screen character actor who appeared in 30 films and who portrays Dick Williams in *Charlie Chan's Secret* (1936).

In films from 1933, handsome, curly-haired leading man Charles Quigley was signed by Columbia Pictures in 1937. There he was groomed as a leading man in the studio's "B"-picture product, appearing as Jimmy Jones in *Girls Can Play* (1937) and as Jim Quinn in *The Shadow* (1937)—opposite another young hopeful named Rita Hayworth. In the end, however, it was Rita who clicked with the public, and Quigley's option was dropped in 1938. He recovered somewhat with a starring role as Gene Townley in the Republic serial *Daredevils of the Red Circle* (1939) and gradually drifted into character roles. Out of films for nearly fifteen years, Charles Quigley died of cirrhosis.

Quigley, Rita (March 31, 1923, Los Angeles, California–) Character actress who portrayed Cole King's variety troupe member Clementine in *The Trap* (1947).

quinine sulfate An alkaloid drug (chemical formula: $C_{40}H_{50}N_4O_8S$) formed by the mixture of quinine and weak sulfuric acid. Quinine is obtained by extraction from the bark of the cinchona tree of South America and Indonesia. The drug was once the sole treatment for malaria, and was also used to allay fever and pain from other diseases and for heart arrhythmias. The alkaloid has fluorescent properties—it emits a blue glow when struck by ultraviolet light.

In *Charlie Chan's Secret* (1936), Charlie Chan uses a chlorine water reagent to determine that a quinine solution was put on the face of the murdered Allen Colby. The solution gives the effect of a glowing apparition when struck by a beam of ultra-violet light during a séance conducted by Professor Bowan and his assistant Carlotta. To find out who might have access to quinine, Charlie sneezes and pretends that he has just caught a bad cold. He asks Ulrich, the caretaker, if he might have some quinine sulfate and if he had given some to Professor Bowan when he also complained of having a cold. *See also* **chlorine water**.

Quon, Marianne Chinese actress who portrays Charlie Chan's Number Two daughter Iris in *Charlie Chan in the Secret Service* (1944).

Quotations from Charlie Chan A small paperback book compiled and edited by Harvey Chertok and Martha Torgue. Published in 1968 by Golden Press (New York), it is no longer in print.

The book contains many (but not all) of the pithy wise words of wisdom quoted in 21 films made by Fox and Twentieth Century–Fox, from *Charlie Chan in London* (1934) to *Castle in the Desert* (1942)—with the exception of *Charlie Chan in Paris* (1935), but includes none of the 17 Monogram films. The compilation is arranged by the editors into 36 categories—e.g., of truth, of superstition, of parents and children, of fortune, etc. *See also* **aphorisms**.

R

"RACE HORSE KILLS PROMINENT TURFMAN" Newspaper headline in the *Honolulu Standard* reporting the death of Major Kent aboard the S.S. *Oceanic* in *Charlie Chan at the Race Track* (1936).

Racine, Dr. Anton Luxor physician and Arnold family doctor (portrayed by Jameson Thomas) who is prescribing medication for

Carol Arnold's depression in *Charlie Chan in Egypt* (1935). When Professor Arnold's body is discovered inside Ahmeti's mummy case, Dr. Racine is called upon to perform the autopsy. Dr. Racine also has a financial interest in Professor Arnold's work as he has loaned Professor Arnold some money to finance his expedition.

radar Acronym for *radio detecting and ranging* (and is spelled the same way both forwards and backwards). Radar is an application of using beamed and reflected radio waves for the detection and location of objects as well as measuring distances, altitudes, and speed of moving objects.

In *The Scarlet Clue* (1945), the Hamilton Laboratory is engaged in secret radar and radio work for the U.S. government, and their inventions allow fighter planes at night to hunt down enemy planes without seeing them.

radium Radioactive metallic chemical element whose symbol is Ra; it is the 88th element in the periodic table. The name is derived from the Latin word *radius*, meaning "ray." At one time radium was extensively employed in the treatment of cancer and for testing metal castings in industrial radiography. Today its medical and technological uses have been supplanted by more readily accessible sources. Radium salts mixed with zinc sulfide form a paste that was once used in luminescent paints for watch and meter dials but has now been replaced by the element promethium (which emits less hazardous radiation).

In *The Shanghai Cobra* (1945), radium belonging to the U.S. government is stored in vault number 210 in the Sixth National Bank and is the target of a planned theft by a gang led by the bank's vice president, Bradford Harris.

Rafferty Bank guard at the Sixth National Bank who is one of three bank employees murdered with cobra venom in *The Shanghai Cobra* (1945).

Rafferty, Officer Policeman (portrayed by Ralph Peters) in *Black Magic* (1944). Rafferty's superior officer is Sgt. Matthews.

Ragin, Dave Cinematographer for *Behind That Curtain* (1929).

Raksin, David (August 4, 1912, Philadelphia, Pennsylvania–) Music conductor and composer who arranged the musical scores for stage, television, ballet, and nearly 60 films, including *Dead Men Tell* (1941). Rakin's best known song is perhaps the theme from *Laura* (1944), even though he was twice nominated for Academy Awards in the Best Music, Scoring of a Dramatic or Comedy Picture category—for *Forever Amber* (1947) and *Separate Tables* (1958).

Raleigh, Alan Alias Kenneth Dunwood (portrayed by James Todd) who is sought by Sir Lionel Grey for a murder in England, in *Charlie Chan's Chance* (1932). Now traced to America, Raleigh murders Grey with a poisonous gas in Barry Kirk's office.

Note: The character Alan Raleigh loosely parallels that of Paul Narvo, alias Keith Jeffrey, in *Murder Over New York* (1940).

Ramullah Paul Narvo's servant and sabotage ring confederate (portrayed by Lal Chand Mehra) in *Murder Over New York* (1940). When Charlie Chan and Inspector Vance look through Hugh Drake's briefcase, they read a Scotland Yard Criminal Identification Bureau report that lists Ramullah as using the aliases Rewa Singh, Rayadrolu Khan, and Gunga Subba.

Narvo's estranged wife, Patricia West, tells Chan that one day she overheard Narvo and Ramullah talking about the murder of a British Air Ministry official, and she feared that both of them were part of a sabotage ring. Now in New York, Ramullah poses as Aga Singh, a dealer in East Indian curios. Following a lineup at the police station, West identifies Singh as Ramullah. Ramullah then tries to escape but is shot in the back by Narvo firing from the window of an adjacent building.

Chan and son Jimmy then search Ramullah's curio shop and find a small chemical laboratory for the creation of tetrogene, a poisonous gas. There they also find stolen plans for the TR-4 bomber which is scheduled to undergo a test flight the next day at the Metropolitan Aircraft Company.

Note: The character Ramullah loosely parallels that of Li Gung in *Charlie Chan's Chance* (1932).

Rand, Willie Radio and television actor at the Cosmo Radio Center (portrayed by Jack Norton in his second of three *Charlie Chan* roles) in *The Scarlet Clue* (1945). Rand is murdered during a television performance by Mrs. Marsh after inhaling a gas from a radio actuated gas pellet hidden inside flowers and then smoking a cigarette, the combination of which produces a deadly poison.

Randolph, George Captain Johnson's chief officer on the *Susan B. Jennings* (portrayed by John "Dusty" King) in *Charlie Chan in Honolulu* (1938).

Randolph Apartments Residence of Mary McCoy (Apartment 36) in *Shadows Over Chinatown* (1946).

Ransome, Kate Typist (portrayed by Sheila Ryan) who is a friend of Steve Daniels and is a passenger on the *Suva Star* during the Cocos Island treasure hunt in *Dead Men Tell* (1941). Kate faints after seeing in a magazine a picture of an escaped murderer who is posing as fellow passenger Bill Lydig. After she faints, Lydig puts her inside the iron maiden in the ship's hold.

Raquello, Edward (1899–1976) Actor who portrays Paul Savarin in *Charlie Chan at Monte Carlo* (1937). Savarin loses 50,000 francs to business rival Victor Karnoff in a high-stakes game of chemin de fer at the casino.

Rausch Foreign agent trying to steal radar secrets from the U.S. government, and murdered by Ralph Brett, in *The Scarlet Clue* (1945).

Rawlins, Inspector Charlie Chan's police chief (portrayed by Paul Harvey in his second of two *Charlie Chan* roles) in *Charlie Chan in Honolulu* (1938).

Ray, Albert (August 28, 1883, New Rochelle, New York–February 5, 1944, Los Angeles, California) Film actor, director, producer, and screenwriter for *Charlie Chan in Reno* (1939).

Ray, Bobby Assistant director for *Black Magic* (1944).

***The Red Dragon* (1945)** The seventh *Charlie Chan* film produced by Monogram Pictures Corporation.

Alternate Title: *Charlie Chan in the Red Dragon*. Working Title: *Charlie Chan in Mexico*. Source: based on the character "Charlie Chan" created by Earl Derr Biggers. Original Copyright: Monogram Pictures Corporation, December 22, 1945; LP74. Copyright Renewed: July 17, 1973; R555467. PCA Certificate Number: 11289. Production: early to late September, 1945. Release Date: February 2, 1946. Sound: Western Electric Mirrophonic Recording. Film: b&w. Running Time: 64 minutes.

Producer: James S. Burkett. Director: Phil Rosen. Assistant Director: Eddie Davis. Original Screenplay: George Callahan. Director of Photography: Vincent Farrar. Special Effects: Robert Clark. Technical Director: Dave Milton. Editor: Ace Herman. Musical Director: Edward J. Kay. Sound Recording: Tom Lambert. Production Manager: Glenn Cook.

Cast

Sidney Toler	*as*	Charlie Chan
Fortunio Bonanova		Inspector Luis Carvero
Benson Fong		Tommy Chan
Robert E. Keane		Alfred Wyans
Willie Best		Chattanooga Brown
Carol Hughes		Marguerite Fontan
Marjorie Hoshelle		Countess Irena
Barton Yarborough		Joseph Bradish
George Meeker		Edmund Slade
Don Costello		Charles Masack
Charles Trowbridge		Prentiss
Mildred Boyd		Josephine
Jean Wong		Iris Ling
Donald Dexter Taylor		Walter Dorn
Lucio Villegas*		Chemist
Toni Raimondo*		Woman in powder room
Richard Lopez*		Bellboy
Augie Gomez*		Taxi driver

**Unbilled.*

Plot Summary: In Mexico City an attempt is made to steal the papers of the mysterious Alfred Wyans. His secretary, Walter Dorn, who is working undercover with the United States government, begs Prentiss at the U.S. embassy to send for Charlie Chan. The next day Dorn is shot during a luncheon party at Wyans' apartment, but before he dies he manages to type the cryptic letters TH E$M OST on his typewriter.

After Chan, an old friend of Inspector Luis Carvero, arrives (accompanied by his son Tommy and his chauffeur Chattanooga Brown), Carvero tells him that no gun was found at the scene of the murder and that although the guests only heard one shot, two bullet holes are discovered. Chan tells Carvero that Wyans' papers reveal the discovery of a new 95th element that could be used in a bomb many times more powerful than the atomic bomb. Suspecting that one of the party guests is the murderer, Chan questions each in turn: Marguerite Fontan, with whom Luis is in love; Edmund Slade, a former gunrunner; Joseph Bradish, an international smuggler; the Countess Irena, a singer; and Charles Masack, a Nazi propagandist. Chan then accompanies Inspector Carvero to the police lab and learns that the bullet that killed Dorn has no firing marks, indicating that it was not fired from a gun. Wyans complains to the police that his typewriter has been stolen and Chan warns him to protect his papers.

Later, Chan discloses that Marguerite Fontan has connections in Czechoslovakia, the country from which the papers were stolen from the Allies by Wyans. While all the suspects are at dinner, Chan and Carvero search Wyans' baggage in a basement storeroom but are interrupted by others who have the same idea. After the suspects leave, Chan and Carvero discover the missing typewriter there.

Wyans tells Carvero that he knows how Dorn was killed, but before he can reveal the answer, he is shot in the same manner as Dorn. At the nightclub where Irena sings, Chan reveals that her "Countess" title is not one of nobility, and she is married to Charles Masack who spies for several countries. When confronted with this information, Irena starts to reveal the secret, but she too is killed by the same method. Later, an attempt is made on Chan's life in a similar manner.

Chan is puzzled why a bottle of indelible "Red Dragon" brand Chinese red ink was found on Dorn's desk. Inspector Carvero eventually locates a Chinese artist, Iris Ling, who had visited Wyans' hotel before Dorn's death. Iris tells Chan that she sold Wyans the ink to use on his *banderillas*, which Chan eventually figures out are actually the typewriter ribbons. Going back to Wyans apartment, Chan and Carvero examine the ribbon that Dorn removed from the typewriter before he was killed and find the secret information written upon it in indelible ink.

Chan then clears Marguerite of suspicion when he discloses that her uncle, Joseph Fontan, had discovered the secret 95th element. He then explains that Bradish committed the murders to acquire the information using a remote control device disguised as a thermostat that exploded the bullet that he had earlier slipped into his victims' pockets or purses.

Note: Jon Tuska, in his book *The Detective in Hollywood*, notes that although *The Red Dragon* is set in Mexico City, the neon signs of the nightclubs seen in the film are actually those of Los Angeles nightspots.

Red Dragon Chinese Ink Rare, indelible ink brand sold by artist Iris Ling to Alfred Wyans to write his secret research papers on a typewriter ribbon in *The Red Dragon* (1945). *See also* ***banderilla***.

Red Hornet One of two working titles for *The Chinese Ring* (1947) before its release on December 6, 1947. *See also* ***The Chinese Ring* (1947)**.

Redfordshire Geoffrey Richmond's country house where Capt. Hamilton is murdered, in *Charlie Chan in London* (1934).

Redley, Mr. Stella Essex's uncle (portrayed by Charles Halton) who handles Paul Essex's business affairs in *Charlie Chan at Treasure Island* (1939).

Rednick, Dr. Paul Noted criminologist (portrayed by Ian Keith) who wrote *Murder by Madame*, an account of the Thomas Manning murder, in *The Chinese Cat* (1944). Charlie Chan tells Dr. Rednick that the book explains everything so easily except what happened to the murder weapon. Rednick replies that if his book is wrong, then the murder can't be solved.

Rednick bets $2,000 at 10-to-1 odds that Chan cannot solve Thomas Manning's murder. Charlie accepts the bet (witnessed by Harvey Dennis), telling Rednick that if he loses he will donate $2,000 to the Chinese War Relief; otherwise, Rednick has to give $20,000 to the same cause. Even though Charlie is not a betting man, he mentions that 10-to-1 odds are too good to pass up.

Reef & Palm Hotel Honolulu hotel where both James Eagan and T.M. Brade stay in *Charlie Chan's Greatest Case* (1933). Chan finds Amos Winterslip's dead body on the grounds of the hotel.

Reeves, George (January 5, 1914, Woolstock, Iowa–June 16, 1959, Beverly Hills, California) American stage and screen leading man (real names: born George Keefer Brewer; later George Bessolo when adopted) who appeared in nearly 75 films. Reeves portrays escaped murderer Bill Lydig in *Dead Men Tell* (1941).

George Reeves was born as George Keefer Brewer, but when he was adopted by his stepfather he took the name of George Bessolo. He was raised in Pasadena, California, and educated at Pasadena Junior College. In his youth, Reeves was a musician and aspired to become a boxer, but he gave up this pursuit because his mother was worried that he would be seriously injured.

Attracted to acting, Reeves was an intern at the Pasadena Community Playhouse where he starred in several productions. It was there Reeves was discovered, having now changed his name to George Reeves, and he was selected to play Stuart Tarleton in *Gone with the Wind* (1939). He made an excellent impression in the role and spent the next few years playing roles of varying sizes at Warner Bros., Twentieth Century–Fox, and Paramount.

His career was interrupted by military service in Word War II with the Army Air Corps, for which he made training films. Upon his return to civilian life, however, Reeves found it difficult to gain good roles. He subsequently starred in a few "B" pictures and played the title role in Columbia's *The Adventures of Sir Galahad* (1949), but for the most part was shunted away in ordinary villain roles. In 1951 he starred in *Superman vs. the Mole Men*, playing both the "Man of Steel" and his bespectacled alter ego, Clark Kent.

Career difficulties after the war led to his moving to New York for live television. This led to the immensely popular *Superman* television series, in which Reeves starred from 1953 through 1957. While the Superman series saved Reeves' career, it also permanently typecast him. A chance for a film comeback as Sergeant Maylon Stark in *From Here to Eternity*

George Reeves in his famous role as Superman.

(1953) was scuttled after a preview audience laughed and yelled "There's Superman" when Reeves made his first appearance. In the final release print Reeves appears only fleetingly and without screen credit.

Reeves was unable to get work after the cancellation of *Superman* in 1957, and on June 16, 1959, Reeves died of an apparently self-inflicted gunshot wound. The official ruling was suicide and, since he left no note, it was assumed that Reeves was despondent over his flagging career. Since that time, however, there has been a mounting suspicion, raised by his friends and family, that he was murdered.

Regan, Inspector Los Angeles police chief (portrayed by Guy Usher in his second of two *Charlie Chan* roles) in *Charlie Chan at the Opera* (1936).

Reicher, Frank (December 2, 1875, Munich, Germany–January 19, 1965, Playa del Rey, California) Veteran stage and screen character actor, sometimes credited as Frank Reichert, who appeared in over 170 films after a career as a writer and film director of over 40 silents. In two *Charlie Chan* roles, Reicher portrays Dr. Jaipur in *Charlie Chan in Egypt* (1935) and Mr. Harper in *The Jade Mask* (1945).

Launching his theatrical career in his native Germany, actor-director Frank Reicher worked in London before coming to America in 1899. His entry into the movies was as co-director of the 1915 production, *The Clue*. He continued to direct in Hollywood before returning to the stage in 1921. At the dawn of the talkie era, Reicher was brought back to California to direct German-language versions of American films.

For his first talkie acting role, Reicher was cast in the title role of *Napoleon's Barber* (1928), a Fox Movietone two-reeler which represented the first talkie for director John Ford. At this time, Reicher specialized in humorless authority figures such as college professors, doctors, scientists, and cabinet ministers. In 1933 he was cast as Captain Engelhorn in the classic adventure movie, *King Kong*.

The remainder of Reicher's film career was devoted to brief character roles, often as murder victims. He was killed off at least twice by Boris Karloff (*Invisible Ray* [1936] and *House of Frankenstein* [1944]), and was strangled by Lon Chaney, Jr., at the very beginning of *The Mummy's Ghost* (1944). During the war, Reicher's Germanic name and bearing came in handy for the many anti–Nazi films of the era, notably *To Be or Not to Be* (1942) and *Mission to Moscow* (1944).

Reiner Master spy and saboteur who is a member of the secret police who arrested and killed Kathi Lenesch's father and brother in *Charlie Chan in Panama* (1940). Reiner is now in Panama posing as Miss Jennie Finch, a maiden Chicago schoolteacher, and intends to blow up a section of the Panama Canal while a fleet of U.S. naval ships is passing through it. To prevent her confederate Manolo from being captured while escaping, she kills him.

Reiner, Maxine Actress who portrays trapeze performer Marie Norman in *Charlie Chan at the Circus* (1936).

release dates Release dates for the *Charlie Chan* films are assumed to be national release dates as determined from studio records, release charts, or the *American Film Institute Catalog of Motion Pictures Produced in the United States*. When there is a doubt, the copyright date is given as the release date.

Movie	Release Date
The House Without a Key (serialized)	
1. The Spite Fence	October 1, 1926
2. The Mystery Box	October 1, 1926
3. The Missing Numeral	October 8, 1926
4. Suspicion	December 2, 1926
5. The Death Buoy	December 5, 1926
6. Sinister Shadows	December 14, 1926
7. The Mystery Man	December 18, 1926
8. The Spotted Menace	December 24, 1926
9. The Wrist Watch	December 27, 1926
10. The Culprit	December 29, 1926
The Chinese Parrot	August 24, 1927
Behind That Curtain	June 28, 1929
Charlie Chan Carries On	April 12, 1931
The Black Camel	June 7, 1931
Charlie Chan's Chance	January 24, 1932

Movie	Release Date
Charlie Chan's Greatest Case	September 15, 1933
Charlie Chan's Courage	July 6, 1934
Charlie Chan in London	September 12, 1934
Charlie Chan in Paris	January 21, 1935
Charlie Chan in Egypt	June 21, 1935
Charlie Chan in Shanghai	October 11, 1935
Charlie Chan's Secret	January 10, 1936
Charlie Chan at the Circus	March 18, 1936
Charlie Chan at the Race Track	August 7, 1936
Charlie Chan at the Opera	December 4, 1936 and January 8, 1937
Charlie Chan at the Olympics	May 21, 1937
Charlie Chan on Broadway	September 18, 1937
Charlie Chan in Monte Carlo	December 17, 1937
Charlie Chan in Honolulu	January 13, 1939
Charlie Chan in Reno	June 16, 1939
Charlie Chan at Treasure Island	September 8, 1939
City in Darkness	December 1, 1939
Charlie Chan in Panama	March 8, 1940
Charlie Chan's Murder Cruise	June 21, 1940
Charlie Chan at the Wax Museum	September 6, 1940
Murder Over New York	December 13, 1940
Dead Men Tell	March 28, 1941
Charlie Chan in Rio	September 5, 1941
Castle in the Desert	February 27, 1942
Charlie Chan in the Secret Service	February 14, 1944
The Chinese Cat	May 20, 1944
Black Magic	September 9, 1944
The Jade Mask	January 26, 1945
The Scarlet Clue	May 11, 1945
The Shanghai Cobra	September 29, 1945
The Red Dragon	February 2, 1946
Dark Alibi	May 25, 1946
Shadows Over Chinatown	July 27, 1946
Dangerous Money	October 12, 1946
The Trap	November 30, 1946
The Chinese Ring	December 6, 1947
Docks of New Orleans	March 21, 1948
The Shanghai Chest	July 11, 1948
The Golden Eye	August 29, 1948
The Feathered Serpent	January 8, 1949
The Sky Dragon	May 1, 1949

Renard, Inspector Parisian policeman (portrayed by Minor Watson) and an old friend of Charlie Chan in *Charlie Chan in Paris* (1935). Renard is called in to investigate the murders of Nardi and Albert Dufresne.

Renault Murdered bank messenger (portrayed by Georges Renavent) who carries $1 million in metallurgic bonds belonging to Victor Karnoff to Paris for sale in *Charlie Chan at Monte Carlo* (1937).

Renavent, Georges (April 23, 1894, Paris, France–January 2, 1969, Guadalajara, Mexico) Stage and screen actor, sometimes credited as Georges de Cheux, who portrays Renault, the murdered bank messenger who is carrying $1 million in metallurgic bonds belonging to Victor Karnoff to Paris for sale in *Charlie Chan at Monte Carlo* (1937).

René The niece (portrayed by Virginia Dale) of Simon Lafontaine (who is also her guardian) in *Docks of New Orleans* (1948). From her father, René inherited a one-fourth interest in the Lafontaine Chemical Company where she works as her uncle's secretary.

When Oscar Swendstrom comes to the office and threatens her uncle with a gun for having tricked him when buying his formula for a poisonous gas, René telephones her boyfriend, Capt. Pete McNalley, to come over. When McNalley arrives, however, they find Lafontaine dead in his office.

Reno Western Nevada resort city that is the location setting for *Charlie Chan in Reno* (1939). Reno usually calls itself the "Best Little City in the World."

"REPORT MADMAN IN LOS ANGELES" Newspaper headline of the *Los Angeles Star* about Gravelle in *Charlie Chan at the Opera* (1936).

Retling, Dr. Manderley family physician (portrayed by Steven Geray) in *Castle in the Desert* (1942). Paul Manderley bribes Dr. Retling and lawyer Walter Hartford to quietly take Professor Gleason's body to the Mojave Wells Hotel in the town closest to the castle and make it look as if he died there of a heart attack. Retling, Hartford, and Hartford's wife, Brenda, hire Gleason to pretend to have been poisoned by Manderley's wife, Lucy, to convince Manderley that Lucy is insane and induce him to turn the control of a $20 million estate over to Walter Hartford via power of attorney, and then leave quietly with his wife.

Revier, Dorothy (April 18, 1904, San Francisco, California–November 19, 1993, Hollywood, California) American leading lady (real name: Doris Velegra) of the silent screen, usually appearing as a vamp. She portrays the movie actress Shelah Fane, who murdered actor Denny Mayo three years earlier, in *The Black Camel* (1931).

The daughter of a musician, Dorothy Revier worked as a chorus girl and nightclub dancer before making her film debut as Dorothy Cumberland in *Life's Greatest Question* (1921). The following year she portrayed Vivian Collins in *Broadway Madonna*, which was directed by her first husband, Harry Revier. In 1925 she was chosen by the Western Association of Motion Picture Advertisers as a "WAMPAS Baby Star."

Never a major star, Dorothy Revier nevertheless was a dependable, hard-working leading lady, averaging seven to ten movie appearances per year during the silent era. Perhaps her most celebrated role was Milady de Winter in Douglas Fairbanks' *The Iron Mask* (1929), one of her many vamp or evil-seductress roles.

In making a successful transition to talkies, Revier kept busy at Fox and Universal, continuing in the femme-fatale mode that had earned her fame. By the mid–1930s she was consigned almost exclusively to "B" pictures, earning the far-from-coveted title, "Queen of Poverty Row." After finishing a 1936 Buck Jones western, *The Cowboy and the Kid* (1936), Dorothy Revier retired from films.

Reynolds, Harry Film editor of 35 movies, including three *Charlie Chan* films at Twentieth Century–Fox: *City in Darkness* (1939), *Charlie Chan's Murder Cruise* (1940), and *Dead Men Tell* (1941).

Reynolds, Joan Ken Reynolds' jealous wife (portrayed by Mary Beth Hughes) in *Charlie Chan in Rio* (1941). Joan's husband is the former boyfriend of Lola Dean, and Joan accuses Grace Ellis of Lola Dean's murder, saying, "Put her under a hot light and give her the third degree; she'll talk." When Charlie Chan asks how is she familiar with American police methods, she reveals that she was once married to a cop.

Reynolds, Ken Joan Reynolds' husband (portrayed by Richard Derr) in *Charlie Chan in Rio* (1941). Reynolds is the former boyfriend of Lola Dean.

Reynolds, Sgt. California state policeman (portrayed by Kirk Alyn) who is called in to investigate the murder of Lois in *The Trap* (1947).

Rhadini, Fred Magician and murderer (portrayed by Cesar Romero) who operates the Temple of Magic theater on Treasure Island in *Charlie Chan at Treasure Island* (1939). Rhadini masquerades as the mysterious psychic Dr. Zodiac, who blackmails his clients (some of whom have committed suicide). When Charlie Chan suggests that Rhadini issue a public challenge to Dr. Zodiac, Rhadini has his servant Abdul pose as Dr. Zodiac and then murders Abdul to fool the police into believing that Dr. Zodiac is now dead.

Rhadini, Myra Jealous wife (portrayed by June Gale) of magician Fred Rhadini and former vaudeville knife thrower in *Charlie Chan at Treasure Island* (1939).

"RHADINI CHALLENGES DR. ZODIAC TO TEST" Newspaper headline of the *San Francisco Union Telegraph* about Charlie Chan's plan to use Zodiac's vanity to trap him in *Charlie Chan at Treasure Island* (1939).

Rhodes, Erik (February 10, 1906, El Reno, Oklahoma–February 17, 1990, Oklahoma City, Oklahoma) Comic stage and film actor (real name: Ernest Sharpe) who appeared in nearly 25 films and portrays Max Corday in *Charlie Chan in Paris* (1935).

Erik Rhodes made his film debut as the genial Rodolfo Tonetti in the Astaire-Rogers musical, *Gay Divorcee* (1934), and had appeared two years earlier in the Broadway version. Rhodes portrayed virtually the same

Erik Rhodes (Everett Collection)

part, but as Alberto Beddini, in another Astaire-Rogers musical, *Top Hat* (1935), after which he settled into a short film career, playing mostly gigolos and sharpers. He left films in favor of stage work in 1939, working without interruption (except for wartime service in the Army Air Force) until his retirement in the early 1970s.

Rice Lola Dean's butler (portrayed by Leslie Dennison [billed as Leslie Denison] in his first of three *Charlie Chan* roles) in *Charlie Chan in Rio* (1941). Rice knows that Helen Ashby has just killed Lola, and, to keep him quiet, Ashby gives Rice money and jewels from Dean's bedroom wall safe. When Rice is captured by Jimmy Chan after he is found rummaging through a room and is about to be questioned by Charlie Chan, Ashby suddenly turns off the lights and shoots Rice dead to keep him from exposing her as Lola Dean's murderer.

Richards, Addison (October 20, 1887, Zanesville, Ohio–March 22, 1964, Los Angeles, California) Stage and screen character actor (real name: Addison Whitaker Richards, Jr.) who appeared in over 210 films, often in roles as distinguished authority figures. In two *Charlie Chan* roles, Richards portrayed British agent R.J. Godley in *Charlie Chan in Panama* (1940) and bank guard John Adams, the alias of Jan Van Horn, in *The Shanghai Cobra* (1945).

An alumnus of both Washington State University and Pomona College, Addison Richards began acting as an amateur in California's Pilgrimage Play, and later became associate director of the Pasadena Playhouse. In films from 1933, Richards was one of those dependable, distinguished character players perfectly capable of alternating between respectable authority figures and dark-purposed villains.

On television, Richards was a regular on four series. He was both the narrator and "The Colonel" on *Pentagon USA* (1953), wealthy westerner Martin Kingsley on *Cimarron City* (1958), Dr. Gamble on the video version of radio's *Fibber McGee and Molly* (1959), and elderly attorney John Abbott on the short-lived soap opera *Ben Jerrod* (1963). Richards also appeared in several episodes of *Perry Mason*, *Wanted: Dead or Alive*, and *You Are There*.

Richmond, Geoffrey Alias used by Paul Frank (portrayed by Alan Mowbray), who poses as a wealthy British landowner and who has been under investigation for years by British military intelligence, in *Charlie Chan in London* (1934). Richmond is engaged to Lady Mary Bristol and murders Capt. Hamilton to steal Hamilton's secret plans for an ingenious method to silence war planes. Richmond later murders Lake, his stud groom, and tries to murder Lady Mary because they both knew or suspected that he was involved in framing Paul Gray for Hamilton's murder.

Richmond, Kane (December 23, 1906, Minneapolis, Minnesota–March 22, 1973) American character actor (real name: Frederick W. Bowditch) who appeared in over 70 films. In three *Charlie Chan* roles, Richmond portrays Curtis Whitman in *Charlie Chan in Reno* (1939), Ralph Percy in *Murder Over New York* (1940), and Richard Cabot in *Charlie Chan in Panama* (1940).

Kane Richmond was gainfully employed as a state's-rights film booker when he was invited to appear in films. Richmond's first acting assignment was in Universal's *The Leather Pushers*, a long-running series of boxing two-reelers. Richmond spent the first half of the 1930s playing bits in big-studio films and heroes in basement-budgeted serials like Krellberg's *The Lost Jungle* (1935). In the latter part of the decade he co-starred with juvenile actor Frankie Darro in a series of action films produced at Ambassador and Monogram.

By the 1940s Richmond was firmly established as a serial leading man at Republic. Many probably consider Richmond's dual role of Alan Armstrong (the Spy Smasher) and Jack (his twin brother) in *Spy Smasher* (1942) as his best. Richmond retired from films in 1948 and went on to make a fortune in the fashion business.

The Riders of the Whistling Skull A 1937 film by Republic Pictures whose original story was from a novel written by William Colt MacDonald. The screenplay was written by Oliver Drake and was later reworked by Drake at Monogram as the *Charlie Chan* film *The Feathered Serpent* (1948).

Riders stars Robert Livingston as Stony Brooke, one member of The Three Mesquiteers who accompany an archeological expedition to Lukachuke, a lost Indian city of gold. Livingston also appeared in the *Charlie Chan* remake as Professor John Stanley.

rifling marks Marks that are left on a bullet fired by a gun having spiral grooves cut into the inner surface of the barrel to make the bullet spin when fired. In *The Red Dragon* (1945), forensic examination of the bullets that murdered Walter Dorn and Alfred Wyans show no rifling marks. The police lab technician, Charlie Chan, and Inspector Carvero are then at a loss to explain how a bullet could have been fired without a gun.

Rio de Janeiro Cosmopolitan Brazilian city (whose name means "River of January") which is the location setting for *Charlie Chan in Rio* (1941). Rio, as it is frequently called, is Brazil's second-largest city and was the country's capital from 1822 until 1960.

Rita Female confederate (portrayed by Mary Moore) of H.R. Jarvis who tends the counter of a laundry that hides a hidden entrance to the sewer system leading to the Sixth National Bank in *The Shanghai Cobra* (1945).

Robards, Jason, Sr. (December 31, 1892, Hillsdale, Michigan–April 4, 1963, Sherman Oaks, California) Leading man (real name: Jason Nelson Robards) and character actor of stage and film who appeared in over 120 silent and sound films. Robards portrays Walter Honeywood in *Charlie Chan Carries On* (1931).

Jason Robards studied theater at the American Academy of Dramatic Arts. After establishing himself on the American stage, he began appearing in silents, beginning with his role as Frank Thompson in *The Gilded Lily* (1921). He starred in a number of silents, often as a clean-living rural hero, but in the sound era he began playing character roles, almost always as an arch villain. He was the father of actor Jason Robards, with whom he appeared on Broadway in 1958 in *The Disenchanted.*

Roberts, Mickey Alias used by Mike Rogan in *Shadows Over Chinatown* (1946). Mary Conover knew Rogan as Mike Roberts when she once worked at the Bay City Escort Bureau. There Roberts often annoyed Conover and suggested that it was possible for her to become a wealthy widow. *See also* **Rogan, Mike.**

Roberts, Mike Alias used by Mike Rogan in *Shadows Over Chinatown* (1946). *See also* **Rogan, Mike.**

Roberts, Thayer Actor who portrays the shady Capt. James J. Kelso in *The Chinese Ring* (1947).

Robinson, Dewey (1898, New Haven, Connecticut–December 11, 1950, Las Vegas, Nevada) Barrel-chested stage and screen character actor who appeared in over 120 films and portrays the gangster Salos in *The Chinese Cat* (1944).

Dewey Robinson was much in demand during the gangster cycle of the early 1930s, as few actors could convey muscular menace and mental emptiness as quickly and as well as he did. Although most of his roles were unbilled bits, he was given extended screen time as the polo-playing mobster Butch Zanwutoski in Edward G. Robinson's *Little Giant* (1933), as a bored slave master seen in the outrageously erotic "No More Love" number in Eddie Cantor's *Roman Scandals* (1933), and as a plug-ugly ward heeler at odds with beauty contest judge Ben Turpin in the slapstick two-reeler *Keystone Hotel* (1935). Shortly before his death in 1950, Dewey Robinson had a lengthy (but unbilled) role in *The Jackie Robinson Story* as a Brooklyn baseball fan who slowly changes from a brainless bigot to Jackie's most outgoing supporter.

Robot Murder Working title for *The Scarlet Clue* (1945) before its release on May 11, 1945. *See also* ***The Scarlet Clue* (1946)**.

Rochelle, Kitty The daughter (portrayed by Charlotte Henry) of opera stars Gravelle and Mme. Lilly Rochelle in *Charlie Chan at the Opera* (1936). Kitty attempts to see her mother for permission to marry Phil Childers because she is not of legal age and was told that her father was killed in an opera house fire years ago. As a child Kitty was sent away to boarding schools, since her mother would not publicly acknowledge that she had been previously married and had a child (feeling that if the truth were known it would be an embarrassment to her career as an opera star).

Rochelle, Madame Lilli Star soprano (portrayed by Margaret Irving) and head of the San Marco Opera Company in *Charlie Chan at the Opera* (1936). Lilli was once married to opera star Gravelle, with whom she had a child, Kitty. During a fire at a Chicago opera house, she and her lover, Enrico Barelli, had locked Gravelle in his dressing room and left him for dead. After the fire Kitty Rochelle was sent off to boarding schools and was never publicly acknowledged by her mother because it could hurt her opera career. Lilli has since married Mr. Whitely, whom she never told of her previous marriage to Gravelle and the birth of a child.

Prior to the opening night performance of the opera *Carnival* in Los Angeles, Mme. Rochelle receives a death threat and requests that both the police and Charlie Chan provide protection during the performance. During the performance, Madame Lilli faints at the end of a scene when she realizes that it is her former husband, Gravelle, who is performing as Mephisto instead of Barelli. After she is taken unconscious to her dressing room and momentarily left alone, Mme. Rochelle is murdered by Mme. Anita Barelli, who earlier had murdered her husband.

Rocke, Joe Innocent man who was hanged for a crime he did not commit (based on the testimony of scientific criminologist Dr. Otto von Brom) in *Charlie Chan at the Wax Museum* (1940). Rocke and criminals "Butcher" Degan and Steve McBirney were once partners in an honest business venture. However, Degan framed Rocke for murder in order to gain control of the business.

Rocke, Mrs. Joe Joe Rocke's widow (portrayed by Hilda Vaughn) in *Charlie Chan at the Wax Museum* (1940).

Rockland State Sanitarium Mental institution where Gravelle is confined (suffering from amnesia after being intentionally locked in his dressing room by Mme. Lilli Rochelle and Enrico Barelli during a Chicago opera house fire) in *Charlie Chan at the Opera* (1936). Gravelle escapes from the sanitarium by overpowering an attendant and donning his clothes after seeing an article and picture in a newspaper about an upcoming opera performance in Los Angeles that has triggered his memory of the events just prior to the fire.

Rodin Bank Bank that Stanley Gray is convicted of robbing in *Dark Alibi* (1946). Gray, an ex-convict, is framed by an elaborate scheme whereby his forged fingerprints are left at the crime scene. *See also* **Gray, Stanley**.

Rogan, Mike Real name of a gangster (portrayed by Paul Bryar in his first of two *Charlie Chan* roles) in *Shadows Over Chinatown* (1946). From police records Chan learns that Rogan has used the names Mickey Roberts, Marty Roman, and Mike Roberts as aliases. Rogan is involved in the torso murders and insurance fraud with Jeff Hay, who later kills Rogan before he can be captured by the police.

Rogers, Albert The 35-year-old, Chicago-born former vaudeville dancer (portrayed by George Lynn) who is a bartender at the Hotel Imperial in *Charlie Chan at Monte Carlo* (1937). Rogers blackmails his supposed ex-wife, Joan Karnoff, and acquires $25,000 in bonds from her current husband's safe. He is later murdered by his ex–brother-in-law Gordon Chase.

Rogers, Bruce Portrayed by Thomas Beck in his third of four *Charlie Chan* roles, the secretary to the late Major Kent and fiancée of Alice Fenton in *Charlie Chan at the Race Track* (1936). When Major Kent is killed, Rogers then becomes the secretary to Kent's son-in-law, George Chester.

Rogers, Jean (March 25, 1916, Belmont, Massachusetts–February 24, 1991, Sherman Oaks, California) Blonde, wide-eyed, light leading lady (real name: Eleanor Lovegren) who appeared in over 45 films. Rogers portrays Kathi Lenesch in *Charlie Chan in Panama* (1940) and was originally cast as Laura Thursday in *Dead Men Tell* (1941) but was replaced (by Katharine Aldridge) after shooting began when she became ill with the flu.

Jean Rogers came to Hollywood on the strength of a beauty contest and rose to notoriety as the captivatingly underdressed, ever-imperiled Dale Arden in *Flash Gordon* (1936). She also co-starred in the second *Flash Gordon* film and appeared as Peggy Trainor in both *Ace Drummond* (1936) and *The Adventures of Frank Merriwell* (1936). Jean moved from Universal to Twentieth Century–Fox where she was starred in a series of enjoyable "B" pictures, the best of which was *Heaven with a Barbed Wire Fence* (1939). She appeared in supporting parts in several MGM films of the 1940s and then freelanced in independent productions. Jean Rogers retired from show business in 1951 after her marriage to a successful actors' agent.

Rogers, John (1888, England–1963) British-born character actor who appeared in over 30 films. In four *Charlie Chan* roles, Rogers portrayed Alf Pornick in *Behind That Curtain* (1929), Martin in *Charlie Chan Carries On* (1931), Lake in *Charlie Chan in London* (1934), and the ship steward Mooney in *Charlie Chan at the Race Track* (1936).

Rogers, Mr. R. Fictitious name given by Jan Van Horn (alias John Adams) over the telephone when hiring private detective Ned Stewart in *The Shanghai Cobra* (1945). Rogers instructs Stewart to go to 1055 Harley Street every night, and if a woman named Pauline Webster comes out, to follow her, as she seems to be in danger.

The day after Samuel Black's murder, Stewart receives a letter from an R. Rogers with a postal money order for full payment for services rendered and with instructions to do nothing more about following Pauline Webster. Charlie Chan compares the fingerprints on the letter with those of the bank employees and learns that Mr. Rogers is bank guard John Adams, who is really Jan Van Horn.

Roland, Yvonne Mata Hari–type spy (portrayed by Katherine DeMille) in *Charlie Chan at the Olympics* (1937). Roland works for Charles Zaraka, a diplomat from an unnamed country who wants to acquire a strategic remote control airplane guidance system being developed and tested by the Hopkins Aviation Company.

Roland is identified as the lady with the "white fox fur," whose traces of hair are found in the murdered Miller's hotel room. While traveling on the S.S. *Manhattan* with the

U.S. Olympic Team, she directs her charms at Richard Masters to get information about the remote controlled guidance system and, in so doing, incurs the jealousy of Betty Adams, Masters' girlfriend.

Romaine, J. Prefect of police of Paris (portrayed by C. Henry Gordon in his fourth of five *Charlie Chan* roles) in *City in Darkness* (1939). Romaine is an old friend of Charlie Chan and hosts a 20-year reunion of several friends to commemorate the end of World War I.

Roman, Marty Alias used by Mike Rogan in *Shadows Over Chinatown* (1946). *See also* **Rogan, Mike.**

Romero, Cesar (February 15, 1907, New York, New York–January 1, 1994, Santa Monica, California) Suave, tall, handsome stage and screen actor who billed himself as "The Latin from Manhattan." Romero appeared in over 100 films, usually as a "Latin lover" type, and portrays magician Fred Rhadini in *Charlie Chan at Treasure Island* (1939).

Cesar Romero, "The Latin from Manhattan."

Cesar Romero was born in New York City to parents of Cuban extraction and was the grandson of Cuban patriot-poet José Marti. Known by the nickname "Butch," Romero was a better than average ballroom dancer. He received several Hollywood offers after his appearance in the Preston Sturges play *Strictly Dishonorable* but didn't step before the cameras until 1933 for his first film, *The Shadow Laughs* (although some sources claim that Romero's first movie was 1934's *The Thin Man*, in which he was typecast as a naive gigolo).

Long associated with Twentieth Century–Fox, Romero occasionally cashed in on his heritage to play Latin lover types but was more at home with characters of indeterminate nationalities. Cheerfully plunging into the Hollywood social scene, Romero became one of the community's most eligible bachelors; while linked romantically with many top female stars, he chose never to marry, insisting to his dying day that he had no regrets as a confirmed bachelor. Of his many movie roles, Romero is perhaps best remembered as the Cisco Kid in a brief series of Fox films made between 1939 and 1940. His favorite movie role, and one of his best performances, was as Cortez in *The Captain from Castile* (1947).

When his Fox contract ended in 1950, Romero was wealthy enough to retire but continued to star throughout the decade in cheap "B" pictures, always giving his best no matter how seedy his surroundings. In 1953 Romero starred in a 39-week television espionage series, *Passport to Danger*, which he cheerfully admitted to taking on because of a fat profits-percentage deal. Television fans of the 1960s most closely associate Romero with the role of the white-faced "Joker" on the *Batman* series (19 episodes). While Romero was willing to shed his inhibitions in this villainous characterization, he refused to shave his trademark mustache, compelling the makeup folks to slap the clown white over it. Among his other notable television work were appearances on *Zorro* (in the recurring role as Esteban de la Cruz); *Murder,*

She Wrote; *Wagon Train*; *Alias Smith and Jones*; *Zane Grey Theater*, and *The Love Boat*.

Always elegant and affluent-looking, Romero signed on for the recurring role of Peter Stavros in the late–1980s nighttime soap opera *Falcon Crest*, and in the early 1990s he showed up as host of a series of classic 1940s romantic films on cable television's American Movie Classics. Romero died of a blood clot on New Year's Day, 1994, at the age of 86.

Ronnell, Charlotte Foreign agent (portrayed by Dorothy Tree) who is working with Petroff to smuggle munitions in *City in Darkness* (1939). They both attempt to have a cargo of munitions on the *Medusa* (which is currently docked in Cherbourg) disguised as fruit, for which they need the necessary clearance papers.

When Ronnell cannot find the papers at Petroff's house, she shoots and kills Belescu, who is the middleman. Ronnell then flees to a nearby airport (where she meets the *Medusa*'s captain), intending to head for the border by plane. However, the plane blows a tire, crashes, and is destroyed in flames.

Room 4 Patricia West's room at 21 Washington Square in *Murder Over New York* (1940).

Room 35 Cliveden Compton's room at the Hotel San Pablo in Panama City in *Charlie Chan in Panama* (1940).

Room 104 Charlie Chan's hotel room number in *Charlie Chan in London* (1934).

Room 105 Jeanne Bently's room number at the Hotel Sierra in Reno (where she is found murdered) in *Charlie Chan in Reno* (1939). While working on the case, Charlie Chan wants to stay in the hotel room, telling the hotel's owner, Mrs. Russell, "When searching for needle in haystack, haystack only sensible location."

Room 106 Mary Whitman's room number at the Hotel Sierra in Reno in *Charlie Chan in Reno* (1939).

Room 211 Room number of an office at the Algard Building used by a man named Cooper to transfer incoming calls with the right code word to an unknown leader of an espionage ring in *The Scarlet Clue* (1945).

Room 313 Charlie Chan and son Lee's room number at New York's Carlton Hotel in *Charlie Chan on Broadway* (1937). Billie Bronson pays a hotel employee for a key to Chan's room so that she may retrieve a much sought after diary she previously hid in Chan's luggage when they were traveling on a ship from Europe to New York.

After finding Bronson's body in Johnny Burke's office at the Hottentot Club, Chan learns that Joan Wendall took a picture of the murder scene. The photo shows a key for Room 313, but there is no key at the scene now. Chan and the police then go to his hotel room and find the dead body of Thomas Mitchell. Near the trash can, among other papers that have been strewn all over the floor, Chan finds a page that had been torn out of Billie Bronson's diary.

Room 319 Evelyn Grey's room number at the Hotel Imperial in Monte Carlo in *Charlie Chan at Monte Carlo* (1937).

Room 340 Susie Watson and Paula Drake's room number at the Luani Hotel in *Charlie Chan's Murder Cruise* (1940).

Room 342 Mr. Kenyon's room number at the Luani Hotel (where he was found strangled to death) in *Charlie Chan's Murder Cruise* (1940).

Room 413 Billie Bronson's room number at the Carlton Hotel in New York in *Charlie Chan on Broadway* (1937).

Room 432 Charlie Chan's room number at the Shattuck Hotel in *Black Magic* (1944).

Room 461 Captain Kong's room number at the Palace Hotel in San Francisco in *The Chinese Ring* (1947).

Room 502 Charlie Chan's room number at the Hotel Mazarin in Paris in *Charlie Chan in Paris* (1935).

Room 538 Charlie Chan's room number at the Hotel Francis in San Francisco in *The Chinese Cat* (1944).

Room 702 Room number of radio announcer Wilbur Chester's office at the Cosmo Radio Center building in *The Scarlet Clue* (1945). The office has a hidden control switch used by Mrs. Marsh to open the trap door of the building's service elevator (Marsh uses this to kill Ralph Brett).

Room 703 Office at the Cosmo Radio Center building where Mrs. Marsh uses a teletype to send messages to Ralph Brett in *The Scarlet Clue* (1945). A radio transmitter used to detonate gas pellets is also found in the room by Charlie Chan.

Room 722 Office in the Berkeley Building from which Mrs. Justine Bonner leaves after being hypnotized by Paul Hamlin in *Black Magic* (1944). By coincidence, the office is across the hall from Charles Edwards' magic supply company (Room 726). Mrs. Bonner goes across the street to the roof of the Chalmont Building and walks off the roof to her death while hypnotized.

Charlie Chan is attacked when searching Room 722, the same room in front of whose door he finds Mrs. Bonner's glove prior to her walking off the roof of a building while in a hypnotic trance. When Chan awakes, he is restrained in a chair in a darkened room and is about to be hypnotized by Hamlin's voice.

Room 726 Office in the Berkeley Building for Charles Edwards' magic supply company in *Black Magic* (1944). The office is across the hall from Room 722, in front of whose door Charlie Chan finds Mrs. Bonner's glove prior to her walking off the roof of a building while in a hypnotic trance.

Room A-324 Room in which Charlie Chan, Number Four son Eddie, and Birmingham stay at the Carlton Hotel in *The Jade Mask* (1945).

Rosen, Phil (May 8, 1888, Marienburg Russia–October 22, 1951, Hollywood, California) Russian-born American cinematographer, producer, writer, and director of second features. Sometimes credited as Philip Rosen, Philip E. Rosen, or Phillip E. Rosen, he started working with Edison in 1912 as a cinematographer, where he filmed *Miracle Man.* Rosen later directed over 125 silent and talking films, including six *Charlie Chan* entries at Monogram. Rosen was the first president of the American Society of Cinematographers and served as secretary and board member of the Screen Directors Guild.

Charlie Chan filmography: *Charlie Chan in the Secret Service* (1944), *The Chinese Cat* (1944), *Black Magic* (1944), *The Jade Mask* (1945), *The Scarlet Clue* (1945), *The Red Dragon* (1945).

Rosenberg, Aaron Assistant director and producer of over 50 films, including *Charlie Chan in Shanghai* (1935) and (unbilled) *Charlie Chan at the Race Track* (1936). In 1963 Rosenberg was nominated for an Academy Award in the Best Picture category as the producer of *Mutiny on the Bounty* (1962).

"roses red violets blue sugar sweet so are you" Test sentence typed on Warren Fenton's typewriter by Lee Chan in *Charlie Chan at the Race Track* (1936). Charlie Chan and Lee observe that a warning message given to George Chester onboard the S.S. *Oceanic* was on stationery having the same watermark as the ship's paper and typed on a typewriter which has both a clogged "e" and a letter "r" that is raised slightly above the line.

Lee, working undercover as a ship's steward, searches the staterooms and finds a typewriter having these same characteristics in Warren Fenton's stateroom. While typing, he is startled by Fenton entering the stateroom. When questioned, Lee smiles and responds in Chinese-accented pidgin English, "So solly. Write letter to gilflend."

Ross, Frederick Wholesale jeweler (portrayed by Don Beddoe) in *Charlie Chan's Murder Cruise* (1940). As a member of Dr. Suderman's cruise, Ross romantically pursues Susie

Watson. He is a small-time jewelry fence and is blackmailed by Jim Eberhardt into donning the disguise of a bearded beggar and provide Eberhardt, posing as Professor Gordon, with an alibi.

When Charlie Chan is about to determine the identity of the elusive Jim Eberhardt, Ross is forced to wear the disguise once more and steal incriminating photographic negatives from Chan. After hitting Chan over the head and trying to escape capture, Ross is shot to death at close range in the ship's hold by Eberhardt.

Ross, Harry Makeup-artist for *Shadows Over Chinatown* (1946) and *Dangerous Money* (1946).

Ross, John Alias used by Jim Everhard in *Charlie Chan Carries On* (1931). *See also* **Everhard, Jim.**

Note: The character John Ross (a.k.a. Jim Everhard) loosely parallels that of Professor Gordon (a.k.a. Jim Eberhardt) in *Charlie Chan's Murder Cruise* (1940).

Roth Mr. Harper's butler of 15 years (portrayed by Cyril Delevanti in his first of two *Charlie Chan* roles) in *The Jade Mask* (1945).

Roth, Gene (January 8, 1903, South Dakota–July 19, 1976, Los Angeles, California) Burley utility actor (real name: Eugene Stutenroth) who appeared in over 200 films, sometimes credited as Eugene Roth or Gene Stutenroth. In two *Charlie Chan* roles (billed as Gene Stutenroth), Roth portrays Philipe von Vegon (alias Luiz Vega) in *Charlie Chan in the Secret Service* (1944) and the gangster Morgan in *The Shanghai Cobra* (1945).

Gene Roth was initially billed under his given name of Gene Stutenroth, but he shortened his surname in 1949. Most often cast as a hulking villain, Roth growled and glowered through many westerns and serials but also appeared in several Columbia two-reel comedies, starting with the Shemp Howard and Tom Kennedy film, *Society Mugs* (1946). Also a frequent foil of The Three Stooges, Roth extended his association with *The Three Stooges Meet Hercules* (1962). A prevalent television actor, Roth was frequently cast as a judge or bailiff on the *Perry Mason* series and portrayed two roles in the 1961 *Twilight Zone* classic, *Shadow Play*.

Roxbury House Located on Sutton Place, the New York residence (Apartment 44) of actress June Preston in *Murder Over New York* (1940).

Roy, Gloria Actress who appears in seven *Charlie Chan* films: as Arlene Compton in *Charlie Chan's Greatest Case* (1933), an unbilled player in both *Charlie Chan in Paris* (1935) and *Charlie Chan in Egypt* (1935), the psychic Carlotta in *Charlie Chan's Secret* (1936), Catherine Chester in *Charlie Chan at the Race Track* (1936), an unbilled hat check girl in *Charlie Chan on Broadway* (1937), and an unbilled hostess in *Charlie Chan in Panama* (1940).

Royal Hawaiian Hotel Well-known Honolulu hotel where Tarneverro is staying in *The Black Camel* (1931). It is also the hotel where Richard Masters, Hopkins, Arthur Hughes, and Cartwright all are staying in *Charlie Chan at the Olympics* (1937). The real Royal Hawaiian Hotel is located at 2259 Kalakaua Avenue in Honolulu.

Royal Theater Honolulu theater venue where Robert Fyfe, the actor and ex-husband of Shelah Fane, is appearing in a stage play in *The Black Camel* (1931).

Royce, Lionel (March 30, 1886, Dolina, Poland–April 1, 1946, Manila, Philippines) Stage and screen actor who appeared in 30 films, often as sinister Nazi-type spies. Royce portrays Dr. Rudolph Grosser in *Charlie Chan in Panama* (1940).

A Teutonic villain assignment as Hintze in *Confessions of a Nazi Spy* (1939) typecast Lionel Royce for the rest of his Hollywood career. Among his many other assignments, the actor proved to be a memorable threat for Bob Hope as Monsieur Lebec in *Road to Zanzibar* (1941) and Karl in *My Favorite Blonde* (1942). Fans of Republic's films will remember Royce for his dual characterization of a kindly Sultan and the despicable Baron Von Rommer in *Secret Service in Darkest Africa* (1943). Lionel Royce died while on a USO tour of the Philippines in 1946.

Royer Costume designer for almost 30 films, including three *Charlie Chan* entries: *Charlie Chan's Greatest Case* (1933), *Charlie Chan's Courage* (1934), and *Charlie Chan in London* (1934).

Rozelle, Rita Actress who portrayed Luana, the native Hawaiian girlfriend of an artist-beachcomber named Smith, in *The Black Camel* (1931).

Ruark, Lt. Mike San Francisco homicide detective (portrayed by Tim Ryan) in three *Charlie Chan* films—*The Shanghai Chest* (1948), The *Golden Eye* (1948), and *The Sky Dragon* (1949).

Ruby Member of Cole King's variety troupe (portrayed by Helen Gerald) in *The Trap* (1947).

Rue de Monterpan 117 Apartment address (117 Monterpan Street) of Victor Descartes in *Charlie Chan in Paris* (1935).

Rue de Pont 17 Address (17 Bridge Street) of crippled beggar Marcel Xavier (obtained from bank records) in *Charlie Chan in Paris* (1935). Latouche tells Charlie Chan that the address is in "a rather nasty neighborhood." Chan and Victor Descartes go to the address, look around inside, and find a secret exit to the underground sewer system which leads them to another door, behind which is a printing press, engraving tools, and counterfeit bonds of the Lamartine Bank.

Ruhl, William American character actor who appeared in over 50 films, often in one-scene assignments as detectives and lawyers. In three unbilled *Charlie Chan* roles, Ruhl portrays Gregory in *The Shanghai Cobra* (1945), Mr. Thompson, the police lab technician in *Dark Alibi* (1946), and a jailer in *The Shanghai Chest* (1948).

Running Times Running times are obtained from *American Film Institute Catalog of Motion Pictures Produced in the United States. The Shanghai Chest* is the shortest *Charlie Chan* movie—at 56 minutes. Of the talkies, *Behind That Curtain* is the longest—at 91 minutes.

Running Times
for *Charlie Chan* Movies

Movie	*Length*
The House Without a Key (1925)	10-part serial
The Chinese Parrot (1927)	unknown
Behind That Curtain (1929)	91 min
Charlie Chan Carries On (1931)	76 min
The Black Camel (1931)	71 min
Charlie Chan's Chance (1932)	73 min
Charlie Chan's Greatest Case (1933)	70 min
Charlie Chan's Courage (1934)	71 min
Charlie Chan in London (1934)	79 min
Charlie Chan in Paris (1935)	70 min
Charlie Chan in Egypt (1935)	72 min
Charlie Chan in Shanghai (1935)	70 min
Charlie Chan's Secret (1936)	71 min
Charlie Chan at the Circus (1936)	72 min
Charlie Chan at the Race Track (1936)	70 min
Charlie Chan at the Opera (1936)	66 min
Charlie Chan at the Olympics (1937)	71 min
Charlie Chan on Broadway (1937)	68 min
Charlie Chan at Monte Carlo (1937)	71 min
Charlie Chan in Honolulu (1938)	65 min
Charlie Chan in Reno (1939)	70 min
Charlie Chan at Treasure Island (1939)	64 min
City in Darkness (1939)	75 min
Charlie Chan in Panama (1940)	67 min
Charlie Chan's Murder Cruise (1940)	75 min
Charlie Chan at the Wax Museum (1940)	63 min
Murder Over New York (1940)	65 min
Dead Men Tell (1941)	60 min
Charlie Chan in Rio (1941)	60 min
Castle in the Desert (1942)	63 min
Charlie Chan in the Secret Service (1944)	63 min
The Chinese Cat (1944)	65 min
Black Magic (1944)	64 min
The Jade Mask (1945)	69 min
The Scarlet Clue (1945)	65 min
The Shanghai Cobra (1945)	64 min
The Red Dragon (1945)	64 min
Dark Alibi (1946)	61 min

Movie	*Length*
Shadows Over Chinatown (1946)	64 min
Dangerous Money (1946)	66 min
The Trap (1947)	69 min
The Chinese Ring (1947)	68 min
Docks of New Orleans (1948)	64 min
The Shanghai Chest (1948)	56 min
The Golden Eye (1948)	69 min
The Feathered Serpent (1948)	60 min
The Sky Dragon (1949)	64 min

Russell, Mrs. Owner of the Hotel Sierra (portrayed by Kay Linaker in her second of four *Charlie Chan* roles) in *Charlie Chan in Reno* (1939). Charlie Chan finds out that Jeanne Bently stole Mrs. Russell's husband, Wayne, about five years ago. When Mrs. Russell sees that Jeanne Bently is going to ruin Mary Whitman's life just as she did hers, Mrs. Russell attempts to disfigure Bently's face with nitric acid taken from Dr. Ainsley's office. However, Bently wrestles the acid bottle away.

Note: In the Call Bureau Cast Service lists, Mrs. Russell's name was originally Alice Williamson.

Russell, Wayne Deceased ex-husband of Mrs. Russell in *Charlie Chan in Reno* (1939). In 1935 Jeanne Bently, a New York socialite, persuaded Wayne Russell to divorce his wife and marry her. In 1936 Jeanne Bently murdered Wayne, and Dr. Ainsley (the attending physician) falsified the death certificate to indicate that Russell died from a heart attack.

Rutherford Mansion Pacific Ocean waterfront beach house at 624 Malibu Drive in Malibu Beach which is rented by Cole King for his variety troupe in *The Trap* (1947). Although San Toy gives Birmingham the address as 26 Malibu Drive over the telephone, the house number is displayed as 624.

Ryan, Sheila (June 8, 1921, Topeka, Kansas–November 4, 1975, Woodland Hills, California) Perky brunette leading lady (real name: Katherine Elizabeth McLaughlin) who appeared in 35 films. Ryan portrays typist Kate Ransome in *Dead Men Tell* (1941).

In 1940 Sheila Ryan was signed by Twentieth Century–Fox, where she played Susan Wetherby in *The Gay Caballero* (1940) and Connie Earle in *Dressed to Kill* (1941). She also appeared in two *Laurel and Hardy* movies, *Great Guns* (1941) and *A-Haunting We Will Go* (1942). Her best opportunity at Fox came in the role of Vivian Potter in *The Gang's All Here* (1943), in which she was not only permitted to sing but was afforded a special-effects curtain call in the film's finale.

By the late 1940s, Ryan's career had dwindled to "B" pictures at other studios. While co-starring with Gene Autry as Carol Bannister in *Mule Train* (1950), Sheila fell in love with Autry's sidekick, Pat Buttram. They were married shortly afterward and remained that way until her death.

Ryan, Tim (July 5, 1899, Bayonne, New Jersey–October 22, 1956, Hollywood, California) American comedy supporting stage and screen actor who appeared in over 75 movies and was very good at portraying drunks and dumb cops. In five *Charlie Chan* film appearances, Ryan portrays Red Eye (unbilled) in *Dead Men Tell* (1941), Foggy in *Dark Alibi* (1946), and police detective Lt. Mike Ruark in *The Shanghai Chest* (1948), *The Golden Eye* (1948), and *The Sky Dragon* (1949). In addition, Tim Ryan wrote some of the dialogue for *The Shanghai Chest*.

S

79P666 California license plate number of the Manderley Castle car in *Castle in the Desert* (1942).

605 Number of the Yellow Cab Company taxi driven by Birmingham Brown in *The Chinese Cat* (1944). Because Charlie Chan is reopening the investigation of Thomas Manning's murder, Salos places a bomb with an alarm clock timer in the taxi to kill Chan. The cab blows up, but only after Birmingham tells Chan that he hears two ticking sounds, one of which is the taxi fare meter. Chan, son Tommy, and Birmingham stop and quickly get out of the cab before the explosion.

670 Birmingham Brown's taxi driver's license number in *The Chinese Cat* (1944).

1692 Year the Galt Building was built in *Behind That Curtain* (1929).

750,000 francs Amount received by Joan Karnoff from a pawn shop in Nice in exchange for some jewelry (intended as a blackmail payment to Albert Rogers) in *Charlie Chan at Monte Carlo* (1937).

$60 million Estimated value of the treasure thought to be buried on Cocos Island in *Dead Men Tell* (1941).

6:04 p.m. Time stamp on a warning note delivered to George Chester onboard the S.S. *Oceanic* in *Charlie Chan at the Race Track* (1936).

7:30 Time that Charlie Chan, Paula Webb, and Ned Stewart meet at the Lotus Garden Café in *The Shanghai Cobra* (1945). Paula reads the newspaper story that Ned Stewart has been arrested for the murder of Samuel Black and then telephones Chan to meet her at the restaurant at 7:30 where she gives Chan information that clears Ned of the murder charge.

sailor's knot A type of knot Capt. Johnson uses to tie a scarf (with which he strangles Elsie Hillman—alias Mrs. Carol Wayne) in *Charlie Chan in Honolulu* (1938).

St. Francis Hotel Charlie Chan's San Francisco hotel in *Charlie Chan at Treasure Island* (1939).

St. Louis Sun Herald Newspaper for which reporter Bill Lydig works in *Dead Men Tell* (1941).

Salisbury, Stuart Real name of Thomas Gregory (portrayed by Douglass Dumbrille in his second of three *Charlie Chan* roles) in *Charlie Chan at Treasure Island* (1939). Salisbury is a private investigator for the Granville Insurance Company and is investigating three recent suicides and Paul Essex's death, as they were all clients of Dr. Zodiac.

Salos Gangster (portrayed by Dewey Robinson) in *The Chinese Cat* (1944). With fellow gangsters Catlen, Salos, and the twin brothers Carl and Kurt Karzoff, Salos is part of a jewelry theft and smuggling ring led by Thomas Manning and Webster Deacon.

Because Charlie Chan is asked to reopen the investigation of Thomas Manning's murder, Salos places a bomb with an alarm clock timer in Birmingham Brown's taxi cab. The cab blows up, but only after Birmingham tells Chan that he hears two ticking sounds, one of which is the taxi fare meter. Chan, son Tommy, and Birmingham quickly stop and get out of the cab.

samba The national dance of Brazil. In *Charlie Chan in Rio* (1941), Jimmy Chan asks Lola Dean's maid, Lili Wong, to teach him the samba.

Samoa A group of volcanic islands in the South Pacific Ocean, divided into American Samoa and Western Samoa, that are located about halfway between Honolulu and Sydney, Australia. American Samoa comprises six islands, and its capital, Pago Pago, is located on the island of Tutuila. The capital of Western Samoa is Apia and is on the island of Upolu.

In 1722 the Dutch explorer Jacob Roggeveen was the first European to discover the islands. The United States and Germany divided them in 1900. New Zealand administered Western Samoa from 1914 until it became independent in 1962.

In *Dangerous Money* (1946), the S.S. *Newcastle* is heading from Honolulu to Pago Pago, Samoa, and then on to Australia.

San Francisco Northern California city that is home to Charlie Chan in many of the films made at Monogram.

San Francisco Union Telegraph San Francisco newspaper, whose reporter, Pete Lewis, joins magician Fred Rhadini on a crusade to expose fake psychics in the San Francisco area (with Dr. Zodiac as their primary target) in *Charlie Chan at Treasure Island* (1939).

San Marco Opera Company Opera company, headed by soprano Mme. Lilli Rochelle, that produces the opera *Carnival* in *Charlie Chan at the Opera* (1936).

San Pablo Small Mexican village on the way to Mexico City which serves as the location setting for *The Feathered Serpent* (1948).

San Quentin The point extending into San Francisco Bay, north of the city, and the location of the well-known California state prison and its gas chamber. In *Dead Men Tell* (1941), a convicted murderer, posing as newspaper reporter Bill Lydig, is mentioned in a magazine article to have escaped from San Quentin. In *The Shanghai Chest* (1948), Tony Pindello is executed in San Quentin prison.

Santa Anita Race Track Race track in Arcadia, California, where the racing scenes for *Charlie Chan at the Race Track* (1936) were filmed. In the movie, the track uses the name Santa Juanita Race Track. *See also* **Santa Juanita Race Track.**

Santa Juanita Handicap Sixth race at the Santa Juanita Race Track in which Avalanche, owned by George Chester, is the odds-on favorite in *Charlie Chan at the Race Track* (1936). A racetrack gambling ring has tried to fix the race by switching Avalanche with Gallant Lad, as the two horses look alike when some coloring dye is applied. However, Charlie Chan notices the switch and is able to switch the horses back just before the race begins so that they run under their true names.

Riding Avalanche (with the promise from Chester of a $10,000 bonus if he wins), Brill wins the race, but the horse stumbles and falls immediately after crossing the finish line from the effects of a tranquilizer dart fired from the three-quarter mile pole. Fortunately, both Brill and Avalanche are later found to be uninjured.

Prior to the start of the race, the movie displays several continuity errors. Just before the horses are brought to the starting gate, the odds board gives the following racing information for eight horses:

Post	Horse	Jockey	Odds
1	Golden Fleece	Adams	3–1
2	Money Maker	Engle	10–1
3	Schrapnel	Jackson	4–1
4	Blue Boy	Saxton	8–1
5	Court Jester	Farley	12–1
6	Gallant Lad	G.H. Roy	20–1
7	Avalanche	Patten	3–5
8	Pico	Burroughs	30–1

When the horses bolt from the starting gate, there are at least 12 horses shown in the film. In addition, the odds board lists Patten as Avalanche's jockey, but because of the publicized threats against Avalanche, none of the jockeys are willing to ride Avalanche in the race. Eddie Brill steps up to George Chester and offers to ride the horse. Another error occurs when the horses are parading in front of the stands and the track announcer gives the name of Honey Girl—a horse that is not even listed on the odds board.

Santa Juanita Race Track Fictitious California racetrack in *Charlie Chan at the Race Track* (1936). The racetrack scenes were actually filmed at the Santa Anita Racetrack in Arcadia, California. *See also* **Santa Juanita Handicap**.

Santelle, Louis Locksmith (portrayed by Leo G. Carroll) who makes fake passports in *City in Darkness* (1939). Because of the possibility of war being declared very soon, Santelle sells a boat ticket to Panama to Marie Dubon for an outrageous price of 15,000 francs. Dubon later goes to Santelle's shop to pay him for a fake passport that will identify her husband, Tony Madero, as Antonio Castillo so he won't be noticed by the police when boarding the boat. She starts to pay Santelle the 10,000 francs he quoted earlier, but he now wants 50,000 francs.

When Charlie Chan visits Santelle's shop to investigate, he notices that Santelle has lots of equipment and supplies that could be used for purposes other than locksmithing. Santelle's assistant, Pierre, strangles Chan with a rope, rendering him unconscious, and then ties Chan to a chair.

sarsaparilla Aromatic liquid extract made from the roots of several species of tropical vines of the genus *Smilax* in the lily family *Liliaceae*. It was once employed as a tonic and as a treatment for rheumatism and is now used to flavor medicines and soft drinks. Sarsaparilla plants, having large perennial vines with short, thick, underground stems, are native to tropical America and grow in jungles from Mexico to Peru. Sarsaparilla derives its name from the Spanish *zarza* ("bramble") and *parrilla* ("little vine") and was introduced into Europe as a medicinal tonic in the 1500s.

Charlie Chan rarely drinks anything other than tea, but when he does, especially in a bar, he orders sarsaparilla. In *Charlie Chan in Shanghai* (1935), Chan tries to order sarsaparilla when he is with the U.S. government agent impostor, James Andrews, in the Versailles Café. He also orders sarsaparilla in *Charlie Chan at the Race Track* (1936).

Saturnia, Mme. Fortune teller and astrologer (portrayed by Ethel Griffies in her second of two *Charlie Chan* roles) who is also referred to simply as Lily in *Castle in the Desert* (1942).

Savarin, Paul The scheming business rival (portrayed by Edward Raquello) of Victor Karnoff in *Charlie Chan at Monte Carlo* (1937). Savarin bribes Karnoff's chauffeur, Ludwig, to tip him off when Karnoff will be shipping $1 million in bonds to Paris for sale, a move that would financially hurt Savarin.

Savoy Hotel Col. John Beetham's London hotel in *Behind That Curtain* (1929).

Sayre, George Wallace Screenwriter for almost 20 films, including *The Shanghai Cobra* (1945).

***The Scarlet Clue* (1945)** The fifth *Charlie Chan* film produced by Monogram Pictures Corporation.

Alternate Title: *Charlie Chan in the Scarlet Clue*. Working Title: *Robot Murder*. Source: based on the character "Charlie Chan" created by Earl Derr Biggers. Original Copyright: Monogram Pictures Corporation, April 1, 1945; LP13234. Copyright Renewed: October 25, 1972; R538950. PCA Certificate Number: 10372. Production: January, 1945. Release Date: May 11, 1945. Sound: Western Electric Recording. Film: b&w; 5,808 feet. Running Time: 65 minutes.

Producer: James S. Burkett. Director: Phil Rosen. Assistant director: Eddie Davis.* Original Screenplay: George Callahan. Director of Photography: William Sickner. Editor: Richard Currier. Musical Director: Edward J. Kay. Sound Recording: Tom Lambert. Technical Director: Dave Milton. Production Manager: Wm. Strohbach.

Cast

Sidney Toler	*as*	Charlie Chan
Mantan Moreland		Birmingham Brown
Ben Carter		as himself
Benson Fong		Tommy Chan
Virginia Brissac		Mrs. Marsh
Robert E. Homans		Capt. Flynn
Jack Norton		Willie Rand
Janet Shaw		Gloria Bayne
Helen Devereaux		Diane Hall
Victoria Faust		Hulda Swenson
Milt Kibbee*		Herbert Sinclair
I. Stanford Jolley*		Ralph Brett
Reid Kilpatrick*		Wilbur Chester
Charles Sherlock*		Sergeant McGraw
Leonard Mudie*		Horace Carlos
Charles Jordan*		Nelson
Kernan Cripps*		Detective

Plot Summary: Charlie Chan, working as a federal agent, is on the trail of a spy ring intent on stealing government radar plans. Chan enlists the aid of Captain Flynn of the New York police. Unfortunately, Flynn follows Chan's lead to one of the spies, a foreign agent named Rausch, too closely and Rausch is murdered by Ralph Brett on orders of his mysterious, unknown boss.

Discovering that the murderer escaped in the stolen car belonging to Diane Hall, a radio performer, Chan, his son Tommy, and chauffeur Birmingham Brown, go to the Cosmo Radio Center. There they find a footprint identical to one left at the murder scene. Meanwhile, Ralph Brett, the studio manager, telephones the spy ring leader, who

*Unbilled.

uses the Western Union teletype machine to warn Brett to be more careful or he will meet the same fate as Rausch.

Chan then goes to the Hamilton Laboratory (which is located in the same building as the radio center) and is told of numerous—but unsuccessful—attempts to break in and steal the radar plans from the laboratory's safe. Chan then places phony radar plans in the safe in case the spies are more successful in the future.

Radio actress Gloria Bayne realizes that her boss, Brett, stole Diane's car (and suspects that he killed Rausch) when she finds a book of her personalized matches that she recently gave Brett in Diane's car. Gloria then blackmails Brett into giving her better acting parts and higher pay, but she is later killed by an unidentified poison. Brett now worries that Chan is onto him and asks his boss for help in escaping. The unknown spy kills Brett instead by using a trap door in the service elevator.

Upon finding the murdered studio manager, Chan formulates a plan using a voice impersonator to call the spy leader. The unknown leader, thinking that Brett is still alive, then orders him to use the service elevator once more, but Chan, Tommy, and Birmingham escape the trap. Chan then questions the studio people who worked with Brett and Gloria but learns nothing new.

Later, Willie Rand, an actor, is murdered while doing a television show after telling Chan that he may have uncovered some information. Laboratory chemical analyses show that both Gloria Bayne and Willie Rand were killed by inhaling some kind of poisonous gas which was activated by smoking a cigarette.

They search the building and find the mysterious spy leader's office. The leader tries to escape but mistakenly takes the service elevator with its trap door set to open. Like Brett, the spy drops to the basement and is killed instantly. There Chan discovers the dead body of Mrs. Marsh, the ruthless radio sponsor and the leader of the spy ring.

Schneider, Samuel Assistant director for *Charlie Chan on Broadway* (1937).

Schneiderman, George (September 20, 1894, New York–November 19, 1964) Cinematographer for nearly 60 silent and sound films, including *Charlie Chan Carries On* (1931).

Schrock, Raymond L. (1892, Goshen, Indiana–December 12, 1950, Hollywood, California) Screenplay writer of over 80 silent and sound films, including *Shadows Over Chinatown* (1946).

Scorpio The eighth sign of the zodiac, representing the scorpion (symbol: ♏). Scorpio corresponds to the dates October 23 to November 22 and is the southern constellation of stars between Libra and Sagittarius.

In *Charlie Chan at Treasure Island* (1939), mystery writer Paul Essex receives a disturbing radiogram during a China Clipper flight from Honolulu to San Francisco which reads, "Sign of Scorpio indicates disaster if Zodiac obligations ignored." Essex then asks Charlie Chan which month is Scorpio, and Charlie replies, after thinking, "October… tomorrow is first day of scorpion symbol on Chinese calendar."

As Paul Ellson, Essex was in prison for three years for stock swindling, a secret known by Dr. Zodiac, whose message now threatens blackmail. When the plane begins to land, Jimmy and Charlie find Essex dead, having committed suicide with poison. *See also* **zodiac.**

Scott, Mr. (Chief) Charlie Chan's police chief superior (portrayed by Andrew Tombes) in *Charlie Chan at the Olympics* (1937). Although he is credited as such, he is never referred to as "Chief Scott," only as "Mr. Scott."

Scott, Professor Archeologist (portrayed by Erville Alderson in his second of two *Charlie Chan* roles) in *The Feathered Serpent* (1948). Scott and Professor Henry Farnsworth find the lost Aztec Temple of the Sun, but both are captured and tortured by Professor John Stanley and his gang.

Scott eventually escapes and is found, exhausted, by Charlie Chan, sons Lee and Tommy, and Birmingham while on their vacation near the village of San Pablo. After treatment by a doctor, Scott is somewhat irrational as he starts to tell Chan and others the details of finding the Aztec Temple of the Sun and his escape from his captors there. Before he can say much, however, Professor Stanley quickly blows out a candle as a distraction and Scott is killed by Sonia Cabot with an Aztec sacrificial knife.

Sea Tide Art Company Company owned by Webster Deacon in *The Chinese Cat* (1944). Wu Song looks in his record book and tells Charlie Chan that he sold some small figurines and one of a large black cat to the Sea Tide Art Company.

Seaborg, Glenn T. (April 19, 1912, Ishpeming, Michigan–February 25, 1999, Lafayette, California) American chemist who shared the 1951 Nobel Prize for chemistry with Edwin McMillan for his participation in the discovery of most of the transuranium elements.

Glenn Seaborg received his Ph.D. in 1937 from the University of California at Berkeley, where he remained and did his early work on the isotopes of common elements. He later worked with McMillan who, in 1940, isolated neptunium (element number 93), the first element beyond uranium. Seaborg and his associates later isolated the next transuranium element, plutonium. They also found a plutonium isotope that promised to yield more fission energy than uranium.

In 1942 Seaborg moved from Berkeley to the University of Chicago to find ways of producing plutonium for the atomic bomb project. In 1944 his group discovered two new elements, americium (95) and curium (96). In 1946 he returned to Berkeley, and during the next 12 years he and his colleagues discovered six more transuranium elements—berkelium (97) in 1949, californium (98) in 1950, einsteinium (99) in 1952, fermium (100) in 1953, mendelevium (101) in 1955, and nobelium (102) in 1958.

In 1958 Seaborg was named chancellor of

Dr. Glenn Seaborg (left) and Dr. Edwin McMillan on the day they were notified that they had won the Nobel Prize for Chemistry in October 1951 (Courtesy the Lawrence Berkeley National Laboratory).

the Berkeley campus. From 1961 to 1971 he was the first scientist to be chairman of the Atomic Energy Commission. In 1974, at the Lawrence Berkeley Laboratory, scientists discovered element number 106, which was named seaborgium in his honor. *See also* **95th element.**

séance A meeting or session at which people try to communicate with the spirits of the dead using a medium or spiritualist. Fake séances are part of the plot of three *Charlie Chan* films—*Charlie Chan's Secret* (1936), *Charlie Chan at Treasure Island* (1939), and *Black Magic* (1944).

Second Assistant (1) Nickname Charlie Chan uses for Birmingham Brown in *The Scarlet Clue* (1945). Chan's Number Three son Tommy is "First Assistant." *See* **Brown, Birmingham.**

Second Assistant (2) Title given Chattanooga Brown by himself in *Dangerous Money* (1946). Brown refers to Jimmy Chan as Charlie Chan's "First Assistant."

The Secret of the Pigmy Arrow Mystery novel, written by Paul Essex, about a fake mystic who blackmails his clients in *Charlie Chan at Treasure Island* (1939).

Seeton, Capt. Real name of Phillips the butler, who is working undercover for British military intelligence, in *Charlie Chan in London* (1934).

Seiler, Lewis (1891, New York, New York–January 8, 1964, Hollywood, California) Film director of over 65 films, including *Charlie Chan in Paris* (1935).

Sekhmet From Egyptian mythology, the lion-headed goddess who is the mistress of war and sickness and who represents the destructive power of the sun's heat. Sekhmet was part of the Memphis Triad, with the gods Ptah (her consort) and Nefertem (the son by Sekhmet and Ptah).

In *Charlie Chan in Egypt* (1935), Professor John Thurston, having murdered Professor Arnold and discovered the secret entrance to a vast treasure storeroom in Ahmeti's tomb, often uses a headmask of Sekhmet that glowed and sparkled in the dark to scare intruders away from the tomb.

The use of Sekhmet echoes a plot point from the 1930 Philo Vance novel *The Scarab Murder Case* in which a man is found dead in a museum, his head crushed beneath a Sekhmet statue. In *Charlie Chan in Egypt*, Charlie Chan is told that Barry Arnold was permanently crippled when a wall guarded by a statue of Sekhmet collapsed on his leg.

September 15, 1923 Date of Chicago opera house fire when Gravelle was intentionally locked in his dressing room and left to die by his wife, Mme. Rochelle, and Enrico Barelli in *Charlie Chan at the Opera* (1936).

Seroff, Muni (January 8, 1903, Kishinev, Russia– *) Actor in Yiddish- and English-language films who portrays Peter Laska in *Charlie Chan in the Secret Service* (1944).

Seward, Billie (* –1982) Character actress who appeared in 20 films and portrays Bessie Sibley in *Charlie Chan at Treasure Island* (1939).

Seward, Ed Corrupt lawyer (portrayed by Tristram Coffin) in *The Shanghai Chest* (1948). Seward is the lawyer who unsuccessfully defends Tony Pindello in a murder case tried before Judge Wesley Armstrong and prosecuted by District Attorney Frank Bronson. After the trial, Seward becomes the personal lawyer of Judge Armstrong.

Seward and Tony Pindello were once partners in an insurance swindle. However, Seward became greedy and framed Pindello for murder. After Pindello is found guilty and executed, a commission, which includes Seward and Judge Armstrong as members, is set up to investigate the insurance swindles. New evidence now surfaces that might prove Tony Pindello was innocent, and Seward embarks on a plan involving forging Pindello's fingerprints and successively murdering Judge Armstrong, Frank Bronson, and Thomas Cartwright while leaving Pindello's fingerprints at each murder scene to give the mysterious impression that a man who died six months earlier is responsible for the murders.

***Shadows Over Chinatown* (1946)** The ninth *Charlie Chan* film produced by Monogram Pictures Corporation.

Working Titles: *Corpus Delecti* and *The Mandarin's Secret*. Source: based on the character "Charlie Chan" created by Earl Derr Biggers. Original Copyright: Monogram Pictures Corporation, July 5, 1946; LP420. Copyright Renewed: January 28, 1974; R569474. Production: mid– to late March, 1946. Release Date: July 27, 1946. Sound: Western Electric Mirrophonic Recording. Film: b&w. Running Time: 64 minutes.

Producer: James S. Burkett. Director: Terry Morse. Assistant Director: William Calihan, Jr. Original Screenplay: Raymond Schrock. Photography: William Sickner. Technical Director: Dave Milton. Supervising Film Editor: Richard Currier. Editor: Ralph Dixon. Musical Director: Edward J. Kay. Recordist: Tom Lambert. Makeup: Harry Ross. Production Manager: Glenn Cook.

Cast

Sidney Toler	*as*	Charlie Chan
Mantan Moreland		Birmingham Brown
Victor Sen Young		Jimmy Chan
Tanis Chandler		Mary Conover [alias Mary McCoy]
John Gallaudet		Jeff Hay [alias for Craig Winfield]
Paul Bryar		Mike Rogan
Bruce Kellogg		Joe Thompson [alias Jack Tilford]
Alan Bridge		Capt. Allen
Mary Gordon		Mrs. Conover
Dorothy Granger		Joan Mercer
Jack Norton		Cosgrove
George Eldredge		Chief Brannigan
Tyra Vaughn		Miss Chalmers
Lyle Latell		Police clerk
Myra McKinney		Kate Johnson
Gladys Blake		Myrtle
George Chan,* James B. Leong*		Chinese Americans
Jack Mower*		Hobart
John Hamilton*		Pronnet, San Francisco–bound lawyer
Harry Depp*		Dr. Denby
Charles Jordan*		Jenkins
Louise Franklin*		Maid
Frank Mayo*		Police lieutenant
Kit Catson*		Hotel clerk
Doris Fulton*		Angie
Jimmy Dugan*		Police driver

*Unbilled.

Plot Summary: Charlie Chan, his son Jimmy, and chauffeur Birmingham Brown are all on a bus traveling to San Francisco to investigate a murder case involving a torso without its head, arms, or legs. A short time later, when the bus breaks down during a heavy rainstorm, several passengers notice that they have been robbed. While waiting for the bus to be fixed, the passengers are joined in the bus station by a U.S. Marine who calls himself Jack Tilford. After the bus is fixed and the passengers go out to the bus to resume their journey, Chan speaks privately to Cosgrove, a pickpocket, and suggests that if he returns all the stolen items, his crime will not be revealed. Grateful, the pickpocket promises to return the favor in the future.

Back on the bus, Chan learns that Mrs. Conover is traveling to San Francisco to search for her missing granddaughter, Mary. After they arrive in San Francisco, Chan, Jimmy, and Birmingham visit the Bureau of Missing Persons where Chan reveals to Captain Allen that he has two purposes. The first, on behalf of an insurance company, is to discover the identity of the torso. The second is to learn the whereabouts of Mary Conover. Before arriving in San Francisco, Chan had suspected that the torso belongs to a former showgirl named Grace Gortner, whose wealthy husband, Homer B. Pendleton, died after taking out a large insurance policy.

On Allen's desk Chan spots a photograph of AWOL Marine Corporal Joe Thompson and recognizes him as Jack Tilford. Chan then returns to the hotel where Mrs. Conover is staying with her friend Kate Johnson. He reassures Mrs. Conover that the body, which has an appendectomy scar, cannot be Mary's. Now hungry, Chan and Jimmy lunch in the hotel's restaurant where Chan recognizes that their waitress is Mary Conover, but with dyed blonde hair. Before Chan can bring her grandmother down to confirm her identity, Mary is also recognized by her former employer, Mike Rogan, and flees the restaurant. Jimmy and Birmingham follow her, but when Chan later meets them at Mary's apartment, they are joined by private detective Jeff Hay who tells Chan he has followed their bus driver, who is actually Mike Rogan, to this location.

Inside Mary's apartment they discover Kate Johnson's body, and Chan suspects that the killer mistook her for Mary. Chan returns to the Bureau of Missing Persons and learns that Grace Gortner had once been in love with a man named Craig Winfield before her marriage to Pendleton. Thompson is then picked up by the police and explains that he went AWOL to find Mary, with whom he was in love. Thompson further explains that Mary worked at the Bay City Escort Bureau and was frightened of her employer, Rogan.

Chan returns to his hotel where Hay is waiting with information that he has found Rogan in Chinatown. But when they arrive there, Rogan is dead. Then Mary is picked up by the police and explains that Rogan discovered that Thompson's father was wealthy and suggested that she marry Joe, take out a large insurance policy, and soon become a wealthy widow. Mary and her grandmother are reunited, and Chan asks Mary to help him set a trap for the owner of the escort bureau. At the escort bureau, Mary meets Jeff Hay, but when he learns that she is part of a police trap, he kidnaps her. In the meantime, a photograph has come over the police bureau's wire service that identifies Hay as Winfield.

Following a hunch, Chan finds Hay and Mary in Chinatown. Although Hay tries to shoot Chan, Cosgrove has removed the bullets from Hay's gun. Chan then explains that Hay killed Kate Johnson, mistaking her for Mary, and also killed Rogan to blame him for the other deaths.

Note: *Shadows Over Chinatown* marks the return of Victor Sen Young (formerly Sen Yung) to the series (as Jimmy Chan) after an absence of eight films.

Shang Dynasty Ancient Chinese dynasty, also called the Yin Dynasty in its later stages, that ruled northern China from the 16th century to about 1027 B.C. The Shang civilization is characterized by an advanced system of writing, sophisticated bronze metallurgy, the first Chinese calendar, and cities.

In *Charlie Chan's Murder Cruise* (1940), Charlie Chan gives son Jimmy a history lesson about his ancient ancestors, stating that the "Golden Era" was during the Shang Dynasty of northern China. This corrects information that Professor Gordon, a fake archeologist, told Chan earlier, when Gordon claimed that the Han Dynasty was "Golden Era of southern China" and that he had made quite a study of it. *See also* **Han Dynasty**.

Shanghai Leading Chinese industrial seaport city at the confluence of the Huangpu and Wusong Rivers. Shanghai is the location setting for *Charlie Chan in Shanghai* (1935).

***The Shanghai Chest* (1948)** The fourteenth *Charlie Chan* film produced by Monogram Pictures Corporation.

Working Title: *Murder by Alphabet*. Source: based on the character "Charlie Chan" created by Earl Derr Biggers. Original Copyright: Monogram Pictures Corporation, July 11, 1948; LP13021. Copyright Renewed: October 2, 1975; R615168. Production: early February to mid–February, 1948. Release Date: July 11, 1948. Sound: Western Electric Recording. Film: b&w; 5,872 feet. Running Time: 56 minutes.

Producer: James S. Burkett. Director: William Beaudine. Assistant Director: Wesley Barry. Screenplay: W. Scott Darling and Sam Newman. Original Story: Sam Newman. Additional Dialogue: Tim Ryan. Photography: William Sickner. Camera Operator: William Margulies.* Stills: James Fullerton.* Art Director: David Milton. Editor: Ace

**Unbilled.*

Herman. Supervising Film Editor: Otho Lovering. Set Decoration: Raymond Bolt, Jr.* Music Director: Edward J. Kay. Sound Recordist: Frank McWhorter. Hair Stylist: Lela Chambers.* Production Supervisor: Glenn Cook. Screenplay Supervisor: Jules Levy.* Grip: Harry Lewis.*

Cast

Roland Winters	*as*	Charlie Chan
Mantan Moreland		Birmingham Brown
Tim Ryan		Lt. Mike Ruark
Victor Sen Young		Tommy Chan
Deannie Best		Phyllis Powers
Tristram Coffin		Ed Seward
John Alvin		Victor Armstrong
Russell Hicks		District Attorney Frank Bronson
Pierre Watkin†		Judge Wesley Armstrong
Philip Van Zandt		Joseph Pindello
Milton Parsons		Mr. Grail
Olaf Hytten		Bates
Erville Alderson		Walter Somerville
George Eldredge		Pat Finley
Charlie Sullivan*		Officer Murphy
Eddie Coke*		Thomas Cartwright
William Ruhl*		Jailer
Lois Austin*		Landlady
Chabing*		Receptionist
John Shay*		Stacey
Paul Scardon*		Cemetery custodian
Willie Best*		as himself

Plot Summary: In San Francisco, Judge Wesley Armstrong is stabbed to death in his study by an intruder, and Victor Armstrong, the judge's nephew who has come to see him, is slugged unconscious by the same assailant. Police lieutenant Mike Ruark is alerted by the judge's secretary, Phyllis Powers, and arrives to find Victor recovering consciousness—but with a knife in his hand.

Meanwhile, Tommy Chan and Birmingham Brown, Chan's chauffeur, are walking home from a movie when they spot an apparent burglar entering a house by a window. When it turns out that the burglar was the house's owner, District Attorney Frank Bronson, they both end up spending the night in jail.

Later, Bates, the judge's butler, tells Bronson that the judge had denied Victor entrance to the house and Victor had sneaked in through a window. Phyllis then admits to Bronson that she overheard Victor, her boyfriend, and the judge arguing about an unwise stock deal in which Victor had invested $30,000. The judge then called his lawyer, Ed Seward, and arranged to meet him the following morning to draw up a new will that would exclude Victor, his sole heir. Victor would have been totally disinherited, thus making it appear that he had every motivation to kill his uncle.

When Chan comes to see Bronson to apologize about Tommy and Birmingham, Bronson and Lt. Ruark are notified that two sets of fingerprints were found on the knife—Victor's and Tony Pindello's. Aware that Pindello was sentenced by Judge Armstrong for a framed murder and was executed in the San Quentin gas chamber six months earlier, Lt. Ruark asks for Chan's help with the case. Later, someone shoots and kills Bronson and removes papers he was examining that are related to the Pindello case. Ruark tells Chan about Bronson's murder and that Pindello's fingerprints were found on Bronson's desk.

At Judge Armstrong's office, Chan and Lt. Ruark discover Walter Somerville, the judge's clerk of court, going through the judge's papers in a filing cabinet. While Chan and Ruark examine the judge's papers, Ed Seward arrives and tells them that before he became the judge's personal attorney, he defended Pindello in his murder trial. In the judge's home safe the detectives find papers pertaining to a commission investigating racketeering in the insurance business (a commission on which Seward is serving). They also find a letter addressed to Victor (to be opened only in the event of the judge's death) which states that he had uncovered evidence suggesting that Tony Pindello may have been framed and that he intended to inform Bronson of this.

Chan learns that Pindello was buried in a local cemetery. When Chan, Ruark, Tommy, and Birmingham go there, they discover that the coffin has been removed. Chan then requests that all members of the Pindello jury be placed under police protection, as he now

**Unbilled. †Billed as Pierre Watkins.*

fears for their safety. However, Lt. Ruark fails to locate one juror, Thomas Cartwright. Chan tells Ruark that he thinks there may be a connection between the Pindello case and the insurance swindle. Pat Finley, Ruark's assistant, locates Cartwright's new address, but before he can reach him, someone enters Cartwright's room and slugs him. When Finley arrives, he finds Cartwright dead by hanging, and once again Pindello's fingerprints are found at the crime scene.

Chan has the police department perform some experiments and discovers that it is possible to forge fingerprints. He then asks Ruark to arrange a meeting with Phyllis, Victor, and Seward at the judge's home. While they are in the study, the lights go out and a masked gunman locks them in a closet and then leaves. They manage to break out only to find that all the papers related to the Pindello case are gone. Later, Chan discovers that Mr. Grail, the director of a funeral parlor, has recently reburied a sealed coffin, and Chan obtains the address of the man who arranged for the burial. Chan breaks into the man's room but is surprised by Joseph Pindello, Tony's brother.

Later, Lt. Ruark assembles all the principals in the case, and Chan explains that Pindello's brother, Joseph, was in jail when Tony wrote to him telling him that he was about to be executed for a crime he had not committed. According to Chan, when Joseph got out of jail, he dug up his brother's body and intended to kill everyone associated with his execution. As Chan explains this, Joseph enters, holds everyone at gunpoint, and says that he simply intended to give his brother a proper burial. Before he can continue, Joseph is tackled from behind by Tommy and is taken prisoner.

Chan tells the group that Joseph is not the murderer of Armstrong, Bronson, or Cartwright, but that Seward is. Although Seward denies it, Chan states that Seward was involved with Tony Pindello in an insurance swindle, but Seward wanted all the money and framed Tony for murder. Fearing that Armstrong and Bronson were about to discover this, Seward murdered them and added Cartwright to make it look like a series of alphabetical killings. Seward grabs Joseph's gun and explains how he used copies of Tony's fingerprints to divert attention from himself. Chan then reveals that Joseph is part of the set-up they have just gone through, and that the gun is not loaded. As Seward tries to flee, he collides with Birmingham and is captured.

***The Shanghai Cobra* (1945)** The sixth *Charlie Chan* film produced by Monogram Pictures Corporation.

Alternate Title: *Charlie Chan in the Shanghai Cobra*. Source: based on the character "Charlie Chan" created by Earl Derr Biggers. Original Copyright: Monogram Pictures Corporation, August 5, 1945; LP56. Copyright Renewed: October 25, 1972; R538953. Production: January, 1945. Release Date: September 29, 1945. Sound: Western Electric Recording. Film: b&w; 5,797 feet. Running Time: 63–64 minutes.

Producer: James S. Burkett. Director: Phil Karlson. Assistant Director: Eddie Davis.* Screenplay: George Callahan and George Wallace Sayre. Original Story: George Callahan. Director of Photography: Vincent Farrar. Art Directors: Vin Taylor* and Dave Milton.* Editor: Ace Herman. Musical Director: Edward J. Kay. Recordist: Tom Lambert. Production Manager: Glenn Cook. Technical Director: Ormand McGill.*

Cast

Sidney Toler	*as*	Charlie Chan
Mantan Moreland		Birmingham Brown
Benson Fong		Tommy Chan
James Cardwell		Ned Stewart
Joan Barclay		Paula Webb [alias Pauline Webster]
Addison Richards		Jan Van Horn [alias John Adams]
Arthur Loft		Bradford Harris [alias for Special Agent Hume]
Janet Warren		Lorraine
Gene Stutenroth		Morgan
Joe Devlin		Taylor
James Flavin		H.R. Jarvis
Roy Gordon		Walter Fletcher
Walter Fenner		Inspector Harry Davis

**Unbilled.*

George Chandler*	Joe Nelson
Mary Moore*	Rita
Cyril Delevanti*	Larkin
Stephen Gregory*	Samuel Black
Bob Blair*	Corning
Bill Ruhl*	Gregory
Andy Andrews*	Policeman
Karon Knight*	Telephone supervisor
Diane Quillan*	Telephone operator
Dick Richardson*	Mailman

Plot Summary: After bank employee Samuel Black is killed by a cobra bite, Inspector Harry Davis of the New York City homicide squad telegrams his old friend Charlie Chan for help. Davis knows that Chan had captured accused murderer Jan Van Horn in Shanghai eight years earlier, and that Van Horn had been accused of using cobra bites on his victims.

Chan, now working as a government agent, arrives in New York City and quickly learns that Black and two similar victims were employed by the Sixth National Bank, whose vault holds millions of dollars worth of the government's radium. With the help of his son Tommy and his chauffeur Birmingham Brown, Chan learns that Ned Stewart, a novice private detective, had been seen with Black on the night of his death. Stewart tells Chan that he had been hired (his first case) by an unknown man to watch Paula Webb, the bank president's secretary (who confirms his story).

Meanwhile, Larkin, a police undercover agent working at the Sixth National bank, disappears after calling Davis for help. Soon thereafter, Davis learns that gangsters Morgan and Taylor were seen in the office of bank president Walter Fletcher. Tommy and Birmingham follow the hoodlums into a nearby laundry where they find a secret passageway from the laundry into the sewers. There Tommy and Birmingham uncover Larkin's murdered body, and an autopsy reveals that Larkin was killed by cobra venom. Chan then reasons that there must also be a secret passageway into the bank.

Back in the sewers, Chan, Stewart, and Inspector Davis discover a secret entrance into Paula's office. The investigators then go to a nearby coffee shop, whose proprietor, Joe Nelson, tells them that he purchased his video jukebox from a man named Jan Van Horn. Recognizing the jukebox operator's voice from the bank, Chan and Davis search the office of chemical engineer H.R. Jarvis and find Lorraine operating the jukebox from a secret room.

Chan quickly discovers that Black and the other victims were poisoned by cobra venom placed on a needle that appeared when they requested change from the jukebox. As part of a plan which he hopes will force the gangsters to act, Chan then feeds a fabricated story to the local newspapers that the government plans to remove its radium supply from the bank the next day. While Chan checks the bank's vault, Tommy and Birmingham follow Morgan into the laundry and become caught in the sewer after the gangsters attempt to blow open the vault. Chan becomes trapped when a section of the sewer caves in, but he uses the telephone lines to send a message in Morse code to Davis.

The police arrive at the bank in time to capture the gangsters and rescue Chan, Tommy, and Birmingham. From fingerprints, Chan determines that John Adams, a bank guard, is actually Jan Van Horn, and that Paula is his daughter. Van Horn then tells how he followed Jarvis to America, believing that he was one of the men who framed him for murder in Shanghai. Chan then recognizes bank officer Bradford Harris as Special Agent Hume of the Shanghai police, who is arrested as the real killer and leader of the gang.

*Unbilled.

"Shanghai is an unhealthy place for you." First sentence of a warning written on a piece of paper that is not too skillfully shoved into Charlie Chan's coat pocket while Chan chats with a missionary on a ship bound for Shanghai in *Charlie Chan in Shanghai* (1935). The remainder of the warning reads: "If you are wise you will not leave this ship."

Shanghai Maid Name of Capt. Kong's ship in *The Chinese Ring* (1947).

Shattuck Hotel Charlie Chan's hotel (he stays in Room 432) in *Black Magic* (1944).

Shaw, C. Montague (March 23, 1882, Adelaide, Australia–February 6, 1968, Woodland Hills, California) Dignified stage and screen character actor who appeared in over 50 films and had roles in three *Charlie Chan* films. Shaw portrays Hilary Galt in *Behind That Curtain* (1929), the doctor (unbilled) that treated Lady Mary Bristol after she was thrown from her horse in *Charlie Chan in London* (1934), and Inspector Duff in *Charlie Chan's Murder Cruise* (1940). Shaw has the distinction of being only one of six actors who appeared with three different actors playing Chan.

Shaw, Janet (1921, Beatrice, Nebraska–) Character actress (real name: Ellen Clancy) who appeared in over 45 films. In two *Charlie Chan* roles, Shaw portrays radio actress Gloria Bayne in *The Scarlet Clue* (1945) and Miss Petrie in *Dark Alibi* (1946).

Janet Shaw played a variety of minor roles before receiving her first big break as Dee, the daughter of Bette Davis in *The Old Maid* (1939). Unfortunately, this assignment led only to a few nondescript heroine roles. In 1940 she became a contract player at Universal, playing parts of all sizes (though usually small). Shaw was memorable as the girlfriend of Alderman Thurston Hall in the opening scenes of Abbott and Costello's *Hold That Ghost* (1941), and even more so as Louise, the sluttish waitress in Hitchcock's *Shadow of a Doubt* (1943). She spent the mid-1940s at Monogram, appearing in two *Charlie Chan* pictures as well as contributing a pleasing cameo as Gladys in *Johnny Doesn't Live Here Anymore* (1944).

Sheffield, Reginald (February 18, 1901, London, England–December 8, 1957, Pacific Palisades, California) British-born stage and screen character actor (real name: Reginald Sheffield Cassan) who appeared in nearly 50 films. Sheffield portrays RAF Flight Commander King (unbilled) at the Farnwell Aerodrome in *Charlie Chan in London* (1934).

Sherlock, Charles American character actor who appeared in over 35 films, often as unbilled reporters and cops. Sherlock portrays Sgt. McGraw in *The Scarlet Clue* (1945).

ships Many of the *Charlie Chan* films use ships of various kinds as a setting. The following ships are mentioned in the series.

Ship	Movie
Medusa	*City in Darkness* (1939)
President Pierce	*The Chinese Parrot* (1927), *Charlie Chan Carries On* (1931)
Presidente	*Docks of New Orleans* (1948)
Shanghai Maid	*The Chinese Ring* (1947)
S.S. *Manhattan*	*Charlie Chan at the Olympics* (1937)
S.S. *Nestor*	*Charlie Chan's Secret* (1936)
S.S. *Newcastle*	*Dangerous Money* (1946)
S.S. *Oceanic*	*Charlie Chan at the Race Track* (1936)
Susan B. Jennings	*Charlie Chan in Honolulu* (1938)
Suva Star	*Dead Men Tell* (1941)

In *Charlie Chan in Shanghai* (1937), *Charlie Chan on Broadway* (1937), and *Charlie Chan's Murder Cruise* (1940), the names of the ships are not mentioned.

Shore End Pier San Francisco waterfront amusement pier location of a funhouse hideout for the diamond theft gang (and the location of the Sea Tide Art Company owned by Webster Deacon) in *The Chinese Cat* (1944). Wu Song tells Charlie Chan that the pier is closed for the end of the war (World War II).

Shores, Lynn American film director who directed *Charlie Chan at the Wax Museum* (1940).

Sibley, Bessie Confederate (portrayed by Billie Seward) of Dr. Zodiac who originally persuaded psychic mind reader Eve Cairo to see Dr. Zodiac in *Charlie Chan at Treasure Island* (1939). Sibley is being blackmailed by Dr. Zodiac, who forces her to supply him with embarrassing information about others.

Sickner, William A. Director of photography for 10 *Charlie Chan* films at Monogram.

Charlie Chan filmography: *The Scarlet Clue* (1945), *Dark Alibi* (1946), *Shadows Over Chinatown* (1946), *Dangerous Money* (1946), *The Chinese Ring* (1947), *Docks of New Orleans* (1948), *The Shanghai Chest* (1948), *The Golden Eye* (1948), *The Feathered Serpent* (1948), and *Sky Dragon* (1949).

signatures Term used by the police fingerprint technician (portrayed by James T. Mack) for latent fingerprints in *Charlie Chan's Secret* (1936).

Silverheels, Jay (June 26, 1912, Six Nations Reservation, Brantfort, Ontario, Canada–March 5, 1980, Woodland Hills, California) American Indian actor (real name: Harold J. Smith) who appeared in over 50 movies and portrayed the Indian whom many recognize as The Lone Ranger's faithful companion, Tonto. Silverheels portrayed the Aztec Indian Diego in *The Feathered Serpent* (1948).

Jay Silverheels as The Lone Ranger's faithful Indian companion, Tonto.

Jay Silverheels was born on a reservation in Canada to a Mohawk chief. U.S. government records give Silverheels' birthdate as June 26, 1912, though virtually all cinema references disagree and give the year as 1919. He was a star lacrosse player and also excelled at wrestling, horse racing, football, boxing, and hockey. With the help of actor Joe E. Brown, Silverheels entered films in 1938 as a stuntman and extra. Following military service in World War II, Silverheels returned to film work and began landing small, often stereotypical roles as Indian warriors in westerns (that sometimes credited him as Harry S. Smith or Silverheels Smith). John Houston used him as one of the fugitive Osceola brothers in *Key Largo* (1948).

In 1949 Silverheels would work in a movie called *The Cowboy and the Indians* (1949) with another "B"-movie actor named Clayton Moore. It was later that same year that Silverheels was hired to play the faithful Indian companion, Tonto, in the television series *The Lone Ranger* (1949–57). He appeared as Tonto in all the episodes except for those that he missed when he had a heart attack (with Tonto being replaced by the Ranger's nephew, Dan).

Together with Moore, Silverheels reprised the role of Tonto in two big screen color movies—*The Lone Ranger* (1955) and *The Lone Ranger and the Lost City of Gold* (1958). After the series ended he became an outspoken activist for Indian rights, a spokesman to improve the portrayal of Indians on television, and a respected teacher within the Indian acting community. In the late 1970s his health failed and Silverheels died of a stroke in 1980.

Silvernail, Clarke (1892–September 22, 1930, Los Angeles, California) Screenwriter who (with Sonya Levien) wrote the screenplay for *Behind That Curtain* (1929).

Simmonds, Rona English tourist (portrayed by Gloria Warren) who is engaged to George Brace in *Dangerous Money* (1946). Simmonds tells Charlie Chan that she is going to Apia to visit the Robert Louis Stevenson shrine. Brace has falsified her travel visa, for which Rona is now being blackmailed by P.T. Burke (who knows about the fraud). She pays Burke off with a valuable necklace of hers.

Chan finds out that Rona's father was an Australian who was stranded during the war in Manila with valuable art objects that were stolen from bank vaults during the Japanese invasion. Rona is now trying to discover their whereabouts.

Simpson, Ivan F. (February 4, 1875, Glasgow, Scotland–October 12, 1951, New York, New York) Character actor who appeared in nearly 100 silent and sound films and portrayed T.M. Brade in *Charlie Chan's Greatest Case* (1933).

Sinclair, Herbert Henpecked assistant (portrayed by Milton Kibbee) to Mrs. Marsh in *The Scarlet Clue* (1945).

Sing Sing Prison State prison located in Ossining, New York, with its electric chair used for capital punishment. In *Charlie Chan at the Wax Museum* (1940), Steve McBirney is convicted of murder and sentenced to death at Sing Sing Prison during the week of December 9.

Singh, Aga Alias for Paul Narvo's servant and confederate Ramullah (portrayed by Lal Chand Mehra) in *Murder Over New York* (1940). Ramullah poses as a New York dealer in East Indian curios and uses part of his shop as a chemical laboratory to create tetrogene, a new poisonous gas. Following a lineup at the police station, Narvo's estranged wife, Patricia West, identifies Singh as Ramullah. When Ramullah tries to escape, he is shot in the back by Narvo through a window from an adjacent building. *See also* **Ramullah**.

Sister Teresa *see* **Teresa, Sister**

Sistrom, William Associate producer for *The Black Camel* (1931).

Sixth National Bank Distribution center of radium for hospitals, factories, and laboratories in *The Shanghai Cobra* (1945). The radium is stored in safety deposit box number 210 in a special vault rented by the U.S. government. The bank president is Walter Fletcher, and Bradford Harris is the vice president. In the past four months, three bank employees have been murdered with cobra venom by Harris, who is the leader of a gang that plans to steal the radium.

***The Sky Dragon* (1949)** The seventeenth *Charlie Chan* film produced by Monogram Pictures Corporation.

Alternate Title: *Charlie Chan in the Sky Dragon*. Working Title: *Murder in the Air*. Source: based on the character "Charlie Chan" created by Earl Derr Biggers. Original Copyright: Monogram Pictures Corporation; May 1, 1949; LP2407. Copyright Renewed: June 21, 1976; R635328. PCA Certificate Number: 13645. Production: December, 1948. Release Date: May 1, 1949. Sound: Western Electric Recording. Film: b&w. Running Time: 63–64 minutes.

Producer: James S. Burkett. Director: Lesley Selander. Assistant Directors: Wesley Barry and Ed Morey, Jr.* Screenplay: Oliver Drake and Clint Johnston. Story: Clint Johnston. Photography: William Sickner. Camera Operator: John Manin.* Gaffer: Bob Campbell.* Stills: Bud Graybill.* Special Effects: Ray Mercer. Technical Director: David Milton. Supervising Film Editor: Otho Lovering. Film Editors: Roy Livingston and Ace Herman.* Set Decoration: Raymond Boltz, Jr.* Musical Director: Edward J. Kay. Recordists: Tom Lambert and John Kean.* Makeup: Webb Overlander.* Hair Stylist: Lela Chambers.* Production Manager: Allen K. Wood. Screenplay Supervisor: Ilona Vas.* Grip: Harry Lewis.*

Cast

Roland Winters	*as*	Charlie Chan
Keye Luke		Lee Chan
Mantan Moreland		Birmingham Brown
Noel Neill		Jane Marshall
Tim Ryan		Lt. Mike Ruark
Iris Adrian		Wanda LaFern
Elena Verdugo		Connie Jackson [alias Marie Burke]

**Unbilled.*

Milburn Stone	Tim Norton
Lyle Talbot	Andy Barrett [alias Andrew J. Smith]
Paul Maxey	John Anderson
Joel Marston	Don Blake
John Eldridge	William E. French
Eddie Parks	Jonathon Tibbetts
Louise Franklin	Lena Franklin
Lyle Latell*	Ed Davidson
Gaylord Pendleton*	Ben Edwards
Emmett Vogan*	Doctor
Edna Holland*	Demanding old woman passenger
Joe Whitehead*	Stage doorman
Lee Phelps*	Detective at airport gate
Charles Jordan*	Stage manager
Suzette Harbin*	Second maid
George Eldredge*	Stacey
Bob Curts*	Watkins
Frank Cady*	

Plot Summary: Inside the cockpit of a commercial jetliner, pilots Tim Norton and Don Blake talk with insurance couriers Ben Edwards and Ed Davidson, who are carrying a shipment of $250,000. Norton goes to the back of the cabin for some coffee just as flight attendant Marie Burke begins seating the passengers. Marie, a former racketeer whose real name is Connie Barrett, notices that two of her past accomplices, Andy Barrett and follies star Wanda LaFern, are among the passengers. When they accuse her of stealing $60,000 from them, Marie denies it and begs them not to ruin her chance at a new life.

Minutes after drinking the coffee, everyone onboard the plane falls asleep, including the crew. Lee Chan is currently studying to become a commercial airplane pilot and is the first to awake. He notices a limp hand protruding from the cockpit door, and discovers that Davidson has been murdered and the insurance money stolen while everyone was asleep. After Lee wakes his father and the other passengers, John Anderson introduces himself as an investigator for the insurance company that insured the money shipment.

When the plane lands in San Francisco, Lt. Mike Ruark of the police and William E. French, the owner of the insurance company, question the passengers and crew but do not find out much information about the theft and killing. Norton and Blake go to the Gayety Theatre where Wanda LaFern is currently performing as a follies star. Reaching her dressing room door, they eavesdrop on a conversation in which Wanda accuses Marie, her sister, of stealing the insurance money. Chan, Lee, Lt. Ruark, and Chan's chauffeur Birmingham Brown also go to the theater where they now find Don Blake unconscious with a fractured skull. When Lt. Ruark sees Norton running away, he arrests him while Blake is rushed to the hospital.

Barrett later breaks into Charlie Chan's house to talk to Chan. While he holds a gun on Chan and is about to tell Chan some important information, he is shot by Anderson, who had been following Barrett. Chan and Lee search the marriage records of many of California's counties for information on Barrett's marriage years ago and eventually find the entry.

Chan and Lee go to the home of Jonathon Tibbetts, the justice of the peace in Humbolt County who officiated at the Barretts' wedding years ago. As an amateur photographer, Tibbetts always took pictures of the weddings he performed, and Chan asks to see the negatives of the wedding photos. When Tibbetts goes into the garage to get them, a shadowy figure knocks him out and sets the negatives on fire. Birmingham sees smoke coming from the garage and they rescue Tibbetts, but all the negatives are destroyed. However, Tibbetts checks his order book and notes that he sent prints of the wedding to the LaFern sisters, Connie and Wanda. Later, Chan and Lee find a photograph of the LaFern sisters in the newspaper and recognize Connie as Marie Burke.

With Lt. Ruark's help, Chan summons all of the remaining suspects back onto the plane. Chan then asks Connie, Wanda, and Tim Norton to take their places next to the coffee pot where they had been standing just prior to the robbery. Chan tells all the suspects about Don Blake's attack at the theater, and Lee, impersonating Blake wrapped in

**Unbilled.*

head bandages, boards the plane. As he raises his arm to point toward the thief, Connie grabs a gun from her purse. Before Connie can fire, however, Anderson shoots and kills her.

Chan describes how Anderson passed the money to French, his accomplice, in the lining of his overcoat after the plane landed. When Lt. Ruark tries to arrest them, French also draws his gun and Anderson, an experienced pilot, locks the cabin door and takes off. With the plane's sole parachute on his back, Anderson shuts off the plane's fuel and locks the cockpit door. Realizing that he has been double crossed, French struggles with Anderson, but both are grabbed by the police. Chan suspected something like this would happen and had a spare key to the cockpit door with him. After Norton opens the cockpit and restores fuel to the engines, Norton turns the controls over to Lee to safely land the plane.

Note: *The Sky Dragon* was the last movie in the *Charlie Chan* series made by Monogram.

Slade, Edmond A gunrunner suspected of murder (portrayed by George Meeker) who has escaped from one country and now poses as an agent for a firm that sells farm machinery in *The Red Dragon* (1945). Like Brandish, Countess Irena, and Masack, Slade is trying to obtain secret research papers held by Wyans describing a new 95th element.

Slade, Jimmy Convict number 8251 (portrayed by Anthony Warde in his second of two *Charlie Chan* roles) in *Dark Alibi* (1946). Slade is a convicted forger and prison trustee who is employed in the prison's fingerprint bureau file room. As part of an elaborate scheme concocted by prison guard Hugh Kenzie, Slade's job is to remove fingerprint cards of previous inmates at the prison which are then smuggled out by Kenzie. The fingerprints are then forged by Mr. Johnson to frame ex-convicts Steven Brill, Stanley Gray, and Thomas Harley of bank robbery and murder.

When Slade finds out that Charlie Chan suspects him of being part of the bank robbery and forgery scheme, Slade tries to escape with a gun given to him by Kenzie. Slade is cornered in the prison baling shed and tries to shoot Chan, but his gun explodes and he is killed (the gun barrel having been purposely plugged by Kenzie).

Slade, Mr. Charlie Chan's Secret Service boss (portrayed by George Lessey) in *Charlie Chan in the Secret Service* (1944).

Slippery Sam Name of hobby horse ridden by Frederick Ross in the hobby horse races in *Charlie Chan's Murder Cruise* (1940). For the final night's entertainment on his around-the-world cruise, Dr. Suderman organizes a series of hobby horse races with Charlie Chan as the judge. Susie Watson is the owner of Slippery Sam, who wins the first race.

"A smart gambler knows a dead horse can't win" Warning message in a note left for professional gambler Denny Barton in *Charlie Chan at the Race Track* (1936). Charlie Chan has Number One son Lee secretly distribute different warning messages to Warren Fenton, Bruce Rogers, George Chester, and Barton as part of a plan to identify the leader of a racetrack gambling ring.

Smiles, Frank Finch Actor of silent and sound films who portrayed Hilary Galt's clerk (credited as Finch Smiles) in *Behind That Curtain* (1929).

Smith Artist-beachcomber (portrayed by Murray Kinnell in his first of four *Charlie Chan* roles) in *The Black Camel* (1931). Smith tells Robert Fyfe he overheard Shelah Fane admit that she killed Denny Mayo. Smith then blackmails Fyfe by forcing him to "buy" one of his paintings for $300, but is soon shot in the back by Jessop.

Smith, Andrew J. Alias of Andrew Barrett in *The Sky Dragon* (1949). *See also* **Barrett, Andrew.**

Snowshoes Tom Evans' hired hand (portrayed by Stepin Fetchit) in *Charlie Chan in Egypt* (1935). Snowshoes tells Charlie Chan a hard-to-believe story that Evans had won him in a crap game. He then accompanies Professor Arnold's expedition to Egypt on the word of a fortune teller in Mississippi who tells him that his ancestors came from Egypt.

Sojin, Kamiyama (January 30, 1884, Sendai, Japan–July 28, 1954, Tokyo, Japan) Japanese stage and screen actor who appeared in over 35 silent and sound films, sometimes simply credited as Sojin. He was the second person to portray the character of Charlie Chan—in *The Chinese Parrot* (1927).

Kamiyama Sojin (the screen's second Charlie Chan) with Edmund Burns in *The Chinese Parrot*.

Note: The obituary in the August 4, 1954, issue of *Variety* gives the actor's name as Sojin Kamiyama, even though cinematic sources list the name as Kamiyama Sojin.

Somerville, Walter Clerk of the court (portrayed by Erville Alderson) for Judge Armstrong in *The Shanghai Chest* (1948).

Song, Wu Chinese artisan (portrayed by Luke Chan in his second of two *Charlie Chan* roles) who is noted for making items that contain secret compartments in *The Chinese Cat* (1944). Wu Song has sold some of his figurines to the Sea Tide Art Company (owned by Webster Deacon) which are used to conceal diamonds stolen in Chicago one year earlier.

Soueida, Fuad Fez-wearing Luxor police official (portrayed by Paul Porcasi) in *Charlie Chan in Egypt* (1935). When the body of Professor Arnold is discovered inside the mummy case of Ahmeti, Soueida is called in to take charge of the investigation.

Souto, Chief Captain of Police in Rio de Janeiro (portrayed by Harold Huber in his last of four *Charlie Chan* roles) in *Charlie Chan in Rio* (1941). With the assistance of Charlie Chan, Souto is about to arrest Lola Dean for a murder she committed several years ago in Honolulu.

Spaulding, George L. (1881–August 23, 1959, Hollywood, California) Actor who portrayed Dr. Hickey in *The Chinese Ring* (1947).

"SPY PLOT SUSPECTED!" Newspaper headline of the *Honolulu Post Dispatch* about the missing remote controlled test plane in *Charlie Chan at the Olympics* (1937).

S.S. *Manhattan* Steamship that is transporting the U.S. Olympic Team to Germany in *Charlie Chan at the Olympics* (1937).

S.S. *Nestor* A ship that was lost in a storm and sunk off the coast of Hawaii in *Charlie Chan's Secret* (1936). A headline in *The Daily Post* recorded that there were 30 passengers onboard and 27 were rescued in lifeboats.

Seven years later Charlie Chan is hired by Henrietta Lowell to determine if the body of the heir to the Colby estate, Allen Colby, is among the sunken wreckage. Divers recover two bodies, leaving only one person unaccounted for, presumably Allen Colby. Although Colby's body was not found in the water, a briefcase with the initials A.C. is recovered. Inside are Allen Colby's passport and a diary which tells of an attempt on his life after he had cabled his family that he was coming home. Colby writes: "It seems that the prodigal son isn't welcome."

"S.S. NESTOR LOST IN STORM OFF HAWAII!" Newspaper headline of *The Daily Post* story in *Charlie Chan's Secret* (1936). *See also* ***S.S. Nestor.***

S.S. *Newcastle* San Francisco–based steamship commanded by Capt. Black that is traveling from Honolulu to Samoa and Australia in *Dangerous Money* (1946). The passengers gather in the ship's salon for a ceremony to celebrate the crossing of the equator, and Scott Pearson, an undercover U.S. Treasury agent, is killed by a thrown knife before he can pass on information to Charlie Chan about the sudden appearance of money and artworks stolen from Philippine banks during the Japanese invasion.

S.S. *Oceanic* Steamship, commanded by Capt. Blade, traveling from Australia to Los Angeles, via Honolulu, in *Charlie Chan at the Race Track* (1936). Warren Fenton and George Chester are transporting their racehorses for the Santa Juanita Handicap.

Stable Murder Case The name of the case of the murder of Capt. Hamilton (which takes place in the stables of Geoffrey Richmond's country house) in *Charlie Chan in London* (1934). Paul Gray, Richmond's hunt secretary, is found guilty of the premeditated murder and sentenced to hang.

Stacey San Francisco policeman (portrayed by George Eldredge in his last of four *Charlie Chan* roles) who assists Lt. Ruark in *The Sky Dragon* (1949).

Stack, William Actor who appeared in almost 35 films and portrays James Eagan in *Charlie Chan's Greatest Case* (1933).

Stanley, Edwin (1880–December 24, 1944, Hollywood, California) Stage and screen actor who appeared in over 60 films, often as military officers, theatrical producers, and other dignified, take-charge characters. In three *Charlie Chan* roles, Stanley portrays the police lab technician (unbilled) in *Charlie Chan on Broadway* (1937), a police lab chemist (unbilled) in *Charlie Chan in Reno* (1939), and Col. D.C. Webster in *Charlie Chan in Panama* (1940).

Stanley, Professor John Aztec archeologist and antiquities smuggler (portrayed by Robert Livingston) who is engaged to Joan Farnsworth) in *The Feathered Serpent* (1948). Stanley and Sonia Cabot are part of a gang smuggling ancient Aztec artifacts out of Mexico. When Sonia's fiancé, Professor Farnsworth, and associate Professor Scott discover the lost ancient Aztec Temple of the Sun, Stanley and his gang capture and torture them. Scott eventually escapes but, before he can tell others of what he knows, is killed by Sonia (with help from Stanley). Because Sonia is unhappy about Stanley's engagement to Joan Farnsworth, Stanley murders Sonia to keep her from talking about their smuggling activities.

Stanton, Paul (December 21, 1884–October 9, 1955) Character actor who appeared in more than 80 films and portrays circus owner Joe Kinney in *Charlie Chan at the Circus* (1936).

Stardust Racehorse who initially finished second to Avalanche in the Melbourne Cup in *Charlie Chan at the Race Track* (1936). Because Avalanche's jockey, "Tip" Collins, is ordered to foul Stardust, Avalanche is subsequently disqualified and Stardust is made the winner of the race.

Starkey, Tom Séance assistant (portrayed by Charles Jordan in his first of five *Charlie Chan* roles) in *Black Magic* (1944). Starkey and his wife Vera help William and Justine Bonner with their phony séances. Before vaudeville faded away, both were magician's assistants.

Starkey, Vera Séance assistant (portrayed by Claudia Dell) in *Black Magic* (1944). Starkey and her husband Tom help William and Justine Bonner with their phony séances. Before vaudeville faded away, both were magician's assistants.

Statue of Liberty Ceramic statue brought to George Melton's house by Mrs. Winters as a going away present for Inez Arranto in *Charlie Chan in the Secret Service* (1944). As the German master spy Manleck, Mrs. Winters hides George Melton's torpedo plans inside the statue, plans which were stolen by her confederate, von Vegon, whom she murdered.

Stevens, Charles (May 26, 1893, Solomonsville, Arizona–August 22, 1964, Hollywood, California) Character actor who appeared in over 100 silent and sound films. In two *Charlie Chan* roles, Stevens portrays the fisherman-spy with a camera (unbilled) in *Charlie Chan in Panama* (1940) and the villainous henchman Manuel in *The Feathered Serpent* (1948).

A grandson of the legendary Apache chief Geronimo, Charles Stevens (often billed as Charles "Injun" Stevens) made his film debut as an extra in *The Birth of a Nation* (1915). The close friend and mascot of cinema idol Douglas Fairbanks, Sr., Stevens appeared in all but one of Fairbanks' starring films, beginning with *The Lamb* (1915). He was often seen in multiple roles, never more obviously than in Fairbanks' *The Black Pirate* (1926). His largest role during his Fairbanks years was Planchet in *The Three Musketeers* (1921) and its sequel *The Iron Mask* (1929).

In talkies, Stevens was generally cast as a villain, usually an Indian, Mexican, or Arab. Outside of major roles in early sound efforts like *The Big Trail* (1930) and *Tom Sawyer* (1930), he could be found playing menacing tribal chiefs and bandits in serials and "B" pictures, and seedy, drunken "redskin" stereotypes (invariably named Injun Joe or Injun Charlie) in big-budget films like John Ford's *My Darling Clementine* (1946). He was also much in demand as a technical adviser on Native American lore and customs.

Stevens, Landers (February 17, 1877, San Francisco, California–December 19, 1940, Hollywood California) Film producer and stage and screen character actor (real name: John Landers Stevens) who appeared in over 30 silent and sound films. In two unbilled *Charlie Chan* roles, Stevens portrays a bank attendant in *Charlie Chan in Paris* (1935) and the coroner in *Charlie Chan's Secret* (1936).

Stevenson, Robert Louis (November 13, 1850, Edinburgh, Scotland–December 3, 1894, Samoa) Scottish novelist, travel writer, poet, and essayist who is the author of the popular romantic adventure stories *Treasure Island* (1883) and *Kidnapped* (1886), and the alarming psychological fable *Dr. Jekyll and Mr. Hyde* (1886). After becoming a successful writer, Stevenson and his wife sailed from San Francisco to the islands of the South Pacific in 1888, and Samoa became his permanent home in 1890, where he died in 1894.

In *Dangerous Money* (1946), Rona Simmonds tells Charlie Chan that she is traveling to Apia to visit the Robert Louis Stevenson shrine.

Stewart, Ned Private detective (portrayed by James Cardwell) in *The Shanghai Cobra* (1945). As the sole employee of the Apex Detective Agency, Stewart is hired by a Mr. Rogers, a fictitious name given by Jan Van Horn (alias John Adams), over the telephone. Rogers instructs Stewart to go to 1055 Harley Street every night, and if a woman named Pauline Webster comes out, to follow her, as she seems to be in danger.

As the case progresses, Stewart quickly feels romantically attracted to Paula Webb and even buys an engagement ring. When he shows it to Charlie Chan, Chan tells Stewart not to offer the ring to Paula until the case is closed.

Stone, Arthur (November 28, 1884, St. Louis, Missouri–September 4, 1940, Hollywood, California) Make-up artist and stage and screen character actor who appeared in over 40 films and portrays the dragoman in *Charlie Chan in Egypt* (1935).

Stone, John (September 12, 1888, New York, New York–June 3, 1961, Los Angeles, California) Producer or associate producer (real name: Jack Strumwasser) of 15 *Charlie Chan* films with Twentieth Century–Fox, as well as *Mr. Moto's Gamble* (1938), a reworked

Associate producer John Stone, Warner Oland, William Demarest, and director "Lucky" Humberstone going over the script of *Charlie Chan at the Opera*.

version of the never-completed *Charlie Chan at the Ringside*.

John Stone was educated at DeWitt Clinton High School, College of New York, and New York University, and had no stage training when he signed on as a staff writer at Fox studios in 1925. He wrote for most of the Fox stars, including William Farnum, Dustin Farnum, William Russel, Shirley Mason, Buck Jones. Stone also wrote two *Zane Grey* films, *Nevada* (1927) and *Drums of the Desert* (1927), for Paramount.

Stone worked two years for Tom Mix, writing films such as *No Man's Gold* (1926), *The Great K & A Train Robbery* (1926), *Hard Boiled* (1926), *Arizona Wildcat* (1927), and *Daredevil's Reward* (1928). Stone then switched to the production end of the business when he became director of foreign productions at Fox in 1930 to 1931. In 1931 he was appointed as an assistant to Fox vice president Winfield Sheehan and then weathered Sheehan's dismissal by latching onto Sol Wurtzel's "B"-picture unit.

In 1933 Stone produced *Smoky* for Sol Wurtzel, and then three of the early *Charlie Chan* films in 1934–35. After the merger with Twentieth Century in 1935, Stone was made the associate producer for 12 more Chan films and also produced most of the *Mr. Moto* series. When he moved to Columbia in 1940, John Stone became the producer of the *Boston Blackie* features.

Charlie Chan filmography—as producer: *Charlie Chan's Courage* (1934), *Charlie Chan in London* (1934), and *Charlie Chan in Paris* (1935).

Charlie Chan filmography—as associate producer: *Charlie Chan in Shanghai* (1935), *Charlie Chan's Secret* (1936), *Charlie Chan at the Circus* (1936), *Charlie Chan at the Race Track* (1936), *Charlie Chan at the Opera* (1936), *Charlie Chan at the Olympics* (1937), *Charlie Chan on Broadway* (1937), *Charlie Chan at Monte Carlo* (1937), *Charlie Chan in Honolulu* (1938), *Charlie Chan in Reno* (1939), *City in Darkness* (1939), and *Charlie Chan's Murder Cruise* (1940).

Milburn Stone as "Doc" Adams from his *Gunsmoke* days (Everett Collection).

Stone, Milburn (July 5, 1904, Burton, Kansas–June 12, 1980, LaJolla, California) American stage and screen character actor who appeared in over 110 films, usually as a villain or tough hero. Stone portrays airplane pilot Tim Norton in *The Sky Dragon* (1949).

Milburn Stone got his start in vaudeville as one half of the song 'n' snappy patter team of Stone and Strain. He worked with several touring theatrical troupes before settling down in Hollywood in 1935, where he played everything from bits to full leads in the "B"-picture products ground out by such studios as Mascot and Monogram. One of his few appearances in an "A" picture was his unbilled but memorable role as Stephen A. Douglas in John Ford's *Young Mr. Lincoln* (1939). During this period he was also a regular in the low-budget but popular *Tailspin Tommy* series. He spent the 1940s at Universal in a vast array of character parts, at one point being cast in a leading role only because he physically matched the actor in the film's stock-footage scenes.

Full stardom would elude Stone until 1955 when he was cast as the irascible Dr. Galen "Doc" Adams in television's *Gunsmoke*. Milburn Stone went on to win an Emmy for this colorful characterization, retiring from the series in 1972 due to ill health.

Strang, Harry Character actor who appeared in over 115 films, including three *Charlie Chan* entries. Strang portrays the impostor chauffeur of Shanghai police commissioner Col. Watkins in *Charlie Chan in Shanghai* (1935), a policeman in *Charlie Chan on Broadway* (1937), and the guard stationed in front of Mr. Pendleton's cabin in *Charlie Chan's Murder Cruise* (1940).

Strange, Philip Actor who portrays Eric Durand in *Behind That Curtain* (1929).

Strasser, Inspector Typical Prussian-styled Berlin police inspector (portrayed by Frederick Vogeding in his second of three *Charlie Chan* roles) in *Charlie Chan at the Olympics* (1937). Strasser is very good at saluting while clicking his heels, and tends to exclaim, "Things like this cannot happen in Berlin!"

"Streamline" Jones *see* **Jones, "Streamline"**

Strohbach, William Production manager for *The Jade Mask* (1945) and *The Scarlet Clue* (1945).

Strong, Michael Mr. Harper's mute chauffeur and handyman (portrayed by Lester Dorr in his second of two *Charlie Chan* roles) in *The Jade Mask* (1945). Strong is murdered by Lloyd Archer with a poison dart before he can give Charlie Chan clues about Harper's murder.

Stutenroth, Gene *see* **Roth, Gene**

Suderman, Dr. Cruise tour conductor (portrayed by Lionel Atwill in his second of two *Charlie Chan* roles) in *Charlie Chan's Murder Cruise* (1940). After five members of his cruise are murdered, Suderman becomes part of Charlie Chan's plan to uncover the elusive Jim Eberhardt, who is responsible for the murders.

Note: The character Dr. Suderman loosely parallels that of Dr. Lofton in *Charlie Chan Carries On* (1931).

Slim Summerville (Everett Collection)

Summerville, Slim (July 10, 1892, Albuquerque, New Mexico–January 5, 1946, Laguna Beach, California) Tall comedic character actor (real name: George J. Summerville) and former Keystone Kop who appeared in nearly 130 silent and sound films. In two *Charlie Chan* roles, Summerville portrays a prospector in *The Chinese Parrot* (1927) and Sheriff "Tombstone" Fletcher in *Charlie Chan in Reno* (1939).

Susan B. Jennings Freighter ship piloted by Capt. Johnson in *Charlie Chan in Honolulu* (1938). The ship is headed from Shanghai to San Francisco with a cargo of wild animals for a San Francisco zoo. Besides the animals and crew, the freighter carries an eclectic group of six passengers—Judy Hayes, Carol Wayne, Johnny McCoy, Detective Arnold, Dr. Cardigan, and Al Hogan.

Sutton, John (October 22,1908, Rawalpindi, India–July 10, 1963, Cannes, France) Stage and screen actor who appeared in nearly 60 films, often cast as a villain. Sutton portrays saboteur Keith Jeffrey (an alias for Paul Narvo) in *Murder Over New York* (1940).

Like Errol Flynn, John Sutton led an adventuresome pre–Hollywood life in the British colonies, working at various junctures as a hunter, plantation overseer, and rancher. Unlike Flynn, Sutton was not immediately perceived as the dashingly heroic type, and he worked first not as an actor but as a technical consultant in films with British themes. It wasn't until 1936, when he portrayed an unbilled British officer in *The Last of the Mohicans*, that he stepped in front of the camera.

He spent most of the 1940s as a "utility Englishman" at Twentieth Century–Fox in both sympathetic and sneering roles. He portrayed Lord Crewe in *Hudson's Bay* (1940), Dr. Rivers in *Jane Eyre* (1943), and Cecil Graham in *The Fan* (1949). Sutton also played the leading roles of Dr. Phillip Rossiter in *Moon Over Her Shoulder* (1942), Geoffrey Carter in *Tonight We Raid Calais* (1943), and the Duke of Buckingham in MGM's remake of *The Three Musketeers* (1948).

Contrary to some published sources, Sutton never played Bulldog Drummond in Paramount's *Drummond* series of the 1930s, although he did have minor roles in three of the films and portrayed Inspector Tredennis twice—in *Arrest Bulldog Drummond* (1939) and *Bulldog Drummond's Bride* (1939). Sutton died of heart failure at the age of 54 shortly after playing (unbilled) Kinsford in *Of Human Bondage* (1964).

Suva Star Ship commanded by Captain Kane which is chartered for a treasure hunt cruise to Cocos Island by Miss Nodbury in *Dead Men Tell* (1941).

***Swan Lake* (Opus 20)** Popular ballet music, written in 1877 by Pyotr Ilyich Tchaikovsky (1840–1893), which is the opening music in *Charlie Chan in Egypt* (1935) in addition to several other movies of the 1930s, including *Dracula* (1931).

Swendstrom, Dr. Oscar Scientist and inventor (portrayed by Harry Hayden in his second of two *Charlie Chan* roles) in *Docks of New Orleans* (1948). He sells the formula of a poison gas he had developed to the Lafontaine Chemical Company for $500.

Upon learning of a major shipment of the gas to South America, Swendstrom feels that he has been swindled by Simon Lafontaine and his two partners. With his wife as an accomplice, Swendstrom ingeniously murders Lafontaine, Henri Castanaro, and Theodore Von Scherbe using the same poison gas he had sold to Lafontaine's company.

The gas is contained in a radio vacuum tube whose glass shell breaks when music of a certain pitch is played over the radio. The radio is tuned to receive the radio broadcast hosted by Mrs. Swendstrom, who plays the required music to break the glass.

A similar method of placing a poison gas in a thin-walled glass tube and using it as a murder weapon is employed by Professor Thurston in *Charlie Chan in Egypt* (1935) to kill his nephew Barry Arnold while playing his violin.

Swenson, Hulda Swedish cleaning woman at the Cosmo Radio Center (portrayed by Victoria Faust) in *The Scarlet Clue* (1945). Swenson is really Janet Carter, an undercover government investigator placed at the building by Charlie Chan to watch people coming from and going to the Hamilton Laboratory.

Sze, Field Marshal Chun Chinese warlord who is the brother of Princess Mei Ling in *The Chinese Ring* (1947).

T

$2.00 (1) Price of a hotel room (without breakfast) at the Mojave Wells Hotel that is quoted to Jimmy by Hank Wigley, the hotel owner, in *Castle in the Desert* (1942).

$2.00 (2) Amount Charlie Chan pays for the book *Murder by Madame* in a bookstore in *The Chinese Cat* (1944). *See also* **Murder by *Madame*.**

2W 590 California license plate number on a car belonging to George Bently in *Charlie Chan in Reno* (1939). The license plate also bears the inscription "California's World Fair 39."

10 Number for the song "The Blue Danube" requested by Samuel Black from the jukebox located in Joe's Coffee Shop in *The Shanghai Cobra* (1945). When a different song is played instead, Black tells Lorraine, the voice from the jukebox, that the song is not what he requested. Lorraine then tells Black to push the coin return button and his money will be refunded.

12th Precinct New York police district of both Capt. Flynn in *The Scarlet Clue* (1945) and homicide squad chief Inspector Harry Davis in *The Shanghai Cobra* (1945).

$20 (1) Amount Charlie Chan gives son Lee as spending money in *Charlie Chan on Broadway* (1937). Lee asks for a couple of weeks allowance in advance, as he only has $1 to see the town. Almost as quickly as Lee puts the money in his pants pocket, a pickpocket bumps into Lee and takes it from him. Chan then suggests that Lee lock himself in the hotel room before his dinner suit is snatched from his body.

$20 (2) Fee for consultation with Dr. Zodiac requested from Charlie Chan by Abdul the Turk in *Charlie Chan at Treasure Island* (1939). When Pete Lewis and Fred Rhadini, who are with Chan, complain about the fee, Chan philosophically replies while paying Abdul, "If request music, must be willing to pay fiddler."

20 francs Amount of bet made by Lee Chan at the roulette wheel on the number 25 (red) in *Charlie Chan at Monte Carlo* (1937).

21st Dynasty Ancient Egyptian dynastic period (1085–945 B.C.) which marked the end of the New Kingdom and the beginning of the Third Intermediate Period. The succeeding royal governments of the 21st Dynasty ruled from the city of Tanis and abandoned all claims to Nubia.

The known pharaohs that reigned during

this dynasty were Smendes (1085–1044 B.C.), Amenemnisu (1040 B.C.), Psusennes I (1040–992 B.C.), Amenemope (993–984 B.C.), Osorkon (984–978 B.C.), Siamun (978–959 B.C.), and Psusennes II (959–945 B.C.). Psusennes II's successor, Sheshonq I, founder of the 22nd Dynasty, married Maarkare, Psusennes' daughter. The little light that is thrown on the 21st Dynasty comes largely from biblical records, since this period coincides with the struggle of David in Israel to unite the tribes and destroy the Philistines, exemplified initially in the story of David and Goliath.

In *Charlie Chan in Egypt* (1935), Tom Evans clarifies some ancient Egyptian history for Charlie Chan when he tells Chan that the mummy found in the tomb is that of Ahmeti, who was one of the most powerful High Priests of the 21st Dynasty.

21 Washington Square, Room 4 Address of New York rooming house residence of Patricia West in *Murder Over New York* (1940).

22 Box number in the Olympic Stadium (in a section reserved for the diplomatic corps) which belongs to Charles Zaraka in *Charlie Chan at the Olympics* (1937). Charlie Chan receives a ticket for the opening ceremonies, and when son Lee points out to his father he has never met Zaraka, Charlie replies, "Have never met Santa Claus either, but accept gifts from same."

25 Losing roulette wheel bet repeatedly made by Lee Chan in *Charlie Chan at Monte Carlo* (1937). Lee chooses the number 25 (red) by noting a series of coincidences to his father—they are staying in Room 125 in a hotel in Nice; Lee is 25 years old; today's date is August 25; and the current year is 9325 on the Chinese calendar.

25¢ (1) Price of admission to the Kinney & Gaines Combined Circus' "Greatest Show on Earth" in *Charlie Chan at the Circus* (1936).

25¢ (2) Price of admission to Dr. Cream's Crime Museum in *Charlie Chan at the Wax Museum* (1940).

$25 (1) Amount of money Charlie Chan reminds Number One son Lee that Lee borrowed from him the previous week when Lee asks Charlie for some money to bet at the casino in *Charlie Chan at Monte Carlo* (1937).

$25 (2) Amount that Jimmy Chan is charged for the taxi ride to Manderley Castle in *Castle in the Desert* (1942). Jimmy has only $20, but the taxi driver (portrayed by George Chandler in his second of four *Charlie Chan* roles) says that he will trust him for the rest.

26 Malibu Drive Malibu Beach waterfront address of the Rutherford Mansion, a beach house rented by Cole King for his variety troupe, in *The Trap* (1947). Although San Toy gives Birmingham the address as 26 Malibu Drive over the telephone, the house number nevertheless is displayed as 624.

28 CG 321 License plate number of Max Corday's car in *Charlie Chan in Paris* (1935). Lee Chan follows Max Corday (disguised as Marcel Xavier, a crippled beggar), who takes a taxi from the Lamartine Bank and, five miles later, transfers to a car with license plate number 28 CG 321. Later that evening, while watching Albert Dufresne's apartment, Lee sees the same car pull up to the front entrance and disgorge Max Corday and Renee Jacquard.

210 Safety deposit box number of a special vault in the Sixth National Bank in *The Shanghai Cobra* (1945). The vault is rented by the U.S. government and contains radium for hospitals, factories, and laboratories.

349 Dexter Street Address of William Bonner's house where he and his wife Justine hold phony séances in *Black Magic* (1944).

$2,000 at 10-to-1 odds Challenge made by Dr. Paul Rednick to Charlie Chan in *The Chinese Cat* (1944). Rednick bets Chan that he cannot solve Thomas Manning's murder, which was the basis for Rednick's book *Murder by Madame*. After checking the family finances and being told by Tommy that all of the members of the family are now working,

Charlie accepts the bet, witnessed by Harvey Dennis. Chan tells Rednick that if he loses, Chan will donate $2,000 to the Chinese War Relief; otherwise, Rednick has to give $20,000 to the same cause. Even though Charlie is not a betting man, he mentions that 10-to-1 odds are too good to pass up.

$10,000 (1) Amount Warner Oland was paid for his role in *Charlie Chan Carries On* (1931). Because of the success of this picture, Oland was paid $12,500 per movie for the next nine pictures, although he had asked for more.

$10,000 (2) Amount George Chester promises to pay jockey Eddie Brill as a bonus if he rides Avalanche to victory in the Santa Juanita Handicap in *Charlie Chan at the Race Track* (1936). Because of publicized threats against Avalanche, none of the jockeys are willing to ride the horse in the handicap race. However, Eddie Brill steps up to Chester and offers to ride the horse. Appearing grateful, Chester then promises Brill a bonus of $10,000 to "see that specialist about his leg" if he wins the race.

10,000 francs Amount of money Nardi writes in her diary that Albert Dufresne lost in a gambling house in Montparnasse in *Charlie Chan in Paris* (1935).

$20,000 (1) Amount Warner Oland was paid per movie for *Charlie Chan at the Circus* (1936), *Charlie Chan at the Race Track* (1936), and *Charlie Chan at the Opera* (1937).

$20,000 (2) Amount Warren Fenton offers to George Chester to retire Avalanche in *Charlie Chan at the Race Track* (1936).

$25,000 Amount of three metallurgic bonds, 250,000 francs each, missing from Victor Karnoff's safe in *Charlie Chan at Monte Carlo* (1937).

$30,000 Amount Warner Oland was paid per movie for *Charlie Chan at the Olympics* (1937), *Charlie Chan on Broadway* (1937), and *Charlie Chan at Monte Carlo* (1937).

226574 Identification number on Morgan's mug shot, whose police record is shown to Charlie Chan by Inspector Davis in *The Shanghai Cobra* (1945). *See also* **Morgan**.

$300,000 Amount that Judy Hayes is instructed by her employer, John Emery, to give to an unknown man (who then is to give her a wedding ring as a receipt) in *Charlie Chan in Honolulu* (1938).

The unknown man is R. Hillman, who is in the process of getting a divorce from his wife. Hillman and his lawyer, John Emery, plan to get $300,000 out of China and avoid a property settlement. Emery is to have his secretary, Judy Hayes, travel from Shanghai to San Francisco on the freighter *Susan B. Jennings* with a package containing $300,000.

After the man is murdered, Judy Hayes puts the money in an attaché case in a trunk in her cabin, but it later goes missing. The money is stolen by Capt. Johnson, who hides the attaché case in one of the ship's lifeboats, but it is later discovered by Johnny McCoy.

347762 Identification number on Taylor's mug shot, whose police record is shown to Charlie Chan by Inspector Davis in *The Shanghai Cobra* (1945). *See also* **Taylor**.

2 million francs Amount of money Albert Dufresne receives at the Lamartine Bank from receipts of the counterfeit bonds in *Charlie Chan in Paris* (1935). Dufresne packs the money (which is wrapped in envelopes, each sealed with a wax seal of the bank) in his suitcase and plans to escape to Switzerland on a midnight plane.

10:00 p.m. Time that Emil Manolo sets the timer to explode on a bomb placed at the Miraflores Power Control Station in *Charlie Chan in Panama* (1940).

12:00 midnight (1) Time of an airplane flight on which Albert Dufresne plans to flee to Switzerland with 2 million francs received from the sale of bogus bonds in *Charlie Chan in Paris* (1935). However, he is shot in the back by Max Corday (disguised as the crippled beggar, Marcel Xavier), who then takes the money.

12:00 midnight (2) Time that Billie Bronson tells Speed Patten to meet her in her hotel room for her to give him a hot story in *Charlie Chan on Broadway* (1937).

12:00 noon Deadline given Joan Karnoff by Albert Rogers to repay him $25,000 for the metallurgic bonds she took from his room in *Charlie Chan at Monte Carlo* (1937).

tagara The Sanskrit name for the plant *Valeriana wallichi*, which is a perennial, herbaceous plant indigenous to India and found in the temperate Himalayan region. The dried rhizome and rootlets are used for medicinal purposes as an analgesic and tranquilizer. Used in too large a dose, however, it may produce liver disease.

In *Castle in the Desert* (1942), Dr. Retling tells Charlie Chan that the root of the tagara weed is used for treatment of insomnia. Professor Gleason and Arthur Fletcher drink wine containing root of tagara weed and pretend to have been poisoned by Lucy Manderley, a descendant of the infamous Borgias who were known to have poisoned their victims. This is part of a scheme concocted by Dr. Retling and Walter Hartford to convince Lucy's wealthy husband that Lucy is insane and should turn the control of a $20 million estate over to Hartford via power of attorney. Mme. Saturnia mentions to Charlie Chan that Juliet drank tagara, but what Juliet drinks is never specified in Shakespeare's *Romeo and Juliet*.

Tait, Patrick Elderly criminal lawyer (portrayed by William Holden) who is a member of Dr. Lofton's world tour in *Charlie Chan Carries On* (1931).

Talbot, Lyle (February 8, 1902, Pittsburgh, Pennsylvania–March 2, 1996, San Francisco, California) Square-built American leading man (real name: Lisle Henderson) in over 170 films and television. Talbot portrays Andrew Barrett (alias Andrew J. Smith) in *The Sky Dragon* (1949).

Lyle Talbot (Everett Collection)

Born into a family of traveling show folk, Lyle Talbot toured the hinterlands as a teenaged magician. Talbot went on to work as a regional stock-company actor, pausing long enough in Memphis, Tennessee, to form his own troupe, The Talbot Players. Like many other barnstorming performers of the 1920s, Talbot headed to Hollywood during the early talkie era. Blessed with good looks, he started out as a utility lead at Warner Bros.

Talbot worked steadily throughout the 1930s, playing heroes in "B" pictures and supporting parts in "A" pictures. During a loanout to Monogram, he was afforded an opportunity to co-star with Ginger Rogers in a series of entertaining mysteries—as Winston in *The Thirteenth Guest* (1932) and as Theodore Rand in *A Shriek in the Night* (1933).

In 1933 Talbot and 23 other film players organized the Screen Actors Guild. To the end of his days, he could be counted upon to proudly display his SAG card number four at the drop of a hat. As his hairline receded and his girth widened, Talbot became one of Hollywood's busiest villains. He worked extensively in serials, playing characters on both sides of the law. In 1949 alone, he could be seen as Commissioner Gordon in *Batman and Robin* and as villain Lex Luthor in *Atom Man vs. Superman*.

Seemingly willing to work for anyone who met his price, Talbot had no qualms about appearing in low-budget horror films in the 1950s. He was prominently cast in two of Edward D. Wood's "classics," *Glen or Glenda* (1953) and *Plan 9 from Outer Space* (1955). When asked what it was like to work for the untalented Wood, Talbot would recall with amusement that the director never failed to pay him up front for each day's work with a handful of stained, crinkled ten-dollar bills.

Appearing on television, his better-known assignments were as Ozzie Nelson's irksome neighbor Thorny Thornwell on *The Adventures of Ozzie and Harriet* (1952–66) and Bob Cumming's lascivious air force buddy Paul Fonda on *Love That Bob* (a.k.a. *The Bob Cummings Show*; 1955–59).

Tarneverro the Great Hypnotist and fortune-teller (portrayed by Bela Lugosi) whose real name is Arthur Mayo in *The Black Camel* (1931). Tarneverro arrives in Honolulu (at Shelah Fane's request) to advise on a marriage proposal from Alan Jaynes. While in Honolulu, Tarneverro tries to get proof that Fane murdered his brother, the well-known movie actor Denny Mayo, three years earlier.

In a meeting in a hotel lobby, Charlie Chan tells the mystic that the Honolulu police take a dim view of fortune-tellers. Tarneverro assures Chan that he is not in Honolulu professionally and tells Charlie that, "We are both detectives. You look backwards; I look forward."

Note: The character Tarneverro loosely parallels that of Alfredo Marana in *Charlie Chan in Rio* (1941).

Taylor Gangster (portrayed by Joe Devlin) who is involved with Bradford Harris, H.R. Jarvis, and Morgan in a plan to steal radium belonging to the U.S. government from the vault at the Sixth National Bank in *The Shanghai Cobra* (1945).

Taylor, Donald D. Actor who portrayed Alfred Wyans' murdered secretary, Walter Dorn, in *The Red Dragon* (1945).

Taylor, Forrest (December 29, 1883, Bloomington, Illinois–February 19, 1965, Garden Grove, California) Veteran character actor (real name: E. Forrest Taylor) who appeared in over 180 silent and sound films, most often cast as a businessman or a lawyer (sometimes on the shadier side of the law). Taylor portrays Mr. Manning in *The Golden Eye* (1948).

Taylor, Vincent A. Film set decorator and production designer for nearly 30 films. Taylor was the set decorator for *The Jade Mask* (1945) and the art director (unbilled) for *The Shanghai Cobra* (1945).

The Temple of Magic Performance venue of "The Great Rhadini" located on San Francisco's Treasure Island in *Charlie Chan at Treasure Island* (1939).

Teresa, Sister The nurse (portrayed by Evelyn Brent) hired from a nearby mission by Mrs. Driscoll at a doctor's request to administer needed around-the-clock medication (opiates) to the critically injured Mr. Manning in *The Golden Eye* (1948). The nun is an impostor and is part of the gold smuggling gang.

Charlie Chan deduces that the nun is an impostor when she momentarily bends over near Manning's sickbed and her habit's hemline lifts a bit, showing that she is wearing high heeled shoes and nylon hose. He then confirms his suspicion by asking her a medical question, with the phony nun showing her medical ignorance by not knowing about tetanus.

tetrogene A new poisonous gas that kills with one whiff and evaporates quickly, leaving a harmless scent. In *Murder Over New York* (1940), Charlie Chan and son Jimmy search Ramullah's curio shop and find a chemical lab and a piece of paper on which is written the chemical formula for tetrogene. David Elliot, a chemical engineer who owns a chemical research company, is secretly experimenting with tetrogene as the basis for a powerful explosive.

Confined in a glass pellet, tetrogene is used by Paul Narvo (masquerading as Keith

Jeffrey) to murder Hugh Drake in George Kirby's library. Narvo later murders Kirby by placing some tetrogene in a glass of brandy that Kirby is drinking from, and also tries to kill Herbert Fenton (before he can tell Chan Paul Narvo's true identity) by placing tetrogene in a cup of water from which Fenton is about to drink.

TH E$M OST Letters typed as a dying clue by Alfred Wyans' secretary, Walter Dorn, after being shot in *The Red Dragon* (1945). The letters are supposed to spell "THERMOSTAT," referring to the murder weapon—a disguised radio transmitter that remotely triggers an explosive that fires a bullet. The fake thermostat is virtually unnoticed when attached to a wall by a small spike and is easily removed by the murderer (Joseph Brandish) before anyone would notice it.

Thacker, Detective Sgt. The by-the-book British county police constable (portrayed by E.E. Clive) in *Charlie Chan in London* (1934). Thacker is called in to investigate the murder of Lake and is first suspicious of Chan, an outsider, whom he calls "Mr. Chang." However, Thacker soon appreciates Chan's superior methodical deductive abilities.

"Thank you, so much" (多謝, dúo xiè) Charlie Chan's ever-present polite words of thanks. In *Charlie Chan in Paris* (1935), Chan even politely bows and gives thanks to a wooden cuckoo clock bird for leading him to a hidden diary.

"They Met in Rio" Title of song sung by Lola Dean during her nightclub act at the Carioca Casino in *Charlie Chan in Rio* (1941). The music was written by Mack Gordon, with lyrics by Harry Warren.

"THIRD COBRA KILLING" Newspaper headline read by police inspector Harry Davis in *The Shanghai Cobra* (1945). The murder of bank guard Samuel Black is the third such killing in the last four months, and all three victims were employees of the Sixth National Bank.

"Thirty days has September, July, and August" Word code combination spoken by Mr. Harper that opens a voice-actuated door to a hidden room in *The Jade Mask* (1945). The room contains secret papers about Harper's inventions. The papers are kept inside a desk that, when opened, releases gas in the room and closes the door. To escape, the correct words have to be spoken in Harper's voice. When Lloyd Archer intentionally traps his wife, Stella Graham, alone in the room, Charlie Chan uses a cylinder recording of Harper reciting the correct phrase to open the door and rescue Graham.

thirty pieces of silver Thirty silver dimes in a small pouch seen in *Charlie Chan's Murder Cruise* (1940). The dimes are recognized by Charlie Chan as a symbol of ancient betrayal, referring to the biblical betrayal of Jesus by Judas.

In *Charlie Chan's Murder Cruise*, two bags of 30 dimes appear. The first bag is found in the hands of the murdered Mr. Kenyon, who is mistakenly killed due to having earlier changed hotel rooms with Gerald Pendleton, the intended victim. The second bag is dropped through the door vent of Gerald Pendleton's cabin room. Nervous and scared, Pendleton tells Chan that his wife once received a similar bag five years earlier; he had no idea of its meaning then, but now considers it a warning of death—his. Chan later learns that Pendleton's wife was once married to a jewelry thief and smuggler named Jim Eberhardt, whom she turned in to the police, and that Eberhardt then swore to take revenge.

"This is your last chance. Withdraw Avalanche before it is too late." Warning message George Chester receives prior to the Santa Juanita Handicap in *Charlie Chan at the Race Track* (1936). To divert suspicion away from himself as both the murderer of Major Kent and the leader of a racetrack gambling ring, Chester surreptitiously sends this message to himself at his hotel and requests that J.L. Lansing, the Santa Juanita Race Track association's secretary, provide him and his horse Avalanche additional security.

Thomas, Jameson (March 24, 1888, London, England–January 10, 1939, Sierra Madre, California) Film director and stage and screen character actor who appeared in over 35 films and portrays Dr. Anton Racine in *Charlie Chan in Egypt* (1935).

A London stage actor from the early 1900s, Jameson Thomas made his film debut in *Chu Chin Chow* (1923). With few exceptions, such as his role as Samuel Sweetland in Hitchcock's *The Farmer's Wife* (1928), Thomas was dissatisfied with the British phase of his film career. He remained philosophical, observing that, "If one wants to live by playing in British films it is better to be miscast than never to be cast at all."

Moving to Hollywood in the early talkie era, he was largely confined to minor roles until his death in 1939. His larger assignments included the role of Claudette Colbert's fortune-hunting husband, King Westley, in *It Happened One Night* (1934) and Charles Craig in *Jane Eyre* (1934).

"THOMAS P. MANNING MYSTERIOUSLY SLAIN" Newspaper headline of the October 8 "Late Edition" of the *Star Dispatch* about the murder of Thomas P. Manning in a locked room in his own house in *The Chinese Cat* (1944).

Thomasson, Jed Retired Baltimore coin dealer and double murderer (portrayed by Donald Douglas in his second of two *Charlie Chan* roles) in *Dead Men Tell* (1941). Thomasson is a passenger on the *Suva Star* for the Cocos Island treasure hunt.

Years ago, under different names, Thomasson and Captain Kane went on a treasure hunt to Cocos Island, but Thomasson left Kane there to die. Believing that his former partner would not be able to resist returning to Cocos Island, Kane arranges the journey for Miss Nodbury's treasure hunt so that he can find and kill Thomasson. Miss Nodbury fears that someone is trying to steal her treasure map, so she tears it into four pieces, sending Thomasson one of the pieces.

When aboard the *Suva Star*, Thomasson masquerades as the ghost of Black Hook. When Miss Nodbury sees what she believes to be the ghost of Black Hook, she has a fatal heart attack and the murderous Thomasson takes her piece of the map. Charlie Chan uses himself as bait to trap Thomasson, who Captain Kane reveals as his former partner, and Thomasson admits to killing Miss Nodbury and Bill Lydig.

Note: The *American Film Institute Catalog of Motion Pictures Produced in the United States* describes Thomasson as being a mortician, not a numismatist as Steve Daniels tells Charlie Chan.

Thompson, Joe Marine corporal who uses the alias of Jack Tilford when dressed in civilian clothes in *Shadows Over Chinatown* (1946). Portrayed by Bruce Kellogg in his first of two *Charlie Chan* roles, Thompson goes AWOL to find his girlfriend Mary Conover who he thinks may have been murdered. After reaching Los Angeles, he visits the local Bureau of Missing Persons and removes a photograph of Mary Conover from the files.

Thompson, Mr. (1) Police lab technician (portrayed by William Ruhl in his second of three *Charlie Chan* roles) in *Dark Alibi* (1946). At Charlie Chan's request, Thompson tries to determine how fingerprints are able to be forged and left at the crime scenes of three bank robberies in the last two years. He first tries a thin mixture of olive oil, but it runs; he is later successful when he uses a mixture of vegetable and mineral oils.

Thompson, Mr. (2) The office manager for the Lafontaine Chemical Company (portrayed by Rory Mallinson) in *Docks of New Orleans* (1948).

Thompson, Tommy Set decorator for *The Chinese Cat* (1944).

Thorn, Mrs. Wardrobe mistress of Cole King's variety troupe (portrayed by Lois Austin in her first of three *Charlie Chan* roles) in *The Trap* (1947). Mrs. Thorn is

King's ex-wife who deserted him by running away with a dancer. When she wants to return to him, he humiliates her by offering her a job as his wardrobe mistress. She then kills Lois and Marcia and frames King to ruin him and make him suffer. She is killed in a car accident while trying to escape from Charlie Chan.

Thorne, Martin P.J. Madden's secretary (portrayed by Hobart Bosworth) in *The Chinese Parrot* (1927). Thorne, Jerry Delaney, and "Shaky" Phil Maydorf are all part of a scheme to steal the Phillimore pearl necklace by having Delaney impersonate Madden.

In *Charlie Chan's Courage* (1934), a remake of *The Chinese Parrot* (1927), Thorne is J.P. Madden's assistant (portrayed by Murray Kinnell in his second of four *Charlie Chan* roles). As with *The Chinese Parrot*, Thorne, Jerry Delaney, "Shaky" Phil Maydorf, and Henry Maydorf (alias Professor Gamble) are all part of a scheme to steal the Phillimore pearl necklace by having Delaney impersonate the real Madden, who has bought the pearls and is awaiting their delivery.

Thursday, Charles Alias for Charles Parks (portrayed by Paul McGrath) in *Dead Men Tell* (1941). Parks, a well-known movie star, and his wife Laura are traveling incognito as Mr. and Mrs. Thursday, having just been married, and are passengers on the *Suva Star* for the Cocos Island treasure hunt.

Thursday, Laura The wife (portrayed by Katharine Aldridge) of actor Charles Parks, both of whom are traveling incognito on the *Suva Star* as the just-married Mr. and Mrs. Thursday in *Dead Men Tell* (1941).

Note: Jean Rogers, who portrayed Kathi Lenesch in *Charlie Chan in Panama* (1940), was originally cast as Laura Thursday but was replaced after shooting began by Katharine Aldridge when Rogers became ill with the flu.

Thurston, Professor John Archeologist-businessman (portrayed by Frank Conroy) in *Charlie Chan in Egypt* (1935). Professor Thurston is in Luxor as part of an expedition headed by his brother-in-law, Professor Arnold, who he murders for the hidden treasure in Ahmeti's tomb.

Because Professor Arnold cannot be found when Charlie Chan arrives in Egypt, Chan asks Thurston for an explanation as to why some treasures of the Ahmeti tomb have recently found their way to the Berlin Museum (as well as several private European collections) in violation of the agreement between Professor Arnold and the French Archeological Society that financed the expedition. Thurston explains that Arnold is an archeologist not a businessman, and that the expedition had run low on funding. To raise some additional funds, Thurston tells Chan that he took it upon himself to sell a few of the more minor pieces, an act which supposedly infuriated Arnold. Professor Thurston then tells Chan that Arnold, after discovering the Ahmeti tomb, had found evidence of a royal burial ground at Napata in the Upper Nile. The last letter received from Arnold was from Napata, although Arnold is already dead in Luxor.

Fearing that his nephew Barry Arnold has information that could expose him, Thurston ingeniously murders Barry by placing a thin-walled, sealed glass tube containing poison gas inside Barry's violin. When Barry plays a certain note, the vibration from the violin's sound breaks the glass and the poison gas escapes through the sound vents. Inhaling the gas, Barry dies instantly.

Thurston's final murder attempt as he tries to keep the hidden treasure room inside Ahmeti's tomb a secret occurs when Tom Evans, Chan, and Snowshoes discover the treasure in the secret room. When alone in the secret chamber, Evans is shot by Professor Thurston who wears a headmask of the goddess Sekhmet as a disguise.

Tibbetts, Jonathon The hard-sell, talkative owner of the Orange Blossom Manor (portrayed by Eddie Parks) in *The Sky Dragon* (1949). As a Justice of the Peace in Humbolt County, he married Connie Jackson and Andrew Barrett on July 21, 1941.

When Charlie Chan and son Lee visit the wedding chapel to see if Tibbetts married the couple and had a picture of the wedding, Tibbetts looks in his records, confirms that a marriage took place, and says that as an amateur photographer he always takes at least one picture just in case the couple wants one later. Charlie wants to see the picture to identify Barrett's wife, Connie Jackson.

Tibbetts then goes to the garage to look for the negative but is knocked unconscious by a shadowy figure, probably William French. The mugger then sets the garage contents afire to destroy any photographic evidence. Birmingham sees the smoke from the garage and, with help from Charlie and Lee, puts out the fire and rescues Tibbetts.

Tilford, Jack Civilian alias for Marine corporal Joe Thompson in *Shadows Over Chinatown* (1946). *See also* **Thompson, Joe**.

timing head Electronic timing device that shoots a light beam at a photoelectric cell across a racetrack. In *Charlie Chan at the Race Track* (1936), professional gambler Denny Barton and track technician Al Meers explain to Charlie Chan that timing heads are located every quarter of a mile around the track and are used to electronically time the race.

Meers is part of a racetrack gambling ring that is betting on Gallant Lad—actually Avalanche, as he was earlier switched with Gallant Lad to obtain better odds—to win the Santa Juanita Handicap race. To help make sure that the bogus Gallant Lad wins, Meers plans to use a special timing head that has a tranquilizer dart and is set to fire at any horse that is in front of "Gallant Lad" when approaching the three-quarter mile pole.

Tinling, James S. (1889–1955) Film director of over 50 films who directed *Charlie Chan in Shanghai* (1935) and *Mr. Moto's Gamble* (1938), the remake of *Charlie Chan at the Ringside*.

TMB Initials of T.M. Brade found on a strongbox that contained jewels and gold stolen by Dan Winterslip 35 years ago in *Charlie Chan's Greatest Case* (1933). During a stopover in San Francisco, John Winterslip's uncle, Roger, gives him a strongbox marked with the initials "TMB" and instructs him to throw it into the Pacific Ocean the next day, as per Dan's orders.

As John is about to toss the box into the sea, he is tackled by Koahla, Dan Winterslip's houseboy, who steals the box. Koahla then admits that he knew of his master's fear of Brade and stole the box in San Francisco to blackmail his master.

Todd, James (1908–1968) Character actor who appeared in 20 films and portrays Kenneth Dunwood in *Charlie Chan's Chance* (1932).

Toler, Sidney (April 28, 1874, Warrensburg, Missouri–February 12, 1947, Beverly Hills, California) Following the death of Warner Oland in 1938, Sidney Toler became the fifth person cast in the role of Charlie Chan.

After graduating from the University of Kansas, Sidney Toler took to the stage in Kansas City at the Ninth Street Theatre in *The Master Man*. He eventually appeared on stage in Brooklyn and then Broadway in 1903 in *The Office Boy*. Besides appearing on the stage, Toler was an accomplished baritone

Sidney Toler, the screen's fifth Charlie Chan, played the role 22 times.

opera singer and also wrote several plays, such as *Golden Days* and *The Exile*, both of which appeared on Broadway.

At the age of 55 Toler went to Hollywood where his first role was Merivel in *Madame X* (1929). For the next decade he appeared in numerous supporting roles, generally playing such abrasive characters as detectives, sea captains, and stage managers. During this period Toler appeared with Cary Grant and Marlene Dietrich in *Blonde Venus* (1932), with Kate Hepburn in *Spitfire* (1934), and with Laurel and Hardy in *Our Relations* (1936).

When Warner Oland died on August 6, 1938, the call went out for actors to be screen-tested for the new Charlie Chan. Both Noah Beery and Leo Carrillo had been tested and even J. Edward Bromberg had been considered as a replacement when Oland was ill, but associate producer John Stone chose Toler on October 18, 1938, after seeing him play Dr. Chang Ling in the Paramount film *King of Chinatown* (1938). Prior to his selection, Sidney Toler had already appeared in nearly 50 films and was the thirty-fifth actor tested for the role. Production for *Charlie Chan in Honolulu* began two weeks later on October 31.

When Oland died and the series continued with Toler, Keye Luke left the series and his role was replaced with the character of Jimmy Chan, portrayed by Sen Yung (later Victor Sen Young). Although he was never in a *Charlie Chan* film with Toler, Keye Luke and Toler did appear together in *Adventures of Smilin' Jack* (1943), with Toler playing General Kai Ling and Luke playing Captain Wing.

With a few exceptions, such as his role as Wong in *White Savage* (1943) and *It's in the Bag* (1945), Toler played the Charlie Chan role exclusively in 22 films. In 1942 Sol M. Wurtzel and Twentieth Century–Fox decided to end the *Charlie Chan* series with *Castle in the Desert*. Toler then obtained the rights to the character from Earl Derr Biggers' widow and made 11 more *Charlie Chan* features at Monogram before he died.

Compared with Oland, Toler's characterization of Charlie Chan was a more abrasive and bullying character. Like Oland, however, Toler was a heavy drinker, and director "Lucky" Humberstone told Toler to have a few drinks before the day's shooting, which he felt gave Toler a better characterization.

Toler was very ill during the making of his last films, such as *Dangerous Money* (1946) and *The Trap* (1947), so much so that he could barely walk. On Wednesday, February 12, 1947, he died at his Hollywood home of intestinal cancer.

Charlie Chan filmography: *Charlie Chan in Honolulu* (1938), *Charlie Chan in Reno* (1939), *Charlie Chan at Treasure Island* (1939), *City in Darkness* (1939), *Charlie Chan in Panama* (1940), *Charlie Chan's Murder Cruise* (1940), *Charlie Chan at the Wax Museum* (1940), *Murder Over New York* (1940), *Dead Men Tell* (1941), *Charlie Chan in Rio* (1941), *Castle in the Desert* (1942), *Charlie Chan in the Secret Service* (1944), *The Chinese Cat* (1944), *Black Magic* (1944), *The Jade Mask* (1945), *The Scarlet Clue* (1945), *The Shanghai Cobra* (1945), *The Red Dragon* (1945), *Dark Alibi* (1946), *Shadows Over Chinatown* (1946), *Dangerous Money* (1946), and *The Trap* (1947).

Note: While Sidney Toler's birth year is often reported as 1874, a certified copy of his marriage license to Vera Tattersall Orkow in Ventura County, California, November 9, 1943, shows him having been 54 years old on that date.

Tom, Layne, Jr. (Los Angeles, California–) Chinese-American juvenile actor who at various times plays three of Charlie Chan's sons. Tom portrays Charlie Chan, Jr., in *Charlie Chan at the Olympics* (1937), Number Five son Tommy Chan in *Charlie Chan in Honolulu* (1938), and Number Seven son Willie Chan in *Charlie Chan's Murder Cruise* (1940). He is now a very successful architect.

Tombes, Andrew (June 29, 1885, Ashtabula, Ohio–March, 1976) Bald-headed character actor who appeared in nearly 110 films, often as genial individuals but just as often as weak-willed, shady types. Tombes portrays Charlie Chan's Honolulu police chief, Mr. Scott, in *Charlie Chan at the Olympics* (1937).

tonga Poison that Charlie Chan states is used by Borneo headhunters. In *Charlie Chan at the Wax Museum* (1940), Chan mentions that "Butcher" Degan's signature is the use of tonga poison on a bamboo dart fired with a goose-quill toothpick as a blow gun. Degan, now posing as Tom Agnew, murders Dr. von Brom with this method just before von Brom is about to reveal the real solution to the Joe Rocke Case.

Tonopah Small Nevada town located about 230 miles southeast of Reno. In *Charlie Chan in Reno* (1939), Sheriff Fletcher, frustrated that Charlie Chan solves the case, tells Reno police chief King that he is going to Tonopah as, "they have an easy case of cattle rustling over there and I know I can pin it on the guilty guy because they found him under the cow!"

Tony An Australian talking parrot at the Madden ranch who repeats phrases in English and Chinese in both *The Chinese Parrot* (1927) and its remake, *Charlie Chan's Courage* (1934). The parrot was given to Madden several years ago by a sea captain. One night, Tony is heard making comments suggestive of a murder, but is later discovered dead, having been poisoned with arsenic in his feed.

Torrence, David (January 18, 1880, Edinburgh, Scotland–December 26, 1942, California) Scottish-born actor (real name: David Torrence Tayson), often appearing in roles as governmental and aristocratic officials in over 75 silent and sound films, including two *Charlie Chan* entries. Torrence portrays Home Secretary Sir Lionel Bashford in *Charlie Chan in London* (1934) and Sir Stanley Woodland in *Charlie Chan in Shanghai* (1935).

"torso" murders A series of murders being investigated by Charlie Chan for an insurance association in *Shadows Over Chinatown* (1946). In these murders, wealthy older men who married young women mysteriously die on their honeymoons, and the widows, as beneficiaries, disappear after the death benefits are paid. Chan notes that the nature of the murders are similar to the "New Orleans trunk murders," whereby the headless body of the victim is often unable to be identified.

towels While in their stateroom aboard a ship bound from Europe to New York in *Charlie Chan on Broadway* (1937), Charlie Chan notices that Lee has a lot of towels in his luggage. When asked about the towels, Lee replies, "Some people pick up soap or ashtrays, but I like towels best." In searching through the suitcase, Charlie is disturbed to see towels from Hotel Sheffield, Chateau Paris, Rhine Inn, and the ship they are on. Although it is too late for Lee to return the towels to the hotels, Charlie tells his son to take the ship's towel from his suitcase.

Toy, Ming Name, meaning "daughter of happiness," given by Charlie Chan to U.S. Army carrier pigeon, number 13576, which belongs to the U.S. Army's Signal Corps and has been entrusted to Jimmy Chan in *Castle in the Desert* (1942). Chan tells Jimmy that he prefers a briefer name and names the pigeon Ming Toy, "daughter of happiness." When Jimmy tells Charlie that it is a boy pigeon, Chan responds that Ming Toy is a temporary alias while on the case. *See also* **carrier pigeon**.

Toy, San Member of Cole King's variety troupe (portrayed by Barbara Jean Wong) who discovers Lois' dead body in *The Trap* (1947).

Toy, Su Circus contortionist dubbed "the human knot" (portrayed by Shia Jung) in *Charlie Chan at the Circus* (1936). Because she is both pretty and Chinese, she attracts the attention of Charlie Chan's Number One son Lee.

TR-3 bomber Test bomber developed by the Metropolitan Aircraft Company that crashes due to sabotage in *Murder Over New York* (1940).

TR-4 bomber Test bomber flown by Lt. Cooper in *Murder Over New York* (1940).

Trans Panama Air Lines Name of company that operates the seaplane in *Charlie Chan in Panama* (1940). Charlie Chan obtains the following reservation list of those passengers who flew on the seaplane with R.J. Godley, an American diplomat who was murdered: R. Starkey, pilot; C.W. Johnson, co-pilot; Cliveden Compton (Seat 1); Dr. Rudolph Grosser (Seat 2); Kathi Lenesch (Seat 3); Richard Cabot (Seat 4); Emil Manolo (Seat 5); Achmed Halide (Seat 6); Jennie Finch (Seat 7); R.J. Godley (Seat 8).

Note: The sign on the dock in Balboa gives the airline's name as Trans Panama Airways.

***The Trap* (1947)** The eleventh *Charlie Chan* film produced by Monogram Pictures Corporation.

Source: based on the character "Charlie Chan" created by Earl Derr Biggers. Original Copyright: Monogram Pictures Corporation, November 26, 1946; LP728. Copyright Renewed: June 24, 1974; R579843. Production: late July to mid–August, 1946. Release Date: November 30, 1946. Sound: Western Electric Sound System. Film: b&w. Running Time: 69 minutes.

Producer: James S. Burkett. Director: Howard Bretherton. Assistant Director: Harold Knox. Original Screenplay: Miriam Kissinger. Director of Photography: James Brown. Technical Director: Dave Milton. Supervising Film Editor: Richard Currier. Editor: Ace Herman. Set Decorations: Raymond Boltz, Jr. Musical Director: Edward J. Kay. Recordist: Tom Lambert. Makeup: Harry Ross. Production Manager: William Calihan, Jr.

Lobby card for *The Trap*, with Sidney Toler, Victor Sen Young, and Mantan Moreland. *Inset:* Rita Quigley, Anne Nagel, Barbara Jean Wong, Bettie Best, and Margaret Brayton (Everett Collection).

Cast

Sidney Toler	*as*	Charlie Chan
Mantan Moreland		Birmingham Brown
Victor Sen Young		Jimmy Chan
Tanis Chandler		Adelaide
Larry Blake		Rick Daniels
Kirk Alyn		Sergeant Reynolds
Rita Quigley		Clementine
Anne Nagel		Marcia
Helen Gerald		Ruby
Howard Negley		Cole King
Lois Austin		Mrs. Thorn
Barbara Jean Wong		San Toy
Minerva Urecal		Mrs. Weebles
Margaret Brayton		Madge Mudge
Bettie Best		Winifred
Jane Bryant		Lois
Walden Boyle*		George "Doc" Brandt

Plot Summary: Cole King's variety troupe, along with press agent Rick Daniels and Mrs. Thorn, the wardrobe mistress, are renting a Malibu, California, beach house to relax for a few days. When Adelaide, a showgirl, criticizes Marcia, the bossy star of the show and King's girlfriend, Marcia threatens to reveal that Adelaide is secretly married to George Brandt, a physiotherapist and dietitian for the troupe, and also hints that she knows Brandt's real identity.

Marcia then forces showgirl Lois to steal letters from Adelaide's trunk by threatening to tell King that Lois is under eighteen. Lois agrees because she says she really needs the job. Later that evening, Marcia disappears and Lois' body is discovered by Chinese troupe member San Toy. Because Lois has been strangled by a garrote, a murder technique said to be favored by both the Chinese and the French, both San Toy and Adelaide are under suspicion. Thinking like a press agent, Daniels suggests that they try to make Lois' death appear to be a drowning so that the troupe would not be drawn into what could be a publicly embarrassing situation. Because she knows she is innocent, San Toy, who is a friend of Jimmy Chan, calls Jimmy and asks him to investigate, as his father is not at home at the time. When Charlie does return, he sees the note left by Jimmy and heads to the beach house.

The troupe is having a cookout on the beach to relieve the tension caused by the previous events. Clementine trips over Marcia's body, which has washed up on the beach with a silk cord wrapped around its neck. Chan searches the grounds and spots Daniels burying Marcia's bathrobe. When Chan reveals that the cord from her robe was used in one of the murders, Daniels claims that the robe was planted on Cole King to frame him. Now becoming mentally unstable, King accuses Daniels of murdering the women and trying to hide the evidence.

Privately, Chan reveals that he knows that "Doc" Brandt was once accused of his wife's murder and, although the charges were dropped, his career was ruined. Brandt then went to war and met and married Adelaide in Paris, where Marcia first met them and learned of his past. Brandt then admits that he found Lois' body and removed the letters, but denies killing her.

Chan then decides to set a trap for the killer. That night King confesses that he took a box from Brandt's suitcase that contained incriminating papers, and Jimmy later finds the missing box in the furnace. Jimmy then sees someone try to strangle San Toy and intervenes without thinking, spoiling Chan's trap and allowing the attacker to escape in a car. Chan, Jimmy, and Birmingham chase the assailant, who fails to negotiate a section of the highway and crashes into a ditch. They run up to the car and the unknown attacker is revealed to be Mrs. Thorn. With her dying breath, she tells how, years ago, she had deserted King, her husband, and when she wanted to return to him, he humiliated her by offering her a job as his wardrobe mistress. She confesses that she then killed the two women and framed Cole to make him suffer. Her letters were in the box that King stole from Brandt. Chan then assures Brandt that the Board of Medical Examiners will reinstate his license and he will be free to practice under his own name.

Note: *The Trap* marked the last film appearance of Sidney Toler, who died on February 12, 1947. Roland Winters was then

**Unbilled.*

selected for the role of Charlie Chan in *The Chinese Ring* (1947).

Treasure Island Artificial island halfway in the bay between San Francisco and Oakland, California; it is the location setting for *Charlie Chan at Treasure Island* (1939). The San Francisco–Oakland bridge has a support on the island, which was the site of one of two World's Fairs held in 1939. The "Western" fair was called the Golden Gate International Expedition (New York City was the other location) and was held from February 1939 to October 1940. The island was originally built to accommodate San Francisco's new airport. Then in 1939, while it was used as the base for Pan Am's China Clippers, San Francisco held the Golden Gate International Expedition there. Until it closed in 1997, the site was a U.S. naval station.

Tree, Dorothy (May 21, 1906, Brooklyn, New York–February 12, 1992, Englewood, New Jersey) Brunette character actress (real name: Dorothy Estelle Triebitz) who appeared in almost 40 films. Tree portrays foreign agent Charlotte Ronnell in *City in Darkness* (1939).

Dorothy Tree was a versatile general purpose actress, playing everything from a middle-class housewife to a Nazi spy. After graduating from Cornell and working extensively on Broadway, Tree came to Hollywood for a part in the Fox musical comedy *Just Imagine* (1930). She remained in films for the next twenty years, appearing in such roles as Elizabeth Edwards in *Abe Lincoln in Illinois* (1940) and Teresa Wright's mother in *The Men* (1950), which was Marlon Brando's first film. Given her expertise at dialects and subtleties of intonations, Tree later became a top vocal coach, writing a public speaking guide titled *A Woman's Voice*.

Trent, Jack (August 24, 1896, Texas–August 1, 1961, Los Angeles County, California) Actor who portrays Victor Jordan in *The Chinese Parrot* (1927).

Trevor, Edward Character actor who portrays murderer Fred Gage in *Charlie Chan's Secret* (1936).

Troffey, Alex (1895–September 11, 1978, Woodland Hills, California) Movie editor, sometimes credited as Alexander Troffey, of 30 films, including six *Charlie Chan* entries at Twentieth Century–Fox: *Charlie Chan's Chance* (1932), *Charlie Chan's Greatest Case* (1933), *Charlie Chan's Courage* (1934), *Charlie Chan at the Opera* (1936), *Charlie Chan at the Circus* (1936), and *Charlie Chan in Rio* (1941).

Tropic Hotel Honolulu hotel residence of Miller, an aviation mechanic, in *Charlie Chan at the Olympics* (1937). Suspecting Miller of murder and hijacking a test airplane with a valuable new remote controlled guidance system invention, Charlie Chan and the aviation company's owner search Miller's room at the Tropic Hotel, finding Miller dead in one of the closets.

Trowbridge, Charles (January 10, 1882, Vera Cruz, Mexico–October 30, 1967) Former architect and stage and screen character actor who appeared in over 170 films. In two *Charlie Chan* roles, Trowbridge portrays a judge (unbilled) in *Charlie Chan at the Wax Museum* (1940) and Prentiss, a U.S. embassy official, in *The Red Dragon* (1945).

Charles Trowbridge was born in Mexico to American parents. An architect for ten years, Trowbridge then turned to stage acting. Silver-haired even as a young man, Trowbridge was generally cast in kindly but authoritative roles, usually as doctors, lawyers, professors, and military officers. He also had a bad habit of being killed off before the film was half over. In 1940 Trowbridge had the distinction of being murdered by Lionel Atwill and George Zucco respectively in two separate Universal horror films—*Man Made Monster* and *The Mummy's Hand*.

While he was active until 1957, Charles Trowbridge was best known to millions of wartime servicemen as the cautionary military doctor-narrator in John Ford's venereal disease prevention film *Sex Hygiene* (1941).

Tse, Ling Chinese girl (portrayed by Tashia Mori) who sells cigarettes, film, and flash bulbs at the Hottentot Club in *Charlie Chan on Broadway* (1937).

Tucker, Richard (1864, Brooklyn, New York–December 5, 1942, Woodland Hills, California) American stage and screen actor who appeared in 150 silent and sound films. Tucker portrays Wilkie Ballou in *The Black Camel* (1931).

Prosperous-looking American actor Richard Tucker went from the stage to the Edison Company in 1913, where he played romantic leads before the cameras. Even in his youth, the tall, regal Tucker exuded an air of corporate success, and was best suited to roles as bankers and stockbrokers. After World War I service, Tucker resumed his film career as a character man. In talkies, the newly mustachioed, grey-haired Tucker was seen in innumerable small, authoritative roles. His two best-known assignments from this period were in the serial *Flash Gordon* (1936), in which he played Flash Gordon's scientist father, Professor Gordon, and in the Laurel and Hardy feature *Pack Up Your Troubles* (1932), wherein Tucker was the bank president who turned out to be Mr. Smith, the grandfather of the orphan girl Stan and Ollie are protecting.

Turner, Florence (January 6, 1885, New York, New York–August 28, 1946, Woodland Hills, California) Stage and screen actress who appeared in 45 silent and sound films and portrays the middle-aged Sally Phillimore in *The Chinese Parrot* (1927).

At age three Florence Turner began appearing in stage productions, and was already a veteran actress when she joined Vitagraph in 1906 at the of 21. Credited only as the "Vitagraph Girl," she became one of the screen's first stars. In 1913 she went to England with Larry Trimble, her frequent director and long-time friend. They performed together in London music halls and formed Turner Films, their own production company.

Turner sometimes co-wrote and or directed her own films. However, her popularity had greatly decreased as the popularity of films boomed, and she went on to play secondary roles and eventually had to beg for work. In the 1930s she was put on the MGM payroll, but it was an act of charity as she was used only as an extra and in bit parts.

Twentieth Century–Fox Film Corporation American production and film corporation formed by the merger of Joseph Schenck's Twentieth Century Pictures and William Fox's Fox Film Corporation, which was publicly announced on May 29, 1935. Shares in the new company were divided equally between the Fox shareholders (613,264 shares) and the Twentieth Century trio of Darryl F. Zanuck (183,979 shares), Schenck (214,642 shares) and William B. Goetz (214,642 shares). The new company had Darryl F. Zanuck as the production head at an annual salary of $260,000 plus ten percent of the gross of his films. The only Fox Film executive kept on after the merger was Sol M. Wurtzel, who became the executive producer in charge of the "B"-pictures unit.

At first, Twentieth Century's films would be distributed by Fox Films' organization. Fox Films then took out ads in *Variety* to announce their product for the 1935-1936 season. However, there quickly arose some confusion over the company name. In some *Variety* articles, the company was referred to as Fox-Twentieth; in others, as Twentieth-Fox. On September 18, 1935, the issue was put to rest when a full-page ad in *Variety* announced the new trademark of Twentieth Century–Fox.

Until Monogram Pictures Corporation took over filming the series' final 17 films in 1944, Twentieth Century–Fox made 18 *Charlie Chan* movies following the merger, with each picture generally budgeted between $250,000 and $275,000. When the Fox and Twentieth Century studios merged, Oland was paid $12,500 for *Charlie Chan's Secret* (1936). Starting with *Charlie Chan at the Circus* (1936), he was then able to get $20,000 for the next three films. When his option was picked up again, Oland received $30,000 for each of his last three pictures.

Charlie Chan Filmography: *Charlie Chan's Secret* (1936), *Charlie Chan at the Circus* (1936), *Charlie Chan at the Race Track* (1936), *Charlie Chan at the Opera* (1936), *Charlie*

Chan at the Olympics (1937), *Charlie Chan on Broadway* (1937), *Charlie Chan at Monte Carlo* (1937), *Charlie Chan in Honolulu* (1938), *Charlie Chan in Reno* (1939), *Charlie Chan at Treasure Island* (1939), *City in Darkness* (1939), *Charlie Chan in Panama* (1940), *Charlie Chan's Murder Cruise* (1940), *Charlie Chan at the Wax Museum* (1940), *Murder Over New York* (1940), *Dead Men Tell* (1941), *Charlie Chan in Rio* (1941), and *Castle in the Desert* (1942).

Note: Cinematic sources disagree as to which was the first *Charlie Chan* film made by Twentieth Century–Fox. Although the production of *Charlie Chan in Shanghai* began after the merger (from July 11 to August 3, 1935) and the film was released on October 11, 1935, the opening credits nevertheless list the Fox Film Corporation. Production of the next entry, *Charlie Chan's Secret*, occurred from August 26 to September 21, 1935, and the picture was released on January 10, 1936, but it was the first film of the series to list Twentieth Century–Fox in the opening credits.

Twitchell, A.R. "Archie" (November 28, 1906, Pendleton, Oregon–January 31, 1957, Pacoima, California) Actor (real name: Michael Brandon) who appeared in over 35 films and portrays attorney Carter Lane in *Charlie Chan at the Wax Museum* (1940).

"TWO DEAD IN DIARY MURDER" Newspaper headline of the *New York Globe* about the murder of Thomas Mitchell, the estranged husband of Marie Collins, in *Charlie Chan on Broadway* (1937). His death is somehow thought to be linked with the death of Billie Bronson, who supposedly kept a diary with details about the rackets and politics.

Tyler, Lelah Character actress who portrays Mrs. Winters, an alias for the master spy Manleck, in *Charlie Chan in the Secret Service* (1944).

U

Ulrich Surly caretaker of Colby House (portrayed by Egon Brecher) in *Charlie Chan's Secret* (1936). Allen Colby was once engaged to Ulrich's daughter, but Allen broke off the engagement when he left home after a disagreement with his father. Heartbroken, Ulrich's daughter committed suicide and Ulrich blamed Allen Colby for her death.

ultraviolet light Also known as black light, a source of electromagnetic radiation (invisible to the human eye) having wavelengths shorter than visible light but longer than X rays. The ultraviolet region of the electromagnetic spectrum was discovered in 1801 by John Ritter in the course of photochemical experiments. Fluorescent and mercury-vapor lamps produce large amounts of ultraviolet light which is filtered out when the lamps are intended for optical use. On the other hand, visible light can be filtered out instead to achieve black-light effects through the induced luminescence of objects by ultraviolet light.

In *Charlie Chan's Secret* (1936), Charlie Chan discovers that a hidden ultraviolet lamp is used in the séance to illuminate the face of the dead Allen Colby. A solution of quinine sulfate, which was put on Colby's face, gives the effect of a glowing apparition when struck by ultraviolet light in the dimly lit room during the séance.

Ung, Florence (April 20, 1918, Los Angeles, California–) Chinese-American actress who appeared in uncredited roles in two *Charlie Chan* films. Ung portrays one of Charlie's 12 children in *Charlie Chan at the Circus* (1936) and Ling, the Number One daughter and expectant mother in *Charlie Chan in Honolulu* (1938). Florence Ung is a first cousin of both Layne Tom, Jr., and Barbara Jean Wong, who also appear in several *Charlie Chan* films.

University of Southern California (USC) University attended by Jimmy Chan in *Charlie Chan in Reno* (1939).

Urecal, Minerva (September 22, 1894, Eureka, California–February 26, 1966, Glendale, California) Character actress who appeared in over 130 films and portrays the Olympic matron (unbilled) in *Charlie Chan* *at the Olympics* (1937) and the housekeeper, Mrs. Weebles, in *The Trap* (1947).

Actress Minerva Urecal once claimed that her last name was an amalgam of her family hometown of Eureka, California. Making the transition from stage to screen in 1934, Urecal appeared in innumerable bits, usually as cleaning women, shopkeepers, and hatchet-faced landladies. In "B" pictures and two-reelers of the 1940s, she often portrayed society dowagers and housekeepers.

With the emergence of television, Urecal achieved top billing as "Tugboat" Annie Brennan in the sitcom *Tugboat Annie* (1958). She also replaced Hope Emerson as Mother for the 1959-60 season of the weekly detective series *Peter Gunn*. Minerva Urecal was active up until the early 1960s when she enjoyed some of the most sizable roles of her career, notably as Brenda, the easily offended Swedish cook in *Mr. Hobbs Takes a Vacation* (1962), and as Kate Lindquist, the town harridan who is turned to stone in *Seven Faces of Dr. Lao* (1964).

Note: Although the Call Bureau Cast Service lists Minerva Urecal as Mrs. Foss in *Dark Alibi* (1946), production information in the Academy of Motion Picture Arts and Sciences (AMPAS) library states that she was replaced by Edna Holland, who is listed in the on-screen credits.

Usher, Guy (1875–June 16, 1944, San Diego, California) Stocky American stage and screen character actor who appeared in over 90 films, often as a policeman. In two *Charlie Chan* roles, Usher portrays the Shanghai Chamber of Commerce president (unbilled) in *Charlie Chan in Shanghai* (1935) and Inspector Regan in *Charlie Chan at the Opera* (1936). Usher also appears as District Attorney Hamilton Burger in the early *Perry Mason* film *The Case of the Black Cat* (1934).

V

Valerie, Joan (1914, Rheinlander, Wisconsin–January 30, 1983, Long Beach, California) Attractive character actress (real name: Helen Vlahakis) who had roles in two *Charlie Chan* films. Valerie portrays Lily Latimer in *Charlie Chan at the Wax Museum* (1940) and actress June Preston in *Murder Over New York* (1940).

Vallin, Rick (1920, Russia–August 31, 1977, United States) Handsome Russian-born leading man (real name: Richard Vallin) who appeared in nearly 60 films and portrays smuggler Tao Erickson in *Dangerous Money* (1946).

Handsome and personable enough for leading roles, Richard Vallin was also an effectively sinister villain when the occasion arose. He spent the bulk of his career at such "B" studios as Republic, Monogram, and PRC. He was a semi-regular in the *East Side Kids* films of the 1940s, and later showed up in several of the 1950s *Bowery Boys* films. Additionally, Vallin was a fixture of the Columbia Pictures serial unit, playing Sandy Sanderson in *Brick Bradford* (1947), Barry Brown in *Batman and Robin* (1949), and the dual roles of Stan and Boris in *Blackhawk* (1952).

Vance, Inspector New York policeman (portrayed by Donald MacBride in his second of two *Charlie Chan* roles) in *Murder Over New York* (1940). Vance is called in to investigate the murder of former Scotland Yard inspector Hugh Drake in George Kirby's apartment.

Note: The character Inspector Vance loosely parallels that of Inspector Flannery in *Charlie Chan's Chance* (1932).

Van Horn, Jan Man accused and arrested by Charlie Chan in 1937 for bank robbery and murder in Shanghai in *The Shanghai Cobra* (1945). Before his capture Van Horn could be readily recognized by his dark black hair with an unusual white streak. However, he was injured during a Japanese bombing raid on Shanghai and his face and hands were burned, requiring plastic surgery. After being put on a launch for a boat to take him to Singapore for trial, Van Horn jumps off the launch into the water and escapes.

Claiming he was innocent and was framed, Van Horn follows H.R. Jarvis (who was also on the launch from which he escaped) to find the leader of the criminal gang. When Jarvis takes an office on the second floor of the Sixth National Bank Building, Van Horn (with dyed hair, a new face, and an alias of John Adams) finds work in the bank as a guard. To help gather evidence, he gets his daughter, Paula Webb, a job in the bank as secretary to the bank's president, Walter Fletcher.

Van Zandt, Philip (October 3, 1904, Amsterdam, The Netherlands–February 16, 1958, Los Angeles, California) Dutch-born character actor (real name: Philip Pinheiro) who appeared in almost 100 films and portrays Joseph Pindello in *The Shanghai Chest* (1948).

Varconi, Victor (March 31, 1891, Kisvarde, Hungary–June 16, 1976, Santa Barbara, California) Hungarian-born actor (real name: Mihály Varkonyi) who appeared in over 60 films. Varconi portrays Robert Fyfe, the actor and ex-husband of Shelah Fane, in *The Black Camel* (1931).

Born on the Hungarian-Rumanian border, Victor Varconi began his acting career in Transylvania, playing leads with the Hungarian National Theater in Budapest. He made his first film, the Hungarian *Sargá Csikó* (Yellow Boy), in 1913. The ever-shifting political climate of Europe convinced Varconi to try his luck in America where he was signed by Cecil B. DeMille's company on the strength of his performance in the German-made *Sodom und Gomorrah* (1922). Under DeMille's direction, the handsome Varconi played wealthy American tin factory manager William Silver in *Triumph* (1924), a bookkeeper in *Feet of Clay* (1924), Prince Dimitri in *The Volga Boatmen* (1926), and Pontius Pilate in *The King of Kings* (1929). His last major silent role was as Lord Nelson in *The Divine Lady* (1929).

In talkies it was revealed that Varconi had a pleasant but pronounced Hungarian accent, which limited his range of portrayals. He played many a continental adventurer and roguish gigolo during his sound career and also starred in English-language versions of Anglo-German co-productions. World War II resulted in a boost for Varconi, permitting him to play a variety of Axis agents. One of his last roles was Lord of Ashdod in *Samson and Delilah* (1949), directed by his old boss Cecil B. DeMille.

Vaughn, Hilda (1897–December 28, 1957, Baltimore, Maryland) Character actress who portrays Mrs. Joe Rocke in *Charlie Chan at the Wax Museum* (1940).

Vega, Luiz Philipe Traveling salesman for an exporting company in Smyrna (portrayed by Gene Roth [billed as Gene Stutenroth] in his first of two *Charlie Chan* roles) in *Charlie Chan in the Secret Service* (1944). *See also* **von Vegon, Philipe.**

Verdugo, Elena (April 20, 1926, Hollywood, California–) Hispanic-American actress of films and television. Verdugo portrays Connie Jackson (alias Marie Burke) in *The Sky Dragon* (1949).

Educated by studio tutors, Elena Verdugo

Elena Verdugo (Everett Collection)

spent her teen years playing Mexican peasants, gypsy girls, harem handmaidens, and exotic South Sea islanders. Her co-stars ranged from Lou Costello in *Little Giant* (1946) to Lon Chaney, Jr., in *House of Frankenstein* (1945). She appeared in several television series, most notably as Millie Bronson in *Meet Millie* (1952–56), Audrey in *The New Phil Silvers Show* (1964), and nurse Consuelo Lopez in *Marcus Welby, M.D.* (1969–76).

Vernon, Wally (May 27, 1904–March 7, 1970, Van Nuys, California) Pop-eyed comic actor who appeared in over 40 films and portrays Fred Rhadini's assistant, Elmer Keiner, in *Charlie Chan at Treasure Island* (1939).

Wally Vernon started performing in show business at the age of three. With extensive experience in minstrel shows, burlesque, vaudeville, and the legitimate stage, Vernon began his film career in the early 1930s, showing up in two-reelers produced at Sennett, RKO, MGM, and Universal. As a contract player at Twentieth Century–Fox in the mid–1930s, Vernon displayed his salty dialogue delivery in such films as *Sharpshooters* (1938) and *The Gorilla* (1939).

During the late 1940s to early 1950s, Vernon was the omnipresent comedy relief in many Republic westerns. From 1948 through 1956 Vernon co-starred with Eddie Quillan in a lively series of 16 two-reel comedies produced by Columbia Pictures. Back at Fox in the 1960s, Vernon was one of many Hollywood old-timers given good supporting roles in the Shirley MacLaine comedy *What a Way to Go* (1964). Wally Vernon was killed by a hit-and-run driver near his Van Nuys home in 1970.

Versailles Café Sleazy Shanghai waterfront bar to which Lee Chan trails the taxi driver that kidnapped him earlier in *Charlie Chan in Shanghai* (1935). Based on Lee's information, Charlie Chan and the impostor posing as U.S. government agent James Andrews go there to investigate, and a trap is set for Charlie.

Vessey, Inspector San Francisco policeman (portrayed by Stanley Andrews in his first of two *Charlie Chan* roles) in *Dead Men Tell* (1941). Vessey is called in to investigate the murder of Miss Patience Nodbury aboard the *Suva Star*.

Visaroff, Michael (1892, Moscow, Russia–February 27, 1951, Hollywood, California) Burly Russian actor who appeared in over 60 films, often cast as innkeepers and European-type characters. Visaroff portrays criminologist Dr. Otto von Brom in *Charlie Chan at the Wax Museum* (1940).

Like many of his fellow Russian expatriates, Michael Visaroff claimed to be of noble lineage, which enabled him to land such roles as Count Bosrinov in *Disraeli* (1929). From the early 1930s until his death, he was usually cast as innkeepers, most memorably in Universal's *Dracula* (1931) and *Mark of the Vampire* (1935), and in *Laurel and Hardy*'s film *The Flying Deuces* (1939). Perhaps Visaroff's funniest film appearance was as the homicidal maniac ("She's the first wife I ever killed!") who shares a jail cell with W.C. Fields in *Man on the Flying Trapeze* (1935).

Vogan, Emmett (September 27, 1893–November 13, 1969) Veteran character actor (real name: Charles Emmett Vogan) who appeared in almost 200 films, including *Charlie Chan* entries. Vogan portrays a wirephoto technician (unbilled) in *Charlie Chan at the Opera* (1936), a ship's officer (unbilled) in *Charlie Chan at the Olympics* (1937), the prosecuting attorney (unbilled) in *Charlie Chan at the Wax Museum* (1940), the absentminded Professor Martin in *Dangerous Money* (1946), Henri Castanaro in *Docks of New Orleans* (1948), and a doctor (unbilled) in *The Sky Dragon* (1949). Vogan has the distinction of being only one of six actors who appeared with three different actors playing Chan.

Comedy fans will recognize Emmett Vogan as the engineer partner of nominal leading man Charles Lang in W.C. Fields' *Never Give a Sucker an Even Break* (1941) and as the prosecuting attorney in the flashback sequences of *Laurel and Hardy*'s film *The Bullfighters* (1945).

Vogeding, Frederick (March 28, 1887, Nijmegen, The Netherlands–April 18, 1942, Los

Angeles, California) Dutch-born character actor (real name: Frederik Wilhelm Vogeding) who appeared in 40 films. In three *Charlie Chan* roles, he portrays Ivan Marloff (incorrectly credited as "Burke") in *Charlie Chan in Shanghai* (1935), Berlin police inspector Strasser in *Charlie Chan at the Olympics* (1937), and the shady boat captain of the *Medusa* in *City in Darkness* (1939).

Frederick Vogeding began his career as a cabaret singer in Holland and as an actor in Germany. He left for the U.S. in 1920, and his first American film was *Below the Sea* (1933), in which he had several good scenes as a grim U-boat commander. His stiff-necked bearing and humorless demeanor came in handy for "Nazi" characterizations in such pre-war productions as *Confessions of a Nazi Spy* (1939) and *Four Sons* (1940).

von Brom, Dr. Otto Scientific criminologist (portrayed by Michael Visaroff) who has a photographic memory and is formerly of the Berlin Police Department in *Charlie Chan at the Wax Museum* (1940). Based on von Brom's evidence, Joe Rocke was convicted and hung for a murder he didn't commit.

During the weekly *Crime League* broadcast that revisits the Rocke Case, Dr. von Brom, whose evidence was used to convict Joe Rocke, now sees he was wrong and says he will reveal the real solution. Before he can do so, however, von Brom is murdered with a poison tipped bamboo dart, an occurrence which Charlie Chan claims points to the fact that "Butcher" Degan is still alive.

von Czardas, Baroness Kathi Real name of Kathi Lenesch, a Czechoslovakian aristocrat whose brother and father are murdered by the secret policeman known as Reiner, in *Charlie Chan in Panama* (1940). *See also* **Lenesch, Kathi.**

von Kirbach, Arthur L. Sound engineer for over 30 films and *Charlie Chan at the Circus* (1936).

Von Scherbe, Theodore A business partner (portrayed by Stanley Andrews) of Simon Lafontaine and Henri Castanaro in a syndicate to ship a poisonous gas to South America in *Docks of New Orleans* (1948).

Charlie Chan learns from Mr. Thompson that Von Scherbe is an embezzler and is wanted by three South American countries. Like his two partners, Von Scherbe is the third murder victim of Oscar Swendstrom using the same poison gas he had sold for $500 to Lafontaine's chemical company (Swendstrom feels that he was tricked when selling his poison gas formula).

von Vegon, Philipe Electrical engineer, author, and war refugee (alias Luiz Vega) who poses as a traveling salesman and is a confederate of German master spy Manleck in *Charlie Chan in the Secret Service* (1944). Inventor George Melton is electrocuted by von Vegon when Melton pulls the light chain to turn on a closet light. Then von Vegon takes the secret torpedo plans from Melton's coat pocket.

When searching Melton's house, Charlie Chan notices a book titled *Magnetic Properties of Electricity*, written by a Philipe von Vegon. Chan also notes the similarity of the Vega and von Vegon names. Chan looks in a scientific *Who's Who*, sees von Vegon's picture, and recognizes that Luiz Vega and Philipe von Vegon are the same person. Fearing that von Vegon will talk about his killing George Melton, Manleck (alias Mrs. Winters) kills von Vegon with a noiseless spring gun activated by a powerful magnetic field.

W

W Monogrammed letter on a handkerchief belonging to Paul Wagner, the ex-husband of Lola Dean, that is found near her dead body in *Charlie Chan in Rio* (1941).

waffle Breakfast entrée that Charlie Chan orders in *Charlie Chan at Monte Carlo* (1937). The French waiter at first does not understand what "waffle" is in English, and Number One son Lee's assassination of the French language is no help either (the French word for waffle is *gaufre*). Charlie then draws a picture of it—a big circle with crisscrossed lines, representing squares inside—telling Lee that "picture still worth a thousand words!" The waiter then indicates that he knows what Charlie wants and shortly brings him an American book of crossword puzzles, proudly proclaiming, "Waffle!"

Wagenheim, Charles (1895–March 6, 1979, Los Angeles, California) Diminutive, frequently mustached stage and screen character actor who appeared in over 65 films and portrays the crime museum night watchman, Willie Fern, in *Charlie Chan at the Wax Museum* (1940).

After making the transition from stage to screen around 1940, Charles Wagenheim's most memorable role was probably that of "the runt" in *Meet Boston Blackie* (1941), a part taken over by George E. Stone in the subsequent Boston Blackie "B" films. Generally cast in unsavory bit parts, Wagenheim's on-screen cunning was showcased in roles ranging from the assassin in Hitchcock's *Foreign Correspondent* (1940) to the (unbilled) sneak thief who nearly gives away the hiding place of the Frank family in George Stevens' *Diary of Anne Frank* (1959). In 1979 Wagenheim was bludgeoned to death by an intruder in his Hollywood apartment five days before another veteran actor, Victor Kilian, met the same fate.

Wagner, Lola Real name of Lola Dean in *Charlie Chan in Rio* (1941). *See also* **Dean, Lola.**

Wagner, Max (November 28, 1901, Mexico–November 16, 1975, West Los Angeles, California) Muscle-bound, Mexican-born character actor who appeared in over 75 films, usually as thugs, sailors, bodyguards, cabbies, and moving men. In three *Charlie Chan* roles, Wagner portrays the taxi driver that kidnaps Lee Chan in *Charlie Chan in Shanghai* (1935), Joe (unbilled) in *Charlie Chan at the Race Track* (1936), and a U.S. soldier (unbilled) in *Charlie Chan in Panama* (1940).

Wagner, Paul Lola Dean's ex-husband (portrayed by Truman Bradley in his second of two *Charlie Chan* roles) in *Charlie Chan in Rio* (1941). Although divorced from Lola three years earlier, Wagner still has strong feelings for Lola and sends some orchids and a note to her dressing room at the Carioca Casino. When he is about to leave Rio de Janeiro for good, Wagner tries one more time to win her back, but is told by Lola's secretary, Helen Ashby, that Lola isn't going to see anyone now that she has just become engaged to Clark Denton.

Still wanting to see her, Wagner goes to her house and climbs in through a window. After talking with her, he accidentally drops his monogrammed handkerchief. Later, this handkerchief is found near Dean's dead body. Seeing this as a possible clue, Chief Souto has the police go to the Continental Hotel to have Wagner picked up for questioning.

Note: The character Paul Wagner loosely parallels that of Robert Fyfe in *The Black Camel* (1931).

"walk softly, go far" English translation of the Chinese characters embroidered on a pair of slippers that were once given to Col. John Beetham by the emperor of China for distinguished service and are now found on the feet of the murdered body of Hilary Galt in *Behind That Curtain* (1929).

Walker, Ray (August 10, 1904, Newark, New Jersey–October 6, 1980, Los Angeles, California) Stage and film character actor who appeared in over 90 films. Walker portrays traveling salesman Mr. Danvers in *Dark Alibi* (1946).

Wall, Geraldine (1912–June 22, 1970, Woodland Hills, California) Character actress who appeared in over 30 films and portrays Harriet Green in *Black Magic* (1944). Besides films, Wall appeared occasionally on television, including nine episodes of *Perry Mason* (1957–66).

Wallace, Morgan (July 26, 1888, Lompoc, California–December 12, 1953, Tarzana, California) Stage and screen actor who appeared in almost 75 films and portrays The Honorable Charles Zaraka in *Charlie Chan at the Olympics* (1937).

After considerable experience on the New York stage, Morgan Wallace entered films at D.W. Griffith's studio in Mamaroneck, Long Island. His first screen role of note was as the lecherous Marquis de Praille in Griffith's *Orphans of the Storm* (1921). Thereafter he specialized in dignified character parts, such as James Monroe in George Arliss' *Alexander Hamilton* (1931). Wallace was a favorite of comedian W.C. Fields—perhaps because he was born in Lompoc, California, one of Fields' favorite comic targets—and he portrayed Jasper Fitchmuller, the customer who wants kumquats and wants them *now*, in Fields' *It's a Gift* (1934).

Walters, Jeremiah and Sarah Strange husband and wife team (portrayed by Charles Middleton and Claire DuBrey, respectively) who are passengers of Dr. Suderman's cruise in *Charlie Chan's Murder Cruise* (1940). Mr. Walters is a tightlipped, puritanical religious fanatic, and his wife claims to be psychic.

Walton, Douglas (October 17, 1910, Toronto, Canada–November 15, 1961, New York, New York) Stage and screen character actor (real name: Douglas Duder) who appeared in almost 40 films. Walton portrays condemned murderer Paul Gray in *Charlie Chan in London* (1934).

WAMPAS Baby Star Title given by the Western Association of Motion Picture Advertisers each year from 1922 to 1934 to 13 Hollywood actresses perceived as the most likely to succeed. There were five actresses who appeared in *Charlie Chan* films that were WAMPAS Baby Stars: Sally Blane (1929); Mary Brian (1926); Sally Eilers (1928); Marian Nixon (1924); Dorothy Revier (1925).

Wang, James (1853–April 20, 1935, Los Angeles, California) Chinese actor, sometimes credited as Jimmy Wang or Jim Wang, who portrays Kee Lin in *Charlie Chan's Chance* (1932) and Louie Wong in *Charlie Chan's Courage* (1934).

Warburton, John (October 20, 1887, Huddersfield, England–October 27, 1981) Actor who appeared in nearly 30 films and portrays John Quincy Winterslip in *Charlie Chan's Greatest Case* (1933).

Ward, E. Clayton Sound engineer for three *Charlie Chan* films: *Charlie Chan in London* (1934), *Charlie Chan at the Olympics* (1937), and *Charlie Chan at Treasure Island* (1939).

Warde, Anthony (November 4, 1908, Pennsylvania–January 8, 1975, Hollywood, California) American stage and screen character actor who appeared in nearly 80 films. In two *Charlie Chan* roles, Warde portrays the gangster Catlen in *The Chinese Cat* (1944) and convict Jim Slade in *Dark Alibi* (1946).

Often seen with a pencil-mustache, Anthony Warde excelled in unsavory characterizations, usually in serials and low-budget crime and western films. He played Killer Kane in the 1939 chapter play *Buck Rogers* and "Killer" Mace in *The Masked Marvel* (1943). Active in films until 1964, Warde also made a number of television appearances in the 1950s, including a brief turn as a counterfeiter in an episode of *Amos 'n' Andy*.

Warner, H.B. (October 26, 1875, London, England–December 21, 1958, Woodland Hills, California) Distinguished British stage

H.B. Warner

and screen actor (real name: Harry Byron Charles Stewart Warner-Lickford) who appeared in nearly 140 silent and sound films, sometimes credited as Henry B. Warner. Warner portrays Inspector Fife of Scotland Yard in *Charlie Chan's Chance* (1932).

H.B. Warner was the son of Charles Warner and the grandson of James Warner, both prominent British stage actors. A tentative stab at studying medicine was abandoned when he took drama lessons in Paris and Italy and then joined his father's stock company. After touring the British empire, Warner made his first American stage appearance in 1905. A leading man in his younger days, Warner starred as Warren Jarvis in the first stage and screen versions of *The Ghost Breaker* (1914). His most celebrated silent-film role was as Christ in Cecil B. DeMille's *The King of Kings* (1927), and he remained extremely busy as a character actor in the 1930s and 1940s.

A favorite of director Frank Capra, Warner appeared as Chang in *Lost Horizon* (1937), for which he was nominated for an Academy Award in the Best Supporting Actor category, and as old man Gower in the Christmas-themed *It's A Wonderful Life* (1946). Warner also played Inspector Col. J.A. Nielsen in several of the *Bulldog Drummond* pictures of the 1930s. H.B. Warner's final screen appearance was as Amminadab in DeMille's remake of *The Ten Commandments* (1956).

warning messages

Charlie Chan in Paris (1935)

To Charlie Chan: "The purpose of your visit is known. If you place the least value on your life, leave France tonight. This will be your only warning."

Charlie Chan in Shanghai (1936)

To Charlie Chan: "Shanghai is an unhealthy place for you. If you are wise, you will not leave this ship."

Charlie Chan at the Race Track (1936)

To Warren Fenton: "A dead horse isn't worth $20,000."

To Denny Barton: "A smart gambler knows a dead horse can't win."

To George Chester: "Don't enter Avalanche in the Santa Juanita Handicap—A Dead Horse can't win a race."

To Bruce Rogers: "It's dangerous to know too much about other people's business."

To George Chester: "This is your last chance. Withdraw Avalanche before it is too late."

To George Chester: "Withdraw Avalanche from the Santa Juanita Handicap. This is your last warning."

Charlie Chan at the Opera (1936)

To Mme. Lili Rochelle: "YOU WILL DIE TONIGHT"

Charlie Chan at the Olympics (1937)

To Charlie Chan: "If you wish news of your son, be in your same seat in the Olympic Stadium alone and unguarded."

Charlie Chan at Treasure Island (1939)

To Charlie Chan: "Do not challenge the supernatural unless you are prepared to visit your ancestors."

To Paul Essex: "Sign of Scorpio indicates disaster if Zodiac obligations ignored."

Castle in the Desert (1942)

To Charlie Chan: "A wise man does not visit a Borgia if he values life."

Warren, Gloria Wilmington, Delaware–born singer and actress who portrays Rona Simmonds in *Dangerous Money* (1946).

Warren, Harry (December 24, 1893, Brooklyn, New York–September 22, 1981, Los Angeles, California) Composer and song writer (real name: Salvatore Guaragno) who has written nearly 300 songs for over 70 films. Warren wrote the lyrics for the song *They Met in Rio* used in *Charlie Chan in Rio* (1941).

Although born Salvatore Guaragno, composer Harry Warren changed his name while working as a drummer and pianist in various traveling bands. Writing the music for the Eddie Cantor musical *Roman Scandals* (1933), Warren so impressed the film's choreographer Busby Berkeley, that Berkeley brought Warren with him to Warner Bros. for the film *42nd Street* (1933).

Working in collaboration with Al Dubin,

Warren composed tunes like "Shuffle Off to Buffalo," "Young and Healthy," and the title song for *42nd Street*. Films like *Footlight Parade* (1933) yielded songs such as "By a Waterfall," "Honeymoon Hotel," "Shanghai Lil," and the film *The Gold Diggers* (1933) featured "We're in the Money." The list of Harry Warren songs is virtually a shorthand history of movie musicals and includes such well-known songs as "I Only Have Eyes for You," "You Must Have Been a Beautiful Baby," "Jeepers Creepers," "Chattanooga Choo Choo," "The More I See You," "That's Amore," "I've Got a Gal in Kalamazoo," and "Down Argentine Way."

Despite the familiarity of his output, Harry Warren's name was never a household word. Warren's one chance for posthumous acclaim was squelched when producer David Merrick, utilizing over a dozen Warren songs for his 1983 Broadway musical *42nd Street*, perversely refused to put Warren's name on the advertising or in the programs. In recent years, singer-pianist Michael Feinstein has worked diligently to bring the invaluable contributions of his late friend Harry Warren to the attention of audiences who'd grown up humming "Shuffle Off to Buffalo" or "By a Waterfall" without ever knowing who had put the notes on paper in the first place.

In his career, Warren received 11 Academy Award nominations in the Best Music (Song) category, winning three of them:

*"Lullaby of Broadway" (*Gold Diggers of 1935*, 1935)
"Remember Me" (*Mr. Dodd Takes the Air*, 1937)
"Jeepers Creepers" (*Going Places*, 1938)
"Down Argentine Way" (*Down Argentine Way*, 1940)
"Chattanooga Choo Choo" (*Sun Valley Serenade*, 1941)
"I've Got a Gal in Kalamazoo" (*Orchestra Wives*, 1942)
*"You'll Never Know" (*Hello, Frisco, Hello*, 1943)
*"On the Atchison, Topeka and Santa Fe" (*The Harvey Girls*, 1946)
"Zing a Little Zong" (*Just for You*, 1952)
"That's Amore" (*The Caddy*, 1953)
"An Affair to Remember" (*An Affair to Remember*, 1957)

**Academy Award winner.*

Warren, Janet Character actress, sometimes credited as Elaine Morey, who appeared in two *Charlie Chan* films at Monogram. Warren portrays radio actress Jean Kent in *The Jade Mask* (1945) and Lorraine, the voice in the jukebox, in *The Shanghai Cobra* (1945).

Warwick, Robert (October 9, 1878, Sacramento, California–June 6, 1964, Los Angeles, California) Film editor of 13 westerns and a stage and screen character actor (real name: Robert Taylor Bien) who appeared in over 175 films, often as military officers, politicians, and judges. In two *Charlie Chan* roles, Warwick portrays Dan Winterslip in *Charlie Chan's Greatest Case* (1933) and Charlie Chan's police chief (unbilled) in *Charlie Chan at the Race Track* (1936).

Washington, D.C. Location setting for *Charlie Chan in the Secret Service* (1944) and most of the early Monogram Chans.

Note: One of the best known errors of the series occurs in this film when Charlie Chan walks out of a federal building where his Secret Service office is located, and the flag flying on the flagpole in front of the building is that of the state of California. The same scene and error is repeated in *The Shanghai Cobra* (1945).

Washington Street San Francisco Chinatown street address of the Chan Family Society in *The Golden Eye* (1948). Curio shop owner Wong Fat tells Mr. Manning where to reach Charlie Chan.

Watkin, Pierre (December 29, 1889, Sioux City, Iowa–February 3, 1960, Hollywood, California) Tall, imposing American actor with a well-trimmed white mustache who appeared in almost 250 films, particularly in roles as bankers, lawyers, judges, and doctors. Watkin (incorrectly billed as Pierre Watkins) portrays Judge Wesley Armstrong in *The Shanghai Chest* (1948) and also the district attorney in *Mr. Moto's Gamble* (1938), a reworked version of the never-completed *Charlie Chan at the Ringside.*

Watkins An airplane pilot (portrayed by Bob Curtis) in *The Sky Dragon* (1949). Charlie Chan tries to reconstruct a murder and the theft of money during Flight 17, and Watkins takes the place of pilot Tim Norton (who Lt. Ruark considers to be one of several possible suspects).

Watkins, Col. Shanghai commissioner of police (portrayed by Halliwell Hobbes) in *Charlie Chan in Shanghai* (1935). Watkins and Charlie Chan are friends, having first met in London at Scotland Yard at the time of Sir Lionel Bashford's murder.

Watkins, Linda (May 23, 1908, Boston, Massachusetts–October 31, 1976) Character actress who portrays Gloria Garland in *Charlie Chan's Chance* (1932).

Watson, Minor (December 22, 1889, Marianna, Arkansas–July 28, 1965, Alton, Illinois) American stage and screen actor who appeared in over 100 films, often as lawyers or kindly fathers. Watson portrays Paris police inspector Renard in *Charlie Chan in Paris* (1935).

Minor Watson was fond of saying, "I'm a stage actor by heart and by profession. I was a movie star by necessity and a desire to eat." Though never a true "movie star" per se, he remained gainfully employed into the 1950s in choice character roles. One of Minor Watson's largest and most well-rounded screen assignments was the part of Brooklyn Dodgers manager Branch Rickey in *The Jackie Robinson Story* (1950).

Watson, Susie Flighty society matron (portrayed by Cora Witherspoon) who is romantically pursued by Frederick Ross in *Charlie Chan's Murder Cruise* (1940). She and her secretary, Paula Drake, are members of Dr. Suderman's cruise.

Wayne, Mrs. Carol Alias used by Elsie Hillman (portrayed by Claire Dodd) while a passenger on the *Susan B. Jennings* in *Charlie Chan in Honolulu* (1938). Wayne tells Charlie Chan that she was recently widowed and is taking a trip for relaxation. However, Mrs. Wayne's purpose in traveling on the ship is to prevent her estranged husband, from whom she is getting a divorce, from receiving a package containing $300,000 in cash (money that Mr. Wayne intends to keep out of the property settlement). Mrs. Wayne is later found dead in Judy Hayes' cabin, having been strangled with a scarf tied with a sailor's knot, which points Charlie Chan toward Capt. Johnson as her murderer for the $300,000.

WD Initials on a gun Charlie Chan takes from Catlen in the fun house on the amusement pier in *The Chinese Cat* (1944). Chan explains to Leah Manning and Det. Harvey Dennis that Webster Deacon used this gun to shoot and kill Thomas Manning.

Weaver, Marjorie (March 2, 1913, Crossville, Tennessee–December 1994, Austin, Texas) American leading lady, especially of second features, who appeared in over 30 films. In two *Charlie Chan* roles, Weaver portrays Paula Drake in *Charlie Chan's Murder Cruise* (1940) and Patricia West in *Murder Over New York* (1940).

Educated at the University of Kentucky and the University of Indiana, Marjorie Weaver was a band singer, model, and stock-company actress before making her first film appearance in *Transatlantic Merry-Go-Round* (1934). From 1936 to 1942 Weaver was under contract to Twentieth Century–Fox, where she played any number of nice but no-nonsense leading ladies. She co-starred with Henry Fonda in *Young Mr. Lincoln* (1939), in which she played Mary Todd.

Webb, Paula Secretary (portrayed by Joan Barclay) to bank president Walter Fletcher in *The Shanghai Cobra* (1945). Webb is the daughter of bank guard Jan Van Horn, who uses the alias of John Adams.

Webster, Col. D.C. Governor of the Panama Canal Zone (portrayed by Edwin Stanley in his third of three *Charlie Chan* roles) in *Charlie Chan in Panama* (1940). *See also* **Panama Canal Zone**.

Webster, Pauline Alias used by Paula Webb in *The Shanghai Cobra* (1945). Ned Stewart, a private detective, is hired by a man calling himself Mr. Rogers to follow a woman named Pauline Webster.

Wednesday, September 2, 1936 Date of S.S. *Oceanic* log entry noting the accidental death of Major Kent at the ship's location of 12° N latitude, 167° W longitude (southwest of Hawaii) on its voyage from Australia to Honolulu and Los Angeles in *Charlie Chan at the Race Track* (1936). It is first thought by both the ship's captain and doctor that Kent was accidentally kicked to death by his horse, Avalanche, in the stable located in the ship's forward hold.

Weebles, Mrs. Temperance-minded housekeeper (portrayed by Minerva Urecal in her second of two *Charlie Chan* roles) of the Rutherford Mansion (rented by Cole King for his variety troupe) in *The Trap* (1947).

Weldon, Robert Actor who portrays Steve Daniels in *Dead Men Tell* (1941).

Wells, Conrad (c. 1897–January 2, 1930) Cinematographer (real name: Abe Fried) for *Behind That Curtain* (1929).

Wells, Vivian Social director of Reno's Hotel Sierra (portrayed by Phyllis Brooks in her second of two *Charlie Chan* roles) in *Charlie Chan in Reno* (1939). Wells is very fond of Dr. Ainsley and murders Jeanne Bently out of jealousy and self-defense.

Wendall, Joan Wisecracking, aggressive freelance photographer (portrayed by Joan Marsh) who is a friend of reporter Speed Patten in *Charlie Chan on Broadway* (1937). Wendall recognizes Billie Bronson, who was once "hot" in New York, getting off a boat and takes her picture. She then takes the picture to Murdock, managing editor of the *New York Daily Bulletin*, who says that he already has a dozen pictures of Billie Bronson and offers to pay $50. Wendall then claims that she knows a dozen editors who would like to know that she took this picture that afternoon, to which Murdock agrees to pay her asking price of $100 and tells her to forget that she ever took this picture. Wendall responds, "My mind's a complete blank," and Murdock comments, "I suppose you haven't forgotten the way to the cashier's office?" Wendall then replies, "And how!"

West, Patricia Paul Narvo's estranged wife (portrayed by Marjorie Weaver [incorrectly credited as Patricia Shaw]), in *Murder Over New York* (1940). West had played in a show with June Preston in London five years before she married Narvo, who then made her quit the show.

One day she overhears Narvo and his servant Ramullah talking about the murder of a British Air Ministry official, and she guesses that both of them are part of a sabotage ring. She then flees England and skips around the globe trying to get away from Narvo. Now in New York and engaged to David Elliot, West lives in Room 4 of a rooming house at 21 Washington Square. Through information obtained from June Preston, Charlie Chan locates West and gets her to help him find Narvo and Ramullah.

Note: The film's credits list Marjorie Weaver as playing Patricia Shaw, but nowhere in the film is she mentioned as such. The mailbox of her rooming house lists her as Patricia West. When Charlie Chan and Police Inspector Vance search through Hugh Drake's briefcase, they see a Scotland Yard Criminal Identification Bureau report that gives Mrs. Paul Narvo's maiden name as Miriam Shaw, with aliases of Lucy Millard, Dorothy Cochran, and Patricia West. Furthermore, the character Patricia West loosely parallels that of Shirley Marlowe in *Charlie Chan's Chance* (1932).

"What happened in London the night of October 5th, 1935?" Question repeatedly asked during a séance conducted by William and Justine Bonner in *Black Magic* (1944). Pretending to be in a trance, William Bonner is startled by the question from an unknown voice, after which a scream is heard. When the lights come on, Bonner is found dead, killed by a bullet than can't be found and shot by a gun no one heard or can find.

When in London years ago Bonner was

an assistant to a magician, Chardo the Great. The magician's wife, Justine, ran off with Bonner and married him. Charlie Chan finds out from Scotland Yard that Chardo, in trying to follow his wife, was injured in an automobile crash on that date and was in a hospital for one year.

"What no man hears, no man ever knows" Words spoken by Sir Frederic Bruce to Eve Durand and Col. John Beetham upon hearing that Eric Durand has been killed at the Cosmopolitan Club while resisting arrest in *Behind That Curtain* (1929). Eve had always feared the embarrassment if it became publicly known that her estranged husband was a murderer.

"What will Confusion say?" Question that is occasionally asked by Charlie Chan's chauffeur, Birmingham Brown, who thinks the name of Confucius is pronounced "Confusion." In *Dark Alibi* (1946), Tommy Chan tries to correct Birmingham by saying, "It's not Confusion—*Confucius*," to which Birmingham replies, "Every time you open your mouth it's confusion to me."

Whelan, Arleen (September 16, 1914, Salt Lake City, Utah–April 8, 1993, Orange County, California) Character actress who appeared in over 20 films and portrays Brenda Hartford in *Castle in the Desert* (1942).

Whipple, Mrs. The alias used by Joseph Murdock, who is dressed as a woman and posing as the wife of Rev. Whipple, in *Dangerous Money* (1946). *See also* **Murdock, Joseph**.

Whipple, Rev. The alias used by Theodore Lane, posing as a missionary and traveling to Samoa, in *Dangerous Money* (1946). Rev. Whipple is traveling with Joseph Murdock, who is dressed as a woman and posing as his wife. The Whipples are leaders of a gang planning to sell artworks stolen from Philippine banks during the Japanese invasion. *See also* **Lane, Theodore M.**

white fox fur Stylish fur boa worn by Yvonne Roland in *Charlie Chan at the Olympics* (1937). When searching the hotel of an aviation mechanic named Miller, who is suspected of hijacking a test plane and murdering Edwards, its test pilot, Charlie Chan finds clues indicating that a woman was once in the room and that she wore white fox fur.

Even though it is a clue, the "white fox fur" becomes something of a comic gag for the remainder of the film. While at the Pan American Airlines ticket counter, Chan is checking over the passenger list of the Clipper ship that left Honolulu for San Francisco. Number Two son, Charlie Junior, more than once points out to his father women wearing white fox fur boas as possible suspects. Irritated at being interrupted from his train of thought, Chan warns his son that if he mentions "white fox fur" one more time, "very bright junior son walk home." When the ticket agent at the Pan American Airline office remembers that there was such a woman wearing white fox fur, Charlie Junior again reminds his father about the connection, forcing Charlie to make good on his threat.

When Chan meets up with Number One son Lee and the U.S. Olympic Team in Germany, Lee tells Charlie about the suspicious Yvonne Roland and her activities aboard the S.S. *Manhattan*. While the two are searching Roland's stateroom, Lee yells, "Look, here's a swell clue—her white fox fur!" In turn, Charlie immediately slaps Lee on his behind, saying, "Have heard enough of white fox fur!"

White, Lee Roy "Lasses" (August 28, 1888, Wills Point, Texas–December 6, 1949, Hollywood California) Stage and screen actor who portrays the prospector named Pete in *The Golden Eye* (1948).

White, Marjorie (July 22, 1908–August 20, 1935) Comic actress who appeared in nearly 15 films, including two *Charlie Chan* roles. She portrays Sadie Minchin in *Charlie Chan Carries On* (1931) and Rita Ballou in *The Black Camel* (1931).

Comedienne Marjorie White spent the late 1920s in vaudeville, appearing in an act with husband Eddie Tierney. In 1929 White was signed by Fox Studios, where she appeared in several of the early Fox musicals, including *Sunny Side Up* (1929) and *Just Imagine* (1930). Her first assignment outside of Fox was arguably her best, when she played the aggressive vampish Dolores in the Wheeler and Woolsey farce *Diplomaniacs* (1933). The following year she starred in the two-reel Columbia musical novelty *Woman Haters* (1934), in which she was supported by a trio called Howard, Fine, and Howard, later to be known as The Three Stooges. Marjorie White's promising film career ended with tragic suddenness when she was killed in a car crash in 1934.

White, Robertson Screenwriter (with Lester Ziffren) of *Charlie Chan's Murder Cruise* (1940).

Whitehead, Joe Actor who appeared in two *Charlie Chan* films. Whitehead portrays Dr. Samuel R. Peabody in *The Jade Mask* (1945) and the Gayety Theatre stage watchman (unbilled) in *The Sky Dragon* (1949).

Whitely, Mr. Mme. Lilli Rochelle's jealous husband (portrayed by Frank Conroy in his second of two *Charlie Chan* roles) in *Charlie Chan at the Opera* (1936). Whitely is convinced that his wife is having an affair with baritone Enrico Barelli and hires a private detective to have her followed. He is never told by his wife that she had been married to Gravelle and had a child.

Whitman, Curtis Mary Whitman's estranged husband (portrayed by Kane Richmond in his first of three *Charlie Chan* roles) in *Charlie Chan in Reno* (1939). As an old friend of Charlie Chan, Whitman asks Chan to fly with him to Reno to prove his wife's innocence, even though they are getting a divorce and he had plans to marry Jeanne Bently, the woman Mary is accused of killing.

Whitman, Mary Wife (portrayed by Pauline Moore in her second of three *Charlie Chan* roles) of Curtis Whitman in *Charlie Chan in Reno* (1939). She and her husband (who are old friends of Charlie Chan) have separated and are getting a divorce. Mary then travels to Reno, Nevada, to establish the necessary residency at the Hotel Sierra.

In the hotel she runs into Jeanne Bently, also at the hotel for the same reason; Bently plans to marry Curtis when the divorce is final. Later that evening, however, Bently is murdered by the hotel's social director, Vivian Wells, and Mary Whitman is accused of the murder.

Wiles, Gordon (1902, St. Louis, Missouri–1950) Film director for *Charlie Chan's Secret* (1936). Gordon won an Academy Award in the Best Art Direction category for *Transatlantic* (1931).

Wilkie House detective of the Luani Hotel (portrayed by James Burke) in *Charlie Chan's Murder Cruise* (1940).

Williams, Charles B. (September 27, 1898, Albany, New York–January 3, 1958, Hollywood, California) Short stage and screen character actor, playwright, and screenwriter who appeared in almost 80 movies and two *Charlie Chan* films. Williams portrays an unbilled reporter in *Charlie Chan at the Race Track* (1936) and was Johnny Burke's lawyer, Meeker, in *Charlie Chan on Broadway* (1937). In addition, Williams portrays Gabby Marden in *Mr. Moto's Gamble* (1938), a reworked version of the never-completed *Charlie Chan at the Ringside*.

Short of stature, high-pitched of voice, and usually sporting a toothbrush mustache and coke-bottle glasses, Charles Williams was the perfect nerd in many Hollywood films. Williams began his career at Paramount's New York studios in 1922, dabbling in everything from writing to assistant directing. When talkies arrived, Williams found his true calling as a supporting actor, seemingly cast as a nosy reporter or press photographer in virtually every picture produced in Hollywood.

Williams, Dick Newspaper reporter for *The Globe* (portrayed by Charles Quigley) who is engaged to Alice Lowell in *Charlie Chan's Secret* (1936).

Wilson Paul Manderley's butler (portrayed by Eric Wilton) in *Castle in the Desert* (1942).

winch shoe Metallic, horseshoe-shaped murder weapon used by George Chester to murder his father-in-law, Major Kent, aboard the S.S. *Oceanic* in *Charlie Chan at the Race Track* (1936). It is originally thought that the horse Avalanche accidentally kicked Kent in the head while in its stall because the winch shoe resembles a horseshoe. However, Charlie Chan observes that the pattern of the blood stains on the sides of the stall indicate that Kent was murdered.

While docked in Honolulu, a search of the ship by Charlie Chan and son Lee find the winch shoe. They deduce that it is the murder weapon by the bits of hair and blood on it. Chan fingers Chester as Kent's murderer and leader of a racetrack gambling ring after Avalanche is struck by a tranquilizer dart during the running of the Santa Juanita Handicap. At this, Chester foolishly blunders when he accuses Fenton of murdering Kent with a winch shoe. Chan then remarks that only three people besides himself knew the identity of the murder weapon—the ship's captain (Capt. Blade), the chief of police, and the murderer.

Winfield, Craig The former manager of the Bon Ton Burlesque Company in *Shadows Over Chinatown* (1946). Now, 12 years later, Winfield poses as Jeff Hay, a private detective who secretly runs the Bay City Escort Bureau.

Winifred Member of Cole King's variety troupe (portrayed by Bettie Best) in *The Trap* (1947).

Winters, Mrs. Alias of German master spy Manleck (portrayed by Lelah Tyler) in *Charlie Chan in the Secret Service* (1944). Her chauffeur is Birmingham Brown, who makes his first appearance in a *Charlie Chan* film. *See also* **Manleck**.

Winters, Roland (November 22, 1904, Boston, Massachusetts–October 22, 1989, Englewood, New Jersey) The sixth actor to portray the role of Charlie Chan, Winters appears in Monogram's final six films in the series.

The youngest of the Chans, Roland Winters squinted his eyes and wore a black hairpiece.

Born Roland Winternitz to a concert violinist father, Roland longed for something exciting to do and shipped out on the United Fruit Lines for two summer tours while in his teens. When 16, a friend got Winters interested in a little theater group in Boston. From there he graduated to stock companies and landed on Broadway in 1924. Roland Winters was 19 when he played his first important character role—in the New York theatrical production of *The Firebrand*, which was being produced by a classmate of his brother.

Besides theater, Winters became a staff announcer on Boston's WNAC radio, sportscasting 154 games for the Red Sox and the Boston Braves. In addition to sportscasting, he also served as announcer on the shows of Kay Kyser, Kate Smith, and Henry Aldrich until his film debut as Van Duyval in *13 Rue Madeleine* (1946), with Jimmy Cagney.

When Sidney Toler died on February 12, 1947, Monogram was searching for a replacement for their *Charlie Chan* series. Having already screen-tested 46 actors, producer

James Burkett asked Winters to test for the role. Immediately after he did a trial scene, Burkett told him he had the part, and filming on *The Chinese Ring* began on August 21, 1947. Unlike Warner Oland and Sidney Toler, Winters' prominent nose and blond hair would have never allowed him to pass for an Oriental without some adjustments. Winters would squint to give his eyes a slanted appearance, and to reduce the prominence of his nose, Winters always looked straight into the camera (if he were talking to someone at his side, Winters would merely move his eyes right or left).

While Winters' six low-budget entries are generally disliked by *Charlie Chan* movie buffs, it can now be seen that Winters brought a much needed breath of fresh air to the flagging film series with his self-mocking, semi-satirical interpretation of Charlie (which was very close to the Charlie Chan in Biggers' novels). As the youngest of the "big three" actors who play Chan, he was the least energetic.

Roland Winters was a good friend of James Cagney, and once Monogram had ended the Charlie Chan series, Winters showed up in several of Cagney's films of the 1950s, notably *A Lion Is in the Streets* (1953) and *Never Steal Anything Small* (1959). He continued to flourish in colorful supporting roles into the 1960s and was also seen as a regular on television sitcoms like *Meet Millie* (1952), *The New Phil Silvers Show* (1963), and *The Smothers Brothers Show* (1965). In the late 1960s Winters even returned to the Broadway stage in the musical *Minnie's Boys* and appeared as Mr. Gimble in the television version of *Miracle on 34th Street* (1973). Roland Winters died of a stroke at the Actors' Fund Nursing Home in Englewood, New Jersey, on October 22, 1989, at the age of 84.

Charlie Chan filmography: *The Chinese Ring* (1947), *Docks of New Orleans* (1948), *The Shanghai Chest* (1948), *The Golden Eye* (1948), *The Feathered Serpent* (1948), and *The Sky Dragon* (1949).

Winterslip, Amos The moralistic brother (portrayed by Frank McGlynn) of Dan and Minerva Winterslip who is murdered by Harry Jennison in *Charlie Chan's Greatest Case* (1933).

Winterslip, Barbara Dan Winterslip's daughter (portrayed by Virginia Cherrill), who plans to marry Harry Jennison, in *Charlie Chan's Greatest Case* (1933). Both Jennison (Dan Winterslip's lawyer) and Barbara are traveling back to Honolulu by boat and telegram her father with the news. Instead of congratulating the couple, her father's reply contains a warning to Jennison that unless he breaks off the engagement, Barbara will be disinherited.

Winterslip, Dan The ingrate brother (portrayed by Robert Warwick) of Amos and Minerva Winterslip in *Charlie Chan's Greatest Case* (1933). Thirty-five years ago Dan stole jewels from T.M. Brade's father when he was a mate on Brade's ship. At Dan's home, his sister Minerva sees a prowler and then discovers Dan dead in the den, stabbed in the heart (by Harry Jennison) and with a broken arm.

Winterslip, John Quincy The cousin (portrayed by John Warburton) of Minerva, Dan, and Amos Winterslip in *Charlie Chan's Greatest Case* (1933).

Winterslip, Minerva Sister (portrayed by Clara Blandick) of Dan and Amos Winterslip in *Charlie Chan's Greatest Case* (1933). At Dan's home in Honolulu, Minerva Winterslip sees a prowler (Harry Jennison) and then discovers Dan dead in the den. Charlie Chan questions Minerva, who remembers only one identifying characteristic of the prowler—a glow-in-the-dark wristwatch with a blurred numeral two.

"Withdraw Avalanche from the Santa Juanita Handicap. This is your last warning" Warning message in a note to George Chester secretly dropped by Lee Chan in *Charlie Chan at the Race Track* (1936). Charlie Chan has Lee distribute different warning messages while onboard the S.S. *Oceanic* to Warren Fenton, Bruce Rogers, Denny

Barton, and Chester as part of a plan to identify the leader of a racetrack gambling ring.

Witherspoon, Cora (January 5, 1890, New Orleans, Louisiana–November 17, 1957, Las Cruces, New Mexico) American stage and screen character actress who appeared in over 40 films, often as bossy society matrons, domineering maiden aunts, and henpecking housewives. Witherspoon portrays the middle-aged spinster Susie Watson in *Charlie Chan's Murder Cruise* (1940). Of all her roles, she is perhaps best recognized as Agatha Souse, W.C. Fields' sloppy wife, in *The Bank Dick* (1940).

Wong, Anna May (January 3, 1905, Los Angeles, California–February 2, 1961, Santa Monica, California) American-born Chinese stage and screen actress (real name: Wong Liu Tsong) who appeared in over 50 films and portrays the Nautch dancer in *The Chinese Parrot* (1927).

Anna May Wong began playing small parts in her preteen years. Her first role of consequence was as a slave girl in Douglas Fairbanks' lavish *The Thief of Baghdad* (1924). Shortly afterward, she played Tiger Lily in the first film version of *Peter Pan* (1924). While she had several large roles in subsequent Hollywood films, it wasn't until she went to Europe in 1929 that she was taken seriously as an actress.

Anna May Wong

Once back in Hollywood, however, it was back to exotic Oriental stereotypes with little opportunity for romantic roles, as there were still many prohibitions against racial intermingling in films of the 1930s. Her best film assignments included Josef von Sternberg's *Shanghai Express* (1932), in which she appeared as Hui Fei with Charlie Chan's Warner Oland, as Mme. Pyke in the *Sherlock Holmes* film, *A Study in Scarlet* (1933), and a string of Paramount second features in the late 1930s, notably (as Lan Ying Lin) *Daughter of Shanghai* (1937).

Anna retired from films in 1942, thereafter making only occasional stage appearances in the Los Angeles area. She died of heart failure at the age of 56, just before she was to begin work on the screen version of the Rodgers and Hammerstein Broadway hit *Flower Drum Song* (1961).

Wong, Barbara Jean (March 3, 1924, Los Angeles, California–November 13, 1999, Tarzana, California) Chinese-American actress who portrays Cole King's variety troupe member San Toy in *The Trap* (1947).

Wong, Choy Jeanne Bently's maid (portrayed by Iris Wong in her first of two *Charlie Chan* roles) in *Charlie Chan in Reno* (1939).

Note: In the Call Bureau Cast Service lists, Choy Wong's name originally was Sung Li.

Wong, Iris (1920, Watsonville, California–September 2, 1989, Honolulu, Hawaii) Chinese-American actress who portrays Jeanne Bently's maid Choy Wong in *Charlie Chan in Reno* (1939) and Lola Dean's maid Lili Wong in *Charlie Chan in Rio* (1941).

Wong, Jean Chinese-American actress who appears in two *Charlie Chan* films at Monogram. Wong is the Chinese artist Iris Ling in *The Red Dragon* (1945) and Princess Mei Ling in *The Chinese Ring* (1947).

Wong, Lili Lola Dean's Chinese maid (portrayed by Iris Wong) in *Charlie Chan in Rio*

(1941). When Charlie Chan and Number Two son Jimmy begin talking to each other in Chinese, Bill Kellogg asks Lili what they are saying. She responds, "I don't know. It's all Chinese to me," and explains that she was raised in an American orphanage in San Francisco and doesn't speak the language.

Wong, Lilly Mae Portrayed by Chabing in her first of two *Charlie Chan* roles, the maid to Princess Mei Ling in *The Chinese Ring* (1947). She is murdered by Mr. Armstrong with a poison dart shot from a European air rifle.

Wong, Louie Cook and caretaker of the Madden ranch. In *The Chinese Parrot* (1927) Wong is portrayed by George Kuwa. In *Charlie Chan's Courage* (1934) the role of Louie Wong is portrayed by James Wang in his second of two *Charlie Chan* roles. Wong has been away from the ranch for a short while and, upon his return, is murdered by "Shaky" Phil Maydorf before he can identify Jerry Delaney as the one who is impersonating his boss, P.J. Madden/J.P. Madden.

Wong, Mr. Polite Chinese detective who is the basis for a series of six movies from 1938 to 1940 at Monogram. The character is taken from stories by Hugh Wiley. The *Mr. Wong* series was created to compete with Twentieth Century–Fox's Japanese detective Mr. Moto and the well-liked *Charlie Chan* series. The first five films feature Boris Karloff as James Lee Wong, a detective whose manners and humility often paralleled that of Warner Oland's Chan. The final film, *Phantom of Chinatown* (1940), has Keye Luke in the main role and is the first time an Oriental actor was cast in the major role of an Oriental detective.

Boris Karloff as Mr. Wong.

Monogram later reworked the first two *Mr. Wong* films into similar *Charlie Chan* episodes. *Mr. Wong, Detective* (1938) became *Docks of New Orleans* (1948), and *Mr. Wong in Chinatown* (1939) became *The Chinese Ring* (1947).

Mr. Wong filmography: *Mr. Wong, Detective* (1938), *Mr. Wong in Chinatown* (1939), *The Mystery of Mr. Wong* (1939), *The Fatal Hour* (1940), *Doomed to Die* (1940), and *Phantom of Chinatown* (1940).

Wong, Sun A leading Chinese merchant (portrayed by Moy Ming [unbilled]) who makes a brief welcoming speech in Chinese at a dinner honoring the visit of Charlie Chan to Shanghai in *Charlie Chan in Shanghai* (1935).

Wood, Allen K. Production manager and supervisor for over 45 films, including *The Feathered Serpent* (1948) and *The Sky Dragon* (1949).

Wood, Helen (1917–1988) Actress who portrayed Alice Fenton, the daughter of racehorse owner Warren Fenton, in *Charlie Chan at the Race Track* (1936).

Woodbury, Joan (December 17, 1915, Los Angeles, California–February 22, 1989, Desert Hot Springs, California) Tall, seductive actress who appeared in nearly 50 films and had roles in two *Charlie Chan* entries. Woodbury portrays nightclub dancer Marie Collins in *Charlie Chan on Broadway* (1937) and Leah Manning in *The Chinese Cat* (1944).

Joan Woodbury was a professional dancer

in the Los Angeles area before entering films in the early 1930s. Almost exclusively confined to "B" pictures, she had few pretensions about her abilities and disdained any sort of star treatment. Woodbury was proudest of the time, while playing the lead role in *Brenda Starr, Reporter* (1945), she prevented the film from going over budget by performing a complicated five-minute scene in a single take, which earned her a spontaneous round of applause from the crew members. After retiring from films in the 1960s, she organized and maintained the Palm Springs–based Valley Players' Guild, staging plays which featured other veteran performers.

Woodland, Diana Sir Stanley Woodland's niece from Canada (portrayed by Irene Hervey) in *Charlie Chan in Shanghai* (1935). Her uncle had never confided in her about the operations he was involved in, except that he was working with an American agent named James Andrews.

When Charlie Chan sees her to offer his condolences the morning after her uncle's murder, she tells Chan that her uncle had been nervous of late and did not wish to be alone. As part of a plan by Charlie and the police to find out who is involved in the opium smuggling ring, Diana helps Sir Stanley's secretary, Philip Nash, escape from the police station where he is being held as a suspect in Sir Stanley's murder.

Woodland, Sir Stanley Secret agent for the British government (portrayed by David Torrence in his second of two *Charlie Chan* roles) in *Charlie Chan in Shanghai* (1935). Woodland is working with James Andrews, a U.S. government agent, on an opium smuggling operation in Shanghai.

At a dinner honoring the visit of the famous Charlie Chan to Shanghai, Sir Stanley wants to tell Charlie why he wasn't at the dock to meet him earlier that day, having made an important discovery concerning the opium smuggling operation he was investigating. Chan cautions Woodland that they should talk later and that there are "two ears for every tongue." Apparently Charlie is not in Shanghai by accident but at the request of Sir Stanley, who thinks that Chan's knowledge of the Chinese language and customs would be of help in the case.

When Sir Stanley rises to make a speech, he is shot by a small gun triggered to fire when he opened a wooden chest containing a handwritten scroll he was to read to commemorate Charlie's visit. Although it is later learned that the opium smuggling ring is responsible for the murder, it is Sir Stanley's secretary, Philip Nash, who is first arrested.

Woods, Donald (December 1, 1904, Brandon, Manitoba, Canada–March 5, 1998, Palm Springs, California) Handsome second lead actor (real name: Ralph L. Zink) who appeared in over 70 films. In two *Charlie Chan* roles, Woods portrays Bob Crawford in *Charlie Chan's Courage* (1934) and newspaper reporter Speed Patten in *Charlie Chan on Broadway* (1937).

Donald Woods came from the stage to films in 1934 and played a few unremarkable roles before rising to prominence as Charles Darnay in *A Tale of Two Cities* (1935). He spent the 1940s and 1950s heading the cast of "B" productions and serials. Woods was one of four actors to portray Erle Stanley Gardner's defense lawyer Perry Mason—in *The Case of the Stuttering Bishop* (1937), 20

Donald Woods (Everett Collection)

years before Raymond Burr made the character famous on television.

Among his appearances on television, Woods played the title role in the 1952 syndicated series *Craig Kennedy, Criminologist* and played a dignified recurring role as John Brent on the 1965 sitcom *Tammy*. He also hosted several television series, such as *The Orchid Award* (1953–54), *Damon Runyon Theater* (1955), and *Hotel Cosmopolitan* (1957–58). Throughout his career, Woods supplemented his acting income as a real estate broker.

Woods, Nancy Alias of Norma Duncan (portrayed by Helen Beverley) in *Black Magic* (1944). *See also* **Duncan, Nancy**.

Woolstenhulme, Charles (1892–May 24, 1960, Glendale, California) Assistant director to Irving Cummings for *Behind That Curtain* (1929).

working titles *see* **alternative titles**

Worlock, Frederick (December 14, 1886–August 1, 1973, Woodland Hills, California) Stage and screen character actor, sometimes credited as Frederic Worlock, who appeared in over 50 films. Worlock portrays Hugh Drake in *Murder Over New York* (1940).

As a dignified British stage actor, Worlock came to Hollywood in 1938. During the war years, Worlock played many professorial roles, some kind, some villainous. As a semi-regular in Universal's *Sherlock Holmes* series, he portrayed roles such as Geoffrey Musgrave in *Sherlock Holmes Faces Death* (1943) and Colonel Cavanaugh in *Dressed to Kill* (1946). Active until 1966, one of Worlock's final assignments included the voices of both Horace Badun and Inspector Craven in the Disney cartoon feature *101 Dalmatians* (1961).

Wright, Cobina (August 14, 1921, New York, New York–) Actress and former model (real name: Cobina Carolyn Wright) who appeared in over 10 films, sometimes credited as Cobina Wright, Jr. Wright portrays the jealous Grace Ellis in *Charlie Chan in Rio* (1941).

Wright, George A. Dialogue director for *Castle in the Desert* (1942).

Wright, Joseph C. Art director and set director for almost 70 silent and sound films. He served as set director for *Charlie Chan Carries On* (1931). In his career, Wright received 12 Academy Award nominations, winning two of them:

Art Direction (Black-and-White)

Lillian Russell (1940)

Art Direction (Color)

Down Argentine Way (1940)

Art Direction–Interior Decoration (Color)

Blood and Sand (1941)
**My Gal Sal* (1942)
The Gang's All Here (1943)

Art Direction–Interior Decoration (Black-and-White)

**This Above All* (1942)

Art Direction–Set Decoration (Black-and-White)

Come to the Stable (1949)
The Man with the Golden Arm (1955)
Days of Wine and Roses (1962)

Art Direction–Set Decoration (Color)

On the Riviera (1951)
Guys and Dolls (1955)
Flower Drum Song (1961)

Wurtzel, Sam (c. 1896–March 12, 1967, Hollywood, California) Assistant director (unbilled) for *The Black Camel* (1931), and the brother of Sol M. Wurtzel.

Wurtzel, Saul (1912–November 19, 1984, Los Angeles, California) Assistant director for six *Charlie Chan* films, and the nephew of Sol M. Wurtzel.

Charlie Chan filmography: *Charlie Chan in Monte Carlo* (1937), *Charlie Chan in Honolulu* (1938)†, *Charlie Chan in Panama* (1940)†, *Charlie Chan's Murder Cruise* (1940)†, *Dead Men Tell* (1941)†, and *Castle in the Desert* (1942)†.

**Academy Award winner.* †*Unbilled.*

Wurtzel, Sol M. (September 12, 1881, New York, New York–April 9, 1958, Westwood, California) Movie producer and director of over 700 films. Wurtzel was either the executive producer, producer, associate producer, or assistant director for ten *Charlie Chan* entries at Twentieth Century–Fox. He was also the producer (unbilled) of *Mr. Moto's Gamble* (1938), a reworked version of the never-completed *Charlie Chan at the Ringside*.

American production executive Sol Wurtzel spent his entire professional career at one single studio. In 1914 Wurtzel joined the new Fox Film Company as private secretary to William Fox, eventually surviving Fox's ouster from the company in 1930. Wurtzel's long-standing loyalty was rewarded when, in 1933, he was promoted to producer, turning out several of Fox's best Will Rogers and Spencer Tracy films. When Fox merged with Darryl F. Zanuck's Twentieth Century company in 1935, several of the old guard were let go, but Wurtzel was one of the survivors. However, he was demoted from "A" pictures to executive in charge of Fox's "B" unit, where he remained until his retirement in 1949.

Under Wurtzel, Twentieth Century–Fox turned out several profitable series, among them were the *Charlie Chan*, *Mr. Moto*, and *Michael Shayne* detective pictures, the *Jones Family* domestic comedies, and the *Jane Withers* musicals. Wurtzel developed several cast-in-stone theories during the late 1930s. Among them was the notion that no film is successful without a villain. He also was convinced that his "B" films would post a profit no matter how much time or money was spent on them, so why endeavor to make his films any better? This approach resulted in four of the weakest *Laurel and Hardy* comedies ever produced, but all were box office successes. His brother Sam Wurtzel was the assistant director (unbilled) for *The Black Camel* (1931) and his nephew Saul Wurtzel was the assistant director for six *Charlie Chan* films.

Charlie Chan filmography: *Charlie Chan's Greatest Case* (1933) [Producer], *Charlie Chan in Paris* (1935) [Executive Producer],* *Charlie Chan in Honolulu* (1938) [Producer],* *Charlie Chan at Treasure Island* (1939) [Executive Producer],* *City in Darkness* (1939) [Executive Producer],* *Charlie Chan in Panama* (1940) [Executive Producer], *Charlie Chan's Murder Cruise* (1940) [Executive Producer], *Murder Over New York* (1940) [Executive Producer], *Dead Men Tell* (1941) [Assistant Director], *Charlie Chan in Rio* (1941) [Executive Producer].

**Unbilled.*

WXK9X Call sign of the experimental television station at the Cosmo Radio Center in *The Scarlet Clue* (1945). Willie Rand is murdered in Studio Number One during his performance of an interpretation of *Dance of the Spirits*.

Wyans, Alfred Researcher (portrayed by Robert E. Keane) who mysteriously acquires secret research papers that describe atomic secrets and the discovery of a new 95th element in *The Red Dragon* (1945).

Wyatt, Dave Convict who Thomas Harley knew in prison eight years ago in *Dark Alibi* (1946). When Harley is arrested for the robbery of a bank and the murder of one of its guards, Harley claims to have been locked in the Carey Theatrical Warehouse for four hours. To prove his story, he shows the policemen a typed note from Dave Wyatt asking him to meet him there. The police discount the note, telling Harley that Wyatt has been dead for eight years.

Wylie, Philip Author of *Death Makes a Decree*, a story that serves as the basis for *Charlie Chan in Reno* (1939).

X

XABH Identification number of the airplane on which Charlie Chan, Number Three son Tommy, and Chattanooga Brown fly to Mexico City in *The Red Dragon* (1945).

Xavier, Marcel Crippled beggar who is an ingenious disguise employed by Henri

Latouche and Max Corday in *Charlie Chan in Paris* (1935). Both Latouche and Corday take turns masquerading as the fictitious Marcel Xavier to provide each other with perfect alibis.

When outside the Café du Singe Bleu, Latouche (disguised as Xavier) runs into Charlie Chan and Corday, begging for money. Inside the café, Xavier murders Charlie Chan's undercover agent, Nardi, while Charlie is sitting at a table with Corday. At the Lamartine Bank, Latouche has an argument with Xavier (Max Corday in disguise) in front of Charlie, with Xavier claiming that the bank is cheating him of his money. Latouche apologizes to Chan, saying that Xavier is "hardly human, an unfortunate relic of the war—shell shock."

Note: The use of a disguise as the basis for establishing an alibi is repeated in *Charlie Chan's Murder Cruise* (1940).

Y

Yamaoka, Otto Japanese actor who portrays Charlie Chan's overzealous but inept policeman assistant Kashimo in *The Black Camel* (1931).

Yarborough, Barton (1900–December 19, 1951, Hollywood, California) Actor who portrays triple murderer Joseph Brandish in *The Red Dragon* (1945).

Yellow Cab Co. Taxi cab company for which Birmingham Brown works in *The Chinese Cat* (1944). Birmingham drives cab number 605, which blows up from a time bomb that is placed in the cab by Salos.

"You are Murderer" Well-known Charlie Chan accusation, spoken when all the suspects that are still alive are gathered together for the reconstruction of the crime. In *Charlie Chan in London* (1934), Chan points out that this is the method used by French police. Step by step, the evidence is presented and Chan concludes with the accusation in the following films: *Charlie Chan in London* (to Geoffrey Richmond); *Charlie Chan in Paris* (to Henri Latouche); *Charlie Chan at the Opera* (to Mme. Anita Barelli); *Charlie Chan at the Olympics* (to Cartwright); *Charlie Chan on Broadway* (to Speed Patten); and *Charlie Chan at Monte Carlo* (to Gordon Chase).

"YOU WILL DIE TONIGHT" Warning message to Mme. Lili Rochelle written on a card with a bouquet of flowers in *Charlie Chan at the Opera* (1936).

Young, Robert (February 22, 1907, Chicago, Illinois–July 21, 1998, Westlake, California) Handsome American leading man of film and television who was cast in amiable, dependable roles in almost 100 films. His sole *Charlie Chan* film appearance, as well as his film debut, is as the publicity director Jimmy Bradshaw in *The Black Camel* (1931).

Robert Young grew up in California and had some stage experience with the Pasadena Playhouse before entering films in 1931. His movie career consisted of characters who were charming, good-looking, and bland. His screen image was such that he usually never got the girl. Louis B. Mayer would say, "He has no sex appeal," but he had a work ethic that prepared him for every role that he played. He had a role of some note as the spy in

Robert Young (Everett Collection)

Hitchcock's *Secret Agent* (1936), but it would be in the '40s when he would have some of his best roles, such as Langdon Towne in *Northwest Passage* (1940), Richard Blake in *Western Union* (1941), and Harry Pulham in *H.M. Pulham, Esq.* (1941).

In 1949 Young started a radio show called *Father Knows Best* in which he played Jim Anderson, an average father with average situations. This program ran for five years on radio before it went to television in 1954. After a slight fall in the ratings and a switch from CBS to NBC, it would become a television mainstay until it was canceled in 1960. Robert Young perhaps was best known as Dr. Marcus Welby in the *Marcus Welby, M.D.* series which ran from 1969 to 1976. After the series ended, there were two television movies in which he would reprise his role as Dr. Welby: *The Return of Marcus Welby, M.D.* (1984) and *Marcus Welby, M.D.: A Holiday Affair* (1988).

Young, Victor Sen (October 18, 1915, San Francisco, California–November 9, 1980, North Hollywood, California) Chinese-American actor who was once a chemical salesman and who thought he'd like to get into movies. Young's original name was Sen Yew Cheung, and in his early appearances as Jimmy Chan opposite Sidney Toler he is credited as Sen Yung.

During the series at Twentieth Century-Fox, Sen Yung appeared in all his films with Sidney Toler—with the exception of *City in Darkness* (1939). However, when Monogram took over the series in 1944, Yung left the series for a while, being replaced by Benson Fong as Tommy Chan, Charlie's Number Three son. With Yung now having changed his name to Victor Sen Young, he was reunited with Sidney Toler for Toler's last three Chan pictures. Following Toler's death, Roland Winters continued the role of Charlie Chan, and Young was now mysteriously cast as Tommy Chan for five of the six final Monogram films. To add confusion to his billing, he was credited as Victor Sen Yung in *The Feathered Serpent* (1948). In five films from Monogram, the character of Tommy Chan was upgraded to Number Two son status for no known reason.

Besides appearing in 18 *Charlie Chan* films, Young also appeared in over 35 other films, such as *The Letter* (1940), *Across the Pacific* (1942), and *Flower Drum Song* (1961). In addition, he appeared in several television shows. He was Chuen in *Kung Fu* (1972), Charlie Fong in *Bachelor Father* (1957–62), and was perhaps best recognized as the ranch cook Hop Sing on *Bonanza* (1959–73). He died on November 9, 1980, in his North Hollywood home of accidental asphyxiation from carbon monoxide poisoning as a result of an apparent gas leak.

Charlie Chan filmography—Sen Yung as Jimmy Chan: *Charlie Chan in Honolulu* (1938),* *Charlie Chan in Reno* (1939),* *Charlie Chan at Treasure Island* (1939), *Charlie Chan in Panama* (1940), *Charlie Chan's Murder Cruise* (1940), *Charlie Chan at the Wax Museum* (1940), *Murder Over New York* (1940), *Dead Men Tell* (1941), *Charlie Chan in Rio* (1941), *Castle in the Desert* (1942), *Shadows Over Chinatown* (1946),* *Dangerous Money* (1946),* and *The Trap* (1947).*

Charlie Chan filmography—Victor Sen Young as Tommy Chan: *The Chinese Ring* (1947), *Docks of New Orleans* (1948), *The Shanghai Chest* (1948), *The Golden Eye* (1948), and *The Feathered Serpent* (1948)†.

Yuen, Fu Panama hat shopkeeper (an alias for Charlie Chan) in *Charlie Chan in Panama* (1940). In Panama City, Chan works undercover to gain information about a reported plot to sabotage U.S. military ships that will be traveling through the Panama Canal.

Yung, Sen *see* **Young, Victor Sen**

Yung, Victor Sen *see* **Young, Victor Sen**

YWCA Place where Susie Watson tells Charlie Chan he can always find her, day or night, in *Charlie Chan's Murder Cruise* (1940).

**Billed as Victor Sen Young. †Billed as Victor Sen Yung.*

Z

Zaraka, Charles Diplomat of an unnamed foreign country (portrayed by Morgan Wallace) in *Charlie Chan at the Olympics* (1937). Aided by Yvonne Roland, Zaraka tries to obtain (by whatever means necessary) a new remote controlled guidance system invention that is of strategic importance to the U.S. military.

Once Charlie Chan recovers the stolen invention in Berlin, Zaraka sends Chan a ticket to be his guest in Box 22 at the Olympics' opening day ceremonies. Both then play a cat and mouse game, and Zaraka warns Chan that there is a struggle for world supremacy in a more sinister field, and that, "It's not a game for amateurs." The diplomat then asks Chan if it wouldn't be advisable to turn over the invention to him and return to Honolulu, and gives Chan the remainder of the game's opening ceremonies to think about it. To increase the pressure on Chan to hand over the guidance system control box, Zaraka orders his henchmen to kidnap Chan's Number One son Lee just outside the Olympic Stadium during the opening day's ceremonies.

Ziffren, Lester Screenplay writer for four *Charlie Chan* films: *Charlie Chan in Panama* (1940), *Charlie Chan's Murder Cruise* (1940), *Murder Over New York* (1940), and *Charlie Chan in Rio* (1941).

zodiac Derived from the Greek *zoion* (meaning "animal"), an imaginary belt in the heavens that is divided into 12 equal regions or signs (each 30 degrees in width) representing the annual cycle of the sun. The signs coincided with the zodiacal constellations of about 2,000 years ago.

The first sign of the zodiac, Aries, was given approximately the first twelfth of the year, beginning from the spring equinox, March 21. The other 11 signs were assigned the succeeding one-twelfths of a year, and each sign was attributed characteristics of its own. Because of the precession of the Earth's axis, the vernal equinox has moved westward by about 30 degrees since that time. The signs have moved with it and thus no longer coincide with the constellations. However, the signs are considered to be of great importance by astrologers. The following table lists the signs of the zodiac and their corresponding dates.

Sign	Symbol	Dates
Aries	♈	March 21–April 20
Taurus	♉	April 21–May 20
Gemini	♊	May 21–June 21
Cancer	♋	June 22–July 22
Leo	♌	July 23–August 22
Virgo	♍	August 23–September 22
Libra	♎	September 23–October 22
Scorpio	♏	October 23–November 22
Sagittarius	♐	November 23–December 21
Capricorn	♑	December 22–January 20
Aquarius	♒	January 21–February 19
Pisces	♓	February 20–March 20

In *Charlie Chan at Treasure Island* (1939), mystery writer Paul Essex receives a disturbing radiogram during a China Clipper flight from Honolulu to San Francisco that reads, "Sign of Scorpio indicates disaster if Zodiac obligations ignored." Essex then asks Charlie Chan which month is Scorpio, and Charlie replies, "October ... tomorrow is first day of scorpion symbol on Chinese calendar."

Zodiac, Dr. Mysterious, heavily masked psychic who is really magician Fred Rhadini in *Charlie Chan at Treasure Island* (1939). Dr. Zodiac blackmails his clients, some of whom have committed suicide. *See also* **Rhadini, Fred.**

Zucco, George (January 11, 1886, Manchester, England–May 28, 1960, Hollywood, California) Actor who appeared in over 80 films and is best known as a villain in horror pictures. In his sole *Charlie Chan* role, Zucco portrays the eccentric psychiatrist Dr. Cardigan in *Charlie Chan in Honolulu* (1938).

Although born in England, George Zucco launched his theatrical career in Canada in 1908. He eventually established himself as a leading actor in England in the 1920s. Zucco entered films with *The Dreyfus Case* (1931), and portrayed Disraeli opposite Helen Hayes in *Victoria Regina* (1935). He finally found his villainous niche in the role of the learned

George Zucco as master criminal Professor James Moriarty in the *Adventures of Sherlock Holmes* (1939).

but deadly Professor Moriarty in *The Adventures of Sherlock Holmes* (1939).

Throughout the 1940s Zucco apparently took every role that was offered him, playing mad scientists, master criminals, and occasional red herrings, such as Dr. Alfred Morris in *The Mad Ghoul* (1943) and Leo Grainger in *Fog Island* (1945). Zucco portrayed the fanatical Egyptian priest Anhodeb in *The Mummy's Hand* (1940) and, though supposedly killed in that film, appeared in the sequel, *The Mummy's Tomb* (1942). When not starring in horror films, Zucco was also cast in roles requiring quiet whimsy, such as Officer Barret in *Lured* (1947) and the judge in *Let's Dance* (1950).

References

During the encyclopedia's preparation, the following sources were consulted:

Books

Alvarez, Max Joseph. *Index to Motion Pictures Reviewed by Variety, 1907–1980.* Metuchen, NJ: Scarecrow Press, 1982.

Bartelt, Chuck, and Barbara Bergeron. *Variety Obituaries.*

Volume 1: 1905–1928. New York: Garland Publishing, Inc., 1988.
Volume 2: 1929–1938. New York: Garland Publishing, Inc., 1988.
Volume 3: 1939–1947. New York: Garland Publishing, Inc., 1988.
Volume 4: 1948–1956. New York: Garland Publishing, Inc., 1988.
Volume 5: 1957–1963. New York: Garland Publishing, Inc., 1988.
Volume 6: 1964–1968. New York: Garland Publishing, Inc., 1988.
Volume 7: 1969–1974. New York: Garland Publishing, Inc., 1988.
Volume 8: 1975–1979. New York: Garland Publishing, Inc., 1988.
Volume 9: 1980–1983. New York: Garland Publishing, Inc., 1988.
Volume 10: 1984–1986. New York: Garland Publishing, Inc., 1988.
Volume 11: Index (1905–1986). New York: Garland Publishing, Inc., 1989.
Volume 12: 1987–1988. New York: Garland Publishing, Inc., 1989.
Volume 13: 1989–1990. New York: Garland Publishing, Inc., 1992.
Volume 14: 1991–1992. New York: Garland Publishing, Inc., 1993.
Volume 15: 1993–1994. New York: Garland Publishing, Inc., 1995.

Bogle, Donald. *Toms, Coons, Mulattoes, Mammies, & Bucks.* New York: Continuum Publishing Company, 1989.

Chertok, Harvey, and Martha Torge (eds). *Quotations from Charlie Chan.* New York: Golden Press, 1968.

DeAndrea, William L. *Encyclopedia Mysteriosa: A Comprehensive Guide to the Art of Detection in Print, Film, Radio, and Television.* New York: Prentice Hall, 1994.

Dixon, Wheeler W. *The "B" Directors, A Biographical Dictionary.* Metuchen, NJ: Scarecrow Press, Inc., 1985.

Everson, William K. *The Detective in Film.* Secaucus, NJ: The Citadel Press, 1972.

Gevinson, Alan (ed.). *The American Film Institute Catalog. Within Our Gates: Ethnicity in American Feature Films, 1911–1960.* Berkeley: University of California Press, 1997.

Hanke, Ken. *Charlie Chan at the Movies: History, Filmography, and Criticism.* Jefferson, NC: McFarland & Co., Inc., 1989.

Hanson, Patricia Kay (exec. ed.). *The American Film Institute Catalog of Motion Pictures Produced in the United States. Feature Films, 1931–1940* (Volume F3). Berkeley: University of California Press, 1993.

Hurst, Walter E., and Richard D. Baer (ed.). *Film Superlist: Motion Pictures in the U.S. Public Domain, 1894–1939* (Vol. 1). Hollywood: Hollywood Film Archive, 1994.

______, and Richard D. Baer (ed.). *Film Superlist: Motion Pictures in the U.S. Public Domain, 1940–1949* (Vol. 2). Hollywood: Hollywood Film Archive, 1994.

Katz, Ephraim. *The Film Encyclopedia* (2nd Edition). New York: HarperCollins, 1994.

Munden, Kenneth W. (exec. ed.). *The American Film Institute Catalog of Motion Pictures Produced in the United States. Feature Films, 1921–1930* (Volume F2). New York: R.R. Bowker Company, 1971.

Osborne, Robert. *65 Years of the Oscar*. New York: Abbeville Press, 1994.

Palmer, Scott. *British Film Actors' Credits, 1895–1987*. Jefferson, NC: McFarland & Co., Inc., 1988.

Parish, James Robert (ed.). *The Great Movie Series*. South Brunswick, NJ: A.S. Barnes and Company, 1971.

_______, and William T. Leonard. *Hollywood Players: The Thirties*. New Rochelle, NY: Arlington House Publishers, 1976.

Pitts, Michael R. *Famous Movie Detectives*. Metuchen, NJ: Scarecrow Press, Inc. 1979.

_______. *Horror Film Stars* (2nd Edition). Jefferson, NC: McFarland & Co., Inc., 1991.

Ragan, David. *Who's Who in Hollywood 1900–1976*. New Rochelle, NY: Arlington House Publishers, 1978.

Solomon, Aubrey. *Twentieth Century–Fox: A Corporate and Financial History*. Metuchen, NJ: Scarecrow Press, Inc., 1988.

Steinbrunner, Chris, and Otto Penzler (eds). *Encyclopedia of Mystery and Detection*. New York: McGraw-Hill Book Company, 1976.

Truitt, Evelyn Mack. *Who Was Who on Screen*. New York: R.R. Bowker Company, 1984.

Tuska, Jon. *The Detective in Hollywood*. Garden City, NY: Doubleday & Company, 1978.

Vazzana, Eugene Michael. *Silent Film Necrology: Births and Deaths of Over 9,000 Performers, Directors, Producers, and Other Filmmakers of the Silent Era, Through 1993*. Jefferson, NC: McFarland & Co., Inc., 1995.

Walker, John (ed.). *Halliwell's Filmgoer's Companion* (12th Edition). New York: Harper Perennial, 1997.

Wallechinsky, David. *The Complete Book of the Olympics*. New York: Viking Press, 1988.

Zinman, David H. *Saturday Afternoon at the Bijou*. New Rochelle, NY: Arlington House Publishers, 1973.

Magazines

Charles P. Mitchell. "A Guide to Charlie Chan Films, Part One—Warner Oland and the First Chans." *Classic Images*, September, 1997 (Vol 267), pp. 28–32, C-1.

_____. "A Guide to Charlie Chan Films, Part Two—Sidney Toler at Fox." *Classic Images*, October, 1997 (Vol 268), pp. 20–22.

_____. "A Guide to Charlie Chan Films, Part Three." *Classic Images*, November, 1997 (Vol 269), pp. 24–28.

_____. "A Guide to the Mr. Moto Films." *Classic Images*, April, 1998 (Vol 274), pp. 32, C-1—C-4.

Walsdorff, Robert. "Charlie Chan." *Movie Marketplace*, March/April, 1991, pp. 58–59.

Internet Resources/Databases

Because of the rapidly changing nature of the Internet/World Wide Web, the following URLs may change or be removed without notice.

Academy Awards Search. http://group.lightside.com/~w3design/search.htm

Charlie Chan Message Board. http://www.charliechan.net/webbs/index.cgi

Internet Movie Database (IMDb). http://us.imdb.com

Library of Congress. http://lcweb.loc.gov/catalog/browse/prem.html

TV Guide Movie Review Database. http://www.tvgen.com/movies

Index

Entries that begin with numbers (in numerical form) are placed in numerical order at the beginning of the particular letter.